Fundamentals of Sociology

Richard Holmes
CONSULTING EDITOR

 Holt, Rinehart and Winston of Canada, Limited
Toronto

Canadian Cataloguing in Publication Data
Main entry under title:

Fundamentals of sociology

Bibliography: p.
Includes index.
ISBN 0-03-922554-2

1. Sociology. I. Holmes, Richard (Richard Gordon).

HM51.F86 1988   301   C87-094366-9

Cover: *Streetcar Embarking/Disembarking* by Lorie Schinko 1983,
acrylic on canvas 36″ × 24″

Ms. Schinko is a graduate of Ontario College of Art.

Reproduced by permission of Ms. Lorie Schinko. From the
collection of the Corporation of the City of Toronto.

Publisher: Susan Lilholt
Developmental Editor: Dennis Bockus/The Editorial Centre
Editor: Tessa McWatt
Publishing Services Manager: Karen Eakin
Editorial Co-ordinator: Edie Franks
Copy Editor: Brenda Missen/The Editorial Centre
Cover and Interior Design: Peter Maher
Typesetting and Assembly: Compeer Typographic Services Limited
Printing and Binding: John Deyell Company

Printed in Canada
1 2 3 4 5   92 91 90 89 88

Preface

The typical introductory sociology course of twenty years ago is not quite so typical today. Many courses last only one semester instead of the traditional two. They are no longer offered only in our universities but have now become an important part of the curricula in the community colleges. An increasing number are being presented in such non-traditional formats as independent and individualized study where the student is much more responsible for his or her own learning. These new types of courses represent a challenge to the discipline, the teachers, and the students of sociology. This new text has been designed to accommodate this new diversity.

Fundamentals of Sociology is intended to meet the needs of community college students, university students in one- or two-semester courses, and all students studying in non-traditional formats.

Each of the 14 chapters in the text is authored by a recognized Canadian sociologist who is a specialist in the area. Each chapter can be seen as an overview of the major areas of sociology and covers the fundamental concepts as well as current research interests and findings. The chapters have been succinctly edited to ensure continuity of style and suitable length for a variety of courses.

Consistency and balance across the chapters have been maintained by approaching each area using the three basic sociological perspectives and by comparing and contrasting these perspectives throughout the text.

The book has been specially designed to ease student learning and understanding. It is written in a clear, direct, and highly readable style which is suitable for both community college and university students. Each chapter includes learning objectives to focus the student's attention, two types of boxed inserts to illustrate major ideas (a cross-cultural focus and "everyday sociology" items), bold-faced type for sub-headings and two-colour design for ease of reading. A summary at the end of each chapter outlines the major points. Glossaries and reference indexes simplify the search for definitions. A special writing appendix has been included which will guide students in their written assignments.

The instructor's manual contains two banks of test questions available on computer disks as well as ideas for essays, research projects, and films appropriate to illustrate the text.

My gratitude goes to the co-authors of this text. The quality of their contributions and their patience with the editing made my task not only easy but enjoyable.

I would also like to express my appreciation to the following people for their thoughtful reviews of the manuscript and their helpful suggestions: Tom Callaghan of St. Clair College, Helen Douglas of Okanagan College, Richard Gilbert of John Abbot College, Walter Goffin of Niagara College, William Hanigsberg of Dawson College, Bert Headrick of St. Lawrence College, Doug Hudson of Fraser Valley College, Hugh Lautard, University of New Brunswick, Jane McAvity of Lambton College, Neil Morrison of Cariboo College, Jeffrey G. Reitz, University of Toronto, Barry Smith of Red River College, René Souéry of Centennial College, Les Takahashi of Humber College, and Jean Veevers, University of Victoria.

Special thanks must go to Dennis Bockus of The Editorial Centre whose creative energy is responsible for the final form of the book.

Richard Holmes
Mohawk College of Applied
Arts and Technology
August, 1987

Publisher's Note to Instructors and Students

This text book is a key component of your course. If you are the instructor of this course, you undoubtedly considered a number of texts carefully before choosing this as the one that will work best for your students and you. The authors and publishers of this book spent considerable time and money to ensure its high quality, and we appreciate your recognition of this effort and accomplishment.

If you are a student, we are confident that this text will help you to meet the objectives of your course. You will also find it helpful after the course is finished, as a valuable addition to your personal library. So hold on to it.

As well, please don't forget that photocopying copyright work means the authors lose royalties that are rightfully theirs. This loss will discourage them from writing another edition of this text or other books, because doing so will simply not be worth their time and effort. If this happens, we all lose — students, instructors, authors, and publishers.

And since we want to hear what you think about this book, please be sure to send us the stamped reply card at the end of the text. This will help us to continue publishing high-quality books for your courses.

Contributors

Reginald W. Bibby
University of Lethbridge

Jean Leonard Elliott
Dalhousie University

Patricia Fitzsimmons-LeCavalier
Concordia University

Ellen Gee
Simon Fraser University

A.R. Gillis
Erindale College
University of Toronto

John Hagan
University of Toronto

Robert Hagedorn
University of Victoria

R. Alan Hedley
University of Victoria

Karen Jakob
Humber College

Guy LeCavalier
Concordia University

Marlene Mackie
University of Calgary

R. Ogmundson
University of Victoria

John F. Peters
Wilfrid Laurier University

Terrence H. White
University of Alberta

Contents

Detailed Contents

I The Field of Sociology

**Chapter 1
What Is
Sociology?**

This first section looks at the nature of sociology. We see what sociologists study and pay particular attention to current perspectives in sociology and their historical development.

The theoretical perspectives of sociology are the lenses through which sociologists see. Is a group of people a collection of individuals, or does a group have properties of its own? Is society stable or changing? Do we share basic values, or are we essentially in conflict? The answers to these questions define sociological perspectives. These perspectives determine what you will measure and what you will look for. These, in turn, determine what you find.

In sociology there are three major perspectives:

1. structural functionalism;
2. symbolic interaction;
3. conflict.

These are discussed in the first chapter and are used throughout the book.

1
What Is Sociology?

The purpose of this chapter is to introduce you to the discipline of sociology and to the methods of social research. Be sure, when you are finished, that you are able to

1. summarize the basic viewpoints of
   (a) Durkheim,
   (b) Marx,
   (c) Weber;

2. distinguish among the following sociological perspectives :
   (a) structural-functionalism,
   (b) conflict theory,
   (c) symbolic interaction;

3. list and explain the characteristics of science;

4. outline the steps in sociological research;

5. define *dependent variable* and *independent variable*.

Right now you may be asking yourself: What am I getting into? What is this book about? What is sociology?

To many people, sociology is the most exciting subject on earth, a fresh, lively, coherent, and valuable way of understanding people and the world in which we live. For some people, sociology is so compelling that they invest their entire professional careers in learning it, teaching it, and doing it. As Figure 1-1 shows, people trained in sociology work in a wide variety of jobs, where their knowledge and research influence many decisions that affect our everyday lives.

Sociology is important because it deals with the details of everyday life—but in a new way. The smallest details of human interaction and the largest events of the evening news take on new meaning and make more sense in the light of sociological insights. You will learn that our behaviour is affected by social forces beyond our control. Not only do we, as individuals, influence society; society also influences us.

For some of you, this may seem trivial. Of course, you say, society influences us. In many ways, the essential insights of sociology, and many of its discoveries, seem deceptively like common sense. Common sense tells you that the more severely you punish people, the less likely they are to repeat the forbidden act. Common sense tells you that reading pornography increases the

FIGURE 1-1. Employment of Sociology Bachelor Graduates

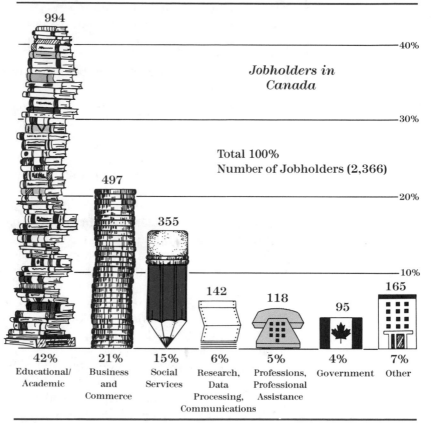

Jobholders in Canada

Total 100%
Number of Jobholders (2,366)

994	497	355	142	118	95	165
42%	21%	15%	6%	5%	4%	7%
Educational/ Academic	Business and Commerce	Social Services	Research, Data Processing, Communications	Professions, Professional Assistance	Government	Other

SOURCE: "The job market for bachelor degree holders" by Hedley R. Alan and Susan M. Adams, 1982, *The American Sociologist, 17* (3).

likelihood of sex crimes. Common sense tells you that capital punishment will reduce crime. Common sense tells you that these statements are obvious. What is not so obvious is that each of these statements is false. Far from being trivial, sociological insight, with its emphasis on groups and social interaction, increases human knowledge, extends our awareness of ourselves as human beings, and can expand our power over our own destinies.

Each of the chapters that follows will add to your awareness of the social forces that affect your destiny. In them you will encounter a broad range of important social issues—power and the political process, life in the city, the growth of large organizations, crime, discrimination, poverty and wealth, class conflict, to name only a few. More important, you will see how these issues influence your life. Consider the following questions:

1. How does a person become a criminal?
2. Can an individual have feminine qualities and masculine qualities at the same time?
3. Why don't more women study math and science?
4. Do all people have the same chance to succeed in their careers?
5. If I marry, what are the chances my partner and I will be happy?
6. Why do people join religious cults?
7. Will I get a good job when I graduate?
8. What motivates people to work hard?

The answers to some of the questions may surprise you. Sociology can give you important insights into the forces that shape you and your world.

Most sociologists agree on the importance of their work and on this basic sociological insight: human behaviour is shaped by social groups. But many disagree among themselves as to precisely what they should study and how they should study it. These disagreements can be examined from three basic perspectives.

Before we look at these three sociological perspectives, however, we need to define sociology itself. Sociology describes and explains social behaviour, social structures and social interaction.

In the balance of this chapter, you will study the three basic sociological perspectives around which this book is organized, the three early theorists whose ideas underlie these perspectives, and some examples of how the different perspectives contribute to sociological knowledge.

Three Early Viewpoints

Each of the three theorists to be discussed—Durkheim, Weber, and Marx—is seen by different people as the most important sociologist. What follows is a description of how these theorists viewed the world, with emphasis on how their viewpoints have affected current sociology. As you read, remember that we are less concerned with the "rightness" or the "wrongness" of one viewpoint or another than with the established usefulness of all three in shedding light on the social world around us.

Emile Durkheim, 1858-1917

Durkheim's main concern was to establish sociology as a discipline and as a science separate from psychology. He defined sociology as the scientific study of **social facts**, of things that are outside the individual but that *coerce* or *constrain* him or her in some way.

French-born Emile Durkheim is considered by many to be the father of modern scientific sociology and the originator of the functionalist approach. He is probably best known for *Suicide* (1897), which is a model of empirical research and statistical reasoning.

SOURCE: The Bettmann Archive

Sociology: What We Study. Most of you would agree with the the following statements:

1. Canadians wear clothes in public.
2. Rich people's opportunities are different from poor people's.
3. Priests behave differently from football players.
4. Large classes are different from small classes.

If, in your explanations for these statements, you refer to custom or law or to the differences that income, occupation, and class size make, you are referring to social facts. For Durkheim, the key characteristics of social facts are that they are *outside (external* to) individuals and yet *constraining* upon them.

Because they are external, Durkheim claimed that social phenomena could not be studied using psychological methods. He argued that any psychological explanation for sociological phenomena was automatically false (Durkheim, 1938, originally published in 1895).

Durkheim's study of suicide is a good example of his view of sociology. A psychologist might study suicide by examining records of interviews with people who had later committed suicide. The words and behaviour of the individual would be of prime importance. Durkheim, on the other hand, treated suicide in strictly sociological terms. He studied suicide rates for various segments of the population. The suicide rate is the number of suicides in one year for a specific group of people, divided by the total number of people in that group, and multiplied by some constant—usually 100 000. As an example, if we look at the number of single Canadian males who committed suicide in 1985, divide that figure by the total number of single males in Canada, and multiply by 100 000, we get the suicide rate for single Canadian males (26.3). Durkheim observed that certain rates of suicide were stable over time and across countries. He found that rates for married persons were lower than rates for divorced persons and that Catholics had lower rates of suicide than Protestants. He argued that since the rates were stable—that is, since Protestants everywhere and at different times committed more suicides than Catholics—you could not explain the rates by the psychological motivations of individual Protestants and Catholics. Durkheim insisted that you must look at social facts for the explanation of suicide rates. Specifically, you must look at the extent to which the groups are integrated into the society. What explained these suicide rates, he argued, was the social fact of integration: in the Europe of his time, both married people and Catholics were more integrated into society than divorced people or Protestants.

Durkheim's key suggestion, then, was that social facts external to the individual can offer an explanation for social behaviour. He isolated what he saw as unique to sociology. Not only is a society more than the sum of its parts; it is constraining on those parts. We can see this in the position of prime minister in Canada. The position exists independently of a specific individual—external to any individual. It is a social fact. Further, it is constraining upon any individual who is elected to the position. What is important for us in Durkheim's thought, and therefore worth repeating, is the suggestion that social structure, or social facts, can offer explanations for social behaviour and for other social facts.

Sociology: How We Study It.   Durkheim believed that social facts could be studied and explained in the same way we study the physical and biological world—that is, scientifically. For Durkheim, to explain social facts you must establish both what causes them and how they function. Durkheim wanted both *causal* explanations and *functional* explanations. An example that he gives is: "The social reaction that we call 'punishment' is due to [caused by] the intensity of the collective sentiments which the crime offends; but, from another angle, it has the useful function of maintaining these sentiments at the same degree of intensity, for they would soon diminish if offenses against them were not punished" (Durkheim, 1938, originally published 1895). This quotation suggests that, for Durkheim, the more intense the collective feelings about a certain crime, the more severe the punishment. This is a fairly obvious statement of cause and effect. But he also notes that punishment serves the purpose of maintaining this feeling within the group. This is the function of punishment.

It is clear, throughout Durkheim's works, that he wanted to establish sociology

1. as a distinct subject that could not be explained by other disciplines—especially psychology;
2. as a science, because social facts could be explained scientifically.

Furthermore, Durkheim believed that science could determine the best goals that a society should aim for. He asked: Why strive for knowledge of society if this knowledge cannot serve us in life? Durkheim's view was that science can determine what society's goals (*ends*) should be, as well as the *means* of achieving those ends. As we will see, sociologists are still asking Durkheim's question of why we should strive for knowledge of society. But most of those who accept sociology as a science reject Durkheim's answer, that science can determine goals.

Max Weber, 1864-1920

There are certain fundamental differences between Weber's and Durkheim's approaches to sociology. These may be seen most clearly by contrasting their definitions of sociology.

The German academic Max Weber exercised a profound influence over European and North American sociology. Weber directed the thrust of many of his major works to the criticism or elaboration of what he regarded as simplistic elements in Marxian thought. He is probably best known for his classic *The Protestant Ethic and the Spirit of Capitalism* (translated in 1930). His work has been of particular influence among symbolic interactionists.

Sociology: What We Study.   Weber (1947) defined sociology as "a science which attempts the interpretive understanding of social action in order thereby to arrive at a causal explanation of its course and effects." *Action* here, refers to all human behaviour to which an actor attaches subjective meaning. Here is an example of what Weber meant: a traveller was at a museum in Spain and wanted to find a particular painting that he thought was in another building. He asked the guard for directions, and the guard put his arm out, palm down, and moved his hand up and down. The traveller thought this meant, "Go away from me," that is, toward the other building. But as he went toward the other building, the guard moved his hand up and down more violently. When he got to the door, he saw that the building was closed. He looked back at the guard, who was still moving his hand wildly. Then he remembered that in Spain this motion didn't mean "Go away." It meant "Come forward." The guard and the traveller had misunderstood each other because the same hand motion meant something different to each of them—each had a different subjective meaning for the same motion. The only way to understand their *social action* would be to know what these subjective meanings were.

A **social action** occurs between two individuals when each person takes into account the actions of the other—for example, the traveller and the guard. For Weber, sociology was concerned with the subjective meanings that guide people in their social conduct. The purpose of sociology for him, then, was to achieve an objective understanding of how people evaluate, use, create, and destroy their social relationships.

In this view, the *individual* is the basic unit of analysis. For Weber, sociologists studying a nation should concern themselves with what it means to its individual members because it is from the members that a nation gets its reality. For example, Canada probably means quite different things to someone in Rimouski, Québec and to someone in St. John's, Newfoundland. Contrast this with Durkheim's view of the nation as a reality in and of itself (a social fact), which therefore cannot be explained by its parts, that is, by its individual members.

Sociology: How We Study It.   Two of Weber's major statements concerning science have had a great impact on contemporary sociology. The first describes a method for studying social action, which he called *Verstehen* (the German word for "understanding"). The second sees science as *value-free* that is, having no connection with the question of what is morally right or wrong.

For Weber, one way we understand people is by what they do

Meanings of Gestures in Different Cultures

On his first trip to Naples, a well-meaning American tourist thanks his waiter for a meal well-served by making the "A-Okay" gesture with his thumb and forefinger. The waiter pales and heads for the manager. They seriously discuss calling the police and having the hapless tourist arrested for obscene and offensive public behaviour.

What happened? Most travellers wouldn't think of leaving home without a phrase book of some kind, enough of a guide to help them say and understand "Ja," "Nein," "Grazie," and "Ou se trouvant les toilettes?" And yet, while most people are aware that gestures are the most common form of cross-cultural communication, they don't realize the language of gestures can be just as different . . . and just as likely to cause misunderstanding as the spoken word.

Consider our puzzled tourist. The thumb-and-forefinger-in-a-circle gesture, a friendly one in America, has an insulting meaning in France and Belgium: "You're worth zero." In parts of Southern Italy it means "ass-hole," while in Greece and Turkey it is an insulting sexual invitation.

There are, in fact, dozens of gestures that take on different meanings as you move from one country or region to another. Is "thumbs up" always a positive gesture? Absolutely not. In northern Greece and Sardinia it has the insulting meaning "Up yours." Does nodding the head up and down always mean "Yes?" No! That gesture may indicate "no" in parts of Greece and Turkey.

SOURCE: "The International Language of Gestures" by Paul Ekman, Wallace V. Friesen, and John Bear. *Psychology Today*, May 1984, p. 64. Copyright 1984 by the American Psychological Association. Reprinted by permission.

and how they do it. We can use scientific methods to set up general laws about these phenomena.

In Weber's view, general laws explaining human behaviour are possible but inadequate. Just as we can observe natural objects, such as plants, stars, and chickens, we can also observe from the outside how people behave and explain the regularities in their behaviour by abstract scientific laws. But with humans we can do more than with natural objects. Humans think, feel, and pursue goals. We can come to understand the subjective meanings people attach to their own behaviour and the behaviour of others. But how do we study motives?

In order to understand what is unique to humans, we need a different approach from that offered by the methods of physical science. This new approach for Weber was **Verstehen**, or the interpretive understanding of social behaviour. Weber suggested that this type of understanding could be achieved in two ways:

1. by reproducing in ourselves a person's *purpose*;
2. by having *empathy* for a person.

Purpose is a simple concept. If we see a woman walking with a book under her arm, we might conclude that her *purpose* is either to read the book or to return it to the library. A more important way of understanding is *empathy*. To achieve empathy, sociologists try to put themselves in the other person's place in order to see things as the other person sees them. For example, a sociologist today who wanted to study the use of marijuana could begin by finding out who smokes, how often different people smoke, and the age and social class of smokers. Then the sociologist would see if there are any general trends—for example, if rich people smoke more than poor people do.

But this is not enough. Our sociologist would also have to find out what smoking marijuana means to the people who use it, what motivates them to try it, and why they continue with it. To do this, the sociologist would talk to marijuana users, observe them, and try to experience their situation as they experience it. The only way the researcher can get at what is uniquely sociological is through this kind of empathy. Weber stated that this approach is scientific.

Weber's second major statement concerning science is that science, by its very nature, avoids value judgments, and is, therefore, **value-free**. He believed that social scientists can gather information that is not affected by their values. An atheist, for example, can gather accurate data on religious beliefs. Weber also believed that scientific data and theories, in and of themselves, contain nothing that tells the scientist what *should* be done. If we accept his viewpoint, we would claim that there is nothing in the theory of relativity, for example, that tells the scientist that it is bad to drop atomic bombs. Good and bad, right and wrong—they are beyond science. To Weber, the physician's only job is to cure the patient. It is not the physician's job to say whether or not life is worth living. We can ask science, "What should we do?" But we will get no answer for, on questions of value, science is mute.

Karl Marx, 1818-1883

Durkheim and Weber were both directly concerned with creating a separate, distinct field of sociology, so they took great pains to define what sociology is. Because of this, most of their contributions are directly related to sociology. Marx is different.

Sociology: What We Study.   Marx had an impact on the whole world. He wrote books, articles, and speeches. He was a scientist and a revolutionary. Marx called himself a philosopher, but every social science has some members who claim him as one of their own.

Not only did Marx want a science of society, he also wanted to change society. Therefore, his ideas about society are not just theory—they are also a revolutionary program.

Essentially, Marx argued, everything that happens in society is caused by economic relationships. In his view, capitalist society consists of two basic economic classes of people with unequal power: the **bourgeoisie**, who own the wealth, and the **proletariat**, or working class, who produce the wealth. The inequality of power is the result of the differences in their relationship to the *means of production*, such as land, factories, and so on. The bourgeoisie own the means of production (the land and the factories) and can, therefore, employ labourers in exchange for wages. The proletarians do not own the means of production and are, therefore, forced to sell their labour in order to survive. The result is that the masses of workers are exploited by a small privileged elite that manages to control most of the wealth without actually producing it themselves. The opposition this exploitation creates is called **class conflict**. Periodically, the exploited

Born and educated in Germany, Karl Marx went to England after the failure of the socialist revolution of 1848 and spent the remainder of his life there. He collaborated with Friedrich Engels in writing *The Communist Manifesto* in 1848. With V.I. Lenin, Marx is generally considered the father of modern communism.

SOURCE: Miller Services

class revolts and in turn becomes the exploiting class. As Marx put it: "The history of all hitherto existing society is the history of the class struggle" (Feuer, 1959).

Marx saw revolution as necessary for social change, since those who have power—in this case the bourgeoisie—will not give it up voluntarily. In this evolutionary stage, the workers revolt against the bourgeoisie and become the owners of the means of production. The result, in theory, is a *classless society*. (Classes are based on ownership of the means of production being in the hands of a chosen few; after the revolution, the workers own the means so there are no more classes.)

Marx also saw the economic system as a major influence on other elements—law, politics, religion, art, and philosophy. These elements are also affected by their relationship to the means of production. They can also affect each other. In an often-quoted statement, Marx referred to religion as "the opium of the people," because religion urged workers to do without rewards in this life and to concentrate on building up rewards in an after-life. Thus in Marx's view, religion merely justified and prolonged the current economic system (Bottomore, 1964).

Marxist concepts that have influenced present-day sociology include:

1. the view of society as constantly changing, and change as inevitable (a contrast to theories that stress the stability of society);
2. the importance of economic structures as they determine other structures in society and as they determine an individual's economic standing, life-chances, values, and behaviour;
3. a stress on the interrelations among parts of the society's superstructure, so that any one part, to be understood, must be seen in relation to the others, especially economic institutions.

In more general terms, Marx has contributed to our understanding of the roles of conflict and power as major elements of society.

Sociology: How We Study It.   Marx considered himself a scientist and attempted to construct a historical science separate from philosophy. He believed that his theories were based on scientific fact, not just opinion, and that his conclusions were soundly based on the study of history and society. He also tried to construct a theory of social structure and social change. Marx also felt that scientists should apply their knowledge in the service of humanity. In this, he was directly opposed to Weber, for whom science was value-free.

In sum, Marx, Durkheim, and Weber each saw himself as a scientist and believed that a science of society, human behaviour, and history was possible. They meant very different things, however, by the term science. The major questions they posed were:

1. Can we set up general laws of social behaviour?
2. Can we use the methods of natural science to study social behaviour and social structure? If so, are these methods enough?
3. Can and should scientists use their knowledge for the betterment of humanity?
4. Is science value-free?

These questions are still with us, and sociologists are still divided in their answers.

Current Perspectives

In a sense, a perspective is a pair of glasses for viewing a part of the world. The world is seen and interpreted through the perspective used. A high rate of suicide, for example, can be seen as the result of many factors. One perspective might relate the high suicide rate to the failure of some people to integrate into society. Another might see it as the outcome of a capitalist economic structure. By stating what sociology is, each of our three perspectives is also suggesting what questions its followers will ask in conducting their research.

What part of the world you look at and what questions you ask about that part of the world are therefore largely determined by the perspective you use. For example, all sociologists would agree that human behaviour is shaped by social groups. But what behaviour is shaped, how it is shaped, and what groups are central to the shaping process are viewed very differently, depending on the sociologist's perspective.

In spite of their various specific disagreements, there is general agreement that the views of Durkheim, Weber, and Marx form the basis of three of the current perspectives in sociology:

1. structural functionalism, which is traced to Durkheim;
2. symbolic interactionism, which is traced to Weber;
3. conflict theory, which is traced to Marx.

The Structural-Functional Perspective

Most sociologists who use this approach agree on the assumptions that

1. a society or group is a system of integrated parts;

2. social systems tend to be relatively stable, and change is usually gradual;
3. each part of a society contributes to and has an effect on the whole society;
4. a society or group cannot survive unless its members share some common beliefs and values.

The concept of social system is central to the structural-functional perspective. The **social system** can be defined by four characteristics:

1. boundaries;
2. interdependence of parts;
3. needs or requirements;
4. equilibrium.

A system must have *boundaries* so that you can identify what parts are in the system and what parts are outside it. An example would be your college. The buildings, the programs, and the people who are members are all parts of the college system. Nonmembers are not part of the system and are not bound by its rules.

The parts of this system are interrelated, or *interdependent*. What happens to one part in the system affects the other parts. For example, if student membership declines, all parts of the system (number of faculty, number of programs, standards, budget) are affected.

The college system has needs or requirements if it is to survive (for example, no students, no college). The college also needs funds for its programs and salaries for its teachers and other personnel. And it must have some control over its members to see that they perform at an acceptable level.

When, at a particular time, the college has adequate funds and adequate numbers of students, faculty, and staff, it is in a state of *equilibrium*, or balance. If this equilibrium is threatened (if, for example, the number of students increases very rapidly), then the system will be obliged to adapt itself to a new set of circumstances.

Equilibrium in social systems changes over time. The college grows. As it grows, an equilibrium—more money, more faculty, more students—is maintained. **Dynamic equilibrium** is the structural functionalists' term for this condition.

This kind of analysis is called *structural* because it sees society as a system (or structure). It is called *functional* because it sees the parts as functioning in terms of that system. The parts of a system can be

1. functional;

2.   dysfunctional; or
3.   non-functional.

A part of a system is **functional** if it helps meet the needs of the system, if it helps contribute to the adjustment of the system. A part that is harmful to the rest of the system is **dysfunctional.** A part that is of no importance within the system is **non-functional.** Gans (1972), for example, in his functional analysis of poverty, concluded that poverty persists when it is functional for the rich and dysfunctional for the poor, and that it will persist as long as the elimination of poverty would create dysfunctions for the rich. In the same way, job discrimination against women is dysfunctional for women, but functional for men, and non-functional for the retired.

Functional analysis sees the system as being in a state of equilibrium, or balance, when the needs of the system are being met and the parts are interdependent. This analysis also assumes that societies have value systems that are shared by their members. If most of the people in a society did not agree on the values of that society, the society would fall apart. From the structural-functionalist perspective, agreement on the major values, such as laws, is seen as a requirement of a social system.

Thus, the structural-functionalist perspective stresses order and stability in a society. Institutions such as the family, education, and religion are analysed according to the way they help meet the needs of society, the role they play in maintaining society's stability. Education, for example, teaches the basic values and skills necessary in an industrial society and tries to fit children into what are seen as appropriate societal positions. The educational system matches individuals with various positions or jobs. In this way, society gets the doctors, nurses, travel consultants, technicians, machinists, and engineers that it needs. Not everyone can be an engineer, and the educational system identifies those who can and want to be, as well as those who can't and don't have the desire. The general view is, therefore, that modern education serves positive functions for society. The maintenance of social order is one outcome of education.

Other social institutions and their functions, as seen by structural-functionalists, would include

1.   the economic system, which operates to produce and distribute necessary goods;
2.   the family, which performs the functions of early socialization, sexual regulation and satisfaction, and the rearing of children;
3.   the political system, which provides an orderly way to decide who will hold power.

Symbolic Interactionism

This perspective is summed up in the following example. Suppose we are walking down a garden path and, turning a corner, suddenly see a large snake. You might say: "Hey, that snake will be a great addition to my dance act!" or "Wow, here comes dinner!" I might say, "Poor snake, it could get hurt on this path." The point is that we can both agree that this is a snake—a fact—but our responses to it depend on the meaning we attach to it. A snake may mean good luck or bad, may seem beautiful or ugly, may cause curiosity or fear. Symbolic interaction theorists insist that social facts are relevant only to the extent that people attach meaning and significance to them. What matters is what you as an individual *think* about these facts.

Symbolic interactionism is the second of the main contemporary sociological perspectives. Everyday statements that reflect symbolic interaction are: "I know how she feels, because I have gone through it"; "I understand his depression, because I, too, have worked on an assembly line"; and "I once lost my job, so I can understand the feelings of those who are forced to retire." In other words, symbolic interactionists try to understand how individuals are feeling in order to understand why they act the way they do.

Much sociological research on delinquency, attitudes, company morale, job satisfaction, and social values stems from Weber's notion of social action. (Remember the story of the tourist in Spain.) Weber saw humans as feeling, thinking beings who attach meaning to the situations they are in and behave according to that meaning. In Weber's perspective, people are creators of society—not just puppets acting out society's attitudes. Not only are they capable of learning the attitudes of their society, but they also discover, invent, and initiate new attitudes. They create, interpret, plan, and control their values and their environment. People not only react, but act.

One of the ways people act and react is through the use of symbols. A **symbol** is something that stands for something else. Language, gestures, and flags are symbols. Symbols get their meanings from the people who create them. For the symbolic interactionist, what makes human beings unique among all other forms of life is our use of language. What makes us human is our ability to represent ourselves, each other, ideas, and objects in symbols. To a great degree, humans rely on symbols to adapt and survive. Humans can communicate effectively because we can agree on and share the meanings of symbols. Furthermore, because meanings of symbols are learned through interaction, they are necessarily social. We communicate and interact

George Herbert Mead introduced the concept of symbolic interaction, showing how people interact through symbols, especially language. His book, *Mind, Self, and Society*, deals with the process of interaction and human beings' ability to anticipate the responses or viewpoints of others. Role taking, the process by which we develop self-awareness, is the basic process by which interaction occurs.

SOURCE: The Granger Collection

by interpreting the symbols that others convey. In this process of interaction, we learn to anticipate each other's responses and to adjust to each other.

This ability to anticipate the responses of others, or to imagine the viewpoint of others has been called **role taking**. The concept was formulated by George Herbert Mead, who published a key work on the subject in 1934.

We take on roles such as mother, bully, best friend, manager. In a sense, we see ourselves from the outside, and we try to behave as other people would expect someone playing that role to behave. Symbolic interactionists believe that we develop an awareness of self—of who we are—through role taking. This development of the self through the process of role taking is a central concept of the interactionist perspective. It shows how our humanness and our individual identities are dependent on interaction with other members of society.

Symbolic interactionists focus on social behaviour in everyday life, trying to understand how people create and define the situations they experience. A useful way to summarize the symbolic-interactionist perspective is to look at the basic assumptions that most symbolic interactionists accept:

1. humans are acting, thinking, feeling beings who make choices about how to act;

2. humans' responses to the acts of others depend on the situation in which the acts occur and what they think the underlying motives are;

3. humans create and use symbols. Human interaction is greatly influenced by the symbols humans use to conceptualize the "real world";

4. through symbolic interaction with others, humans develop a concept of self, including a conception of what kind of self is acceptable in the community;

5. society is a process in which human beings construct or negotiate social order.

The Conflict Perspective

Like the structural-functionalist perspective, the **conflict perspective** assumes that social structure affects human behaviour. But where structural functionalism emphasizes integration, shared values, and social stability, the conflict perspective stresses conflict, power differences, and social change. While conflict theorists do not necessarily follow the class conflict assumptions of Marx, they do follow his general orientation.

There are four basic elements (adapted from Dahrendorf, 1959) in the conflict perspective:

1. societies are always changing;

2. conflict and disagreement are always present in every social system;

3. there are elements or parts of every social system that contribute to change;

4. coercion is always present in society; that is, in every society some people have more power than others.

In the conflict perspective, society is seen as a delicate balance of power groups trying to hang onto or improve their positions. Structural functionalists tend to view institutions and groups as working together. Conflict theorists, by contrast, suggest that such groups usually work at cross purposes; the goals of one group are frequently at odds with the goals of another. Conflict is everywhere. When there is stability, it occurs during (usually brief) periods in which one group dominates the rest or some groups have a balance of power.

SOURCE: Miller Services

Modern conflict theorist Ralf Dahrendorf was director of the London School of Economics. Dahrendorf is a major influence on modern conflict theory that focuses on conflict, power differences, and social change.

The conflict perspective also tends to see values, ideas, and morality as inventions of the existing power groups that allow them to continue their control. Thus, the way to change society is to change its structure—not its individuals.

By the same token, power is seen as a result of social position, rather than as a result of individual characteristics. The prime minister, for example, has power because he or she is prime minister, not because of any individual characteristics he or she might have. Additionally, people are seen as having power because they control resources, such as money or the means of production.

A conflict theorist studying education would likely view modern mass education in the following manner:

1. it teaches the values and skills of the dominant groups in society in the hope that their values will be accepted and that these dominant groups will not be challenged;
2. it selects individuals so that the power structure of society will stay the same.

To illustrate the three sociological perspectives, we can ask ourselves how each might be used in studying the students in a classroom. A structural functionalist, focusing on what is common to classrooms, might analyse the functions of tests. A symbolic interactionist might want to determine how the individual students interpret the class, or what effect the teacher has on the development of their self-images. A conflict theorist could look at the effects of the power differences between teacher and students.

An Overview

These, then, are the major sociological perspectives. Which is right? A better question is: Which of them has been useful in helping us come to an understanding of society? And the answer to that is all of them. They are each based on different assumptions, but each has provided a useful way of viewing part of the social world.

Strangers in a Familiar World

Anthropologists use the term "culture shock" to describe the impact of a totally new culture upon a newcomer. In an extreme instance such shock will be experienced by the Western explorer who is told, halfway through dinner, that he is eating the nice old lady he had been chatting with the previous day—a shock with predictable physiological if not moral consequences. Most explorers no longer encounter cannibalism in their travels today. However, the first encounters with polygamy or with puberty rites or even with the way some nations drive their automobiles can be quite a shock to an American visitor. With the shock may go not only disapproval or disgust but a sense of excitement that things can *really* be that different from what they are at home. To some extent, at least, this is the excitement of any first travel abroad. The experience of sociological discovery could be described as "culture shock" minus geographical displacement. In other words, the sociologist travels at home—with shocking results. He is unlikely to find that he is eating a nice old lady for dinner. But the discovery, for instance, that his own church has considerable money invested in the missile industry or that a few blocks from his home there are people who engage in cultic orgies may not be drastically different in emotional impact. Yet we would not want to imply

that sociological discoveries are always or even usually outrageous to moral sentiment. Not at all. What they have in common with exploration in distant lands, however, is the sudden illumination of new and unsuspected facets of human existence in society.

People who like to avoid shocking discoveries, who prefer to believe that society is just what they were taught in Sunday School, who like the safety of the rules and the maxims of what Alfred Schuetz has called the "world-taken-for-granted," should stay away from sociology. People who feel no temptation before closed doors, who have no curiosity about human beings, who are content to admire scenery without wondering about the people who live in those houses on the other side of that river, should probably also stay away from sociology. They will find it unpleasant or, at any rate, unrewarding. People who are interested in human beings only if they can change, convert or reform them should also be warned, for they will find sociology much less useful than they hoped. And people whose interest is mainly in their own conceptual constructions will do just as well to turn to the study of little white mice. Sociology will be satisfying, in the long run, only to those who can think of nothing more entrancing than to watch men and to understand things human.

SOURCE: *Invitation to Sociology: A Humanistic Perspective* (p. 23) by P. I. Berger, 1963, New York: Doubleday.

Early in the chapter, we suggested that sociology describes and explains social behaviour and social interaction. It tries to understand the social structures and how they affect behaviour. Sociology also studies people's perceptions of their social environment. Think about how all three approaches contribute to that definition.

Having considered what sociology is and how we study it from various points of view, we will now consider the matter of sociology and science.

Sociology as a Science

For sociology to be considered a science, the scientific method must be applied to the study of social behaviour. Science is basically a method for collecting and explaining facts. The primary goal of the scientific method is to construct scientific laws; a scientific law is a hypothesis that has been supported repeatedly by empirical tests. Therefore the goal of the science of sociology is to discover patterns of social behaviour and to explain these patterns by developing scientific laws. Scientific laws contain predictions that certain effects will occur under certain specified conditions. To form hypotheses and establish laws, we must assume that there is order in the physical and social universes, and that systematic relations exist that can be observed and formulated into laws. The task for sociologists, then, is to find the order in social phenomena and express it using the scientific method.

Characteristics of Science

How do we construct scientific laws? A law must be accurate, objective, and without bias. Scientists construct a law in three ways:

1. by verifiability;
2. by unbiased observation;
3. by unbiased interpretation.

Verifiability means that an observation can be confirmed by independent observers. An observation can be verified when several other observers have made the same observation. We can then say it is a **fact**. A fact exists when several qualified observers, after careful observation, achieve the same results.

It should be clear that, for science, *observation* is what counts. Consequently, science can answer only questions on phenomena that can be observed. Science is restricted to problems that deal with the observable world. Therefore, some very important problems and concerns cannot be resolved by the scientific method: What is beauty? Is there a God? These are questions and statements that cannot be resolved by observation. We may use logic, tradition, authority, common sense, revelation, faith, or intuition to answer these questions, but we cannot answer them by observation.

Conflicts between religion and science can occur only over questions of fact—that is, questions that have to do with the world of observation. In this perspective, science is objective or unbiased. Science assumes that it is possible to make observations that are unaffected by beliefs, values, or preferences.

In restricting science to the realm of the observable, scientists are limited to studying facts: satellite photos show the earth *is* round; crime rates are increasing; a higher proportion of women were in the labour force in 1980 than in 1960. Factual statements are different from statements or questions of preference or values. For example, sociologists cannot, as scientists, state that capital punishment is right or wrong. They can say that there is no clear relationship between capital punishment and a reduction in the homocide rate. They can also state that a poll (Gallup, 1981) showed that as many as 74 percent of the Canadians surveyed favoured the return of capital punishment for certain crimes. Sociologists can study scientifically what people *do* want, but there is nothing in this method that enables them to tell individuals what they *should* want.

Unbiased observation, the second way we reach our goal of constructing laws, assumes that the researchers' values can be controlled adequately in doing social research. The amount of bias can be determined by other independent observers. If your poll has the NDP winning and mine has the Progressive Conservatives winning, we do not know who is right. However, if several other pollsters support your findings, then the evidence suggests either that I did a bad job of polling or that my biases affected my observation.

Unbiased interpretation, the third way we reach our goal, has the same pitfalls. Our biases frequently affect our interpretations. The problem here is that most facts or relationships can be interpreted in more than one way.

The solution to this problem is to require testing of the interpretation. In other words, the interpretation becomes a hypothesis, a testable statement asserting a relationship between two or more variables. An interpretation must be stated so that observations can determine whether the statement is true or false. Some interpretations are by definition not able to be tested. If I state that the plague was caused by God's anger, for example, there is no way that I could test this statement to determine whether it is scientifically true or false.

The ability to test whether one interpretation or another is correct is a way of controlling for bias in interpretations of observations. Another aid is the fact that science is public. When something is public, if it is wrong, sooner or later someone will point this out. It may take time, especially when a given theory fits the biases of most people. In this case, there may be a time gap before the error is identified, because most people want to believe it. Another possible explanation is that the scientist who made the statement is very powerful or has a great deal of prestige in the discipline.

Scientists can and must try to keep their values and preferences from affecting what they see and how they interpret what they see. Science is value-free, although scientists are not. Therefore, by keeping to the rules of science, scientists can reduce the effects of values. By verification and retesting they can determine the extent to which values may have intruded upon their research.

We have just considered some of the qualities that sociology must have or acquire to be considered a science. Is sociology now, or can it be, a science? Opinions vary; sociologists differ. It is probably true that most sociologists accept scientific standards as a goal, at the same time realizing that it is extremely difficult to exclude personal values from social research.

There is no one right way to view the world. In a book such as this, written by many people, it is necessary that you be aware of diverse perspectives, since in various chapters you will encounter all of them.

This chapter has presented an overview of the discipline of sociology. Necessarily, much has been omitted and simplified. The stress has been on the value of using multiple viewpoints, as opposed to one right way of seeing society.

Summary

1. Durkheim and Weber defined sociology in opposite ways. For Durkheim, sociology was concerned with *social facts*, which are external to individuals and which constrain their behaviour. Weber, on the other hand, believed that what was uniquely sociological was our ability to understand the *subjective states of individuals*.

2. Marx did not define sociology, but his influence has been direct and profound. For Marx, society is seen largely in terms of the relationships people have to the means of production and the class conflict that results. Change and conflict, in his view, are fundamental characteristics of society.

3. Three major current perspectives are derived from these three classical thinkers: structural functionalism is traced to

Durkheim; symbolic interaction is clearly related to Weber; and conflict theory stems from Marx.

4. Structural functionalism stresses order and stability in society. This perspective emphasizes that a society cannot survive unless its members share some common values, attitudes, and perceptions; that each part of the society contributes to the whole; that the various parts are integrated with each other; and that this interdependence keeps societies relatively stable.

5. Symbolic interaction focuses on people and how they create, use, and communicate with symbols, especially language.

6. The conflict perspective emphasizes that societies are always changing; that conflict and disagreement are always present in society; that parts of every society contribute to change; and that coercion is always present in society because some people have more power than others.

7. Sociology aspires to be a science; consequently, most sociology is based on objective, verifiable data.

Further Reading

Gouldner, A. W. (1963). The sociologist as partisan: sociology and the welfare state. *American Sociologist, 3*, 103-17.
One of the best statements on why science cannot be value free.

Hagedorn, R., & Labovitz S. (1973). *Sociological orientations.* New York: John Wiley.
A slightly different view of the major perspectives on schools of sociological thought.

Merton, R. K. (1968). *Social theory and social structure.* Glencoe, IL.: Free Press.
A clear statement of what functionalism is and what it isn't. See especially pp. 19-84.

Mills, C. W. (1967). *The Sociological imagination.* New York: Oxford University Press.
A classic introduction to sociology from the conflict perspective.

Ritzer, G. (1975). *Sociology: Multiple paradigm science.* Boston: Allyn and Bacon.
A more advanced discussion of theories in sociology, which is compatible with this chapter.

Rudner, R. S. (1966). *Philosophy of social science.* Englewood Cliffs, N.J.: Prentice-Hall.
Chapter four is a clear statement on why social science can be value-free.

Stryker, S. (1980). *Symbolic Interactions.* Menlo Park, Cal.: Benjamin/Cummings.
Excellent statement of this approach and the differences among symbolic interactionists.

Appendix on Social Research

In everyday life, you are constantly evaluating the results of research. Reading your daily newspaper, purchasing a car, writing or evaluating reports in your work, even buying a bottle of aspirin all require you to arrive at some judgment or conclusion. A knowledgeable appreciation of how the facts were researched is essential to a sound interpretation of what they mean. An understanding of basic research procedure can be very useful in making any kind of evaluation. It will also be helpful in your reading of other sections in this book.

Planning Research

You are reading a newspaper article on juvenile delinquency. You observe that most delinquents reported in the article have addresses in the predominantly poor areas of your city. On the basis of this casual observation, you speculate that poverty is a contributing factor to delinquency. This is your hypothesis.

Hypotheses and Variables. A **hypothesis** is an idea you expect to be true, but which remains to be proven as a result of scientific research. Like researchers in the physical sciences, social scientists try to design research that will test the truth or validity of their hypotheses.

A hypothesis states a relationship between two or more **variables**. There are two general kinds of variables that scientists consider when designing an experiment:

1. dependent variables;
2. independent variables.

A **dependent variable** is a factor that depends on or is caused by some other factor. In your hypothesis, delinquency is a dependent variable because it depends on income level; that is, you are speculating that the lower the level of income, the greater the likelihood that delinquency may occur. The **independent variable** is the factor that causes the dependent variable. In this case, the independent variable is poverty.

A hypothesis can only be tested if you can measure the variables. How do you measure poverty and delinquency?

Measurements and Indicators. Measurement is the weakest link in the research process. Research results are only as good as the measurements used to produce them. **Indicators** are the empirical measurements used for variables in the same way that a thermometer is used to measure temperature. For any one variable, there are potentially a variety of indicators to measure it.

Independent and Dependent Variables

A **variable** is a measurable dimension of a concept that takes on two or more values; for example, sex, education, and income are commonly used variables. Two types of variables—independent and dependent—are important because the independent variable is the only way to tell what sociological perspective is being used.

A *dependent variable* is what you are trying to explain or the question you are seeking to answer. For example, if you ask, "What causes alcoholism?", alcoholism is the dependent variable. An *independent variable* is the variable that you think explains or causes the differences in the dependent variable. You can think of the independent variable as the cause and the dependent variable as the effect. Or you can think that what happens to the dependent variable *depends* upon changes in the independent variable.

In order to know what sociological perspective is being used, it is necessary to know what the independent variable is since, in many instances the dependent variable is the same. This is demonstrated in the writings of Durkheim, Marx, and Weber in that they were all concerned with explaining the changes in society and the changing relation of individuals to society, the dependent variable.

Durkheim argues that the independent variable, the cause of these changes, was the division of labour. The occupational specialization that occurred during industrialization resulted in a new type of social cohesion. For Marx, the independent variable was the relationship of individuals to the means of production. In capitalist societies this would result in the development of two classes and, eventually, class conflict. The means of production, an independent variable, is seen as determining the relation of the individual to society, the dependent variable. Weber suggested that it is the values people have, especially about authority, that is the independent variable.

Remember your original observation in the newspaper. Because you know your city well and, consequently, where the rich and the poor live, your measure, or indicator, of poverty in this case is residential area. Your indicator of delinquency is the arrests of juveniles reported in the paper.

Validity.   Experiments are designed to test the **validity** or truth of your hypothesis. Achieving valid results is a major goal of all research. In sociology, validity is the result of having measured what you had intended to measure. This sounds simple enough, but it is one of the most elusive goals in research, because we can never be certain that we are indeed measuring what we want. Too often there are other factors that get in the way.

Classical design.   Social scientists try to design experiments to eliminate competing explanations for how the results were obtained. The best technique to use is the **classical design**. Two equivalent groups are selected. It is important that the two groups be similar in every controllable way.

One group, called the experimental group, is subjected to the independent variable. The other group, the control group, is treated identically to the experimental group, except that it is not subjected to the independent variable.

Both groups are measured before and after the experiment. Provided that the groups are equivalent at the outset, and that they are treated identically in every respect except for the intro-duction of the independent variable to the experimental group, any difference in result between the two groups can only be a result of the independent variable. Thus, the classical design allows the researcher to isolate and actually determine the effect of the independent variable on the dependent one.

Cross-Sectional Design. Perhaps the most used design in soci-ological research is the **cross-sectional design.** Two or more groups with varying degrees of an independent variable are measured at one time to determine how they compare with respect to a dependent variable. For example, much research has

What is love? Sexual attrac-tion, companionship, a physical sensation, or a spiritual communication? For social researchers, defining what they observe and how they measure it is essential.

SOURCE: H. Armstrong Roberts/Miller Services

been undertaken on the effects of university education (independent variable) on the values of students (dependent variable). Common in these studies is a comparison of representative groups of students from each year of university. To the extent that groups vary in the predicted direction (for example, in a value such as conservatism), it is concluded that university education is primarily responsible.

In order for this conclusion to be appropriate, however, it must be assumed that each group was equivalent at the beginning of its university education. The assumption cannot be validated with this type of design, and thus competing explanations must be considered as possible alternatives. For example, changes in student values could be because of the aging process of the students and not because of university education. Is the hypothesis necessarily wrong? No. The point is that circumstances frequently force sociologists to go with a less than ideal design.

In sociology, we are often faced with situations for which it is difficult or impossible to set up control groups. Independent variables, such as the changing of school boundaries, the closing of a plant, or the occurrence of a tornado, happen without sociologists' advance knowledge. We may wish to study their effects on individuals, but it is impossible to know what these people were like or how they felt before these events. Also, we have no way of knowing whether the groups we are comparing were equivalent prior to the occurrence of these independent variables.

Most researchers keep the classical experimental design in mind when planning their studies. Though it is often impossible to apply these ideal designs, knowledge of the particular discrepancies between the researchers' own designs and these ideals allows them to anticipate difficulties.

Population and Sampling

In sociology, a **population** is the total body of people whom you are interested in studying. Many times, it would be impossible or prohibitively expensive to study a whole population, so a sample is selected. A **sample** is a smaller group, chosen to represent the whole population.

A sample should be *representative* of the particular population from which it is drawn. It should include those characteristics that relate directly to the problem being studied. For example, because the rate of delinquency is known to be higher for boys than for girls, the distribution of males in a sample used to test our hypothesis should match the distribution of males in the population. Otherwise, the results of the sample may be misleading.

Most samples used by scientists are random samples from the population being studied. A **random sample** is a sample in which each person within the population has an equal chance (probability) of being selected. An essential aspect of random samples is that the population being used must be explicitly defined or identified. In order for each element to have an equal probability of selection, all elements must be listed. Suppose that you wished to take a random sample of your class or your town.

First, you identify the population. It is necessary to make a list of all the people that comprise this population. In many cases, lists already exist (class lists, voting lists, city directories, telephone books, tax records). But you must ensure that these lists correspond to your target population, that is, to the population about which you want to make generalizations. Voting lists contain only adults; telephone books contain only those people with listed telephones, and therefore probably exclude the very poor, the highly mobile, and those who desire privacy.

Second, you select a sample from that population. A number of specialized techniques have been developed by researchers to ensure that samples are representative of the whole population. When the sample has been chosen, you can begin to gather information.

Data Collection

Sociologists gather data in three ways.

1. they ask people for information;
2. they observe people's behaviour;
3. they observe the results of people's behaviour.

Consider an illustration of these methods. If you are interested in the drinking patterns of a community, you could ask a sample of the residents how much and how often they drink. Or you could observe them in bars, homes, and liquor stores. You could also gather evidence by counting the bottles in their garbage cans.

There are two ways of asking people for information—by questionnaires and by interviews.

Questionnaires. A questionnaire is a series of questions to be answered by the *respondent*. It may be handed out at work or school or mailed directly to a person's home. The questionnaire will include a letter informing the person of the purpose of the questionnaire, how she or he was chosen, reasons encouraging the person to respond, and, usually, assurance of anonymity.

Interviews. Since interviewing involves human interaction, the potential for problems is greater than with questionnaires—mainly because personal characteristics of researchers and respondents must be considered. Research using face-to-face interviews must be designed so that the results of the study are not the consequence of the interviewer's influence. Age, sex, race, dress, general appearance and behaviour, a raised eyebrow, a vocal inflection—all can influence the respondents' answers.

The interview itself may vary from a brief, structured session to a lengthy, complicated, unstructured one lasting a few hours. The structured interview uses a schedule, which is essentially a questionnaire that is read to the respondents in a specified order. In an unstructured interview, the interviewer is allowed to explore the respondents' answers.

One advantage of interviews over questionnaires is that in conducting interviews, the populations are less restricted. The respondents need not be able to read or write, but merely be able to understand the language of the interviewer. Also, the response rate is usually higher and the identity of the respondents is known. Because personal interviews can be expensive to conduct, telephone interviewing is becoming increasingly popular.

Observation. Both questionnaires and interviews measure opinions, attitudes, and perceived behaviour. But they do not measure actual behaviour, and what people actually do may be crucial for some studies. **Observation** is the term applied to methods of gathering data without direct questioning.

Participant observation is a common sociological method of gathering data, by which the observer is part of the social setting that is being observed. This technique has led one sociologist to participate in the activities of street gangs (Whyte, 1943) and another to spend long hours watching the interactions in a school classroom (Richer, 1979). In most studies of this kind, people know they are being studied, so there is the possibility that their behaviour could be affected by that knowledge.

Whatever data collection methods are used, statistical techniques have been developed to help compile and interpret the thousands of bits of data that are accumulated in most sociological studies. The area of data analysis is best dealt with in statistics courses, a subject required for students majoring in sociology.

Part of the use of observation to study behaviour involves the quantification of information.

"The man by the door sneezes 18 times a minute, the man in the middle hiccups 21 times a minute, and this man here says 'you know' 23 times a minute."

The Value of Research Methods

Knowledge of what is involved in the research process enables consumers of research findings to assess the results and arrive at their own conclusions. Depending on how the research was undertaken, what kind of design was used, and how the sample was selected and the data collected, the results may be more or less valid. As you read research studies or summaries of their conclusions, you should ask yourself questions such as the following:

1. How do you know?
2. Can any other factors explain this result?
3. Under what conditions does this assertion hold?

Use the information in this
appendix to evaluate what
you read about society, both
for this course and in your
reading about current
events.

SOURCE: H. Armstrong Roberts/Miller Services

To the extent that you develop this critical appreciation of
research, you will not be obliged to accept the claims of others
on faith. Keep this attitude in mind as you read the rest of this
book.

Appendix Summary

1. Hunches, personal problems, observations, conversations, and theory are all sources of research problems. Whatever the source, the steps in researching a problem are similar: dependent and independent variables are identified and a hypothesis is formulated that states a relationship between them.

2. The purpose of a research design is to eliminate alternative explanations for the results. The ideal (although not perfect) design is the classical experimental design.

3. In sociology, most research involves a sample rather than the total population. The major concern in sampling is attempting to make the sample representative of the population. To achieve a representative sample, random sampling procedures are usually employed.

4. All data collection is based on asking or observing. The most commonly used techniques in sociology are structured questionnaires, structured interviews, and participant observation. All data collection techniques have advantages and disadvantages that determine their usefulness for a particular research problem.

II The Individual in Society

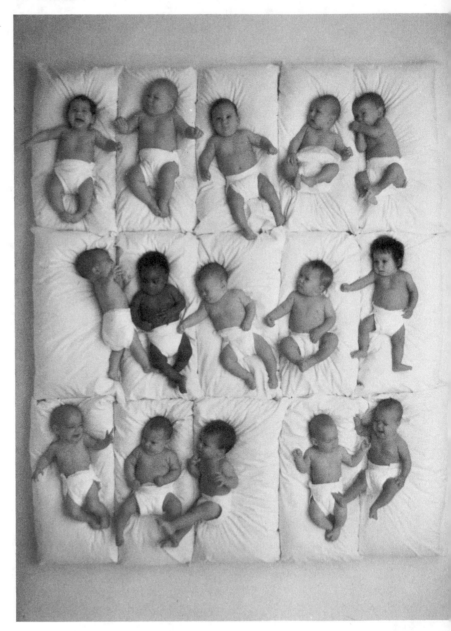

At birth we are colour coded, blue or pink. We are usually tagged with names that tell people whether we are male or female. Sooner or later we are toilet trained, introduced to eating schedules, and taught the proper way to eat. We learn to be polite. We learn whom and what to love, and whom and what to fear. We are born into a world that has a social order, and much of our early education is an effort to teach us to adapt to that order.

Every society has beliefs that are generally accepted and beliefs that are almost universally rejected. There are accepted patterns of behaviour and accepted values. Every society has rules governing matters such as who is responsible for taking care of children, who is an eligible marriage partner, how to behave when our parents die, and what to eat and how often. Chapter 2, Culture, discusses the variations and uniformities in these rules and values. Implied here is the notion that human beings are systematically taught how to behave, feel, and think. This process of learning to become a member of society continues throughout life. What we learn is part of our culture; how we learn it is called *socialization*, which is discussed in Chapter 3.

Chapter 4 talks about gender: how sex has been used to categorize people, what this means, what the consequences of gender roles are, and how they are changing.

Every society has deviants. These are people who break the rules. Law-breakers are deviants, but so are people who break unwritten rules. The question of what is deviant, the puzzle of who becomes a deviant, and the attempts to explain deviance are the topics of Chapter 5.

2
Culture

The purpose of this chapter is to introduce you to the very essence of sociological thinking: the concept of culture. Make sure that when you have completed this chapter you are able to

1. define and give examples of the following concepts:
    (a) symbols,
    (b) values,
    (c) norms,
    (d) subcultures;

2. compare and contrast ethnocentrism and cultural relativity;

3. outline the impact on society of the changing technologies of mass communication.

I know a lot about you. For instance, when you go out of your house, you wear clothes. You have never eaten worms or grubs and usually eat three meals a day at specified times; you would be embarrassed to spit food on your plate or to eat mashed potatoes with your hands in a restaurant; most of you believe in God, and you own a radio. On the average, you have spent more than 15 000 hours watching television, during which you have seen 18 000 murders and 350 000 commercials. You will get married and have children. I also know that you hate to waste time, plan to work even if you don't need the money, and that you drive on the right-hand side of the road. I know these things because you are Canadians. My knowledge of Canadian culture enables me to predict your behaviour.

A simple but adequate definition of **culture** is everything we think, believe, do, and have as members of a particular society. Since human behaviour is not controlled genetically, what does control it, and why are there patterns of behaviour? Part of the answer is to be found in the concept of culture. If the people in groups or societies learn to think, act, feel, and do things in roughly the same way, we can make some general statements concerning the group. Culture is our social inheritance, which gives structure to our lives.

Culture is learned, transmitted, shared, and normative.

Characteristics of Culture

Culture is Learned.   The fact that culture is *learned* has several implications:

1. We are born into a culture; it exists prior to any given individual, and continues beyond one's life span.
2. Unlike insects who inherit their ways of behaving, humans do not rely solely on instinct or biological heredity, but mostly on learning and their social heritage. As we will explain in Chapter 3, we are taught the values, beliefs, and rules of our society.
3. Because culture is learned, there will be greater differences among and between human groups than we would find in other forms of life, which rely on biological inheritance. In other words, because it is a learned process, the content of various cultures can and does *vary* greatly.

Culture is Transmitted.   A major aspect of culture is that it is transmitted symbolically. A **symbol** is something that stands for something else. Flags, smiles, and words are symbols. Because the meanings attached to the symbol are arbitrary conventions, a swastika means very different things to westerners than it does to the people of India. A cross means something different to Christians than to non-Christians. Words are also symbols—they represent objects or actions or qualities. Culture is transmitted primarily through language, that is, through word-symbols and the rules for their combination.

For most social scientists, it is the fact that people are *symbol users*, that we are the only animals with an involved language system, that makes us unique. Our libraries, schools, and technology are based on our ability to use language. Without it, each of us would have to learn from direct experience, by trial and error. We would each have to develop our own explanations for why apples fall. Instead, because knowledge and science can be accumulated and stored, we can learn the theory of gravity or the theory of combustion engines and can continue where others have left off.

> When we talk to one another, we accomplish a commonplace miracle; commonplace because we do it so effortlessly and so often; miraculous because how we do it remains largely a mystery (Keesing, 1976).

One way of seeing the importance of language is in its relation to perception. It is generally agreed that the categories and distinctions that are part of our language introduce perceptual dis-

Canadians welcome former Prime Minister Trudeau to St. Lucia. We use the maple leaf flag as a symbol of our Canadian identity.

tortion. They act as filters between us and the world we perceive. The Inuit see and name many more types of snow than we do. The Philippine Hanunoo tribe has more than 1800 distinct species labels for the plants in their environment, while western scientists class them into less than 1300. The categories and models we use that determine what we see and name are learned and transmitted throughout our culture.

Culture Is Shared.   It will now be clear that culture is a product of group experience. This means that we learn our culture from others, or, stated another way, that we are socialized by parents, teachers, peers, and the mass media into the culture in which we are born. No society leaves this process to chance. In every society someone or several people or institutions are designated as those to teach and pass on certain values, skills, and ways of behaving. According to some anthropologists, *shared meanings* is the essence of culture. It is the sharing of meanings and of the rules of the game that make social life possible. Without shared customs and conventions we could not get through the day. These shared meanings give order and pattern to life, as well as to the goals we strive for. When we talk about culture, we are not referring to unique ideas and beliefs, but rather to those things held in common. We may share these with all members of society or only a few, but they are nevertheless shared. Even in a highly diverse society such as ours, some beliefs and values can be characterized as "Canadian" and are true of almost all of us.

Culture Is Normative.   Normative refers to the moral and social order—what is right or wrong, good or bad, the shoulds and oughts we live by. You wear clothes to school because in our culture you should, and you would be very uncomfortable if you were forced to sit naked in class. This kind of knowledge has been used to help break down or brainwash prisoners of war. We learn that nudity is all right in certain situations and wrong in others. The goals and values we should pursue, how we should pursue them, what is moral, what God(s) to believe in, what is sinful, shameful, or embarrassing are all parts of the normative aspect of culture.

Cultural Universals and Cultural Diversity

Because culture is learned, transmitted, shared, and normative, different societies and different groups in the same society can and do learn, transmit, and share different norms and values. It is the normative dimension of culture that is primarily involved in four important aspects of culture. These four are

1.   cultural universals;
2.   cultural diversity;
3.   ethnocentrism;
4.   cultural relativism.

Cultural Universals.   There are biological, ecological, and sociological pressures that limit human variability. Humans live in a world that has many common features: mating, birth, infancy, growth, work, and death. Night and day, the lunar cycle, heat and cold, rain, storms, and so on are conditions we all face. There are enough common elements to ensure some cultural universals. **Cultural universals** are features common to all cultures. Murdock (1945) has listed several. Among them are athletic sports, courtship, division of labour, education, funeral rites, family, marriage, language, sexual restrictions, and religious rituals. However, there are no specific practices found in all societies. For example, every society may have the family institution, but the variation in family patterns among cultures can be striking.

Cultural Diversity.   One way to see the diversity among cultures is to look at what is considered food. In Peru, Ecuador, and Bolivia, the native Indians rear guinea pigs, which often form the main source of meat. In Liberia, monkey meat sells for much more than beef, and in Nigeria meat from the giant rat is more expensive than mutton. Nigeria is also domesticating the giant African land snail, and the University of Chile is looking into ways of rearing the wild toad. It follows that whether an animal is seen as a pet or as a delectable dinner is a matter of cultural values.

Human sacrifices, cannibalism, homosexuality, necrophilia, infanticide, head hunting, eating worms, genocide, slavery, torture—all of these behaviours have been the custom for many peoples. It seems as if somewhere at some time anything can be worshipped, any sexual practice accepted, any substance a delicacy, any behaviour moral or immoral. Whether a schizophrenic ends up as a mental patient or a religious prophet depends on time and place. What is pornographic to you may be normal to someone else; what is normal to you may be pornographic in some other culture.

Ethnocentrism. People have a strong tendency to be **ethnocentric**, to judge or evaluate other cultures in terms of their own cultural values. People with religious beliefs different from our own are sometimes labelled pagans and heathens whom we should convert. People who lend their wives to their guests for sexual purposes are "weird," infanticide is ugly, and starving to death amidst healthy cows is "crazy" by our values. This raises the questions, "Should we impose our values and standards on another society?" and "Should they impose their standards on ours?"

Cultural Relativism. **Cultural relativism** argues that each society's way of life can be evaluated only by its own standards of right and wrong. All cultures are different, and no culture is "better" than another. This view suggests that values and norms that work well for some particular culture may, with equal grounds, be rejected by another culture. This view is easy to accept when you think, for example, of which side of the road it is correct to drive on. It also may be acceptable when you consider that out of 458 societies, 115 strongly prohibit premarital sexual relations, 163 freely permit them, and the rest fall somewhere in between these two extremes. It doesn't seem too difficult to understand that in some societies virginity is very important, while in other societies it is unimportant, and that either value works equally well for those societies. However, cannibalism, infanticide, or slavery seem "morally" wrong, and societies that practice them seem not as good as those that don't.

Cultural relativism argues that certain practices make sense in certain societies. According to this view there are no universal standards that can be used to evaluate the norms and values of societies. Cultural judgments are relative. This view alerts us to be cautious in interpreting other cultures and encourages a tolerant attitude and a greater effort toward understanding them. However, cultural relativism also poses a dilemma. Because racism and genocide have been the custom in many societies, are we then to say, "it is just their way of doing things" and "it works for them"? On the other hand, much of the conflict and injustice in the world has been the result of people imposing their ways and their standards on others. The dilemma is between moral impotence—everything is O.K.—and moral imperialism—my way or else.

It seems that we are stuck either with being ethnocentric (using our standards to evaluate others) or with making no evaluation at all. But be aware of the problem of ethnocentrism. Be cautious in judging others and realize that some values and norms that seem morally wrong to you may make sense within a given culture at any given time.

Components of Culture

Culture is usually defined as having three main elements:

1. the material;
2. the cognitive;
3. the normative.

The material, comprised of objects and physical things, includes anything that humans make or use. Archaeologists use the material culture (for example, pottery and tools) as their basic data. The cognitive refers to beliefs and knowledge, while the normative includes norms and values, the rules of the game, and moral order of society.

Sociologists have stressed three culturally-related concepts:

1. values;
2. norms;
3. technology.

Values and norms belong to the normative dimension. Technology includes both knowledge (the cognitive dimension) and physical objects (the material dimension).

Values

Values are the generally accepted standards of desirability of a society or group and, as such, are often synonymous with goals. A value held by all Canadians is good health. We all want to be healthy. We worry about our health, talk about staying in shape, and occasionally do something about it. Health foods, vitamins, gyms, spas, diet books, and sporting goods all attest to our concern with being healthy. If you could devise a way to attain fitness and health without effort, your fortune would be made.

Every society has certain dominant values, and it is the knowledge of these values and their consequences that is the concern of sociologists.

Individuals and groups are likely to hold many values simultaneously, and inevitably some values conflict with others. For example, people may value both pacifism and patriotism—because they are both nonaggressive and loyal to their country. However, if their country goes to war, this will cause a value conflict because they will have to decide whether to fight or to be conscientious objectors. To resolve a value conflict, we must choose one value over another; that is, we must rank our values in order of importance.

Importance of Values. The front page of any newspaper attests to the importance of values. Nine Irish prisoners starve themselves to death to obtain the status of political prisoner; Muslems fight Muslems; Christians fight Buddhists; one Christian denomination opposes another. We encounter nationalism, sexism, racism, and affirmative action. People who suffer or even die for their values, and groups whose values conflict with those of other groups—these are shaping forces in our lives. Commonly shared values help hold society together, as well as set it apart from other societies. Sociologists consider it important to determine what each society values.

Canadian Values. One way to determine Canadian values is to look at those symbols that stand for the nation. Every country has its flag and its national anthem. On February 15, 1965, the maple leaf became our official flag, replacing the Union Jack. In 1967, "O Canada" replaced "God Save the Queen" as our national anthem.

Other important symbols of a country are those documents, such as the Magna Carta, that guarantee the rights of a country's citizens. On April 17, 1982, by an act of the British Parliament, Canada received a new constitution, which included a Charter of Rights and Freedoms. This is in addition to the British North America Act, which was signed into effect July 1, 1867, creating the Dominion of Canada.

Another set of symbols controlled by the federal government is money. Most countries use their coins and paper money to display national symbols, usually people who have historically or are currently important to that country. What is obvious with these national symbols of Canada is their newness. This newness suggests a nation symbolically becoming rather than one that has arrived. The oldest uniquely Canadian national symbols are the Maple Leaf, the Mountie, and the Beaver. It has been suggested that Canada is the only nation in the world that has a policeman as a national symbol. One interpretation of the symbolism of the Beaver is "an allegorical representation of what Her Majesty's Canadian subjects are meant to be: diligent, industrious, tranquil, apolitical. . . well nourished but with few independent thoughts or questions of their own" (Bodemann, 1984).

Other symbols of a nation are represented by its heroes and heroines. A nation's heroes are usually warriors, politician-statesmen, or adventurer-explorers. There is no Canadian concensus on such heroes. The only Canadian hero universally agreed upon is Terry Fox. What is it that makes him a unanimous choice? What does Terry Fox symbolize? A hero is a person of distinguished courage admired for brave deeds. A martyr is one who is put to death or who endures great suffering on behalf of a cause. It is interesting that our only hero is a martyr. Was it necessary for him to be a martyr to be a hero? In one sense, Terry Fox could be seen as representing a set of values of a people who have fought an inhospitable environment: "the great white north." The values of courage, perseverence, effort, and sacrifice against a natural enemy—these may be characteristic Canadian values.

Chief Clifford Big Plume of the Sarcee Indian Band presents Rick Hansen with an eagle feather, traditional tribal symbol of courage. Only time will tell whether Hansen's qualities will establish him alongside Terry Fox as a true national hero.

SOURCE: Canapress Photo Service

Give Us Liberty? No Thanks

*The main themes in this article—self-depreca-
tion, reluctance to take risks, regionalism, linguistic divisions, and government
intervention—are all frequently seen as Canadian characteristics. The implicit contrast to
Americans is also typical of how we go about
defining who we are.*

If Canada had been offered the Statue of Liberty first, by no means would it have been a
sure thing that we would have accepted it.
This is Canada.

The first thing we would ask is: Why? Why
would anyone want to give us a gift like that?

To honour the finest nation in the world?
Come on. Even Canadians don't believe that.
Self-delusion is not one of our faults. Canadians see Canada for exactly what it is, which is,
if I might paraphrase Groucho Marx (an American): We wouldn't want to belong to a club
that would have us as a member.

The second thing we would want to know is :
Is there something wrong with it? If nothing,
then what do they want in return?

Not only do we look gift horses in the mouth,
we also take them to the veterinarian before
taking possession. Put it down to enlightened
self-interest. Canadians do not want the world
to admire them, Canadians want the world to
buy their lumber and wheat.

We are an adept trading nation and see nothing wrong with a mutually profitable deal dis-
guised as good will. If they asked us for, say,
the symbolic gift of 400 million bushels of
wheat in return, we could understand their
motive.

If Canada had been offered the Statue of Liberty first, where would we put it?

The French Canadians would want it in Quebec, overlooking the St. Lawrence River. They
would point out that it had been designed by
Frenchmen and was being offered by the
French government, and therefore had
obviously been built with them in mind. They
would also argue that such a sublime work of

art would be wasted on English Canadians.
They would also demand that Quebec ship-
yards dismantle the statue, then rebuild it,
because they need the work.

The English would be inclined to put it
either in Ottawa, for emmigrating bureaucrats,
or in Toronto, because Toronto fields the biggest number of seats in the House of Commons. If the Torontonians got the statue, they
would put it in the suburbs so as not to
upstage the CN Tower. They would put a restaurant on top of the statue's head.

Vancouver would not get the statue. Vancouver city council would pass a height-restriction
bylaw designed to keep the statue outside city
limits so as not to spoil the view of the
mountains.

A site would eventually be picked by a royal
commission, after hearing submissions from
lobby groups during a six-month cross-country
tour. Commissioners would receive $600-a-day
dinner allowances and, at the end of their fact-
finding trip, would recommend that the statue
be placed in the exact geographic centre of Canada, which is approximately located on King
William Island in the Keewatin section of the
Northwest Territories.

The federal government would give its
approval because the damn thing, which was a
headache all along, would then be out of sight
and thus out of mind. The government could
go on to other business, like raising bail for
cabinet ministers.

If we accepted the statue, the federal government would ask the public to submit appropriate names. It goes without saying that "Statue
of Liberty" would be rejected. Scathing cri-
tiques complaining that the name lacked sub-
tlety would be written by members of the
Canadian intelligentsia from their villas in
Majorca, where, on their government-funded
sabbaticals, they would be writing a history of
the Canadian intelligentsia. Artists in their
group, rejecting outdated symbolism and the
internalized turmoil of neo-expressionism,

would suggest a neo-realist name like "Big Woman Holding A Light."

The name would finally be decided on by the prime minister's wife, which would have been the plan all along. She would call it the "Statue of Peace and Love and Good Things." It would be known popularly as The Big Beaver.

Feminist groups would demand removal of the statue's seven-pointed crown, maintaining that it could be interpreted as a depiction of bondage, the spikes recognizable as instruments of torture. They would also complain that the statue is too statuesque and therefore stereotypical of women.

Finally, Canadians would ask the builders of the statue to make one adjustment. We would ask that the writing on the tablet the statue is holding be in both official languages, just to keep everybody happy.

SOURCE: "Give Us Liberty? No Thanks." by P. McMartin, July 7, 1986, *Vancouver Sun.*

Another way to determine national values is to look at empirical research. A few studies have investigated general Canadian values (Lambert *et al.*, 1979, Blishen and Atkinson, 1980, and Atkinson and Murray, 1980). Lambert studied several different child-rearing values, including "insolence," interpreted here as valuing politeness; "temper control," interpreted as valuing non-aggression towards objects (we do not want children destroying property); and "social temper," interpreted as non-aggression toward people (we do not want children to hit or beat up other people).

According to the study, while all Canadians disapprove of "insolence," English-Canadians treat it more harshly than French-Canadian parents. Put another way, English-Canadian parents demand more politeness than do French-Canadian parents.

Lambert found that Canadians are harsh in their response to potential aggression, whether against things or people. He also found that Canadians are much more strict toward girls than boys when they display aggression. As Lambert states, "Apparently we are dealing here with a broadly shared point of view in Canada. Canadian parents, in general, appear to bring girls up so that they will not be socially aggressive" (Lambert *et al.*, 1979:67). "Apparently Canadian parents feel that to survive in the aggressive world, boys must be given more opportunities than girls to learn to take care of themselves" (Lambert *et al.*, 1979).

The other two studies used a modified version of a common measure of values. The first of these studies was done by Blishen and Atkinson (1980). Over 70 percent of their representative sample of Canadians felt that all but three of the values shown in Table 2-1 are very important or of utmost importance. The three exceptions were: excitement (55 percent), spiritual understanding (47 percent), and prosperity (36 percent). The three top-ranked values were: family security (93 percent), economic stability (88 percent), and love (84 percent). While it is arbitrary at what percentage level it can be said that a value is a value for the

TABLE 2-1. Personal Values

Prosperity	Having plenty of money to afford the better things in life
Excitement	Having a stimulating and active life
Friendship	Having close friends and companions
Independence	Controlling your own life, free from interference from others
Spiritual understanding	Living a life based on religious principles
Achievement	Having a sense of accomplishments, being successful
Love	Having the affection and romantic love of a man or a woman
Economic stability	Having a steady secure income to provide for your basic needs and those of your family
Self-development	Being able to improve your skills and abilities, to keep improving yourself
Helping others	Serving other people who need your help
Family security	Providing love and care for family members

SOURCE: Bernard Blishen and Tom Atkinson, 1980, p. 7.

entire country, it seems reasonable to assume that if 70 percent of a population states that a value is very important or of utmost importance, then it is a national value. Most Canadians rank these values the same, with family security first, economic stability second, and love third. The rank order of the values and the percentage that sees these values as very important or of utmost importance suggest a high degree of consensus on nine of these values and a very high degree of consensus on three of them.

Comparison of Values of Different Societies.   So far, we have discussed studies with a focus on values within Canada. Another approach is to study values by comparing the same set of values in different societies. A great deal of research on Canadian values has been concerned with how our values are different from those of the United States. The following is a list taken from a wide variety of sources—novels, professional journals, and newspapers—describing Canadian values in comparison to American values: Canadians are more elitist (referring to either respect for authority or concern with status), more conservative, traditional, law abiding, and accepting of government intervention, less materialistic, nationalistic, and patriotic, and less inclined to take risks than are Americans. We are also seen as self-denying, having an inferiority complex, and being more concerned with survival, including survival as a nation. Our southern neighbours are perceived as patriotic, high-achieving, self-oriented, materialistic, and risk-taking, a people for whom "winning isn't everything, it is the only thing." Most of the research on values has started with the thesis that while the differences are small, they are theoretically interesting.

Using the same Canadian sample and value set as in the study by Blishen and Atkinson (1980), Atkinson and Murray compared Canadians with a probability sample taken in the United States in 1971. They found that Canadians valued love and marriage more so than Americans, while work had a greater value for Americans than for Canadians. If work is seen as an indicator of achievement, then Americans value achievement more than Canadians. They found no support for the assertion that Americans are more materialistic than Canadians. In general, Canadians ranked these values in the following order of importance: love/marriage, financial situation, leisure, and work. The ranking of importance that Americans gave to these values was: leisure, work, love/marriage, and financial situation. Several other studies have shown that Americans are more religious and more traditional in moral attitudes.

One way a group develops values and an identity is by comparing itself to another group and being seen as different from it. If this is correct, some Canadian values may reflect an attempt to distinguish Canadians from Americans. Out of belief that there are dominant values that characterize Canada, I offer the following set of values for discussion. This list is based on the values of English Canada, although I suspect it holds more or less for French Canada, too.

1. **Effort**, trying, doing your best: winning is not beating the other person, or reaching a goal, it is in doing your very best. To know that you have given your all, it is necessary to overcome great odds. This is why Rick Hansen crossed Canada in his wheelchair in the winter. If he had wanted to maximize achieving his goal, Hansen would have done it in the best weather possible, but that is not the Canadian way. It seems that surviving the worst that nature can throw at us, including our own physical disabilities, is highly valued—and valued more than just beating the other person. This may be why our Canadian soccer team was lauded by the press in the 1986 World Cup playoffs, even though they did not win a game or score a goal. They did their best in a situation where no one expected them to win.

2. **Politeness**, courtesy, or, stated negatively, lack of rudeness or insolence: Canadians are politely curious people and polite

The Survival of Canadian Culture

The most studied society is that of the United States. Canadians must decide how much of that research is applicable to Canada. There is an ongoing debate about whether Canada has its own culture or is merely a branch of American society. Barbara Amiel, a contributing editor for Maclean's *magazine in Canada, is one voice against the existence of a distinctive Canadian culture.*

Fears about the Americanization of Canadian culture always resurface when issues like free trade heat up. But that particular fear seems a non sequitur since Canada and America share the same culture, and so the question of domination seems beside the point—except in an economic sense. The warning cries about selling our culture to the Americans reflect only the interests of a small but vociferous lobby of Canadian businessmen and intellectuals who want to protect themselves from American competition. Their fears have little to do with the intrinsic nature of Canadian culture. Even in the face of a free trade agreement, most of Canada's public and private cultural entities would remain; the CBC would continue and so would the Canadian Opera Company and the National Ballet. Cultural businessmen may feel the bite in some areas, inefficient Canadian publishers may go under, but the good ones will survive as, more importantly, will Margaret Atwood, Robertson Davies, Alice Munro, and the successors.

In fact, the concept of an exclusive Canadian culture or indeed a distinct Canadian identity under threat from America is a fabrication. The roots of it can be traced to the battle of Pierre Trudeau against Québec, when it was thought necessary to postulate a synthetic Canadian identity to counter the very genuine cultural nationalism of the French Canadians. In truth, there is very little to distinguish Anglo-Canadians from Americans. We are about as different from them as the people of Montana are from New Yorkers or Albertans from Ontarians. Canadians and Americans share a virtually indistinguishable language, system of values, ethnic composition of founding and immigrant groups (with the exception of a sizable black community in Canada), lifestyle, cultural assumptions, and expectations. This common North American identity left those wishing to establish Canadian nationalism in a bit of a quandary. It became necessary to invent a "Real Canadian identity," different from the Coca-Cola and Hollywood culture to the south.

The result was predictable. Canadian nationalism, being mainly political, artificial, and synthetic, could express itself only in negatives—the rejection of what it regarded as American values. This is where the economic goals of the nationalists to protect their businesses from American competition happily coincided with their political left-liberalism. To be anti-American was to be against the great American values of individual liberty, limited government, and a system based on the economic concept of free enterprise. Canadian nationalism, with Trudeau's Liberals behind it, turned a cold cheek to those values, and a left-liberal philosophy developed in this country that has become the standard approach to cultural and social policy questions by all political parties.

Little of this was apparent to ordinary Canadians, however. They were blissfully unaware of the political thrust of Canadian nationalism. Occasionally, they may have complained when an American TV channel was moved off the dial, but otherwise life seemed pretty much unchanged and, anyway, what could be wrong with a decent dose of patriotism? Meanwhile, the nationalists saw their policies institutionalized in the enormous bureaucracies that sprang up to regulate Canadian content in almost every area of human endeavor.

Ironically, the nationalists failed in the one area that they claim was their real target—the battle against American culture. In spite of all the grants, the incentives and the regulations, Canadians continued to prefer *Dallas* to *The Beachcombers*.

Which seems to me to pose little threat to the political entity we all love and know as Canada.

SOURCE: "The Survival of Canadian Culture" by Barbara Amiel, April 20, 1987, *Maclean's*, p. 9.

neighbours. Even our protests are usually polite. On those occasions when our protests are not polite or when they are expressive, they usually make front page news. Lambert's study, referred to earlier, suggests that Canadian parents do not put up with insolence or aggression. Politeness is a virtue.

3. **Financial security:** financial security has been seen by Blishen and Atkinson (1980) to be highly valued by Canadians. To strive for security means you will not likely take great risk. Many people have pointed to the high savings rate of Canadians and to the fact they tend to take out much insurance and invest in bonds and safe stocks, as opposed to playing the stock market and thereby risking their capital.

4. **Insecurity:** Canadians seem hesitant to take pride in Canadian people and institutions. We seem very reluctant to recognize our own writers, painters, dancers, musicians, academics, industrialists, and statesmen. A reasonable argument could be put forth that insecurity is an enduring legacy of colonialism.

   We seem to doubt our ability to be the best, the very best. This value, plus the value of financial security, probably explains Canada's reluctance to take risk, to remain hewers of wood and drawers of water. Are we willing to buy back our economy, to insist on manufacturing our natural resources? Do we risk our secure position and end up, as one student suggested, like Mexico? To take risks requires a belief that we will succeed. We just may not have that belief, yet.

5. **Conformism:** Canadians play by the rules. Like many sociologists, especially the functionalists, Canadians believe that most people most of the time will behave as they should. Large percentages of Canadians vote because good citizens should. We obey the law. If we are arrested, we are not "read our rights," because our system assumes either that we are guilty or that we will be released. The invoking of the War Measures Act in October, 1970, which denied Canadians many civil rights, did not result in an outburst of anger because we believed the police would not abuse their power, but would behave correctly. If the Mountie is a symbol of Canada to Canadians, he is not a symbol of authority but rather of the law—a basic set of rules we try to follow. Canadians are not tolerant of law-breakers or those who violate clear community norms.

6. **Pragmatism:** Canadians judge acts in a practical way, as opposed to an ideological or moralistic way. Because we have no national myths, no single abiding faith in a national destiny, there is no "Canadian way" in the sense that there is a

British, French, or American way. Our abiding principle is, "If it works and is beneficial, do it." It makes no difference whether the government, which reduces tax benefits to the rich, nationalizes the ferries, and increases or decreases government corporations, is Conservative, Liberal, or NDP. There is no logical contradiction in the terms red-tory or conservative-liberal. This is not to deny that there are political party differences in policies or promises, only that no one is really surprised by what is actually done, since policy is probably changed for practical reasons and accepted as such. Because there is no one "right way," compromise is more easily achieved in Canada than in most other countries.

Beliefs are an important part of culture. In some fundamentalist religious groups, children and adults alike dress in sombre clothing that de-emphasizes individualism and worldly concerns. These people believe that they should be more concerned with spiritual reality than with outward appearance.

SOURCE: Victor Rolan/Miller Services

Norms

In Thailand, it is a grave insult to point your food at someone's head. In Arab countries, a guest at a banquet should refuse the offered dishes several times before he accepts them. Fortunately, the host repeatedly urges acceptance. In Canada, to repeatedly offer a dish may seem pushy and, consequently, an Arab at a Canadian table is likely to go home very hungry. Latin Americans stand significantly closer together when conversing than do Canadians. Arriving 30 minutes late is quite normal in some countries, but to a Canadian businessman to whom time is money, such behaviour requires an explanation.

People around the world are characterized by such differences, although similarities are also common. Europeans and Canadians, for example, are mostly monogamous—that is, are married to only one person at a time. Differences and similarities among and within groups are a major concern of sociologists. Norm, like value, is a major concept used to describe and explain these differences and similarities.

Norms are standards of conduct, rules for behaviour. Norms tell us how we should and should not behave. In a general way, norms are usually derived from values. We value honesty; therefore we should not lie, cheat, or steal. We may value marriage, but norms tell us how we should behave as a husband or wife. In this sense, norms act as blueprints for behaviour. We learn norms that tell us how to be a good citizen, a good person, a polite person. Like values, many of these norms are internalized, and in conforming to norms, behaviour becomes patterned. To illustrate, in every society only certain of its members are possible marriage partners. How you obtain a spouse is determined by the norms of your society. It may be by capture, by mutual consent of the individuals involved, by parental arrangement, or by purchase. In any given society, only one or a specified combination of these ways will be appropriate. Once norms have developed, they become not just one way of doing things but the right way and the only way.

Once the norms of behaviour have emerged, they exert pressure on people to conform. In Durkheim's terms, they are social facts. According to this view, most people behave as they should most of the time. Consequently, it is the sharing of these social norms that accounts both for patterns and uniformity within a society and for the differences between societies.

To see how norms work, we can look at what societies define as food. Lice, lizards, ants, grubs, worms, and dogs have each been defined as good to eat by different groups. To the Inuit, seal eyes, the entrails of whales, and seal blood are considered delicacies; mushrooms, however, are feared. While the need to eat is biological, what we eat (like who we can marry, what or whom we worship, or whether we have one God or many) is not. These are norms that are learned, and they vary from society to society and within society over time.

Importance of Norms.   Without rules and standards—that is, social norms—order and predictability would break down. We simply would not know how to behave, and each situation would have to be worked out separately. For example, in the classroom, we would not know whether to sit quietly, talk incessantly, hold a seance, smoke, or just stretch out and go to sleep. Norms define appropriate and inappropriate behaviour and, by doing so, hold society and its social relations together.

Besides giving order to social relations, norms are considered important for the following reasons. The sharing of norms is a source of social cohesion, serving as one basis of assuring the conformity without which society could not exist. Norms also serve as a basis for evaluating others, as well as ourselves. For example, most of us believe that mate swapping is morally wrong and disapprove of married men and women having extramarital affairs. Consequently, when others behave in violation of these norms, we say they are not "good" wives, husbands, or mothers. Similarly, if we believe in these norms but violate them ourselves, we are likely to judge ourselves harshly.

We have been taught that there are some things we should never do and some things we should always do. Many norms are internalized; that is, they have become so much a part of us that we evaluate ourselves in terms of our conformity to them. These internalized norms can become a source of guilt; for example, during the school year you will likely have a vacation. You will plan to do a great deal of studying and catching up, or to write that term paper, or prepare for that exam. So you will take your books and notes with you but you will not look at them nearly as often as you had planned. And you will feel guilty. Some norms, however, become so internalized that we simply could not violate them. How many of you would eat human flesh to stay alive? If our country was attacked, how many would refuse to fight? How many of you could sit in a classroom naked?

Another reason why norms are important is that they reduce conflict among those sharing the same norm. The gradual acceptance of the idea that people should be free from the need to breathe in other people's cigarette smoke limits confrontations between many individual smokers and non-smokers.

A final reason why norms are important is that they define what is "deviant" behaviour. Individuals are deviant if they violate the laws, customs, etiquette, or manners (that is, the norms)

No Smoking on the Job

The order was one of the most extreme actions in a growing North American clampdown on smoking. Last week officials of a Chicago-based building products manufacturer announced that they may fire any employees at their nine U.S. plants who refuse to stop smoking—on or off the job. But USG Acoustical Products Co.'s plan to extend a smoking ban into the personal lives of 1300 employees provoked angry responses from workers, civil liberties spokesmen, and tobacco industry representatives. Declared William Matten, a shipper—and nonsmoker—at a USG Minnesota plant: "What's next? You can't drink at home? That's the feeling some people have." Added Scott Stapf, a spokesman for the Tobacco Institute, a Washington-based lobby group: "This would easily be the most punitive or asinine proposal we have seen. Obviously there is just an incredible invasion of privacy."

USG's edict was one of the latest in a series of restrictive actions against smokers across the continent. In Calgary officials at Petro-Canada's head office announced last week that smoking was no longer permitted in public areas in any of the company's offices and plants. In addition, public school board officials in that city said they would ban smoking by all staff and students at its 215 schools by 1988. Similarly, Ontario's ministry of health has announced that, as of March 2, cigarette smokers among the ministry's 12 000 employees will have to light up in specially designated areas. And 2.3 million U.S. civil servants face similar restrictions: early next month smokers in 7500 federal buildings will have to indulge their habit in clearly posted locations.

Some U.S. lawyers said that USG's proposal constituted an invasion of privacy. But most acknowledge that federal and state laws provide U.S. companies with sweeping powers to set conditions of employment. Declared Donald Cohen, the co-chairman of the American Bar Association's committee on employee rights in the workplace: "As immoral as this appears, it is not illegal. Unless you can prove that an employer has violated a statute, you are out." Added Jay Miller, executive director of the American Civil Liberties Union in Chicago: "We think it is outrageous but we are somewhat helpless. We could try to get a law passed, but frankly I am not optimistic."

Still, the growing body of evidence of tobacco's harmful effects practically guarantees more prohibitions against smoking. In one important development, the 1986 report of the U.S. Surgeon General states that secondhand smoke—the inhalation of cigarette smoke by nonsmokers—can cause cancer and other diseases. As a result of such findings the smokers among USG's plant employees have become reluctant conscripts in the widening war against tobacco.

SOURCE: "No smoking on the job" by Michael Salter, February 2, 1987, *Maclean's*, p. 71.

of their society. Whether a man who kills is considered a criminal or not depends on whether or not there is a law against such behaviour and on how the law is defined.

Classification of Norms.   Given the importance of norms to the field of sociology, it is not surprising that there have been many attempts at their classification. One early attempt is important because its terminology has become part of most people's vocabularies and because it points to some important elements in the study of norms. In his book Folkways (Sumner,

1906), William Graham Sumner made a basic distinction among three types of norms: **Folkways** are informal customs or etiquette that do not have harsh sanctions associated with their violation. If you dress oddly or use the wrong spoon, there may be disapproval, but you are not likely to be severely punished. **Mores** (pronounced mor-aze) are customs that a society considers to be right, obligatory, and even necessary for group survival. As such, they often form the basis of laws. The transgression of mores—which would include such violations as rape, incest, murder, and child molesting—is, therefore, harshly sanctioned. For Sumner, it was the severity of the sanction and the related importance of the norm to the group that formed his classification of folkways and mores. **Laws,** however, were classified as "enacted"—that is, formally made by legislative bodies, for specific purposes, to regulate specific forms of behaviour, with punishment clearly stated and carried out by the state. Because of these characteristics, while most mores are governed by laws, laws can be enacted without support from mores or folkways, resulting in regulations to which there is little feeling attached. Many of the laws governing the operation of automobiles are of this nature, and we obey the law largely only if we think we are going to get caught. There is little feeling of wrong-doing or guilt attached to speeding.

Changing Values and Norms.   It is very difficult to determine the extent of change in values and norms. There is a great deal of discussion about the sexual revolution, changing sex roles, more liberal attitudes toward drugs, changes in the family, and the meaning of work. However, the evidence for Canada shows surprising continuity between generations. In a recent study of a representative sample of Canadian teenagers, ages 15 to 19, it was found that they saw the following values as "very important": being loved (87 percent), honesty (85 percent), success (78 percent), a comfortable life (75 percent), working hard (69 percent), and family life (65 percent). In terms of norms regarding moral issues—that is, how we should behave—80 percent of teens and 74 percent of adults agree that sex before marriage is all right when people love each other; 86 percent of both teens and adults agree that it should be possible to obtain a legal abortion when a female has been raped; only 12 percent of the teens and 21 percent of the adults agree that it is sometimes all right for a married person to have sexual relations with someone other than their marriage partner; and 28 percent of both the teens and the adults agree that the use of marijuana should be legalized. Thirty-nine percent of the teens and 43 percent of the adults see themselves as religiously committed. From this study it appears that those values and norms held by adults are also held by a majority of young people. In short, there is little evidence of a revolution in values and norms (Bibby and Posterski, 1985).

Nevertheless, there is evidence of some changes. In the areas of bilingualism, French-English relations, and attitudes towards racial and ethnic groups, teens are more tolerant than adults (Bibby and Posterski, 1985). The fact that 30 percent of the teens admit to using drugs while 46 percent see drug use as a serious problem raises questions about the relationship between values and norms and their utility.

The interrelationship of norms and values and their utility can be illustrated by examining these in relation to behaviour, subcultures, and countercultures. The last two can be understood only in terms of norms and values.

Norms, Values and Behaviour. The relationship of norms and values to behaviour can be seen by looking at marriage as a value and divorce rates as behaviour. Most Canadians say a good marriage is extremely important and most expect to get married. Yet roughly 38 percent of first marriages end in divorce. The situation is this: most want to marry and will, and expect to stay married to the same person, but one in three won't. This clearly suggests that many people do not behave consistently with their values.

Subcultures. A **subculture** is a group that is part of the overall culture but has its own distinctive norms, values, and lifestyle. Ethnic minorities concentrated in a specific location, such as a Chinatown or a little Italy, are examples. While greatly affected by the dominant culture, they maintain some of their language and old customs and, fortunately, their styles of cooking. Some subcultures that have been studied by sociologists include the adolescent culture, lower class, mental hospitals, various occupational groups, and ethnic and deviant subcultures.

Countercultures. A **counterculture** is a subculture that is opposed to certain norms, values, or lifestyles of the larger culture. Revolutionary groups, the hippie movement, with its rejection of the work ethic and success-striving, and delinquent gangs are examples of countercultures.

Technology

I was raised in a world without refrigerators, microwave ovens, electric typewriters, word processors, calculators, personal computers, hi fi, video cassettes, high-speed computers, transistors, microchips, satellites, atomic energy, nuclear energy, lasers, particle beams, robots, radar, hydrofoils, jet aircraft, electric trains, space travel, penicillin, organ transplants, Salk vaccine, the pill, genetic engineering, or wash-and-wear clothes. There were no "silicone valleys," no aerospace or computer industries. These are only some of the technological changes that have occurred recently. Some of them are so recent that they weren't even part of your own world as young children. And the rate of change is increasing dramatically. According to Corwin, "It is estimated that one-half of the jobs now available to high school graduates were not in existence when they were in the sixth grade, and they will not be in existence in ten years" (Corwin, 1965:124). For example, eventual automation of computer programming could mean that computer programming may be a one-generation career.

Technology is the application of tools, machines, and knowledge to the material resources of the environment. Historically the process has been from muscle power, to animal power, to machines. Put another way, we walked, then rode, and now fly. Technological change has brought about the agricultural revolution, the industrial revolution, and, some claim, the post-industrial society and the "information age."

Importance of Technology.   The importance of technology can be seen in its consequences for society. The article on the introduction of a steel ax into a society that used stone axes illustrates the dramatic changes produced in a social system by the introduction of a single piece of technology. Ogburn listed 150 social effects of the automobile (1933, pp. 153-156). In a similar vein, Cottrell traced the history of a town that had grown and prospered because of the steam engine only to "die" when steam was replaced by diesel engines (Cottrell, 1951, pp. 358-365).

The importance of technology is seen in many aspects of our society: transportation, sports, industry, work, agriculture medicine, communication. When people talk about "rapid change," they are usually referring to technological charge. To gain some understanding of the consequences of technological change, we will look at mass communication.

Mass Communication.   Communication networks—telephone, telegraph, teletype, radio, TV, computer communication, satellites, fibre optics, microwave, radio relay systems, home computers, and word processors—are central to the modern state.

Because of revolutionary changes in communication technology, a middle-class home may soon have a video-phone that can

The Steel Ax Among the Yir Yoront

This excerpt demonstrates how technological inventions—in this case a steel ax—can have dramatic effects on social structure.

Even the introduction of less sophisticated technology—such as, for example, the steel ax—can create far-reaching and unforeseen effects in other aspects of the social system. Consider the example of the Yir Yoront tribe of southeastern Australia, who depended on the stone ax as their most basic and essential tool for many centuries (Sharp, 1952). For them the ax was more than a tool; it was a symbol of status, of male dominance, and of basic rights of ownership. It played a role in religious ceremonies and was considered as one of the tribe's most valued objects. When a person needed an ax, he would approach one of the leaders to ask permission to use it. Only if the leader considered him worthy would permission be granted. Therefore, the very scarcity of the valuable tool made access to it a considerable privilege and . . . a means of social control.

Then came the white man, bringing modern technology in the form of steel axes. But instead of progress, the introduction of the steel ax resulted in a drastic upheaval of the social structure of the tribe. It had the following effects:

1. In order to get a steel ax, it was necessary to go to the mission or to a trader and act "deserving, industrious, and dependent." That resulted in a decrease in self-reliance.

2. The ax has been considered as a status symbol and as a sign of manhood, but the white man at times gave axes directly to young men and children, resulting in the upset of status relations between the young and the old.

3. Similarly, in the past no woman could own an ax. Europeans often gave axes to women to use as their own, thereby upsetting the status relations between males and females.

4. Prior to the introduction of the ax, there was no overall leader or chief of the tribe. However, when dealing with the whites, it was necessary to appoint one or two spokesmen, who gradually acquired more power than they were entitled to traditionally, creating a leader group form of organization in the tribe.

5. Easy access to axes diluted the entire notion of ownership and upset the norms of ownership, thus resulting in an increase in the incidence of stealing and trespassing.

6. Members of the tribe explained the origins of every major artifact they possessed with some myth showing how the article was given to them by a distant mythical ancestor. Since they had very few artifacts and the technology was virtually stagnant, it was quite easy to believe in these stories. However, there was no mythical explanation for the origins of steel axes; the source was obvious. The result was to cast suspicion on the other myths and on the old structure of the religion.

SOURCE: *Social Change* by Steven Vago, 1982. Toronto: Holt, Rinehart and Winston.

be used for conference calls, a computer, an electronic mail terminal, two-way cablevision, and a video recorder and player. The British post office has set up one telephone network in Scotland that permits people to dial a number to have railroad timetables displayed on their TV screens. The network can also be used to send messages from the TV of one subscriber to the TV of another. In the United States, experiments are being made with news delivery on computers and with a computer version of a citizen-band radio. In some of these systems it will be possible for customers to place orders at stores via computer using credit cards.

Let us focus here on the mass media with particular reference to television. The **mass media** include newspapers, books, magazines, radio, cinema, and television. Before the invention of the printing press and the production of inexpensive paper, a book manuscript took half a year to copy onto quality parchment. The invention of the rotary press and newsprint gave us the penny newspaper and cheap books. Today, a typical middle-class home has a telephone, radio, stereo, tape deck, and television. Canada is a mass communication society.

Unlike face-to-face communication, mass communication is typically a one-way process, with the audience reading, listening and watching. You may occasionally swear at a news writer's views or at your TV set—but it is still a one-way communication. One very important fact about the mass media is that they have the capacity to present the same images and viewpoints to millions of individuals simultaneously. Never have so many people listened, read, and watched the same things at the same time. We read the same news and the same comics, see the same movies, and watch the same television programs. These media constantly create images that become shared symbols of their times, such as the Fonz, Rambo, Snoopy, Watergate, and Tunagate. To the degree that the mass media present common values, attitudes, and symbols, they not only entertain and inform, but also produce or create culture. The term **mass culture** refers to cultural elements, symbols, knowledge, beliefs, values, attitudes, and norms transmitted by the mass media and, therefore, generally shared in standardized form by very large numbers of people. **Mass medium** is the technology; **mass culture** is the content.

We can expect the mass media to affect us in the following general ways:

1. To inform us about social roles, sex roles, family roles, and political roles;
2. To present certain values and to selectively show some as good and some as bad;
3. To foster identification with role models such as Superman and She-ra;
4. To give an order of importance to world events.

By selectively presenting to its audience a particular view of the world, the media establish a sense of what is important and not important. By presenting a limited and recurring range of images and ideas (for example, sex roles and racial stereotypes), the media not only influences the way we order our world but also may create part of our world for us. It is very likely that to the extent we are presented with a consistent picture attended to by a large audience, the mass media will be effective in establishing or maintaining cultural values and norms.

Television has become the most pervasive medium. In 1936 there were four TV broadcasting stations in the United States; by 1976 there were 764 (Kando, 1980, p. 242). In 1976 approximately 7 billion dollars were spent on television advertising (Kando, 1980, p. 254). The three largest networks had an income (profit) of 406 million dollars. These data are relevant because 71 percent of the viewing time of English-Canadians is spent watching foreign, mostly American, programs. For French-language viewers, it is 65 percent of their viewing time. Further, 60 percent of the time, we watch English-Canadian stations for foreign programs.

In 1974 Canadians watched television an average of 3 hours and 36 minutes a day, Monday through Friday. The average for children 2 to 11 was 3 hours, for teens 3 hours and 12 minutes, women 18 and over, 4 hours and 24 minutes, and men 18 and over, 3 hours and 24 minutes (Canadian Radio-Television and Telecommunications Committee, 1977, p. 14).

Evidence suggests that people watch TV as much as they used to but are enjoying it less. In 1974, 46 percent of a sample of the population said it was their favourite leisure time activity; in 1977 only 30 percent affirmed this, even though the time spent watching TV remained roughly the same (Social Indicators III, 1980, pp. 558-561).

The pervasiveness of television in our lives has also affected the other mass media. Williams and Boyes state that "children who watched more television reported reading fewer books and listened less to the radio and records, but did more comic reading" (Williams and Boyes, 1986, p. 241). A similar effect on mass magazines has been that the general all-purpose magazines such as *Look* and *Life* have all but disappeared. This decline in sales is the result of lack of sponsors because TV advertising is cheaper in terms of the number of people reached.

Television has also had a great impact on radio. Gone are the adventure, detective, and mystery plays, the soap operas, the comedy, and the variety shows. In the 1930s, radio was the home entertainment centre that TV has become today, and many of those earlier radio programs are now on TV. Radio has become primarily a source of music and news.

Given the wide use of television, it is useful to look at some of its special qualities. The Singers (1981, pp. 8-12) list the following as special qualities of television:

1. *Attention demand.* "It is almost impossible to ignore a TV set if you are in the same room even if the sound is turned off and only the picture is visible" (p. 8).

2. *Brief sequences.* "Commercial television in this country has involved a style of extremely brief sequences of events." (p. 8). "There are reasons to believe that rapidity of sequences can have an arousing quality and may produce hyperactivity in the young child" (p. 9).

3. *Visual orientation.* "It is possible that the ease of viewing is enhancing a strong preference for or reliance on global visual representations that makes children and later young adults more impatient with the effort required to process purely auditory verbal material . . . or to deal with reading materials" (p. 11). Related to this is the danger that the electronic media and other pictorial devices will result in less reading of anything. Also, several studies suggest that television may slow down the acquisition of reading skills.

4. *Emphasis on action and violence.* "By its very format American television presents a set of models for vigorous motion that can spill over even in play toward direct aggression" (p. 11).

The Singers, along with other researchers, have also found that television contains excessive materialism, commercialism, and racial stereotypes, and has failed to develop extensive children's programming that emphasizes sharing, cooperation, and altruism. The special characteristics of television and its content, plus the amount of time spent watching TV, make it a very important and pervasive form of the mass media.

One media development that is expected to have important sociological implications is public-access TV and community TV. With public-access channels you can broadcast live discussions via television; for example, viewers can phone in and participate in town meetings or civil council meetings. Another example is access channels programmed by and for children. In community television, groups work together to produce and distribute films and tapes on local public issues, for example, a documentary on the pollution of a river shown on television to instigate court action or to facilitate audience involvement in local issues. Some universities offer courses to train community organizations in the use of video as a tool for community development.

Several effects of the mass media and particularly television have been researched and discussed by many social scientists.

Some of the more noteworthy consequences that show the importance television has on us include the following:

1. *Politics and Mass Media.* Some of the effects of the mass media in the area of politics seem to be a decline in the importance of the face-to-face political campaign, more attention paid to the personality of the leader, an opposition between parties that stresses image rather than beliefs and ideological differences, a greater emphasis upon opinion polls, and a recognition by politicians that the mass media is extremely important to their visibility. It is also suggested that the merger of politics with the mass media has resulted in the reduction of politics to marketable entertainment. Political candidates are treated as a commodity to sell, like detergent, automobiles, or beverages. Politics has become show business.

2. *Violence and TV.* After reviewing 67 studies done between 1956 and 1976 on TV violence and viewer aggression, Andison (1977, p. 323) concluded that there is "at least a weak positive relationship between watching violence on television and subsequent aggression displayed by viewers of the violence." More recent evidence supports this conclusion. The Singers (1981) state, "our results confirm the link between viewing action shows, aggressive cartoons, and overt aggressive behaviour." This evidence rules out the widespread belief that watching aggressive programs is simply a consequence of an aggressive tendency in the child (Singer, 1981, p. 131). Another study, which included interviewing children and parents in one town before they had television and then interviewing them after television was introduced, found that "children displayed more aggression two years after the introduction of television" and that "boys and girls, children initially high and low on aggression, and those watching more or less TV were equally likely to show increased aggressive behaviour" (Joy *et al.*, 1986, p. 339).

    Another consequence of watching frequent aggression on television and in movies seems to be that aggression may become a more acceptable way of resolving problems.

3. *View of the World.* The Singers (1981, p. 152) suggest that a major consequence of television viewing is the creation of a "common consciousness" and that television viewing is related to the viewers' conception of reality. That is, those who watch the most TV are more likely to give television-based responses to questions about conceptions of social reality. A general theme in the research on mass media and particularly television is that our view of the world is

increasingly "mediated," (that is, comes from the mass media) and that more people now receive a similar version of the world than ever before. This has raised three general questions: what view of the world is presented by television? (That is, what is the content of television?) Who controls television and other mass media? And what are the consequences of such control?

We have seen that many researchers have been concerned with one aspect of television content: namely, violence. Another consequence of the content of action-adventure programs and the news is the presentation of a terrifying view of the world, which results in moderate-minded viewers grossly over-estimating the dangers in their lives. As stated by Gerbner (1979, p. 196), "the most significant and recurring conclusion of our long-range study is that one correlation of television viewing is a heightened and *unequal* sense of danger and risk in a mean and selfish world." A similar and interesting conclusion was reached in a study of the viewing of United States TV programs by Australians. It was found that despite actual differences in the amount of violence and crime in Australia and the United States, Australian children who watched U.S. programs see the two countries as about the same in this regard. The study concluded that "cultivation of beliefs about the world, at least in this case about violence and crime, does occur even when the messages are imported from another country" (Pingree, 1981, p. 104). Given the wide distribution of American films and television in other countries, this finding, if it proves to be true in general, has serious implications.

4. *Social Control.* If our world view is affected by the mass media, the content that is selected for television becomes important. It is clear that what we see on TV news programs represents somebody's viewpoint; if that is the only "news" we get, it is most likely to become our viewpoint as well. Moreover, the vast majority of cities are dominated by single-media operations. This is also true for the other mass media. From the huge quantity of information available, people in the mass media must select those items that they will present to the public. Whatever they select represents their own point of view.

Some may intentionally "slant" the news, but even those with the most noble motives cannot avoid selecting and presenting what we read, hear, and see, and they therefore have a great impact on what we accept as "fact." A good deal of what we know beyond first-hand experience is based on what we see on TV. Therefore, it is important to be aware of the media processes by which our "facts" are created for us. Many studies suggest that the mass media are more effective in creating new attitudes than in changing old ones.

A basic concern we are now faced with is that big corporations—unfamiliar and little interested with public communications—have become involved in the mass media. The media may suffer if they are controlled by people whose main concern is the business of making a profit rather than communicating information. The problem is stated by Johnson (1970):

> In general, I would urge the minimal standard that no accumulation of media should be permitted without a specific and convincing showing of a continuing countervailing social benefit. For no one has a higher calling in an increasingly complex free society bent on self-government than he who informs and moves the people. Personal prejudice, ignorance, social pressure, and advertiser pressure are in large measure inevitable. But a nation that depends upon the rational dialogue of an informed electorate simply cannot take any unnecessary risk of polluting the stream of information and opinion that sustains it. At the very least, the burden of proving the social utility of doing otherwise should be upon him who seeks the power and profit which will result.

It should be remembered that the average Canadian does have a vast array of media available from which to select and that "we can turn the set off." However this does not change the fact of biased reporting: editors select what is "newsworthy" and in this sense are our "gate keepers."

Sociological Perspectives on Culture

Conflict Perspective.   Conflict theorists view the normative order, ideas, and symbols as dependent variables. This perspective sees culture as constantly in a state of flux or change.

For the Marxist, the stress is on the means of production or other types of economic variables as they affect the norms and values of a culture. From a Marxist point of view, norms and values represent the interests of the dominant group and are used to retain its power. The mass media, in this view, are powerful weapons for holding the masses in voluntary submission.

Other types of conflict theorists see culture in a similar vein; that is, its norms and values are viewed in the context of powerful groups trying to impose their values and norms by persuasion or force on the least powerful. Since control over technology affects the distribution of wealth, knowledge, and values, this variable is frequently used by conflict theorists as an independent variable.

Structural-Functional Perspective. The sharing of norms and values is an essential element in the structural-functionalist viewpoint. They are the glue that holds society together. We are born into a world with norms and values "out there." Through the process of socialization, we are systematically taught these values; they become part of us and become the only way to believe and behave. In this way, social order is possible because norms and values are shared. Because they are seen as "out there," existing before us and remaining after we are gone, they are seen as external and, therefore, structural variables. According to this view, norms and values are also compatible or integrated with each other and are functional for society, in that they have positive consequences for society. The norms and values are also seen as relatively stable, with any change coming largely from outside. For example, one culture may introduce something new into another culture, which effects changes in the values and norms of that society.

For many structural functionalists, social order is possible because people have culture, a set of common values and norms. Values function to legitimize the institutions of society, and the norms derived from these values function to integrate society. As stated by Parsons, "That a system of value-orientations held in common by the members of a social system can serve as the main point of reference for analysing structure and process in the social system itself may be regarded as a major tenet of modern sociological theory" (Parsons, 1960). In this perspective, values are the independent variable, and social structure is the dependent variable.

Symbolic-Interactionist Perspective. In this view, the meanings of events are flexible and dynamic and arise out of an interpretive process. People are not passive animals who just accept the values and norms "out there." They can influence culture, as well as be influenced by it. They can change cultural meaning by creative actions.

Crucial topics in the study of culture for symbolic interactionists are the study of culture and subculture as systems of meanings that shape the individual's world and the study of individual definitions of the situation that produce unique responses to that situation.

While we learn many meanings that are common to the group, we also remain flexible and capable of developing and communicating new meanings when the established ones are outmoded or inappropriate. We use existing meanings to interpret events and we use events to evaluate those meanings. If on meeting you for the first time I put out my hand and you shake it, we are sharing the same meanings or definitions of the situation. If, however, I put out my hand and you step on my foot, I must evaluate this event. I was taught to open doors for women, but these days I find that some women reject this behaviour, defining it as "chauvinistic," and consequently I must "negotiate" this interaction.

One of the more interesting developments in the study of culture using a symbolic-interactionist approach is the study of popular culture. A generally acceptable definition of popular culture is elusive. "It consists largely of everyday activities, habits, beliefs, and tastes often shared by *many* people but occasionally by a small, fringe subculture" (Kando, 1980, p. 41).

Popular culture studies tend to focus on norms and values involving the telephone, TV dinners, roadside restaurants, coffee breaks, and other elements in everyday life, as well as an examination of subcultures (Truzzi, 1968). An example is the subculture of those who use and work in hotels (Prus and Irini, 1980). The symbolic interactionist studies of popular culture attempt to discover the subjective meanings that a given element (for example, the telephone) or a particular popular subculture has, for the people who engage in it.

Summary

1. Culture is everything we think believe, feel, and do as members of society. Culture is learned, transmitted symbolically, and shared by members of society. Culture is normative; that is, we are systematically taught how we ought to feel and behave.

2. There are a number of general cultural universals but no specific practices found in all societies. Cultures are diverse. This means they vary widely in terms of values, beliefs, norms, and behaviour.

3. There is a strong tendency for people to be ethnocentric, judging other cultures in terms of their own. It is important that social scientists adopt a stance of cultural relativism, in order to try to understand other cultures in their own terms.

4. Values are what society considers to be desirable, including the goals we should pursue. Subcultures and countercultures are distinguished from the main culture primarily by the values they hold.

5. Norms are standards of conduct; how we should and should not behave. Norms are basic to the patterns of behaviour we find in society. They enable us to get through the day without having to see our daily life as a set of unique problems to be solved. Folkways, mores, and laws are three types of norms.

6. The relationship among values and norms and behaviour is complex. Sometimes we behave consistently with our values and norms and sometimes we do not.

7. The third component of culture stressed by sociologists is technology—the application of tools, machines, and knowledge to the material resources of the environment. The importance of technology is seen in its impact on occupations and the effects of the mass media on society, especially television.

8. Conflict theorists see culture as constantly in flux due to unstable power relationships. Structural functionalists see shared norms and values as the glue that holds society together. Symbolic interactionists theorize that individual action can change culture as well as be influenced by it.

Further Reading

Bibby, R. W., & Posterski, D. C. (1985). *The emerging generation.* Toronto: Irwin.
  A readable account of an extensive survey of attitudes, values, and beliefs of Canadian teens.

Brake, M. (1985). *Comparative youth culture.* London: Routledge and Kegan Paul.
  Treats youth subcultures in England, Canada, and the United States.

Keesing, R. (1981). *Cultural anthropology: A contemporary perspective.* (2nd ed.) New York: Holt, Rinehart and Winston.
  An excellent source for an understanding of culture by an anthropologist. See especially Part II, pp. 65-100.

Lambert, W. E., Hamers, J. F., & Frasure-Smith, N. (1979). *Child-rearing values.* New York: Praeger.
  A very interesting study comparing child-rearing values within and between countries. Among other concerns, it compares native groups with comparable immigrant Canadian groups—for example, Portuguese in Portugal with Canadian Portuguese.

Ogburn, W. F., & Nimkoff, M. F. (1955). *Technology and the family.* Cambridge, MA: Houghton Mifflin.
  Chapters 12 and 13 contain a good discussion of the possible

future effects of invention and scientific discoveries on the family.

Williams, T. M. (Ed.). (1986). *The impact of television.* New York: Academic Press.

An extensive longitudinal study of the impact of television on three towns in B.C..

3
Socialization

The purpose of this chapter is to ask how we, the animal we call *homo sapiens*, become human. If to be human is to have culture, how do we get it? Socialization is a lifelong learning process. We are continually "becoming" human. This chapter examines some of the theories that describe this lifelong process.

When you have completed this chapter, be sure you are able to

1. distinguish among the four basic types of socialization;

2. briefly outline the theories of
   (a) Piaget,
   (b) Freud,
   (c) Cooley,
   (d) Mead;

3. summarize the importance of the following agents of socialization:
   (a) family,
   (b) peers,
   (c) school,
   (d) mass media;

4. explain the idea of "oversocialization."

Human beings must eat to stay alive. For infants, the matter is quite straightforward. They experience hunger; they cry; a parent responds; they suck. Adult satisfaction of this basic physiological need is more complicated. Canadians consider some things proper food (steak, hamburgers), but gag at the thought of eating equally nutritious alternatives (caterpillars, horsemeat). A taste for sauerkraut or blintzes is likely to mark someone as a member of a minority ethnic group (Anderson and Alleyne, 1979).

Eating is surrounded by rules. Even when people are ravenous, for example, they are not supposed to attack the apple pie before the spinach. Plucking an interesting item from a neighbour's plate will result in raised eyebrows. So will scratching one's tonsils with a fork.

How, then, does the carefree infant become transformed into the disciplined adult? Sociologists have a one-word answer to this question—socialization. The answer is simple, but the concepts covered by that one word can be quite involved.

Socialization is a complex, lifelong learning process. Through socialization, we develop our sense of self. We acquire the knowledge, skills, and motivations that we need in order to participate in social life. Socialization is the link between the individual and society and may be viewed from the perspectives of each.

The newborn infant is utterly helpless. The newborn's abilities are limited to crying, sucking, eliminating wastes, yawning, and a few other reflexes. It has no self-awareness. Though it has the potential for becoming human, it is not yet human. The physical care, emotional response, and training provided by the family transform this noisy, wet, demanding bundle of matter into a functioning member of society. It learns language, control of impulses, and skills. It develops a self. It acquires knowledge of both the physical world and the social world. The child learns whether it is male or female. It becomes capable of taking on social roles with some commitment. It internalizes, or accepts as its own, the norms and values of, first, the family and, later, the wider society.

Effective socialization is as essential for the society as it is for the individual. Untrained members disturb the social order. For example, small children frequently ask embarrassing questions in public. Furthermore, Canadian society could not continue to exist unless the thousands of new members born each year eventually learned to think, believe, and behave as Canadians. The continuity of our society requires that each generation come to embrace societal values as its own.

Cultural breakdown occurs when the socialization process no longer provides the new generation with valid reasons to be enthusiastic about becoming members of that society (Flacks, 1979). However, individual members may redefine social roles and obligations, as well as accept them as they stand. In this way, social change occurs over time (Bush and Simmons, 1981).

The diverse, or heterogeneous, nature of Canadian society complicates the socialization process. Although many values and norms are shared by all Canadians, there are differences that relate to language, region, ethnicity, religion, social class, and urban or rural residence. The perpetuation of these distinctive Canadian groups depends on children learning the relevant subcultural norms and values. Thus these variations in social environment bring with them variations in the content of socialization. For example, the Danish-Canadian community cannot continue in any meaningful fashion unless children of this ethnic background learn to view themselves as Danish-Canadians and learn the traditions and perhaps the language of this group. Similarly, the continuation of the unique features of the Maritime region requires that Canadians who live there acquire, by means of specialized socialization, the identity of Maritimers and the special norms, values, and history of that region.

Historical events, such as the Great Depression, World War II, and the protest era of the late 1960s mean that successive generations of Canadians have different socialization experiences (Mannheim, 1953). For example, people who grew up during the Depression often learned what it meant to go hungry, to give up career plans, to delay marriage. We would expect their perspective on life to contrast sharply with that of earlier and later generations (Elder, 1974).

The socialization process explains how commitment to the social order is maintained. Paradoxically, most people find their own fulfilment as individuals at the same time they become social beings. However, it is important to note that socialization for deviance also occurs. Some people learn to forge cheques, to crack safes, and to snort cocaine.

Types of Socialization

There are four basic types of socialization:

1. primary socialization;
2. adult socialization;
3. anticipatory socialization;
4. resocialization.

Primary Socialization.   **Primary socialization** is the basic socialization that occurs in childhood. It involves:

1. the development of language and individual identity;
2. the learning of cognitive skills and self-control;
3. the internalization of moral standards and appropriate attitudes and motivations;
4. some understanding of societal roles.

Adult Socialization.   **Adult socialization** occurs beyond the childhood years. Primary socialization lays the foundation for later learning, but it cannot completely prepare people for adulthood. For one thing, our society confronts people with new role expectations as they move through life. Moving beyond the family or daycare centre into the neighbourhood, entering school, becoming an adolescent, choosing an occupation, marrying, bearing children, encountering middle age, retiring, and dying all involve new lessons (see the accompanying article, "Learning to Die," for a glimpse at how this final stage is being addressed in one institution).

Learning to Die

This is where one comes to die.

On a hill overlooking the St. Lawrence River sits a new two-story yellow-brick building, the Maison Michel Sarrazin. Canada's only free-standing hospice, a residence for people soon to die of cancer, it opened its doors a year ago.

A pilot project of the Québec Government, built on leased Government land, it is supported by private donations, volunteer labour and $1-million in provincial funds being provided over five years.

The only patients allowed to enter will not leave again. Most have only a few weeks remaining in their lives and they know it.

Fifty patients, ranging in age from 22 to 92, have come and gone. Most are in their 60s and stay about 22 days.

Recognizing and accepting the fact of one's imminent death is a condition of entry—which is why several of the 15 beds regularly remain unfilled. Many patients, refusing to accept their prognosis, choose to stay at home or in a hospital, surrounded by the possibility of further treatment, however futile.

"The name Michel Sarrazin frightens some people," says Dr. Louis Dionne, a cancer specialist and medical professor at Laval University who is founder and director of the hospice. "It's almost the first step to the cemetery."

"A person's death, as tragic as it may be in itself, is as natural as his birth. . . . This project hopes not only to rehabilitate (the notion) of death, but attempts, above all, to give his remaining life the quality and place it deserves, up to the very last minute," Dr. Dionne writes in the 10-page statement of philosophy and objectives offered every visitor to the hospice.

"Death is as much a process of personal growth as birth, childhood, adolescence, adulthood and old age. The dying person is someone who is entering the final chapter of his human condition. During this phase, life offers him a final chance to grow, to integrate all the dimensions of his existence and to become even more human."

Three values are names as priorities at the Maison Michel Sarrazin: dignity, honesty, and respect for the dying patient, basics often brushed aside in the rush for defibrillating paddles to jolt to heart back into a final beat, the injection of one more shot of morphine into a body too exhausted to protest.

Patients who choose to come to Michael Sarrazin—named for the first North American to perform a mastectomy, a seventeeth-century French-Canadian physician famed for his use of natural remedies—are beyond needing such dramatic interventions.

They simply want to die in peace, something modern-day hospitals, built and run to respond to the needs of the curable, rarely allow.

Yet even as they are dying, patients here are very much alive, which is shown in myriad details. Fresh tulips on the granite mantle over the fireplace; the small library with leather armchairs; relaxed groups of friends and family seated on the comfortable velvet sofas; a colour television turned down low in a corner; a bridge-table by the picture window.

All costs are covered by regular provincial medical insurance. It is not, as many patients and doctors still suspect, a private refuge for the rich.

Staff members say they have learned much about their own skills, about co-operation with other health professionals in a non-hierarchical and multidisciplinary team, about the possibilities for a rich and joyous end to life that few had seen offered in other medical settings.

Head nurse Nicole Gagnon has had 13 years of experience watching hospitals dismiss the special needs of the dying.

"One night, I was sitting with a dying woman in her 60s who wanted me to hold her hand while she prayed. But a doctor who was trying to attach the electrodes for an electrocardiogram told me to get out of the way," she says.

Caring for terminal cancer patients in a regular hospital setting is difficult for other reasons. It is physically exhausting and emotionally demanding—bones are so brittle that a leg can be fractured just by being moved. Human care requires more time than many over-burdened hospital nurses are able to give, Mrs. Gagnon says.

"Here, we have a maximum of four patients—in hospital we would have eight or nine. We have much more time to do everything. We ease their pain, we pay attention to the way we handle their bodies.

Because the care-giving team is small, tightly knit and non-authoritarian, the grief that members feel at a patient's death is openly acknowledged at weekly meetings.

"Here it's easier for (patients and staff) to express their feelings. This work calls on us to be as human as we can be."

A year ago, 54-year-old Jean-Guy Landry, a chemist with Reed Paper, entered the Maison Michel Sarrazin as one of its first six patients. He lived there for 29 days—with his wife, Marthe, beside him day and night.

Freed from domestic responsibilities, Mrs. Landry slept beside her husband on a cot. Their three grown sons would stay and talk sports far into the night. Unlike hospitals, the hospice welcomed Mr. Landry's family members and encourage them to participate in his care.

The sons gave their father massages. Mr. Landry held his 3-month-old grandson in his arms, feeding him a bottle in his bed.

"We lived our family life. It was an extraordinary experience. It was almost a retreat, a meditation," Mrs. Landry says.

Jean-Guy Landry died listening to his favourite classical music on the radio. His wife stayed in the room with his body for three hours, though she could have gone down the hallway to a small room designed for that moment—an airy solarium full of plants, with a long view over the fields to the river—to sit with him.

In French, an animal that has become tame and lost its shyness of people is considered *apprivoise*.

This is what death means at Maison Michel Sarrazin. It has lost its sting.

"Nous avons apprivoise la mort," Marthe Landry says.

SOURCE: Extracted from "Life before Death" by Caitlin Kelly, May 6, 1986, *The Globe and Mail*.

Also, society changes, and people must therefore equip themselves to cope with new situations (for example, microtechnology and technological job obsolescence, war, and changes in sexual mores).

Finally, some people have to deal with specialized situations, such as geographical and social mobility, marital breakdown, physical handicaps, and so on. These all require further socialization (Brim, 1966).

Anticipatory Socialization. **Anticipatory socialization** occurs in advance of the actual playing of roles. This rehearsal for the future involves learning something about role requirements (both behaviour and attitude) and visualizing oneself in the role. For example, children begin to practice being pupils before they ever enter school. Law students mentally try on the role of practicing lawyer. We think about being married, being parents, and being retired before we actually assume these roles.

Resocialization. **Resocialization** occurs when a new role or a new situation requires a person to replace established patterns of behaviour and thought with new patterns (Campbell, 1975). Old behaviour must be unlearned because it does not fit in some way with new role demands. Usually, resocialization is more difficult than the original socialization; the established habits interfere with new learning. Fortunately, though, human beings retain the capacity for change across the entire life span. Indeed, thousands of organizations, from Alcoholics Anonymous to Zen training centres, are designed to help individuals resocialize (Brim and Kagan, 1980).

Resocialization is more characteristic of adult socialization than of primary socialization. However, as youngsters mature, they, too, are expected to discard former behaviour. Block printing is fine for a first-grade pupil, but a fourth-grade pupil must learn to write. A two-year-old boy may cry when he is frightened, but a twelve-year-old boy who climbs into his mother's lap and whimpers is thought to be odd.

Resocialization necessarily confronts the individual with contradictions between old and new behaviour that are sometimes confusing and sometimes painful. The fact that the non-responsible, submissive, asexual child must become the responsible, dominant, sexually active adult (Mortimer and Simmons, 1978) illustrates one huge difference between childhood and adulthood.

The resocialization involved in new situations entails contradictions for adults as well. For example, the women's liberation movement has resulted in redefinitions of the ways men and women relate to each other. Can either sex initiate a date? Should husbands help with the housework? Even more dramatic contrasts between old and new selves are experienced by individuals who get caught up in extreme instances of resocialization, such as brainwashing, religious conversion, and programs in prisons and mental hospitals.

The Lifelong Process

We have noted that socialization is a lifelong process. Despite some anticipatory socialization during childhood, primary socialization simply cannot prepare people for roles and situations that either are unforeseeable at the moment or that lie far ahead in the future.

Adult socialization is particularly necessary in the complex, changing society inhabited by most Canadians. Here, a comparison may be made with the Hutterites, who constitute a culture that has remained very much the same for some 450 years. Hutterites live out their lives in small rural colonies in western Canada. Everybody knows everybody else. There are few secrets; therefore, nearly all adult roles are open for the Hutterite children's inspection (Mackie, 1975). Eventually, the children will inherit those very roles they see enacted before them. In cases such as these, adult socialization can be less extensive than in Canadian society generally.

The primary socialization provides the groundwork for all later learning. The major structures of personality are formed in childhood. In addition, the lessons learned during this impressionable period are the first lessons, and learning comes easily (unlike resocialization, which is difficult because old behaviour must be unlearned before new behaviour can be acquired). Finally, it should be noted that primary socialization channels and sets limits for adult socialization. For example, a person who emerges from childhood without a strong motivation to achieve is unlikely to excel in medical school.

A number of fundamental differences exist between primary socialization and adult socialization (Brim, 1966), in addition to those just considered.

1. With some exceptions, adult socialization concentrates on overt behaviour, rather than on values and motives. Society assumes that adults already hold the values appropriate for a given role and that they are motivated to pursue that role. Colleges, for example, do not worry about motivating students to work hard—they assume the motivation is already there. Prisons, on the other hand, encourage prisoners to resocialize, but their high rates of recidivism (of individuals lapsing into crime after release from prison) illustrate that it is not easy to alter basic values and motives.

2. While primary socialization tends to be idealistic, adult socialization tends to be realistic. Children are taught how society ideally operates and how people ideally behave. They are shielded from knowledge of how society actually operates and how people actually behave. At the same time that parents urge children to be honest, they protect children from awareness of corruption in government and their own "fudging" of the truth. Part of growing up, then, involves substituting sophistication for naïvete.

3. The content of adult socialization is more specific than the content of primary socialization. Although there are exceptions, children learn general knowledge, skills, and behaviour relevant to many roles. Adults, on the other hand, acquire information specific to particular roles. For example, children learn to read and to write. This knowledge is useful in a wide range of roles and situations. By contrast, adults learn to diaper a baby or to wire a circuit board. Such infor-

The First Hockey Game

Games teach youngsters about social life. When they learn the rules of the game, they are also learning something about the rules of society. A father describes taking his five-year-old son to see his first hockey game.

"After the face-off both teams skated hard, the lead changed back and forth, and—well, it turned out to be a pretty good game . . . , with no ugly stuff and, as pro hockey goes, relatively few penalties. I think this must have been a disappointment for my son, for, aside from eating, the aspect of hockey that seemed to appeal to him most was the penalty box. I decided that it must answer powerfully to something basic in a five-year-old's ideal of justice: immediate, *brief* punishment, and then return to one's peers without shame or guilt. Anyway, he leaned forward expectantly each time the ref blew his whistle, and whenever a player was sent off he appeared to take a stern, Calvinist pleasure in making certain that the offender didn't attempt to return to the ice an instant before his sentence had expired."

SOURCE: "The Talk of the Town," *The New Yorker*, December 27, 1982.

mation pertains to the parent and the electronic-technician roles, and not elsewhere.

4. As a general rule, adults are socialized by formal organizations (schools, corporations), while children are socialized in informal contexts (the family, babysitters, peer groups). This distinction, however, reflects a general tendency rather than a rule. The school, for example, although it is a formal organization, is an important primary socialization agency. Also, the actual socializing of adults within organizations is often done through primary relationships. For example, the impact of inmate subculture on prisoners' experience of being incarcerated and their responses to treatment programs is well-documented (Ekstedt and Griffiths, 1984, p. 220).

5. The nature of the relationships between socializer and socializee differs in primary and adult socialization. The family is the major socializer of the child. Because of the emotionally charged familial context and the power of the parents to hand out rewards and punishments, parents have a tremendous impact on the child.

On the other hand, the relationship between adult socializer and socializee is usually more emotionally neutral and more equal in terms of power. The adult socializee is often in that position voluntarily. One *chooses* to be an apprentice welder or a college student.

These three prisoners were involved in a hostage-taking incident in a British Columbia prison. Prisoners may be more influenced by inmate subculture than by official resocialization programs.

SOURCE: Canapress Photo Service

Socialization Theories

Although socialization occurs throughout life, the learning that takes place during the formative years of childhood has been of special concern to psychologists and sociologists. The family, which bears the major responsibility here, has therefore received considerable attention from these social scientists. This section considers the principal ideas involved in three theoretical approaches to childhood socialization:

1. Piaget's cognitive developmental approach to moral thought;
2. Freud's psychoanalytic theory;
3. symbolic-interactionist views on development of the self.

These theoretical perspectives vary in their emphases on how learning occurs and what socialization is, but, for the most part, they are complementary, rather than opposed sets of ideas. All of them can contribute to our understanding of childhood socialization.

Piaget's Cognitive Developmental Approach to Moral Thought

Jean Piaget's (1896-1980) general theory (1928) considers how children think, reason, and remember. The development of moral thought—a sense of right and wrong, an understanding of societal values—is a particularly important dimension of his theory (Piaget, 1932).

In his research, Piaget observed children playing marbles and asked them to explain the game to him. He in turn talked to them about such ethical concepts as stealing, cheating, and justice. In many respects, childhood games are small-scale analogies of society. When children learn about the rules of the game, they are learning, at their level, about the norms of society. Similarly, when they learn to play game roles, they are also learning something about playing societal roles.

Primary socialization occurs during childhood. An important part of childhood learning involves developing rules about what is acceptable behaviour. Piaget found that when children learn about the rules of a game, they are learning, at their level, about the norms of society.

SOURCE: H. Armstrong Roberts/Miller Services

From his observations and discussions, Piaget concluded that two stages of moral thought exist. Children from four to eight years display the more primitive stage of morality, **moral realism**. The second stage, **moral autonomy**, develops after the age of eight. Several characteristics are associated with each stage.

The **moral realist** judges wrongdoing entirely in terms of the outcome of the act, disregarding extenuating circumstances or the intentions of the wrongdoer. For example, Piaget told stories about two boys, John and Henry, and asked them to decide which boy deserved the more severe punishment. John was called to the dinner table. He came immediately. As he entered the dining room, he accidentally knocked over a teacart that had been left behind the door. Fifteen cups broke. The other boy, Henry, had been forbidden by his mother to eat jam. When his mother left the room, Henry climbed up to the cupboard to reach the jam and knocked a cup to the floor.

Children in the moral realism stage believed that John should be punished more severely. After all, John had broken fifteen cups while Henry had broken only one. However, the older children, the **moral autonomists**, were more concerned with the boys' *reasons* for acting than with the *consequences* of the acts. These older children felt that Henry deserved the greater punishment, because his offense had been committed while disobeying his mother's order. John's offense, on the other hand, had been accidental.

The moral realist believes that all rules are unchangeable absolutes. Rules are handed down by adult authority and must be obeyed to the letter. The moral autonomist, by contrast, views rules as somewhat arbitrary social conventions. Older children involved in a game, for example, may agree that certain rules are appropriate or inappropriate to that particular game. When the players consent to change, new rules can be adopted.

More specifically, when asked why the child who knocks the most marbles out of a circle gets the first turn, the moral realist would answer: "That's the rule. That's the way things are done." The moral autonomist would also agree that turns are decided by this preliminary trial. However, this child would explain the procedure differently: "Well, the first turn has to be decided somehow. There are probably other ways to do it, but we decided to do it this way, and it works fine."

Piaget believed that moral thought develops along with the capacity for cognitive thought. This cognitive development results from the interaction between the child's genetic makeup and his or her social experiences. According to Piaget, the child's interaction with peers—not with parents—provides crucial social experiences for the development of morality. For one thing, freewheeling games with other children show that rules are conventions that arise out of cooperation and discussion. Parents, on the other hand, are often reluctant to discuss the reasons for their rules. This authoritarian stance underscores the younger child's view of rules as arbitrary and unchangeable.

Many studies have borne Piaget out, showing that children from different cultures and social class backgrounds do in fact go through a stage of moral realism before they reach moral autonomy.

Freud's Psychoanalytic Theory

Psychoanalytic theory, as formulated by the Viennese physician Sigmund Freud (1856-1939), is both a theory of personality and a system of therapy. Freud's writing has been reprinted in *The Complete Psychological Works of Sigmund Freud* (1953). Freud's theory views socialization as society's attempt to tame the child's inborn animal-like nature. He believed the roots of human behaviour lie in the irrational, unconscious dimensions of the mind. He assumed that the entire adult personality is the product of the child's early experiences within the family.

Freud saw the personality as composed of three energy systems: the Id, the Ego, and the Super-ego. The **Id** is the biological basis of personality, the **Ego** is the psychological basis of personality, and the **Super-ego** is the social basis of personality (Shaw and Costanzo, 1970).

The Id is the reservoir of inborn, biological instincts. This "seething cauldron of sex and hostility" is wholly unconscious. It seeks immediate pleasure. The selfish, impulsive Id is not in contact with the reality of the external world.

If all of the Id's desires were gratified, the Ego would never emerge. Unlike the Id, the Ego develops out of the child's learning experiences with the environment. The Ego includes thought, perception, and memory. It also contains the defense mechanisms (such as rationalization, repression, projection) that have emerged from the Ego's previous contact with reality. Part of the Ego is conscious and part is unconscious. The Ego's primary purpose is to direct the personality toward realistic goals; it is oriented toward the reality principle. Therefore, the Ego is a go-between among the demands of the Id, the Super-ego, and the external world.

The Super-ego, or conscience, emerges as a result of the child's identification with her or his parents. Through reward, punishment, and example, the parents communicate society's rules to the child. When these social values and behavioural standards have been adopted as the child's own standards, the Super-ego censors the Id's impulses. This internal authority also guides the Ego's activities.

Symbolic-Interactionist Views of Cooley and Mead

Symbolic interactionism is more sociological than the two perspectives on primary socialization discussed so far. It emphasizes the impact of the social environment on the child, rather than the unfolding of the child's biological capacities.

The term "symbolic" in the title also signals the focus of attention of this theoretical perspective. A "symbol" is something that stands for something else. A red light means stop. A five-dollar bill symbolizes buying power. Though there is some physical reality "out there," people respond not directly to this "objective reality," but to a symbolic interpretation of that reality (Charon, 1979, p. 36). These interpretations are called *definitions of the situation*. Definitions of the situation may be personal (idiosyncratic) or cultural (standard meanings embedded in a community's culture, and learned through socialization) (Stebbins, 1967). Symbolic interactionists are especially interested in how human beings attach meanings to the actions of other people as they attempt to make sense of both themselves and their social worlds.

Although the symbolic interactionists are interested in many facets of socialization, we will concentrate here on the question of how the child acquires a self. We will consider the work of two pioneer theorists—Charles H. Cooley and George Herbert Mead.

Cooley's Looking-Glass Self.   Cooley (1864-1929) was an American sociologist who derived many of his ideas about socialization from observing and recording the behaviour of his own children at the turn of the century. He used the metaphor of the looking glass to illustrate his point that children acquire a self through adopting other people's attitudes toward them. The self is social; it emerges out of interaction with the people who are important to the child. Its content reflects how children interpret others' judgments about what kind of people they are.

The **looking-glass self** has three elements:

1. how we imagine we appear to the other person;
2. how we imagine the other person judges that appearance;
3. how we feel as a result—e.g., proud, ashamed, and so on (Cooley, 1902).

Notice that what is important here is the child's *interpretation* of other people's attitudes. This interpretation may or may not be accurate. A little boy may pick up messages from his parents that they think he is short, fat, and clumsy, and that they think being short, fat, and clumsy is deplorable. If this message is not countered by other sources of opinion, the boy has little choice but to define himself as short, fat, and clumsy and to see these as negative.

Mead's Theory of the Self. In formulating his ideas about how the child acquires a self image, Cooley's contempory, Mead (1863-1931), elaborated upon many of Cooley's insights. Mead's major work on the self is contained in *Mind, Self, and Society* (1934). In order to specify what he meant by the "self," Mead made three fundamental assumptions:

1. The newborn infant does not come equipped with a self. Although the infant is born with the potential to reach this goal eventually, the self is acquired, not innate.

2. To have a self is to have the ability to think about oneself and to act socially toward oneself. When we congratulate ourselves for an honest act or blame ourselves for a piece of stupidity, for example, we are acting *toward* ourselves.

3. The self is a process, not a "thing." The self consists of the processes of thinking and acting toward oneself.

For Mead, the self includes two aspects or dimensions: the "I" and the "Me." The "I" is the spontaneous, creative aspect of the self. It is the acting, unique, unfettered self. The "Me," the social self, consists of internalized societal attitudes and expectations.

Unlike the Freudian Id, Ego, and Super-ego, the "I" and "Me" work together. The "I" provides individuality and initiative for behaviour, while the "Me" provides direction for that behaviour according to the dictates of society. Mead was particularly interested in the development of the "Me," the social self.

Mead's complex explanation of how the child acquires a self can be summarized in two central ideas.

1. The development of the self depends upon development of the capacity to use language. According to Mead, language and self develop together. As a first step in developing self-awareness, the child must differentiate himself or herself as a separate "thing" from the many other "things" in the environment. Through language, the child learns the names of things. This object is called a "chair"; that one is called "Mommy." The child learns his or her name along with other

object names: there is an object called "George." The child also learns the characteristics of objects. Fire is hot and dangerous. Chairs have four legs and are intended for sitting. Similarly, George learns what sort of object he is—a boy, little, someone who likes cookies. (See Chapter 4 for an application of this theory to gender socialization in particular.)

2. Both language and development of the self require "taking the role of the other." In order to communicate with another person, it is necessary to take the role of the other, that is, to adopt the other's point of view about what is being said. Suppose you greet me Monday morning by asking, "How are you?" Before I can reply properly, I have to put myself in your shoes and arrive at my definition of the situation. I must decide whether you really want to hear all about my physical and psychological well-being or whether you are merely being polite. In the first case, I will tell you at great length how I am feeling. In the second, I will answer, "Fine, thank you."

The development of the self requires this ability to take the role of the other. The self is social and the child must be able to adopt the perspective of other people toward himself or herself. Having a self means viewing yourself through the eyes of other people.

According to Mead, the ability to indulge in role play and the consequent forming of the self occur through two main stages (Meltzer, 1978):

1. the play stage;
2. the game stage.

During the **play stage**, the child begins role playing. The little girl pretends she is a mother or a teacher or a store clerk. She is demonstrating the ability to adopt the mother's role, for example, and to act back upon herself from the perspective of this role. In pretending that she is the mother scolding her imaginary child for lying, the little girl is placing herself in her own mother's shoes and reacting to her own behaviour. This type of play indicates that the self is forming. However, at this stage the self is fragmentary because the child is taking the role of only one person at a time. A person who has a significant influence on the formation of a child's values is called a **significant other** for that child.

A coherent self develops during the **game stage**, when the child becomes capable of taking a number of roles simultaneously. Mead used the game of baseball to explain this process. When you play baseball, you have to adopt several different roles at the same time. Being a catcher involves understanding the roles of pitcher, shortstop, umpire, opposing team member up to bat, and so on. The events in a particular game must be understood from all of these perspectives.

Girls and boys in late childhood encounter increasingly divergent expectations; peers and teachers join family members as authorities. They begin to play many more roles (daughter, pupil, friend, Boy Scout). Through experience, children eventually develop a clear understanding of how all these roles—their own and other people's—fit together in social life. Mead called the composite view of this last stage the **generalized other**. During the play stage, the child might think, "Dad says I am bad when I tell lies." During the game stage, the child thinks, "*They* say lying is wrong." Behaviour thus comes increasingly to be guided by an abstract moral code (a generalized other) rather than the opinion of one or two significant others.

In Mead's view, self-development does not stop in childhood. As the person adopts new roles and encounters new situations, the self continues to evolve (Bush and Simmons, 1981).

Theoretical Overview

The ideas of Piaget, Freud, and the symbolic interactionists all contribute to our understanding of childhood socialization. Our brief discussion has touched on only a few of the important ideas of these theorists. Their work should be seen as complementary—not as competing—systems of thought. Piaget's work analyses the development of morality. Both Freud and Mead are also concerned with the question of how society's notions about what is proper are internalized by the child. However, their theories address other questions as well. Freud emphasizes emotions, sexuality, and the unconscious. His theory focuses on the role played by specific family members in socializing the child. Finally, Mead and Cooley stress the social context of child development. Their emphasis on the linkage between the emergence of self-awareness and the acquisition of language was an important insight.

Socialization: The Contemporary Context

What does it mean to grow up in the 1980s? As mentioned earlier, individuals who were born about the same time and who have similar experiences during their formative years share characteristics throughout their lives that distinguish them from other generations. In this section, we discuss major factors affecting the experiences of Canadians currently ten to twenty years old.

Each generation is influenced by *demographic*, or population, characteristics (see Chapter 6). Take generation size. There is more room for this generation in classrooms, for example, than there was for the "baby-boomers" of the late fifties and sixties. The trends of decreased fertility, later marriages, and postponed births (Statistics Canada, 1985a) mean that youngsters have fewer siblings or none at all. Previously viewed as "jealous, egotistical, selfish, spoiled little brats who grew into lonely, neurotic adults" (Pappert, 1983), only children have now become commonplace and, hence, respectable. Also, because parents have fewer children, the potential exists for their relationships with the children they do have to increase in intensity (Luxton, 1980).

Declining death rates also involve changes in socialization. The probability of a child's being orphaned or growing up without grandparents has diminished (Sullivan, 1983). Since Canada is an "aging society," children will be increasingly familiar with the elderly. However, death is no longer the commonplace family event it once was. Living in a society that isolates the dying in hospitals and nursing homes leaves young people inadequately prepared to cope with death when it touches their lives.

National economic circumstances during the past 15 years or so—inflation, recession, regional disparities in employment levels—have also affected the socialization experiences of Canadians. Many wives and mothers have sought employment outside the home. Many families have migrated across the country in search of jobs. Barnett Richling, a professor at Mount Saint Vincent University, studied the migration between Newfoundland and the mainland. He quotes a migrant who had recently returned to Newfoundland:

> Up there [in Toronto] it's hard to save money since you owe so much in rent and all. At least here a house is reasonable enough ... with a regular job you could save money. You could hardly find three Newfoundlanders up there who wouldn't go back home, but what's the good of it to return without jobs? (Richling, 1985, p. 247)

Technological developments affect socialization as well. Children are experiencing computerized learning and computerized play. In this high-tech era, "for the first time, many youngsters know more than their elders and are now teaching their elders in ways that parents have traditionally encultured children" (Williams, 1983). While children of the past may have been preoccupied with the "knife, compass, 36 cents, a marble, and a rabbit's foot" in their pockets (Winn, 1983), today's children turn to electronic amusements. They spend hours in the space-age atmosphere of video arcades. They cocoon themselves in Walkman headphones. At home, they live in a constant bombardment of noise from radio and stereo. Listening to music, especially rock music, is the favourite leisure activity for Canadian adolescents (Bibby and Posterski, 1985, p. 36). Younger children slump passively in front of the television.

Changes in marriage and family patterns have serious implications for socialization. Many children are growing up in single-parent families. The Canadian divorce rate has risen steadily since liberalization of the divorce legislation that took place in 1968 (McKie *et al.*, 1982). Warner Troyer, who interviewed 400 of these children for his book, *Divorced Kids* (1979), says: "Divorce is like escaping from a burning house. . . . If a whole family jumps out of the second-story window, everyone's bound to be hurt a little" (Landsberg, 1982). However, one in ten Canadian single parents has never been married (Davids, 1985, p. 3). Despite the decline in teenage pregnancy and an increase in abortions, an estimated 80 percent to 90 percent of all teenage mothers are keeping their children (Schlesinger, 1985, p. 35).

Growing up in a single-parent home has many consequences. Single parenthood typically means single motherhood. Families headed by women often experience poverty (Ambert, 1985). The custodial parent is frequently overwhelmed with responsibility

Technology can influence socialization. Many children know more than their parents about computers, a circumstance that sometimes reverses the normal flow of information about culture.

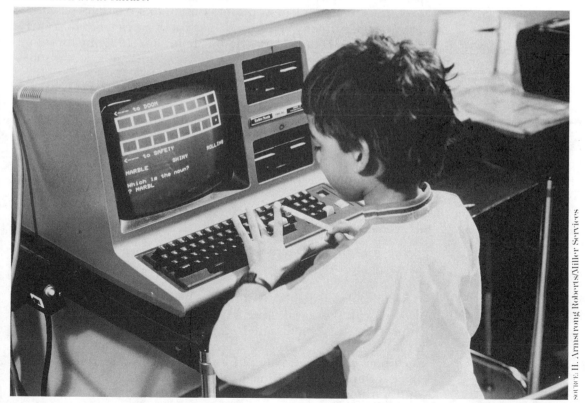

for earning a living and may treat the child as a pseudoadult equal, loading the child with many responsibilities of the missing parent—for example, expecting him or her to serve as a listening post.

In addition, many children are growing up in blended families with step-parents and siblings unrelated to them by blood. Sociologists are just beginning to understand the nature of socialization in such reconstituted families. Take the thorny issue of discipline. During courtship of the children's mother, the step-father often tries to be popular with the youngsters, to be an "easygoing pal." With marriage, his perceptions of his role tend to change. As well as striving to love the children, he now also strives to exercise firm control over them. The children are apt to resent this discipline, especially if it differs from that of their mother or biological father (Spanier and Furstenberg, 1987, p. 427).

By 1984, more than half the mothers of preschoolers were in the labour force (Labour Canada, 1986, p. 22). As a result, a majority of Canadian children are now cared for by someone other than a parent (Eichler, 1983, p. 249). Children are increasingly involved with age peers, television, and secondary socialization agencies, such as schools, daycare centres, or YMCA and YWCA groups. Although it is now more common to see fathers pushing baby strollers, many studies, such as those carried out by Lupri and Mills (1987) in Calgary and by Michelson (1985) in Toronto, conclude that when wives go out to work, husbands do *not* substantially increase their share of child care.

Agents of Socialization

The socialization process involves many different types of influence on people throughout their lives. This part of our discussion will concentrate on four major socialization agents:

1.   the family;
2.   the peer group;
3.   the school;
4.   the mass media.

These agents affect almost every Canadian. In addition, they all exert a powerful influence during the impressionable childhood years.

Society has charged two of these agencies, the family and the school, with the socialization of children. Although much of the impact they have upon children is unintentional, both the family and the school also deliberately set out to equip children with the knowledge required to fit into adult society. The influence of the peer group and the media, on the other hand, is frequently unintentional.

Family

Although the contemporary family now shares some functions with other agencies, the family's impact upon the child is foremost. In Clausen's words (1968, p. 132): "the 'widening world of childhood' spirals out from the parental home." Learning occurs rapidly during those years of early childhood when the family has almost exclusive control. Moreover, learning takes place in the context of close emotional bonds. The family touches every sphere of the child's existence. The family lays the foundation for the later and lesser influences of the other socialization agents. Chapter 10 offers more details about the nature and content of socialization by the family.

There is a second reason why sociologists stress the importance of the family. The particular family situation affects the child in specific ways. For example, growing up in a one-parent or blended family is different from growing up in a more conventional family. Also, by being born into a particular family, the child automatically becomes part of a larger family—grandparents, aunts, uncles, cousins.

The Bad Kangaroo

Children learn many of their socialization lessons through imitating their parents.

There was a small Kangaroo who was bad in school. He put thumbtacks on the teacher's chair. He threw spitballs across the classroom. He set off firecrackers in the lavatory and spread glue on the doorknobs.

"Your behaviour is impossible!" said the school principal. "I am going to see your parents. I will tell them what a problem you are!"

The principal went to visit Mr. and Mrs. Kangaroo. He sat down in a living-room chair.

"Ouch!" cried the principal. "There is a thumbtack in this chair!"

"Yes, I know," said Mr. Kangaroo. "I enjoy putting thumbtacks in chairs."

A spitball hit the principal on his nose.

"Forgive me," said Mrs. Kangaroo, "but I can never resist throwing those things."

There was a loud booming sound from the bathroom.

"Keep calm," said Mr. Kangaroo to the principal. "The firecrackers that we keep in the medicine chest have just exploded. We love the noise."

The principal rushed for the front door. In an instant he was stuck to the doorknob.

"Pull hard," said Mrs. Kangaroo. "There are little globs of glue on all of our doorknobs."

The principal pulled himself free. He dashed out of the house and ran off down the street.

"Such a nice person," said Mr. Kangaroo. "I wonder why he left so quickly."

"No doubt he had another appointment," said Mrs. Kangaroo. "Never mind, supper is ready."

Mr. and Mrs. Kangaroo and their son enjoyed their evening meal. After the dessert, they all threw spitballs at each other across the dining-room table.

SOURCE: *Fables* by Arnold Lobel (p. 28), New York: Harper & Row.

The family's social class position means that the child will learn one set of values rather than another. The opportunities of a child born into an upper-middle-class family are considerably different from those of a child born into a working-class family. The ethnic background and the geographical location of the family are other important determinants of the content of socialization. For example, growing up in Toronto and growing up in a Newfoundland outport are quite different experiences (Firestone, 1978).

Social Class. Canadian society, like all other large societies, is socially stratified. (For a detailed discussion of the nature of stratification in Canada, see Chapter 7.) The best indicator of a Canadian family's social class position is the occupations of the parents, and this position influences the child's socialization experiences and consequent opportunities.

Growing up in a lower-class (as opposed to a middle-class) home means less money. Satisfaction of such basic needs as housing, diet, medical and dental care, clothing, and so on is less adequate. Poor people are more likely to grow up in overcrowded homes. The experience of overcrowding is associated with poor physical and mental health, poor child care, and poor social relations in the home (Gove, Hughes, and Galle, 1979).

The amount of income at the family's disposal also determines less tangible aspects of socialization. Opportunities to read a wide variety of books, to visit museums, to travel, to attend camp, and so forth all widen the growing child's intellectual horizons, and all tend to narrow the parental purse. If the parents in a lower-class home are vulnerable to job lay-offs and unemployment, their feelings of powerlessness and insecurity will be communicated to their children.

Members of different social classes, by virtue of experiencing different conditions of life, develop different world views and different conceptions of social reality (Gecas, 1976; Kohn, 1977). Distinctive occupational backgrounds are related to parental values. According to a Hamilton, Ontario study (Pineo and Looker, 1983), white-collar families consider their children's self-direction to be more important and obedience to parents to be less important than do blue-collar families.

Recently, a cross-national study of child-rearing values was carried out among French- and English-speaking Canadian parents (as well as parents in the United States, Japan, and six European countries). Working-class parents almost everywhere were more likely than middle-class parents to be intolerant of children's insolence and temper, to restrict their independence, to insist on good manners, and to maintain male-female distinctions (Lambert *et al.*, 1980).

Moreover, the class origins of a child remain important as the child matures. They are a significant influence on the occupation that a person will eventually choose. Indeed, evidence suggests that children are very likely to achieve a class position similar to that of their parents (McRoberts, 1985). Lower-class children are relatively less successful in school, leave school earlier, and have lower occupational aspirations. Middle-class parents are more likely to socialize their children to value the individualism and high motivation that success in school requires (Pike, 1975). However, the impact of social origin on educational attainment has declined through the century. Social origin now plays a decreasingly important role in high school completion, but it still affects the probability of attaining some post-secondary experience (Guppy *et al.*, 1984).

Ethnicity.   Canada is not a melting pot that culturally homogenizes its people, so ethnicity exerts a major influence on many families. Although most Canadians share a common core of experiences and values, their socialization may also reflect ethnic differences in values, norms, and identity. The matter is further complicated by the fact that ethnic background and social class position are frequently related.

The role of ethnicity in primary socialization varies enormously. The experiences of the non-English-speaking recent immigrant from Vietnam, for example, differ from those of the fourth-generation Ukrainian-Canadian raised in this country. Ethnicity means something different to the black child from Jamaica than to the child from Germany, who is physically indistinguishable from Caucasian Canadians. Ethnicity is a different proposition for native Canadians—Indians and Inuit—than for more recent arrivals (Peters, 1984). Clearly, the term "the Canadian family" represents an abstract oversimplification (Ishwaran, 1976).

Socialization by Siblings.   Brothers and sisters play an important role in socializing one another. An older sibling can provide a role model. Children learn many of their socialization lessons through imitation. Also, a younger sibling gives the older child the opportunity to try on for size some part of the parental role. Guiding and protecting a younger brother or sister helps the child internalize his or her parents' perspective. Much of the older child's influence is, of course, quite unintentional.

Sibling interaction provides practice in co-operation and competition. As Freud observed, sibling rivalry is one of the more emotional experiences encountered in growing up. All children are concerned about how smart, how big, how worthwhile they are. Children with siblings near their own age arrive at some of these answers by comparing themselves with brothers or sisters.

It is common for siblings to compete for attention from parents. But at times, brothers and sisters also provide useful allies against parents. Siblings appear to organize themselves into twosomes, bound together by love or hate; these sibling pairs result from situations such as being close in age or sharing a bedroom (Bank and Kahn, 1982). Indeed, Canada is moving toward the two-child family as the model family (Eichler, 1983). The more adult-oriented only child benefits from the exclusive attention of the parents, but, lacking siblings, may be somewhat unskilled in social relations with peers.

Peers

After the family, **peers**—other children approximately the same age—constitute the second most powerful socialization agency.

Peer Influence Throughout Life.   From early childhood through life, people attach a great deal of importance to peer relationships (Brenton, 1974). Even young infants stare at each other with fascination. By the age of two, children play alongside each other. By three or four years old, this parallel play becomes shared play. Most parents know that companionship with other children is a necessity, not a luxury. They take pains to find little companions for their child and worry if their offspring does not seem to make friends. Within a few years, children are able to relate to groups of children. (Recall the emphasis both Piaget and Mead placed on games for the child's social development.) By eight or nine years, most children are concerned with having one special friend. Many of us may remember being rejected by a best friend as one of the tragedies of childhood.

A national study of Canadian teenagers (Bibby and Posterski, 1985, p. 112) found that "many teenagers tend to find high levels of gratification from friends rather than from their mothers and fathers. They consequently place more value on friendship than they do on family life." However, other researchers (Davies and Kandel, 1981) conclude that when the issues concern teenagers' future life goals and educational aspirations, rather than current lifestyle matters such as fashions and music, parents are a more important influence than peers (Davies and Kandel, 1981).

Adolescence is the high point of peer group influence. The teenager reaches out for the companionship, opinions, and tastes of age-mates. This process helps to bridge the gulf between childish dependence on the family and adulthood. Peer relations continue to matter a great deal to people in the middle adult years and on into old age (Matthews, 1986). Although adults have more inner resources than children, they remain sensitive to the opinions of their friends.

Content of Peer Socialization.   What do children learn from one another? Contact with peers provides opportunities to practise social roles and to develop interaction skills. For example, children gain experience in leader and follower roles. During Mead's game stage, they learn the meaning of all the interdependent roles involved in games, such as baseball. They learn to cooperate and to compete.

As symbolic interactionist theorist Gecas (1981) notes, egalitarian peer relations provide frequent opportunities for role making, as opposed to role taking. Role taking involves adapting to roles that are explicitly predefined in the culture. In such cases, there is little opportunity for the idiosyncratic needs of the particular role taker. Role taking is particularly likely in hierarchical social relationships, such as those within the military. By contrast, role making refers to situations in which roles can be either created or substantially modified to the actor's own specifications through interaction (Turner, 1962). The role of clown or wit in a friendship group is a good example.

Children's comparison of their appearance and abilities with those of their peers influences their attitudes towards themselves (Kagan, 1984, p. 273). For example, classmates' clothing or skateboarding abilities may be critical in a sixth grade boy's assessment of his own worth. To say this another way, the looking-glass self (mentioned earlier) reflects the child's interpretation of peer, as well as familial, judgments.

Peers are a source of information. Children interpret the world for one another in a manner adults cannot possibly duplicate. Adults are ignorant of many aspects of reality that matter greatly to their children, such as the latest trends. Moreover, some sensitive topics are more easily discussed with peers than with adults, such as how babies are born or how to behave on dates. The fact that much of this peer information might be the wildest *mis*information in no way minimizes its importance to the young people in question.

Peers influence one another's values and attitudes. Piaget was well aware of the impact of peer experiences on moral development. Such ethical abstractions as rules, fair play, and honesty become meaningful in the give-and-take of peer interaction. Similarly, children teach each other attitudes toward such diverse subjects as TV programs, heavy metal music, athletics, cigarette smoking, future occupations, and homosexuality.

School

Industrialized nations such as Canada assign to the school a major role in preparing children for adulthood. The knowledge and skills required to function effectively in urbanized, industrialized societies are too extensive and too complex for parents to convey to their offspring.

Most children are eager to begin school. For many, enrolling in school is their first encounter with a formal institution. This significant step beyond the family or babysitter represents "being grown up." In school, the child is treated not as a unique individual but as a member of a group. For example, when recess comes, Suzy will march out to the playground with the other pupils—whether she feels like it or not. (At home, on the other hand she could probably have gotten away with refusing to go out and play.) At school Suzy is "processed" as one of a "batch." Experiences such as this prepare children for adulthood, where the demands of organizations often take priority over the individual's own wishes.

Some of the content of socialization is consciously planned; some is incidental to the school's stated goals. In addition, no two children have precisely the same school experiences. A variety of factors all influence what happens there, such as the child's ability and temperament; the teachers; the parents' attitudes toward academic success and their particular social class position; and the child's relations with the peer group. To children from some ethnic minorities or from very poor environments, the school may be an alien place that devalues what they have learned in their families (Gecas, 1981).

Nonetheless, it is possible to offer some generalizations about the content of school socialization:

1. Formal Knowledge. The most obvious purpose of the school is to provide students with some of the information and skills required to function in society.

2. Values. Educational systems attempt to transmit some appreciation of the sentiments and goals considered important in our society. These include motivation to achieve, individual responsibility, and respect for other people's rights. In addition, the school plays a vital role in orienting the child to Canadian society as such—a society that contains strong regional and ethnic identities and consumes American mass media.

3. Interpersonal Skills. Because elementary school represents most children's first experience in coping with the demands

of a formal organization, new social skills are developed. Young pupils are confronted with impersonal rules for behaviour—waiting your turn, being on time, co-operating—that are not rooted in parental or peer authority.

4. Self-Evaluation. Throughout childhood and adolescence, interaction at school provides reflections for the looking-glass self. The child needs to know what sort of person she or he is, relative to others of the same age. Educational authorities attempt to judge all children according to universal criteria.

Although it is possible to comment in general terms on the school as socialization agent, Canadian schools provide young people with a wide variety of socialization experiences. Here are two samples:

1. Royal Military College, founded in Kingston, Ontario, in 1876, demands a 16½-hour day of military discipline, ceremonial drills, sports, and bilingual classes of their uniformed (male and female) cadets.

2. A Linden, Alberta, Mennonite group that objected to the "lack of discipline . . . permissive moral atmosphere, and neglect of the Bible" in the public schools formed their own "Christian" school. This school stresses religion and bans movies, television, and competitive sports (Levy, 1979).

When considering these two rather extreme examples, we should remember that "school" is an abstraction and that children are really socialized by teachers, textbooks, and other pupils. We have already considered the role of other pupils, or peers; now we will consider the role of teachers and textbooks.

Teachers. When you think back to your days in elementary and junior high school, many of your thoughts revolve around particular teachers. Some are remembered as heroes or heroines and some as villains. Sometimes, you liked a particular subject, or school in general, because you had a warm, talented teacher that year. In contrast, perhaps your attitude toward school was soured by contact with an unpleasant teacher. Teachers are powerful socialization agents because they are the human point of contact between pupils and the formal organization of the school (Martin and Macdonell, 1978). Although the teacher-student relationship is not devoid of emotion, the tie is considerably more impersonal than the parent-child relationship.

The teacher exercises influence on the child in several ways.

He or she acts as the major vehicle for transmitting the school curriculum and associated values. The teacher interprets the wider society. In addition, the teacher sets up the rules of expected behaviour and hands out punishment when these are broken. Finally, the teacher is a potential role model. Richer (1979) observed that the female teacher of an Ontario kindergarten class was a powerful role model for the girls, but not the boys. The girls initiated physical contact with the teacher—hand holding, caressing, leg hugging. Often, one of the girls would sit on the piano stool (the teacher's territory), book in hand, and pretend to read to the class.

Textbooks.   Schools also socialize through textbooks, as well as computers, films, and videotapes. Their content adds to the information conveyed by teachers. As pupils advance through the educational system, an increasing proportion of their new knowledge is obtained through this more impersonal source.

Texts have considerable potential for conveying social attitudes along with factual material. For this reason educators have been concerned to provide children with Canadian, not American, texts. Canadian parents are understandably disturbed when their children are more familiar with the president of the United States, the Fourth of July, and "The Star Spangled Banner" than with their Canadian counterparts.

Mass Media

The mass media—television, radio, newspapers, magazines, books, movies, records, tapes—are impersonal communication sources, and they reach large audiences. If you try to imagine a week in Canada without any of these media, you will gain some idea of the important part they play in the lives of most Canadians. The media act as direct agencies of socialization. Television, the "universal curriculum" (Gerbner and Gross, 1976), is a major transmitter of culture and information (see Chapter 2).

The media reflect nearly every aspect of society, but these reflections are, of course, not necessarily accurate. Children see or hear world news. Their country is presented visually, along with its political leaders, diverse cultures, arts, and sports. Situation comedies picture what happens in other people's families. "Cops and robbers" programs present children with an astonishing number of violent crimes per evening. Media advertisements show children all the paraphernalia supposedly required for them to be happy, healthy, and respectable.

In providing children with common interests and experiences, the media also function as indirect socialization agencies. Being part of this "community of discourse" (Tuchman, 1979) amounts to a vital dimension of peer socialization. From coast to coast, Canadian youngsters are familiar with this chant: "Alligator pie, alligator pie / If I don't get some I think I'm gonna die" (Lee, 1974). Older children share delight in Judy Blume's (1972) *Tales of a Fourth Grade Nothing*, the story of Peter, whose unbearable little brother swallows Dribble, his pet turtle. (Some parents worry that the turtle-swallowing idea might be catching! [McNulty, 1983])

Television and music are even more vital parts of young people's subculture. Being television-wise brings prestige on the playground (Ellis, 1983). Children discuss what they have seen on television and act out the roles of TV characters in their fantasy play (Fouts, 1980). A national poll asked 2000 American eighth graders to name their "top heroes":

> Not a single world leader, government official, business figure, or scientist appeared among the 30 individuals listed. Instead, the list consisted almost exclusively of television and film stars and a few sports personalities made famous by their appearance on television (Ellis, 1983).

Child development experts have been particularly concerned about television as a socialization agent. Television has been called the "plug-in drug" (Winn, 1977), the Phantom Babysitter, and the Great Leveller, "mowing down all the bright young minds to the same stunted level (Landsberg, 1982). No other experience in a child's life "permits quite so much intake while demanding so little outflow" (Winn 1977). The average television set is on seven hours a day. Many children are zombie viewers, who watch anything and everything, "silent, immobile, mesmerized" (Goldsen, 1979). Television reaches 87 percent of all Canadian children two to eleven years old. These children watch an average of 21 hours of TV per week (Singer, 1986, p. 80).

Television "crowds out" other uses of time (Condry and Keith, 1983). Sleeping is the only activity that commands more of children's time. Television time is replacing hours of playtime, through which, as we have seen, children learn both societal norms and social skills. Children watch television rather than read, and reading is a skill that requires practice (Singer and Singer, 1981). By the age of 18, children will have spent more time in front of the television than anywhere else, including school. Even schools also make extensive use of television and other media as teaching devices.

The ability of television to influence children has become an extremely important issue. If children can learn to read from

SOURCE: H. Armstrong Roberts/Miller Services

Child development experts are concerned about television as a socialization agent. Most children watch so much television that it crowds out other uses of time.

educational television, if they pressure parents to buy heavily advertised toys and breakfast cereals, and, worse, if they learn to solve problems through violent means from watching crime shows, then this medium has almost unbelievable power for socialization.

Unfortunately, tracing the direct effects of the media is a very difficult research task. One reason for this is that when the media operate in the natural environment, their influence is only one factor among many other factors. For example, if Peter behaves aggressively, is this because of the type of television programs he watches, his family, or his nasty temperament?

In general, research on specific media effects shows that children are indeed influenced by their media consumption. But one major factor reduces this influence: children are exposed to media content in a social context. What they see and hear is monitored, at least to some extent, by parents. Similarly, their interpretation of media content is molded by the opinions of parents, teachers, and friends. Parents may forbid watching violent television series or recommend an educational series. They can offer their own opinions on fighting as a way of solving differences of opinion, or on the advisability of spending the contents of a piggy bank on a heavily advertised toy. "When parents encourage their youngsters to think about and evaluate content and to consider alternative actions, the impact of negative or antisocial contents is considerably reduced" (Fouts, 1980).

Research shows that although children as young as four can distinguish television commercials from programming (through cues such as use of jingles, faster pacing of material, and adult voiceovers), the majority of first-graders cannot explain the selling intent of commercials (Singer, 1986, p. 83).

However, Frazer and Reid (1979) report that, with parental help, even young children can learn to become skeptical about commercials. Here is one example. Charlie, a preschooler, is watching a Purina Cat Chow commercial featuring a number of cats dancing to the jingle, "Chow, Chow, Chow." He says: "That's dumb. Cats can't dance like that, 'cause Barney [the family cat] eats the stuff [Purina Cat Chow] and don't dance like that." His father responds: "You are very smart. You remember what we told you about TV advertising." Charlie answers: "Yeah. They don't always tell the real truth, do they?"

We now turn to more specific considerations of the media as agents of socialization.

Violence and the Media. Most of the research on media influence upon children has been concerned with possible negative effects of exposure to violence. (For a discussion of the influence on children of the mass media's portrayal of gender roles, see Chapter 4.)

What messages, for example, do children take away from their Saturday morning cartoon sessions? Week after week, they see cartoon characters such as the coyote in "Road Runner" being smashed with giant mallets, blown up with dynamite, and crushed by trains. It has been well established that violence is a staple in the television diet of Canadian children. Waters and Malamud (1975) claim that by the time the average child is 16 years old, that child will have witnessed more than 13 000 television killings.

The Ontario Royal Commission on Violence in the Communications Industry (Thatcher, 1978) also found cause for concern in the way newspapers report violence. Newspapers tend to focus on the violence in isolation from the context or issues involved. One case the Commission examined concerned the reporting of a labour strike. Angry confrontations between striking workers and scabs were described in detail. However, the issues leading up to the dispute remained somewhat obscure.

Similarly, Huggins and Straus (1978) did a content analysis of 125 recommended children's books, for the period 1850 to 1970.

They found that the typical children's book had two violent incidents for every 15 pages. A third of these violent incidents involved someone being killed. These researchers found that the amount of violence remained the same over the 120-year period studied.

Learning psychologists have shown that children imitate the behaviour of adults on film. Bandura, Ross, and Ross (1963) exposed nursery-school children to an adult who modelled unusual forms of physical and verbal aggression toward an inflated Bobo doll. The children themselves later displayed precisely the same responses toward the doll. Bandura, *et al.* report that filmed models were as effective as live models.

Critics of the Bobo doll experiment have pointed out that the doll was the type of toy that invited aggression. Also, since the filmstrip used in the experiment lacked a plot, it contained no justification for the adult's violence. Therefore, its similarity to a television program has been questioned. Many other experiments, however, do support the conclusion that children are susceptible to examples of violence presented to them through the media.

There are two opposing positions on the effect of media violence. The observational-learning position takes its cue from research such as that by Bandura, *et al.* (1963)—the Bobo doll study. This position holds that the media encourage children to solve their problems by violent means. Constant exposure to media violence normalizes violence. The opposite position holds that violence in the media provides a *catharsis*; that is, the individual's frustrations are relieved or purged through watching media violence. Alfred Hitchcock's humorous defense of his own television program (quoted in Schellenberg, 1974) illustrates the catharsis position:

> One of television's great contributions is that it brought murder back into the home where it belongs. Seeing a murder on television can be good therapy. It can help work off one's antagonisms. If you haven't any antagonisms, the commercials will give you some.

Available research tends to support the observational-learning position rather than the catharsis position. Both the Ontario Royal Commission on Violence in the Communications Industry (1977) and the United States Surgeon General's Advisory Committee report, *Television and Growing Up: The Impact of Televised Violence* (1972), expressed grave concern about violence in the media. Although other variables are involved, televised violence is one factor in the production and maintenance of violence in our society (Murray and Kippax, 1979). Different methods of

There is considerable debate over the influence that portrayal of violence in the media may have on the socialization of children. Many psychologists and sociologists think that films like *Rambo* encourage children to try to solve problems by violent means.

SOURCE: Canapress Photo Service

investigation all point to an association between viewing violence and subsequent aggression (Eysenck and Nias, 1978). "TV violence has a large effect on a small percentage of youngsters and a small effect on a large percentage of youngsters" (Liebert *et al.*, 1982). The "large effect" refers to isolated incidents when modelling effect, personality, and circumstances come together:

In Crewe, England, a few years ago, a 14-year-old boy burned himself to death on the school's rugby field. As dozens of helpless friends and teachers watched, Andrew Potter poured alcohol over himself and set himself on fire. The youth left a suicide note saying that he was under pressure at school, hated homework, and resented the examination system. Potter had told a friend that he had been fascinated by a horror film in a television series called Theatre of Blood, which ended in a gruesome self-immolation (Calgary Herald, 24 January, 1979).

The "small effect" refers to the fact that televised violence makes children more tolerant of aggression in other children and less emotionally responsive to violence in themselves. In the words of an 11-year-old interviewed by *Newsweek* (Waters, 1977): "You see so much violence that it's meaningless. If I saw someone really get killed, it wouldn't be a big deal. I guess I'm turning into a hard rock" (quoted in Greenfield, 1984, p. 51).

Television's Beneficial Effects. Researchers have also been interested in finding out what positive socialization effects the mass media have on children. For example, television has been studied as an agent of anticipatory socialization for work roles. The main conclusion is that television does provide a wider perspective on work roles, but it also oversimplifies what the real world of work is like. (Peterson and Peters, 1983). While television exposes young people to career models beyond their own experiences, its portrayal of occupations has definite limitations. Occupations with high prestige occur much more frequently and occupations with low prestige much less frequently than is the case in the actual job market. Moreover, DeFleur and DeFleur (1967) found that the information television provides children about occupations tends to be superficial and misleading. It is full of stereotypes: clever unethical lawyers; temperamental, eccentric artists; burly, aggressive truck drivers, and so on.

The discussion of television's contribution to occupational socialization illustrates its unintentional influence on children: children go to television to be entertained, but while being entertained, they absorb much incidental information about their society. For example, "The Cosby Show" communicates attitudes such as respect for parental authority and tolerance of racial groups. We can hypothesize that TV programs that feature single-parent or blended families, or families with adopted children or youngsters with physical handicaps help children with similar experiences to feel comfortable. Attempts have been made to harness television's potential to benefit children. Since educators recognized the importance of youngsters' pre-school experiences for their later educational development, programs such as "Sesame Street" were developed to provide pre-school experiences at home. Research (Bogatz and Ball, 1972) showed that frequent "Sesame Street" viewers had improved skills, such as reading and alphabet recitation, and were rated by teachers as better prepared for school than infrequent viewers. Yet although it was hoped that "Sesame Street" would narrow the gap between economically advantaged and disadvantaged children, it turns out that the children who are more likely to watch "Sesame Street" are from advantaged homes. Therefore, any cultural or intellectual gap might be widened rather than decreased (Liebert *et al.*, 1982).

Attempts have been made to influence positively children's attitudes and behaviour, as well as their skills. For example, 30-second TV spots tried to show children that there are non-aggressive alternatives for solving problems. In one spot, two children are running toward the one empty swing in a playground. They arrive at the same time, and each child grabs an end of the swing. Impasse. The kids must either fight or find some other way to resolve the problem. Finally they decide to take turns. Both kids are winners; nobody loses.

Although the evidence clearly shows that television has great potential power to socialize, the actual socialization process is complex. For example, studies show that although pro-social episodes in programs such as "Mister Rogers' Neighborhood" have pro-social effects, the influence is limited to situations that are quite similar to those presented in the program. In addition, while a single exposure to a pro-social episode has immediate specific effects, these effects do not last even for a day. Finally, critics raise the questions, "Should television entertainment be consciously designed to socialize the young?" "Does such programming amount to subtle brainwashing?" (Liebert *et al.*, 1982).

An Overview

This section has dealt with the influence of major socialization agents: the family, the peer group, the schools, the mass media. Children are, of course, also socialized by other people, such as babysitters and daycare workers, by such institutions as Sunday school and the church, and by community organizations such as the YWCA and the YMCA.

As children mature into adults, they encounter an increasing diversity of socialization agents, which help them to learn relatively more specialized roles. For example, a considerable amount of occupational socialization occurs on the job. Young interns learn how to be effective doctors partly by attending medical school and partly by practising on hospitalized patients (Chappell and Colwill, 1981). Newly divorced adults are often socialized into the single role through self-help groups such as Parents Without Partners.

Many colleges and universities offer non-credit courses on topics such as effective parenting, coping with divorce and widowhood, and re-entry into the labour market by women who have been full-time housewives for many years. On the whole, adult socialization agencies tend to be impersonal, formal organizations such as universities, colleges, corporations, social welfare agencies, and the like. Nonetheless, family and peers continue to be important influences throughout adult life.

Over-socialization

Throughout this chapter, we have argued that the socialization process serves both society and the individual. Society's order and continuity depend upon its members learning to share values, norms, and language. Interaction and role playing rest upon these common understandings. On the other hand, socialization also allows individuals to realize their potential as human beings.

Because socialization is such a powerful process, there is a danger that those who read about it will end up with what sociologist Dennis Wrong (1961) called the "oversocialized conception of man." By this phrase, Wrong meant that we are mistaken if we think of people as being completely molded by the norms and values of their society. If this were the case, there would be no free will and people would not be responsible for their actions.

But this does not happen. It is quite true that people brought up in a particular society speak the same language, value much the same things, and behave in a similar fashion. And yet they are not all identical products turned out by an all-powerful socialization factory. There are many reasons why absolute conformity just does not occur.

To begin with, each person is biologically unique. The raw materials of temperament and inborn aptitudes leave considerable room for individuality. In addition, human beings possess the ability to question norms and values and to make changes. (The theorists of socialization also allowed for some measure of independence. Mead acknowledged the spontaneous, creative "I," as well as the socialized "Me." Similarly, Freud's personality structure theory contained the impulsive, selfish Id, as well as the conventionalized Super-ego.) Individuals also *make* roles as well as take roles, as they modify situations to suit themselves.

Furthermore, although nearly everyone is socialized within the family, the actual content of children's socialization varies from family to family. Even brothers and sisters brought up in the same home experience growing up somewhat differently. In addition, the fact that parents and children represent two different generations ensures two different perspectives on the lessons of socialization (Yoels and Karp, 1978).

The societal norms and values that make up the content of these lessons are really only abstractions until they are interpreted by specific agencies of socialization. The people responsible for teaching the child to fit into society have differing interpretations of these norms and values. Finally, socialization is carried out by a variety of agencies, so that the person being socialized is exposed to different perspectives.

All of this means that although we can speak about Canadians in general, and in so doing distinguish them from Japanese or Brazilians, we are talking about characteristics that make Canadians similar, not identical. The existence of at least some deviant behaviour within every society, including our own, demonstrates that no system of socialization is perfectly efficient.

Summary

1. Through socialization, individuals develop selfhood and acquire the knowledge, skills, and motivations required for them to participate in social life. This learning process is functional for both the individual and the society. From the individual's point of view, interaction with adult caretakers allows the infant to realize its human potentialities. From society's point of view, socialization equips the person to handle societal roles and ensures that commitment to the social order is maintained over time.

2. Sociologists have distinguished four types of socialization. "Primary socialization" refers to the learning that occurs in childhood. It lays the foundation for all later learning. "Adult socialization" describes the socialization that takes place beyond the childhood years. "Anticipatory socialization" is the role learning that occurs in advance of the actual playing of roles. "Resocialization" occurs when a new role or situation requires that a person replace established patterns of behaviour with new patterns.

3. Major theoretical approaches to childhood socialization include Piaget's cognitive-developmental approach, Freud's psychoanalytic theory, and Mead's and Cooley's symbolic interactionist theories. Piaget's work focuses on the development of morality. Freud's approach analyses the development of personality structure. The symbolic interactionists emphasize the child's acquisition of language and self. These approaches are complementary, rather than competing, systems of thought.

4. There are four major agents of childhood socialization: the family, the school, the peer group, and the mass media. Because society has given the family and the school a mandate to socialize youngsters, both of these agencies deliberately attempt to equip them with the knowledge and values required to fit into adult society. The influence of the peer group and the media is, for the most part, unintentional.

5. Socialization is a lifelong process. Primary socialization cannot possibly equip individuals for all the roles and situations they will encounter throughout their lives. Compared to primary socialization, adult socialization tends to concentrate on overt behaviour (as opposed to values and motives). It tends to be realistic, rather than idealistic; to be more specific in content; and to occur in formal organizations, rather than informal contexts. In addition, the relationship between socializer and the one socialized in the adult situation is marked by lower levels of feeling and power than in the childhood situation.

6. Socialization does not mold members of society into identical products. Fortunately, there is considerable room for spontaneity and individuality.

Further Reading

Bank, S. P., & Kahn, M. D. (1982). *The sibling bond*. New York: Basic Books.
The first major attempt to unravel the complex and lifelong relations among sisters and brothers.

Bogdan, R. (1972). Learning to sell door to door. In B. Geer (Ed.), *Learning to work*. Beverley Hills, CA: Sage Publications.
Focuses on the role of persuasion in the context of occupational socialization.

Brim, O. G., Jr., & Kagan J. (Eds.). (1980). *Constancy and change in human development*. Cambridge, MA: Harvard University Press.
An analysis of the extent to which childhood experiences constrain adult behaviour.

Elkin, F., & Handel, G. (1984). *The child and society: The process of socialization*. (4th ed.) New York: Random House.
A compact overview of the subject of socialization.

Freeman , D. (1983). *Margaret Mead and Samoa: The making and unmaking of an anthropological myth*. Cambridge, MA: Harvard University Press.
A controversial discussion of whether or not adolescence is a universally difficult phase of life.

Goffman, E. (1961). *Asylums: Essays on the situation of mental patients and other inmates.* New York: Doubleday Anchor.
How total institutions, such as mental hospitals and prisons, attempt resocialization, and how the inmates fight back.

Haas, J., & Shaffir, W. (1978). *Shaping identity in Canadian society.* Scarborough, Ont.: Prentice-Hall.
A book of readings that deals with ethnic and occupational socialization from a symbolic-interactionist perspective.

Synnot, A. (1983). Little angels, little devils: A sociology of children. *The Canadian Review of Sociology and Anthropology, 20* (1), 79-95.

4
Gender Relations

The purpose of this chapter is to explore one of the most important distinctions human beings make of each other—the classification as male or female. Many of the differences, especially in how we treat each other, are not biological in origin, but social, and things social are learned rather than inherited.

After completing this chapter, be sure that you are able to

1. distinguish gender from sex;

2. briefly describe some of the basic male-female differences;

3. explain the anthropological approach to male-female differences;

4. describe the importance of gender stereotypes;

5. outline the differences in life experience between Canadian men and women;

6. explain the concept of women's liberation;

7. explain the concept of the countermovement toward men's liberation.

Female. Male. The difference that makes a difference. She can identify 25 colours, including taupe and magenta. He can identify 25 cars, including Aston-Martin and Lamborgine. He defends against danger. She is afraid to go out alone after dark. She smiles more. He does more of the talking and is more likely to interrupt her remarks (Thorne and Henley, 1975). Except for anger, she finds it easier to express her innermost feelings (Jourard, 1964). He thinks sexual humour is funny (Brodzinsky, Barnet, and Aiello, 1981). She prefers jokes that make fun of the status quo between the sexes.

Consider marriage. In our society, it is still the sign of the successful woman, while occupational achievement is the sign of the successful man. It is women who show primary (though not exclusive) interest in makeup, fashionable clothing, cosmetic surgery for wrinkles and jowls, health spas, Weight Watchers' meetings, and fashion shows.

Men, on the other hand, take responsibility for initiating contact with women (and the risk of rejection). The burden of decision-making and economic support within marriage is carried disproportionately by men. Society expects men to achieve, to compete, to be aggressive. These "men of iron" do not have the option to be unemployed or to fail occupationally. On the other hand, the children belong to the women. Wives receive custody of three-quarters of the children involved in divorce (Statistics Canada, 1985, p. 3).

Educational and economic experiences also differ by sex. Since the mid-1960s, female enrolment in Canadian universities has increased steadily. Women now represent slightly more than half of full-time university undergraduates. Nevertheless, they continue to enrol in the type of educational programs that lead to the traditionally lower-paid women's occupations (Buchland, 1985, p. 138).

Old age is not easy for either sex. Compared to older men, older women are more likely to be poor and widowed, to be living alone, or to be institutionalized (Dulude, 1987). Elderly men, on the other hand, tend to lack the occupational prestige, income, physical strength, and sexual prowess that are associated with masculinity in our society (Abu-Laban, 1980). In recent years, destitute women have joined homeless men on the Skid Rows of our cities (Ross, 1982).

Men and women differ in their experience of physical and mental health. Women are ill more often than men; however, their illnesses are relatively mild (Nathanson, 1984), and the average woman outlives the average man by seven years (Statistics Canada, 1985). There are more females than males with the diagnosis of depression, phobia, anxiety, hysteria, and chronic schizophrenia. There are more males than females with the diagnosis of personality disorders, such as alcoholism and drug addiction, and psycho-physiological disorders, such as ulcers, heart, and respiratory illness (Al-Issa, 1980). At every age, Canadian males are more likely than Canadian females to kill themselves (Cumming and Lazer, 1981). In short, the male gender role "may be dangerous to your health" (Harrison, 1978). Women and men are socialized differently, play different roles, and have different thoughts and experiences (Bernard, 1981). They live out their lives in social worlds that are separate at some points and overlapping at others. "Men and women march to different drummers"; in some respects, "they are not even in the same parade" (Bernard, 1975).

Sociology of Gender Relations

This chapter explores one central question: what does it mean to be male or to be female in contemporary Canadian society? Human social life always and everywhere has been built around the relationships between the sexes. Changes in these relationships thus affect the entire social structure.

Some Definitions

Note that the term *gender relations* is not a code-word for women. Although the women's movement stimulated sociology to analyse previously ignored female behaviour, sociologists soon recognized that it was pointless to study one sex in isolation from the other. Masculinity and femininity derive their meaning from the relation of one to the other. The roles most influenced by gender (for example, husband and wife) are interdependent roles. Moreover, the changes currently taking place in female roles inevitably affect male roles as well.

Let us define *gender* and distinguish it from the closely related word, *sex*. **Sex** refers to the physiological differences between males and females. **Gender**, on the other hand, is what is socially recognized as femininity or masculinity (Gould and Kern-Daniels, 1977). The cultural norms of a particular society identify some ways of behaving, feeling, and thinking as appropriate for females, and others as appropriate for males. Gender is a set of social attitudes that vary greatly from culture to culture and that change over time.

The Importance of Gender

Our argument for the importance of gender rests upon two major points. First, in Canadian society, as in all human societies, the genders are *differentiated*. A great fuss is made over the biological distinctions between female and male. Elaborate sets of meanings are built upon them. Gender's impact upon the individual begins at birth and continues until death. The parents of a newborn infant ask: "Is it a boy or a girl?" Even though at this stage the infant is little more than a bundle of tissue with potentiality, members of society immediately begin to react to it in terms of its gender. It will likely be wrapped in a pink or blue blanket. It will also be given a name that usually signals its sex. Thus begins a sorting process into different socialization streams (Goffman, 1977).

Sex-typing begins even before birth. Aberle and Naegele (1952) reported that fathers expect their daughters to be pretty, fragile, sweet, and delicate, and their sons to be athletic and aggressive. Rubin *et al.*, (1974) interviewed 30 pairs of parents at a Boston hospital within 24 hours of the birth of their first child, selecting the parents of 15 daughters and 15 sons. Infant girls were described by the parents as "softer," "finer-featured," "littler," and "prettier," boys as "bigger," "stronger," "firmer," and "more alert."

Throughout life, gender permeates every social relationship

cathy®   by Cathy Guisewite

and every sphere of human activity. There are girls' games and boys' games; there is women's work and men's work. Being a male student is not the same as being a female student. Being a wife, mother, divorcé, widow, or elderly woman is not the same as being a husband, father, divorced male, widower, or elderly man. The male-female distinction serves as a basic organizing principle for every human society (Bem, 1981). Family, work, religion, politics, and sports have traditionally employed a division of labour along gender lines.

A second reason for gender's importance is that society values men's characteristics and activities more than women's (Lipman-Blumen, 1984). The sexes are ranked. As a category, males have more status, power, influence, and resources than females. When parents ask the doctors which sex their newborn infant is, in all likelihood they are hoping for a particular answer. If the baby is their first child or intended to be their only child, research shows that parents, especially fathers, tend to prefer a boy (Williamson, 1976). Which sex would you prefer to be? Chances are that if you are female, you sometimes wish you were male and, if you are male, you are quite satisfied to remain that way.

Why do people permit—even admire—the masculine behaviour of a twelve-year-old girl and dislike the feminine behaviour of a twelve-year-old boy? Even the labels for these children, "tomboy" and "sissy," convey society's attitudes. The answer to this question, and many more just like it, is clear: society values males more highly than females.

Female-Male Similarities and Differences

In our society people tend to view physiological distinctions (sex) and the cultural elaborations upon them (gender) as equally natural. Therefore, it makes sense to determine just what these differences really are. Possible origins of such differences are explored in later sections.

Loss of Equality for !Kung Women

The !Kung* have lived as hunters and gatherers in the Kalahari Desert of South Africa for at least 11 000 years, but recently they have begun to settle in agrarian villages near those of the Bantus. Settlement began about 15 years ago, and all but about five percent of the 30 000 !Kung now live by farming and keeping herds of domestic animals.

One aspect of this change has been the loss of equality for these newly agrarian women. The remaining !Kung hunter-gatherer women enjoy a higher status because of the role they play in contributing to the band's food supply. Since they gather at least half the group's food, these women, of necessity, are as mobile as the men, who make up the other half by hunting. Women and men leave the camp equally often to obtain food. Those who do not seek food on a given day, women and men, remain in the camp and share in taking care of the children.

The women in the new !Kung farming settlements, however, have far less mobility than the men and contribute less to the food supply. The men leave the village to clear fields, raise crops, and care for the cattle of their Bantu neighbours; the women remain in the village where they prepare food and take care of the shelters.

Since the men work for the Bantus, they learn the Bantu language. Thus when the Bantus deal with the !Kung, they deal exclusively with the men. This practice, together with the men's emulation of the male-dominated Bantu society, contributes to increasingly subservient roles for !Kung women.

---

*The exclamation point refers to an alveolar-palatal click. The tongue tip is pressed against the roof of the mouth and drawn sharply away, producing a hollow, popping sound.

SOURCE: "!Kung hunter-gatherers: feminism, diet, and birth control" by Gina Bari Kolata, 1974, *Science, 185.*

Misleading Female-Male Comparisons

Because so much emotion and mystery surround male-female relations, it is not surprising that many notions about sex differences have been biased (Tresemer, 1975). We dwell on the differences between males and females and ignore their similarities. Men and women are seen as *either* this *or* that, not both. We are fascinated with the anatomical differences. However, we tend to overlook the fact that males and females really share much the same body blueprint.

Psychological traits provide another example. Deaux (1984) analysed a decade's research on gender in the field of psychology and concluded that the main effect sex differences are "surprisingly small." We assume—correctly, as it happens (Maccoby and Jacklin, 1974)—that males are more aggressive than females. But this does not mean that *all* males are aggressive while *all* females are passive. Males and females vary between being highly aggressive and being very unaggressive. Although the group average for males is somewhat higher, a substantial number of females will be as aggressive as, or more aggressive than, a substantial number of males.

Gender Differences

With regard to psychological characteristics, "the sexes are more alike than different" (Maccoby, 1980). To date, research has established that females have superior verbal ability, while males have superior mathematical ability and visual-spatial skills. As mentioned earlier, males tend to be more aggressive than females. Females do better at understanding non-verbal communication. Finally, some evidence suggests that females are more likely than males to conform to group pressure. Other psychological traits are being studied, such as possible differences in moral thinking (Gilligan, 1982). These differences, however, are slight and can be significantly altered by training (Deaux, 1985).

Researchers' inventory of female-male distinctions grows longer when consideration is given to some of the following:

1. fashion (trousers and hair length are no longer reliable guides);
2. etiquette and demeanor (who drives the car on dates? who lights cigarettes for whom?);
3. language (which gender is more often likened to food—a dish, tomato, peach, cookie, honey, cheese cake? [Eakins and Eakins, 1978]);
4. non-verbal communication (women gaze at men [Lamb,

1981] and are touched by men [Henley, 1975] more than vice versa);

5. social roles (nurses versus soldiers, mothers versus fathers);
6. spheres of existence (the domestic world of women versus the public world of men).

Up to this point, we have concentrated on enumerating differences rather than explaining them. The sections that follow will consider the causation of gender.

Biological Explanations of Gender

To what extent are men masculine and women feminine because they were born that way? In particular, is women's social subordination a reflection of their biological inferiority? These questions have concerned researchers in many academic disciplines.

The Anthropological Approach

Anthropologists have provided a perspective on the question, "To what extent do women's and men's psychological characteristics and social behaviour have their source in their physical differences?" If a certain type of behaviour is found in many different cultures, then anthropologists assume that the behaviour is determined by, or at least connected with, heredity and the biological differences between women and men. If, however, social arrangements in one culture are different from the social arrangements in another culture, then anthropologists assume that the behaviour is socially determined or learned.

Recent debate has centred upon two interrelated and apparently universal aspects of the anthropological record: evaluation of the sexes and male dominance (Rosaldo, 1974). The first universal refers to the fact that all cultures value males more than females. If a particular area of activity is defined as exclusively or predominantly male, it is valued.

The second universal is related to the first. Although women sometimes have a good deal of informal influence, "societies in which women are consistently dominant do not exist and have never existed" (Friedl, 1978). Even the Iroquois, whose society was the closest to the hypothetical form called a *matriarchy* (rule by women), were not actually ruled by women. Iroquois women might install and depose their chiefs, but the chiefs were men (Rosaldo, 1974).

Anthropologists locate the source of universal gender inequality in the most important biological sex difference: women bear children and men do not (Sayers, 1982). In pre-literate societies, the division of labour built upon biological sex meant that women were responsible for the domestic sphere, especially the feeding and care of children. Women were usually responsible for agriculture, cooking, and food gathering—all tasks that were performed at home (Ambert, 1976). Men, by necessity, filled the more public roles of hunting, politics, military, and religion (Rosaldo, 1974). When class societies developed and goods were produced for exchange, rather than for sharing, women's child-care responsibilities made them economically dependent on men (Sayers, 1982).

Two polarities of personality are thought to have developed as a result of this division of labour. Socialization pressures encouraged women to focus on feelings, communion with others, and nurture. These pressures encouraged men, on the other hand, to develop task mastery, competition, and strong ego boundaries (Bardwick, 1979).

The significance of physiological distinctions between the sexes in reproductive function, size and strength has been exaggerated through cultural interpretations. Men's monopoly of the public domain gave them privileged access to resources and symbols that enhanced their power. As primary culture-makers, males produced religion, philosophy, literature, science, laws, and so on, which assumed and upheld male dominance. Both sexes have been socialized to accept as true these definitions of the situation.

The real issue, then, is cultural meanings, not reproductive capabilities. Ideas are human products and are thus subject to revision (Richardson, 1981). The notion of male superiority is therefore open to question; moreover, technology permits humans to transcend biology. Through the use of modern birth control methods, for example, technology has made it possible for women in industrialized nations to decide when, or if, to bear children. In addition, inventions such as bottle feeding and day-care centres have made the child-rearing function separable from the childbearing function. Assigning of domestic tasks to women and public tasks to men can no longer be justified on biological grounds. In short, male dominance is not inevitable (Richardson, 1981).

Psychosexual Deviations

Gender identity (a person's conviction of being male or female) and genitals usually match. Children born with penises believe themselves to be males and display male personalities and behaviour. Similarly, children born with vaginas develop female gender identities and feminine characteristics. Occasionally, ambiguous genitals occur through birth defects or accidents. People with psychosexual abnormalities provide some insight into the question of whether biological or social causation is more important in the development of gender. Evidence on both sides has been reported (Singleton, 1986). However, the case described below reinforces the importance of gender as social assignment.

In the 1960s, the parents of perfectly normal seven-month—old twin boys took their children to a hospital to be circumcized. The physician elected to use an electric cauterizing needle instead of a scalpel to remove the foreskin of the one who chanced to be brought to the operating room first. When this baby's foreskin didn't give on the first try, or on the second, the doctor stepped up the current. On the third try, the surge of heat from the electricity literally cooked the baby's penis. Unable to heal, the penis dried up, and in a few days sloughed off completely, like the stub of an umbilical cord (Money and Tucker, 1975).

Doctors recommended that the boy's sex be reassigned and that female external genitals be surgically constructed. The child's name, clothes, and hairstyle were feminized as the parents made every effort to rear the twins—one male and one female. As the following anecdotes concerning the twins at age 4½ show, both parents and children successfully developed gender-appropriate attitudes and behaviour. The mother, talking about the boy, reported: "In the summer time, one time I caught him—he went out and took a leak in my flower garden in the front yard, you know. He was quite happy with himself. And I just didn't say anything. I just couldn't. I started laughing and I told daddy about it."

The corresponding comments about the girl went this way: "I've never had a problem with her. She did once when she was little, she took off her panties and threw them over the fence. And she didn't have no panties on. But I just gave her a little swat on the rear, and I told her that nice little girls didn't do that, and she should keep her pants on" (Money and Ehrhardt, 1972). For Christmas, the girl wanted dolls, a doll house, and doll carriage. The boy wanted a toy garage with cars, gas pumps, and tools.

This case and others suggest that sex by assignment outweighs biological factors in determining gender identity. However, gender reassignment is usually unsuccessful after the age of 18 months (Money and Ehrhardt, 1972). By then, the child has the ability to understand verbal labels for gender and to view the world from a "female" or "male" perspective.

By permission of Johnny Hart and North America Syndicate, Inc.

Conclusions

A variety of arguments has been used to decide whether or not Canadian society's estimation of males as superior and the importance of gender in the societal division of labour have a biological foundation. The anthropological approach and psychosexual differences were reviewed above. Additional approaches exist, such as comparing sex/gender in animals and humans, and studying and operation of sex hormones upon unborn foetuses. Unfortunately, space limitations make it impossible to discuss all these ideas in detail. (See Archer and Lloyd [1985] for a review of this research.)

Every approach to the problem of the biological foundation of female-male differences raises more questions than it answers. Biology may be directly involved in cognitive differences and aggressiveness, and indirectly involved in the gender division of labour. The secondary sex characteristics of male size and strength may also contribute indirectly to gender differences. For instance, in a culture such as ours, which values "sheer bigness," the generally greater male body size may translate into status (Garn, 1966). Superior male strength is obviously also an ingredient in the traditional gender division of labour. More important, however, is the implicit or actual physical threat that males present to females. As Goffman (1977) points out: "Selective mating ensures that generally husbands are bigger than wives and boyfriends are bigger than girlfriends."

The biological differences between females and males are really very slight in comparison with the immense gender differences built upon this substructure. To search for either biological *or* environmental causation of gender patterns is a misleading and simplistic formulation of a complex question. In gender patterns, as in social behaviour in general, both biology and environment are involved. Biochemical and genetic factors set the stage, but culture and history provide the script (Kunkel, 1977).

The fact that socialization often emphasizes "natural" sex differences further complicates the situation. For example, our society provides more athletic facilities and opportunities for the physically stronger males. However, because most of the gender differences between the sexes involve learning in one way or another, let us look at socialization as an explanation of gender.

Socialization Explanations of Gender

Chapter 3 defined *socialization* as the complex, lifelong learning process through which individuals develop selfhood and acquire the knowledge, skills, and motivations required to participate in social life. **Gender socialization** involves the particular processes through which people learn to be masculine and feminine according to the expectations current in their society. As we have already seen, there exist a number of theoretical approaches to socialization: the Piagetian, Freudian, and symbolic-interaction perspectives. Symbolic-interactionism will be emphasized here.

Each society has its scripts (Laws, 1979) for femininity and masculinity. Children's emotions, thoughts, and behaviour are shaped in approximate conformity with these **gender scripts.** Gender stereotypes and occupational sex-typing tell us something about our society's gender scripts.

Gender Stereotypes

Imagine yourself talking with a friend who describes two people you have never met. One person is said to be independent, adventurous, and dominant, while the other is described as sentimental, submissive, emotional, and affectionate. Would it be easier to picture one of these persons as male and the other as female? If you visualize the first person as male and the second as female, you have demonstrated your knowledge of gender stereotypes. What is more, you could be Canadian, American, Peruvian, Nigerian, Pakistani, or Japanese. Cross-cultural research shows that citizens of 30 nations share similar general beliefs about the sexes (Williams and Best, 1982). **Gender stereotypes** capture folk beliefs about the nature of females and males generally. Many studies show that, despite the activities of the women's movement, gender stereotypes are "widely held, persistent, and highly traditional in content" (Ward and Balswick, 1978). When researchers (Broverman *et al.*, 1972) ask respondents to describe the average man and the average woman, the gender traits fall into two groups: a masculine *instrumental* cluster and a feminine *expressive* cluster. The masculine **instrumental** group includes such characteristics as being independent, active, competitive, and ambitious. A relative

Sex and Temperament in Three Primitive Societies

More than fifty years ago, anthropologist Margaret Mead set off to New Guinea to discover whether North American sex differences in temperament were innate or learned. Her analysis of three New Guinea societies is a classic argument for cultural conditioning of sex differences. Mead visited three primitive tribes located within a 160-kilometre area on the island of New Guinea: the gentle, mountain-dwelling Arapesh; the fierce, cannibalistic Mundugumor; and the headhunters of Tchambuli.

Arapesh men and women alike displayed an unaggressive, maternal personality that would seem feminine in our society. The mild-mannered Arapesh "see all life as an adventure in growing things, growing children, growing pigs, growing yams and taros and coconuts and sago, faithfully, carefully, observing all the rules that make things grow." An Arapesh boy "grew" his wife. The girl was betrothed when she was seven or eight to a boy about six years older. Although the marriage was not consummated until both reached sexual maturity, the Arapesh male's greatest claim on his wife was that he had contributed the food that became the flesh and bone of her body. Later, both parents participated in childbirth. Conception was believed to require repeated sexual union in order to feed and shape the child in the mother's womb. Both parents lay down to bear the child and observed the birth taboos and rituals. Mead said that "if one comments upon a middle-aged man as good-looking, the people answer: 'Good-looking, Y-e-s? But you should have seen him before he bore all those children.'"

Aggressiveness was eschewed by both sexes. The ideal Arapesh male never provoked a fight, and rape was unknown. Males considered leadership to be an onerous duty.

Mead found that the Mundugumor tribe offered a striking contrast to the Arapesh. Whereas the Arapesh standardized the personality of both men and women in a mold that, out of traditional bias, we would describe as womanly and maternal, the Mundugumor went to the opposite extreme. Again, ignoring sex as the basis for establishing sex differences, they standardized the behavior of both men and women as actively (almost pathologically) masculine. Both sexes were expected to be violent, aggressive, jealous, competitive, and active.

The structure of the Mundugumor family system appeared to be the source of these insecure, aggressive personalities. Here, the social organization was based on a "theory" of natural hostility among members of the same sex. Because father and daughters formed one rival group (called a "rope") and mother and sons another, neither parent welcomed pregnancy. The resulting offspring could abet the forces of the opposing group. The infant, regardless of sex, was not cherished by its mother. For example, weaning consisted of slapping the child. Hostility existed among siblings. All this unpleasantness was intensified by the fact that polygyny (a man having more than one wife at a time) was the ideal. Although wives brought wealth, additional marriages fuelled hostility and jealousy. Sex often took the form of a rough-and-tumble athletic tryst in the bushes. The delights of these bush encounters could be enhanced by copulating in other people's gardens, an act that would spoil their yam crops. The fact that this society was rich was the reason that it managed to exist at all, with so little of its structure based on genuine co-operation.

Among the lake-dwelling Tchambuli, Mead found that the gender roles and the accompanying temperament reversed western notions of normalcy. The woman was the "dominant, impersonal, managing partner, the man the less responsible and the emotionally dependent person." The Tchambuli derived their greatest satisfaction from art. Economic affairs were relegated to the women, while the men devoted themselves to art and ceremony. The women worked together in amiable groups and enjoyed the theatricals the men put on, "whereas the lives of the men are one mass of petty bickering, misunderstanding, reconciliation, avowals, disclaimers, and protestations accompanied by gifts, the lives of the women are singularly unclouded with personalities or with quarrelling."

The Tchambuli women were described as "solid, preoccupied, powerful, with shaved unadorned heads" and the men as having "delicately arranged curls," "handsome pubic coverings of flying-fox skin highly ornamented with shells," "mincing steps and self-conscious mien." The women were more "urgently sexed" than the men. And from early childhood, males continued to be emotionally dependent on the women.

From her observations of the three New Guinean tribes, Mead arrived at this conclusion: "The material suggests that we may say that many, if not all, of the personality traits which we have called masculine or feminine are as lightly linked to sex as are the clothing, the manner, and the forms of head dress that a society at a given period assigns to either sex. . . . [The] evidence is overwhelmingly in favor of the strength of social conditioning." Nevertheless, Mead's conclusion has not gone unchallenged.

SOURCE: *Sex and Temperament in Three Primitive Societies* by Margaret Mead, 1935, repr. 1950, New York: Mentor Books.

absence of these traits is supposed to characterize women. In other words, relative to men, women are seen to be dependent, passive, non-competitive, and not ambitious.

The feminine **expressive** group, on the other hand, consists of such attributes as being gentle, quiet, sensitive to the feelings of others. Relative to women, men are perceived as lacking these traits. In addition, gender stereotype studies (Broverman *et al.*, 1972) report that many more of the characteristics valued in western societies are considered to be masculine rather than feminine traits.

It appears that beliefs about gender develop, at least in part, from people's observations of women and men playing these traditional social roles. For example, children are more likely to encounter women taking care of babies and men wielding authority in the workplace than vice versa. It is natural for them to conclude that the characteristics thought to be necessary for child care (nurturance, warmth) and for success in the labour force (dominance, objectivity) are typical of each sex. Therefore, it is likely that gender stereotypes "will not disappear until people divide social roles equally; that is, until child care and household responsibilities are shared equally by women and men, and the responsibility to be employed outside the home is borne equally" (Eagly and Steffen, 1984).

Meanwhile, the gender stereotypes themselves, functioning as self-fulfilling prophecies, constitute one important impediment to social change. If women are assumed to be less competent, their performance may be judged less successful than it actually is. Or, if women are assumed to be less competent, they may be given fewer opportunities to assert themselves (Deaux and Wrightsman, 1984).

Occupational Sex-Typing

The sex-typing of occupations is a central element of the societal script for masculinity and femininity that children learn. Many occupations have a majority of either female or male workers, a condition known as, **occupational segregation**. For example, most nurses are women and most lawyers are men. As you will learn, this kind of sex-segregation in the work force is, in part, responsible for the large differences between Canadian men and women with respect to income, job security, and opportunities for advancement (Boyd, 1984).

Occupational sex-typing refers to the tendency to regard sex-segregated occupations as more appropriate for one sex or the other. Kindergarten teaching has traditionally been regarded as women's work, while university teaching has been viewed as men's work. Beliefs that men are better suited for certain occupations and women for others are backed up by reference to gender stereotypes. Thus, women may be considered suited to nursing because they are nurturant and men to law because they are logical (Williams and Best, 1982).

Occupational sex-typing has left men as pilots on airliners while women served meals to passengers. These traditional segregations are changing, but Judy Cameron will not meet many other women in the pilot's lounge at commercial airports.

SOURCE: Canapress Photo Service

A study of elementary school children in Saskatchewan and Québec (Labour Canada, 1986) suggests that these traditional ideas are undergoing some change. A high proportion of the children believed that most occupations could be undertaken by both sexes. However, there is a stronger expectation that traditionally masculine occupations will attract both men and women than that traditionally feminine occupations will attract men. As the study points out, attempts have been made to attract girls into science-based careers, such as engineering. However, no comparable efforts have been made to interest boys in becoming secretaries or nurses. Besides, the relatively low salaries paid in predominately female occupations militates against attracting men into them.

The children were asked, "What do you want to be when you grow up?" Their own occupational aspirations showed both persistence and change in traditional notions. Ninety-three percent of the boys chose a traditionally male occupation. Only one percent chose traditionally feminine careers. No boy wanted to be a dental assistant, librarian, nurse, or hairdresser. Forty-three percent of the girls also chose traditionally masculine occupations. The jobs they had in mind were professional ones requiring a high level of education, such as dentistry or medicine. Some boys (but no girls) mentioned mathematician, stockbrocker, astronomer, or air traffic controller.

Many of the girls seemed to believe that equality of the sexes does not apply to them personally. Many of them seemed to be saying, "Yes, women can become doctors, but I expect to be a nurse," "Bank managers can be women as well as men, but I am going to be a teller" (Labour Canada, 1986, p. 55).

The Role of the Mass Media in Gender Socialization

Concerns about the effects on children of violence in the mass media led to the studies described in Chapter 3. Since the advent of the women's movement, a parallel concern has been voiced over the impact of the media on the development of gender attitudes and behaviour. The Royal Commission on the Status of Women in Canada (1970) accused the media of perpetuating stereotyping of both sexes. It was especially critical of the "degrading, moronic" depiction of women in advertisements. The Commission argued that although men as well as women are stereotyped, the results may be more damaging for women because advertising encourages females to be dependent—to live in a dream world instead of acting to achieve what they hope for. More than a decade later, the Canadian Radio-television and Telecommunications Commission (1982) registered similar concerns about gender stereotyping in both commercials and programming.

Among the recommendations of the Canadian Radio-television and Telecommunications Commission (1982) are the following:

1. Broadcasting should include a wide variety of images reflecting the diversity of women in our culture—women of all ages, women of differing ethnic groups, and women of differing physical appearance.

2. Broadcasting should present women engaged in a wide variety of activities, including athletics.

3. Women should not be used as sexual stimuli, or as attention-getting, but otherwise irrelevant, objects.

4. When families are presented, the diversity of lifestyles that exist today should be reflected (for example, single parents and extended families).

5. Women should be more adequately represented as news readers, reporters, and hosts.

6. A balance of female and male perspectives should be represented in stories, issues, topics, and images, as well as in writing, editing, directing, and producing.

The gender-relevant content of television has certainly changed since the Royal Commission on the Status of Women (1970) brought the matter to the attention of Canadians. From time to time, various feminist issues, such as provision of daycare, are aired on educational panels and dramas. Female newscasters, business commentators, and disc jockeys are now present in significant, if not representative, numbers. The gender scripts portrayed in TV sitcoms show some change. Mrs. Huxtable on "The Cosby Show" is a lawyer; Mrs. Keaton on "Family Ties" is an architect. Alexis on "Dynasty" and the three "Golden Girls" challenge the notion that only young women belong on television.

Nevertheless, systematic analysis of television's content demonstrates that traditional patterns are still there. Most areas of TV entertainment feature twice as many males as females. The stars are more likely to be males. Despite departures from stereotypical depiction, such as those mentioned above, the males are apt to be autonomous and aggressive, the females nurturant, dominated by others, and defined by their relationship to males (Durkin, 1986). Even when women hold professional jobs, their first concern is their family and home. (We see Dr. Huxtable in his medical office much more often Mrs. Huxtable in her law office.) While females are still typically young and attractive, middle-aged and older males are commonplace. Moreover, Joan Collins and the "Golden Girls" are expensively groomed, attractive women, not grandmotherly figures.

Advertising continues to sell stereotyped messages about the sexes along with products (Singer, 1986). Men predominate as voices of authority. Ads portray women as trivial and infantile. Males remain rugged individualists, dressed for success (Wernick, 1987). Although a consumer-oriented image of both sexes is portrayed, women especially seem "born to shop." Both sexes are now being sexually exploited (Posner, 1987). As ads such as the Calvin Klein "Obsession" campaign demonstrate, the emphasis in now on sexuality under the guise of liberality. Even the Miss Mew cat food commercial features "a buxom feline complete with false eyelashes and sultry voice being lusted after by a variety of toms" (Posner, 1987, p. 187).

In the late 1980s, two matters concern people who are worried about the role the media play in gender stereotyping. First, how is the Canadian Radio-television and Telecommunications Commission to enforce the recommendations outlined above? Second, how is the issue of sexually explicit and violent portrayal of females in pornographic videotapes and magazines to be handled?

The Symbolic-Interactionist Perspective on Gender Socialization

Symbolic interactionists, such as Cooley and Mead, view "reality" as a matter of social definition. Socialization involves the development of a self, which is also socially defined. "Because gender consists of social constructions built upon female-male physiological differences, symbolic interactionism seems a particularly appropriate theoretical approach to the questions we have been asking in this chapter" (Mackie, 1987).

Development of Gender Identity.   As a first step to self-awareness, the child differentiates herself or himself from other objects in the environment. As you learned in Chapter 3, Mead hypothesizes that the capacity to use language allows the child to learn the meaning of all these things, including himself or herself. Names form a basis, then, for the development of the self. A given name individualizes the infant and classifies it by gender; that is, naming a child "Barbara" simultaneously separates this infant from other infants and signifies its femaleness.

This gender classification influences the way caregivers interact with the infant as a boy or as a girl. For example, for the first six months or so, male infants are touched more, while female infants are talked to more (Lewis, 1972). Later, the male toddler is tossed into the air ("How's my big boy?"), while the female child is tickled under the chin ("How's my sweet little girl?") (Richmond-Abbott, 1983).

Although the child's adult socializers place it in a gender class at birth, some time must pass before the child responds to its own self in terms of gender. By the age of three years, a child can accurately and consistently answer the question: "Are you a girl or a boy?" At the same age, children show preferences for either "girl" or "boy" toys and activities (Kessler and McKenna, 1978).

Socialization agents, such as the family, peers, mass media, and school, teach children what sorts of traits and behaviours go along with the female-male distinction. Parents admonish that "Boys don't cry" and "Girls don't sit with their legs apart." Richer's (1979) observational study of Ontario kindergarten classrooms shows how the teacher provided cues to enable children to classify "properly" the two sexes. The teacher found gender to be a practical means of organizing the children. For example, children lined up by gender to move from one activity to another—going to the library or the gymnasium, retrieving food from their lockers, preparing to go home. Also, gender was used to motivate participation: "The girls are ready, the boys are not," or "Who can do it the fastest, the boys or the girls?" During coordination exercises, commands were given by gender: "Boys, put your fingers on your nose; girls, put your hands in your laps; boys, touch your toes." When someone slipped up here, the teacher's admonishment sometimes took this form: "Are you a girl? I thought all along you were a boy." Richer (1979) tells us that such situations left the child squirming with embarrassment. Likely, part of the reason was loss of status associated with his "demotion" from boy to girl. Be that as it may, the various socialization agents teach children both gender identity—awareness of being a member of one gender or the other—and the differential evaluation of females and males. Let us turn now to some examples of how language reinforces the ranking of the sexes.

Language and the Ranking of the Sexes.   The English language (among others) puts women down, while it asserts male superiority. Therefore, children unwittingly learn sexism along with language.

The "problem of the generic masculine" labels the way in which the English language fails to speak clearly and fairly of both sexes (Spencer, 1985). Here, language excludes women through generic masculine terms that are supposed to refer to people in general: "he," "mankind," "man, the social animal," "men of good will." Some grammarians argue that the generic masculine applies to both sexes—that "man" means "woman" as well. Feminists claim that the generic masculine is both ambiguous and discriminatory. For instance, Ritchie's (1975) survey of 200 years of Canadian law concluded that the ambiguity of the generic masculine allowed judges to include or exclude women under statutes and regulations, depending on the climate of the times or their own personal biases (Martyna, 1980). If the law says "he," does it mean "he" or "he/she"?

Another way language treats the sexes differently is by regarding the female as a sex object (Eakins and Eakins, 1978). Language conveys the impression that women are completely defined by their sexuality, while men are well-rounded human beings, sexuality only a part of their identities. Research on sexual terms reveals that terms for men carry more positive associations and reflect, perhaps, the social double standard.

Sexual Terms

Women: nympho hooker tramp whore slut

Men: Casanova Don Juan letch stud
(Eakins and Eakins, 1978).

The process works the other way around as well. Probably, men fare worse in this trade-off. Labelling a woman "mannish" is less insulting than labelling a man "womanish" or "sissy." Indeed, "there are surely overtones of praise in telling a female she runs, talks, or, most especially, *thinks* 'like a man.'"

Then, there are "praise him/blame her" pairs of words.

Praise Him / Blame Her

He	She
bachelor	old maid
chef	cook
discusses	chatters
reminds	nags
complains	bitches
forgetful	scatterbrained
has character lines	has wrinkles

(Eakins and Eakins, 1978).

The point to be emphasized is that as girls and boys learn their language, they also learn something about women's place and men's place.

Parents as Significant Others.   Lynn (1959; 1969) emphasizes the importance of parents in gender socialization. Lynn argues that, because of the greater availability of the mother and the relative absence of the father during early childhood, little girls easily develop their gender identity through imitation and positive reinforcement. Little boys, on the other hand, must shift from their initial identification with the mother to masculine identification. Because male models are scarce, they have greater difficulty than females in achieving gender identity.

According to Lynn, males must learn by gradually piecing together what society's definition of masculinity is. Some of the boy's information comes from stereotypes in the media. The boy has less to go on than the girl because the male gender role tends to be "so strongly defined in terms of work and sexuality, both of which are usually hidden from the eyes of children" (Colwill, 1982).

As a result, masculine behaviour is rarely defined positively as something the boy *should* do. He is more likely to be told *not* to do something associated with feminine behaviour (Hartley, 1959). Consequently, males remain anxious about gender. Females freely imitate males (in fashion, for example), but not vice versa. As adults, men are more hostile toward both the opposite sex and homosexuals than women are. Relationships with others are all-important to girls and women. Males, on the other hand, see the world in terms of autonomy, hierarchy, and conflict. Intimacy threatens them (Gilligan, 1982).

The Role of Peers.   Children's experience with age-mates is also important in learning masculine or feminine behaviour. Boys and girls have different friendship patterns and different forms of play. Consequently, they acquire different sorts of social skills that may well have implications for their later adult behaviour. In addition, peer activities reinforce the notion that males are more important than females (Richer, 1984).

After formal schooling begins, children's play becomes increasingly sex-segregated. The size of children's sex-segregated play groups differs according to gender (Eder and Hallinan, 1978). Girls tend to play in small groups, especially two-person groups. Boys prefer to congregate in larger groups. Therefore, in general, girls learn the type of interpersonal skills required by small, intimate groups, such as sensitivity to others' feelings, the ability to disclose information about themselves, and the ability to show affection. In general, boys, on the other hand, learn something about group leadership and decision making. In addition, girls protect their exclusive groups against the advances of newcomers, while boys tend to welcome new members.

The difference between the type of play that boys enjoy and the type that girls enjoy partly explains the size difference of their friendship groups (Lever, 1978). Although such differences seem to be diminishing somewhat, boys tend to play competitive games requiring teams of interdependent players with definite roles and specific rules. (Hockey is a good example.) In comparison, girls prefer to converse or to engage in physically undemanding activities in an indoor setting. Playing dolls or board games requires few participants and does not demand the coordination of effort that hockey or baseball does. Thus girls learn different types of skills and, again, these are very likely to carry over into adulthood.

Boys acquire the ability to co-ordinate their actions, to cope with impersonal rules, to work for collective as well as individual goals, to deal with competition and criticism. Girls learn to be imaginative, to converse, and to be sensitive to others' feelings. All these social experiences would be valuable for both sexes.

Conclusions

Many social scientists are convinced that the traditional gender stereotypes are arbitrary and even damaging gender scripts for socialization. During the 1970s, some became intrigued with the possibility of making androgyny rather than sex-typing the goal of socialization. The term **androgyny** combines the Greek words for male (andro) and female (gyne), and it refers to the presence of both feminine and masculine elements within individuals of both sexes (Laws, 1979).

In a utopian society where gender has been transcended, each child would be taught that the meaning of girl/boy, female/male is exclusively biological. The multitude of sociocultural elaborations on sex would disappear. Personality traits, interests, hobbies, toys, clothing, occupations, domestic division of labour—none would any longer be a function of sex (Bem, 1983).

Social-Structural Explanations of Gender

According to the social-structural perspective, gender is the result of societal, not individual, characteristics. The functionalist and conflict perspectives on gender are reviewed below.

The Structural-Functionalist Explanation of Gender

Structural-functionalist theorists such as Parsons and Bales (1955) ask how societal arrangements, such as those involving male-female distinctions, contribute to the stability and survival of the social system. The family institution is seen as functional for the society because it performs such crucial tasks as satisfaction of sexual needs, procreation, child care, and socialization.

Role specialization of the adult family members enhances the ability of the family to perform these functions. The father-husband assumes the *instrumental role*, meaning that he connects the family to the wider society. (In our society, this implies bringing home income from an outside job.) The mother-wife, on the other hand, assumes the *expressive role*. She looks after the relationships within the family.

According to Parsons and Bales (1955), these roles developed from a biological base. The female is the sex that bears and nurses children. Pregnancy, lactation, and human children's long period of helplessness restrict women's activities outside the home. Therefore, it is convenient for women to carry out the family's expressive functions. Men perform the instrumental tasks almost by default. Someone has to perform the instrumental role, and men's biology does not restrict their movements in the outside world. The structural functionalists are in agreement with the feminist anthropologists (Rosaldo, 1974; 1980), whose views were discussed earlier in this chapter.

Structural functionalists have been severely criticized for putting forth scientific arguments that seem to justify the traditional view that women's place is in the home (Friedan, 1963). However, just because it is functional for women to stay home does not mean that women *must* stay home. Arrangements that were convenient in pre-literate societies do not necessarily make sense in modern societies. For one thing, women need no longer be constantly pregnant to ensure survival of the species. For another, social inventions such as daycare facilities free women from constant childcare. Also, male physical strength matters much less in our society than it did in earlier societies. Anyone can "man" a computer. Moreover, newer research shows that the role segregation discussed by the structural functionalists is not a universal feature of family life in other cultures.

The Conflict Perspective

The analysis of the inequality of the sexes in *The Origins of the Family, Private Property, and the State* by Karl Marx's associate, Friedrich Engels (1884), provides the starting point for a conflict theory of gender (Fox, 1982; Smith, 1977). The main idea is that females and males are tied to the economic structure in different ways, and this difference explains why males are the more powerful gender (Nielsen, 1978).

In capitalist societies, men and women constitute two separate classes. The reason for this is that classes are defined by their relation to the *means of production*, and the sexes have a unique relation to these means. In a society such as our own, which is based on **commodity production** (products created for exchange in the market place), household labour, including child care, is not considered real work because it lies outside the marketplace. Men have primary responsibility for commodity production, women for the **production of use-values** (things produced in the home). This is the source of women's inferior status.

> In a society in which money determines value, full-time housewives are a group who work outside the money economy. Their work is not worth money, is therefore valueless, is therefore not even real work (Benston, 1969).

Women's unpaid work in the home, nevertheless, serves the capitalist system. To pay women for their work would require a massive redistribution of wealth. Statisticians value household work in Canada at approximately one-third of the Gross National Product, that is, between 121 billion and 139 billion dollars (Swinamer, 1986).

Women who are employed outside the home also have a different relation to the economic structure than do men. For one thing, women can be used as a "reserve army of labour" (Morton, 1972). They can be called into the labour force when they are needed (during wartime for example) and sent home when the need disappears (Glazer, 1977).

Women's primary allegiance to the family is used by the capitalist system as an excuse for confining them to menial, underpaid jobs. Women are supposedly untrained, unreliable workers because their families come first. They require less money than men because they are secondary workers anyway. Or so the argument goes.

Women's unpaid labour directly and indirectly subsidizes men's paid labour (Eichler, 1978). Women entertain husbands' business acquaintances, type, and help with husbands' small businesses and farms—all without compensation. All of these services cost money when someone outside the family performs them. These free services allow husbands to devote their efforts to full-time paid work.

In general, the conflict perspective explains the inequality of Canadian women in these structural terms:

> A glance at the Canadian social structure indicates that it is men who own and control the essential resources. . . . Ownership of the most important resource, the means of production, is mainly in the hands of a few men. . . . Men also have control of the next most important resource, access to the occupational structure and control of policy making in the major areas of social life (Connelly and Christiansen-Ruffman, 1977).

Gender Relations in Canadian Institutions

This section presents a brief over view of some of the ways in which female and male experiences differ in selected Canadian institutions.

The Family

Marriage and the family affect men and women differently. Indeed, Bernard (1971) argues that each family unit actually contains two families—his and hers. What evidence supports this claim?

His and Her Priorities.   Females are expected to give priority to the family and males to their occupation. Through recent cultural changes, women may now combine the wife-mother and career roles. However, even when the woman works outside the home, she is still expected to be committed to her family first, her work second (Coser and Rokoff, 1971).

This cultural mandate, or expectation means that for a woman in early adulthood, locating and marrying a suitable man takes precedence over investment of time and money in extensive job training.

The fact that women marry 2.1 years earlier than men (Statistics Canada, *Vital Statistics*) is one indication of this cultural mandate. Looking ahead, the young woman's decision is not between family and work, but between family and *demanding* work. Baker (1985) conducted a national study of the aspirations of Canadian teenagers. Although she found males and females equally likely to want to continue their education beyond high school, females made their occupational choices within a narrower range of jobs. These choices tend to relegate women to lower paid and unpaid jobs and to continue their financial dependence on men and government assistance. Baker concludes:

> After interviewing 150 adolescents, we found that many held notions of the future that did not tally with the likely outcome of their adult lives. In the eyes of many of these adolescents, there is no unemployment in their future, no divorce, no poverty. Only interesting jobs, adequate incomes, loving husbands, trouble-free children, home ownership, and international travel were on their horizons (Baker, 1985, p. 165).

Greenglass and Devins (1982) report that, although 85 percent of a sample of Canadian university undergraduate women plan to combine career and family in the future, only ten percent anticipate working while they have preschool children. These students' plans reflect our society's gender attitudes. They do not reflect the reality of women's labour force participation in the 1980s. In 1982, 54 percent of a national sample felt that married women with young children should not take a job outside the home (Boyd, 1984).

The cultural mandate has directed men to focus much of their energy on fulfilling the breadwinner role in the nuclear family: "As the chief breadwinner, a man's success and ultimately his definition of masculinity has been primarily judged by how well he provides for his family's needs and wants" (Doyle, 1983). Studies of the male life-cycle (Levinson, 1978) report priority shifts over time. Men, during their twenties and thirties, during the early years of marriage and family formation, remain "largely passive spectators in the home setting." In mid-life, there tends to be a shift from this high centrality of work to a greater investment in family (Rossi, 1980). This life-cycle change happens because of some combination of age, stress, and perceived failure in work. At the same time, the full-time housewife-mother in mid-life often becomes interested in achievement outside the home (Rubin, 1979).

Division of Labour.   Sociologists have shown considerable interest in who does the work around the home. In the traditional marriage, husbands and wives have distinctive responsibilities. If life is to proceed smoothly, someone has to prowl supermarket aisles in search of food, someone has to cook dinner, someone has to scrub toilet bowls, someone has to wipe children's noses. That someone is usually the wife. Outside work does not let women "off the hook": they carry two jobs. Recent studies (Lupri and Mills, 1987; Michelson, 1985) conclude that when wives go out to work, husbands do not substantially increase their share of housework. The weight of child-rearing responsibility also continues to fall on the mother's shoulders. A Flin Flon, Manitoba mother has this to say:

> I know that when my children are small they need me. But sometimes I think I'll go nuts if I don't get out of this house and meet some grown-ups. I find I'm starting to talk like a three-year-old all the time now (Luxton, 1980).

One result of the familial division of labour is inequality in power between husband and wife. Because our society values and rewards occupational achievement, the husband's power status in the outside world typically spills over into the family. In contrast, the bargaining position of the dependent wife, especially one encumbered with young children, is minimized.

Marital Dissolution.   When marriages are dissolved, separation and divorce affect men and women quite differently. First,

In most Canadian homes, the principal responsibility for raising the children falls on the mother's shoulders.

SOURCE: Canapress Photo Service

custom but not the law favours women in regard to child custody. The mother gets child custody in over 75 percent of the cases (Statistics Canada, 1985). Second, the economic implications of marriages ending are often different for husband and wife. Divorce often spells downward economic mobility, even poverty, for women (Ambert and Baker, 1984). There are a number of reasons for this situation:

1. Women generally earn less than men. Divorced and separated women suffer from the widespread assumption that men are the chief breadwinners and women merely secondary earners.

2. Women returning to the labour market after years of full-time housewifery are unlikely to be well trained.

3. Often, the woman is supporting children and must pay for child care while she works.

4. Husbands often hold back on child-support payments. Until recently, the law failed to recognize the financial contribution to the marriage of the wife who chose to be a full-time housewife or to work in a family business.

Divorced women are less likely to remarry than divorced men. Four-fifths of divorced men versus two-thirds of divorced women remarry (Ambert, 1980). The double standard of aging is the major factor involved here, with women's age being a greater barrier to their remarriage than dependent children. Older women have less chance of remarriage, because custom says they must marry someone at least their own age. In comparison, even much younger women are considered suitable marriage partners for divorced men.

Death still ends most marriages, and widowhood has different consequences for men and women. First of all, there are many more widows than widowers. In Canada, widows outnumber widowers by nearly five to one (Matthews, 1987). Because men choose younger wives and women outlive men by seven years, widowers have many more opportunities for remarriage. Another difference is that widows are more likely to be poor. The reason is that they likely devoted their lives to their families without pay; in other words, they obeyed the cultural mandate mentioned earlier.

Work Outside the Home

It is not surprising, on the basis of the previous discussion, that the labour force experiences of women and men differ.

Labour Force Participation. Although there are more men than women who work for pay (77 percent versus 54 percent in 1985; Lindsay and McKie, 1986, p. 2), the participation of women in the labour force has risen dramatically since World War II. A high percentage of the increase has been among married women and mothers of young children. Between 1975 and 1985, the labour force participation of women with children under three years of age rose from 31 percent to 54 percent (Lindsay and McKie, 1986, p. 3).

How is this rising labour force participation to be explained? Women's increasing education, and consequent higher earning capabilities, is one reason (Gunderson, 1976). Also, though marriage and children still reduce women's labour force participation, the figures cited in the previous paragraph show that they are weaker deterrents now than in the past. In addition, women are having fewer children. The economic circumstances of the past decade—first inflation and then recession—have forced many women to enter the labour force. More clerical and service jobs have become available in the post-World War II economy, and women have qualified for them. Finally, there has been a dramatic growth in part-time employment. In 1985, 72 percent of all part-time employees were women. More than one out of every four employed women worked part-time, compared with eight percent of employed men (Burke, 1986, p. 10).

Sex Segregation of Work. Although the female participation rate in the Canadian labour force has risen sharply, corresponding changes have not occurred in the nature of women's work.

Occupational segregation by sex means that the majority of

employees in the occupation are one sex. For example, 99 percent of stenographers and typists and 95 percent of nurses are women, while 92 percent of dentists and 85 percent of lawyers and notaries are men (Armstrong and Armstrong, 1984). Women are considerably more occupationally segregated than men. Women tend to work in a relatively few traditionally "female" jobs (for example, clerical, health, teaching, and service occupations). Since women hold about 75 percent of all clerical jobs, the office is a "female job ghetto" (Lowe, 1980). Although considerable publicity is given to female physicians, lawyers, dentists, and pharmacists, in 1981 each of these professions involved a tenth of one percent (or less) of all female workers (Armstrong and Armstrong, 1984a). The concept of occupational sex-typing, which was discussed earlier, reflects the idea that certain jobs are quite properly women's work or men's work.

Income. The money women derive from their work represents a key indicator of progress toward equality. The facts are straightforward: employed women earn considerably less money than their male counterparts. In 1983, Canadian women employed full-time earned 59 percent of the average income of Canadian men. Married women earned about 46 percent as much as married men, but single, divorced, or widowed women earned about 89 percent as much as unmarried men (Women's Bureau, Labour Canada, 1986). Women in other categories earned about 60 percent as much as men in these same categories (Block and Walker, 1982). These differences are accounted for by women's cultural mandate to give their families priority, by their consequent greater involvement in part-time work and career interruptions, by discrimination, and by the lower-paying jobs available to them.

Additional Characteristics of Women's Work. Women's work is more unstable than men's work. The female unemployment rate is slightly higher than the male rate. In 1985, the unemployment rate for women 25 to 44 years of age was 10.3 percent, compared to 8.9 percent for men of the same age (Lindsay and McKie, 1986, p. 5). Men are benefiting from computers more than women are, because women are clustered in clerical jobs in which computers are replacing people, (Menzies, 1984). Also, because women have lower labour force participation and earning levels than men, they receive fewer employment benefits, such as pensions (Women's Bureau, Labour Canada, 1986).

Women are much less likely than men to occupy authority positions in work organizations (Symons, 1986). As University of Alberta sociologists Lowe and Krahan (1984, pp. 127-128) point out, "True enough, we can now point to some 'high profile'

Pay Equity Legislation

*There are ample data to show that women
earn lower incomes than men, on average.
Most people consider this situation unjust. But
when it comes to designing affirmative action
programs that will correct the imbalance, controversy invariably erupts. The following article gives some glimpses of the debates that
preceded the passing of a pay equity law in
Ontario in 1987.*

The first law in North America to force private sector companies to upgrade low-paying
jobs held by women is expected to be passed
today by the Ontario legislature.

Seven months after Attorney General Ian
Scott introduced the pay equity bill, all three
parties are expected to join together to give
third and final reading to the historic and controversial legislation. The bill, trumpeted by
the minority Liberal government as a landmark reform, will get royal assent later this
week.

The law will make Ontario the first jurisdiction on the continent to compel private sector
employers to end wage discrimination between
men and women for different but comparable
work.

And it will be closely watched by other provinces and U.S. states that are considering enact-
ing similar legislation but are concerned about
the potential impact on business.

Under the equal pay principle, workers
receive the same wage for jobs that, while not
necessarily the same, are considered to be of
equal value to the employer.

To implement the principle, employers must
set up written job descriptions—taking into
account skill, experience and responsibility—
on which pay equity formulas could be based.
In addition, wages cannot be lowered for male
workers to give pay increases to underpaid
female employees.

Liberal Chris Ward, who shepherded Bill 154
through months of often bitter wrangling in
committee, called the legislation a "balanced"
law that aims to eliminate the 36-percent wage
gap between men and women resulting from
occupational segregation and wage
discrimination.

Many businessmen, however still see the bill as
stacked against them, and they argue that it's

intrusive, too costly and will create a moun-
tain of red tape.

"It may take years; but this is an issue that
will come back and sting the Liberals," pre-
dicts John Bulloch, president of the 76 000-
member Canadian Federation of Independent
Business.

The opposition Conservatives and New Democrats also have reservations, but they say
they'll hold their noses and support the bill
when it comes up today for final debate and
vote.

New Democrat Evelyn Gigantes, who waged
a losing battle to broaden the scope of Bill 154,
called it a "a lousy piece of legislation" that
will leave half of Ontario's estimated two million working women uncovered.

This number includes about 238 000 employed
in companies of fewer than 10 workers and
another 500 000 part-timers who Gigantes
expects may find themselves classed as casual
or on-call workers as employers try to evade
terms of the bill.

The Tories, meanwhile, are worried about
the size of bureaucracy that will be created
under a government tribunal set up to oversee
pay equity plans and the impact the law will
have on business.

Companies will be required to study their work-
force, determine whether women are underpaid and then come up with a plan to end the
discrimination.

Under the legislation, a tribunal called the
pay equity commission will also be set up to
ensure the government and a broad segment of
the private sector implement pay equity
programs.

Ward said Bill 154 is by far the most comprehensive attempt by any American or Canadian
government to redress the wage gap between
men and women.

The federal, Québec and Manitoba governments as well as some U.S. states have pay
equity laws, but they don't go nearly as far as
the Ontario bill.

The federal government and Québec have
pay equity laws that apply to both the public
and private sectors.

But unlike Ontario's legislation, they don't
force companies to devise pay equity plans to
redress the wage imbalance.

SOURCE: "Ontario to pass women's pay equity law today." June 15, 1987, *Calgary Herald*, p. A3. Copyright Canadian Press. Reprinted by permission.

women in corporate and government organizations and in male-dominated occupations and professions, but they are usually the exception." Although women's lack of qualifications is an explanatory factor, just as important are discriminatory employer policies based on the assumption that women are unfit to supervise others (Wolf and Eligstein, 1979).

Fewer Canadian female workers are unionized: 32 percent versus 42 percent of Canadian male workers in 1984 (Women's Bureau, Labour Canada, 1986). The main reasons are that white-collar workers and part-time workers are difficult for unions to organize (Marchak, 1975) and that unions have not given women's issues a high priority (Baker and Robeson, 1986). However, "women have dominated union membership growth in recent years . . . almost doubling their share of organized workers over the last two decades" (Armstrong and Armstrong, 1983).

Religion

Church organization has traditionally assigned different roles to women and to men. With few exceptions, men are the authority figures: deacons, priests, clergymen, bishops, cardinals, popes. Ceremonial ties with the deity are maintained by men. When women are permitted a role beyond member of the congregation, it is usually a service position. For example, nuns in the Roman Catholic Church teach and nurse, while priests celebrate mass, perform marriage ceremonies, and ordain other priests.

Iona Campagnolo, former Canadian Minister of Amateur Sport, discussing her childhood ambitions, was quoted in *Today* magazine as saying: "I always thought I'd be a missionary of some kind. Because I was a female, I never thought of becoming a minister." Although some of the large Protestant denominations, such as the United Church, have finally agreed to ordain women, the numbers involved are very small. Often, these female clergy are sidetracked from ministerial roles into teaching (Roberts, 1984).

Women's marginal position in the churches has serious implications for gender socialization. Ruether (1974) claims, perhaps extravagantly, that religion is "undoubtedly the single most important shaper and enforcer of the image and role of women." While children might encounter female Sunday School teachers, they again see the important roles as belonging to men and experience only males making ceremonial contact with God (Mackie, 1983). Other consequences are more indirect. As long as women remain outside the church's inner circle, the female point of view is missing on matters of considerable concern to them, such as abortion and birth control (Ambert, 1976).

The religious doctrine presented to children is also male-

SOURCE: Canapress Photo Service

Two rabbis show Old Testament scrolls to Ottawa children. Authority figures in most religions are men.

oriented. For instance, the male image of God—his traditional presentation as father, judge, shepherd, king—serves indirectly to support the idea of male supremacy on earth. If God is male, how can females be made in his image?

Only a handful of studies have attempted to measure the effects of religious socialization on gender attitudes. A recent study of Canadian and American university students (Brinkerhoff and Mackie, 1985) reported on the range of traditional gender attitudes that the greater the religiosity, the more traditional the gender attitudes. Mormons and Fundamentalist Christians hold the most traditional gender attitudes, followed by mainline Protestants, and then Roman Catholics. These findings are consistent with the renewed use of the chador, a traditional woman's garment, in the fundamentalist Muslim society of Iran (see the inset article). People with no religious affiliation are the least conservative of all. It would seem, in general, that religious socialization adds to and reinforces other sources of gender socialization.

The School

Although most Canadian classrooms are not segregated by sex, school is not the same psychological or social environment for girls and for boys. Elementary school is a place where women teachers rule. Seemingly, many approve of the girl students who identify with them and scold boy students for being rambunctious. An observational study of elementary school pupils (Best,

The Chador: Symbol of Modesty or of Male Oppression?

For Middle Easterners and Westerners alike, the chador—the black, ankle-length veil designed to swath a woman's body to near shapelessness—has become a symbol of the conflicts in values occurring today in Iran and similar countries. Modernism and traditionalism, fundamentalism and reinterpretation, feminism and patriarchy, patriotism and colonialism all find expression in battles over whether women should have to wear this innocuous if unglamourous garment whenever they venture outside their own boudoirs.

Ironically, the chador is not mentioned in the Koran or traditional Islamic law. Both emphasize chastity (for members of both sexes), but women are simply urged to behave and dress so as not to provide sexual stimulation or temptation. Historians believe that the custom of veiling originally arose in Persia as a sign of the aristocracy. Only gradually did it come to serve the social purpose of segregating women from men and the religious purpose of public modesty. Eventually many Muslim societies required women to veil at least their faces in certain circumstances, but only the Persian-oriented countries used the full chador.

In Iran the custom was virtually universal for centuries, enforced by religious and civil law (the two are identical in a Muslim state) and by social pressure. Contact with Europeans in the nineteenth century piqued interest in many Western ways, but primarily among the upper classes. Only in the mid-1950s did change come. As part of sweeping modernization and Westernization, the Shah banned the chador. The change was hailed by many women—especially young urban women of the growing middle class, who were in a position to take advantage of the opening of education and the professions to women. But many older women felt stripped, revealed to the eyes of a world that had changed for them without warning. In many rural areas,

social custom proved stronger than edict, and the chador continued to be used "as always."

The Iranian Revolution of 1978-79 brought new ironies. Although the Shah's reforms had seemed to raise the position of women, many felt that the changes were only cosmetic or that the dictatorial regime's violation of civil rights was more important. Thus the revolutionaries who supported the Ayatollah Khomeni, both in exile and then in triumphant return, included many women, especially feminists of leftist persuasion. And it was the feminists who were most vocal in their opposition when the Ayatollah promptly mandated that all women return to *hejab* (modest dress), which, in Iran, means the chador.

Today, acceptance of the ruling appears high, even in the cities. Women must wear the chador in public; if they appear on the street without it, they risk interrogation by the Revolutionary Guards.

Whether compliance is so high in private—especially among middle-class urbanites—is another question. Ross Laver reported in *Maclean's*, 8 March 1987:

At the customs counter of Tehran's Mehrabad airport there are glimpses of the typical middle-class Iranian woman's wardrobe. Suitcases laid open for inspection reveal sequinned dresses, silk blouses, and shoes that would not look out of place on the streets of Paris. One Western resident of Tehran said that he was shocked when he visited an Iranian businessman's home to find that his host's wife—who at their only previous meeting was shrouded from head to foot in a chador—was sunbathing nude in the backyard. In a city with few tall buildings, a 10-foot-high fence was enough to ensure that her private habits would not be condemned by strictly religious neighbours.

1983) observed that when the boys eagerly ran outside to play, the girls fought among themselves for the "privilege" of staying indoors and helping the teacher. Considerable evidence supports the hypothesis that students of both sexes are exposed to a feminizing process in school (Schneider and Coutts, 1979). As a consequence, young boys escape into the macho world of their peers (Best, 1983).

During the early years of school, girls are more successful academically than boys. Girls beginning school are, on the average, two years ahead of boys. They begin to speak, read, and count before boys do. This developmental advantage is reflected in girls' academic achievement. In the early grades, girls are at least equal with boys in mathematical skill (Fink and Kosecoff, 1977). Two to three times the number of boys, as compared with the number of girls, have reading problems. Also, boys seem to have a more difficult time adjusting to elementary school classroom demands for obedience, order, neatness. "Feminine" behaviour seems more appropriate to school. Possibly, girls have already learned at home to be obedient and quiet, while boys have been reinforced for "bouncing about, questioning, being curious or aggressive" (Howe, 1974). Finally, the female authority figure in the elementary grades makes it easier for girls to identify with their teacher, and hence with general academic values (Richer, 1979).

Although the sexes' access to post-secondary education is now nearly equal, women remain concentrated in traditionally feminine fields of study. Most girls want to be teachers, social workers, nurses, secretaries—not chartered accountants, engineers, architects, lawyers. As girls approach the age for entry into the labour market, they lower their aspirations and revise their career goals toward more traditional choices. Many women, planning their careers according to traditional gender patterns, are not developing their human potential.

So in the end, females, the sex most comfortable in school, end up doing less well in the occupational structure. As we saw earlier, most Canadian women who work outside the home are concentrated in a small number of low-skill, poorly paid jobs. Research tells us that gender is a bigger barrier to women's occupational achievement than lack of resources, such as academic ability or socio-economic background (Marini and Greenberger, 1978). Girls "receive less family encouragement to pursue higher education than do boys, but such encouragement, it turns out, is especially critical for girls" (Turritin, Anisef, and MacKinnon, 1983). Girls from poor families, from Indian or Inuit families, and from remote regions of the country, are even more disadvantaged.

Why are women's educational ambitions so modest compared

The Costs of Machismo

Raphaela Best's book, We've All Got Scars: What Boys and Girls Learn in Elementary School *(1983), documents her discovery that alongside the academic curriculum there exists a hidden curriculum in which children teach one another the traditional gender roles and attitudes. Little girls learn to be helpful and nurturant. Little boys learn to distance themselves from the girls, to look down on them. Because society makes inordinate demands on small boys to become instant men, to live up to macho criteria, they seek support from one another. Little girls do not face the same stresses. Society does not expect them to become instant women. Consequently, the female peer group is not so influential. According to Best, so great was the need to be first, to win, and thus to prove themselves real men, that the second-grade boys often got in their own way and lost out entirely. The episode described here illustrates an occasion when machismo was costly for the boys. In later life, the costs mount.*

The second-grade class had their collective eye on an incubator in the room that had been filled with 12 eggs now about to hatch. A chart in the front of the room listed carefully worked out plans that the children were to follow when the long-awaited event finally happened in the spring. All contingencies had been taken into consideration so that the children would derive the greatest benefit from this experience. After what seemed to them an endless amount of time, the day finally arrived when the first eggshell broke and the bill of a tiny chick began to peck its way out. Every ear in the class heard that eggshell break, and the children knew exactly what was happening.

The girls waited at their desks for instructions on how to proceed. The boys didn't wait for anyone or anything. As a group they jumped to their feet and started toward the incubator shouting, "I'm in charge! I'm in charge!" The boys nearest the incubator were pulled away by other boys shouting, "I'm in charge and you can't watch until I say when!"

Then pushing and pulling quickly turned into full-scale fighting. David practiced his karate kick on Sean, who fell to the floor in pain and then got up and delivered an even stronger kick to David. The familiar playground pattern of fighting to determine who would be in charge was working itself out in the classroom. The boys would not listen to the long-term substitute teacher trying to stop the fighting. The noise echoed up and down the halls.

The girls meanwhile did not take part in the fight. They wanted to see the chicks hatch as much as the boys did, but they had no compulsion to be in charge. Now, however, that the careful plans were not being implemented, they had to improvise. One girl climbed onto a table overlooking the incubator and out of range of the fighting, which now occupied the center of the room. Other girls joined her on the table and those for whom there was no room stood on chairs that they pushed into the same area. Their strategy worked, for from their vantage point they could ignore the boys and, totally absorbed, watch the whole process as the chicks hatched. This was, after all, the "moment of truth" for which the entire class had been waiting ever since the incubator had been introduced into the classroom. This was the miracle they had been so long anticipating. The girls saw it all. By the time the boys had fought out the precedence problem, the show was over.

SOURCE: *We've All Got Scars: What Boys and Girls Learn in Elementary School* by Raphaela Best. 1983. Bloomington: Indiana University Press.

to men's? Possibly, men's occupational ambitions are greater because work is a major ingredient of masculine self-esteem, and because they expect to spend a lifetime in the labour market. As they reach adolescence, males take school, the avenue to the "breadwinner" role, more seriously. Many girls have confused images of the future and are unable to formulate realistic plans for their lives (Press, 1985). Although she has been exposed to both the ideal of occupational achievement and her eventual destiny in marriage and family roles, the girl is apt to hold her future in abeyance until the right young man comes along. Although the job plans of males are not sabotaged by dreams of settling down with Mrs. Right and producing babies, obstacles also impede their life course. The majority abandon earlier hopes for university education or technical training (Bibby and Poterski, 1985, p. 161), presumably for economic reasons.

The school is only one of many agents that market gender stereotypes and depress women's ambitions. However, the school reflects the values of the surrounding society; its teachers, curricula (official and hidden), textbooks, and guidance counsellors are all engaged in the business of gender socialization. But things are slowly changing. Because of the women's movement and the demands of the economic climate, women's lives are less determined by the family cycle. The recent trend toward later marriage, later initiation of child-bearing, reduced family size expectation, and the rising number of female-headed families all contribute to women's growing occupational commitment (Garrison, 1979).

Women's and Men's Liberation Movements

The decade of the 1960s was marked by protest and demands for just treatment by Indians, blacks, the poor, university students, and, eventually, women. In 1967, the Royal Commission on the Status of Women was set up to enquire into the situation of Canadian women and "to recommend what steps might be taken by the federal government to ensure for women equal opportunities with men in all aspects of Canadian society" (Royal Commission on the Status of Women in Canada, 1970). The feminist movement in Canada officially began with the federal government's decision to establish the commission (Morris, 1980). Before this political action, women's situation was not regarded as a social problem. Three years later, the commission tabled its report, which contained 167 recommendations concerning the economy, education, the family, taxation, poverty, public life, immigration and citizenship, and criminal law.

Women's problems are far from being solved. Economic equality is still a long way off. To date, several of the commission recommendations have not been implemented—for example, establishing 18 years as the minimum age for marriage. Also, many new issues concern women today that were not evident in 1970; provision of daycare and violence against women are two examples. Therefore, the women's movement remains active.

In 1981, thousands of women across the country successfully organized against opposition from the federal government to achieve recognition of legal equality of the sexes under the Canadian constitution (Kome, 1983). After April 1985, Section 15 of the Canadian Charter of Rights and Freedoms became the basis for legal challenges to inequity, among other things, in society's gender arrangements.

Legal discrimination against women has decreased over the years. However, informal or customary injustices continue. Therefore, feminist groups across Canada are organized around such issues as reproductive freedom and control over their own bodies, pornography and violence against women, provision of daycare, pensions for women, and equality in religious organizations. In addition, women have organized around the more general issues of nuclear disarmament and environmental concerns. Finally, structural changes have involved setting up special institutions for women, parallel to those in mainstream society. Examples include self-help medical clinics, media, and cooperative daycare.

Societal arrangements are also changing for men (David and Brannon, 1976; Dubbert, 1979; Fasteau, 1975; Komarovsky, 1976; Nichols, 1975). Because gender roles are interlocking and complementary, women's dissatisfaction has inevitably affected men. Women's critical scrutiny of the traditional ways the sexes relate forced men also to become conscious of the flaws in the status quo. A few men, mostly middle-class and university educated (Snodgrass, 1974), became involved in heterosexual male liberation groups in the 1970s, but this did not go on to become a popular cause.

The potential social base for a significant men's movement simply isn't there. Males experience psychological oppression from their gender socialization. Nevertheless, "they have not been economically or politically discriminated against because they are *men*" (Richardson, 1981, p. 264; emphasis in original). The contemporary gender stratification system favours men as a group. Not many men would willingly forfeit the power, privileges, and resources that accrue to those at the top of the gender hierarchy. Unfortunately, many males are caught in a "double bind" (Baker and Bakker, 1980). Masculinity exacts high costs, as well as the rewards mentioned above. For example, the traditional linkage between masculinity and work fails to satisfy the needs of many men. "Each day men sell little pieces of themselves in order to try to buy them back each night and weekend with the coin of 'fun'" (Mills, 1951, p. 237). Insistence that males achieve, be aggressive and competitive, and resist emotional expression has been described as the "lethal aspect" of the male role (Jourard, 1964). The higher male suicide rates and earlier death rates appear to be consequences of the masculine role.

Despite the foregoing, social definitions of masculinity are changing. Gay liberation politics continue to call into question the conventional understanding of maleness (Carrigan *et al.*, 1987, p. 139). In the 1980s, small numbers belong to groups seeking equality for men who have lost custody of their children, self-help for their own violent behaviour, or intellectual understanding of "the new man." The flavour of these groups has been therapeutic or concerned with self-improvement. Some, such as the fathers' rights groups, have been anti-feminist. Certainly, there has been a deepening of tensions around male-female relationships. Nonetheless, "a good many men feel themselves to be involved in some kind of change having to do with gender, with sexual identity, with what it is to be a man" (Carrigan *et al.*, 1987, p. 185).

The political and religious conservatism of the 1980s threatens attempts to establish healthier definitions of femininity and masculinity. For example, REAL Women, an anti-feminist organization based in Toronto, champions traditional roles for the sexes and opposes equal pay for work of equal value, affirmative action programs, easier divorce, universal daycare, abortion, and homosexuality (Riley, 1985). We conclude that traditional gender arrangements continue because they are situated in power differences. The ideology that sustains these arrangements is instilled through the socialization process and buttressed by most of the institutions of society.

Summary

1. The sociology of gender relations examines masculinity and femininity across cultures and historical periods. This subdiscipline, which was inspired by the feminist movement, attempts to remedy sociology's previous exclusion of women.

2. Human social life is built on the relationships between the sexes. The sexes are differentiated and ranked.

3. According to the study of the anthropological record and psychosexual abnormalities, biology seems to be directly involved in cognitive gender differences and aggressiveness and indirectly involved in the female-male division of labour. However, both biology *and* environment are involved.

4. Theories based on biology, socialization, and social structure are complementary explanations of gender.

5. The socialization process teaches children society's gender scripts, which include gender stereotypes and occupational sex-typing. As well, children acquire their gender identity through this process.

6. The structural approach assumes that gender results from external social factors, not individual characteristics. The structural-functionalist and conflict perspectives are examples of structural theories.

7. To a great extent, women and men inhabit separate social worlds. Therefore, they have somewhat different experiences in societal institutions, such as the family, work, education, and religious institutions.

8. The feminist movement, the gay liberation movement, and the men's movement have pressed for more egalitarian social arrangements and healthier definitions of gender.

Further Reading

Armstrong, P., & Armstrong, H. (1984). *The double ghetto: Canadian women and their segregated work.* (Revised Edition.) Toronto: McClelland and Stewart.
An up-to-date statistical and theoretical analysis of gender and work.

Bernard, J. (1981). *The female world.* New York: Free Press.
An exploration of the idea that women and men possess worlds of their own.

Boyd, M. (1984). *Canadian attitudes toward women: Thirty years of change.* Ottawa: Women's Bureau, Labour Canada.
Canadian public opinion polls from the 1950s to the 1980s.

Eichler, M. (1980). *The double standard: A feminist critique of feminist social science.* New York: St. Martin's Press.
A discussion of the feminist perspective and proposals for social change.

Lipman-Blumen, J. (1984). *Gender roles and power.* Englewood Cliffs, NJ: Prentice-Hall, 1984.
Presents the proposition that the sex-gender system is the blueprint for all other power relationships.

Mackie, M. (1982). *Exploring gender relations: A Canadian perspective.* Toronto: Butterworths.
A detailed discussion of the many dimensions of gender.

Smith, D. E. (1977). *Feminism and Marxism—A place to begin, a way to go.* Vancouver: New Star Books.
An introduction to the conflict perspective on gender relations.

Steinem, G. (1983). *Outrageous acts and everyday rebellions.* New York: Holt, Rinehart and Winston.
A delightful collection of essays from the feminist editor of *Ms.* magazine.

5
Crime and Deviance

We have looked at how people are socialized to the accepted norms of their society. The purpose of this chapter is to explain why some people "break the rules" and how society reacts when they do. Some of these deviations are defined as crimes, while others are merely considered as eccentricities. After studying this chapter, you should be able to

1. classify the types of deviance;

2. summarize the distribution of deviance;

3. explain the following theoretical approaches to deviance:
    (a) anomie,
    (b) delinquent subculture,
    (c) differential opportunity,
    (d) differential association,
    (e) neutralization,
    (f) dramatization of evil,
    (g) conflict theory;

4. briefly outline how the mentally ill and alcoholics are processed;

5. describe the differing approaches to crime in Canada and the United States.

Deviance involves behaviour that is somehow different from the normal standards of society. To behave differently from most other people is to be deviant. Sociologists speak of this as deviation from a norm (the pattern regarded as typical of a particular society; for example, it's the norm in North America to wave when we're saying goodbye). But the topic of deviance also includes the reactions that deviant behaviour provokes from others. Through the reactions of others, diverse human beings are singled out as both different *and* disreputable. **Deviance** then, is variation from a norm and the societal reaction involved.

Kinds of Deviance

With this definition of deviance in mind, we can identify three distinguishing characteristics (Hagan and Leon, 1977):

1. the severity of the society's response;
2. the perceived harmfulness of the behaviour;
3. the degree of public agreement.

The Severity of Society's Response. We respond to our most serious deviants, including first-degree murderers, with long prison terms or, in some countries, with capital punishment. There are other types of institutional and community responses, including mental hospitalization, probation, fines, and outpatient treatment. These societal responses vary in the degree to which they limit a citizen's freedom. Generally speaking, the more seriously the act of deviance is regarded, the more the freedom of the alleged deviant will be limited.

The Perceived Harmfulness of the Behaviour. Some deviant behaviours, such as aggravated assault and aggravated sexual assault, are regarded as serious because of the harm they are perceived to cause. Most sexual practices between consenting adults, on the other hand, are regarded as inconsequential because little or no perceived harm is done. Between the extremely harmful and the relatively harmless are a number of behavioural deviations from the norm that are thought to be only mildly harmful or whose degree of harm is uncertain. Included here are activities such as prostitution. Morality squads have usually had little support from society at large in suppressing prostitution except in cases in which it causes disturbances in residential neighborhoods.

In general, the more harmful a form of behaviour is perceived to be, the more serious a form of deviance it will be regarded. The key word here is *perceived*: the point is not so much what harm these deviant acts actually do, but what harm they are perceived to do.

The Degree of Public Agreement. Across nations and generations there is a high degree of agreement that some forms of behaviour are indeed seriously deviant (for example, armed robbery, aggravated sexual assault, and premeditated homicide). Yet there are also many forms of behaviour about which there is considerable disagreement. Included among these debated subjects are some types of drug use and many forms of sex. Finally, there are those forms of behaviour about which most of us couldn't care less, fads and fashions such as the new-wave styles adopted by teenagers in the mid-80s. As bizarre as these styles can become, most of us have no strong interest in calling them deviant.

We have briefly considered three related characteristics of deviance. Taken together, these characteristics provide a measure of how serious a particular form of deviance may be regarded. In other words, the most serious forms provoke a severe societal response, are perceived as extremely harmful, and are defined as deviant with a high degree of agreement. Less serious forms of deviance result in more moderate or indeterminant forms of societal response, are perceived as less harmful, and may be the subjects of uncertainty or conflict. Finally, the least serious forms of deviance call forth only mild responses, are perceived as relatively harmless, and are widely ignored.

With these points in mind, we can now attach names to the kinds of deviance we have begun to identify:

1. consensus crimes;
2. conflict crimes;
3. social deviations;
4. social diversions.

Consensus Crimes

Consensus crimes are acts defined by law as crimes (Toby, 1974). The Criminal Code of Canada specifies a large number of such criminal acts, yet only a few are widely regarded as extremely harmful, are severely punished, and are agreed upon by society as deviant.

One such act is first degree murder. In many nations and for many centuries, laws of a similar form have defined this type of behaviour as a crime. Not many acts fall into this category. Other examples are sexual assault and armed robbery. History and anthropology demonstrate that most conceptions of crime and deviance are subject to change. What is called criminal in one time or place may frequently be seen quite differently in another. This changeable character of crime and deviance is an important feature of the kind of deviance we consider next.

TABLE 5-1. Kinds of Deviance

Kind of deviance	Severity of Societal Response	Perceived Harmfulness	Degree of Agreement	Examples
Consensus crimes	Severe	Extremely harmful	Consensus	First degree murder, sexual assault
Conflict crimes	Punitive	Somewhat harmful	Conflict	Victimless crimes (e.g., prostitution, narcotics)
Social deviations	Indeterminant	Potentially harmful	Uncertainty	Mental illness, juvenile delinquency
Social diversions	Mild	Relatively harmless	Apathy	Fads and fashions

Conflict Crimes

Conflict crimes are usually regarded as only marginally harmful and are typically subjects of conflict and debate. In this category are many of the victimless crimes, including prostitution, drug use, and many sexual acts between consenting adults. It is significant that many conflict crimes were once consensus crimes. For example, during much of this century marijuana use was regarded as a serious form of narcotics abuse requiring strict legal control (Bonnie and Whitebread, 1974). Yet today people talk about making it legal. Significantly, this change did not begin until marijuana use became a part of middle- and upper-class youth cultures in the 1960s. What was once a consensus crime is now a subject of conflict.

In contrast to marijuana use, sexual assault seems to be a crime whose roots involved conflict and whose legal definition has only recently become a focus of renewed debate. It can be argued that the historical illegality of rape is grounded in a conflict between the sexes. That is, rape laws may have emerged out of men's efforts to protect their women—not because these women were women, but because these women were theirs. From this viewpoint, rape consisted of the taking of one man's property by another. Consequently, until 1982 a husband could not be convicted of raping his wife. Furthermore, Lorenne Clark (1976) has demonstrated that rape usually results in sentences quite similar to those handed down for robbery. For most of our Canadian experience, these facts have been the subject of apparent consensus and, only recently, has the conflict underlying this law become a topic of public concern.

Social Deviations

Social deviations include many behaviours that are not criminal but are nonetheless subject to official control. Some are dealt with under statutes defining mental illness, others under juvenile delinquency legislation, and still others by civil laws (for example, laws dealing with securities and stock transactions). A common feature of these laws is the vagueness with which they define their subject. In the case of business and professional activities, this vagueness may reflect an attempt to protect the powerful from public harassment—the cases of juvenile delinquency and mental illness, however, it may be that we simply don't have clear notions of what these official categories include.

There is cause for concern that business and professional people may be able to use this vagueness to slip through the law, while people with less power may not. Furthermore, those defined as delinquent or mentally ill may be defined this way on the basis of what people are afraid they may, do rather than any actual harm done. As well, the treatments assigned to them may be of indeterminate length, rather than for a fixed term. All of this comes from the announced desire to help rather than punish the subjects of social deviation. But help is all too often perceived by those on the receiving end as punishment, and it usually constitutes some form of official control. The past history of responses to homosexuality is an unhappy example of the latter point.

Social Diversions

Social diversions are the variations in lifestyles that make our lives more interesting—such as the fads and fashions of speech, appearance, and play. These diversions all involve the pursuit of pleasure, but there is, of course, extreme variation in what is regarded as pleasurable. Joggers brave subzero temperatures and exhaustion in search of the "runner's high," while surfers circle the world and endure the ravages of weather and water in their quest for "the perfect wave." Yet as odd as many of these activities seem to many of us, we typically react with only a mixture of amusement and apathy to the time, energy, and resources expended by such enthusiasts. We are tolerant because these behaviours are neither good nor bad—they are simply different, diverse, and, to their participants, enjoyable.

So far we have given an extended definition of deviance, seeking to answer the question: What is it? Let us now turn our attention to the question: Where do we find it?

Using several approaches, sociologists have attempted to gain some knowledge of how these behaviours are socially distributed. One way of beginning this task is to compare the official statistics of crime and deviance with those gathered through alternative methods. Where the findings of alternative methods agree with the official measures, we can have some confidence in our conclusions. Where disagreement occurs, we can begin to examine possible explanations for the disparities. Often these alternative explanations can tell us a good deal, not only about the social distribution of deviance, but also about those official agencies that control deviance. In the next section, we use the type of comparison just described to consider the distribution of crime and deviant behaviour by sex and by social class in Canada.

Distribution of Crime and Deviance

Criminal and non-criminal forms of deviant behaviour are not randomly distributed in Canadian society. These behaviours occur at different rates among different groups. Accurately identifying sources of the social distribution of crime and deviance is an important first step toward the explanation of these behaviours.

Sex Distribution

Criminal and non-criminal forms of deviant behaviour clearly are not distributed randomly by sex. Men are significantly more likely to be alcoholic (Cahalan, 1970), addicted to illegal drugs (Terry and Pellens, 1970), and involved in the more serious forms of crime (Hindelang, 1978). This does not mean, however, that men in all ways or at all times are necessarily more deviant than women. We know that women tend to take more legally prescribed psychoactive drugs than men (Manheimer *et al.*, 1969) and that higher rates of mental illness are reported for woman than for men (Gove and Tudor, 1973). But when it comes to criminal forms of deviance, males clearly exceed females.

The most fascinating aspect of this situation is the possibility that it may be changing, along with more general attitudes toward gender roles. It has been argued that women are increasing their involvement in all types of offenses and, more specifically, that a new breed of violent, aggressive female offender may be rising (Adler, 1975).

For example, a review of data on crime and deviance indicates that behavioural differences between the sexes are diminishing (Smith and Visher, 1980). Interestingly, this narrowing of the gap is occurring faster for minor deviant acts than for more serious crimes. Serious criminal behaviour is clearly not equally common among men and women. Similarly, while the sex-deviance relationship is declining for both youths and adults, the data indicate that this trend is stronger for youths. It is predictable that shifting perceptions of gender roles would have a greater effect upon the behaviour of younger women—and this is exactly what the data indicate. These patterns of change deserve to be closely watched in the future.

Class Distribution

The relationship between deviant behaviour and class position is a matter of considerable debate. A major reason for this is a pair of seemingly conflicting assumptions. The first assumption is that being a member of the lower class implies a denial of opportunities and a harshness of circumstances that tend to produce deviant behaviour. The second assumption is that prejudice and discrimination on the part of official control agents and agencies lead them to pick on members of the lower class. The argument will be made in this and a later section that both assumptions are correct.

The official statistics of crime and delinquency make one point rather clearly: people *prosecuted* for criminal and delinquent offenses are disproportionately members of the lower class (Braithwaite, 1981). Is this official sampling of criminals and delinquents representative of the population from which it is drawn, or have the statistics been selected from one class more than from another? The answer to this question seems to depend in part on the type of deviance we are considering.

Data from **self-report surveys** (surveys that are anonymously answered by adults and adolescents) have often been compared with official records to examine the class distribution of crime and deliquency. These comparisons tend to concentrate on the less serious and most frequent types of deviant activity (Hindelang *et al.*, 1979), because the more serious forms of crime and delinquency seldom show up in self-reports. A summary of 47 of these reports shows that 25 of them indicated a relationship between class and deviance and 22 indicated no relationship at all (Braithwaite, 1981). On the other hand, official statistics have traditionally shown a definite relationship between class and deviance.

The implication here is that some class bias exists in the official reports of the most frequent forms of crime and delinquency. One Canadian study (Hagan *et al.*, 1978) reinforces this conclusion, noting that the police in particular tend to feel that dense, lower-class areas of the city most need police patrols. More telephoned complaints come from these areas, for example, and the police develop a probably exaggerated idea of the amount of crime and deliquency occurring there. The police then step up police resources to patrol these areas and, as a result, record higher rates of crime and delinquency—simply because more police are looking for, and responding to, more deviance.

Recently, more serious forms of crime have tended to be studied through surveys of victims. In the United States, nationwide surveys reveal a substantially greater involvement of blacks in the crimes of rape, robbery, and assault (Hindelang, 1978). Insofar as race and class are strongly related, this American research suggests that there is a relationship between social class and criminal behaviour for serious forms of crime.

It bears repeating that the concept of what constitutes a serious form of deviance is subject to change. We saw this earlier with regard to marijuana use. Within one generation, marijuana

Criminals? Or merely deviants? No matter which, these people's common interests and group identity may affect their relationships with society in general and the police in particular.

use has changed, in many people's view, from the alleged cause of "reefer madness" to a kind of status symbol. Related to this change, we now see higher levels of marijuana use in the middle and upper classes than in the lower ones (Barter *et al.*, 1970; Suchman, 1968). Changes in the use of hard drugs, such as heroin, however, have been less substantial (Berg, 1970). These hard drugs have been and continue to be used more extensively in the lower class, and their use is still generally regarded as a serious matter. Statistics show a higher representation of alcohol abuse and mental illness in the lower class (see Bailey *et al.*, 1965; Cahalan, 1970; Dohrenwend and Dohrenwend, 1975).

The conclusions we can draw are that serious crimes, hard drug use, alcohol abuse, and mental illness are found more frequently in the lower class, while less serious and more frequent forms of crime, delinquency, and drug use are more evenly distributed across the social classes. It is in these less serious crimes that official statistics appear most questionable, because here the lower class is disproportionately selected for official attention. To some extent, doubt or confidence in a given deviance statistic depends on how such deviance was measured.

Legislation of Crime and Deviance

Why are some forms of difference and diversity outlawed while others are not? Part of the answer to this question is that some individuals and groups may have interests that encourage them to lobby for the official control of certain types of deviant behaviour. Let us therefore turn our attention next to the issue of crime and deviance legislation.

Moral entrepreneurs is the term Becker (1963) uses for those individuals most active in striving for official control of deviance. These are the people whose initiative and enterprise are essential in getting the legal rules passed that are necessary to "do something" about a particular type of deviant behaviour. Often these individuals seem to be undertaking a moral crusade—they see some activity as a moral evil in need of legal reform (Gusfield, 1963).

Narcotics and Alcohol

The moral entrepreneur most responsible for the passage of Canada's first narcotics laws was none other than Mackenzie King (Cook, 1969). King became aware of Canada's "opium problem" when he discovered that opium could be bought over the counter in Vancouver. This knowledge came to him accidentally. As Deputy Minister of Labour, he had been sent to Vancouver to supervise the payment of compensation to Chinese and Japanese businessmen who had suffered losses during the anti-Asiatic riots of 1907. Two of the compensation claims came from Chinese opium-manufacturing merchants. King was shocked by his accidental discovery and prepared a report to the government, which led in a short time to the Opium Act of 1908.

Along the route to becoming prime minister, King made a small career out of this particular moral crusade. He was selected as part of a five-person British delegation to attend the Shanghai Opium Commission in 1909. In 1911, as a member of Laurier's Cabinet, he introduced a stiffer Opium and Drug Act. By 1920, calls for even stiffer legislation were coming in the form of sensational articles in such periodicals as *Maclean's* magazine. Several of these articles were authored by Mrs. Emily Murphy (1920; 1922), a juvenile court judge in Edmonton who ultimately went on to expand her views in a book titled *The Black Candle*. The background of these efforts tell us much about the way in which moral crusades can be generated.

During the period leading up to our first narcotics legislation, Canadian doctors were probably as responsible for addiction as the Chinese opium merchants. Medications containing opiates were routinely prescribed by physicians and used by patients of all classes. In fact, syrups containing opiates were frequently given to mothers for their infants. In other words, it was not just fear of the drug, but also hostility toward Asian immigrants, that lay behind much of the narcotics legislation. This hostility resulted in large part from the immigration of Asian labourers to Canada. Much of the parliamentary debate that preceded the first Opium Act dealt with Oriental immigration and a proposed trade treaty with Japan that was to allow Japanese immigration.

A dramatic example of how the totally separate and distinct issues of opium and Asian immigration were tied together occurred in the 1922 narcotics debates, when the following remarks of the secretary of the Anti-Asiatic Exclusion League were read:

> Here we have a disease, one of many directly traceable to the Asiatic. Do away with the Asiatic and you have more than saved the souls and bodies of thousands of young men and women who are yearly being sent to a living hell and to the grave through their presence in Canada (House of Commons Debates, 1922).

Others, such as Murphy (1922), spoke of "Chinese peddlers" bringing about the "downfall of the white race." Hostile attitudes toward a minority group were an important part of the efforts that resulted in Canada's first narcotics legislation.

The prohibition against alcohol offers an interesting comparison with drug legislation. The drug legislation worked; the alcohol legislation did not. Alcohol prohibition in the United States followed from the well-organized lobbying activities of the Women's Christian Temperance Union and the Anti-Saloon League. Their efforts constituted a moral crusade to protect an established way of life that was perceived as threatened by the immigration of new Americans into the nation's cities during the early part of this century. Joseph Gusfield (1963) argues that alcohol prohibition was a response to the fears of middle-class Protestant Americans that their established positions in American life, and this style of life itself, were endangered by the increasing abuse of alcohol by urban immigrants. As with drugs, a concerted effort was made to link alcohol with poverty, minorities, crime, and insanity. Alcohol prohibition was only partly successful, however, and resistance to it began to emerge, particularly in the ranks of organized labour.

Timberlake (1963) observes that although wage earners were unable to prevent temperance legislation, they were strong enough to ensure its ultimate failure. He notes that many working men opposed prohibition because it seemed to them like paternalism and class exploitation. To them it was a hypocritical and insulting attempt to control their personal lives in order to gain greater profits for their employers. The employers themselves had no intention of abstaining. Indeed, it is estimated that as much as 81 percent of the American Federation of Labour was "wet."

In summary, it seems that alcohol prohibition failed because it attempted to define as criminal what too large and well-organized a part of the poor, as well as the rich, were doing. By contrast, narcotics legislation focused more narrowly, and more successfully, on minorities of the poor who had no way to oppose being defined as criminal.

Juvenile Delinquency

The work of moral entrepreneurs is often associated with the growth of professional organizations that have their own bureaucratic interests to develop and protect. An example of this is the development of juvenile delinquency legislation and a resulting juvenile court bureaucracy staffed in large part by probation officers trained in social work. The efforts that led to the separate designation of juvenile delinquency and to the development of the juvenile courts were often called "child-saving" (Platt, 1969). Parker (1976) points out that, on the contrary, the real history of

Repeal of prohibition laws in December 1933 was the signal for celebrations. Prohibition failed because it defined as criminal what a majority of the adult population was doing.

SOURCE: Canapress Photo Service

child-saving in the twentieth century is a history of probation. It has little to do with improving children's general life conditions—most of those battles have already been won. It has less to do with history of juvenile institutions—these changed little after the early reformers.

Probation was a new idea at the beginning of this century. Its attraction was the prospect of keeping young offenders in their homes and out of institutions. The emphasis on probation within the juvenile court movement reflected a concern for the family that was typical of the early part of this century. The use of probation also extended the range of control efforts, however, and this control was imposed largely on the families of the urban poor, often outside court. The results of these activities can be seen in Canada and the United States. One of the results was the development of a bureaucracy, staffed in large part by probation officers (Hagan and Lean, 1977).

Theories of Crime and Deviance

So much for what deviance is, where it is found, and how and why it is legislated against. Our chief remaining question is: How do we account for the actual phenomenon? How, that is, do we explain deviance? Accordingly, we now turn to attempted theoretical explanations of class differences in criminal and deviant behaviour.

Structural Functionalism and Deviance

Structural-functionalist theories regard deviant behaviour as the result of a strain or breakdown in the social processes that are aimed at producing conformity. These theories focus on institutions (such as the family and school) that socialize individuals to conform to the values of society. They focus also on the ways in which this process can go wrong. The approach assumes that there is wide agreement, or consensus, about what the prime values of our society are and tries to explain why some individuals, through their deviant behaviour, come to challenge this consensus. The structural functionalist asks, "Why do some people violate the values that nearly all of us are assumed to hold in common?"

Anomie. The roots of functionalist theory are in Durkheim's notion of anomie (1964, originally published 1897). **Anomie** at first meant an absence of social regulation, or normlessness. Merton (1938; 1957) revived the concept, making it refer to the consequences of a faulty relationship between culturally defined goals (such as monetary success) and legitimate means of attaining them (such as education). The problem, according to Merton, is that in our society, success goals are widely shared, while the means of attaining them are not. Merton's theory is intended to explain not only why people deviate, but also why some people deviate more than others. In particular, members of the lower class are most affected by the gap between shared success goals and means to attain them. The result is a high rate of deviant behaviour.

Merton outlined a number of ways in which individuals adapt to inadequate means of attaining their goals. The common feature of these separate patterns is that they all represent adaptations to failure—failure to achieve goals through legitimate means.

Delinquent Subculture.   The adaptations to failure mentioned above occur socially as well as individually. One form of social adaptation is represented in the **delinquent subculture**. Cohen (1955) suggests that members of the lower class (potential members of a delinquent subculture) first experience a failure to achieve when they enter school and are judged by a "middle-class measuring rod." The heart of the problem is that working-class children are not prepared to satisfy middle-class expectations. By adolescence, therefore, they may turn to the delinquent subculture as an alternative set of criteria, or values, that they can meet.

The delinquent subculture completely rejects middle-class standards. It expresses thoroughgoing contempt for a middle-class lifestyle by embracing its opposite—as if to say, "we're everything you say we are and worse." The result, according to Cohen (1955), is a delinquent subculture that is "non-utilitarian, malicious, and negativistic"—a total reversal of middle-class values.

This is one possible type of subcultural reaction to the frustration of failure. The theorists we consider next go on to suggest three other reactions.

Differential Opportunity.   When legitimate opportunites are denied, illegitimate opportunities may be the only game in town. Cloward and Ohlin (1960) argue that to understand the different forms that criminal and delinquent behaviour can take, we must consider the different types of illegitimate opportunities available. Different types of community settings, and the different illegitimate opportunities they offer, produce very different subcultural responses. Cloward and Ohlin suggest that three types of responses predominate:

1.   a stable criminal subculture;

2. a conflict subculture;
3. a retreatist subculture.

The stable criminal subculture, as the name suggests, is the best organized of the three. According to Cloward and Ohlin, this subculture can emerge only when there is some co-ordination between people in legitimate and illegitimate roles (for example, between politicians or police and people in the underworld). One pictures the old-style political machine, with protection provided for certain preferred types of illegal enterprises.

The **conflict subculture** arises in slum locations where legitimate and illegitimate enterprises do not co-exist. Violence and conflict, after all, are a threat to both types of enterprise. The conflict subculture gives rise to street gangs and violent crime, making the streets unsafe for more organized crime.

The **retreatist subculture** includes those people who fail in their efforts in both the legitimate and the illegitimate opportunity structures. These "double failures" may resort to drug abuse and other forms of escape.

Symbolic Interaction and Deviance

In the approaches we have considered thus far, values play some role in causing deviance. The presence of success goals or values without the means to obtain them is seen as producing deviant behaviour. The symbolic-interactionist theories of deviance, by contrast, are concerned less with values than with social meanings and definitions. These theories assume that social meanings and definitions can affect behaviour. Early versions of symbolic-interactionist theory focused on how these meanings and definitions were acquired by individuals from others. Later versions of the theory have focused on the role of official control agencies in imposing these meanings and definitions *on* individuals. The significance of this difference in focus will become apparent as we consider the development of the symbolic-interactionist approach.

Differential Association. A pioneer in the North American study of crime was Edwin Sutherland (1924). Sutherland argued that people behave criminally only when they define such behaviour as acceptable. There is thus a connection between people's actions and their ideas, or definitions. The hypothesis of **differential association** is that a person learns criminal behaviour by associating with people who define that kind of behaviour favourably and having little contact with those who define it unfavourably. If the weight of favourable definitions is greater

Banks and Organized Crime

It is now recognized by international law enforcement organizations that the only successful way to identify and prosecute organized crime figures is to trace the proceeds of crime from the source to the ultimate beneficiaries. The kind of co-operation between people in legitimate and illegitimate roles described in the following article is necessary for organized crime to exist.

New York—On Nov. 11, 1980, Salvatore Amendolito, 52, a well-dressed, distinguished-looking Italian with salt-and-pepper hair, walked into the Bank of Nova Scotia in Nassau, Bahamas, and deposited $233 387.20 cash in small bills.

The next day he deposited another $329 983.12, this time in money orders, travellers' cheques and cashiers' cheques all under $10 000.

Those deposits, Amerdolite told a U.S. federal court recently, were a small fraction of the millions of dollars in "dirty money" the Mafia gave him to launder through Canadian banks in the Bahamas.

Amendolito, who turned informer when police agreed to drop charges against him, is a key witness in a trial here of 22 people charged in a heroin ring and money-laundering operation known as the Pizza Connection.

The trial began six months ago and is expected to continue for several more months.

Court records show that the Mafia used the Bank of Nova Scotia and the Royal Bank in Nassau and other international financial institutions to launder money—give it a clean history—and send about $13 million U.S. to Switzerland in 1980-81.

The New York Mafia also funnelled $20.5 million U.S. to Switzerland from March to September 1982 through currency-trading accounts at the New York offices of brokerage companies E. F. Hutton and Merrill Lynch records show.

The banks and brokerage firms have not been charged with any crime.

Defendants in the case—labelled the Pizza Connection because pizzerias were used to hide drug trafficking and money laundering—also attempted in 1983 to launder unspecified amounts of cash through unnamed Montréal boutiques, controlled by somebody they called "Anna Maria of Montréal," FBI wiretaps indicate.

According to court documents and a 130-page indictment, Anna Maria of Montréal flew from Montréal to La Guardia airport in Queens, where she met Gaetano Mazzara and Francesco Castronovo, two restaurant-business partners from New Jersey, who are among the Pizza Connection defendants. Police said they cannot reveal more information on this connection.

Banks and similar institutions are the first step in giving dirty money a clean history, and Canadian banks—which handle 80 percent of the banking business in the Bahamas—have been key instruments in laundering money.

Laws that forbid Bahamian bankers to disclose records ensure protection from investigation by foreign narcotics and tax agents.

And once a drug trafficker has deposited his cash into a Bahamian bank, he can wire it anywhere in the world, no questions asked.

SOURCE: "Mafia Informer Describes Link between Banks, Dirty Money" by William Marsden, April 24, 1986, [Montreal] *Gazette*.

than the weight of unfavourable definitions, the person will engage in criminal behaviour.

Sutherland (1949) applied his hypothesis in a famous study of white-collar crime, arguing that individuals become white-collar criminals because they are immersed with their colleagues in a business ideology that defines illegal business practice as acceptable. A student of Sutherland's, Donald Cressey (1971), went on to apply a form of this hypothesis to the specific crime of embezzlement. Cressey interviewed more than 100 imprisoned embezzlers and conluded that they had committed their crimes after they had redefined or rationalized them, using such lines as:

> "Some of our most respectable citizens got their start in life by using other people's money temporarily."

> "All people steal when they get in a tight spot."

> "My interest was only to use this money temporarily so I was 'borrowing' it, not 'stealing.'"

> "I have been trying to live an honest life, but I have had nothing but trouble, so 'to hell with it.'"

Techniques of Neutralization.   As Sykes and Matza (1957) have shown, the same subtle process of justification takes place among lower-class delinquents as well. Sykes and Matza list four of these ways of justification:

1. denial of responsibility (for example, blaming a bad upbringing);
2. denial of injury (for example, claiming that the victim deserved it);
3. condemnation of the condemners (for example, calling their condemners prejudiced);
4. an appeal to higher loyalties (for example, citing loyalty to friends or family as a cause of their behaviour).

Sykes and Matza's point is that crime in the underworld, like crime in society at large, is facilitated by this type of thinking.

Dramatization of Evil.   Why are underworld crimes more frequently made the subjects of official condemnation? The beginning of an answer to this question appears in the early work of Franklin Tannenbaum (1938). Tannenbaum points out that some forms of juvenile delinquency are a normal part of adolescent street life—aspects of the play, adventure, and excitement of being young. But to some people, such activities are seen as a nuisance or a threat, and they are likely to call the police.

Tannenbaum argued that police intervention begins a process of change in the way the individuals and their activities are perceived. He suggested that there is a gradual shift from the definition of specific acts as evil to the definition of the individual as evil. Here, the individual's first contact with the law is central. This first contact is a "dramatization of evil" that separates the child out of his or her group for specialized treatment. Tannenbaum goes on to argue that this "dramatization" plays a greater role in making the criminal than perhaps any other experience.

Once singled out as delinquents, individuals go on thinking of themselves as delinquents—and behaving as delinquents behave.

Primary and Secondary Deviance.   Sociologists in recent years have expanded on Tannenbaum's version of the interactionist perspective. For example, Lemert (1967) suggests the terms primary and secondary deviance to distinguish between those acts that occur before and after society's response. Acts of **primary deviance** happen before a social or legal response has occurred. They may be incidental or even random aspects of an individual's general behaviour. These initial acts have little impact on the individual's self-concept. **Secondary deviance** follows the societal response and involves a transformation of the individual's self-concept. From this point on, the individual takes on more and more of the "deviant" aspects of his or her new role. The societal response has, from this point of view, succeeded only in confirming the individual in a deviant role (Becker, 1963).

The Labelling Process.   As we have developed our discussion of the interactionist perspective, it has focused more and more on the official societal reactions to deviant behaviour, what many analysts of deviance call "the labelling process." Societal labelling applies not only to crime, delinquency, and drugs, but also to mental illness. Scheff (1966), for example, has suggested that our society uses the concept of mental illness in much the same way that other societies use the concepts of "witchcraft" and "spirit possession."

Scheff (1966) observes that from childhood we are all aware of the stereotyped behaviour that is associated with insanity. On the basis of this knowledge, Scheff (1966) suggests that when a person finds that society is reacting to him or her in terms of the insanity stereotype, that person's behaviour will tend to conform to the stereotype, that is, become like the behaviour of others who have been classified as mentally ill. In other words, the labelling process of mental illness may help to create the very kind of secondary deviance it is attempting to cure.

In the end, symbolic interactionists do not insist that all, or perhaps even most, deviant behaviour is caused by officially imposed labels. They do note, however, that official labels can create problems for the individual they are applied to, often increasing the chances that additional deviant behaviour will follow. The point is that not only the *actors* but also the *reactors* participate in creating the meanings and definitions involved in deviant behaviour. The poor are more likely than the rich to get caught up in this process—a point further emphasized in conflict theory, which we consider next.

Conflict Theory and Deviance

Why and how do dominant social groups impose legal labels on members of subordinate social groups? To answer, we must pay at least as much attention to the labellers as to the individuals receiving the labels.

Crime as Status. For conflict theorists, behaviour gets the status of *crime* by being labelled that way. Crime is a status imposed by one group on the behaviour of another. Turk (1969) suggests that "criminality is not a biological, psychological, or even behavioural phenomenon, but a social status defined by the way in which an individual is perceived, evaluated, and treated by legal authorities." The task, then, is to identify the group(s) involved in the creation and application of this status.

Turk (1969) undertakes this task by observing that there are two types of people in society: "There are those. . . who constitute the dominant, decision-making category—the authorities—and those who make up the subordinate category, who are affected by but scarcely affect law—the subjects." In short, authorities make laws that in turn make criminals out of subjects. The difference is a matter of relative power. Authorities have sufficient power to label some subjects' behaviour as criminal. It is the poor who have the least power, and we can therefore expect the poor more likely to be labelled criminal.

Legal Bureaucracy. Determining which groups in society will be more criminal than others is in large part a matter of determining which laws will be enforced. Chambliss and Seidman (1971) observe that in modern, complex, stratified societies such as our own, such issues are handed over to bureaucratic agencies. At this point there is set in motion a "primary principle of legal bureaucracy." According to this principle, laws will be enforced when enforcement increases the reward for the agencies and their officials; they will not be enforced when enforcement is likely to cause organizational strain.

Chambliss and Seidman (1971) conclude, therefore, that because the poor are least likely to have the power and resources necessary to create organizational strain, they become the most rewarding targets for the legal bureaucracy's activities. In summary, the poor make up a disproportionate part of our crime statistics more because of a class bias in our society and the realities

Willing to Try Heroin

The obvious question now becomes how a straight-looking girl from the North End ever managed to get familiar with Eastside, considering that Eastside is closed society and people down there don't even know how to talk to someone from the middle-class world, and they automatically dislike them besides. To answer that question is to tell how she started using smack.

I learned Eastside and smack from a boyfriend who grew up there. Unless a girl wanted to change identities and become one of them herself, which is to say become a scuzz, the only way she could get in would be through a boyfriend. I met the guy on a farm in Oregon. I was the cook and he was a farmhand. I was up there because I was on the road and he was up there because he busted out of juvy hall and had relatives in Fallsville. I'd been traveling around the country for a couple of years, but that's another story. Because of a fortuitous combination of circumstances I ended up back here in school, the guy followed, turned himself in, did about a year, and got out with the intention of turning middle-class. He and I and a buddy of his from Eastside used to go around together a couple of nights a week, usually not doing much except getting loaded—smoking marijuana or maybe dropping reds or rainbows—none of which I much liked except that it was a rather different social activity.

Then the buddy got a girlfriend who was a hype from way back. She was 28, an ex-hustler, and a veteran of many habits, especially coke. I never knew anyone who took so much dope. All she cared about was getting loaded and that's all she ever did. My boyfriend and I often dropped by their pad after the library closed. One night they had just bought some smack and offered us some. My boyfriend demurred but I said, "Hell, yes, I want some, just because that's about the only thing I'd never done. Everyone was rather surprised at my willingness (there was another hype there with really awful tracks on his arms), but they shrugged, advised me that I might heave or get sick since it was my first time, discussed who should fix me up (I can't remember which one they decided on), and described the procedure to me. One guy took off his belt and tied me off, another cooked the stuff and hit me.

The rush was terrific. I wasn't expecting it. The others were asking me if I felt it yet, since they hadn't been sure how much to give me and thought they were erring on the short side instead of the heavy side. They gave me plenty though, because I stood up, maybe to unkink or flex my arm or something, since finding a vein on my arm takes some probing, and when the rush did hit me it practically knocked me off my feet. My head reeled so I could hardly even sit up, let alone stand or walk. I hadn't expected such an overwhelming experience, but I thought it was fun, a really wild sensation. The others were checking, asking me if I felt okay, and I assured them I felt better than fine. My attitude was like, "Wow, this stuff sure does it to ya! Spectacular."

SOURCE: From *Deviance: Field Studies and Self Disclosures* (pp. 60-61) by Jerry Jacobs, 1974, Palo Alto, CA: National Press Books.

of our bureaucratic legal system than because of the behaviour of the poor themselves. We will see that the conflict theorists agree with that assessment and build on it.

A New Criminology.   The types of arguments set forth in the preceding paragraphs have recently resulted in the call by a group of British researchers for a "critical" or "new" criminology (Taylor *et al.*, 1973; 1975). The **New Criminology** represents the re-emergence of a Marxian theory of crime and deviance. This group argues that the roots of our modern crime problems are intertwined with those of western capitalism. They argue further that the capitalist ideology is so strong a force that it has conditioned the very way we conceive of crime.

For example, the New Criminologists observe that our thinking about crime focuses primarily on one group of individuals, the poor, making them the chief targets of criminal law and penal sanctions. Advantaged people, on the other hand, are generally bounded only by a civil law that seeks merely to regulate their competition with one another. The New Criminologists argue that the result of this type of arrangement is to create two kinds of citizenship and responsibility. The more advantaged group tends to be "beyond incrimination" and, therefore, above the law (see also Hagan *et al.*, 1980).

The Processing of Crime and Deviance

The symbolic-interactionist and conflict perspectives on crime and deviance have underscored the role that official agencies play in determining what is called criminal or deviant. This increased awareness has stimulated new kinds of research that focus on decision making in official agencies, including, for example, decisions made about mental hospital admissions, police arrests, plea bargaining, and judicial sentencing. The results have often suggested that biases in official decision making do exist.

Processing Mental Illness

Doubting the accuracy with which psychiatrists distinguish the sane from the insane, Rosehan (1973) designed a unique study to see what it takes to get in and out of a mental hospital. How skilful are the diagnoses? In this study, Rosehan and eight other people—with no background of mental disorders—sought admission to twelve different psychiatric hospitals. Each person complained of fictional symptoms (hearing voices saying "empty, hollow, thud") resembling no known form of mental illness. Even though the symptoms were fake, all of the "patients" were diagnosed as schizophrenics. Immediately following admission, these "patients" stopped reporting symptoms and went back to behaving normally. After an average period of more than two weeks, all of the "patients" were released as "schizophrenics in remission." None of the individuals, in other words, was discovered to be *sane*. These results do not indicate, of course, that there are no differences between the sane and the insane, but they do suggest that mental hospital personnel may often overlook or mistake these differences.

Canada's troubled youth the real victim of society?

Adolescents—economically and politically powerless—are becoming society's scapegoats. The Special Senate Committee Report on Youth, seriously under-reported in the media, paid scant attention to mental-health needs of a growing number of under-serviced, psychiatrically impaired young people. And now we have the spectacle of a well-salaried Minister of Youth, Andrée Champagne—with no mandate and no program—who is as impotent and powerless as her constituents.

Our abrogation of values is leading to the victimization of a disenfranchised group. It is clear that disturbed adolescents reflect the frustrations and frictions of society most acutely. Statistics painfully catalogue the fact that although the population of 15- to 21-year-olds may be decreasing in absolute terms, the severity and frequency of their problems are not. Over a 20-year period, between 1961 and 1981, the teen-age suicide rate in Canada increased fivefold, crimes in this age group increased eightfold and motor vehicle deaths increased by 81 percent for males, 47 percent for females. In an average week in 1983, more than 800 000 young people were either unemployed or not attending school. It is estimated that by 1990, half the children under the age of 18 will have experienced divorce or separation. Some 14 percent now live below the poverty line. Some 15 percent in non-family settings.

Psychiatric research is debunking the notion that "adolescent turmoil" is normal, transient and benign. Those who are symptomatic don't simply grow out of it; trends toward more serious psychopathology are becoming apparent.

A recent study at one Toronto hospital, for instance, found roughly one-third of adolescent patients in a sample suffered from schizophrenia and two-thirds from personality disorders. A second research project involving Toronto adolescents is revealing that in a representative population of "normal," non-clinical teen-agers, 46 percent of the sample have some degree of disturbed personality. Of these, more than half fall into a cluster comprised of quiet, introverted and anxious types, while nearly three out of 10 are characterized by anti-social tendencies.

Such trends lead the informed observer to predict increases in average length of stay in hospital or residential care and increases in the rate of re-admissions. At the same time, pressures toward "deinstitutionalization" have created greater needs for community treatment for this age group.

It is clear that manpower and services are inadequate to meet this demand. Data collected by a committee examining adolescent bed demand in Toronto found that 85 percent of requests for admission were considered appropriate, but places could be found for only 41 percent. The most important symptoms leading to the requests for admission were depression or suicidal behaviour, anti-social or dangerous behaviour and bizarre thinking or behaviour. The study concluded that the system may not be able to meet the demand for adolescent beds—whether they be for crisis, intermediate stay or long-term placements.

At treatment centres in Toronto, waiting lists for adolescents needing residential treatment can often be six to nine months. Some psychiatrists, in emergency situations, may have to resort to admitting adolescents to adult wards. As a result, 16-year-olds are sometimes being forced into programs with chronic alcoholics or demented geriatric patients. Toronto has only 30 to 40 acute-care beds for 13- to 18-year-olds. The situation for 18- to 21-year-olds is often worse. They fall between the cracks—too old for children's services and too young for adult programming.

In terms of psychiatric resources, the University of Toronto, which has the second-largest child psychiatry training program in North America, graduates only eight to 10 child psychiatrists a year, not all of whom choose to treat adolescents. This leaves a painfully inadequate number of therapists and consultants, whose waiting lists are so long that minor problems escalate into major ones, or patients become demoralized and give up seeking help. As a result, although 10 percent of children in Ontario are in need of psycho-social assistance, only 1 percent receive it.

Society faces a dilemma as to whether it should try to recapture the status quo, by preserving traditional institutions and values, or support alternative lifestyles, cognizant of changes in our psycho-social fabric that may be irreversible.

Prostitution, child abuse, alcoholism, vandalism, violence, suicide, and depression are symptomatic of social malaise. Escalating divorce rates, increased mobility, changing social conventions, the erosion of institutional supports of church and school, all contribute to a sense of rootlessness and anomie.

In terms of preventive solutions, measures should include support for parents of adolescents and for high-risk people such as single unwed mothers.

On the educational front, topics such as suicide, depression, sex abuse, and alcohol dependence should be introduced into secondary school curricula. Students who have experienced these problems could be used as "tutors" (similar to the Alcoholics Anonymous model). Adolescents should be educated on parenting, through health education or life-skills programs.

Teachers, who are in an ideal position to detect psychological problems at their onset, should be supported through additional training in adolescent psychological development and have greater access to consultation with mental-health professionals.

General practitioners and pediatricians should be given supplemental educational programs on the mental-health needs and problems of adolescents. Provincial governments and universities should provide funding for more psychiatric residency posts in adolescent psychiatry. This is necessary if manpower is to approach the recommended one child psychiatrist per 25 000 of the population.

More money should be directed to research in: normal adolescent development and the natural history of individual disorders; the psychological impact of divorce and child-rearing in non-traditional families; and the utilization of mental-health services to uncover why adolescents who need treatment fail to get it.

On the service end, an increase in availability of acute-care beds, long-term residential placements, day-treatment programs, and outpatient clinics should be considered. Particular attention should be paid to the older, difficult-to-place adolescent (in the 18-21 category) to fill the existing gap in services. In general and pediatric hospitals, the establishment of "teen clinics" which offer medical and psychological assessment and treatment should be encouraged.

While society appreciates the increased necessity of supporting programs for the geriatric population, legislators need to be mindful that the baby boom's baby boom is upon us— today's young adults are producing tomorrow's adolescents. It is conceivable that the demand for services to this age group will rise, just as the demand in services for the elderly is rising.

The rewards which society could reap by better addressing these needs will be measured by the increased productivity and vibrancy which only young people can contribute to a rapidly changing society.

SOURCE: "Canada's Troubled Youth the Real Victim of Society" by Marshall Korenblum, 1986, March 24, *The Globe and Mail*, p. A7.

Processing Alcoholism

The treatment of alcoholism is another area in which certain official decisions give rise to questions. In this area, there is a marked connection between class background and social response. There is a vast difference in social class between people treated in private clinics and those treated by the Salvation Army. It may be informative to see how members of various classes find their way into these widely varying treatment arrangements.

One way of approaching this problem is to study the admission and treatment practices of a single institution that deliberately attempts to care for people of varying class backgrounds. The purpose of this type of study is to determine if there are patterns suggestive of more general principles in the treatment of alcoholism.

Such a study was carried out by Schmidt *et al.*, (1968) in the Toronto clinic of the Alcoholism and Drug Addiction Research Foundation. One of the major findings of this study is that lower-class alcoholics in the Toronto clinic are more likely to receive drug-related treatment from doctors, while upper-class alcoholics are more likely to receive "talking" therapies from psychiatrists. These class-related differences can not be explained by differences in diagnosis or age.

Even more interesting than these treatment differences, however, are variations in how people from varied social classes are referred to the clinic. Upper-class patients are more likely to find their way to the clinic through private physicians, middle-class persons by way of Alcoholics Anonymous, and lower-class persons through general hospital and welfare agency referrals. Schmidt *et al.* (1968) offer the conclusion that these class patterns can be attributed largely to differences in the drinking patterns of the class. We are particulary interested, at this point, in the role the courts play in responding to these class differences.

We can use the studies of voluntary clinics as a source of clues about what may be happening across agencies. Lowe and Hodges (1972) began a progression along this route in studying the treatment of black alcoholics in the southern United States. They started their research with the operations of a single voluntary clinic, but soon left this course after finding that "any variation in amount of services given to patients within the clinic was insignificant beside the overwhelming fact that so few black alcoholics entered into service at all." This result of their research is eventually explained with the observation that black alcoholics are less likely to view admission to a clinic as offering treatment and, are, therefore unlikely to admit themselves voluntarily into any program.

The unfortunate effect is that black alcoholics find themselves the involuntary subjects of law-enforcement operations. These start with the police, take fatal form in the courts, and end with imprisonment. Lowe and Hodges note that the courts very rarely attempt to reverse this situation with referrals to alternative treatment institutions.

This pattern is apparent for native peoples in Canada as well. Hagan (1974) followed up the treatment received by native and white offenders in Alberta following incarceration. On the basis of either judicial recommendation or inmate request, offenders in Alberta are considered for transfer to an open institutional setting offering a program particularly designed for alcoholic offenders. However, Hagan found that although the target population of problem drinkers is nearly twice as large among native offenders as among whites, more whites than native offenders receive treatment in the open institutional setting. White offenders are more than twice as likely as native offenders to find their way to this treatment setting. There are three plausible explanations for this situation. First, judges may recommend referrals of native offenders to the open institution less often. Second, native offenders may seek and accept such referrals less frequently. Third, correctional personnel may consent to the transfer of native offenders less often. It is important to note, however, that the three possibilities described are certainly not mutually exclusive and, in fact, are probably mutually supportive. In other words, there may be general agreement that in its present form the open institutional setting is less beneficial for native than for white offenders.

Policing Crime and Delinquency

Winding up in a correctional institution represents the end point in a series of outcomes. Most people whose cases enter the first stages of a criminal or juvenile justice system are eventually diverted from the stream that leads to institutionalization. For one thing, the police may decide against arrest; or, if an arrest occurs, the prosecutor may decide to dismiss the case; or, if the case results in conviction, the judge may decide to suspend sentence. Any number of other things may happen along the way that end the case without institutionalization. The concern here is the extent to which these outcomes are random, legally determined, and/or socially biased.

Let's start with decisions made by the police. Some of the most important research in this area has been done by Black and Reiss (1970; Reiss, 1971), who draw a very basic distinction between two ways in which the police are mobilized. *Reactive mobilizations* are citizen-initiated (for example, by a telephoned complaint), while *proactive mobilizations* are police-initiated (for example, in response to an observed incident). Eighty-seven percent of the mobilizations in the Black and Reiss research were reactive, suggesting that the police usually do not seek out deviant behaviour, but rather more often respond to complaints about such behaviour.

However, a recent study by Ericson (1982) in a suburban Toronto jurisdiction raises some important questions about how applicable these findings are in Canada. Of 1323 encounters between citizens and officers in Ericson's study, 47.4 percent were characterized as proactive mobilizations and only 52.6 percent as reactive mobilizations. "On the surface," Ericson (1982) notes, "our data reveal that patrol officers are much more likely to go looking for deviance than the figures provided by Reiss, Black, and others would lead us to believe." Still, when only "major incidents" are looked at in these Canadian data, Ericson reports that more than 82 percent result from reactive mobilizations. In these incidents, complainants may still loom large in the decision-making process.

Prosecuting Crime and Delinquency

Once an individual has been arrested and charged, the image of the court process that we get from the media is that of trial by jury, with prosecution and defence lawyers in a battle for justice. In fact, however, few criminal cases follow this pattern. The typical sequence is for the defendant to plead guilty and give up trial. This is called *plea bargaining*. The defendant's lawyer bargains for reduced charges. Grossman (1969) observes, on the basis of interviews with prosecutors in York County, Ontario, that guilty pleas are an important way of avoiding the time, expense, and uncertainty of trials. The assumption is that plea bargaining is an effective way of increasing court efficiency (Blumberg, 1967). David Sudnow (1965) points out, however, that there are no guidelines for deciding what sort of reduction in charges is appropriate. Thus the possibility of a decision being biased on the basis of class is left open.

Judging Crime and Delinquency

Legislation outlining the sentencing responsibilities of the criminal courts in Canada entrusts to presiding judges almost total freedom in determining minimum sentences. Similarly, a wide range of freedom is allowed in the establishment of maximum penalties. The nature of the problem, however, extends beyond the absence of statutory guides to minimum and maximum sentences. The problem is that there is confusion regarding a basic set of principles to be used in determining sentences. Decore

(1964) notes that even the use of precedents in sentencing is a matter of contradiction and doubt. As a result, sentencing relies heavily on the discretion of the individual judge. This can lead to variation and disparity. An attempt to examine variation in criminal sentences is found in the research of Hogarth (1971).

Hogarth provides data suggesting that in the mid-1960s Canada had one of the highest rates of imprisonment in the western world (see also Cousineau and Veevers, 1972; Matthews, 1972). However, Hogarth also presents evidence of a recent shift in this pattern—suddenly fines have begun to replace the prison sentences.

The most recent evidence on Canada's use of imprisonment is provided in an exceptionally careful analysis by Waller and Chan (1975). This analysis indicates that Canada's overall imprisonment rate is no higher than that of the United States and several other countries, with only the Yukon and the Northwest Territories remaining high relative to most American states. Waller and Chan are careful to emphasize the difficulties of drawing any final inferences from the data they present, and to their cautions we will add several additional comments. First, it is not surprising to find Canada's imprisonment rate per 100 000 population low relative to some other countries, particularly the United States, because Canada's serious crime rate is also relatively low. The more crucial comparisons would involve ratios of incarcerations to occurrences and convictions. Waller and Chan appropriately point out the complications in accurately computing these ratios with current official data. Second, it should be noted that, where imprisonment rates are highest in Canada (that is, in the north), native peoples are most likely to be experiencing the consequences. Finally, we can observe that while efforts to avoid incarceration through the increasing use of fines may be generally successful in Canada, economic and ethnic minorities unable to pay these fines remain at a continuing disadvantage. These comments should discourage any sense of complacency with our condition.

Crime, Race, and Violence in Canada and the United States

Let us consider a topic that most Canadians sometimes think about but less often discuss. The topic is crime, race, and violence in Canada and the United States. There is no doubt that officially recorded rates of violent crime and many other kinds of deviance are higher in the United States than in Canada (see Figure 5-1).

There are differences in kind as well as in amount of criminal violence in the two countries. In the United States, for example, about half of all homicides involve handguns, while in Canada

FIGURE 5-1. Comparative Indices of Violent Offenses Reported by the Police in Rates per 100 000 Population, Canada, U.S.A., 1965–1981*

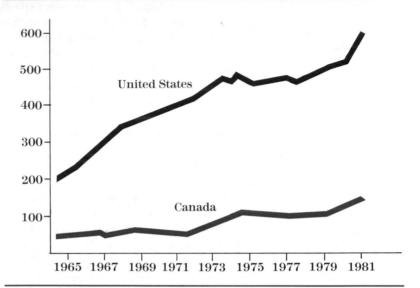

* U.S. violent crimes include robbery, aggravated assault, forcible rape, and murder; Canadian violent crimes include robbery, wounding, rape, murder, attempted murder, and manslaughter.

SOURCES: *Selected Trends in Canadian Criminal Justice: Crime and Traffic Enforcement Statistics—1977–1981;* and *Uniform Crime Reports—1977–1981.* Ottawa: Ministry of the Solicitor General of Canada.

the figure is approximately ten percent. Friedland (1981, p. 1) illustrates this point with some graphic comparisons. In 1971 there were fewer than 60 homicides committed with handguns in all of Canada. Metropolitan Toronto, with more than 2 000 000 people, had only four handgun homicides that year. In contrast, in 1979, handguns were used in almost 900 killings in New York City, 3000 in Metropolitan Detroit, and 75 in Metropolitan Boston. The six New England states had over 200 handgun homicides in 1979; the four Canadian Maritime Provinces did not have a single handgun homicide in 1979. There were over 10 000 handgun homicides in the United States in 1979, almost 20 times the Canadian per capita rate.

The racial character of American criminal violence is another difference between the two national experiences. While blacks constitute about twelve percent of the American population, they have accounted for over half of the arrests for murder for most of the last two decades (Nettler, 1978, p. 145). While there is some evidence that native people in Canada and the United

States also have high rates of assault and alcohol-related crimes (Jensen *et al.*, 1977; Hagan, 1985), there is no indication that the connection between race/ethnicity and serious crimes of violence is nearly as strong in Canada as it is—particularly for blacks—in the United States.

Why are patterns of criminal violence so different in the United States and Canada? And how are these differences connected to issues of race? With regard to violence generally, these national differences are widely thought to have a base in the settlement of the American and Canadian west. Quinney (1970) observes that on the American frontier, local authorities were free to develop their own law enforcement policies or to ignore the problem of crime altogether.

Canada intended to be different. This is one of the reasons Canada chose to have a federal criminal code. The North-West Mounted Police (NWMP), with powers unparallelled by any other police force in a democratic country, were given responsibility for establishing "peace and order." Kelly and Kelly (1976, p. 21) argue that the NWMP of the 1890s "attended to the health and welfare problems of Indians and Eskimos," whereas Brown and Brown (1973, p. 10) write that "the NWMP were established as a semi-military force designed to keep order on the prairies and to facilitate the transfer of most of the territory of the region from the Indian tribes to the federal government with a minimum of expense and bloodshed."

Whichever of the above accounts of the role of the NWMP is the more accurate, it is clear that Canada's native peoples were treated in a significantly different way than were native peoples in the United States. America's treatment of both its black and native minorities was extraordinarily violent. Canada's treatment of its native peoples was, and still may be, socially and economically poor, but it has not been nearly so violent. It seems likely that this difference in the form of mistreatment would have had behavioural consequences—for example, in rates of violent crime.

A more general point can be made before we conclude. This point involves the very different policies the two countries have adopted to accomplish quite similar goals. These alternative policies are reflected in what have been called the "due process" and "crime control" models of law enforcement (Packer, 1964). Societies vary in their commitment to these models, and it can be argued that Americans tend toward the due process model, while Canada is characterized by a more explicit commitment to a crime control model.

The **due process model** is greatly concerned with safeguards to protect people from being unjustly punished. Advocates of the due process model prefer that guilty people go free before innocent people are found guilty.

In contrast, the **crime control model** places heavy emphasis on repressing criminal conduct. This view holds that the only way society can guarantee individuals' personal freedom is by ensuring order. Therefore, advocates of crime control are less anxious than the supporters of due process to presume the innocence of accused persons and to protect them against mistaken findings of guilt. It is not that the crime control model favours the unfair treatment of individuals, but rather that it is willing to tolerate a certain amount of mistreatment when the measures involved are seen as generally necessary for the maintenance of social order.

A final example, involving national differences in the control of guns, may help to bring together the threads of this discussion. Canada has long had tighter and more effective gun control legislation than the United States. This difference is one expression of the different attitudes toward the rights of individuals in the two countries. We have also noted the rather different histories of treatment of racial and ethnic minorities in the two countries. The United States violently suppressed its black and native minorities within a society that makes a rather democratic instrument of violence—handguns—freely available. Canada socially and economically suppressed its native peoples (but much less violently than was done in the United States) and made access to instruments of violence, particularly handguns, difficult.

These are very different national experiences, and they could be expected to produce different behavioural effects. For example, it might be expected that Canada's native peoples should be less violent in their criminal behaviour than are native peoples in the United States. Such comparisons may hold a key to a deeper understanding of the dramatic differences in crime rates that characterize the United States and Canada.

Meanwhile, it is interesting to speculate more generally about the consequences that may follow from Canadian and American strategies for dealing with crime and deviance. The consequences for the socially advantaged of both countries are much the same: both nations possess a legal order that allows the relatively safe and stable conduct of social and economic affairs. The consequences for the socially disadvantaged in each country are, however, somewhat different. Overall, crime rates are significantly higher in the United States than in Canada, and we have shown evidence that this gap is widening. Because it is the poor who are far more likely to be arrested and convicted in both countries, it is the poor who are most affected by this difference (see Hagan and Albaonetti, 1982).

Summary

1. Deviance involves behaviour that varies from a norm and society's reaction to that behaviour.

2. There are several kinds of deviance: consensus crimes, conflict crimes, social deviations, and social diversions. These can be distinguished according to their socially determined seriousness.

3. Whether or not different kinds of deviant behaviour come under official control is influenced by the activities of moral entrepreneurs and various interest groups.

4. The structural-functionalist theories of deviance argue that the presence of success goals or values without the means to attain them can produce deviant behaviour.

5. The symbolic-interactionist theories of deviance are concerned with the role of social meanings and definitions in the production of deviant behaviour.

6. The conflict theories of deviance have focused on the role of dominant societal groups in imposing legal labels on members of subordinate societal groups.

7. Consideration of the processing of various kinds of crime and deviance indicates that social as well as legal factors influence when, where, and upon whom deviant labels are imposed.

8. Two societal strategies for maintaining legal order are the due process and crime control models of law enforcement. Canada tends more toward a crime control model than does the United States.

9. Serious forms of crime and deviance are more common in the United States than in Canada. The social and historical roots of this difference may reflect an important part of what is unique about the Canadian experience.

Further Reading

Black, D. (1976). *The behavior of law.* New York: Academic Press.
   One of the most widely read of recent theoretical works on the way criminal and other kinds of law actually operate in real legal settings.

Boydell, C. L., & Connidis, I. A. (1982). *The Canadian criminal justice system.* Toronto: Holt, Rinehart and Winston.
   An up-to-date and comprehensive collection of readings.

Brannigan, A. (1984). *Crimes, courts & corrections: An introduc-*

tion to crime and social control in Canada. Toronto: Holt,
Rinehart and Winston.

This book focuses on the criminal justice system, giving particular attention to the police, courts, and corrections. New perspectives on these institutions are offered, while common assumptions of the past are questioned.

Chambliss, W., & Seidman, R. (1982). *Law, order and power.*
Reading, MA: Addison Wesley.

A conflict perspective on criminal law and its enforcement. This book deals with all aspects of the criminal justice system and with the development of criminal law.

Durkheim, E. (1964). *Suicide.* J. A. Spalding and G. Simpson (Trans.). Glencoe, IL: Free Press.

The classic work on this form of deviant behaviour. Durkheim anticipated much of what is thought modern in sociological theorizing about crime and deviance, including anomie theory and the labelling perspective.

Ericson, R. (1982). *Reproducing order: A study of police patrol work.* Toronto: University of Toronto Press.

This volume presents the results of the most comprehensive field study of policing done in Canada.

Griffiths, C. T., Klein, J. F., & Verdun-Jones, S.N. (1980). *Criminal justice in Canada.* Vancouver: Butterworths.

This volume provides a concise yet comprehensive introduction to the Canadian criminal justice system, with particular attention to the police, courts, and correctional subsystems.

Hagan, J. (1984). *The disreputable pleasures.* 2nd ed. Toronto: McGraw-Hill Ryerson.

An integrated textbook treatment of crime and deviance with a twist: it is argued that crime and deviance can be pleasurable, albeit disreputable, pursuits.

Shearing, C. (1982). *Organizational police deviance.* Toronto: Butterworths.

This book brings together a collection of articles that broadens that subject of police misbehaviour from simple corruption, which can be dismissed as a private moral failing, to pervasive patterns of official action—referred to as "structural deviance"—such as arresting, charging, harassing, and warning, which can have organizational roots.

III The Social Base

The social base of a society has a great deal to do with what life is like for its members. Many factors make up a society's social base:

1. the density and distribution of population;
2. the ways in which society is stratified or divided into levels;
3. the size and distribution of various ethnic groups;
4. the number and nature of formal organizations.

Consider that Canada is larger than the United States but has roughly the population of California. Consider also that the world's population is expected to double in approximately 40 years—to more than ten billion people by the first quarter of the next century. Chapter 6 examines the causes and consequences of societal population characteristics such as these.

Every society is stratified, or ranked, in several ways—leaders and followers, rich children and poor children, vice-presidents and junior clerks. The ways in which societies are stratified and the degree of mobility between levels, or strata, are the concerns of Chapter 7.

The interaction of various ethnic groups is particularly important in Canada, where we are committed to maintaining the identities of these groups. Chapter 8 discusses the concepts of ethnicity and race, and their importance in understanding Canadian society.

Modern societies are increasingly arranged into large, formal organizations. Today, most of us are born and educated, work and die in formal organizations. Chapter 9 examines some of the causes and consequences of formal organizations.

6
Population

The purpose of this chapter is to describe some of the kinds of data that sociologists acquire about human populations, and to discuss how sociologists predict changes in population. The chapter will look at a number of Canada's demographic characteristics. Be certain that you are able to

1. explain demographic transition theory;
2. explain how to measure
    (a) fertility,
    (b) mortality,
    (c) migration;
3. briefly outline how the patterns of fertility, mortality, and migration have changed historically in Canada;
4. outline the consequences of these changes;
5. discuss predictions of future changes in Canada's demography.

How much is a population changing in size, and why? What are the consequences of population growth or decline—for you, your society and the world? Does the timing of your birth affect your life chances? Does the type of society you live in determine what you are likely to die from, and, if so, how? Do immigrants have positive or negative consequences for the economy? These are some examples of the types of questions that the study of demography seeks to answer.

Demography is the scientific study of human population. Demography describes and explains the characteristics of population as well as the processes underlying those characteristics. Neither society nor the population can be understood apart from each other.

There are three major characteristics of population:

1. size;
2. composition;
3. distribution.

Size refers to the number of people in a given area. **Composition**

relates to the characteristics of the people in the population, particularly age and sex. **Distribution** refers to the geographical location of people in a population. These are the ways in which population can change. We now turn to the most obvious aspect of demographic change over the past few centuries—population growth.

Population Growth

We tend to think of population change in terms of increase, but it is important to keep in mind that populations also decrease. Populations can grow quickly or slowly. World population increased relatively slowly until about 1650 when the total number of people was approximately 500 million. By 1987, world population was over five billion. Rapid population growth is unique to the twentieth century.

Underlying the huge increase in the world's population is a changing growth rate. **Growth rate** refers to the number of people added to (or subtracted from) a population in a given time frame for every 100 or 1000 people in the population. Often, growth is expressed as an annual rate per 1000 population.

The growth rate plays an important role in determining how fast a population will change in size. Often, demographers measure the pace of population increase in terms of doubling time.

FIGURE 6-1. A Schematic Representation of the Increase in the Human Species

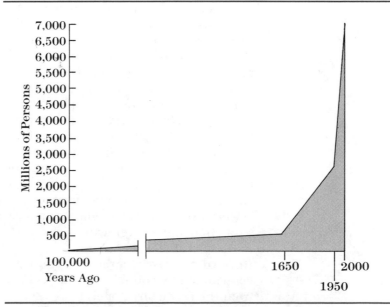

SOURCE: From *Population*, 3rd ed. (p. 9) by W. Peterson, 1975, New York: Macmillan.

Doubling time is the number of years it will take for a population to double in size, assuming that the current growth rate remains unchanged. If the 1987 annual growth rate (17 per 1000 population) were maintained, the world's population would double in approximately 40 years. In such an event, the world would contain more than ten billion people in the year 2027.

Today, non-western, developing nations are growing at a much faster pace than western populations. The annual growth rate in the developing nations is about 21 per 1000 population; in the developed world, it averages 5 per 1000.

Components of Growth

In order to understand the causes of growth—both in the world population and in the different societies comprising it—we must examine three demographic components of growth:

1 fertility;
2. mortality;
3. migration.

Fertility refers to actual childbearing in a population. **Mortality** refers to the deaths occurring in a population. **Migration** is the movement of people from one geographical location to another.

World population increase is a direct result of the extent to which births (*fertility*) outnumber deaths (*mortality*). The excess of births over deaths is termed **natural increase**. (If deaths exceed births, the term natural decrease is used.) In addition to natural increase, a population can change in size as a result of migration. **Net migration** refers to the difference between the number of in-migrants (people moving into an area) and the number of out-migrants (people moving away). Net migration is positive when in-migrants outnumber out-migrants, and negative when out-migrants outnumber in-migrants.

For the world as a whole, only natural increase is involved in population growth, because no one, at least so far, has been able to leave the earth's surface for any appreciable length of time, and no people from another planet have moved in. In some parts of the world, however, including Canada, net migration does play a role in population growth.

Rate of Natural Increase   The **rate of natural increase** is determined by subtracting what is termed the crude death rate from the crude birth rate.

The **crude birth rate** is the number of births per 1000 population and the **crude death rate** is the number of deaths per 1000 population. Birth rate varies considerably from society to society.

In 1987, the highest level was recorded in Malawi and Rwanda: 53 births per 1000 population. The lowest rate, ten, was registered in West Germany. In general, the crude birth rate is related to the level of economic development; that is, developed societies have low birth rates, while developing societies have much higher birth rates.

Variations in the crude death rate bear no such clear-cut relationship to the level of economic development. Many nations in the developing world have very low death rates. On the other hand, western European societies, all highly industrialized, do not experience particularly low death rates. For example, Sweden's death rate in 1987, at 11, was more than double that of Singapore's. This is, in part, a reflection of differences in the age compositions of the two countries. Sweden has an older population than Singapore has and, therefore, has more deaths relative to its population size than does Singapore.

Story in a map

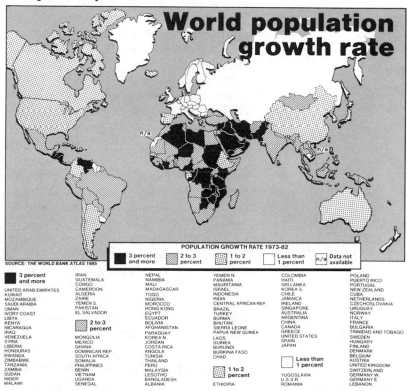

SOURCE: THE WORLD BANK ATLAS 1985

POPULATION GROWTH RATE 1973-82

3 percent and more — 2 to 3 percent — 1 to 2 percent — Less than 1 percent — n/a Data not available

3 percent and more		2 to 3 percent		1 to 2 percent	Less than 1 percent	
UNITED ARAB EMIRATES	IRAN	NEPAL	YEMEN N.	COLOMBIA	POLAND	
KUWAIT	GUATEMALA	NAMIBIA	PANAMA	HAITI	PUERTO RICO	
MOZAMBIQUE	CONGO	MALI	MAURITANIA	SRI LANKA	PORTUGAL	
SAUDI ARABIA	CAMEROON	MADAGASCAR	ISRAEL	KOREA S.	NEW ZEALAND	
OMAN	ALGERIA	TOGO	INDONESIA	CHILE	CUBA	
IVORY COAST	ZAIRE	NIGERIA	INDIA	JAMAICA	NETHERLANDS	
LIBYA	YEMEN S.	MOROCCO	CENTRAL AFRICAN REP.	IRELAND	CZECHOSLOVAKIA	
KENYA	PAKISTAN	HONG KONG	BRAZIL	SINGAPORE	URUGUAY	
NICARAGUA	EL SALVADOR	EGYPT	TURKEY	AUSTRALIA	NORWAY	
IRAQ		ECUADOR	BURMA	ARGENTINA	ITALY	
VENEZUELA	2 to 3 percent	BOLIVIA	BHUTAN	CHINA	FRANCE	
SYRIA		AFGHANISTAN	SIERRA LEONE	CANADA	BULGARIA	
LIBERIA	MONGOLIA	PARAGUAY	PAPUA NEW GUINEA	GREECE	TRINIDAD AND TOBAGO	
HONDURAS	MEXICO	KOREA N.	LAOS	UNITED STATES	SWEDEN	
RWANDA	GHANA	JORDAN	GUINEA	SPAIN	HUNGARY	
ZIMBABWE	DOMINICAN REP.	COSTA RICA	BURUNDI	JAPAN	FINLAND	
TANZANIA	SOUTH AFRICA	ANGOLA	BURKINA FASO		DENMARK	
ZAMBIA	SOMALIA	TUNISIA	CHAD		BELGIUM	
SUDAN	PHILIPPINES	THAILAND		Less than 1 percent	AUSTRIA	
NIGER	BENIN	PERU			UNITED KINGDOM	
MALAWI	VIETNAM	MALAYSIA	1 to 2 percent	YUGOSLAVIA	SWITZERLAND	
	UGANDA	LESOTHO		U.S.S.R.	GERMANY W.	
	SENEGAL	BANGLADESH	ETHIOPIA	ROMANIA	GERMANY E.	
		ALBANIA			LEBANON	

BERNARD BENNELL The Globe and Mail

By the year 2050, the world's population is expected to be about 14 billion — three times its present size. China with more than one billion people, and once a symbol of rampant population expansion, now grows at the rate of 1.2 per cent a year, the same as Canada. India, with three-quarters as many people, is expanding at 2.3 per cent a year, and should overtake China as population leader by the middle of next century. By heavy emphasis on family planning (and expelling many migrant workers) East and West Germany and Switzerland cut populations a little each year. For other reasons, Lebanon's population dips .3 per cent a year.

The highest rates of natural increase occur in Africa and Latin America. The lowest rates occur in Europe; some European countries—for example, West Germany—are currently experiencing natural decrease. Newer societies with a predominantly European heritage, such as Canada, the United States, and Australia, have low rates as well, although these rates are somewhat higher than those in Europe.

Natural Increase and Net Migration: The Canadian Case

Growth in the Canadian population has resulted from a combination of natural increase and net migration; natural increase, however, has played the dominant role. For most decades throughout Canada's history, the contribution of natural increase to population growth has far exceeded that of net migration. The particular role played by migration has varied over time. As you can see in Table 6-1, migration has functioned to increase our size at certain times (for example, from 1901 to 1910) and to lessen it at other times. As a result, the patterns of migration account for much of the unevenness in Canadian population growth, although fluctuations in fertility have been influential as well.

While natural increase has been the major factor in Canada's growth until now, projections concerning the future growth of our population present a very different picture. If we assume that fertility remains at its current low levels and that annual net migration averages 50 000 (from 1981 to 1986, net migration averaged 50 680), then after the year 2000, net migration will make a larger contribution to population growth than natural increase. Indeed, given these assumptions, net migration will be the only contributor to Canada's growth after 2015. After 2021, annual net migration will be exceeded by natural decrease, and the total Canadian population will begin to decline (Employment and Immigration Canada, 1984). We do not know if population decline implies social and/or economic crisis. However, this "unknown" is causing apprehension, so that the Canadian government has increased its annual quota of immigrants for 1987 to between 115 000 to 125 000 (compared to 85 000 to 90 000 for 1985).

Demographic Transition Theory

Much contemporary writing on population growth arises from *demographic transition theory*. This theory is based on the study of changes in population growth in western European societies

TABLE 6-1. Natural Increase and Net Migration in Canada[a], 1851-1986

Census Year	Population (in thousands)	Average Annual Growth Rate (per 1000)	Rate of Natural Increase (per 1000)	Rate of Net Migration (per 1000)
1851	2,436	–	–	–
1861	3,230	29	22	6
1871	3,698	13	18	–4
1881	4,325	16	17	–1
1891	4,833	11	14	–3
1901	5,371	11	13	–2
1911	7,207	30	16	13
1921	8,788	20	16	4
1931	10,377	17	14	2
1941	11,507	10	11	–1
1951	14,009	17	15	1
1956	16,081	28	20	8
1961	18,238	25	20	6
1966	20,015	19	16	3
1971	21,568	15	10	4
1976	22,993	13	9	3
1981	24,343	12	8	4
1982	24,632	12	8	4
1983	24,885	10	8	2
1984	25,124	10	8	2
1985	25,360	9	8	1
1986	25,591	9	8	1

[a]Excludes Newfoundland prior to 1951.

SOURCES: Adapted from "Canada's Population Growth and Dualism" (p. 6) by Roderic P. Beaujot, 1978, *Population Bulletin, 33*(2), Washington, DC: Population Reference Bureau, Inc.; *Canada's Population Outlook* (p. 4) by David K. Foot, 1982, Toronto: James Lorimer and Canadian Institute for Economic Policy; and *Current Demographic Analysis: Report on the Demographic Situation in Canada in 1986*, cat. 91-209E, Ottawa: Minister of Supply and Services.

(for summaries, see Coale, 1973; Stolnitz, 1964). It provides both a description and an explanation of historical changes in population growth.

According to **demographic transition theory**, a population undergoes three major stages in its transition to a modern pattern. These stages are

1. pre-transition;
2. transitional growth;
3. completion of transition period.

In the pre-transition stage, the population is characterized by high fertility and high mortality. Birth rates are constantly high. Death rates are high on average, but rise and fall somewhat in response to external conditions, such as famines, epidemics, and other natural disasters. Because both birth and death rates are high, population grows slowly, if at all.

Stage two, transitional growth, consists of two substages. In the first substage, the death rate declines, but the birth rate remains at the high level characteristic of stage one. As a result, the population grows rapidly. In the second substage, the birth rate begins to decline while the death rate continues to decrease. Because decline in death rate has had a head start, the death rate remains lower than the birth rate, so that a high rate of population growth characterizes this substage as well.

In stage three, the transition to low birth and low death rates is complete. The rate of population growth, then, slows in comparison with stage two. The completion of "transition" implies *zero population growth*, or what demographers call a *stationary population*—at least in the long run. The rates of population growth in stage three and stage one are similar therefore, but are achieved differently.

In stage three, death rates do not rise and fall; they are constantly low because means exist to control short-term crises, such as epidemics. Birth rates, however, do rise and fall in accordance with wider trends in society, such as booms and recessions in the economy. The low, but varying, fertility level of this stage is accomplished through deliberate control of childbearing.

The theory of demographic transition (outlined in Figure 6-2) explains this succession of demographic events in terms of changes in the wider social and economic environment, particularly industrialization and urbanization. The demographic

FIGURE 6-2. *Model of Demographic Transition*

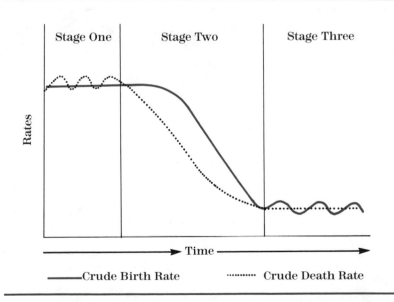

characteristics of stage one result from pre-industrial society's inability to control mortality. Given a threatening environment, the predictable response is to maximize fertility. However, high fertility represents more than a reaction to high mortality. In a pre-industrial society, children are important economically: from a young age they can work in the fields and tend the flocks, and as they mature, they are a source of economic security for aging parents. The costs of child rearing, on the other hand, are minimal. The economic utility of children is reinforced by a system of social beliefs that place a value on children.

Technological advances improve the production and distribution of food, sanitation, and medical treatment. As a result, death rates decline and the first phase of transition begins.

Fertility, however, responds more slowly to modernization; decreases in fertility are more difficult to achieve than decreases in mortality. The pre-industrial beliefs and values that supported high fertility tend to persist after technological development has made them irrelevant.

Nevertheless, modernization eventually lowers fertility. Declining mortality, for example, serves to suppress the birth rate. The increased survival rate of the young acts to reduce fertility by making "insurance" births less crucial. Furthermore, urbanization is a key facet of modernization, and children are less useful in an urban setting. At the same time, because the costs of child rearing and education rise in an urban setting, big families are perceived as liabilities.

Fertility

Demographers use the term *fertility* to refer to the actual childbearing of a woman or group of women. Women can consciously limit their fertility by deliberately preventing a conception or a birth. Deliberate fertility control measures may be used at different times during an individual's reproductive years. Such measures may be used to postpone family formation, to space children at desired intervals, or to prevent births altogether. The conscious limitation of fertility, by any of these techniques and for any of these reasons, depends on societal attitudes. Fertility control may not be viewed as desirable or morally acceptable. Fertility control also depends on knowledge of effective means of control and on the availability and proper use of those means.

Fertility Measurement

The crude birth rate is a measure of fertility; it is the number of births occurring in one year divided by the total population, often expressed as births per 1000 people. For the purpose of assessing the extent to which births contribute to natural increase and, hence, to population growth, the crude birth rate is an adequate measure of fertility. For other purposes, however, more refined rates are required.

The crude birth rate is an unrefined measure because its denominator, the total population, includes people (such as males of all ages, children, and the female aged) who do not bear children.

Fertility Change in Twentieth-Century Canada

Over the course of this century, the level of fertility in Canada has declined. The trend, however, has not been smooth. Fertility rates fell to low levels during the Depression of the 1930s, peaked for a 15-year period following the end of World War II, and declined again during the 1960s, reaching unprecedented low levels by the end of the 1970s. The period of post-war peak fertility (1946 to 1961) is commonly termed the *baby boom*. The present low levels have been referred to as the *baby bust* (Grindstaff, 1975).

The baby-boom era is a major exception to this century's trend of overall declining fertility. What factors account for this disruption of the trend? Specifically, why did the baby boom occur?

One important factor is the timing of childbearing. During the baby boom, women had their children at younger ages than did women of earlier and later eras. A trend toward childbearing at a younger age gives rise to increasing fertility rates. A change in the timing of childbearing affects the level of fertility, because there are more younger women than older women in a population. Thus, if proportionately more women bear children at younger ages, more babies will be produced for the simple reason that there are more younger women. The high fertility of the baby-boom period reflected a shift toward younger childbearing; the present trend of low fertility reflects, in part, a shift back to older childbearing.

Another important factor is age at first marriage. For both sexes, age at marriage is younger now than in the past. For example, the mean age at first marriage for women in Canada in the twentieth century until World War II was over 25. By 1951, the median had declined to approximately 22 and in 1961 it had dropped still further. It rose again, but by 1985, the median age was still under 24.

The essence of the baby boom, then, was a change in the timing of events in the life spans of women. The mothers who produced the baby boom married earlier than women before them, and they had their children shortly after marriage.

These women did not have significantly more children than did earlier groups. The increased fertility of the baby boom signified a change in the childbearing pattern in Canada, and not an increase in completed family size. Similarly, the low fertility of the baby bust reflects, to some degree, a change in the age patterns of childbearing. Today, women marry at relatively young ages but do not bear children immediately. Their behaviour reflects changing social norms, an economic recession, and the availability of effective contraception. We cannot assume that the completed family sizes of these women will be as low as present fertility levels suggest, although it does seem likely that we will have smaller families than earlier generations had, perhaps approximating, on average, two children per ever-married woman.

Factors Affecting Fertility

Fertility levels are determined by a number of interrelated factors. Three types of factors are particularly important:

1. demographic;
2. socio-economic;
3. governmental.

We will look at each factor separately, but it is important to keep in mind that these factors interact.

Demographic Factors. Two important population-related variables affect the fertility level:

1. infant mortality;
2. marriage pattern.

Usually measured by the *infant mortality rate*, **infant mortality** refers to the number of deaths among children under one year old in a population. For the world as a whole in 1987, the infant mortality rate was 81: in other words, nearly eight percent of all children born in 1987 died in the first year of life. Rates varied from a high of 183 (in East Timor, in Southeast Asia) to a low of 5.7 in Iceland. The 1987 rate in Canada was 7.9.

When the level of infant mortality is high, the level of fertility is high. A high incidence of infant death fosters a situation in which women produce many babies in order to ensure some surviving children. Insurance births result; that is, extra babies are produced "just in case."

The marriage pattern in a population also affects fertility level. When virtually all women marry, and at young ages, there is a greater likelihood of producing children. This is so not only because more women are married for a longer period of time, but also because more women are married at the time of peak child-bearing, that is, at ages 30 and under.

Socio-economic Factors.   All developed countries have low levels of fertility, while developing countries have much higher levels. Also, within individual societies, groups of high socio-economic status are characterized by low fertility, and vice versa. The interrelated social and economic factors that are important determinants of fertility behaviour are

1.   type of economic production;
2.   female participation in the labour force
3.   mobility opportunities;
4.   educational attainment.

Type of economic production.   As mentioned earlier, in an agricultural mode of production, children are economic assets. They begin work at a young age and provide economic support for elderly parents. At the same time, children in an agricultural setting are not expensive to raise, as food and housing are more readily available than in urban regions. This means that the economic benefits of children outweigh the costs.

In an industrial setting, on the other hand, children are economic liabilities. The types and structures of jobs in an urban, industrial setting are unsuitable for children. Participation in the labour force depends on skills obtained through education. Children are no longer "workers"; they are "students." As such, they are expensive: they do not contribute to family earnings and their education is costly.

Female participation in the labour force.   While women in all societies work, *where* they work varies according to the level and type of economic production. Women in urban environments are more likely to work outside the home than are women in rural settings. Also, the higher the level of economic development of the society as a whole, the greater the likelihood of female employment outside the home.

Societies with a high rate of female labour force participation have low fertility levels, and vice versa. Also, at the individual level, women who work outside the home have fewer children than women who stay home. The statistics do not indicate whether it is employment in the labour force that affects lowered fertility, or whether women with fewer children are more likely to work outside the home. The two factors probably influence

one another. We may assume, however, that the conflict between
the worker role and the traditional female childbearing and
child-rearing role has some effect. As both roles are demanding,
women may choose to reduce the conflict by minimizing the
number of children they bear. In contrast, women often choose
to keep their work within the confines of the household so that
it is easier to co-ordinate that work with child-rearing tasks.

Mobility opportunities. If people are trying to progress
socially and economically , they may limit the number of children as a means of pursuing those goals. Economic betterment
can more easily be attained with a small family.

The mobility opportunities existing for people in a society are
not equally distributed; people with higher socio-economic status have more opportunities open to them than people of lower
socio-economic status. These differential opportunities may
explain why families at the upper end of the economic scale tend
to have fewer children than families at the lower end.

Educational attainment. A vital factor determining fertility
behaviour is level of education, particularly among women.
High levels of education are associated with low levels of fertility.
This relationship is prevalent both across societies, and within
societies.

There are several factors underlying the relationship between
fertility and education. With increasing education, people come
to define themselves and their world in a certain way. Education
enhances the individual's sense of self. Also, education facilitates
the viewpoint that an individual can control the environment.
Education not only encourages people to exercise control over
their lives; it also provides the tool for that control: knowledge.

In terms of fertility behaviour, therefore, increased educational
attainment breaks down traditional barriers to fertility-limita-
tion practices, making fertility control an acceptable behaviour.
At the same time, the increased knowledge gained through education can be applied directly to reproduction, increasing the
likelihood of effective use of contraception.

Governmental Factors. Governments intentionally (and
sometimes unintentionally) act in ways that can affect fertility
level.

Historically, in western societies, governmental attempts to
influence fertility have sought to increase the number of births.
Mirroring a "bigger is better" mentality, this stance is reflected
in a number of strategies designed to encourage reproduction.
These strategies fall into two major categories: negative measures

Tokyo commuters are packed into train by pushers. Tokyo's population is over nine million.

SOURCE: Canapress Photo Service

and positive measures. Negative measures include the outlawing of birth control, the criminalization of abortion, and strict legal barriers to divorce. Until fairly recently, Canada used all three types of negative measures.

Positive measures include family allowances and tax exemptions for larger families. Despite these measures, however, the birth rate in Canada fell throughout the twentieth century, except during the baby boom. The Canadian case, then, illustrates government failure to influence the birth rate. Indeed, all western societies show that government is powerless to alter the course of fertility decline. If people are highly motivated to limit their fertility, they will do so, regardless of governmental obstacles to the attainment of that goal.

While the history of western societies demonstrates government attempts to increase fertility, the situation in today's devel-

Romania Struggles against Falling Birth Rates

Following the lead of the USSR and other Eastern European countries, Romania legalized abortion on request in September 1957. By 1965 the abortion ratio had soared to about 4000 per 1000 live births and the birth rate had dropped to 14.6 per 1000 population.

To reverse these trends, legal abortion was suddenly and drastically restricted and the import of contraceptives curtailed in October 1966. Abortion was authorized only for victims of rape or incest, for women over 45 or with four living children, where there was a chance that the child would be handicapped, and under a few other special mental and physical conditions.

The following year, in 1967, abortions dropped to about the 1958 level and the birth rate surged to 27.4. However, the trends reversed again and by 1983 the birth rate had dropped to 14.3 and abortions were up to 1300 per 1000 births—most of them provided on "mental health" grounds. In March 1984, President Nicolae Ceausescu announced dramatic new pronatalist measures:

• Doctors who perform abortions other than under the strict terms of the 1966 law (only for women over 45 or with four living children and for medical reasons) are subject to 25 years' imprisonment or even death.
• The minimum age at marriage for women was lowered to 15.
• Childless couples will be taxed an extra 5 percent on top of a surcharge already levied.
• All women aged 20 to 30 must regularly undergo a pregnancy test, followed by a monthly checkup in the event of pregnancy.

The official target is a fertility rise to four children per woman. This number is now held up as "the most sublime duty toward the nation and its people." Women who do not meet the target risk their careers.

SOURCES: "Romanian Population Policy," *Population and Development Review*, Vol. 10, No. 3 (September 1984) pp. 570-537; "In Brief: Romania," *People*, Vol. 11, No. 4 (1984) p. 35; "How Romania Tries to Govern Fertility," *Population Today*, February 1987.

oping countries is radically different. For the most part, the governments of developing nations seek to limit fertility.

The strategies used to limit fertility are as varied as the measures intended to increase it. However, fertility-limiting strategies are of two basic kinds: family planning programs and legal measures. Family planning programs represent an organized effort to educate people about available techniques of contraception, to disseminate contraceptive products, and to propagandize the benefits of small families. Evidence suggests that family planning programs are successful in many developing countries; fertility is being reduced at a faster rate than would be expected as a result of modernization alone (Tsui and Bogue, 1978).

Legal measures to reduce fertility include the endorsement of contraceptive devices, abortion, sterilization, and legal restrictions concerning age at marriage. In the People's Republic of China, all of these legal strategies have been employed to retard population growth. The evidence available to us indicates that these legal strategies are effective—fertility is declining (Aird, 1978).

Mortality

As noted earlier, *mortality* refers to the occurrence of deaths in a population. Fertility and mortality are the two components of natural increase: fertility determines how many people will be added to a population and mortality determines how many people will be subtracted. While human beings have considerable choice about childbearing and can choose to bear no children, they have no choice about dying and cannot postpone it indefinitely. Nevertheless, social and economic factors are still important in determining mortality within populations.

Mortality Measurement

At the simplest level, mortality is measured by the *crude death rate*. For many parts of the world, data are so limited that it is not possible to measure mortality in a more sophisticated way. The crude measurement of deaths is subject, however, to the same limitations as is the crude measurement of births.

The **life table** is a mathematical model used to estimate the average number of years that people of a given age and a given sex can expect to live, assuming that mortality rates continue at current levels. The most commonly used statistic derived from the construction of a life table is the estimation of life expectancy at birth. Correctly interpreted, this is a particularly meaningful statistic. It tells us the average number of years that a newborn baby can expect to live under current mortality conditions.

Mortality Variation

Contemporary death rates are not as variable as birth rates, but substantial differences do exist, globally, in terms of life expectancy at birth (see Figure 6-3). For the world as a whole in 1987, the average life expectancy was 63. The range was from 41 (in Ethiopia, Guinea, and Somalia) to 77 (in Iceland, Sweden, and Japan).

In past centuries, all populations were subject to conditions that resulted in a short life expectancy. Only in the twentieth century has mortality been controlled to allow for an average world life expectancy at birth of 63 years. In earlier centuries, mortality was high for three main reasons (Thomlinson, 1965):

1. acute and chronic food shortages;
2. epidemic disease;
3. poor public health standards.

FIGURE 6-3. Life Expectancy at Birth, 1987

Country	Life Expectancy (in years)
World	63
Africa	51
Egypt	59
Niger	44
Ethiopia	41
Asia	61
Bangladesh	50
India	55
Japan	77
China (Peoples' Republic)	67
North America	74
Canada	76
United States	74
Latin America	66
Mexico	67
Venezuela	69
Argentina	70
Europe	74
United Kingdom	74
France	75
Spain	76
West Germany	75
Poland	71
Oceania	72
Australia	76
USSR	69

SOURCE: *World Population Data Sheet*, Washington, D.C.: Population Reference Bureau, Inc., 1987.

Recent increases in life expectancy are due to the partial control we have achieved over these traditional killers. As a population's mortality rate falls, the causes of death change. When mortality rates are high, communicable or infectious diseases are the primary cause of death. When mortality decreases occur, it is largely the result of the control of communicable diseases. Once such diseases are controlled or wiped out, new ones emerge as the chief threats to life—in particular, cardiovascular diseases and cancer. These new killers gain in prominence, at least in part, because the avoidance of communicable diseases allows people to live to greater ages, when the risks of heart disease and cancer are also greater.

Mortality Differentials

Almost universally, women outlive men. The gap in life expectancy favouring women is greater in developed societies than in developing societies. Also, in the developed world, this gap has increased over time. For example, in Canada 50 years ago, female life expectancy at birth exceeded that of males by approximately two years; now, the gap is about eight years.

The male-female gap in mortality in developed countries is not equal at all ages. The difference is particularly great for those in their twenties, where the death rate for males is approximately four times that of females. The major factor involved is death by accident. In 1985, the death rate for males 20 to 24 years as a result of accidents was 72.7 per 100 000; the comparable figure for females was 17.3. One possible reason for this large difference is that men seem to find themselves in, or put themselves into, riskier situations. Men are more likely to have jobs where the risk of accidental death is high. Also, the traditional male gender role and "give 'em hell" attitude (David and Brannon, 1976) can place men in situations of high risk.

Married people have a better chance of surviving than single people. The reasons for lower mortality among the married are not well established, but two factors are probably involved. One is marital selectivity. It is possible that marriage selects healthier people; that is, the unhealthy and the disabled are less likely to get married. Another explanation centres on the advantages of married life: behaviour patterns are more stable; each spouse is available to care for the other in the event of illness; and a couple may lead a more cautious lifestyle in recognition of their dependence upon one another. In other words, marriage provides a more secure and stable type of existence. On the other hand, in a couple-oriented society such as ours, people who do not have a partner may suffer psychological stress, making them more susceptible to illness and death.

Within any society, different levels of mortality are often found

George Burns on
Making Life Expectancy Rates Work for You

"The point is, with a good positive attitude and a little bit of luck, there's no reason you can't live to be 100. Once you've done that, you've really got it made, because very few people die over 100."

SOURCE: *How To Live To Be 100 or More* by George Burns, New York: Putnam, 1983.

among various ethnic and racial groups. In all likelihood a combination of factors is involved:

1. hereditary factors;
2. inequality in the availability of medical services and facilities;
3. differences in socio-economic status;
4. differences in socialization affecting the motivation to sustain good health.

In Canada, one group has a particularly high mortality level and a short life expectancy at birth: native peoples (Indians and Inuit). Their level of infant mortality is nearly twice the Canadian average. Also, provincial averages of life expectancy at birth for both males and females are lowest for Québec. Similarly, in the United States, a consistent differential in mortality exists between the black population and the white population, a differential favouring whites.

Native peoples, the French in Canada, and blacks in the United States all have one thing in common, aside from a higher mortality than the national average. They are all minority groups, that is, groups excluded from full participation in the social and economic life of the wider society. This is particularly so for native peoples and blacks, whose mortality levels are considerably higher than the average for the societies of which they are a part.

Migration

Migration that crosses national boundaries is called *international migration*. If, on the other hand, the movement occurs within the confines of a society, the migration is said to be *internal*. We noted earlier that for both types of migration, there are two kinds of migrants: people moving into a given geographical area (in-migrants) and people moving out (out-migrants). In the case of international migration, these two types are termed *immigrants* and *emigrants*, respectively. *Net migration* refers to the difference between the number of in-migrants and the number of out-migrants.

International Migration in Canada

Four major periods of immigration can be identified in Canada. During the first period, Canada was settled by the French. The bulk of French immigration to the colony of New France spanned the years 1608 to 1760. The total volume of French immigration was quite small, probably less than 10 000 (Beaujot, 1978). The second period of immigration brought a new group to Canada, the British. This wave of immigration was much larger in scale than the French. Initial British immigration to Canada was, for the most part, via two distinct routes: from the United States and from Great Britain. From the United States, United Empire Loyalists entered Canada during the American Revolution. From Great Britain, direct immigration in significant numbers occurred during the early years of the nineteenth century.

The British-origin population in Canada was further augmented by an influx of Irish escaping famine in the 1840s. During the nineteenth century, other western European groups, particularly Germans, also immigrated to Canada. The total volume of immigrants during this period is uncertain; from 1851 to 1901, estimates range from 1.3 million to 2.3 million (Kalbach and McVey, 1979).

Canada's third period of immigration comprised the first three decades of the twentieth century, when an unprecedented number of immigrants entered the country. Estimates range from 3.7 million to 4.6 million for 1901 to 1931 (Kalbach and McVey, 1979). For the first time in Canadian history, groups other than western Europeans entered Canada in significant numbers. This was a period of large-scale immigration of eastern Europeans, particularly Ukrainians.

The fourth period spanned the post-World War II years. From 1946 to 1984, approximately five million immigrants entered Canada. During this period, in-migration from non-European countries increased steadily. In the early phase, the nine major sources of immigrants to Canada were the United States and European countries. In 1984, the situation was quite different (see Figure 6-4). Of the ten leading source countries, seven were

FIGURE 6-4. Source Countries of Landed Immigrants, Canada, 1984

Country[a]	Number of Immigrants
1. Vietnam	10,950
2. Hong Kong	7,696
3. United States	6,922
4. India	5,502
5. Great Britain	5,104
6. Poland	4,499
7. Philippines	3,748
8. El Salvador	2,579
9. Jamaica	2,479
10. China (Peoples' Republic)	2,214
All countries	88,239

[a]Country of last permanent residence.

SOURCE: *Immigration Statistics* by Employment and Immigration Canada, 1984, table IM7.

developing nations. Nevertheless, Britain and the United States continue to be leading source countries.

Changes in the ethnic origin of immigrants to Canada reflect alterations in Canadian immigration policy over the years. Until 1962, Canadian immigration policy was based, to a large degree, on ethnic criteria. There were preferred immigrants and non-preferred immigrants. The latter were those of western European origin, people viewed as highly suitable for assimilation into Canadian society.

Beginning in the early 1960s, changes in Canadian policy have been designed to delete race and ethnic origin as grounds for admission. As a result, the percentage of non-western Europeans and non-Europeans entering Canada has increased.

In terms of emigration, the major receiver of Canadians (both foreign-born and Canadian-born) has been the United States. Emigration from Canada was very high from 1861 to 1901, a major concern of the Canadian authorities at the time, because the number of emigrants exceeded the number of immigrants. This situation was reversed briefly in the early decades of this century, as a result of changes in Canadian immigration policy combined with economic expansion. However, until quite recently, more people emigrated from Canada to the United States than came from the United States to Canada. For example, in every year from 1950 to 1970, Canada lost numbers in Canadian-American migration exchanges (Beaujot, 1978).

Perhaps more importantly, Canada was losing trained people to the United States and was not receiving comparable numbers of skilled, well-educated United States immigrants. This phenomenon has been called the *brain drain*. Yet for certain occupational categories—university professors, for example—the opposite was the case. Encouraged by short-term exemption from federal income tax payment, more American professors entered Canada than Canadian professors exited to the States.

In recent years, Canadian immigration policy has favoured the admission of skilled, educated people. Therefore, a reverse brain drain has occurred, with Canada receiving highly educated and skilled people, especially from developing countries.

Internal Migration in Canada

With regard to internal migration in Canada, two aspects are particularly important:

1. western expansion;
2. urbanization.

In 1901, approximately 88 percent of the Canadian population lived in the Maritime Provinces (excluding Newfoundland),

Ontario, and Québec. At that time, the western part of the country (the prairie provinces and British Columbia) counted for less than 12 percent of the population. By 1986, the western provinces' share of the total population had increased to 29 percent. The western expansion of the population has been encouraged by the Canadian government. The settling of the prairies was one reason for the admission of previously non-preferred immigrants into Canada in the early decades of this century.

The second significant aspect of internal migration in Canada is the trend to urbanization, the movement of population from rural to urban areas. In 1901, only 34.9 percent of the population lived in urban centres; by 1986, the percentage was 76. This urbanization has taken place largely along Canada's southern rim; few cities in Canada are a considerable distance from the American border.

Consequences of Fertility, Mortality, and Migration

The levels of fertility, mortality, and net migration in a population affect the characteristics of that population. We have already seen that these three demographic processes operate together to determine growth rate. There are other, equally important effects.

Age Structure

The fertility level in a population is the major determinant of **age structure**, that is, the proportion of people in each age category within the population. Age structure is usually represented in graphs known as population pyramids (see Figure 6-5).

Demographers have identified three major types of population pyramids:

1. expansive;
2. constrictive;
3. stationary.

The *expansive* type, which has a very broad base, reflects a population with a high proportion of children, the result of high fertility levels in the present and in the immediate past. A population with an expansive pyramid is termed a young population.

The *constrictive* type has a base somewhat narrower than the middle of the pyramid. This type of pyramid occurs with rapidly declining fertility levels.

The *stationary* type has a narrow base, with approximately equal percentages of people in each age group and a tapering-off in the older age categories. Stationary pyramids occur when a population has had low fertility levels for a long time and the

FIGURE 6-5. Population Pyramids, Canada, 1881 and 1986

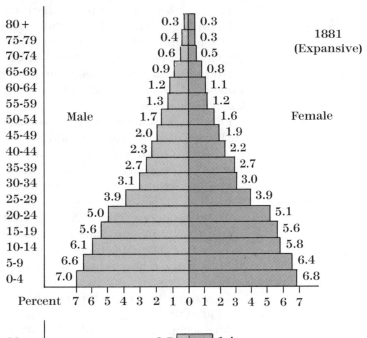

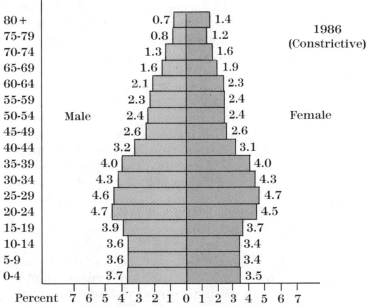

SOURCE: For 1881, Dominion Bureau of Statistics, *1921 Census of Canada*, Vol. 2, table 4; for 1986, Minister of Supply and Services, *Postcensal Estimates of Population by Marital Status, Age, Sex, and Components of Growth, June 1, 1985 and 1986*, cat. 91-921, table 2.

NOTE: The exact percentages appear outside the boxes.

number of births equals the number of deaths. A population with a stationary pyramid is an old population.

Fertility level is the most significant demographic variable affecting age structure. Migration can play a role, although generally a minor one. A population that receives in-migrants will display a pyramid with a bulge in the young working ages. On the other hand, a population that loses people through out-migration will have an indentation at the age groups that are most likely to migrate out.

Figure 6-5 shows age/sex pyramids of the Canadian population in 1881 and 1986. The pyramid for 1881 is expansive, as a result of the high fertility during the nineteenth century. The pyramid for 1986 is constrictive. The declining fertility since the early 1960s has resulted in a relatively small proportion of children in 1983. The bulge in the ages from 20 to 34 years is a direct result of the baby boom. That bulge will continue to show up in Canadian population pyramids until the large segment of the baby boom era eventually dies out. When this happens—assuming that fertility has reached the level of mortality and does not increase substantially in the future—Canada's population pyramid will gradually become that of a stationary population with zero growth.

The social and economic significance of age structure lies in what is termed the *dependency ratio* (or *dependency burden*). The **dependency ratio** is the number of people in the economically dependent age groups compared to the number of people in the productive age groups. Usually, the economically dependent ages are arbitrarily assumed to be under 15 and 65 and over, that is, children and the elderly. The higher the dependency ratio, the more people there are in a population who are economically supported relative to the number of supporters.

Dependency ratio plays an important role in economic and social development. A population with a lower dependency ratio will have a higher per capita output, a better standard of living, greater savings, and more investment capital for development. Also, a lower dependency burden implies that less will be spent per capita on housing and education, especially primary education.

Age structure has a second important implication, apart from dictating dependency burden; it plays an important role in determining future growth of population. A population with an expansive pyramid has, built into it, the potential for substantial future growth. The large numbers of children will age into the childbearing years, resulting in large numbers of potential parents. Even if these parents have small families, the population will grow, because there are so many parents. Therefore, even if

Dependency ratio is the proportion of people who are
economically supported relative to the number of supporters. As the baby boom
generation reaches retirement age our dependency
ratio will rise.

SOURCE: Canapress Photo Service

developing countries substantially reduce their fertility levels,
their populations will continue to grow due to their current age
structures, which have what is termed *demographic
momentum.*

The current Canadian structure also has a built-in demographic momentum. A large percentage of the population is in
the early childbearing ages and constitutes the bulge in our pyramid resulting from the baby boom. Therefore, the number of
babies born is increasing somewhat, not because we are returning to large families, but because there are many people in the
childbearing ages. The slight increase in the percentage of the
population aged zero to four years in the 1986 population pyramid, shown in Figure 6-5, reflects this fact.

Sex Structure

The sex structure in a society is a direct result of the action of
demographic processes, particularly mortality and migration.
Sex structure is usually measured in terms of the **sex ratio**, that
is, the number of males per 100 females. In western populations,
the sex ratio at birth is typically 105. Slightly more male babies
are born than female babies. After birth, however, males lose this

advantage. In later years, women outnumber men by a substantial margin; for example, in Canada the sex ratio at ages 65 and over is approximately 73 (males per 100 females). The main reason for this changing ratio is mortality. As we have already seen, the life expectancy at birth for males is shorter than that for females.

These kinds of differences in life expectancy can have many effects on the wider society. One obvious effect concerns marriage chances. If there is a large excess of one sex relative to the other, the marriage opportunities for the sex with greater numbers will be correspondingly lessened. Some people will have to forego marriage because of a lack of potential mates.

What the Future Holds

We have already seen that, in terms of demographic characteristics, the contemporary world can be divided into two camps—the developed societies and the developing societies. Partly because of the existing differences, these two camps face different demographic prospects and issues in the near future.

Developing Societies

The developing societies are growing very rapidly—some say too rapidly—due to high rates of natural increase. To lower the rate of population growth, there are three scenarios to be considered:

1. heightened mortality;
2. increased emigration;
3. reduced fertility.

The first possibility is not morally acceptable; one does not kill surplus people. The second possibility, increased emigration, is not likely. Where will the emigrants go? In recent years, most developed societies have increased restrictions on immigration. The third possibility, reduced fertility, is the only feasible option.

How is reduced fertility to be achieved? This is a key question for the future of us all. Attempts to answer the question have caused a deep split in both scientific and political circles. Experts disagree on whether demographic actions are more effective than economic development in dealing with the problems facing developing countries.

On one side are those who argue that family planning programs should be implemented where they do not exist and intensified where they do exist. In other words, they define the problem confronting developing countries as a demographic one—too-rapid population growth as a result of too-high fertility levels. On the other side are the proponents of the "development first" school of thought. This side argues that economic development of these countries should be the first priority. Their slogan at the 1974 United Nations World Population Meeting was, "Take care of the people, and the population will take care of itself."

Developed Societies

The demographic situation in the developed world is entirely different from that in the Third World. Our fertility levels have decreased substantially over the past century. As a result, we face stationary or even declining growth and an old age structure. Stationary growth is, in the long run, inevitable.

Here, in the chapter's final section, we will indulge in a little speculation, focusing on some of the economic and social effects likely to appear with an old, no-growth population (Day, 1972).

One set of effects concerns the larger percentage of people in the older age groups. On the one hand, a larger proportion of elderly people implies an increased need for health care facilities. But the relationship between an increasing elderly population and increasing health care does not have to be one-to-one. Much will depend upon our health habits, and possible changes in the organization of our health care system. By focusing on preventive medicine and by increasing options for independent living (rather than institutionalization), we will be able to reduce the health care cost of an aging society.

An older population implies an older labour force, so that opportunities for social advancement may be fewer than at present. One possible way to deal with this problem is the lowering of retirement age. However, this option creates another problem—the income maintenance of retired people.

Our future demographic situation may also influence the status of women in our society. It is not possible to predict this status with any certainty because much depends upon our social and cultural responses, but it does seem that in developed societies such as Canada's, a higher percentage of women will experience fewer and shorter obligations, or none at all, concerning child care. Some of these changes have already occurred, and women have tended to take on other roles, particularly outside the home. A continuation and intensification of female labour participation therefore seems likely; and, as the female gender role changes, so will the male gender role, at least in the long run. In other words, gender equality may be furthered by demographic changes.

In recent years, increasing concern has arisen about the possibility of population decline. Once zero growth is achieved, there

Special Groups of the Aged: A Statistical Picture

Demographics, like many branches of sociol-
ogy, deals with people in very general cate-
gories. For many purposes, however, these
categories must be subdivided. For example,
demographers show that the Canadian popula-
tion is "aging"—falling birth rates and
increased life expectancy mean an increasing
proportion of elderly people. In considering the
implications of this fact for housing, health
care, financial assistance, and social services,
other social scientists are trying to identify the
characteristics of particular groups of seniors.

A comprehensive five-year survey has provided the first statistical portrait of Ontario's
senior citizens. The study, carried out by the
United Senior Citizens of Ontario, identified
seniors with special needs whose life situations
have barely, if ever, been previously
documented.

The survey looked at 846 people aged 62 to
98 not living in institutions.

The Frail elderly
Ten percent of Ontario seniors were members
of a little-recognized group of "frail elderly,"
with special health, housing and social needs.

Geographically, they were more highly concentrated (15 percent) in the city of Toronto
than in the seven other communities surveyed. They were generally older than other
seniors, female, widowed, in the lowest income
group (less than $600 a month); they lived in
apartments, rented their homes and lived with
others. The frail saw doctors and specialists
more often, had the greatest likelihood of
being sent to hospital, used public transportation the least, and had the greatest trouble getting around.

This group had difficulty performing many
routines of daily life, especially bathing, shopping, and heavy housework and were much
more likely (93 percent) to use outside assistance—most frequently from their children.
They were also the most likely to use community agencies and to request more help.

Despite their health problems, the majority—

66 percent— preferred to stay at home with
assistance from agencies.

Seniors over 85
Seven percent of the seniors were 85 or older
(compared to 60 percent aged 62 to 74 and 33
percent aged 75 to 84). They were more likely
to be widowed; to have the lowest income and
fewer than nine years of education; to be
unemployed, rent their housing, and live
alone.

Their health, gauged by seven self-report
measures, was the poorest of all groups, and
they used the health care system the most.
They visited their family doctors more often,
had a 25 percent greater chance of being in
hospital, and, once there, stayed longer.

The majority of the 85-plus group—62 percent—prefer to live at home with the assistance of community services.

The Unmarried
Having no children, never-married seniors,
according to the study, lack the principal
sources of support relied on by most seniors
and are particularly vulnerable to losing their
independence.

"The never-married, who comprised 7 percent of the survey, were concentrated in
Toronto. They were mainly between the ages of
62 to 74 (63 percent), female (68 percent), rent-
ing (61 percent), and likely to live alone (61
percent). They participated in the fewest recreational activities, though they reported the
fewest health problems and the least interfer-
ing health conditions.

This group was the least likely to receive
help with daily tasks. Forty-two percent—more
than any other group—relied on paid help.
Should they become unable to care for themselves, the majority were interested in living in
a supportive housing arrangement.

Childless seniors
Eighteen percent of those surveyed did not
have children. They were more likely to be
women, in the lowest income group, live in

apartments, rent, live alone, and be unmarried. They had less contact with family than those with children—and 7 percent had no contact with family at all.

They were less likely to report that their health interfered with daily activities.

The childless were less likely than those with children to sent to hospital, but, once there, they remained longer.

Fifty-nine percent received no assistance with daily activities, compared to 49 percent of those with children.

Significantly, while those with children received most of their assistance (32 percent) from them, the childless received an equal proportion from paid help and were more likely to rely on friends and neighbours. They were more interested in moving in with friends and less likely to want to stay at home with family or friends to assist.

The study declares, "The absence of offspring, without a significant increase in contacts with friends, greatly reduces the social network of the childless elderly person."

Rural and urban seniors

Although the study found that living conditions vary according to type of community, giving rise to different needs, it also dispels "some preconceived assumptions about how the rural and urban elderly differ."

Rural seniors were more likely to be men, married, with fewer than nine years of formal education, to live in houses and to own their residence. They were the least likely to be in the highest income bracket ($1000 or more a month).

Rural seniors were more likely than their urban counterparts to have frequent contact with children.

While health did not vary dramatically, use of the health care system did: rural seniors visited their doctors more often—37 percent had made ten or more visits in the previous year—but rural seniors were the least likely to see specialists or to be hospitalized.

Rural seniors were the most likely to report heart trouble and more likely than people in the largest urban centres to report heart attacks.

Rural seniors were less likely to rely on family for help and more likely to rely on neighbours and friends.

SOURCE: "Five-Year Study Draws New Picture of Ontario's Aged" by Paula Todd, June 19, 1980, *Toronto Star*.

is no automatic mechanism that will keep fertility at just the right level to ensure an equal number of births and deaths. As pointed out earlier, if fertility remains at its current level and annual net migration approximates 50 000, the Canadian population will begin to decline in size around 2021. The concern is that population decline will lead to economic decline or stagnation.

Summary

1. The study of population, or demography, is intimately related to the study of society. Within demography, the important areas of inquiry are fertility, mortality, and migration. Together, these determine population growth. Singly or in combination, they determine population composition and distribution.

2. The components of growth are natural increase and net migration.

3. Population growth in Canada shows unevenness, historically. Natural increase has been the major component of our

growth, with net migration playing an important role during certain periods.

4. The dominant theory of population growth at present is demographic transition theory. Based on the historical experience of the western world, it provides a three-stage model of population change, with rapid growth occurring in the second stage.

5. Fertility is an important element of population growth, affecting the rate of natural increase.

6. Fertility in Canada declined over the course of this century, with the exception of the period known as the baby boom. Variations in fertility level result from the interaction of demographic factors, socio-economic factors, and governmental factors.

7. Mortality acts simultaneously with fertility in determining rate of natural increase.

8. As a population's mortality rate falls, the causes of death shift from infectious diseases to degenerative diseases.

9. Within societies, differentials in mortality exist. Women outlive men; married people have higher life expectancies than unmarried people; minority groups experience higher mortality than the national average.

10. Migration is the movement of people from one geographical location to another. Migration is of two types—international and internal.

11. Four periods of immigration in Canada can be identified, each differing in volume and type of immigrants. Emigration from Canada, for the most part, has been to the United States.

12. Fertility level is the major determinant of age structure. The three types of age structures, graphically represented in population pyramids, are expansive, constrictive, and stationary.

13. Age structure dictates dependency ratio (or dependency burden), which plays an important role in economic development.

14. In the near future, developing and developed societies face different population issues and prospects. The developing societies face the twin problems of economic underdevelopment and rapid population growth. In developed societies, the future indicates stationary and perhaps declining growth in conjunction with an old age structure.

Further Reading

Beaujot, R., & McQuillan, K. (1982). *Growth and dualism: The demographic development of Canadian society.* Toronto: Gage. An excellent introduction to population issues in Canada, with separate chapters on regionalism and linguistic balance.

Bouma, G. D., & Bouma W. J. (1975). *Fertility control: Canada's lively social problem.* Don Mills, Ont.: Longman. A short, readable inventory of the controversial issues surrounding current birth control in Canada.

Foot, D. K. (1982). *Canada's population outlook: Demographic futures and economic challenges.* Toronto: James Lorimer, in association with the Canadian Institute for Economic Policy. A recent book on Canadian demography, focusing on future demographic characteristics and their relationship to economic and policy issues.

Grindstaff, C. F. (1981). *Population and society: A sociological perspective.* West Hanover, MA: Christopher Publishing. A book about Canadian population that places population variables in the context of the wider society.

Kalbach, W. E., & McVey, W. W. (1979). *The demographic bases of Canadian society.* (2nd ed.) Toronto: McGraw-Hill Ryerson. Provides descriptions of major demographic characteristics of Canadian society, with chapters on ethnicity, religion, education, labour force, family, and housing.

McDaniel, S. A. (1986). *Canada's aging population.* Toronto: Butterworths. An excellent discussion of the causes and possible consequences of population aging in Canada.

Overbeek, J. (1980). *Population and Canadian society.* Toronto: Butterworths. A short book on the Canadian population, describing our major demographic characteristics.

7
Social Inequality

One of the most intriguing questions, one that may have been *the* major motivation for social scientists to study society over the history of sociology, has been the "why" of social inequality and its consequences. After reading this chapter, you should be able to

1. outline the ideas of Marx;

2. describe how structural functionalists explain inequality;

3. outline Weber's attempt to synthesize the radical and conservative perspectives;

4. describe Canada in terms of
    (a) inequality of condition,
    (b) inequality of opportunity;

5. describe how the opportunities available to people are affected by
    (a) ethnicity,
    (b) language,
    (c) gender.

Inequality is apparently a universal characteristic of life in society. **Social inequality** is defined as a situation in which members of a society have unequal shares of resources and unequal opportunities to obtain them. Social inequality takes many forms:

1. economic (some people have more money than others);
2. social (some people are more popular than others);
3. political (some people are more able to have their own way than others);
4. physical (some people are taller, stronger, or more attractive than others).

Students of society have been discussing many forms of inequality for thousands of years, but they have yet to agree on why inequality is an apparently universal characteristic of human societies and what, if anything, can be done to eliminate it. Their disagreement stems from three sources:

1. value judgments;

2. interests;
3. theoretical perspectives.

Value judgments.   Value judgments about inequality differ. Some people feel that there is nothing drastically wrong with the inequality they see around them; therefore, they feel there is no serious need for change. Others disagree, feeling that the inequality around them is thoroughly unfair; these people favour changes.

Those who oppose inequality disagree among themselves about how far inequality should be reduced. Some, for example, would be satisfied with a moderate reduction of some types of inequality (for example, provision of free post-secondary education). Others would be satisfied only if we were all the same in as many respects as possible (for example, all wearing the same clothes and hairstyles, much as was done in Maoist China).

Interests.   People also disagree about inequality because they want to pursue different interests. Those who are well off tend to think that things are fine just the way they are. Those who think they would benefit from a change tend to think that major changes would be a good idea.

The type of change favoured by an individual or group tends to correspond with the interests of that individual or group. For example, your sociology instructors might think it is a fine idea to decrease the salaries of business executives and to increase those of factory workers. It is unlikely, however, that they would favour a reduction of their own salaries so that the salaries of college secretaries could be increased.

Theoretical perspectives.   Yet another basis of disagreement has to do with different theoretical perspectives, the explanations for the causes of social inequality. This is where sociology comes in.

Of the three major sociological theories we have been focusing on, symbolic-interactionist theory is rarely used to explain social inequality. We will, therefore, focus on the structural-functionalist and conflict theories.

It is convenient to divide theories on social inequality into three major perspectives (Lenski, 1966):

1. radical;
2. conservative;
3. synthesis.

Briefly, the **radical** perspective is opposed to inequality; the **conservative** perspective supports it. The **synthesis** approach attempts to create a perspective drawn from the best parts of the radical and the conservative perspectives. We will now expand on each of these perspectives in turn.

The Radical Perspective

The radical perspective emphasizes the divergent interests to be found in any society, the conflict that necessarily results, and the role of force in maintaining social order. This perspective views inequality as the result of the domination and exploitation of some groups by other groups. It emphasizes the injustice of inequality and suggests that something be done to reduce it. As noted in Chapter 1, contemporary sociology labels this perspective *conflict theory*. The two most notable of the conflict theories are **Marxism** and **social democracy**.

Marxism

According to Marxists, economic factors are the key to understanding inequality. They support this position with the following argument: we must eat in order to survive; therefore, our first activity must be economic. Only when our stomachs are full can we worry about relatively secondary matters, such as reproduction, defence, government, or art.

In order to understand economic activity, Marxists find it useful to make a number of distinctions. To begin with, the initial basis of any economic activity may be referred to as the *means of production*. The means of production consist of land (that is, natural resources of all types), labour, and capital. Two other important elements of economic activity, the *forces of production* and the *relations of production*, are also distinguished by Marxists. The **forces of production** are the physical and social technology (tools, machines, technical organization) used in the productive economic activity of a given society. The **relations of production** are the social organization of economic activity. This organization determines who has the authority to give orders and make decisions. In particular, it also determines how the benefits of a society's economic activity are distributed. The combination of these two elements—the technical nature of economic activity (forces of production) and the social nature of economic activity (relations of production)—is referred to by Marxists as the **mode of production** (for example, capitalism, communism).

Marxists argue that throughout written history, a privileged few (emperors, kings, capitalists) have been able to live in the lap of luxury while the bulk of those who do almost all the work (slaves, serfs, workers) have been forced to live in poverty and degradation. Marxists view this inequality as outrageously unjust. Consequently, they argue that the situation should be changed as soon as possible. Some Marxists even argue that such changes are so important and desirable that they justify virtually any bloodshed and disruption necessary in order to accomplish them.

Marxists view change not only as possible, but as inevitable, because each mode of production (for example, feudalism, capitalism) is thought to contain within itself the seeds of its own destruction. In the case of capitalist society, the process of competition forces constant improvements in technology. With these changes in technology (the *forces of production*), it is thought inevitable that the *relations of production* will also change. Thus, just as ancient civilizations gave way to feudalism and feudalism gave way to capitalism, so will capitalism give way to communism.

Marxists are not discouraged by past failures in changing the relations of production. The role of the revolutionary is merely to speed up processes already in motion. In a country such as Canada, Marxists would feel that their task is to speed up the process of transition from the present mode of production (capitalism) to the next mode of production (communism). One of the first steps in doing so is to analyse the capitalist class structure.

Class Structure.   As you will recall from Chapter 1, the dominant class in capitalist societies, according to Marxists, consists of those who own capital and who are thus able to employ other people; this class is called the *bourgeoisie*. The other major class under capitalism consists of those who work for wages, the *proletariat*, or the working class.

The Caste System

A caste is a particular kind of social class in which membership is very strongly fixed. Children automatically become members of their parents' caste. They remain in that caste for life.

The best-known system of social castes existed in India. That system associated caste with specific occupations and attached to that concepts of ritual purity and impurity.

Marxists sometimes see some similarities between a caste system and our own society.

They argue that in our own society, as automation reduces the need for unskilled workers, a castelike "under class" consisting of unemployed, unemployable, or considerably underemployed people is emerging. Lacking both economic and political power, they are forced to live in both urban and rural slums, where they do not have access to the kinds of educational facilities that would enable them and their children to improve their lot.

The relationship between the two major classes—owners and workers—is felt to be the key to an understanding of capitalist society. In Marxist theory, the central economic relationship in capitalist society is that between capital and labour: workers exchange their labour for wages, while capitalists exchange their money for the work done. Marxists argue that the terms of this exchange are always unfair and, therefore, that the entire economic system is based on the exploitation of workers by capitalists. A theory central to the Marxist position on exploitation is the **labour theory of value**, which argues that the value of a commodity is determined by the amount of work that goes into it. If this is so, it follows, according to the Marxist view, that workers should receive virtually all the returns for the value their labour has created.

However, in a capitalist society, the owners appropriate a large part of the benefits for themselves in the form of profit. Consequently, a worker's wages represent only a fraction of the value that worker has created. For example, a worker might produce products worth $100 a day but be paid only $50 a day. Indeed, Marx argues that workers do not receive even a moderate portion of the value they have created, but only enough to keep them alive. The remainder, or what is left after workers get their share, is called the **rate of surplus value**, and it goes to the capitalist.

This very process, so central to the operation of capitalism, is thought likely to contribute ultimately to its downfall. The underpaid workers cannot afford to buy everything they produce, and so capitalism is subject to periodic crises of overproduction. The resulting unemployment leads to recession or depression. This creates a pattern of ruthless competition among capitalists, which eventually reduces their number and concentrates their wealth in fewer and fewer hands. The scene is set for revolution.

Revolution. Marxists predict that revolution will ultimately take place in mature capitalist societies. As the economy evolves, the classes remaining from previous historical periods (the aristocrats and the peasants) will disappear. Most of the people formerly in these classes will become members of a growing proletariat. This leaves the two major classes in a state of outright confrontation—the workers against the bourgeoisie. Then, as the process of competition bankrupts more and more businesses—especially during the periodic economic crises—the capitalist classes will become smaller and more homogeneous. As the competition becomes increasingly ruthless, the rate of profit will fall. In order to survive, the remaining capitalists will have to exploit their workers more efficiently, and the workers' standard of living will deteriorate both economically and psychologically.

As urbanization takes place, the differences in wealth between the workers and their employers will become more visible. Furthermore, the workers, gathered together in large factories and in slum neighbourhoods, will be able to communicate more freely with each other. Gradually, an understanding of their true economic interests will emerge. As they talk among themselves, their concern about their social, ethnic, or gender differences (that is, their **false consciousness**) will dissolve. This false consciousness will be replaced by a **class consciousness** (that is, awareness of their common economic conditions). The workers will come to believe that their position is neither inevitable nor just, and they will band together as an economic and political group in an effort to improve their lives.

As the time for change draws near, Marx (1969, p. 20) predicted, the bourgeoisie itself will begin to fall apart. In particular, some of the brightest and best bourgeois intellectuals will join the proletariat and provide it with intellectual leadership. Sooner or later, all these various factors combine. The result is inevitable—revolution. Capitalism (the private ownership of the means of production) will be replaced by socialism (the collective ownership of the means of production).

After the upheaval of the revolution, Marxists believe there will have to be a brief dictatorship of the proletariat led by party officials and intellectuals who understand what is good for the workers. During this period, *reactionary* , or bourgeois, elements will be eliminated, and the new socialist society set up. After this, however, the state will wither away because there will be no ruling class for it to serve. This new historical period will be unlike all the previous historical epochs. There will be no class division, no class struggle, and no further evolution of the mode of production.

Criticisms of Marxism. Marxists are able to point with pride to many of Marx's predictions that have come true:

1. social groups characteristic of the feudal period in history have certainly declined;
2. capital has become concentrated in the hands of fewer people;
3. urbanization has taken place;
4. there have been many successful Marxist revolutions.

Critics of Marxism, on the other hand, can point to several aspects of the modern world that have not evolved as Marx predicted:

1. the working class has not been economically deprived; instead, its standard of living has risen spectacularly;

2. there is no evidence that working-class people are any more unhappy than they ever were;

3. the working class has become more heterogeneous in terms of its skill and status levels;

4. Marxist revolutions have taken place mainly in underdeveloped countries—not in mature capitalist ones as Marx predicted.

5. Marxist societies have not become classless societies, except in a Marxist sense. The degree of inequality is almost as great in Marxist societies as in capitalist ones (Connor, 1979). In particular, the state in Marxist societies has not withered away but has become much stronger.

To many of these criticisms, Marxists reply that the complete evolution has not yet taken place. They underscore such factors as the initial backward development of most state socialist countries, the nature of their previous cultures, and the pressures created by the international environment. They ask the critic to withhold final judgment.

On some other matters, there is major debate. For example, there is no doubt that a major new social stratum of relatively well-paid and well-educated white-collar workers has appeared. Critics of Marxism consider this to be a new middle class in the social structure of capitalist society. Marxists reply that, since they now work for wages, these people have been "proletarianized" and are now part of the working class.

In both Marxist and capitalist societies, a few people control a large share of the wealth. They direct economic activity, hire workers, and decide wages. With control comes the power to determine the distribution of further wealth.

Social Democracy

In addition to Marxism, there is one other radical theory we should consider briefly: **social democracy**. Social democrats take positions that are, in many respects, very similar to Marxists'. In particular, they share the view that current contemporary inequalities are unjustifiable and that capitalist relations of production are the key to the problem of inequality in capitalist societies. However, the two positions differ considerably in certain value judgments and in theory.

The Marxists view property as an *indivisible* bundle of rights and privileges. It follows that the elimination of the evils believed to be caused by capitalism requires the elimination of the institution of private property. As pointed out earlier, this almost certainly requires revolution. On the other hand, the social democrat views property as a *divisible* collection of separate rights and privileges. It follows from this position that it is possible to eliminate these rights and privileges one by one as the need for change presents itself. Hence, from the social democratic point of view, it is theoretically possible to change the relations of production through a process of reform.

So far as values are concerned, Marxists condone physical and psychological violence as means for achieving their ends. The social democrat, on the other hand, is more reluctant to resort to violence. The Marxist is likely to favour revolution; the social democrat, reform.

The Conservative Perspective

The conservative perspective on social inequality contrasts with the radical perspective. The conservative perspective emphasizes the mutual interests to be found in any society, the cooperation that necessarily takes place, and the role of common values in maintaining social order. It views inequality as being unavoidable—the necessary result of the division of labour required to produce goods and services for the benefit of everyone. In contemporary sociology, the major expression of this perspective is structural functionalism, described in Chapter 1. Here, we review that theory and discuss the structural-functionalist explanation of inequality.

Structural Functionalism

Structural functionalists analyse inequality in much the way we would analyse a piece of machinery, a computer, or a living organism. First, they try to outline the parts of the system and determine how the parts connect (the structure). Then, they try to describe how the system behaves (the process). Finally, they look at a given social phenomenon and decide what function it appears to serve (the purpose).

The structural-functionalist explanation for inequality runs something like this. In order to survive, a society must ensure that certain needs are met. Obviously, one such need is economic—we must eat in order to survive. However, there are other needs as well. There are needs for defence against enemies, for reproduction and the care of children, and for the care of the sick. Furthermore, political, religious, educational, and cultural needs also exist. If these needs are all to be met, people must be assigned specific tasks.

Some of these tasks—such as protecting the country or mining coal—are dangerous; others—such as performing a ballet or removing an appendix—are difficult; and still others—such as cleaning latrines or sweeping out stables—are unpleasant. In all but the most primitive societies, specialized positions are created for the performance of such tasks (for example, soldier, doctor, cleaner). Some of these positions (for example, college president) are more important and/or more difficult than others (for example, janitor). According to the structural-functionalist view, people in all these positions must perform their tasks competently if a society is to prosper. However, it is especially important that those in critical positions, such as general or prime minister, perform well. If this social need is to be met, people must first be motivated to undergo the preparation necessary for the competent performance of difficult tasks and then be motivated to apply themselves conscientiously once they have the job.

The question arises: How are people motivated to undertake the more demanding tasks of a society? The structural functionalists' reply is that motivation for the performance of difficult jobs is provided by unequal rewards. For example, they would say that your work at college or university is motivated, to a large degree, by the belief that you will some day be rewarded for it. The love of knowledge alone, they say, is unlikely to be sufficient to inspire your best performance.

According to the structural functionalist, the unequal rewards given to certain social positions are a result of variations in supply and demand. For example, the demand for people who can shine shoes is low, while the supply of people who can do the job is high. Consequently, rewards for shoe-shiners do not amount to much. On the other hand, the demand for people who can rescue a failing company from bankruptcy or who can write a hit song is high, while the supply of people who can do those jobs is low. Consequently, rewards for such services are substantial.

The structural functionalist also maintains that reward levels for specific occupations differ from one society to another because of societies' different needs. For example, a society that depends on fish as its main source of protein is likely to reward successful fishers relatively well. Similarly, reward levels for entire social groups within a given society may also rise and fall within a given society as the needs of that society change. For example, soldiers are likely to receive greater rewards during times of war than during times of peace. These rewards need not be material; they may also be the psychological rewards of, for example, prestige or popularity. A priest might receive a low income but enjoy high prestige in the community. Nonetheless, inequality of rewards, of whatever kind, is thought to be necessary if performance in key positions is to be adequate. And adequate performance in these positions is necessary if a society is to survive and prosper. Hence, some degree of social inequality is necessary, inevitable, and functionally positive.

Criticisms of Structural Functionalism. There have been many criticisms of the structural-functionalist position. It has been pointed out, for example, that human societies are not nearly so tightly organized as the systems found in machines and bodies; therefore, comparisons can be misleading. Furthermore, contrary to the assumptions of structural functionalism, human society may contain phenomena that are neither necessary nor positive (Merton, 1957). Take slavery, for example. Conservatives used to argue that the universal existence of slavery indicated that slavery was necessary and inevitable. The decline of slavery, however, has proven this argument to be incorrect. Hence, the mere existence of a phenomenon does not prove that it is necessary.

Similarly, the existence of a phenomenon does not mean that it is automatically good for a society. Indeed, it could be unhealthy, or *dysfunctional*. Some critics (for example, Tumin, 1953) point to the inequality of opportunity in most societies as an example of such dysfunction. They argue that key positions can too easily become filled with lazy and stupid children of the privileged, because the bright and energetic offspring of ordinary people are not given a fair chance. Thus, the society suffers because of incompetent leadership, which develops as a result of inequality of opportunity.

Furthermore, these critics continue, even if we grant that some inequality in material reward is necessary to motivate people, it does not follow that this inequality has to be as great as it is in most societies. Therefore, structural-functional theory cannot be used as a scientific justification of extreme disparities of reward.

Finally, various criticisms of a more specific nature have been levelled at structural functionalism. For example, it is argued that to undergo training for highly rewarded positions (for example, to be a college or university student) is no great sacrifice when the alternative is to work for a living like everyone else. Similarly, it has been argued that reward levels often depend on factors other than functional importance. For example, nurses in Canada were able to demand and get much higher salaries after they had unionized. This increase in salary seems to be a result of the increased economic and political power provided by unionization, rather than the increased functional importance of nurses.

Notwithstanding these criticisms, structural functionalists point to the stubborn fact that inequality is everywhere, even in communes, kibbutzim, and revolutionary societies designed to eliminate such inequality. They maintain that this central phenomenon demands explanation, and that their theory is as good as anything yet developed.

Synthesis

The third major approach to inequality is labelled "synthesis." This approach attempts to produce a scientific explanation composed of the best parts of both the radical and the conservative perspectives on social inequality.

Weber

Perhaps the most influential attempt at synthesis is that provided by Max Weber. Weber agreed with Marx on many important matters, including the idea that a basic key to the explanation of human societies lay in economic or material considerations. He also agreed that the relationship of those who own property to those who do not was central. Nonetheless, he was also of the opinion that the Marxist approach oversimplified matters and was, as a result, somewhat incomplete. In particular, Weber felt that Marx overemphasized the role of material factors. In his own work, therefore, Weber attempted to provide a more complete overview of human society.

To begin with, he argued that the employer-worker relationship was not the only significant one in the economic sphere. He maintained that there were at least two other economic relationships of major importance: creditors to debtors and producers to consumers. For Weber, then, the questions of high interest rates ("usury") and the "just price" of products were as likely to be important as the matter of "fair wages."

Furthermore, the practical importance of these economic relationships was likely to vary within a society: Canadian home buyers might be concerned about high interest rates, or the "usury" of the banks; Canadian farmers might be concerned about a "just price" for their produce; and Canadian workers might be concerned about a "fair wage" for their work (Wiley, 1967).

In addition, Weber argued that, aside from economic relationships, there are at least two other very important bases of inequality in human societies—the social and the political. Thus, unlike Marx, who thought there was one basic hierarchy (class), Weber argued there were at least three: class (the economic), status (the social), and power (the political). Social hierarchies based on levels of prestige can be independent of economic hierarchies based on levels of wealth. For example, descendents of aristocrats, intellectuals, or members of certain ethnic groups may feel themselves socially superior to those from other social groups who merely possess money. Consequently, a self-made millionaire with a grade-eight education may find that wealth does not buy acceptance into the social circles of such aristocrats or intellectuals. Common bases of social ranking include gender, race, religion, ethnicity, language, and education. And while Marx thought it was false consciousness to be concerned with such matters, Weber believed that these were an independent issue of major importance.

Similarly, political hierarchies can be independent of both social and economic hierarchies. For example, a labour leader might have considerable political power within a community and access to a number of higher social circles but at the same time make very little money. Here again, Weber disagreed with Marx and argued that political power was an independent dimension of inequality that demanded study in and of itself.

Weber also argued that the key factor in the assessment of a person's position in the overall social hierarchy is not whether that person happens to be an owner or an employee, but rather to what degree he or she is able to enjoy life. That is to say, Weber felt that the *key* issue in society is what you receive, not what you contribute.

This was largely determined by income, but social and political factors were thought to play a role as well. Those working in the Weberian tradition would argue, contrary to Marx, that the key difference between an individual earning $100 000 a year working for someone else and an individual making $10 000 a year working for himself or herself was the difference in their incomes, not the difference in their positions in the relations of production.

Weber saw bureaucratization as the master trend of our time. He foresaw the development of expanding bureaucracies that would increasingly control the lives of ordinary people. In his view, socialist or Marxist revolutions would only serve to hasten this process of bureaucratization and would do little or nothing to reduce inequality.

Lenski

Contemporary American sociologist Gerhard Lenski (1966) has made the most self-conscious attempt to synthesize the traditional viewpoints. In trying to provide an empirically based theory of inequality, Lenski studied our historical experience. His survey of the data indicated that the degree of inequality in human societies varies considerably depending upon the level of technological development (that is, upon what Marxists call the forces of production). Within the limits set by technological level, he found that there seemed to be a predictable range of inequality, which had an apparent average level as well as upper and lower limits.

Lenski's theory gives little comfort to either conservatives or radicals. The fact that the degree of inequality varies substantially in contemporary societies clearly indicates that some reduction in the degree of inequality is possible in most situations. This aspect of the theory displeases conservatives. Conversely, Lenski's study indicates that we cannot eliminate inequality. This aspect of the theory displeases radicals.

Inequality of Condition

Inequality of condition refers to the overall structure of rewards in a society; it involves questions such as: What is the average income? What is the range between the richest and the poorest people? What is the overall distribution of rewards? How equal or unequal is this distribution? In the following sections, we will look at three aspects of inequality of condition:

1. material dimensions;
2. occupational dimensions;
3. political dimensions.

Material Dimensions

A useful way of examining inequality of condition is to consider material factors. In this approach, it is both customary and convenient to look at income distribution. The standard way to do this is to divide the national population into fifths, or quintiles, and to determine how much of the national income each quintile receives. Table 7-1 indicates what happens when you treat Canadian income this way. It is interesting to note that the top 20 percent of the population consistently receives over 40 percent of the national income, while the bottom 20 percent regularly receives about four percent of the national income.

TABLE 7-1. Income Distribution by Quintile, Canada

All Units
(both families and unattached individuals)

	1951[a]	1961[a]	1971	1981
Richest quintile	42.8	41.4	43.3	41.8
Fourth quintile	23.3	24.5	24.9	25.2
Third quintile	18.3	18.3	17.6	17.6
Second quintile	11.2	11.9	10.6	10.9
Poorest quintile	4.4	4.2	3.6	4.6

Despite the difference in income between Canada's poor and rich, Canada's income distribution is relatively equal when compared to most other countries.

[a]Excludes families with one or more farmers.

SOURCE: From *On Social Inequality in Canada* (p. 63) by A. Hunter, 1986, Toronto: Butterworths.

SOURCE: Richard Harrington/Miller Services

SOURCE: Harold M. Lambert/Miller Services

*FIGURE 7-1. Percentage of Income Going to the Top
5 Percent of Households in 24 Countries*

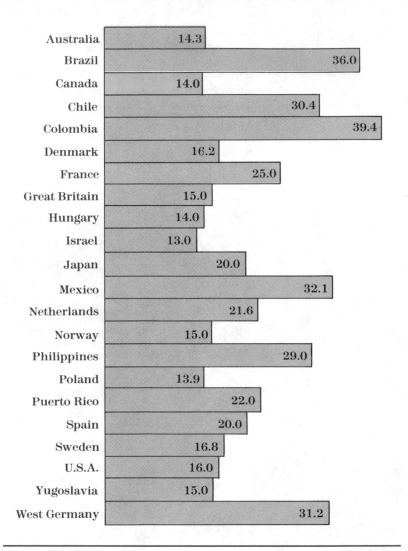

SOURCE: Adapted from Tyree *et al.*, 1979, p. 416.

How should we evaluate these facts? Should we be impressed
by how *equal* or by how *unequal* Canadian income distribution
is? Initially, we might be amazed, perhaps even horrified, by how
unequally income in Canada is distributed. However, in order to
evaluate these figures scientifically, we must put them into historical and comparative perspective. The results of such a comparison are surprising. Canada's income distribution is relatively
equal, even when compared to western European social demo-

The Defeat of Hunger

For most Canadians, hunger means an appetite waiting to be satisfied.

For the billion chronically hungry human beings in less fortunate areas of the world, hunger means intense pain and the erosion of productivity, resistance to disease, and the inability to think clearly. It means death in circumstances that mock the moral values we hold as civilized creatures.

The scale of hunger's global tragedy is staggering. Between 13 million and 18 million die every year from hunger and starvation. Every 24 hours, 35 000 people are killed by hunger—24 every minute, 18 of them children. More people have died of hunger in the last five years than have been killed in all the wars, revolutions, and murders in the last 150 years. This human devastation is roughly equivalent to a Hiroshima-size nuclear bomb being dropped on our planet every three and a half days.

Until recently, it was a generally held view that this carnage was a wretched but unavoidable aspect of the human condition. The best we could do was react with generosity when the media or aid organizations focused attention on a particularly acute disaster, such as the famine in Ethiopia.

Since 1977, The Hunger Project, an international non-profit organization, has dedicated itself to spreading a different message: hunger *can* be eradicated and we have the means to eradicate it by the year 2000. In its recently published reference book, *Ending Hunger: An Idea Whose Time Has Come*, The Hunger Project marshals an impressive array of facts and opinions to hammer home a central theme. "Our world possesses sufficient resources, technology, and proven solutions to achieve the end of the persistence of hunger and starvation by the end of the century. What is missing is commitment."

In an effort to form a grassroots movement powerful enough to forge the concentrated political will necessary to bridge the gulf between possibility and reality, The Hunger Project is asking individuals to commit themselves to the realization of a noble goal.

"Opportunity is not a word we generally associate with a condition that takes the lives of 35 000 of us each day. Yet perhaps it is hunger, more than any of our other concerns or interests, that provides humanity with its greatest opportunity in these last years of the twentieth century."

More than four million people in 152 countries have already declared their commitment to the end of hunger by enrolling themselves in The Hunger Project, which has Canadian offices in Vancouver, Toronto and Montréal. We may hope the number grows.

In a cynical age, it is good to be reminded that human suffering is not inevitable. As Mahatma Gandhi once said, "To believe what has not occurred in history will not occur at all, is to argue disbelief in the dignity of man."

SOURCE: "The Defeat of Hunger," March 24, 1986, *The Globe and Mail*, p. 6.

cracies and to eastern European Marxist societies. This, at least, is the result if one takes the percentage of income going to the top five percent of households as a measure of equality of income distribution (see Figure 7-1).

Historically, the material standard of living in Canada has risen substantially. During the period 1946 to 1974, for example, the income per capita GNP (Gross National Product) rose 237 percent, even with inflation taken into account (Johnson, 1979b).

From this perspective, then, Canadians have reason to be satisfied. On the other hand, it is not at all clear that we have been distributing this increasing wealth any more equally.

Indeed, historical trends in income distribution have been the subject of one of the classic debates in Canadian sociology. In 1974, Leo Johnson, a prominent Marxist historian and sociologist, published a highly influential pamphlet entitled *Poverty in Wealth*, which seemed to prove that income distribution in Canada was rapidly becoming more unequal and that the situation of poor people was deteriorating in a most alarming fashion. Johnson's work, however, became subject to a powerful critique by Richard Hamilton and Maurice Pinard (1977), in which these two McGill sociologists indicated that Johnson was quite mistaken in his analysis and that, if anything, income distribution in Canada was becoming slightly more equal.

Although Johnson (1979a) has subsequently moderated his interpretation of the situation, there is, as yet, no apparent consensus among Canadian sociologists about which of these views is correct (Cohn, 1978). It is interesting to note, however, that researchers in other disciplines hold the view that income distribution in Canada is remaining about the same or becoming slightly more equal, once factors such as the population's changing age distribution are taken into consideration (Reuber, 1978).

Some people have enough money to throw away in gambling casinos. For others, the grim realities of life include six children to feed and colds that last all winter because there isn't any heat.

SOURCE: Harold M. Lambert/Miller Services

Occupational Dimensions

One of the most commonly used measures of social inequality is
occupational prestige. Those who use it argue that this
approach provides a measure of the material and political
rewards that go with an occupational role. Furthermore, they
maintain that the position of an individual or family unit in the
entire social structure is determined chiefly by occupation.
Hence, in their view, the study of occupational prestige is a convenient way to look into the heart of a society's social inequality.

Studies of occupational prestige in Canada have indicated that
white-collar workers have more prestige than blue-collar workers and that higher educational status tends to be associated with
higher occupational prestige. At the top of the scale, professionals have more prestige than managers. However, both managers
and professionals have substantially more prestige than clerical
workers, farmers, and manual labourers. Clerical workers have
slightly more prestige than farmers; farmers have slightly more
prestige than manual workers (see Table 7-2). Indeed, the structure of occupational prestige appears to be very similar in almost
all countries and all time periods for which we have information
(Treiman, 1978; Haller and Bills, 1979). The degree of inequality
in occupational prestige in Canada appears to be about the same
as that found everywhere else.

Political Dimensions

Inequality of condition can also be studied in terms of its political aspects. In a broad theoretical sense, power is found everywhere. Consequently, it would be possible and useful to study the
typical allocation of power in all our social institutions: the
school, the family, friendship cliques, the workplace, the church,
and so on. Here, however, we will concentrate on Canadian society as a whole. We will discuss first the distribution of **authority**
(the recognized right to make binding decisions) and then the
distribution of **power** (the ability to control the behaviour of others, whether such ability is considered legitimate or not).

Authority. Sociologists in Canada have tended to agree that it
is useful to analyse the authority structure of our society in
terms of a number of separate realms: the economic system, the
state system, and the ideological system.

These systems, in turn, can be usefully analysed in terms of
the major institutions within them:

1. business and labour in the economic system;

2.   the legislature, the civil service, the military, and the judici-
     ary in the state system;
3.   the media, the church, and education in the ideological system.

In turn, it is also assumed that authority in each of these areas
is organized as a hierarchy: that is, the people at the heads of
these institutions (corporation directors, union leaders, cabinet

TABLE 7-2 Occupational Prestige Scores

Occupational Title	Canada
Provincial premier	90
Physician	87
County court judge	83
Catholic priest	73
Civil engineer	73
Bank manager	71
Owner of a manufacturing plant	70
Protestant minister	68
Economist	65
Public grade school teacher	62
Social worker	60
Computer programmer	55
Policeman	54
Electrician	52
Bookkeeper	50
Farm owner and operator	49
Machinist	44
Plumber	44
Bank teller	43
Typist	42
Carpenter	42
Barber	40
Automobile repairman	39
Clerk in an office	38
Bus driver	36
Trailer truck driver	36
Restaurant cook	33
Assembly-line worker	30
Clerk in a store	28
Cod fisherman	27
Waitress	23
Bartender	20
Janitor	20
Garbage collector	17

SOURCE: From "Occupational Prestige in Canada" by P. Pineo and J. Porter, 1967,
Canadian Review of Sociology and Anthropology 4(1), pp. 24-40.

ministers, deputy ministers, generals, judges, directors, bishops, university presidents) form an elite that has the authority to make the major decisions for our society (Porter, 1965). Whoever has power in our society must exercise it through these figures.

Perhaps the most notable finding concerning the distribution of authority in Canada is that it is largely, perhaps even mainly, located outside the country. About half the businesses, half the unions, and two-thirds of the media to which Canadians are exposed are externally controlled (Clement, 1975; Watkins, 1973; Ogmundson, 1980a). The military is highly integrated with that of the United States (Warnock, 1970). The economic policy and foreign policy of the Canadian government are substantially limited by agreements with foreign powers (Levitt, 1970). The major churches (except the United Church) have their headquarters elsewhere. In other words, a substantial portion of final authority in almost every realm of Canadian life is located outside the country.

Of the authority that remains in Canada, a great deal appears to be concentrated in relatively few hands. In every institutional sphere, save perhaps education, it is possible to locate at the heads of formal organizations a small group of people who have the authority to make binding decisions for that part of our society. In the economy, just over 100 corporations, with about 1000 corporation directors and senior executives, appear to dominate private business. (See the article on corporate concentration in this chapter and the "Corporations" section of Chapter 9 for an analysis of these holders of economic power.) The labour movement is dominated by about 40 organizations, headed by fewer than 500 people. The media are dominated by about 15 organizations, headed by fewer than 300 people. Religion is dominated by three organizations (the Roman Catholic, Anglican, and United Churches), each in turn controlled by small numbers of people. The civil services and the legislatures are also controlled by a small number of organizations (15, counting the federal government, all the provinces, and the four major cities), which are in turn dominated by a few hundred people (Porter, 1965; Clement, 1975; Olsen, 1977).

In this sense, it is widely agreed that authority is distributed in a rather unequal manner in our society. Yet, if we put the Canadian authority structure into international perspective, it would appear that our situation is more or less normal for capitalist democracies. If we compare Canada to the advanced state socialist countries, such as the USSR, it would appear that authority is distributed more equally in Canada. But the distribution of authority is one issue; the distribution of power is another one. Certain questions come to mind: Who or what has power? Who or what influences or determines the decisions these elite groups make? On these matters, sociologists have been unable to agree.

Social scientists do not agree on who has power in countries such as Canada. Some (for example, Downs, 1957) give the impression that the distribution of power is highly democratic (through public opinion). Others (such as, Dahl, 1961) give the impression that power is moderately well distributed (among the pressure groups). Still others (such as, Miliband, 1969) give the impression that it is distributed in a very unequal manner (controlled by capitalists). Whatever the data available, they are subject to varying interpretations. Let us look at one example.

Earlier research clearly indicated that elite groups in Canada tended to be dominated by a group of well-educated males of British, Protestant, upper-class or upper-middle-class origins (Porter, 1965; Clement, 1975; Olsen, 1977). This pattern appeared to be particularly clear in the case of the business and media elite groups. French Canadians and people of middle-class origin were fairly often found in the church, educational, civil service, and legislative elites, but there still appears to have been a clear over-representation of upper-class Canadians of British origin.

Females, both those of working-class origins and those who were of neither British nor French ethnic ancestry (the *third ethnics*), were hardly to be found in elite groups at all. An exception to this pattern was found in the labour elite, which was more or less representative of the population in class and ethnic background, although it, too, had very few females.

The trend, however, is apparently toward an opening up of the elites to non-British, non-upper-class groups. In particular, French Canadians, Jewish-Canadians, and people of middle-class origin are more and more to be found in the upper levels of our society. Furthermore, one recent study found that third ethnics are actually *over*represented among those individuals who control 100 million dollars or more (Kelner, 1970; Olsen, 1977; Campbell and Szablowski, 1979; Hunter, 1981).

Researchers differ in their interpretation of these data. When the early data indicated very substantial British upper-class dominance of elite groups, radicals argued that this indicated a ruling-class dominance of elite decision making in our society (Clement, 1975). Conservatives replied that the data were not particularly meaningful, because people in these roles performed about the same regardless of their origin and background. Now that the data are changing, the two sides are switching their favoured mode of interpretation. Conservatives view the opening up of the elite structure as proof that democracy works. Radicals (such as, Olsen, 1977) now tend to argue that elite social background is of minimal significance in any case.

Inequality of Opportunity

In the previous section we determined that *power* is distributed unequally. The next set of questions suggests that *opportunity* is distributed unequally as well. How do we decide who gets what? Who said he could be a general when I am a lowly private? Couldn't I be a doctor instead of a nurse? To answer these questions, we must talk about inequality of opportunity, the unequal chances of members of society to get what they want. Also involved is **social mobility**, the upward or downward movement of individuals or groups into different positions in the social hierarchy.

Marxists and social democrats argue that inequality of *condition* is of much greater significance than inequality of opportunity; to them it is more important that the pay differential between managers and workers be reduced than that everyone have a fair chance to be manager.

Others think it is fair that surgeons are paid much more than secretaries, but want people to be placed in these positions on the basis of merit and not on such ascribed bases as age, sex, race, language, religion, ethnicity, or other aspects of social background. People who take this position tend to devote themselves to the study of inequality of opportunity.

*"It's not what you know, it's <u>who</u> you know.
And who do <u>I</u> know? <u>You</u>!"*

Distribution of Opportunity

Research on mobility in Canada has indicated that we have more winners than losers in the area of mobility. A study conducted in 1972 found that 57.5 percent of males aged 25 to 64 years had moved upward in occupation and that only 18.8 percent had moved downward from their father's position. The rest had approximately the same occupation as their parent. For females in the same age group, the figures were even more remarkable; 68.2 percent had experienced upward mobility, while only 17.2 percent had experienced downward mobility (Pineo, 1983: 366).

From a historical perspective, this level of upward mobility is unusually great. It stems mainly from the development of our economy in such a way that the proportion of the occupational structure characterized by better jobs increased, while the proportion of the occupational structure characterized by less desirable jobs decreased. This development created what is known as *structural mobility*. Demand in the job market was such that most Canadians of that generation *had* to move upward to supply products and services for all the consumers born in the baby boom. It seems unlikely that our economy will continue to produce such remarkable transformations. Consequently, it may well be that students reading this chapter will be much less fortunate than those of the previous generation as far as opportunities for upward mobility are concerned.

It is also of interest to consider the manner in which mobility opportunities are distributed internationally. Some studies (Tyree *et al.*, 1979; Hazelrigg and Garnier, 1976) have found that mobility opportunities vary substantially from one society to another. Interestingly, chances for mobility in Canada are apparently among the best in the world (see Table 7-3).

Socio-economic Origins

A central focus of those interested in inequality of opportunity has been the degree to which people's life chances are influenced by the socio-economic status of their parents. A study in Canada, based on a national survey done in 1974, found that less than 15 percent of the variance in the occupational status of a typical Canadian male could be explained by his socio-economic origins. As might be expected, this relationship declines even further when one looks back over three generations. When one compares the status of great-grandfathers to great-grandsons, there is no statistically significant relationship at all. It appears that, if you are a Canadian male, your socio-economic origins will be

TABLE 7-3. Occupational Mobility in 24 Countries

Country	Mobility Index
Israel	−.286
Canada	−.184
Australia	−.141
U.S.A.	−.114
Great Britain	−.102
Hungary	−.068
France	−.056
Sweden	−.045
Netherlands	−.041
Denmark	−.037
Yugoslavia	.003
Norway	.008
Puerto Rico	.013
Belgium	.033
Chile	.048
Japan	.048
Mexico	.051
Spain	.062
Poland	.067
West Germany	.068
Italy	.081
Philippines	.103
Brazil	.133
Colombia	.356

Please note that a negative score indicates a higher rate of occupational mobility. In this table, Canada is second only to Israel in opportunities for occupational mobility.

SOURCE: Adapted from Tyree *et. al.*, 1979, p. 416.

only a minor determinant of your life chances (see Goyder and Curtis, 1979). If you are a female, these origins will probably count even less (Pineo, 1983, p. 367). See the article on Poverty's Children for a description of the immediate reality that some social critics would claim are masked by such statistics.

The findings *do* indicate the importance of education. Privileged parents are able to hand on their status most effectively when they ensure that their children obtain a high level of education. If their children are unwilling or unable to obtain schooling, the influence of their high socio-economic origin is more limited. Finally, data from other countries indicate that the effects of initial social origin diminish even further as one grows older (Matras, 1980).

As always, it is useful to put these data into international and historical perspective. The degree of status transmission in Can-

Poverty's Children

It's lilac time in much of Canada and children romp in schoolyards, feeling the exhilaration of release from the bondage of winter boots and parkas. They look frisky and carefree; adults pause in wistful envy.

Canadian children are among the most fortunate of all the world's young. They live in a country with a social conscience, where citizens support a welfare system designed to protect the helpless and soften poverty. What's more, Canadians believe that they love children.

This being true, and it is, it is baffling that every recent study of poverty in Canada demonstrates that children are hit hardest and that the number of poor children is increasing. Babies born to the poor are twice as likely to die as babies of people with adequate incomes; children of the poor are ill more frequently than other children and require hospital treatment more often; poor children are more likely to be discouraged in school, to drop out early, to be institutionalized, to live all their lives in grinding poverty.

That's not social justice. The whim of chance that puts one infant in the arms of a professional couple who own a home with a teak deck that catches the sun and another infant in the arms of an unmarried woman who works as a waitress should not count so heavily against the second infant.

The two babes are innocents. Viewed through the window of a hospital nursery, they are indistinguishable. Both are stunned and appreciative and fathomless and infinitely dear. They have identical nutritional needs; they each require affection, stability, a stimulating, safe environment. The odds, however, are that only one of them will get that good start. The infant born to the low-income, single-parent is in a high-risk situation. The mother will have difficulty finding affordable housing; she and her baby will live like gypsies, a different bed every few weeks or months. If she works, good child care will be scarce or too expensive; if she goes on welfare to care for her baby herself, she and the child will often be hungry.

A woman who spent ten years supervising a day care centre in an impoverished neighbourhood in Toronto was transferred last winter to a centre where children came from middle-class homes. She thought at first that she had landed among a race of geniuses. Almost every child in the place was a sparkling, verbal, confident, well co-ordinated charmer. After a while she figured it out. These children were only normal; in her previous job, she had grown accustomed to children stunted in development by poverty.

South Riverdale Community Health Centre in Toronto's east end is celebrated for its humane approach to health service. Marianne Cheetham, the primary-care nurse in that setting, tells about the precarious lives of children whose mothers depend on government allowances. In one case the mother was receiving $100 a month in child support from her former husband and this was deducted from her family benefit. When he abruptly stopped paying support, the welfare system was leisurely in restoring her full allowance.

Meanwhile, she and the child had no food.

In another case, a child was in hospital and the mother spent her food money in transportation costs so she could stay with the baby. When the baby was discharged, the mother had no money to feed the child or herself.

In a third case, the children are two years old and six months. They are "so close to the bone," as the nurse puts it, that she weighs them monthly, and she can tell when they have been fed regularly and when, because of a catastrophe like a bill to repair the stove, they haven't.

Children are no longer a phenomenon in line-ups at food banks. The Children's Network, a committee of Toronto City Council, worried last winter about babies and considered establishing a sort of soup kitchen for infants. The scheme was abandoned when it was learned that existing foodbanks already are trying to stock infant formula and baby food, which are in frantic demand. Since a high protein-calorie intake is essential for brain development in the first year of life, it follows that infants of the poor who regularly must survive on watered formula or water alone must be suffering neural damage.

The Toronto Board of Education reasoned some years ago that it can't teach children who haven't eaten. Consequently, an increasing proportion of the education budget is going into food supplements. About 4200 children are being fed daily in 35 elementary schools and four high schools. Teachers have learned to work snacks into daily lessons: for instance, one teaches mathematics while dividing apples.

A new coalition, the Child Poverty Action Group, held a press conference in Toronto last month to announce a scheme of tax reform that would build financial support into parent-child units. Such systems exist in Sweden, West Germany, and France, but the proposal drew little attention here.

Last year the number of children living in poverty in Canada increased by 78 000 while poverty among the elderly declined. Estimates of children living below the poverty line now exceed 1.2 million.

"What is a child?" mused George Bernard Shaw. "An experiment . . . to make humanity divine." In this country, the experiment isn't working well enough.

SOURCE: "Mere Chance Counts Too Heavily against Poverty's Children" by June Callwood, May 14, 1986, *The Globe and Mail*.

ada is generally similar to that found in the United States and in western European countries (Goyder and Curtis, 1979). At least one study (Rich, 1976) has indicated that opportunities for working-class children in Canada to go to college or university are unusually good (see Figure 7-2). There has been some suggestion that status inheritance at the higher levels of Canadian society is greater than that found in other countries (Manzer, 1974; Porter, 1965; Clement, 1975). More recent studies indicate that Canadian elite groups are probably less exclusive than those in other countries (Rich, 1976; Grayson and Grayson, 1978; Campbell and Szablowski, 1979).

FIGURE 7-2. Percentage of University Students of Working-Class Origin in 9 Countries

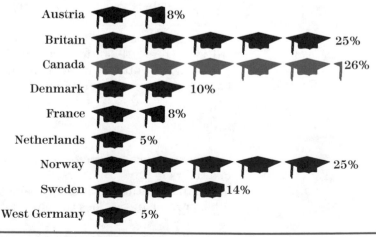

Austria	8%
Britain	25%
Canada	26%
Denmark	10%
France	8%
Netherlands	5%
Norway	25%
Sweden	14%
West Germany	5%

Adapted from Rich, 1976, p. 16.

The historical evidence indicates some decrease in the degree of educational inheritance in Canada since World War II (Manzer, 1974). This means that educational opportunity for the average person, compared to the privileged, has been improving.

Ascribed Status

Students of occupational mobility have also been interested in the degree to which life chances are influenced by such ascribed statuses as ethnicity, race, immigrant status, language, and gender. There is no doubt that many ascribed characteristics are associated with economic standing in Canada. (See Chapter 8 for a discussion of socio-economic standing of various ethnic groups.) It is widely known, for example, that women make less money than men (see Chapter 4) and that Francophones make less than Anglophones. However, there is some question as to how great the differences are, what the trend is, and how much of the difference arises from discrimination stemming from the differing social prestige of people in the various categories. In this section, we discuss several such factors.

Ethnicity

Ever since the publication of John Porter's *Vertical Mosaic* in 1965, it has been widely believed in sociological circles that ethnic origin, or ethnicity, is a major determinant of individual life chances in Canada. It has also been widely believed that the role of ethnicity in Canada is unusually great (Porter, 1965).

Additional work, however, has indicated that the relationship between ethnicity and occupational status is steadily decreasing (Manzer, 1974) and that the relationship was never that strong in the first place (Darroch, 1980). Pineo has concluded that "no more than two percent of the current occupational status of the Canadian male labour force can be said to derive from ethnic origin" (1976, p. 120).

While it may be that ethnicity continues to play some role (Lautard and Loree, 1984), it now appears likely that ethnic background will probably have little or no influence on the life chances of current generations of young Canadians.

Race

Whereas the term *ethnicity* refers to country of origin, the term *race* refers to physical characteristics, most notably skin colour. Unfortunately, the situation in Canada regarding race does not look as promising as does the situation regarding ethnicity.

The living standard of Canada's native peoples, both Indians and Inuit, is very low. Research from about 1960 indicates that almost one out of every five Inuit children died in the first year of life (Manzer, 1974). This was one of the worst rates of infant mortality in the world at that time. The data also indicate that our native people still have "the lowest incomes, the poorest health, and the highest rates of unemployment of any single group in the country" (Valentine, 1980, p. 47).

This situation is of special concern because, unlike the rest of us, native peoples made no choice to take their chances and immigrate to this country. Furthermore, they have been wards of the federal government during most of the history of post-Confederation Canada. Comparative data indicate that our treatment of native peoples has been much less enlightened than that of some other countries (Hobart and Brant, 1966). Hence, as Canadians, we must accept some responsibility for the miserable conditions they face, conditions far worse than those of American blacks—a group for whom Canadians regularly express sympathy. Furthermore, the position of American blacks, unlike the position of Canadian native peoples, has been improving substantially in recent decades (Hogan and Featherman, 1977).

Unfortunately, recent data also indicate that the economic situation of some of our recently immigrated minorities, such as West Indians, is also very poor (Rosenberg *et al.*, 1983, p. 563). There is some hope, however, that these findings reflect factors among the immigrants, such as low educational levels, which may change with their second and third generations in Canada. Only future research will tell.

Immigrants

In this context, it is interesting to look at the position of immigrants in Canadian society. In most countries, it is anticipated that immigrants will come in at lower levels of society and work their way up. It is considered sufficient if they are treated fairly in this process. In Canada, however, a high proportion of immigrants, especially Anglo-Americans, are to be found in the highest levels of the occupational structure. Indeed, partly as a result of Canadian immigration policies, immigrants from many origins generally have a higher socio-economic status than do people born in Canada (Forcese, 1980). If nothing else, this situation of some immigrants contrasts sharply with the situation of our native peoples.

Language

The differing life chances of Anglophones and Francophones have also been the subject of considerable study. Early research clearly indicated that Francophones received a considerably lower income than Anglophones, especially in Québec. For example, in Canada in 1961, the average Francophone income was found to be about 80 percent of the average Anglophone income. Within Québec, the corresponding figure was 64 percent (Morris and Lanphier, 1980). The early research also seemed to show that much of this income differential could be attributed only to discrimination (Dofny, 1970; Beattie and Spencer, 1971). To make matters worse, it appeared that the situation at the managerial-professional level had deteriorated substantially from 1931 to 1961 (Rioux, 1971). As this information spread, it helped to convert many Québécois to the separatist cause.

In this case, however, later research has tended to modify the initial impression of wholesale discrimination. On the one hand, it has become clear that Francophones have contributed in part to their position both through their attitudes toward mobility and through their failure to obtain appropriate educational qualifications (Tepperman, 1975). One study found that a full 60 percent of Anglophone-Francophone differences could be explained by education alone (Manzer, 1974). This, in turn, could be attributed largely to the previous Québec educational system which, until the 1960s, discouraged attendance beyond elementary school (Porter, 1965).

Further research has indicated that the situation in the 1970s and 1980s has substantially improved over the situation in the 1950s and 1960s. By the mid-1970s, research noted that Francophone-Anglophone differences were decreasing (Cuneo and Curtis, 1975; McRoberts et al., 1976). Indeed, one study of engineers and middle-level managers even indicated patterns of discrimination in favour of Francophone Canadians (Armstrong, 1970). A study by Boulet et al. (1983) found a substantial decline in Anglophone-Francophone income differences during the seventies. Nonetheless, significant differences remain, especially in the city of Montréal. If present trends continue, however, Anglophone-Francophone income differentials may well become insignificant before too long.

Gender

There are major differences between the incomes received by males and those received by females in the labour market. Early research clearly showed that women made much less money than men. For example, in 1961, the average annual earnings of female wage-earners were about 55 percent of those of male wage-earners (Manzer, 1974). Furthermore, early research indicated that much of this difference could be attributed only to discrimination (Armstrong and Armstrong, 1978).

The overall incomes of females have been increasing more rapidly than those of males since 1977 (Statistics Canada, 1984b). Female participation in the labour force, in politics, and in the attainment of educational qualification has definitely also been increasing. The symbolically important appointments of females to the Supreme Court and Governor Generalship in 1984 are worthy of note. Indicators such as these seem to suggest a trend toward decreasing discrimination against females in the work place.

Conclusions

In a broad historical perspective, the amount of ethnic, linguistic, and gender discrimination in Canada is probably much less than it used to be. In a broad international perspective, the amount of inequality based on these factors is probably much less here than in most other countries. The situation of immigrants to Canada probably compares favourably with that of immigrants to other countries. On the other hand, the situation of our native peoples is worse than that in many other countries (Hobart and Brent, 1966).

Inequality and Social Change

What the future holds is not at all clear. At the least, it is fair to say that there is no consensus among sociologists. A few dream of the day when the classless society will somehow be created, by evolution or revolution (Marx). Some see the development of new and perhaps worse forms of inequality taking place through a bureaucratization process occasionally assisted by Marxist revolutions (Weber). Others fatalistically take the position that a ruling class will always be with us. Most, perhaps, believe that a certain degree of inequality will always be with us, because the empirical evidence to the present day indicates that this will be so. But these same sociologists would argue that it is always possible to reduce inequality or to eliminate its worst effects through a policy of reform. This suggests that perhaps our future is largely in our own hands. The main purpose of sociology, some feel, lies in the development of theories that will enable our society to guide itself into a more desirable future condition. This raises the issue of *social policy*.

There is no doubt that inequalities of most kinds can be reduced to some degree. Granted, there is some question as to the exact degree, but at present there seems little need to be concerned about whether we are approaching those limits. For example, one study (Hewitt, 1977) has indicated that Canada is among the worst of 17 industrialized western democracies in its success at redistributing income. It is clear that Canadians could reduce some kinds of inequality to some degree if we had the political will to do so.

There are many ideas on how we could reduce inequality. For example, it has been suggested that educational opportunity could be somewhat equalized by such reforms as reduced tuition, increased scholarships, and subsidized housing. Similarly, it might be possible to reduce inequality of condition by suitable revision of our taxation system and by a reduction of regional wage differentials.

Despite the numerous ideas, there are scientific differences of opinion about exactly which reforms are likely to be most effective. On these matters, the experts very clearly disagree. At every point along the way, there are substantial problems with our theories and even with our facts—as we have seen, we are not always sure that we even have the *facts* straight!

There are similar problems with values. What kind of equality do we want? How much equality do we want? How much are we willing to sacrifice in order to achieve it? Probably all of us have some personal limit based on values and interests. Furthermore, it could be that the achievement of equality would involve the sacrifice of other values that are desirable. For example, it is often argued that some equalizing programs reduce freedom. We could insist that all college and university students wear uniforms, so that poorer students would not feel unequal to richer students who can afford to buy more clothes. This would make all students more equal in appearance but would certainly limit their freedom. Would you prefer the equality of uniforms or the freedom of personal clothing choice?

The reduction of one kind of inequality could conceivably increase other kinds of inequality; for example, would you be willing to equalize wages across Canada at the cost of turning more provincial power over to Ottawa? This is the kind of value choice that must be faced.

Finally, there are problems in the differing interests of various segments of our society. Those who think they would benefit from reforms tend to support them. They adopt suitable positions (for instance, the radical perspective) in order to validate their claim for more of society's resources. Those who think they would not benefit from such policies tend to oppose them. They, too, adopt suitable positions (for example, the conservative perspective) in order to defend their interests. Such concerns usually make it difficult to assess policy options in a clear-headed way. What individuals or groups argue is best for the world may in fact, be, what they believe to be best for themselves.

Summary

1. Disagreements about the issue of social inequality stem from three sources: value judgments, interests, and theoretical perspectives. Value judgments have to do with what amount of inequality is judged to be right or wrong. Interests have to do with who stands to benefit or to lose by any changes. Theoretical perspectives have to do with viewpoints on what causes social inequality, how much social inequality there is, and what can be done about it at what cost.

2. Sociological theories on inequality can be divided into three types: the radical, the conservative, and synthesis. Radical theories emphasize the injustice of inequality. Conservative theories emphasize the inevitability of inequality. The synthesis approach attempts to use the best ideas of both traditional approaches and to base conclusions on known facts.

3. Canadians enjoy a very high standard of living by international standards. There is, however, substantial regional inequality in Canada.

4. Income distribution in Canada is relatively equal by historical and comparative standards. There is substantial debate about whether the current trend is toward greater equality or greater inequality. There is also considerable disagreement about how much poverty we have, depending on the definition of poverty adopted.

5. The structure of occupational prestige in Canada is similar to that found in the United States and other developed countries.

6. There is substantial inequality in the distribution of authority in Canada. A very large portion of our authority structure is controlled by foreign interests. Little is known for certain about the distribution of power in Canada.

7. The amount of occupational mobility in Canada appears to be unusually great by international standards. Class origins appear to be a relatively minor determinant of occupational opportunity in this country. This is also true of ethnic background, immigrant status, and language. Gender is strongly related to income. There is also evidence that native peoples are subject to considerable discrimination.

8. Canadians could reduce most kinds of inequality to some degree if they had the political will to do so.

**Further
Reading**

Boyd, M., *et al.* (1985). *Assumption and achievement.* Ottawa:
  Carleton University Press.
  The best source on mobililty in Canada.
Connor, W. (1979). *Socialism, politics, and equality.* New York:
  Columbia University Press.
  An informative comparison of inequality in advanced capital-
  ist and Marxist countries.
Grabb, E. G. (1984). *Social inequality: Classical and contempo-
  rary theorists.* Toronto: Holt, Rinehart and Winston.
  A clear introduction to various theoretical perspectives.
Hunter, A. (1981). *Class tells: On social inequality in Canada.*
  Toronto: Butterworths.
  An informative and recent Canadian text.
Lenski, G. E. (1966). *Power and privilege: A theory of social
  stratification.* New York: McGraw-Hill.
  An ambitious attempt to develop a balanced theory about
  social inequality.
Porter, J. (1965). *The vertical mosaic.* Toronto: University of
  Toronto Press.
  An internationally recognized classic on class and power in
  Canada.

8
Ethnic and Minority Relations

The purpose of this chapter is to explore in more detail one facet of inequality that was touched upon in the previous chapter, the inequality based upon ethnicity.

When you have finished this chapter, make sure that you are able to

1. define the term "ethnic group";
2. explain the concept of ethnic boundaries;
3. define the term "minority";
4. give examples of ethnic stratification in Canada;
5. list the factors that influence ethnic identity;
6. distinguish between prejudice and discrimination.

Racial and Ethnic Groups

How important to you is your racial or ethnic origin? If you speak a language besides English or French or follow customs or celebrate holidays not recognized by your neighbours, you may be more aware than most Canadians of the society your ancestors came from. Nevertheless, we all belong to racial and ethnic groups. What varies is the importance we attach to our membership.

Sociologists have studied race and ethnicity from a variety of theoretical perspectives, with a view to explaining their effects on the individual and society. Before examining some of these perspectives, we should have in mind commonly accepted definitions of race and ethnic group.

Members of one **race** share the same *physical* characteristics—such as skin pigmentation. A racial group may be comprised of many ethnic groups. For example, the Oriental racial group includes Japanese, Koreans, Chinese, and so on. Thus, it would be correct to speak of the country of Japan as being inhabited by an ethnic group such as the Koreans, even though ethnic Koreans and Japanese share the *physical* characteristics we call race. The Koreans in Japan are a distinct **ethnic group** or a "people" if they exhibit at least two of the following defining characteristics:

1. belief in a common ancestry;
2. a common language;
3. shared beliefs and customs (Yinger, 1976).

More than one-third of all Canadians have an ethnic origin other than French, British, Indian, Métis, or Inuit. In other words, the "founding peoples" of Canada currently account for less than two-thirds of the total population. Canada's ethnic mix reflects immigration from all over the world. This makes Canada a *pluralistic* society.

Theoretical Perspectives

Symbolic Interactionism. Symbolic interactionists believe that racial differences affect intergroup relations only to the extent that people attach cultural or symbolic meaning to them. It is not the objective differences that are important in themselves, but how the differences are interpreted by other members of society. The full range of intellectual abilities, for example, is found in all races. And yet slavery was practised in North America on the basis of the false premise that so-called white people were mentally superior to black. This belief in white supremacy legitimized the institution of slavery. Until the abolition of slavery, interaction between the races was determined by skin colour. What social actors believe is symbolized by differences in skin colour will determine what effect those differences have on intergroup relations (Yinger, 1985).

The symbolic-interactionist perspective provides a framework for understanding interethnic as well as interracial relations. Being an Irish Catholic or an Irish Protestant has one set of meanings within Northern Ireland today and an entirely different set of meanings in Canada. In Northern Ireland, there is conflict between these two ethnic groups, while in Canada there is tolerance. Thus, while the ethnic groups may objectively be the same in both countries, their social meaning varies. This meaning, in turn, determines how the two groups interact. Eventually, contact among members of different ethnic groups may change the way the groups view each other. Thus, the social meaning of ethnicity is formed and reformed in recurrent interethnic interactions. Our understanding of our own ethnicity and the ethnicity of others forms as a result of an ongoing process of symbolic interaction.

When ethnic groups interact with each other over a period of time, ethnic boundaries form (Barth, 1969). The **ethnic boundary** is not a *geographical* boundary. Barth coined the term to indicate an invisible *social* barrier that separates ethnic groups, often making interaction between them difficult. We all have a feeling of whether we "belong" or not. When we learn the comfortable limits to our own social interaction, we have, in essence, discovered where the ethnic boundaries are. Ethnic boundaries separate the "we" from the "they."

Since ethnic boundaries are, in effect, social conventions, they may change over time. For example, when a Francophone marries an Anglophone, some people refer to the union as a "mixed marriage." Reactions to this kind of marriage today are mild or nonexistent compared to the reactions of earlier times; the boundaries between these ethnic groups have become less rigid than they once were. Symbolic interactionists view ethnic interaction as a changing, dynamic process because the symbols that give meaning to the process are themselves constantly undergoing review and redefinition.

Conflict Theory.   Conflict theories and symbolic interactionism are not necessarily mutually inconsistent, but they do differ in focus. Whereas the symbolic interactionists study ethnic relations in face-to-face interaction among individuals, conflict theorists attempt to specify the conditions within societies that give rise to co-operation, competition, or conflict. The justification for conflict interpretations is evident when we observe societies such as South Africa and Lebanon, in which there is intense competition among opposing groups for control over land, people, and mineral wealth. On the other hand, there are many examples of relatively harmonious multicultural societies, such as those of Switzerland and Belgium, in which people with different cultures and languages live together within the confines of the nation-state. The broad sociological question is "why do some ethnic groups live harmoniously together when others do not?"

What is the Canadian situation? At the outset, the stage was set for conflict between the indigenous peoples and the settlers with respect to land use and ownership. The question of aboriginal rights today revolves around land and resource control issues. The interests of other Canadians conflict with native land claims. Yet it would be inaccurate to characterize relations between indigenous peoples and immigrant groups in Canada as one of total competition and conflict. It has been said that the early French settlers would not have survived if the natives had not shared their local knowledge and resources with them. Likewise, the Hudson Bay trading company proved beneficial to natives and non-natives alike. Co-operation often took the form of marriage; in fact, the Métis, the descendents of these unions, are a unique ethnic group within Canada.

Some conflict theorists, such as Karl Marx, have predicted that ethnic affiliations will decline in importance with the passage of time. Consequently, they predict that ethnicity will cease to be a basis of social conflict. Conflict will take place between groups with opposing *economic* interests, such as workers and their employers. Marx believed that workers of different ethnic backgrounds will discover that their common interests as workers outweigh other factors. They will organize for their betterment, even though this means opposing a boss who belongs to their own ethnic group. The Marxist conflict perspective emphasizes that for class conflict to take precedence over ethnic conflict, the worker must know his or her "objective interests." To engage in ethnic conflict would be to act against these true interests, or to act with false consciousness.

Structural Functionalism. The structural functionalist, Talcott Parsons, used a different line of reasoning to generate the same hypothesis as that of Marx concerning the decreasing significance of ethnicity in modern societies. Parsons predicted that ethnicity and race will diminish in importance as bases of affiliation because modern societies are based on achievement, not ethnicity and race. Increased consensus on this value in modern society will function to keep potential conflict in check.

The structural functionalists assumed that unbiased merit or achievement criteria would prevail over ethnic judgments. The society that results is a *meritocracy*. In a meritocracy, people are allocated to positions on the basis of skill, not skin colour. Since ethnic and racial prejudice are not functional in a modern society, their decrease was predicted (Parsons, 1951). In fact, Parsons predicted a general decline in social conflicts of all types.

Evaluation. How might we evaluate the theories of Marx and Parsons, given that Marx is predicting conflict and Parsons is predicting the opposite—value consensus? Assuming that Canada has achieved the advanced stage of capitalism and is "modern" as defined by both theories, we observe neither the ascendancy of class conflict over ethnic and racial conflict, as predicted by Marx, nor the rational meritocracy, free from ethnic discrimination, predicted by Parsons.

Marx's theory might receive some support, however, were the data to show a trend over time in the direction of *decreasing* ethnic conflict and *increasing* class conflict. In Canada this would mean a lessening of antagonisms between Francophones and Anglophones and a diminution of ethnic and racial discrimination, on the one hand, and a growth of the labour movement and labour-based parties such as the New Democratic Party, on the other hand.

There is also some evidence in support of the trend toward the meritocracy predicted by Parsons. Entrance examination and various credentials are commonplace prerequisites for entry into today's competitive job market. The Canadian Charter of Rights and Freedoms and provincial human rights legislation attempt to safeguard merit and fairness in such matters as hiring practices. And while it would be naïve to say that the prejudice and discrimination with respect to characteristics such as race and gender have disappeared, we have at least officially recognized that they have no place in modern society. The fact that discrimination persists despite this recognition is not incompatible with the possibility that, in the long run, Parsons' hypothesis may be validated.

Peoples and Nations: Ethnicity in Canada

"Ottawa is the capital of our *two* nations." At first glance, this may seem to be an incorrect statement. In order to judge its validity, we need to know the particular definition of *nation* being used. A leading sociobiologist, Pierre Van den Berghe (1981), theorized that the ethnic group evolved from the kinship bond and that the nation, in turn, evolved from the ethnic group. Using this sense of *nation*, how might the term be applied to Canada?

Events in Canada reveal an uneven growth of nationalism. Fierce regional loyalties and separatist sentiments co-exist with support for a confederated state.

Québec

In his 1838 pre-Confederation report to the monarchy, Lord Durham described Lower Canada (Québec) as "two nations warring in the bosom of a single state." Concern with Québec as a distinct society or as a founding nation is a theme that runs throughout Québec history. In the era of Premier Jean Lesage, the Quiet Revolution of the 1960s, this concern was expressed in the notion that Québec was not "*une province comme les autres*" (a province like the others). Premier Jean Lesage is remembered for the "*maîtres chez nous*" (masters in our own house) doctrine.

In the late 1970s, Québec's claim to be a distinct society within Canada led the Québec government to propose "sovereignty-association." Under this policy, the province would become a separate state but remain associated with Canada. A referendum on this issue was held in 1979 to see if the voters of Québec wanted their government to negotiate sovereignty-association. The "*non*" vote won, and by 1985 a federalist government headed by Liberal Robert Bourassa had returned to power.

Some would argue that Lord Durham's "two nations warring" image applies to Canada today. It was not until 1987, five years after the actual patriation of the constitution, that the Québec

TABLE 8-1. Gender Differences in Income and Education for Black and Chinese Canadians, 1981 Census.

Ethnic Origin by Gender		Average Income (1980) ($)	Education	
			Less than Grade 9 (%)	Some University (%)
Black	Male	14,941	9	23
	Female	9,209	13	13
	Both	11,965	11	18
Chinese	Male	15,068	16	34
	Female	8,915	27	22
	Both	12,201	21	28
Total	Male	16,918	20	18
Canadian	Female	8,414	20	14
population	Both	12,993	20	16

SOURCE: *Socio-economic Profiles of Selected Ethnic/Visible Minority Groups, 1981 Census* (March, 1961), Ottawa: Multiculturalism Canada.

government agreed, in the Meech Lake accord, to sign the Canada Act, the act patriating the constitution. Québec had not signed because the constitution did not recognize Québec as a "distinct society within Canada." This recognition was one of several conditions required for Québec's signature. It should be pointed out, however, that in 1982 the Québec government rejected the Canada Act in spite of constitutional guarantees in the area of minority language rights.

In June 1987, Prime Minister Brian Mulroney and the provincial premiers agreed upon amendments to the constitution recognizing Québec's distinctiveness. The agreement made it more difficult for the federal government to encroach on areas of exclusive provincial jurisdiction. The exact meaning of the accord (when and if it is approved by Parliament and the provincial legislatures) will only become apparent after it has been interpreted by the courts. Still, it would seem that the constitutional recognition of Québec's distinctiveness has produced somewhat increased decentralization of Canadian federalism as it involves *all* provinces.

Even a cursory examination of recent Québec history reveals that the Québécois strongly regard themselves as a people (ethnic group). But they are more than this; because they occupy a homeland in the province of Québec, they are also a nation (Rioux, 1971). A **nation** may be defined as an ethnic group currently occupying a territory or homeland, or associated with a homeland at a previous point in time. Thus, it is sociologically correct to speak of the Québec *nation* within the nation-state of Canada.

French Canada

Returning to the original statement "Ottawa is the capital of our two nations," one might assume that the two nations referred to are Québec and English-speaking Canada. There is, however, another interpretation of the statement: that Ottawa is the capital of our two nations, French-speaking Canada and English-speaking Canada. This second response rests on the distinction between French Canada and Québec. French Canada includes Québec *plus* all the other traditional homelands within Canada such as *l'Acadie* in the Atlantic provinces, the Ontario regions populated by the Franco-Ontarians, and the areas of French-Canadian settlement in Manitoba and Alberta. While *Québec* is the homeland to Québécois, *all of Canada* is the homeland to French Canadians, who make up approximately 30 percent of the Canadian population.

If we follow the second interpretation, Canada is a confederation of English- and French-speaking peoples rather than provinces. The Official Languages Act of 1969 recognized this historical duality by naming both English and French as official languages on the federal level. This means that, among other things, services provided by the federal government must be provided to a citizen in the official language of his or her choice. (New Brunswick is the only officially bilingual province.) It is important to recognize that the interpretation of the "two nations" phrase is a matter of political controversy, with most Québec nationalists adhering to the first interpretation described above and most Canadian nationalists to the second.

Multiculturalism

In order to recognize the contributions of the other ethnic groups in Canada (groups other than the British and French charter groups), the federal government proclaimed a policy of **multiculturalism** in 1971. This policy recognizes that although there are only two official languages in Canada, there are many cultures or ethnocultural communities. The Canadian government asserted that both old and new immigrants were free to preserve their ethnic cultures, even though there would be only two official languages. Individual members are encouraged to have as strong or as weak an attachment to their ethnic group as they wish.

The multicultural policy (House of Commons Debates, 1971) and the Official Languages Act are two pieces of legislation that have no equivalent in the United States on the federal level. Unlike Canada, the United States has had an assimilationist,

SOURCE: N.R. Hoferichter/Miller Services

Canada's policy of multiculturalism encourages ethnic groups to keep their cultural heritage alive as much as they wish to do so.

melting-pot philosophy. (**Assimilation** is a process that results in the lessening of ethnic boundaries. When it occurs, society tends to become more homogeneous with respect to language, culture, and other symbols of identity.) In the United States, it has been assumed that in time all immigrants will speak English and share in the same customs and traditions. This has not always happened. Religious sects such as the Amish and Mennonites settled in America to escape religious persecution, and they have been free to resist the melting pot effect. Some ethnic and racial groups have actually been excluded from fully partaking in the mobility opportunities promised in the American Dream. The Civil Rights Movement in the United States in the late 1960s and 1970s was an attempt on the part of such racial and ethnic groups as blacks, Hispanics, Natives, and Asians to achieve a measure of integration (equal participation), if not full assimilation. People are more likely to seek integration in economic structures; cultural integration has a much lower priority.

In Canada, the image that is contrasted with the American melting pot is the Canadian **mosaic**. The mosaic imagery attempts to convey the idea that assimilation to one uniform, homogenous culture is not our goal. A mosaic is composed of many different pieces—each one beautiful and distinct in its own right. In referring to our society as the Canadian mosaic, we emphasize our diversity.

The mosaic ideal has, however, posed some problems for our representative government. In a liberal democracy such as the United States, all citizens, as individuals, are equal before the law. There are no collective or group rights. It works well in a melting-pot society. For Canada, however, the principle of equality before the law is modified by our recognition of collective rights for certain categories of citizens, such as Francophone and Anglophone minorities and native peoples (Morton, 1985).

Not Only in Canada

Although one thinks of the United States as an English-speaking country, it actually has no official language. Public signs and even drivers' licence applications are bi-or tri-lingual in some areas; during the last 15 years, some school districts have provided primary education in a language other than English. Perhaps a backlash was inevitable. Some two months after the following article appeared, the ballot proposition it describes was passed by a large majority. Although the vote had no legislative force, it did signal the will of the California electorate.

In the Di-Ho shopping mall, signs in large Chinese characters and smaller English letters advertise a fish market, Chinese pastries, books and herbs.

Inside the bookstore, 15-year-old Jenny Pai translates for her 70-year-old grandfather.

"My grandfather says this is an all-American city, different nationalities. It's good if there's a lot of languages."

But Ying Lin Pai's vision of the United States is not shared by a new Monterey Park city councillor, the leader of a majority that swept into power in the spring on an "official English" plank. Three incumbents, two Hispanic men and a woman of Asian descent, were knocked out.

The local battle over language reflects a growing debate throughout the state and the nation about what it takes for immigrants . . . to become good Americans.

"I wonder if these new immigrants would put

their life on the line in Vietnam or Korea or someplace else to defend this great nation," Barry Hatch, a high school teacher and new city councillor, said on a radio show recently.

"All we ask, the sacrifice we ask, is learn English, use it as the official language." A proposal to amend the state constitution will go before the voters in November. It has been an increasingly harsh campaign, characterized by appeals to patriotism on one hand and charges of racism of the other. Monterey Park is the flash point for a statewide campaign to have English declared the official language of California.

Depending on one's point of view, California in the past 20 years has benefited or suffered from a great influx of Hispanic and Asian immigrants, both legal and illegal. . . . Hispanic children, most of them citizens or legal residents, make up 62 percent of the kindergarten population of the Los Angeles school district.

The drive for an offical language has arisen in reaction to that surge of immigrants, with proponents arguing that the country is becoming a "salad bowl" of distinct nationalities rather than a homogeneous melting pot.

The campaign is only the most recent demonstration of nativism in the United States, where foreigners traditionally have been viewed with suspicion. Similar reactions, sometimes with almost identical rhetoric, were prompted by the waves of German and Irish immigrants who arrived in the nineteenth and early twentieth centuries.

The current nationalist movement is spearheaded by a group called U.S. English, based in

Washington, D.C., which is trying to enshrine English as the official language in the Constitution. In the meantime, the organization, headed by Canadian immigrant and former U.S. senator S.I. Hayakawa, has spawned local groups that are pushing for similar changes at the state level.

Related issues of bilingual education and immigration control continue to gather national publicity and remain the focus of legislative efforts in Congress.

A report written for the Washington-based Council for Inter-American Security, an independent think-tank that advises governments, declares: "If we elect to model our society after Canada, then we need a definite statement to that effect.

"Already the education policy is in place to achieve that goal with current bilingual, bicultural practices. . . .

"However, if we desire to preserve our unique culture and the primacy of the English language, then we must so declare rather than sit idly by as a de facto second nation evolves."

For all parties in the debate, Monterey Park has become a testing ground for the wider issues. Forty percent of its 50 000 residents are of Asian descent, 37 percent Hispanic, 22 per-cent Anglo and one percent black.

Until recently, the groups appeared to live in harmony in their well-maintained, prosperous community east of Los Angeles. The city council roughly reflected the community with one Filipino, one Asian, one Anglo and two Hispanic members. Investment money, largely from Hong Kong and Taiwan, created a construction boom. . . .

But, when a few residents began a movement to have English declared the official language, [the city] became a model of racial division and mounting bitterness. . . .

At his modest Monterey Park home, David Almada, former mayor and high school principal, quietly responded to the attack on his Hispanic culture and, in particular, Mr. Hatch's radio attack on the patriotism of minority groups.

"Japanese-American and Mexican-American units had many of the worst losses in the Second World War," he said. "In Vietnam—you go back to Washington, D.C., now and you will see a disproportionate number of Spanish surnames on that black wall [of the Vietnam memorial]. They have no right to question our Americanism."

SOURCE: "English Only: U.S. Salad Bowl or Melting Pot," September 8, 1986, *The Globe and Mail.*

Native Peoples

The Canadian Constitution "recognizes and affirms the existing aboriginal and treaty rights of the aboriginal peoples" (Section 35). Thus, in law, Canada is more than a collection of interchangeably equal citizens. Native people have special rights, called aboriginal rights. While the specific content of these rights has yet to be fully defined, the entrenchment of the rights concept in the Constitution sets these citizens structurally apart from other Canadians.

Rather than viewing Canada as a liberal democracy, it may be more accurate to view Canada as a **consociational democracy**. In a consociational democracy,

. . . the nation-state explicitly acknowledges that it is composed of members who share different linguistic, cultural or ethno-national traditions. It provides mechanisms that help

Killing Seals and Whales

Some of the thorniest issues involving minorities arise when cultural values are diametrically opposed to each other. If you and I must live on the same block and your group believes that public places are for music, laughter, and game-playing while mine holds for decorum, sooner or later you and I are going to clash.

Matters become more serious when people's livelihood is at stake or issues of morality are involved. Problems of this sort abound for Canada's native peoples and are compounded by North America's history of discrimination against the Indians and Inuit. Yet clashes occur even when the opposing groups are well-intentioned.

"You are looking at a smuggler," Finn Lynge of Greenland angrily told delegates and observers to the Inuit Circumpolar Conference. "Our products are outlawed, our culture isn't respected."

Mr. Lynge, who is chairman of the ICC environment committee, was wearing a sealskin vest he had smuggled past U.S. customs authorities in Anchorage. Others in the Greenlandic delegation had their native clothing seized because of U.S. laws against imports of sealskin.

As a result of intense lobbying by environmental groups that oppose the killing of seals, Inuit sealskins are also banned from European community countries.

The Inuit say that ban and others affecting their traditional whale hunting have cost their people in Greenland, Canada, and Alaska millions of dollars and deprived them of the chance to live their traditional life.

"It is unacceptable that Inuit of the Arctic are seldom consulted about their own affairs, yet are part of countries that are always speaking to the world about human rights," Mr. Lynge said.

"We are facing a strange but well-known phenomenon: the urge of the white man to shape us in his image, to make us eat his food, wear his clothes, and lead his life."

Mr. Lynge, who works in Denmark for the ICC, promised a long, aggressive public campaign in Europe and North America to explain why aboriginal peoples should be allowed to continue subsistence hunting and trapping.

The actions of the environmental lobbyists have effectively confined many Inuit to a life of government housing and television, Mr. Lynge said later in an interview.

The irony is that we end up spending our days watching the blood and violence of a people who tell us they cannot stand the shedding of animal blood. And this from the most bloodthirsty civilization on earth. We do not hear them speaking of a total ban on killing and maiming on television, this society that would call us barbarians.

The Inuit were commended for their conservation work by Noel Brown, director of the United Nations Environment Program.

"You have much to teach animal lovers about your love of nature," the Jamaican diplomat told the assembly. "You do not need to apologize to anyone or listen to anyone's lectures on the conservation of nature. It is part of your life and you must defend it by stating your case to the world. For you, interest in nature is not a passing fad."

SOURCE: "Inuit will Campaign to Defend Hunting, Conference is Told," by Matthew Fisher, July 31, 1986. *The Globe and Mail.*

guarantee their survival rather than assimilate them to a common norm (Asch, 1984).

Perhaps this consociational aspect of our democracy, more than any other structural element, differentiates Canadian society from American society with respect to ethnic expression. It makes us more similar to Switzerland than to the United States (Van den Berghe, 1981; Asch, 1984). Given the current movement in the direction of native self-government, it is likely that the consociational aspect of our democracy will become more and more descriptive of the Canadian mosaic as time goes on.

Returning to our original statement concerning Ottawa as the capital of our *two* nations, we can see the complexity involved in giving a full and politically sensitive explanation. Canada contains not merely the partnership between the two founding nations of the French and English, but the nations of the indigenous peoples as well.

The indigenous peoples in Canada and elsewhere constitute a "Fourth World" (Manuel, 1974; Dyck, 1985). The struggle for self-determination among the indigenous peoples of the Fourth World is carried on by nations submerged within nation-states. The nation-states tend to dominate the indigenous nations and hinder their attempts at self-determination. Former B.C. Supreme Court Justice Thomas R. Berger (1981) has referred to native rights in Canada as both the oldest and the most recent human rights issue.

Prior to the patriation of the constitution in Canada, few politicians and citizens were eager to recognize aboriginal rights. In 1969, Prime Minister Trudeau even considered a policy of "termination" with respect to Indians. (A termination policy is the direct opposite of a policy that recognizes aboriginal rights. Any special status the natives enjoyed would have ended.) The Indian Act governing relations between the Indians and the federal government would have been repealed, and natives would have become citizens with the standard rights, obligations and privileges of citizenship.

Although we might expect that termination would have had native support, this was not the case. For the first time in Canada, native communities organized *en masse*, united in their opposition to the proposed termination of their special status. Native leaders believed that the proposed termination policy would lead to forced assimilation and the end of their distinct ethnonational communities (Cardinal, 1969; Weaver, 1981).

The constitutional guarantees hold special significance for the natives in the Northwest Territories, where this group constitutes more than 50 percent of the population. The Inuit are using their aboriginal rights as the basis of their argument for self-government within the Canadian confederation. The Inuit in the Northwest Territories want their own government in their territorial homeland in the Eastern Arctic, which they call *Nunavut* (meaning our land). The government would not be an ethnic government, but a government of all the residents.

Under the same proposal, the Western Arctic would be called

The extent of aboriginal rights in Canada are still being negotiated. This photograph was taken at one of many conferences that have been held on the subject.

SOURCE: Canapress Photo Service

Denedeh (meaning Dene homeland). This territory is the home of the Dene nation. The Dene are Athabaskan-speaking natives of the Mackenzie River Valley. The Dene were the first Canadian natives in modern times to conceive of themselves as a "nation" and to push for land-claim settlements on this basis. Following the lead of the Dene, the name of the National Indian Brotherhood was changed to the Assembly of First Nations.

Asch (1984) is of the opinion that our consociational democracy can eventually accommodate the aspirations of the native people in Canada, as it has those of French- and English-speaking Canadians.

For over one hundred years, Confederation has been incomplete, for it has been organized without the recognition of the special political standing of the aboriginal nations. With patriation of the Constitution . . . Canada took an important step to rectify this situation. But without the entrenchment of the political rights of native peoples, Confederation is still incomplete (Asch, 1984).

In order to become a full-fledged consociational democracy, Canada will have to work out a way of politically incorporating the various indigenous nations into the existing democratic structure. To the extent that Canada succeeds, it will be a country that respects the rights of peoples as "nations," or ethnic groups, that have territorially based homelands within the Canadian nation-state.

Ethnic Social Organization

A Definition of Minority

What do we mean by **minority**? We might adopt a numerical definition and think of a minority as a group with few members. But few in comparison to what? For example, in Alberta, French-speaking people are outnumbered by English-speaking and Ukrainian-speaking residents, but in Québec, they are the majority. A definition should take into account the larger societal context.

A definition of minority implies that there is also another body, the *majority*. We might assume that the majority is the group with controlling political power, but power does not necessarily accompany numerical superiority. The situation in South Africa demonstrates that a relatively small group, such as the white Afrikaaners, can still exert a controlling influence on a society.

Departing from everyday usage, some sociologists define minority status as *subordination*. The superior status of the dominant group defines the subordinate status of the minority. The minority experiences such conditions as poverty and is characterized by a sense of powerlessness and low self-esteem. Thus, a minority group such as the blacks in North America are, by definition, a minority group and would be so even were they to comprise more than 50 percent of the population. The classic definition using this approach was made by Louis Wirth in the early days of sociology:

> A minority group is a group of people who, because of their physical or cultural characteristics, are singled out from others in the society in which they live for differential and unequal treatment and who therefore regard themselves as objects of collective discrimination (Wirth, 1945).

Note the subjective element in this definition. For a group to be a minority, its members must be aware of their own inferior status. Note, as well, that a minority need not be an ethnic or racial group; other societal groups may fit the definition, as well. Physical characteristics could refer to physical disabilities or to gender, as well as to race. Cultural characteristics could refer to the subcultures of such stigmatized groups in society as ex-convicts and gays.

Ethnic Stratification

Ethnic status sometimes influences the way social actors react to each other. People may associate particular personal traits with specific groups. These perceived associations are *ethnic stereotypes*. As a limiting case, one might *refuse* to interact with someone of a certain ethnic background. Reactions conditioned by ethnicity create an ethnic stratification system, a culturally based ranking of ethnic groups.

Ethnic stratification varies in rigidity. At one extreme, the *caste* systems forbid contact with members of certain groups. Typically, ethnic barriers are less rigid, with certain forms of contact allowed and others being discouraged or forbidden.

According to usual measures of stratification—income, occupation, and education—the native peoples are the lowest of all Canadian ethnic strata.

In spite of the prejudice and discrimination that native people have experienced in Canada, they are not a caste. A pure caste system forbids intermarriage between the different strata. Intermarriage between natives and Europeans has been common; in fact, a Canadian ethnic group, the Métis, was formed by the union of native women with the early French and Scots trappers, traders, and explorers.

Official Minorities

A distinctive feature of Canadian ethnic stratification is the existence of **official minorities** as designated by Section 23 of the Charter of Rights and Freedoms. The official minority in Québec consists of the group of English-speakers whose mother tongue was English. Thus, we have what, at first glance, appears to be a rather odd situation—English-speaking people as a Canadian minority.

The "official minority" designation refers only to language rights of Anglophones and Francophones when one of these groups constitutes a numerical minority: "Citizens of Canada whose first language learned and still understood is that of the English or French linguistic minority population of the province

FIGURE 8-1. *Average Income of Non-Native and Native Families with Dependants, Rural and Urban, Canada, 1980*

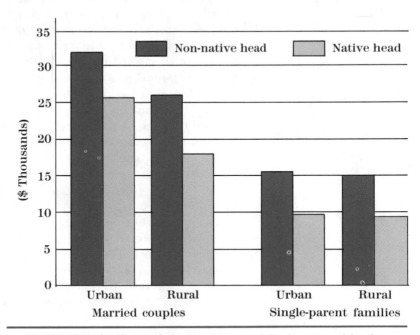

SOURCE: *The Changing Economic Status of Women:* A Study prepared for the Economic Council of Canada (p. 41) by Jac-André Boulet and Laval Lavallée, 1984.

in which they reside . . . have the right to have their children receive primary and secondary school instruction in that language in that province" (Charter, Section 23, 1a).

How inclusive is Section 23? You will note that in order to be protected by this clause, it is necessary that the parent still *understand* the minority language. Suppose that English or French was spoken as a minority language one generation back and that now the parents want to educate their children in that ancestral language even though they no longer speak it. In such cases, they have no legal right to the special instruction. Thus, the right does not extend to all citizens, but only to members of the official linguistic minority population in a province, as defined by Section 23.

The Charter of Rights and Freedoms protects both French and English linguistic communities. But it makes no commitment to provide bilingual education across Canada and thus further Canada as a bilingual nation. Rather, the commitment is to a narrowly defined *group* of Canadians—the official linguistic minority.

Section 23 of the Charter of Rights and Freedoms departs from the majority rule principle in order to aid minorities who wish to resist assimilation. It affirms the "founding nations" principle by giving equal protection to both the English and the French linguistic communities. It also creates a hierarchy by placing the linguistic rights of these two ethnic groups above those of others, an enduring basis for ethnic stratification.

This is not to say that other Canadians are discouraged from speaking the language of their choice. In actual fact, heritage language programs are very popular and well developed in large Canadian cities and on native reserves. Every day in Canada, school children can be found studying Italian, Greek, Cantonese, Hebrew, and Cree—to name only a few of the available languages. Although approximately one-third of the population has ethnic origins that are neither British nor French, the constitutional *right* is extended only to those in the official linguistic minority communities who qualify by the definition set forth in Section 23.

The existence of ethnic stratification—especially when it is officially sanctioned or contrary to official pronouncements—can result in embarrassing contradictions for a society that espouses egalitarian ideals. A classic case of this kind of contradiction was described by the Swedish economist Gunnar Myrdal in a study of American society prior to the Civil Rights Era of the 1960s. He called his work *An American Dilemma* (Myrdal, 1943). The title is significant, as the work points out that the Declaration of Independence was written in the language of equality, yet, in actual fact, Negroes (they were not called blacks in Myrdal's era) were being lynched, denied access to institutes of higher learning, barred from certain occupations, and prohibited from gaining the normal goods and services taken for granted by the white population. This contradiction was the "dilemma" the American people faced.

Note that the ethnic and racial stratification in the United States was different from South African apartheid. Officially, the United States denied the legitimacy of discriminatory treatment. By contrast, there is no pretense of equality in South Africa. The apartheid policy in that country is oriented toward totally separate development. The policy sets forth the conditions under which the three officially recognized races—whites, blacks, and coloured—may mix. Inequality is institutionalized and, for the most part, accepted as the norm by the European settlers. Apartheid is most fervently defended by the white Afrikaaner ethnic group (formerly called the Dutch Boers).

The effects of ethnic stratification in Canada are considered in Chapter 7.

These native children are enjoying their day, but the data on ethnic stratification show that they have less reason to expect a happy, prosperous, and fulfilled life than most other Canadians.

Ethnic Communities

It is important not to confuse ethnic stratification with ethnic neighbourhoods, even when these neighbourhoods are called "ghettoes." Prior to World War II, the term *ghetto* referred to a specific section of a European city in which Jews were forced to live. The modern North American ghetto is not equivalent. Tradition and economic factors may force people to live in certain areas, but residential patterns are not legally enforced in North America. This is not to deny that social pressures do not limit the choices of some members of ethnic groups; witness the Ku Klux Klan's burnings of crosses on the lawns of black interlopers in white neighbourhoods to discourage their continued residence.

People of the same ethnic group may choose to live together for mutual support or camaraderie as, for example, in Vancouver's Chinatown. Ethnic communities may exist without exhibiting ghetto-like qualities; they may be residentially dispersed but still culturally unified. Ethnic groups and communities may exist without being rigidly stratified in relation to the larger society.

The vertical dimension of Canada's mosaic is open to debate (Porter, 1965). In the 1960s, Porter used census data to show a strong correlation between social class and ethnic origin. But more recent data indicate a weakening of the relationship between social class and ethnic origin.

While the existence of two ethnic communities in a city does not necessarily mean that one dominates the other, it is possible for an ethnic group to monopolize the access to jobs in a certain sector of the economy and to exclude others systematically. In such cases, it would be reasonable to speak of ethnic stratification in that particular sector. As new waves of immigrants arrive, the pattern of ethnic stratification is likely to shift in line with the changing ethnic composition of the society.

The positive functions of an ethnic community are numerous. In an exhaustive study of ethnic group survival in Toronto, Reitz (1980) found that there were both economic reasons and cultural reasons for people to identify with and participate in ethnic communities. Ethnic communities differ with respect to their "institutional completeness" (Breton, 1964). Some communities have their own church, newspaper, school, hospital, grocery shops, and businesses. The more institutionally complete a community is with respect to supplying goods and services, the more likely it is that members will live their lives within the community, and the greater the likelihood that the community will survive. Likewise, the more economically viable and culturally vibrant a community is, the more likely it is to be institutionally complete. While it is not essential to reside physically in an ethnic neighbourhood in order to be a member of an ethnic community, the ethnic neighbourhood does aid the preservation of language and the general transmission of culture.

Ethnic neighbourhoods are often located in central sections of our cities. For various reasons (such as the age and condition of housing), these areas are often targets for urban renewal. Municipal governments often conceive of this process narrowly (that is, as physical renovation) and overlook the social fabric of the neighbourhood. Often, when the ethnic group occupying the neighbourhood is low in the stratification system, it is not consulted on the future of its community and is consequently unable to resist disruption.

Until the 1960s, Halifax had a black community called Africville on the shores of Bedford Basin. Africville was a socially cohesive community that approached institutional completeness. It was a classic ethnic community—providing mutual support networks, services, and a sense of identity to its members. But Halifax decided that Africville was in the way of its urban development plan. Consequently, the people were forced to relocate against their will. When the neighbourhood was redeveloped, the people were uprooted. In the end, the people of Africville felt bitter over the loss of their neighbourhood (Clairmont and Magill, 1974). The climate of prejudice existing in the larger society no doubt contributed to the urban renewal policies that destroyed the community.

The Africvillers' experience is similar to that of other urban dwellers who have faced the bulldozers. Those affected are typically the poor and powerless; city administraters know that these people lack the resources to fight city hall. We often regard predicted economic gains as more important than the lives of the individuals who are judged to be in the way.

Ethnic Identity

The chapter on socialization describes the process by which we become members of such social groups as family, peer group, and work group. By participating in a group, we learn the norms and values of the group and our place or role within the group's social structure. Most of us develop an ethnic affiliation through a similar process. We are socialized at a young age to the norms and values of our ethnic group. And just as some of us may wish to abandon our early religious training when we mature, some of us may choose to shed our ethnicity. If one is a member of a "visible minority" such as a racial group, however, this choice may not be available. Those around us—society—may draw the boundaries that define our racial separateness.

In some cases, ethnic identity, like racial identity, may be imposed rather than voluntarily adopted. There is often a gap between *subjective* and *objective* ethnicity, inasmuch as the larger society labels a minority regardless of how the minority feels about itself. For example, at the time of the Nazi Holocaust in Germany, Jews were rounded up for slaughter on the basis of their parentage or **objective ethnicity**. Whether one was an observer of Jewish custom or a religious believer (aspects of **subjective ethnicity**) made no difference. Many assimilated Jews thought they would be exempt because they thought of themselves first and foremost as good German citizens, and only secondarily as Jews. But the Nazi policy was all-inclusive, allowing no room for subjective assessment on either side.

Although we do not always have a choice concerning our ethnic identity because of state policy or early socialization, there are instances in which an individual can exercise a conscious choice with respect to ethnic group affiliation. It is not uncommon for a young person to be ashamed of or embarrassed by ethnic customs that are different from the peer group's customs.

Ethnic and Minority Identities

Children of immigrants often feel "marginal," because they are comfortable neither with the customs of their parents from the Old World nor with the customs of their peers in the New World. Intensifying this marginality may be the fact that Canadian customs in courtship and dress, for example, often conflict with parental notions of proper behaviour and attire. Adolescents with immigrant parents may be subjected to a series of strains and stresses over and above those commonly associated with the "generation gap" between parents and their children. The children in the next generation, on the other hand, may seek their identity through ethnic affiliation. Their voyage of discovery could take the form of language lessons or simply chatting with the elders in the community, in an attempt to piece together their ethnic history. In these ways, the significance of an ethnic identity varies from one generation to the next.

There are some benefits that can be derived from belonging to an ethnic group. Members of an ethnic group may have enough interests in common to warrant their banding together for collective action. In urban areas, ethnic groups act as power bases to advance political awareness or action. If someone is being subjected to racial or ethnic slurs and feels powerless to do anything about it as an individual, he or she may be able to take action through an organization in the ethnic community. A letter to the editor of a newspaper or to a politician bears more weight if it is signed by the executive of an ethnic organization than by an unknown individual. When an ethnic community mobilizes its resources, it maximizes its potential impact on the social structure of the larger society.

Isajiw (1978) describes some reasons that people choose to affirm their ethnicity. Ethnicity provides a psychological anchor, a sense of belonging. Who am I? If I can say "I am Sikh" or "I am Salish," I may not be as psychologically adrift as someone who lacks an ethnic mooring. In today's impersonal, technological society, it is important for the individual to find identity in some primary group, be it the family, a friendship group, or an ethnic group. Isajiw's theory of the ethnic group mediating between society and the individual may help to explain why ethnicity has not disappeared in our mass society, the way both Marx and the structural functionalists forecast that it would.

Newly arrived immigrants often find economic and cultural shelter within the confines of the ethnic community, which provides a bridge between the society of origin and Canadian society. Newcomers have a vital role to play in cultural transmission. New waves of immigrants help to keep a language alive. Chain migration, whereby immigrants come because they already have friends and family in the area, aids group cohesion and injects new blood from the Old World. Some ethnic communities, such as the Ukrainian community, maintain their ethnicity without reliance on immigration—emigration being denied as a matter of policy by the USSR. In time, North American ethnic expression may come to be far removed from Old World practices as it grows and evolves to reflect the circumstances of its present milieu.

Sometimes new ethnicities form in the host society. The development of black ethnicity in Montréal is a case in point. Before the language policy of the Parti québécois government became law, black immigrants from the Caribbean spoke English and sent their children to English-speaking schools. With the new language policy, they had to send their children to French-speaking schools. This development, coupled with emigration from black Francophone countries such as Haiti, has meant that blacks in Montréal are interacting now as Francophones. In time, they may develop a black, Francophone ethnicity unique to the Montréal milieu.

Minority Identity

Minority groups are subgroups; that is, all members of a minority are also members of the larger society. For example, all Filipino Canadians are also Canadians. In consequence, all minority group members are carriers of *two* cultures—their own ethnic *subculture* as well as the culture of the surrounding society.

But when the minority is low in the stratification system (and this is just another way of saying that there is prejudice against it in the majority culture), members of the minority group may be ambivalent (of two minds) about themselves. They will, on the one hand, carry their ethnic community's view of itself as distinctive and worthy, but they may also carry some elements of the disdain felt toward their group by the majority. This inconsistent self-view is a psychological consequence of minority status.

Self-hate and low self-esteem occur when the minority group members take on the values of the larger society even when those values run counter to their own self-interest. It is a basic tenet of symbolic interactionism that we tend to acquire the attitudes that we find expressed by others in their treatment of us (Mead, 1934). If gay people are told that being homosexual or lesbian is wrong, they may come to hate themselves for being so "evil." Some people within the gay community think that "queens" (gays who dress in a sexually provocative or flamboyant manner) deserve to be harassed by the police because they give all gays a "bad name." In this case, gays who dress conventionally share the general societal condemnation of those gays

Canada's Deaf: Signing for Their Rights

Our definition of a minority group emphasizes attitudes towards differentiating characteristics. Members of the majority regard the minority as having low status and thus subject them to discrimination. Members of the minority may lack the power and self-esteem to reject this view, and sometimes they concur in it.

Notice that ill-will on the part of the majority is not a necessary precondition for discrimination. While it is true that disapproval or dislike is sometimes present, often the majority is acting from good intentions, doing what it believes best for people it regards as inferior.

Consider the situation of the handicapped, many of whom are now seeking to change the inferior status awarded them by the majority.

The hands of thousands are finally being heard across Canada. No longer willing to be an all-but-invisible group defined solely by an invisible handicap, more than 80 000 deaf Canadians . . . are emerging as a proud cultural minority, united by a common language and growing determination to take hold of their own affairs.

For the majority of us who have no contact with the deaf community, the change appears very recent, seen largely through the mainstream media. Most notably, there was deaf American actress, Marlee Matlin, winning an Oscar for her role in *Children of a Lesser God*, a film in which her character delivers just one, barely understandable sentence.

There is the current television commercial for the McDonald's restaurant chain, in which two deaf teenagers use sign language for a familiar debate about whether to study or go to the beach—and opt for the surf.

Yet here in Metro [Toronto] there is growing evidence of sign language all around us—a couple signing unobtrusively on the subway, or a largely silent, but nonetheless boisterous, group with flying hands sitting around a table at a popular restaurant.

Even five years ago, the tendency among deaf people was to reflect the attitudes they learned—that their sign language was something that marked them as different from the hearing world, and as such was to be discouraged. . . .

The rationale—expressed by the two-year-old Ontario law, Bill 82, which says that all handicapped students must be integrated into "normal" classrooms as much as possible—is the idea that promotion of the deaf as a bona fide cultural community was tantamount to excluding them from broader society.

The dominant belief, supported most vigorously by hearing parents of deaf children, non-deaf medical experts, and special education bureaucrats, was that deaf children and adults should primarily be taught to function in the hearing world. That meant an educational approach known as "oralism," which stresses lip-reading, mechanical aids to amplify any residual hearing capability, and verbal speech.

Sign language was often ignored or even banned in government schools until recently—much like government and church schools for Canadian Indians and Inuit used to ban their native tongues.

It distracted the deaf from the goal of integration, ran the philosophy. By encouraging them to develop strong ties within their only peer group, use of sign language would only make their chance of surviving in the hearing world that much tougher.

"The native Indian analogy is an excellent one, because we've endured the same kind of paternalistic, we'll-decide-what's-best-for-you systems as native people have," says Gary Malkowski, a leading deaf activist in Metro. "And results have been similar, with too many deaf people being cut off from their own culture and community, too many believing that there was indeed something wrong with stressing their deafness as something to be proud of."

Oralism is still the dominant characteristic of Ontario's deaf education curriculum, although a more balanced concept, known as total communication, means sign language is also being taught now.

But it is based on English structure and grammar, rather than the completely different linguistics of American Sign Language (ASL), as the most expressive deaf signing is called. . . .

"Too often . . . it's the same old story with parents, bureaucracies and school boards deciding what's best," says Fred Walker, executive-director of Metro's Bob Rumball Centre for the Deaf, and a firm opponent of "mainstreaming" deaf children into hearing classrooms for the sake of integration.

He and other deaf advocates complain that despite impressive technical advances in special hardware to help the deaf in the hearing world, Canada lags about 15 years behind the United States in recognition of the existence of a signing-based deaf culture, much like an ethnic minority, [that] has astonished linguists with the depth and structure of sign as a language unto itself. . . .

Despite the ongoing debate, there have been some impressive gains of a more tangible kind for the deaf in Canada. Most recent was the establishment of a special message relay service in Ontario and Québec by Bell Canada,

following a federal government agency's regulatory order, which now provides operators to relay messages between hearing persons and deaf person's TDD (telecommunications device for the deaf) . . . which feature an electronic read-out and a keyboard with telephone lines as the link. . . . [Previously] deaf agencies tried to provide their own relay services—to doctors, lawyers, and the like—but couldn't cope with the demand. Now that Bell has its own, no-charge system, and has included deaf people on an advisory body, communication freedom is vastly improved, they say.

Sign language courses for the hearing are also soaring in popularity, with the Rumball Centre and Canadian Hearing Society programs always full to capacity. . . . The variety of attention-getting flashers to warn deaf people of door knocks, alarm bells, a TDD call and the like are impressive.

Now that it has begun, the younger deaf leaders say, this sense of a minority culture can only snowball as more and more trained deaf professionals get involved. . . .

SOURCE: "Canada's Deaf: Signing for their Rights" by Dan Smith, May 1, 1987, *The Toronto Star*.

---

who do not. By disassociating themselves from that stigmatized group, they are attempting to salvage and protect their own identity.

Low self-esteem is common among minority groups because the general message from the larger society is that the minorities are of low worth. Faced with disagreement and discrimination, some gays may attempt to "pass"—that is, try to fit in to the larger society by giving the impression of "normality." Gays might date members of the opposite sex or even marry in order to keep the appearance of respectability. Passing behaviour is a strategy for survival in a hostile world. It is not unusual for gay people to lose their jobs or face other forms of ostracism when their homosexual identity is revealed. (Only in Manitoba, Ontario, and Québec do the provincial Human Rights Commissions prohibit discrimination on the grounds of sexual orientation, and even there such laws cannot prevent informal discrimination.)

Passing may indicate a reluctance on the part of a gay person to confront his or her "real identity" when society has labelled gays as "unacceptable, sick, and morally perverted." In the wake

The Cosby Show portrays a black family led by an obstetrician and a lawyer. The family's income is well above average. The children go to good schools and universities. The overall image works against low self-esteem that has been part of the minority identity of many black Americans.

SOURCE: Canapress Photo Service

of the increasing AIDS publicity, there is even less incentive for a homosexual male to reveal his sexual orientation. The fear of AIDS has tended to intensify the prejudice against homosexuals that was already present in our culture.

Passing, self-hate, and low self-esteem are not confined to the gay minority. In all instances involving minorities, the psychological dynamics, structural conditions, and resulting behaviour tend to be similar. So we find that some Jews have "Canadianized" their names in attempts to avoid being targets of anti-Semitism. Similarly, some blacks accord higher prestige to members of their community who are least black in appearance. Some blacks, especially during the era of segregation, attempted to straighten their hair and bleach their skin to look "white." Women have written under male pseudonyms and some have gone so far as to disguise themselves as men. These actions are extreme individual attempts to reduce the penalties of minority status or to gain the rewards available only to members of the majority.

Table 8-2 classifies minority group reactions to subordinate status. The minority's goal is cross-classified with a behavioural strategy compatible with the goal. Minorities are classified by the degree to which they accept the dominant society and the degree to which they are willing to relinquish their ethnic identity. The resulting minority action may take a relatively active or passive form and may occur on an individual or a group level.

TABLE 8-2. *Minority Reaction to Subordinate Status*

Minority Goal	Minority Strategy			
	Acceptance of the status quo of the dominant society		Rejection of the status quo of the dominant society	
	passive	active	passive	active
Entry into majority group	assimil- ation	anglo- conformity	involuntary segregation	militant integration
Survival as an ethnic group	accommo- dation	ethno- centrism	voluntary segregation	militant separation

SOURCE: *Minority Canadians*, vols. 1, 2 by J. L. Elliott, 1971, Scarborough, Ont.: Prentice-Hall Canada.

Societal Response

The larger society does not exhibit equal tolerance toward all minorities. The term **social distance** describes differences in levels of acceptance. As early as the 1920s, Bogardus developed scales measuring social distance. He asked people which groups they would be willing to let into their country, or into intimate circles such as the family, and which groups they would exclude. Responses tend to indicate that people will even exclude imaginary groups if these are perceived as culturally different from themselves. Real or imagined, it seems that the foreign or unknown is feared. It follows that those groups that are most often accepted into marriage are those that are perceived to be closest to the respondent in terms of cultural and racial attributes (Bogardus, 1928).

We make a distinction between attitude and action. Ignorant and intolerant attitudes are referred to as **prejudice**. **Discrimination** refers to *behaviour* that results from prejudice. Thus it is possible to have a prejudiced person who does not discriminate. A father may prefer that his daughter not marry a male from a

Cultural Villains

Discrimination against minority groups takes many forms. A common one is stereotyping group members as villainous in the popular media. This attitude is particularly likely to occur when the group in question is perceived as a national enemy. During World War II, the "bad guys" in most comic strips were German or Japanese; a few years later, the villains— sometimes the same characters—were transformed into Russians.

In the following piece, which was feature in The Globe and Mail, *the president of the Canadian Arab Friendship Society pleads for less stereotyping of her ethnic group, one of today's "cultural villains."*

In many a Westerner's view, an Arab is a swarthy, hook-nosed, scheming sheik, robes flowing as he rides a camel through the desert, wielding a scimitar. Other standard descriptions are gun-toting, doped-up lunatics threatening the lives of the innocent. Arabs are arms dealers, wild-eyed terrorists, rapacious barbarians. In addition, there are continual warnings of the "Islamic bomb" that Arab Moslems will explode someday upon the West if their demands are not met. (The media use the words Arab and Moslem interchangeably, but most of the world's Moslems are not Arab. To call all Moslems Arabs is like calling all Roman Catholics Italians.)

The image of the Arab woman is of a docile creature who remains in seclusion, forever submissive to male society, speaking only when spoken to. The Arab female is depicted as the exotic, dark-eyed temptress.

The image of the Arab as one or all of these things has been part of Canadian and U.S. popular culture for so long that it's no longer even recognized as a stereotype. . . .

This is the kind of bigotry faced by Canadians of Arab descent. For Arab Canadians, the anti-Arab bias is a fact of daily life, if not a danger.

The recent mass hysteria and hatred against Libyan leader Moammar Gadhafi, for instance, stirred up sentiments in Canada. Some members of Arab-Canadian organizations received obscene telephone calls—even death threats. "Arabs must die," more than one was told.

Harassment, in the form of lengthy searches of cars and their contents at Canadian Customs, for Arab Canadians returning . . . has become common.

Suspicion of anyone from the Arab world is aroused by cartoons, comics, and television shows that link Arabs with narcotics, white slavery and smuggling. . . .

High school textbooks, dealing with the Arab world, focus on nomads and desert life, with little mention of the modern Middle East or Arab contributions to the West's heritage. Generally, the Canadian educational curricula ignore the centuries of culture and learning that originated and developed among the Arabs and peoples connected with them. . . .

And Arabs in Ontario were not invited to or represented at the Ontario Ministry of Education's conference on Race and Ethnocultural Relations in Education in March this year.

Television, for the most part, has discontinued pejorative characterizations of women and minorities, but Arabs are still maligned. Dynasty's Alexis dallies with the sinister Ahmad Rashid; swarthy and bearded Arab villains have appeared on Charlie's Angels, the Bionic Woman, Hardcastle and McCormick, Hawaii Five-O, Cannon, Columbo, Medical Centre, and Trapper John, M.D. In MASH, Jamie Farr pretends to be a cowardly transvestite who is a Lebanese American from Toledo, Ohio.

Youngsters, too, see the Electric Company, whose Middle Eastern villain, Spell Binder, is always defeated by all-American Letterman. In episodes of Richie Rich, Scooby-Doo, and Transformers, the evil genies out to destroy the universe are characters from the Arab world. . . .

Following the Arab conquest of Spain, the intellectual superiority that arose from Cordova, Seville, Toledo, and Granada pulled the West out of the Dark Ages, with the emergence of translations and scholarly treatises. But these Arab contributions in the fields of medicine, philosophy, mathematics, architecture, literature, law, religious tolerance, and the general development of human civilization are ignored.

Arabs are contemporary cultural villains. Today, no one would dare refer to Jews, blacks, Chinese, Italians or Germans in the way they refer to Arabs.

U.S. oil companies used the 1973 Arab oil embargo as justification for the rapid rise in the price of domestic fuel. If Arabs seek to recover lost territory, they are accused of warmongering. If they seek to exploit their natural wealth, they are accused of threatening the world with economic collapse.

Consider Walter Mondale's U.S. presidential campaign in 1984, when his financial chairman in the Chicago area returned $5000 in donations made by five Arab Americans. They were told it was policy to refuse contributions from Arab Americans. . . .

Arab Canadians are not responsible for the international politics that drive some Arabs to desperate acts. However, given the wrong impressions from stereotyping, some Canadians might be moved to commit violence against innocent fellow Canadians of Arab origin. The fact that few outside the Arab-Canadian community take issue with what is happening adds to the risk.

Multiculturalism is Canadian policy and all Canadians are entitled to partake of it, but the Arab community feels very isolated, and very alone. Arab Canadians are an ethnic group like any other and as such are important to the growth of this nation. They deserve to be recognized that way.

SOURCE: "Arab Canadians Feel the Heat of Being Labelled the Villain" by Muna Salloum, August 7, 1986, *The Globe and Mail.*

certain group, but still be willing to allow that group to enter the country and live and work in Canada on an equal footing with other Canadians. Often, however, there is a strong correlation between prejudice and discrimination.

Even more harmful than individual prejudice and discrimination is that which is institutionally based. Institutions are wide ranging in their impact, and even fair-minded individuals may have to carry out discriminatory practices if they are employees. For example, if the Canadian Forces has a policy that discriminates against women and gays, there is nothing tolerant and progressive administrators can do if their authority is defined by a discriminatory policy. It is possible for tolerant administrators to find themselves in situations that demand discriminatory responses even though these may run contrary to their personal value systems.

In the chapter on social movements, we learn that the prime candidates for movement membership are the dispossessed and powerless. These are the people with little to lose and much to gain. Minorities make up the bulk of membership in social movements; they are the outsiders who are struggling for the price of admission. On the other side, dominant groups in the larger society have an interest in maintaining the status quo. As a consequence of these conflicting goals, the larger society often looks unkindly on minority social movements and seeks to crush or repress them.

SOURCE: H. Armstrong Roberts/Miller Services

Demonstrators demand an
end to institutional discrimination against gays.

Summary

1. Ethnic groups view themselves as having common ancestry
    and usually share religious, linguistic, or other cultural ties.
    Racial groups share genetically transmitted physical charac-
    teristics that are socially defined by the larger society as
    "race." A nation is a race or an ethnic group identified with
    an ancestral homeland, typically submerged within an exist-
    ing nation-state.
2. According to the symbolic-interactionist perspective, our
    perception of our own and others' ethnicity is formed as a
    result of ongoing interaction processes in which we partici-
    pate. Marx and the conflict theorists predict a rise in the
    effects of social class and a concurrent decline in the influ-
    ence of ethnicity. Structural functionalists predict that eth-
    nic ties will ultimately be replaced by cultural uniformity
    based on universal achievement criteria. The persistence of
    ethnicity in modern societies is contrary to the theories of
    both Marx and Parsons.

3. One-third of all Canadians belong to neither the French nor the British "charter group." Since 1971, Canada has had a federal multicultural policy in an attempt to support the ethnicity of all Canadians without weakening Canada's commitment to the original founding nations. Since 1982, the Canadian Constitution has affirmed the aboriginal and treaty rights of the native peoples. In 1987, the Meech Lake accord recognized Québec as a "distinct society" within Canada.

4. Canada acknowledges the "official minority linguistic populations" mentioned in Clause 23 of the Charter of Rights and Freedoms. This clause creates a narrowly defined "official minority" in each province that possesses distinct educational language rights.

5. A minority group has a subordinate status in relation to a dominant group. Some minority groups must contend with the possibility of assimilation into the larger society. Assimilation may lead to acceptance, but it also means the eventual disappearance of the group as a distinct entity.

6. Accommodation to minority status may take individualized forms, such as self-hate, low self-esteem, or passing, or it may take a collective form, such as the formation of ethnic communities and social movements.

Further Reading

Altman, D. (1982). *The homosexualization of America.* Boston: Beacon.
The coming of age of the gay minority is examined with reference to the impact of the gay rights movement on the attitudinal structure of North American society.

Asch, M. (1984). *Home and native land: Aboriginal rights and the Canadian constitution.* Toronto: Methuen.
An insightful discussion of self-determination and self-government on the part of Canadian native peoples with special attention paid to the situation in the Northwest Territories.

Berger, T. R. (1981). *Fragile freedoms: Human rights and dissent in Canada.* Toronto: Clark, Irwin.
A description of the uniquely Canadian successes and failures in our attempt to create a society of tolerance. Events from the Acadian expulsion to the Japanese-Canadian relocation are detailed.

Burnet, J. (Ed.). (1986). *Looking into my sister's eyes: An exploration in women's history.* Toronto: The Multicultural History Society of Ontario.
Women's contributions to Ontario's immigration history are examined from the point of view of their ethnic group ties.

Nevitte, N., & Kornberg, A. (Eds.) (1985). *Minorities and the Canadian state.* Oakville: Mosaic.
An important collection of readings on minority rights and human rights.

9
Formal Organizations

Early in their evolutionary development, humans organized socially in order to survive. This required division of labour, which brought about social interdependencies. The purpose of this chapter is to familiarize you with the importance of social organization and, more specifically, formal organization in our society.

When you have finished this chapter, be sure you are able to

1. distinguish mechanical from organic solidarity;
2. define formal organization;
3. describe the characteristics of bureaucracy;
4. define scientific management;
5. summarize the Hawthorne studies;
6. describe the impact of modern technologies upon workers.

In developed societies, organizations are everywhere. Governments, stores, hospitals, colleges, universities, churches, restaurants, railways, airlines, funeral parlours, and sports clubs are only a few examples of organizations in Canadian society.

Ask a group of people what *organization* means, and you will receive a wide variety of answers. For some, organization will be synonymous with bureaucracy. For others, organization may suggest the dull routine of work, or membership in a ski club. Organization may even have sinister connotations, evoking thoughts of organized crime and the Mafia. Ask sociologists for their views on the subject, and they are likely to respond, guardedly, "Well, that depends; are you talking about voluntary associations, or formal organizations, or complex organizations, or institutions, or what?"

Such a wide range of responses is understandable, because *organization* is a very general term with many possible meanings. So it is necessary to narrow the focus on the term. This chapter examines the nature of organizations and their effects on our lives. In the process, we look at how sociologists study organizations. Our main attention will be on formal organizations. But to avoid narrowing our focus too quickly, let us begin by looking at the role of organizations in the broader social context.

Social Organization

People are *social*—they do not live in isolation from other people. And wherever human beings live as social beings, organizations are bound to develop. Furthermore, when people interact with others, they find that they need each other to make survival easier, and they come to depend on one another for an exchange of services.

If I were a farmer and you were a blacksmith, I might ask you to make a metal plow that would make my plowing easier and more effective. In return for the plow, I could provide you with fresh vegetables and grain for your family. Later, if my horse needed shoeing, I would bring that work to you. In the process of our social interaction with each other, certain mutual dependencies develop. You need the food I grow, and I need your blacksmithing skills. Because we are unable to do everything for ourselves, we divide most of the work so that we tend to do those things we are good at or have special facilities for. As a consequence, we come to rely on others for additional skills, goods, or services; that is, a basic division of labour results. **Division of labour** refers to the tendency for general tasks and roles to become increasingly specialized.

The division of labour, no matter how simple or basic, increases people's dependencies upon one another, which, in turn, reinforces social behaviour. As a society becomes more industrialized, there is a greater specialization in work and, therefore, a more complex division of labour. The various elements that make up this division then need to be co-ordinated, and social organization becomes a necessity.

Durkheim and the Division of Labour

An early scholar who pointed to the link between the division of labour and the necessity for social organization was Durkheim, who, as you'll remember from Chapter 1, is a central figure in the development of sociology. He was interested in how the increasing division of labour affected societies. In *The Division of Labour in Society* (1964a, originally published in 1893), he focused on the question of *social solidarity*—what is it that binds people together in larger social networks?—and on the mechanisms that create social solidarity. He identified two types of social solidarity: *mechanical* and *organic*.

Durkheim suggests that in less complex societies the links between people take the form of **mechanical solidarity**. The society is bound together by a strong system of common beliefs and a simple division of labour. Everyone does the same kind of work to survive (such as hunting and gathering), so each household is self-sufficient. Because people are able to supply most of their own basic needs, they do not depend much on others. As a result, their social bonds are kinship and neighbourliness. Outside of the basic family unit, they get together with other people because they want to, rather than because they need to in order to survive.

Organic solidarity occurs as societies evolve and become more complex. The division of labour increases, and specialization results. No longer is everyone doing relatively similar tasks. Consequently, individual self-sufficiency decreases and greater dependency on others develops. Greater dependency means that people must maintain social relations in order to survive at a desired standard.

Division of labour is the key development that makes the co-ordination and control of social behaviour necessary; that is, as societies become more complex, the need for organization develops.

Organization Defined

Organization is a general term encompassing many interrelated elements. In order to identify the basics of organizations, imagine the following situation. You are driving in the country when you come to a farm where the barn is burning. Wanting to help, you join the farmer and a group of neighbours standing before the blaze. It is necessary to act quickly to limit damage to the barn and prevent the fire from spreading to other buildings. Fortunately, there is a well in the yard, there are some buckets lying around, and there is a ladder close at hand.

Given these particulars, you can easily imagine the next step. Those at the fire start a bucket brigade, moving water from the well to the barn, and up the ladder onto the fire. Each individual performs a specific task, and probably some attempt is made to match people to appropriate tasks. The heavy chore of drawing the water from the well, for instance, is assigned to a well-muscled person, and those afraid of heights are on the ground rather than at the top of the ladder.

Let us step back for a moment and analyse some of the components of this situation—for example, the group's *goals*. The burning barn presents a very clear goal for people on the site: putting out the fire. Without this goal, the people would not become organized. Before an organization can form, there must be a goal or set of goals that each member helps to achieve.

The means for achieving this goal are clear: using the buckets (the *resources*) to move the water from the well onto the fire. This could be done, however, in a number of ways. The men and women could each fill a bucket and run with it individually to the fire. These disorganized and independent actions might be successful if the fire is small and our firefighters are all fairly

Craft Specialization

In nonindustrial societies, where division of labour occurs along lines of age and sex, each person in the society has knowledge and competence in all aspects of work appropriate to his or her age and sex. In modern industrial societies, by contrast, there exists a greater diversity of more specialized tasks to be performed, and no individual can even begin to have knowledge of all those appropriate for his or her age and sex. Yet even in nonindustrial societies there is some specialization of craft. This is often minimal in hunting and gathering societies, but even here the arrow points of one man may be in some demand because of his particular skill in making them. Among people who produce their own food, there is apt to be more in the way of specialization. Among Trobriand Islanders, for example, the artisans of one village specialize in stone blades for adzes, whereas their neighbours may specialize in decorating pots or carving wooden handles for the stone blades.

An example of specialization can be seen among Afar tribesmen of the Ethiopian Danakil depression: they are miners of salt, which since ancient times has been widely traded in East Africa. It is mined from the crust of an extensive salt plain in the north part of the depression, and to get it is a risky and difficult business. L. M. Nesbitt, the first European to successfully traverse the depression, labelled it "the hell hole of creation."[1] The heat is extreme during the day, with shade temperatures between 140 and 156 degrees F not unusual. Shade is not to be found on the salt plain, however, unless a shelter of salt blocks is built. Nor is there food or water for man or beast. To add to the difficulty, until recently, the Muslim Afars and Christian Tegreans, highlanders who also mine salt, were mortal enemies.

Successful mining, then, requires skill at planning and organization, as well as physical strength and the will to work under the most trying conditions.[2] Pack animals to carry the salt have to be fed in advance, for to carry sufficient fodder for them interferes with their ability to carry out salt. Food and water must be carried for the miners, who usually number 30 to 40 per group. Travel is planned to take place at night to avoid the intense heat of day. In the past, measures to protect against attack had to be taken. Finally, timing is critical; a party has to get back to sources of food and water before their own supplies are too long exhausted, and before their animals are unable to continue farther.

[1] L. M. Nesbitt, *Hell-Hole of Creation* (New York: Knopf, 1935).
[2] Haile Michael Mesghinua, "Salt Mining in Enderta," *Journal of Ethiopian Studies*, 1966, 4(2); Kevin O'Mahoney, "The Salt Trade," *Journal of Ethiopian Studies*, 1970, 8(2).

SOURCE: *Cultural Anthropology*, 4th ed. (pp. 204 and 205) by William A. Haviland, 1983, New York: Holt, Rinehart and Winston. Copyright 1983 by CBS College Publishing.

strong and hardy. On the other hand, such unrelated individual actions might result in failure if the fire is big. Imagine people crowded at the well waiting to fill their buckets, people bumping into each other, spilling their water on the way to the fire, and so on. Clearly, the bucket brigade organization is much more likely to achieve the group's goal.

Besides the achievement of goals, the bucket brigade also

involves some additional important concepts. First, it illustrates the use of *technology* in goal achievement. **Technology** is the application of a body of knowledge through the use of tools and processes. In this case, the technology is the application of the knowledge that water can be used to extinguish certain types of fires. The tools in this instance are simply the buckets and the ladder, while the process involves filling the buckets and passing them along a human chain to the fire.

Certain additional resources are required if the technology is to function—the supply of water and people to do the various tasks. Thus, in our elementary organization (the bucket brigade), the resources of water and volunteers are used in a *division of labour*, employing a simple technology to achieve the goal of putting out the fire.

Back to the scene of the blaze. . . . Good progress is being made in getting water to the fire, but a problem has developed, one requiring *co-ordination*: the buckets, once emptied onto the fire, are not being returned to the well so that the process can be repeated. So several uninvolved children are commissioned to return the empty buckets regularly to the well, thus completing the circuit.

An observer of the scene would be impressed, not only by the readiness of the group to solve problems, but also by the *communication* between members of the organization as they pass suggestions among themselves or as they give each other encouragement or criticism for ups and downs in performance. In addition, one person has emerged as a *leader* who co-ordinates the activities of the group and is a key figure in identifying and resolving problems. The reader will be relieved to learn the happy ending of this scene: the fire was speedily doused and only minor damage to the barn resulted.

To sum up, our organization, the bucket brigade, though not as complex as a metropolitan fire department or a large business, does contain the basic elements of an organization:

1. goal(s);
2. resources;
3. technology;
4. division of labour;
5. co-ordination;
6. communication;
7. leadership.

An **organization**, therefore, is an entity in which people and resources are co-ordinated through a division of labour in the use of a technology to achieve a goal. Co-ordination, control, and problem solving are facilitated through communication and leadership.

Spontaneous Organization

Our bucket brigade has disbanded; all the hard-working men, women, and children are enjoying a well-deserved rest. While it was in operation, the brigade constituted a good example of an organization. Furthermore, it was an example of a **spontaneous organization**. The fire was a one-time event. The people who were at the scene of the fire joined together in a co-ordinated activity to achieve a specific goal at a particular time. Once the goal was achieved, the organization dissolved, and the people went their separate ways.

Spontaneous organizations often occur in crises or emergencies. Volunteers, for instance, may band together to fill sandbags and build dikes during a flood. Or the first people to arrive at a car accident may organize to free the victims, provide first aid, and direct traffic. Once police and other regular service personnel arrive, this temporary organization scatters.

Formal Organization

Earlier we referred to the interrelationships among social behaviour, division of labour, and social dependencies. As these links intensified, societies moved, as Durkheim noted, from mechanical to organic solidarity. We have seen that people become increasingly dependent on one another as the division of labour becomes more specialized. To manage the complexity of these links, societies become formalized. **Formalization** is a process by which the informal relationships that characterized early societies are gradually replaced by rules, codes of conduct, laws, and other means of regulation.

In our example of the bucket brigade, the spontaneous organization developed in response to particular circumstances of the moment and disbanded when the task was complete. A more formalized society is likely to decide that fire protection is not something that can be left to the chance that people will happen to appear at the fire scene and that they will organize successfully each time to battle the blaze. Instead, it elects to have in place a ready-made, formal organization to deal with emergencies. Volunteer fire-brigades and full-time fire departments are examples of formal organizations.

You might recall from earlier chapters that a *role* is the behaviour expected of the person occupying a particular position. In a formal organization, the positions necessary in its division of labour are formally stated in the organization's documents, and the requirements of each role are specified in job descriptions. When the fire chief retires, the fire department does not usually disintegrate; instead, a new individual is recruited to fill the vacant and the department continues to meet its goals. Unlike the spontaneous organization of the bucket brigade, the fire department is an enduring organization that normally outlives individual members.

The two main characteristics that distinguish a formal organization from a spontaneous organization, therefore, are *continuity* and *formalized procedures*. We are now in a position to complete our definition. A **formal organization** is a relatively enduring or continuing social entity in which roles and resources are co-ordinated through a division of labour in the use of a technology to achieve a goal or goals. Co-ordination, control, and problem-solving are facilitated through communication and leadership and are formalized through written rules and procedures.

Spontaneous organization is encountered at different times throughout our lives, but the more profound and frequent effects upon us are from formal organizations. These are our focus for the remainder of the chapter.

Authority

There are many possible ways of structuring and administering an organization. From societies to community colleges, one of the great problems in their survival and success is how to co-ordinate social behaviour so that an acceptable degree of social order is maintained and the desired communal goals are achieved. Central to any consideration of social order are the means of control. How does a society or organization get people to co-operate? What power does it have over its members to ensure conformity to established norms? Who is to wield this power?

One of the first scholars to stress the importance of formalization in organizations was Max Weber. Weber was very much intrigued by questions of social order and power. Why, he wondered, do people obey commands from people in authority? Is it a question of *power*—that is, that the person issuing the command is able to achieve his or her objectives in spite of resistance? Or, is it a question of *discipline*—that is, that as a condition of their membership in a group, people are expected to be obedient?

His analyses led him to conclude that one factor people assess before deciding whether or not to obey is the legitimacy of the authority issuing the command. Weber argues that there are three major bases of legitimate authority:

1. traditional;
2. charismatic;
3. legal-rational, or bureaucratic.

The Melanesian Big Man

The qualities for which a leader is chosen reflect the nature of a society and its values. In a primitive agrarian society, leaders must demonstrate some exceptional qualities that relate to that culture. Nonetheless, you may find some qualities of the Big Man of the Kapauku that suggest our own political and economic leaders.

Throughout much of Melanesia there appears a type of leader called the Big Man. The Big Man combines a small amount of interest in his tribe's welfare with a great deal of self-interested cunning and calculation for his own personal gain. His authority is personal; he does not come to office nor is he elected. His status is the result of acts that raise him above most other tribe members and attract to him a band of loyal followers.

An example of this form of political organization can be seen among the Kapauku of West New Guinea. There the Big Man is called the *tonowi*, or "rich one." To achieve this status, one must be male, wealthy, generous, and eloquent; physical bravery and skills in dealing with the supernatural are also frequent characteristics of a *tonowi*, but they are not essential. The *tonowi* functions as the headman of the village unit.

Kapauku culture places a high value on wealth, so it is not surprising that a wealthy individual is considered to be a successful and admirable man. Yet the possession of wealth must be coupled with the trait of generosity, which in this society means not gift giving but the willingness to make loans. Wealthy men who refuse to lend money to other villagers may be ostracized, ridiculed, and in extreme cases, actually executed by a group of warriors. This social pressure ensures that economic wealth is rarely hoarded, but is distributed throughout the group.

It is through the loans he makes that the *tonowi* acquires his political power. Other villagers comply with his requests because they are in his debt (often without paying interest), and they do not want to have to repay their loans. Those who have not yet borrowed money from the *tonowi* probably hope to do so in the future, and so they too want to keep his goodwill.

Other sources of support for the *tonowi* are the apprentices whom he has taken into his household for training. They are fed, housed, given a chance to learn the *tonowi*'s business wisdom, and given a loan to buy a wife when they leave; in return, they act as messengers and bodyguards. Even after they leave his household, these men are tied to the *tonowi* by bonds of affection and gratitude. Political support also comes from the *tonowi*'s kinsmen, whose relationship brings with it varying obligations.

The *tonowi* functions as a leader in a wide variety of situations. He represents the group in dealing with outsiders and other villages; he acts as negotiator and/or judge when disputes break out among his followers.

The *tonowi*'s wealth comes from his success at pig breeding, for pigs are the focus of the entire Kapauku economy. Like all kinds of cultivation and domestication, raising pigs requires a combination of strength, skill, and luck. It is not uncommon for a *tonowi* to lose his fortune rapidly, due to bad management or bad luck with his pigs. Thus the political structure of the Kapauku shifts frequently; as one man loses wealth and consequently power, another gains it and becomes a *tonowi*. These changes confer a degree of flexibility on the political organization, but prevent long-range planning and thus limit the scope of any one *tonowi*'s political power over the rest of the villagers.

SOURCE: *Cultural Anthropology*, 4th ed. (pp. 321-322) by W.A. Haviland, 1983, New York: Holt, Rinehart and Winston. Copyright 1983 by CBS College Publishing. Reprinted by permission.

Traditional Authority

Traditional authority rests on an established belief that certain traditions are sacred and that people exercising authority based on these traditions do so legitimately (Weber, 1947). In ancient monarchies, for example, people believed in the divine right of their king or queen to rule. People accepted the divine right because of a belief that it was a right transferred down through eligible descendents and delegated under certain conditions to members of the official court. Likewise, people accept that in families the parents traditionally exercise authority over their children by virtue of the early dependence of children on parents for survival.

Traditional authority is something we also see in a limited way in Canada with the monarch and his or her representatives—the Governor General and the various provincial Lieutenant-Governors.

Charismatic Authority

Charismatic authority, by contrast, depends on devotion to the actions or personality of a specific individual and the patterns of order that this person requires (Weber, 1947). The authority of charismatic figures derives from the belief that they are special, that they possess some exceptional ability or magic that inspires the loyalty of their followers. Such is the pervasive character of leaders of various religious cults, such as the Moonies. Political charisma has been attributed to Churchill in Britain, Gandhi and Nehru in India, Chairman Mao in China, Hitler in Germany, John Kennedy in the United States, Pierre Trudeau in Canada, and the Ayatola Khoumeini in Iran.

Legal-Rational Authority, or Bureaucracy

By far the most frequent authority pattern we experience is Weber's third type. **Legal-rational authority** is based on a belief that certain patterns of rules are legal and that those in authority under such rules have the right to issue commands (Weber, 1947).

The underlying process of this type of authority is formalization. As a result, legal-rational authority tends to be more systematic and impersonal than either traditional or charismatic authorities. Weber argued in addition that organizations based on rational authority tend to have **bureaucracy**.

Weber identified six common features of bureaucratic organizations.

1. A bureaucracy is governed by a set of *fixed and official rules and regulations.* These rules outline the jurisdictions and responsibilities of each unit and, usually, each position in the organization. In a large hospital, for instance, the housekeeping department is charged with maintenance and upkeep, as

Jeanne Sauvé reads the
Speech from the Throne.
The Governor General is a
representative of traditional
authority in Canada.

SOURCE: Canapress Photo Service

opposed to the nursing departments, which are charged with
patient care. Within the housekeeping department itself, the
tasks of laundry personnel are specified and quite distinct
from those of dishwashers in the kitchen area. Thus, we can
see that a bureaucracy has a set of comprehensive rules that
govern the division of labour in the organization and clearly
fix the duties and jurisdictional areas of each department
and each person within it.

2. There is a *pyramid of authority*. That is, there are various
    levels of authority, with lower offices supervised by higher
    ones. Because there are so many rules and regulations

instructing everyone in the expected practices and outcomes of their offices, an extensive chain of command is necessary to oversee operations. A function of this hierarchy is to make certain that people and departments actually do what they are supposed to do and in the proper manner. Each supervisor has a limited sphere of authority. His or her span of control is confined to particular subordinates, who, in turn, are expected to acknowledge and respond to the authority vested in their immediate supervisor.

3. The management of the organization is based on *written documents.* "Get it in writing" is the key to successful bureaucratic management. These written documents, whether memos, reports, letters, or computer printouts, are all preserved in files for future reference, guidance, or clarification.

4. The written rules and procedures ensure that clients are treated in a *consistent fashion*, without regard to personal considerations. This impersonality of relationships applies not only to clients, but also to other members of the bureaucracy.

5. Because the rules that govern the operation of a bureaucracy are so specific in terms of the duties and responsibilities of each unit and position, there tends to be a relatively *high degree of specialization in tasks.* This high division of labour often means that a prerequisite for people assuming positions in the organization is some degree of specialized training.

"Get it in writing." Reports, memos, and letters are the chief tools of management in the large organization. Written communication ensures clarity, consistency, and objectivity, but makes many managers feel like paper pushers.

SOURCE: H. Armstrong Roberts/Miller Services

6. The presence of extensive operating rules and the impersonal nature of many of the interactions in a bureaucracy are a means of ensuring that people are recruited into the organization and promoted within it on the basis of their performance, competence, knowledge, and ability. Such advancement is based on *achievement criteria*. That is to say, people in a bureaucracy should move ahead because they are best qualified to fill the requirements of the position as outlined in the operating rules and duties of the bureaucracy. Recruitment or advancement involving favouritism or particularism—where the basis is who you know, who you are related to, or other factors unrelated to the demands of the job—are regarded as inconsistent with the underlying principles of bureaucracy.

These six components of bureaucracy are seen to be minimum essentials if the organization is to operate efficiently and endure. Highly bureaucratized organizations are most likely to develop and persist when the nature of the tasks essential to the organization's technology is routine and repetitive. It is also the view of many observers that, as organizations grow and the necessity for control and co-ordination increases, the tendency toward bureaucratization also increases. We shall explore this observation more fully later.

Bureaucracies are more likely to persist when their environments are relatively stable. As we will see, organizations seek to avoid or reduce uncertainty. The formalized rules and authority structures of bureaucracies enable them to operate predictably and consistently. These rules ensure as closely as possible that members will perform in a predictable and consistent fashion.

Department Store Bureaucracy: An Example. We have all experienced the standardizing qualities of bureaucracies. Most people who shop at a department store pay for their purchases with either cash or a credit card. These are the normal procedures; customers who follow them are speedily processed through the cashier's line and on their way.

But if you have ever varied from the norm and used a personal cheque as payment, then you have created a special circumstance. The smooth flow of customers grinds to a halt as you write your cheque (often having to enquire as to the date, the exact amount of the purchases, and other necessary bookkeeping details). Furthermore, accepting a cheque is usually outside of the specified jurisdiction of cashiers. Therefore, this variation from the norm calls into action a series of carefully orchestrated alternative procedures. The cashier rings a bell and waits until the supervisor appears. The supervisor verifies the details of the cheque and asks, "Do you have a valid driver's licence and major charge card?" These documents are carefully scrutinized and appropriate notations made on the cheque. Some stores may have additional procedures such as a further clearance with a central registry, and so on.

In order to avoid bad cheques (and to encourage use of their credit cards), stores and other businesses have highly formalized rules and procedures for dealing with customer payments by cheque. The rules and hierarchy of authority combine to provide a consistent and reliable means of dealing with this variation from the standard expectation. One is given the same treatment throughout the store, regardless of the clerk or the department.

The rules were made in an attempt to anticipate variations from the norm. If there are unanticipated difficulties (such as a person offering a live pig as payment), these are referred up the hierarchy to responsible authorities for a decision. But the more variations an organization regularly experiences, the more difficult it is to anticipate and cover them in the regulations. In other words, in highly changeable and uncertain circumstances, it becomes impossible to incorporate all the exceptions in the rules. If there are too many exceptions, the hierarchy will eventually get clogged with procedural details. We can see, therefore, that a bureaucratic form of organization performs best in situations involving a routine technology in a relatively stable environment.

At about the same time Weber was studying bureaucracy, certain developments were occurring in North America that were to have a profound influence on the study and operation of organizations.

The Organizational Theories

In the 1860s and 1870s, industrialization was well advanced in the United States and slowly beginning to pick up momentum in Canada. With industrialization had come concentrations of workers in plants and factories and the rise of large-scale industrial organizations. A movement in North America was developing that was interested in how organizations might be made more efficient and productive.

An industrial engineer, Frederic Winslow Taylor, believed that the full potential of industrial organization was not being realized because of inefficiency and that the answer to this problem lay in more systematic management. He viewed organizations as large mechanical systems and suspected that much of their inefficiency was a result of a natural tendency of workers to take it easy and not to produce at their peak capacity.

Scientific Management

Taylor's strategy was to make every worker a specialist responsible for a single, narrowly defined task. The key, he argued, was to find the one best way to do each and every task. The means to achieve this state of perfection in productivity was through what he called **scientific management**.

For Taylor, individual workers were simply instruments of production to be employed by management in the same way that the machines of the plant were. The responsibility for finding the one best way of doing a job rests with management.

As the first *time-and-motion* specialists, supporters of scientific management sought to improve organizational productivity through more efficient procedures. To find the one best way of completing a task, they would observe workers who were thought by their supervisors to be the most capable at that job. The work patterns of these superior employees would be analysed and broken down into their basic components, and then rearranged to make them more efficient. The worker was subsequently retrained in the job, doing it in the prescribed best way, and put on an incentive pay scheme to encourage continued use of the desired procedures.

Taylor's method became widely used both because it increased productivity and because workers generally made more money than they had before. His approach was to focus on individual roles in organizations because he believed groups tended to restrict individual productivity.

Scientific management, while successful in many organizations, was not without its critics. The methods were seen to be too employer-oriented; unions felt that greater efficiency would result in fewer jobs. On humanitarian grounds, speeding up work routines was believed to be potentially damaging to health. Highly specialized work was thought to deprive people of meaning in their work. The rapid pace and income geared to exceeding a production minimum put older workers at a considerable disadvantage.

Although Taylor and scientific management advocates were very practically oriented, they tended to have a view of organizations quite similar to Weber's. They saw the organization as an instrument for the co-ordination of human action to achieve specified objectives. All of them saw it as a machine-like instrument, and the objective of scientific management was to fine-tune the efficiency of highly specialized roles by determining the one best way for each.

The Weberian and scientific management conceptions of organizations tended to be rather narrow and limited; they were concerned mainly with an impersonal focus on internal organizational structure and process. But although these perceptions came early in the development of our knowledge about organizations, they continue to have a profound influence over many practitioners today. A broader and more personalized view of organizations began to develop as a result of some chance findings at a large electronics manufacturing plant—the Hawthorne studies.

The Hawthorne Studies

Between 1924 and 1932, a series of important studies was conducted at the Hawthorne Works of the Western Electric Company (Mayo, 1945; Roethlisberger and Dickson, 1947). The original research was undertaken in the scientific management tradition to test the relationship between the quality of the lighting that people worked under and its effects, if any, on their production. The initial results were inconclusive, and the research continued with a total of seven studies exploring a range of physical conditions of work. Of the seven, the Bank Wiring Room Observation Study (Parsons, 1974) is of particular relevance to our considerations.

The work habits of the 14 men in the Bank Wiring Room were observed over time. These three soldermen, nine wiremen, and two inspectors were engaged in complicated wiring and soldering of banks of wires making up telephone exchanges. The men were paid on a piecework basis, which the company intended as an incentive for groups to produce at a maximum pace. The more they produced, the more they would be paid.

The experimenters found that, in this particular group, however, the financial incentives of piecework did not urge workers to ever-increasing levels of production. The group, instead, had informally decided that wiring two exchanges a day was a reasonable output. This constituted for them a "fair day's work," and they produced steadily at that pace with little concern for the piecework incentive.

Not only did the informal work group keep an eye on how much members produced, but they actively sought to bring everyone in line with group norms. If a man worked above the accepted level, he was labelled a "slave" or "speed king"; if he consistently worked below standard, he was known as a "chiseler" because he was making the others in the group carry him. If name-calling didn't work, other group members would give violators a sharp punch on the shoulder in what was called "binging."

These actions were means for workers' groups to control changes in plant routines. It was the workers' belief that, if some of them consistently produced at higher levels, the company would expect that of everyone. Also, they had become comfortable in their relationships with other group members and were convinced that changes in rates of production might put others out of work and lead to the break-up of groups.

Thus, these group norms on productivity in the Bank Wiring Room served to cancel out the effects of the company's piece-work system. The group held its members in check and produced at a steady two units per day. Also, in spite of the rules, soldermen and wiremen rotated their jobs from time to time in order to provide some variety in their tasks and to reduce the boredom of repetition.

These findings were totally unexpected and provided researchers with new and valuable insights into the internal operations of organizations. The Hawthorne Studies turned researchers away from the machine-like view of organizations that Weber and Tayor had held. Instead, researchers discovered that individuals and groups within an organization may act in ways not predicted by formalized rules and structures. This recognition or discovery of informal organization was a significant advance toward a more adequate and balanced understanding of organizations and their operations. The Bank Wiring Room Study demonstrated that there is an important additional dimension to organizational structure—the *social dimension*.

That study and later research (for example, Roy 1952; 1959) kindled an interest in the human side of organizations and served to underscore the point that organizations were not merely structures to produce goods or services. They also contained human beings who were capable of acting and reacting. Human relations in organizations, as a result, became a major preoccupation of organization researchers. The organization became a context in which to view people at work. From this changed perspective, researchers explored such issues as worker alienation, job satisfaction, group cohesiveness, decision-making, and change, to name but a few.

Alienation

In our discussion of the Hawthorne Research, we were introduced to the effects that organizations have on their members. This was an aspect of industrialization and a development of large-scale work organizations that had interested Marx many years earlier. Marx believed that people can find self-fulfillment

Prisons are formal organizations, in which inmates are reluctant participants. Prisons must use extreme authoritarian techniques to achieve their goal—to rehabilitate lawbreakers and return them to society.

SOURCE: H. Armstrong Roberts/Miller Services

only through productive, or creative, labour. Work is a central feature of people's identities and allows them to develop to their fullest potential. As the industrialization process occurs and a capitalist system develops, however, people begin to lose control of their destinies, because they no longer possess the major means of production. Instead, they work in organizations on someone else's machines. The nature of their work is "not voluntary but imposed, *forced* labour. It is not the satisfaction of a need but only a means for satisfying other needs" (quoted in Bottomore and Rubel, 1956). The result is **alienation**, feelings of powerlessness, meaninglessness, and social isolation.

Robert Blauner (1964) was also interested in the impact that technology has on workers—how what a person does in his or her work (the technology) affects that person. In the early 1960s he looked at workers in a number of industries in an attempt to answer the following question: Under what conditions are the alienation tendencies of work organizations the strongest, and under what conditions are they the weakest or least noticeable?

Blauner turned to differences in technology to see if these might explain differences in alienation levels. As a preliminary step, he identified four basic technologies in the industries he studied:

1. assembly-line technology;
2. machine-tending technology;
3. continuous-process technology;
4. craft technology.

The work processes on an *assembly line* are highly particularized, so that each worker has a very small number of routine, specialized tasks to complete. Workers generally have a fixed work station, and the pace of the line determines the speed people work at. The automobile assembly line was Blauner's example of this technology.

In *machine-tending technologies*, work processes are highly routine and workers' tasks consist of watching or tending to the needs of machines. Textile manufacturing is an example of this type of technology. In the production of textiles, large machines spin the fibers, or automated looms weave materials. The worker's role is paced by the machines; when they run out of materials, the worker replaces the spools of fiber, and so on. Simple tasks are completed according to the needs of the machines.

Continuous process is a very advanced form of technology in which a raw material such as petroleum enters one end of the operation and undergoes a number of automated changes. Finished products are derived at various stages along the way. Oil refining and chemical production are examples of this technology. The complexity of the technology requires that workers be highly knowledgeable about its processes, so that operations may be monitored and spur-of-the-moment decisions made when necessary to ensure continuous operation.

Craft technology is characterized by a considerable amount of handwork. It also tends to be relatively unstandardized, because it is difficult to establish routines in a technology in which the products vary considerably. In Blauner's sample, craft technology was represented by printers. Because of the skill involved, printers have judgmental flexibility in the organization and execution of their work.

Blauner arranged these technologies according to the level of control, meaning, and self-expression they allowed the worker. Assembly-line work provides very few of these features, while machine tending contains slightly more of each. Continuous-process technology, he found, provided workers with greater control, responsibility, and meaning in their work than did the previous two. The highest levels of control, meaning, and self-expression were found in craft technology.

Blauner found that feelings of alienation were highest for assembly-line workers and diminished as technologies allowed more control, meaning, and self-expression. For his sample, therefore, alienation was lowest among printers. Blauner's findings are summarized in Table 9-1; similar results were found by Fullan (1970) in a Canadian study.

Whenever individuals, groups, or organizations interrelate, there is, of course, the potential for conflict. Within organizations, labour and management may have differing objectives or views that lead to conflict; the organization may find itself in conflict from time to time with elements in its environment. Research on alienation also serves to remind us that factors within the organization—even its own technology—may stimulate conflict.

Technology remains a major factor for researchers of organizations who examine the conditions that foster the development of alienation. Alienation is likely to be lowest in organizational settings in which members have control, meaning, and opportunities for self-fulfillment in their roles. Many researchers are now exploring the extent to which computers, robots, and related technological innovations generate alienation in the people who work with them.

Group Dynamics

Many researchers have attempted to explore the dynamics of groups in the social structure of organizations and the impact these groups have both on individuals and on the successful attainment of organization goals.

TABLE 9-1. *Blauner's Findings on the Relationship between Technology and Alienation*

Industry	Technology	Control over Work	Meaning in Work	Self-Expression	Alienation
Printing	Craft	Very high	Very high	Very high	Very low
Oil refining	Continuous process	High	High	High	Low
Textiles	Machine tending	Low	Low	Low	High
Automobile assembly	Assembly line	Very low	Very low	Very low	Very high

SOURCE: *Alienation and Freedom* by Robert Blauner, 1964, Chicago: University of Chicago Press.

The Team Concept

Research has shown that highly cohesive work groups frequently result in happier workers and in performance improvements for the organization. One application of this concept is in the form of self-regulating work groups.

For most energy production companies, the design of work has evolved out of requirements of the technology. The typical site design develops out of a business plan that combines, in turn, a production plan and an engineering plan. The distribution of work, in terms of jobs and organizations, is based on principles of engineering design and economies of scale.

Planning for the human operations of new facilities has normally been regarded as a management task. Midway through the engineering design effort, a management representative is asked to develop a plan describing required personnel levels, skill requirements for the operation, work systems, and organization. Shortly before the plant is ready for start-up, the work force is brought on board and oriented.

In the Everdell plant, management took a different approach to operational planning. As before, a manager prepared a preliminary operations plan and reviewed the plan with his management. However, over a nine-month period prior to start-up, this plan was further developed and modified by plant management and a joint team of operators destined to work in the new plant. This design team used the original plan to create a design for the organization of plant work. Rather than build from pre-established personnel levels and skill requirements, their plans aimed at maximizing the quality of work life.

The managers responsible for Everdell decided to fashion the work design around a team concept that emphasized the development of a co-operative, multi-skilled work force. In contrast to the increasing specialization of work found in most plants, operators and maintenance personnel would be expected to work as a single team, carrying responsibility on a shift basis for the whole facility.

Most of the energy behind the team concept came from the manager responsible for a number of production facilities in central Alberta. His image of an effective operation was rooted in his early experiences where conditions and less sophisticated technology had forced co-operation among workers and their learning a variety of skills. This experience led him to believe that a multi-skilled work force would enhance both productivity and employee satisfaction. He pointed out: "We've had some weak spots over the past years. When I ask myself why, the answer is always that we haven't developed the people enough."

Operations management had a number of particular expectations for Everdell. One was that the multi-skilled team would reduce the need for slack resources, particularly in maintenance. Small plants like Everdell have a limited number of mechanical and instrumentation maintenance staff on site. This required that the operating group have the skills to provide effective back-up.

Management also hoped that the team concept would improve the quality of operator decision making.

A third, and related, expectation was that the team concept would reduce traditional conflicts among field and plant operators and between operators and maintenance staff. Lack of co-operation within and among these groups was frequent in larger production plants; in a small plant, it could be disastrous. By cross-training, and by giving a single shift group full responsibility for both plant and field, it was hoped that the negative effects of territoriality could be reduced.

Finally, staff retention was a concern. Plant effectiveness depended on a skilled and experienced work force. Management believed that the increasingly well-educated and mobile work force in Alberta would find traditional operations jobs boring and routine. Compensation limits placed on these jobs would also add to the likelihood of staff turnover. Increasing job variety and employee potential for advancement was seen as a means of offsetting these.

To the group operations manager, trying the team concept was worth the relatively low risk: "The plant is going to run either way. It's a new project and, if it doesn't work, it can always default to the traditional organization."

Management was clear that Everdell's success depended on a willingness of both plant management and workers to make it work. This meant assembling a work force that would be open to a philosophy of increased responsibility and getting plant management to commit themselves to open the decision-making process.

Hiring began with the plant foreman and crew leader. Both were selected on the basis of competence and support for the team concept. They believed that individual operators were under-utilized in traditional work designs, and they saw Everdell as an opportunity to practice a more participative management philosophy. As the crew leader observed:

I've lived under supervisors who didn't tell you anything. They didn't have a clue what was happening so anything you did was wrong. I've lived under supervisors who told you how to do everything and that was the only way you did it. I've lived under supervisors who had everything bolted down shut and, even if you wanted to do something, you couldn't because you couldn't get to the tools.

I figure that if a person is hired and he is given the job then he should be responsible and trusted enough to do the job. There shouldn't be any doors with locks. If you give people jobs to do and let them use their own initiative, many times they will come up with better ways of doing it, ways you never even thought of.

Management also pushed for the early selection of operations and maintenance staff, for planning and training purposes. Field training of plant operators was essential in order to begin functioning without the traditional barriers of separate plant and field operations. Most of the Everdell employees were recruited from other production facilities in Esso Resources, and all were aware they would transfer to Everdell on a full-time basis before start-up. During the months of Everdell design following their selection, these employees were seconded on training assignments and were brought in regularly to assist in the design effort.

SOURCE: "Designing Everdell" by B. Dresner and J.C. Younger, *Quality of Working Life: Contemporary Cases* (pp. 77-105), ed. J.B. Cunningham and T.H. White, Ottawa: Labour Canada, 1984.

People in organizations find themselves in a variety of circumstances. Some people, for instance, work alone, while others work in groups of varying sizes. People working in groups may be dependent on one another to complete a joint task, or they may do their jobs independently but in close proximity to one another. We have already seen (in the Bank Wiring Room example) how groups may act to influence the production standards or levels of their members. But, of course, all groups do not influence their members to the same extent. In attempting to account for these differences, the concept of **cohesiveness**—sticking together—has proven useful.

Groups differ according to how much individuals perceive themselves as members, how much interest they have in belonging to the group, and how highly they regard the other members of the group. When individuals identify themselves as members of the group, when group members want the group to remain together, and when group members have a high regard for each other, there will be a group with high cohesiveness.

Groups vary in the degree to which these characteristics are present, and researchers have investigated what difference, if any, this variation makes. In other words, what variations in behaviour and attitudes normally may be expected when a person belongs to a highly cohesive group as opposed to a low-cohesive group?

Seashore, a social psychologist, looked at this matter in an important study of 228 work groups of various sizes in a machinery factory. His hypothesis was that group cohesiveness depended on how much pressure the group put on the individual to remain a member. Seashore's (1954) major findings were:

1. Members of highly cohesive groups exhibit less anxiety than members of less cohesive groups.
2. Highly cohesive groups have less variation in productivity among members than do less cohesive groups. Highly cohesive groups, such as the Bank Wiring Room, establish and enforce a group standard that is usually missing in less cohesive groups.
3. Highly cohesive groups will differ more frequently and significantly from the plant norm of productivity than less cohesive groups. Highly cohesive groups will tend to have productivity levels either noticeably above or noticeably below the plant norm.
4. Whether the productivity of highly cohesive groups is above or below the plant norm depends on whether the group perceives the plant atmosphere as being supportive or not. Highly cohesive group members who feel secure in their setting are more likely to have productivity above the plant norm than highly cohesive groups who do not.
5. Similarities in members' ages and educational levels are not related to the degree of cohesiveness in a group. Instead, group cohesiveness is positively related to opportunities for interaction by members, and this is most likely to occur in smaller groups of relatively stable composition.

Cohesiveness, alienation, and alienation's positive counterpart, job satisfaction, are examples of the types of research interests that have been pursued since the Hawthorne Studies. The organization is a setting in which to view and seek improved understandings of human behaviour and the social system. One final example that we will consider relates to opportunities for organization members at the lower levels to be involved in decision making.

Decision Making in Organizations

Decision making is a central component in the operation of organizations. In almost every instance of an organization's activity
there are problems to be solved and decisions of the moment to
be made. As we have seen earlier, organizations are structured
with an authority hierarchy that is usually charged with assuming the dominant role in decision making. As a matter of fact, in
many orgainizations this decision-making role becomes a jealously guarded exclusive right of management. As you will see,
decision making figured importantly in the Relay Assembly Test
Room Experiment that follows.

The Relay Assembly Test Room Experiment took place at the
Hawthorne Works of the Western Electric Company from 1927
to 1932. It involved the study of a small group of women making
relay assemblies for telephones. In the tradition of scientific
management and industrial psychology, the researchers were
interested to see if changes in conditions affecting worker
fatigue would result in increased productivity and morale. The
assembly of a telephone relay was completed by a single worker
and required about a minute's time. As a result of the large number of relays produced by a worker each day, it was relatively
easy to observe the effects on productivity of any changes
introduced.

The normal work-week before the start of the experiment consisted of 48 hours and included Saturday mornings. The only
break provided during the day was a brief lunch period. The
changes introduced in the Relay Assembly Test Room Experiment centred largely on rest pauses and the length of the work-
day and work-week. One of the first changes introduced was the
introduction of two five-minute rest breaks during the day; after
five weeks, this was changed to two ten-minute rest breaks; then
after four weeks, six five-minute breaks, and so on. As these
minor changes were introduced, effects on behaviour and attitudes of the women were noted.

During the majority of the changes, the workers' attitudes and
morale remained good, their productivity increased, and their
absenteeism decreased (Parsons, 1974). Most observers tended to
attribute these positive outcomes to the cohesiveness of the work
group. (Before the experiment, the women had been members of
a large department of 100 members.)

But much later, analysts (for example, Blumberg 1968) re-
examined the data of these experiments and argued that,
although the cohesive nature of the work group was an important factor, equally important was the fact that the women in the
experiment had a genuine opportunity to participate in decisions about matters that affected them, an opportunity that they

had not had before in their work. Kahn (1975) put it most suc-cinctly: "Real participation has real effects. When people take a significant and influential part in decisions that they value, the quality of decisions is likely to be improved and their implemen-tation is almost certain to be improved."

Since the Hawthorne Studies, the organization has been the setting in which human behaviour has been examined and the dimensions of the social system explored. In some instances, such as the studies on technology and alienation, the link between the social and the technological systems has been con-sidered. But in general, people, either as individuals or in groups within organizations, have been the main units of analysis. This was clearly the case in the references to group cohesiveness and participatory decision making.

Japanese and Swedish companies have experimented with organizational structures and have derived benefits from cohe-sive and co-operative groups. There have been efforts by Cana-dian hospitals, utilities, and government departments to adapt these techniques. Such programs are known in North America as "Quality of Working Life" (QWL) projects.

Organizations as Open Systems and Task Environments

Most of the materials we have reviewed so far have tended to reflect a very simple view of organizations as **closed systems**. According to this concept, organizations are relatively self-con-tained units in which particular structural arrangements and individual behaviour patterns may be accounted for by factors internal to the organization. Weber, as we saw, viewed organiza-tions or bureaucracies as mechanisms for control of participants, and his overriding interest was with internal mechanisms and operations of bureaucracies. Similarly, the human relations stud-ies we considered were interested in organizations only insofar as they provided a context for assessing attitudes and viewing group and individual behaviour.

But there has been a gradual tendency to regard this closed-system view of organizations as too narrow, because organiza-tions are also part of a larger social system (Barnard, 1938; Selz-nick, 1949; Clark, 1956; Parsons, 1960). Organizations do not operate in a vacuum; they are located in an environment. That is, they are affected by governments and their legislation, by cus-tomers and suppliers, by competitors, and by numerous other external bodies and groups. An organization may attempt to insulate its internal operations, but an organization's environ-ment will ultimately affect even these. Figure 9-1 depicts, in sim-plified form, an organization as an **open system**, in which the organization depends for its viability in part on external inputs and outputs.

FIGURE 9-1. Organizations as Open Systems

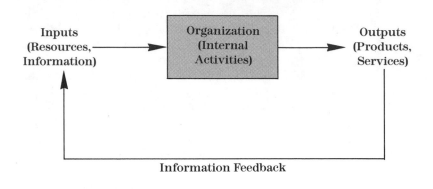

A fish-processing plant, for instance, obtains raw fish from fishers, packaging materials or fuel and so on from suppliers, and its workers from the community. These are inputs from the outside that are necessary for the organization's operation. The organization's internal procedures combine these resources so that the fish are cleaned, filleted, and packaged; they are transformed into a finished consumer package. But, once again, without sales of the products to outside customers, the organization is unlikely to survive. Information about the success of their products or the availability of various input resources, for instance, provides feedback for the organization that is important in determining its future moves.

Task Environment

When we regard an organization as an open system, we take a more realistic but more complex view of it; in order to comprehend its operations, we not only need to understand its internal workings, but we also need to identify those elements in its environment that significantly influence it. We must determine not only how an organization *reacts* to its environment, but also how it *acts* to influence and control its environment.

Furthermore, if we become concerned with an organization's environment, we are confronted with the problem of exactly defining the boundaries of that environment. Is an organization's environment everything external to it? Technically this is the case, but practically speaking there will be elements in the environment that are more important to one organization than to others. A children's daycare centre will be affected by different factors than will a senior citizen's centre. Dill (1958) has suggested that, in analysing organizational environments, it is useful to think of a **task environment**, or those elements in an organization's environment that "are relevant or potentially relevant to goal setting and goal attainment."

Figure 9-2 depicts a typical organization's task environment. In Canadian society, organizations are influenced by a wide range of government legislation, whether at the federal, provincial, or municipal level. Among other things, legislation governs hours of work, pollution and noise limits, safety, union activity, health standards for products or services, taxation, competition practices, exports, imports, and building codes.

In most task environments, suppliers and customers are equally important, and related to these are an organization's competitors. But to determine the components of a task environment accurately, we should also consider four significant subareas:

1. the political;
2. the physical;
3. the economic;
4. the sociocultural.

Political Environment.   The political component of a task environment, through government legislation and regulation, affects in some way or other virtually all of an organization's

FIGURE 9-2. Some Elements in a Typical Task Environment

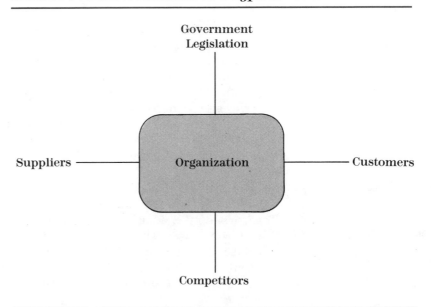

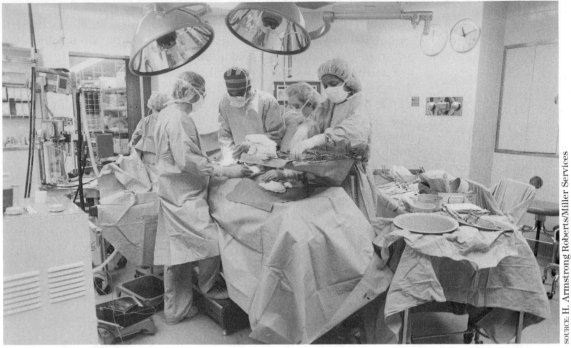

Hospitals are an example of formal organizations in which the responsibilities of each type of employee are specified by regulations, legislations, and collective agreements. The roles in an operating room—who can perform surgery, who can administer anasthetic, who can assist the surgeon, even who must clean up and how—are all governed by formal procedural rules.

activities. Organizations, of course, may and usually do try to influence developments or changes in government legislation by lobbying. **Lobbying** consists of activities by various interest groups wishing to state their cases to politicians in the hope of influencing the course of legislation.

Physical Environment. The physical component of an organization's task environment is often a major consideration. For example, the weather in Canada is frequently a factor in organizational planning. It may affect the location of organizations; fruit and vegetable growers, for example, will establish themselves where there are warm summers, water, and moderate winters. The most visible and negative feature of the interrelationship between organizations and their physical environments is pollution.

Economic Environment. The current economic environment and its impact on organizations underscores its importance. Not surprisingly, managers have generally been ill-equipped to deal with the consequences of a prolonged economic downturn. This is because their outlook was based on theory and research put together during the economic boom years after World War II, when it was assumed that continuous growth would go on forever.

Sociocultural Environment.   The sociocultural features of an organization's task environment are increasingly important. The significance for organizations in Québec of issues relating to language, for instance, is a matter of historical record. The relationship between organizations and their host communities is significant as well (Lucas 1971, Perry 1971), particularly in the large number of Canadian communities that are dominated by a single industry or company.

Figure 9-3 depicts some of the important elements in the task environments of organizations, in these four subareas. The examples given are by no means complete, and their relevance for any specific organization will vary. Also, it is important to realize that, although we have dealt with each of the four task environments separately, what happens in one area may have consequences in another.

If, for instance, public opinion (sociocultural) becomes persuasive about a particular state of pollution (physical), then politicians (political) may be moved to provide pressure or legislation or even funds to force or encourage organizations to take desired action on the matter.

FIGURE 9-3. The Task Environment

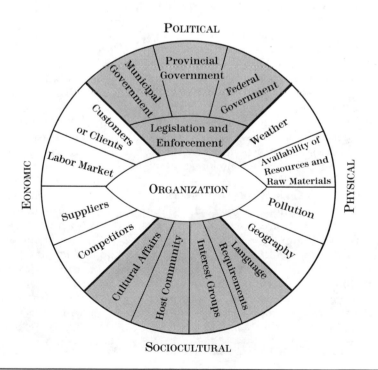

Private Nursing Homes

Nursing homes are one way to provide care to the dependent elderly. If they are run for profit, there is a potential conflict between the goals of making a profit and those of providing good service. The following report deals with this specific issue. The publication of such articles adds a new sociocultural dimension, the mobilization of public opinion behind a demand for government legislation to solve the conflict in goals.

TORONTO (CP)—A crackdown on nursing homes is urgently needed in light of widespread horror stories about the mistreatment of the elderly, a report commissioned by the Canadian Medical Association said.

"The standard of care provided in many nursing homes is grossly inadequate," said the report released last week.

"They provide a life of immobility and tedium and lack any guarantee of adequate basic care."

In the short term, strict standards must be imposed and enforced, the report said.

In the long run, governments should eliminate all nursing homes run privately for profit and establish a system of publicly financed and operated institutions.

"Permitting nursing homes to be run for profit under a lenient system of legislation and an impotent system of inspection is a measure of societal negligence we can no longer allow to continue," the study said.

Joan Watson, chairman of the five-person group which held public hearings across the country, said there were many poignant presentations which highlighted shortcomings in the nursing home field.

A brief by the Concerned Friends of Ontario Citizens in Care Facilities Inc. said some institutions are cockroach-infested, don't provide nutritious meals or enough baths, monitor mail and phone conversations and keep the doors locked.

Some nursing homes are "sterile, friendless and lacking in humanness and warmth, where old people sit and rock, stare at the walls for most of the day, or are led around by the hand like small children by inadequately enlightened staff who refer to them as 'dear,'" said the brief, which is quoted at length in the study group's report.

Other briefs stressed the lack of properly trained staff in some nursing homes.

"If Canadian society were judged by the way it treats its elderly, it would be found wanting," Watson, former host of the CBC-TV consumer affairs show *Marketplace*, told a news conference.

The nursing home system in Ontario, for example, is "disgusting," she said. "It is just not in any way a credit to the Ontario government."

She said the level of care varied from province to province and Ontario was not necessarily the worst but was the one with which the study group had the most experience.

The group emphasized the need to get elderly people out of institutions, especially in light of projections that Canada's aging population is going to cause gargantuan increases in health-care costs.

Perhaps 13 percent of the population will be 65 or older by the turn of the century, a figure that could rise to 18.2 percent—almost double the 1981 rate of 9.7 percent—by the year 2021, the study said.

"If we continue to put old people in institutions at the rate we do now, the costs will not only be prohibitive, we will perpetuate the callous practice of warehousing the elderly."

The study said changes in the makeup of the population alone could increase health care expenditures within the next 40 years by about 75 percent to more than $32 billion.

Thousands more hospital and long-term care beds will be needed unless lower-cost alternatives involving home and community care are developed.

Among the support services which the study group said should be more readily available to allow the elderly to stay at home or live with relatives are: public health nurses, meals on wheels, companions, homemakers, handyman programs, drop-in centres and hospitals where consumers can get medical care without being admitted overnight.

While there will always be some people who will have to stay in institutions, the study said, there should be enough flexibility in the system to let them move from one level of care to another.

Nursing homes, for example, provide higher levels of nursing care than homes for the aged. It said assessment services should be set up to evaluate residents' needs and make sure they are being met.

The group said New Brunswick has had great success with an experimental "extra-mural" hospital, a mobile unit which goes to patients' homes to provide health care in their bedrooms.

This way, hospital admissions are shortened or avoided, the terminally ill can be treated at home and admissions to nursing homes can be postponed.

SOURCE: "Outlaw Private Personal Care Homes, Study Group Urges" by Jane Armstrong, August 20, 1984, *Brandon Sun*, p. 14. Copyright 1984 by the Canadian Press. Reprinted by permission.

Corporations

Canadian federal and provincial governments have large volumes of legislation that relate to organizations within their jurisdictions. This legislation may regulate labour practices, pollution controls, product standards, and a host of other organizational subjects. There is, in addition, a segment of these statutes that is particularly relevant to organizations as such—the statutes concerned with corporations. The corporation is the dominant business mode in Canada. Corporations, of course, are very complex structures. The simplest way to conduct business, after all, is as a **sole proprietor**. A person purchases the necessary local business operating permits and sets up shop. A little video rental shop or small word-processing service will likely be sole proprietorships. These owners use their own resources to establish and develop their businesses. They reap the profits of their efforts but, if they get into financial difficulty, legally they are in a position of *unlimited liability*. This means that not only may the assets of the business have to be sold to satisfy creditors, but "the owner's personal assets such as house, furniture, car, and stocks, may be seized, if necessary, to pay the outstanding debts of his business. Thus a person's life savings could be wiped out by a business failure" (Amirault and Archer, 1976).

Slightly more complex than the sole proprietorship is the **partnership**. The partnership operates in much the same way as a sole proprietorship, but there are additional people and sources of money to base the venture on. Unlimited liability is generally also a feature of partnerships, and one has to be very careful about selecting partners because all are responsible for partnership debts. If, for instance, one partner cannot meet his or her fair share of the debts, the other partners must assume it. The sole proprietorship and partnership are easy and convenient to start, but unlimited liability is a risk that could be very costly for participants.

A **corporation**, on the other hand, is a complex legal entity. The founders incorporate their joint venture with a provincial or the federal government. Operating capital is provided by the sale of shares, and the affairs of the corporation and the rights of shareholders are overseen by a board of directors. The major advantage of the corporation is that it gives the shareholders *limited liability*; that is, they stand to lose only to the extent of their investment in the corporation. Other personal effects are not liable to claims by creditors. There are other advantages for the corporation, such as separation of ownership and management, possibly lower income taxes, and enduring existence (Amirault and Archer, 1976; Smyth and Soberman, 1976).

These advantages have made the corporation the most common organizational form in developed societies; most business organizations in Canada are corporations. Two questions that have been of considerable interest to organization researchers in Canada concern the sources of power and control in Canadian corporations and the patterns of existence for these corporations.

In *The Vertical Mosaic*, Porter (1965) examines power in various sectors of Canadian society. Of particular interest to us is his study of what he refers to as "economic power"—that is, who controls big business. Porter was concerned with how the large corporations were administered and how they formed links with other corporations. Because many of Canada's biggest corporations are largely- or wholly-owned subsidiaries of large American or British corporations, the power probably rests with the board of directors of the parent companies.

In Chapter 7, you learned that economic authority in Canada is concentrated in relatively few hands. That information comes from Porter, who discovered that, among the largest corporations, there is a frequent tendency for a director of one corporation to sit on the boards of others. This tendency creates an interlock between these boards and their corporations. There are striking patterns of interlocking directorships, and key individuals in these networks hold large numbers of such posts. This is particularly true of bank directors.

The central figures identified in this interlocking network form Porter's economic elite. In assessing their backgrounds, he found that in many respects they are a very homogeneous group. They attended similar private schools and universities ; they intermarry; they belong to similar clubs, organizations, and churches; they maintain close ties in their social and political activities.

Clement (1975) provides a more up-to-date analysis and finds similar trends, although the economic elite that he identifies tends to be even more exclusive than previously and shows little evidence of penetration by people of lower social origins. Even more recently, Clement (1977) has extended his view of the corporate elite because "it is no longer possible to provide an adequate understanding of the power structure of Canadian corporations without expanding the horizons of study outside Canada into the United States and, to a limited extent, beyond."

The studies of Porter and Clement provide valuable data and insights for readers on the nature of power in large corporations and the extent to which it is controlled by a relatively small elite group.

White (1978) examined a range of variously sized corporations with different patterns of ownership—Canadian versus foreign, private versus public—to determine how control operates within them. He found that the size of the corporation was not as important as ownership in explaining the activity of corporate boards of directors. For example, boards of independent or parent corporations were more active in control than those of subsidiaries. This is not to suggest that subsidiary corporations are not closely monitored, but that the mechanisms are somewhat different.

A second important factor was the composition of the board. If the board was made up of some directors who were outsiders, rather than employees of the corporation, the board was found to be more active than if it consisted solely of inside directors.

Corporations and foreign ownership remain dominant factors in Canadian life, and organization researchers have only begun systematically to explore their impacts.

Summary

1. The need for organization is consistent with the social nature of humans. Basic divisions of labour result in increasing interdependencies, and, in order to maintain some degree of social order, preliminary forms of organization come into being.

2. The establishment of an organization centres on goal attainment. Its establishment may be spontaneous, left to chance or circumstance, or maintained in a more formalized manner.

3. Early theorists and researchers regarded organizations as closed systems and were mainly concerned with their formal structures and processes. Their primary focus tended to be

on the technical system. Only with the accidental discoveries of the Hawthorne Studies did a more balanced view include the social system as well.

4. According to the scientific management perspective on organizations, individual workers are regarded as instruments of production to be employed by management in the same way as machines. Efficiency is achieved by finding the one best way to do each and every task.

5. Technological or organizational arrangements that fail to give people reasonable control over important aspects of their work and that deprive them of social contacts and meaning in their tasks are likely to result in worker alienation.

6. Every organization interacts with other organizations. Those elements outside the organization that affect its operations or directions make up an organization's environment.

7. Corporations are legal creations that allow people to establish organizations while minimizing their personal liabilities. Most organizations in business and industry are corporations.

Further Reading

Carroll, W. K. (1986). *Corporate power and Canadian capitalism*. Vancouver: University of British Columbia Press.
Builds on the work of Porter and Clement in examining Canadian corporate power and foreign control.

Cunningham, J. B., & White, T. H. (Eds.) (1984). *Quality of working life: Contemporary cases*. Ottawa: Labour Canada.
Looks at some Canadian attempts to change organizations and improve the nature of their working conditions.

Kiesler, Sara B. (1978). *Interpersonal processes in groups and organizations*; MacKenzie, K. D. (1978). *Organizational structures*; Pfeffer, Jeffrey (1978). *Organizational design*; Tuggle, Francis D. *Organizational processes*. Arlington Heights, IL: AHM Publishing.
A series of books that examines contemporary directions in the study of organizations.

Kotter, John P. (1978). *Power and influence*. New York: The Free Press.
A very interesting account of power and influence in organizations.

Ouchi, William (1981). *Theory Z: How American business can meet the Japanese challenge*. Reading, MA: Addison Wesley.
A description of the adaptations Japanese organizations have made of conventional organizational designs for their particular needs and culture.

Peters, Thomas J., & Robert H. Waterman, Jr. (1982). *In search of excellence*. New York: Harper & Row.

An examination of the internal structure and processes of those corporations most successful in adapting to today's environmental uncertainties.

Scott, W. Richard (1987). *Organizations: Rational, natural, and open systems*. (2nd ed.). Englewood Cliffs, NJ: Prentice-Hall.

An excellent overview of major issues and directions in organization research and theory.

IV Social Institutions

Institutions are a central part of social structure. They are developed to solve recurring problems that all societies face.

Family and religion are the social institutions considered in this section of the book. The emphasis here is on Canada, but each chapter also deals with these institutions as they appear in other societies and discusses how the various sociological perspectives have been used to analyse them.

Marriage and the family are the concerns of Chapter 10. This chapter discusses the ways we are socialized into family roles, ethnic differences among Canadian families, getting married, staying married, divorce, and family violence.

Every society defines which religious beliefs are proper, the correct way to honour god(s), and the acceptable procedures involved in becoming a priest or minister. Chapter 11 defines what religion is and why it is important to the individual and society. It also explores the questions of how we explain the universality of and the differences in religion, and what the future of religion is in Canada.

10
Family

The family is a very persistent institution; it appears to have been around as long as human beings have. The purpose of this chapter is to explore the functions of the family, the consequences of being in a family, and the possible future of the family. After studying this chapter, you should be able to

1. define what a family is and list its functions;

2. briefly describe the differing interests of the three perspectives in the area of family studies;

3. explain and give examples of homogamy in mate selection;

4. describe the styles of marital adjustment identified by Cuber and Harroff;

5. list the factors associated with the rising divorce rate;

6. state what changes are likely to occur to the family in the future.

Just as religious and political systems are changing in Canada, so the Canadian family is changing. The typical family no longer consists of a mother, father, and three children, all of whom are happy and well adjusted. Even in the past, of course, most families were not like this. Some families were large, others small. In some families, members supported one another; in others, they did not.

William Stephens has studied the family in many cultures. He defines the family as a social arrangement based on marriage and the marriage contract, including recognition of the rights and duties of parenthood, common residence for husband, wife, and children, and shared economic obligations between husband and wife (Stephens, 1963, p. 8).

Margrit Eichler of the University of Toronto takes issue with this definition, pointing out some serious omissions (Eichler, 1983, p. 3). The definition excludes common-law couples, single-parent families, and families in which children from a previous marriage live in the household. Eichler shows that changes have occurred in the Canadian family and that we need to recognize these changes. It may be that most families have two adults, one of each sex, who have had a ritual marriage ceremony, and who have children, but there are many exceptions to this rather simplistic definition. And we should remember that there were exceptions in Canada through the eighteenth and nineteenth centuries as well.

Although we find William Stephens' definition of family inadequate, his definition of marriage seems acceptable. He states that marriage is an institutionalized mating arrangement between human males and females (Stephens, 1963, pp. 8-10). In most cases there is a public ceremony, some economic co-operation between the partners, and an expectancy of permanence.

Theories of the Family

The family tends to be a conservative institution, resistant to sudden or radical changes in social structure. It should not be surprising, then, to find that structural functionalists have long been interested in the family as an institution, while conflict theorists and symbolic interactionists have been much less concerned with family issues.

Structural Functionalism

Functions of the Family.   The social institution of the family serves several vital functions in society, according to structural functionalists. First, it serves a reproductive function. In order for a society to continue, it must replace those members who die. The family is the accepted and legitimate means for society to replace and increase its membership.

Second, the family serves a socialization function. In Chapter 3, you read how important parents are in teaching young family members how they are expected to act and what they can expect of others. Young family members also receive status through the family. Children receive an identification of race, ethnicity, social class, and religious association through their **family of orientation** (the family they were *born into*). The **family of procreation**, on the other hand, is the family people *create* when they marry and have children.

Third, the family has an economic function in our society. In most cases, parents take the responsibility of providing food and shelter for their children and adolescents. In most countries, law demands this of parents.

Fourth, structural functionalists view the family as a place of physical protection and emotional security. When physical or emotional assaults touch its members, the family provides a refuge. Family members generally develop affectional ties with one another that last long after they are separated geographically. The family is the place where individuals practise interpersonal skills, skills that are particularly crucial in modern society.

As you can see, structural functionalists look at how the family functions in relation to the larger society; this is called analysis on the macro level. Seen from this level, the family plays a vital part, just as other institutions, such as the economy or education, do. Each institution is viewed as essential for maintaining the social structure. When an institution fails in its function, another institution moves in, adaptations are made, and the social system is maintained.

When thousands of people moved from the rural areas to the cities in the 1930s and 1940s, the social structure required considerable readjustment and adaptation. Young single and married people were now living and working away from their families of orientation. Gradually, the government took over some responsibility for temporary housing, new employment, and even financial aid—functions that in the past had been dealt with by the family.

Family Roles.   Structural functionalism views society as a dynamic organism with many parts depending on one another—one of these being the family. The family is also an independent unit, again with interdependence among its parts, or members. This level of analysis—the micro level—recognizes that each family member is expected to fulfil a role: one or more members provide the money for food and housing; one or more prepare the meals; someone drives the younger members to the doctor or to soccer practice; someone washes the car. Each member performs a recognized and approved role, and the family structure is maintained. There is order and some degree of predictability, which gives stability.

Such a system is not static; it is dynamic. The family system accepts change, even on the micro level. For example, when one member becomes ill, others temporarily fulfil his or her role.

One of the strongest supporters of structural functionalism was the Harvard professor Talcott Parsons. In developing his theory, he indicated that wives fulfil an **expressive** role and husbands fulfil an **instrumental** role in the family. The expressive role involves behaviour that is social and emotional in quality. The instrumental role involves work and other physical activities. Professor Parsons' analysis of adult gender roles in the family may have had some general application in the traditional family, but today many critics of Parsons' gender labelling feel that women and men should not be restricted to either expressive or instrumental roles.

Letha and John Scanzoni (1981) described two traditional marriage patterns. The first was the owner-property marriage, in which a married woman was property belonging to her husband. He owned her. She was considered a minor, so that whatever property she might have had before her marriage passed to her husband. At the same time, she played an important function in the economic and social system.

The second traditional pattern was the head-complement marriage, in which the husband was the head of the family and the wife was his complement. He was to show emotional support for her and to be the major breadwinner. She was to please him and care for the needs of the household. In this pattern, the wife had somewhat more authority than in the owner-property marriage pattern.

The Scanzonis state that from these two traditional marriage patterns, two other patterns have evolved or are evolving. In the first, the senior-junior partner marriage, the husband is senior and has more bargaining leverage. The wife in this pattern is employed outside the home, a condition that provides her with some power in marriage matters. But her status is junior—his career is the primary career, while hers is more fluid, allowing her to move in and out of the work force as needs arise in the family cycle. Most Canadian families now have a senior-junior partner marriage pattern.

The second pattern, the equal-partner pattern, is still emerging. In this pattern, each partner is equally committed to a

The head-complement marriage placed the husband at the head of the family and gave him the role of breadwinner. This traditional standard of the 1950s is evolving now into other patterns in which wives are also employed outside the home.

SOURCE: H. Armstrong Roberts/Miller Services

career. The partners practise role interchangeability with respect to the breadwinner and domestic roles. They share roles. They have equal power. Their individual operations are unhindered by gender-role stereotypes.

Nuclear and Extended Families.   Literature on the family refers frequently to the *nuclear* family and the *extended* family. In the past, the **nuclear family** referred to a married man and woman and their offspring. The offspring may be biological, adopted, or children from a previous marriage. The definition excludes single-parent families and families in which the adults are not legally married.

An **extended family** consists of a nuclear family connected or associated with a relative of one or more of its members. Generally, the extended family consists of a young couple and their children who live with their parents until they can establish a home of their own, or an aged parent who is cared for by his or her children. Such families used to be common in Canada and are still the rule in many societies. Where adult family members are not geographically separated, regular family gatherings still occur, although with fewer members (because of smaller family size) and with less frequency than they once did. These gatherings are common among many groups, such as the Mennonites, the Italian-Canadians, and the residents of rural Québec.

The function of the extended family is by no means over. Eugene Litwak (1968) has shown that a better term for our times would be the *modified* extended family, because members of the nuclear family are now more selective in terms of the extended family members they get together with and why. The extended family now functions mainly as a source of baby-sitting help or as a temporary place of residence. In times of crisis, extended family members give emotional support or economic aid.

Symbolic Interactionism

Unlike the structural functionalist, the symbolic interactionist concentrates on interaction among individuals rather than on the social system. Symbolic interactionists have studied communication patterns in families and the ways in which family roles are shaped. Depending on what he has experienced, a young boy may come to regard the role of "father" as caring and gentle, authoritative and demanding, or brutal and violent.

Meaning is modified over time. Interaction is a process. Relationships are not static but dynamic and ever-changing. The

Adult Children, Aging Parents

It's an inevitable fact of family life. Parents' lives begin to wind down as those of their children reach a peak—triggering a major shift in family responsibility.

Women, the traditional care givers, feel the crunch first. Studies show they feel more responsible for their aging parents than do their brothers and that they often feel guilty they're not doing enough.

In most cultures throughout history, the young have cared for the old—and they still do.

But changes in the makeup of today's family are altering the way we care for our aging parents. Although children still feel loyalty to their parents, women in particular now have a host of new and old demands upon them— each clamoring for time.

Some are mothers of teenage children, who demand a special kind of attention. Others are approaching an important career goal that requires steady slogging. Struggling with their own aging process, many may also wonder where *they* fit in.

Often there is the expectation that the roles played by parents and children in family life will simply be reversed. Adult children will begin to "pay back" their parents for the years they spent raising them.

Social service professionals insist this cannot be done.

"You feel you ought to be able to give them everything they gave you as a child," says Carolyn Rosenthal, of the department of behavioural science at the University of Toronto.

"You can't. You will always be their child, and they will always be your parents. You cannot compare the care of an aging parent with the care of an infant."

Pearl Langer, a social worker with Jewish Family and Child Services, says when families reach this stage it's important children remember their parents chose to marry and raise children.

"You don't owe them anything in the sense that it's a given responsibility. Instead, you must figure out how to bring about a shift in your relationship so that you can be there when they need you, but so that you can also be true to yourself," says Langer.

Quite often, she adds, children misread their parents' needs and desires. A real or imagined guilt complex stirs itself up to a frenzied state—but it need not take over your life.

"Older parents usually want to live close by, but not with their children," says Langer. "They want you to be concerned and interested. They often say they don't want to be a burden. They are at a time in their lives when they become very introspective. They begin to wonder if their lives had meaning, if they have succeeded. You should be sensitive to these things, rather than resentful of them.

"They (parents) may be struggling with the idea that they may soon die and their children may be over-vigilant, always trying to protect and preserve them. But maybe parents want to talk about death. They've seen a lot of it at this point in their lives. They may be frightened by it.

"Communicate with your parents. Find out what they really want and show them the limits of what you can do."

But the question all children struggle with still remains: How much is enough?

SOURCE : "Adult Children, Aging Parents" by Leslie Fruman, July 3, 1986, *Toronto Star*, p. D1.

symbolic interactionist's belief in change contrasts with the kind of consistency that the structural functionalist emphasizes. Not only do people change, but roles are reshaped in what are known as **role taking** and **role making**. The young father *takes* the generalized role of father that he learned in his youth. At the same time, he adds to this (or *makes*) his own approach to the role, based on other attitudes he has learned during his life.

Changing roles can create problems in a family. These days it is a common occurrence for a husband to come home at six o'clock with another meeting scheduled for seven. He may find that his wife unexpectedly had to work until 5:30 and that dinner will not be ready until 6:45. The interaction is likely to be explosive in this case, especially if two young children are reminding their parents of their hunger and if the husband considers that it is the wife's role, regardless of her career, to have meals prepared on time.

Marriage and family counsellors find symbolic interactionist analysis significant in their practice. They seek to clarify the perception of family dynamics from the point of view of each individual member. They seek to understand each person's perception of specific family roles, as well as what these perceptions mean in general family communication. Family problems can often be helped if people can understand the symbolic meanings of their actions.

Conflict Theory

Conflict theorists have only recently taken up a study of the family. Conflict theory deals with power, prestige, and property. It is the rise of feminism that has made these matters seem relevant to the interpersonal relationships in the family. Significantly, most of the conflict theory writers and researchers in the field of family studies are feminists. Once feminists proposed that women and children were a subjugated or subordinate people, conflict theory became an appropriate lens for analysis.

Within the family, the husband can be seen as the "bourgeoisie," with excessive power and control. Almost all of the other social structures—such as government, religion, and the economy—reinforce the male's place of power in the social structure. This power is most evident in laws pertaining to divorce, property settlements, and government policy with relation to child care. Stratification by gender is evident everywhere. For many feminists, patriarchial structures in our society are seen to be based in the family, and these structures must be torn down before a new order can be founded. Cronan puts it this way:

"Since marriage constitutes slavery for women, it is clear that the women's movement must concentrate on attacking this institution. Freedom for women cannot be won without the abolition of marriage" (Cronan, 1978, p. 256).

The Family and the Economy

Many family theorists find it appropriate to look at marriage and family from a point of view that involves weighing costs against rewards (Scanzoni and Scanzoni, 1981). The costs are psychological and social in nature, as well as financial.

The financial costs of raising a child fall into two categories: direct costs and opportunity costs. Direct costs include food, clothing, shelter, medical care, and recreation. These costs are estimated to lie somewhere between $45 000 and $75 000 to raise a child to the age of 18 (Espenshade, 1980:11). These costs vary with the social class of the family. The principal opportunity cost is usually the income the family lost because the mother left the work force.

Mothers have always participated in the income of the family. In the days of the rural Canadian farm, the mother worked alongside her husband in the fields and attended to the household and to the raising of children so that they, in turn, could work to supplement basic family needs. For most women, the reward was food and shelter, plus the fulfilment of her role as mother to the children. Industrialization, the Depression, and the war years created extra stress on many families because the instrumental or breadwinning role of the husband and father often meant separation from the family for long periods of time as men travelled far from home to find work in mining, harvesting, railroad construction, or the military.

In the post-war years, married women participated in the work force in increasing numbers. There were at least four reasons for this change:

1. the opportunities for employment were great in the 1950s and 1960s;
2. inflation had raised the cost of living for the average Canadian family;
3. there were rising expectations for the family—better housing and greater opportunities for children;
4. women were seeking greater equality, more independence, and their own identity.

By 1981, 60 percent of families had at least two wage earners. This is a significant jump from the 4 percent recorded in 1931. One estimate shows that by the year 2000, 71 percent of Canadian women will be in the labour force (Townsen, 1980). Overall participation of females in the labour force grew from 20 percent in 1931 to 52 percent in 1985. Their participation was directly related to the level of their education. Male participation in the labour force has remained about the same, at 78 percent.

Speaking from the conflict perspective on the family, radical feminists argue that "sexual oppression is the most fundamental inequity—and the most difficult to eradicate" (Wilson, 1982, p. 41). A considerable part of the sexual oppression that Wilson objects to is linked to the economic system. A wife can be oppressed as long as she is dependent on her husband's income. The wife's entry into the production sphere of society has modified the family considerably. The nuclear family is smaller, and much socialization of children occurs through agents outside the family, such as babysitters, daycare centres, and schools. With the wife's participation in the work force, family dynamics have changed. The wife has increased her independence, as well as her power in family decision making. If this trend continues, more couples will have an equal partner relationship in their marriage.

Socialization

The family is the place where people get their first sense of self. People are proud, ashamed, guilty, or happy, depending to a large extent on the family interactions that took place during their formative years. Ideally, the family is a place where children are accepted regardless of idiosyncracies or quirks.

In the past, individuals in rural Canada learned most of their values, attitudes, and even life skills within the family. Whether formally or unconsciously, mothers taught their daughters how to cook, sew, and care for children. Fathers taught their sons farming skills, much as the Old Order Mennonites and Amish still do today. Other values—relating to religion, honesty, work, education, the arts, cleanliness, sports, charity, and interpersonal relationships—were also overtly or unconsciously taught in large measure by the family. Now, however, since schools have taken over many of these functions and since adolescents are perceived as a special group unto themselves, the values of the parents are often challenged throughout the teen years.

Research on youth shows that socialization does not always flow in one direction—from the superior to the inferior. Young people do in fact teach their parents. This is particularly true in the democratic (rather than authoritarian) family. Study shows that young people have an effect upon their parents' knowledge of politics, sports, leisure, clothing style, attitude toward minority groups and attitude toward sexuality (Peters, 1986). Parents of small children have reported how their children teach or remind them of the very basic and simple things of life. Socialization is bi-directional, with the potential of affecting all involved.

Marriage

Most of us build our lives around the institution of marriage. We spend our early adult years selecting a partner. We adapt our personal goals to the personal goals of our marriage partners. We share possessions, time, and responsibility for children. In ideal marriages, we help each other through the problems of life. Less-than-ideal marriages may cause pain for one or both partners and may end in divorce and the accompanying problems of readjustment and rebuilding. In this section, we will look at some of the sociological details concerning marriage.

Mate Selection

The mate selection process is affected as early as childhood. Parents become role models, and children observe the role played by the male and female partner in an adult relationship. Parents socialize children in how to treat the opposite sex and how to express affection. These perceptions are evaluated through adolescence and modified by the young person's peer group and the media.

Dating is a common prelude to more serious relationships. As one research study shows, when a person chooses a partner to share a common place of residence, the criteria are different than they were during the time of casual dating (Peters, 1980). Traditionally, dating serves four functions:

1. it is recreational;
2. there is socialization with a member of the other sex;
3. it is a means of status grading and status achievement;
4. it provides the social opportunity for courting, which means selecting and developing a relationship for a permanent partner (Skipper and Nass, 1966).

Every society has developed norms regarding the acceptable manner in which a partner is selected. Among the Yanomama of north Brazil, a young man chooses his wife before she is three years old. A male may also request the expected child of a pregnant woman in the correct lineage if a female is born. The bride-preference is for a cross-cousin. Bride payment and bride service are uninitiated and continue through the life of the bride's parents (Peters, 1987). The Yanomama pattern is definitely an owner-property marriage.

In India, marriages are arranged by parents and kin. This is no chance process. Parents spend up to four years seeking an acceptable man for their daughter. Character references are required when the man lives in another locality. Today, educated Indian young people often do see the potential partner briefly

Govind and Asha Saxena's marriage was arranged many years ago. They live happily in Montréal with their two children.

SOURCE: Canapress Photo Service

before the final decision is made, and now have the option to stop further negotiations between the two families. Although the payment of a dowry is illegal, the practice continues. Canadians are sometimes surprised to see an East Indian, educated in the West, travel to India to marry a bride whom he has not seen and whom his parents have found for him. This shows the significance of his earlier socialization and the bond between family members, as well as the trust the young man has in his parents.

Arranged Marriage

In societies where the family is the most powerful institution exercising social control over individuals, marriages tend to be arranged for the economic and political advantage of the family unit, as, for example, in feudal Europe, traditional China and India, and until most recent times, in Japan. The marriage of two individuals who must spend their whole lives together and raise their children together is only incidental to the serious matter of making allies of two families by means of the marriage bond. Marriage involves a transfer of rights between families, including rights to property and rights over the children, as well as sexual rights.

In many societies, marriage and the establishment of a family are considered far too important to be left to the whims of young people. The function of marriage in such cases is often economic in nature and, for wealthy and powerful families, political. Even in our own society, the children of wealthy and powerful families are segregated in private schools and carefully steered toward a "proper" marriage. A careful reading of announced engagements in the society pages of any newspaper provides clear evidence of such family alliances.

SOURCE: *Cultural Anthropology*, 4th ed. (p. 245) by W. A. Haviland, 1983. New York: Holt, Rinehart and Winston. Copyright 1983 by CBS College Publishing.

Arranged Marriage

Arranged marriages are not limited to India. Earlier in Canadian history, they also occurred, as this newpaper report documents.

AKLAVIK, NWT. Lazarus and Catherine Sittichinli had not met each other when their parents decided in 1915 they should marry.

On Saturday night, the Loucheux and Inuvialuit people of the Mackenzie Delta helped the Settichinlis celebrate their 70th wedding anniversary.

Mr. Sittichinli is 95 years old and a living legend of the North. He is an accomplished trapper and hunter and the last survivor of the Royal Canadian Mounted Police's most famous manhunt. As a special constable in the winter of 1931-32, he helped search for the Mad Trapper of Rat River, Albert Johnson.

Mrs. Sittichinli's 87 years on the edge of the treeline, 2000 kilometres northwest of Edmonton, have been extraordinary, too. For dozens of winters, she and her 11 children left Canada's northernmost Indian settlement for the ice-covered delta where she tanned and cured the skins of the muskrat, hare and Arctic fox her husband had trapped.

The celebration began Saturday with an Anglican church service in English and Loucheux— the Sittichinlis are devout Anglicans—and a traditional feast of caribou, moose, fish and muktuk (whale blubber).

After the meal, there were speeches from family members, native and territorial Government leaders and the commanding officer of the RCMP in the Northwest Territories, Chief Superintendent Robert Head. Telegrams were read from Governor-General Jeanne Sauvé, Prime Minister Brian Mulroney, Opposition Leader John Turner and many others.

Sitting with great dignity in their beaded buckskin mocassins and Sunday best during these acknowledgements, the couple seemed lost in their own thoughts. But when the kind words ended, Mr. Sittichinli grabbed the microphone and delivered a speech in Loucheux.

He told the audience of 300 at the Moose Kerr School that when he and his wife were married at nearby Fort McPherson there were no white men in the area.

Later, in an interview, he spoke through an interpreter about the strength of his marriage and why marriages today seldom endure.

"It's been 70 years but it feels like we were married just yesterday," he said. "We were very close and the years went by quickly."

"In my day, the parents paired us. The word was obedience. We did what we were told. Our marriage was very religious and sincere. I had a devoted wife who did not care about (having) a social life. It was until death do us part.

"Nowadays, young people don't take marriage seriously. They have been distracted by television, telephones, education and other southern influences. There is no more family unity. The young women are yappy. They talk too much before marriage. We never said hello before we married."

With his wife, who is less spry, watching with a smile from a chair, Mr. Sittichili eagerly participated in a Dene drum dance and high-stepped a jig to some fast-paced fiddling music.

Nine hours after the party began the NWT's oldest couple returned to their home, where they still care for several members of their extended family.

SOURCE: "Arranged Marriage Lasts 70 Years" by M. Fisher, Dec. 2, 1985, *The Globe and Mail.*

In these two examples, the union of male and female is of primary importance to parents of the bride and groom. In Western societies, we accord more importance to the wishes of the young couple themselves, and their values often diverge from the values of parents. In the romantic love tradition, people love and then marry; in arranged marriages, it is said that they marry and then love. Although the expression of love may be quite different, arranged marriages show the same range of emotional involvement as do romantic marriages. Some couples are intimate and others are emotionally distant.

There are numerous theories relating to why we fall in love and how we select a permanent partner. Some believe in the Hollywood version of love, that when love strikes, people are helpless to fight it. Others suggest that parental image is important at the time of the selection—that a young man seeks a woman with the qualities of his mother and a young woman seeks a man with the qualities of her father. Similar theory—the perfect-image theory—hypothesizes that we seek partners who approximate the ideal images we have constructed. Some people believe that we fall in love with the ones who can best satisfy our psychological needs. If we need affirmation or intellectual stimulation, we look for a partner who can offer us these qualities.

Other theories are more sociological. There have been many studies relating to **homogamy**. This means that a person chooses a mate with similar attitudes and characteristics. Dissimilarity in these areas is termed **heterogamy**. In first marriages, most Canadian couples are homogamous by age. In 1985, the average age was 24.6 for brides and 26.7 for grooms, a mere two years' difference. In terms of their education, couples are also usually homogamous. A person with a grade ten education is not likely to marry someone with a university education. Ethnically, some groups are more homogamous than others. Native people and Francophones tend to marry within their own ethnic groups, while Scandanavians are much more heterogamous. Some of the more homogamous religious groups are Jews, Hindus, Muslims, and Older Order Mennonites. Among Roman Catholics, 58 percent marry within the group (1984). Homogamy is somewhat less for United Church members (24 percent) and Baptists (18 percent). Any investigation of church homogamy must take into consideration two important factors. Some churches are more strict about interchurch marriages than others, and some do not permit marriage heterogamy at all.

Research shows that in past decades true homogamy has not been found with regard to social class. Women tend to marry up, most likely to a level that is close to their own. Inversely, men tend to marry down. This is known as the marriage gradient.

This pattern may change with the higher education and the careers young women are currently pursuing.

Building on the general principles of social homogamy, sociologists have developed *filter theories*, in which couples go through progressive stages in their courting. The most acceptable filter theory is Murstein's SVR (stimuli, value, role) model. In this model, a person is first attracted to another by stimuli: appearance, social characteristics, and symbolic and verbal communication. Having developed this stage, the couple begin to share their values and their attitudes toward such things as money, religion, sports, sex, and children. In the third stage, the role stage, the couple tests the actual and expected behaviour of each other and decides whether this merits a long-term commitment such as marriage (Murstein, 1980).

We conclude this section on mate selection with a discussion of premarital sex. Ira Reiss, a sociologist from Minneapolis, is the expert in this field, having studied the subject for over 20 years. His studies in the United States show two significant changes in the proportion of non-virginal women at marriage. Around the time of World War I, the proportion shifted from 25 percent to about 50 percent. Then, in the 1960s, the proportion rose to almost 75 percent. During that 50-year period, he writes, "... guilt feelings were reduced, public discussion of sex increased radically, probably the number of partners increased, and the closeness to marriage required for coitus to be acceptable decreased" (Reiss, 1972, p. 169).

Before 1960, the double standard was evident. At the turn of the century, men had coitus with a very limited group of women who were in the main considered "bad": prostitutes and lower-class females. These people were not considered acceptable marriage partners. Over the past 20 years, males have become more discriminating in their sexual encounters. There are likely few university or college males who solicit the services of a prostitute. Males have increasingly sought coitus with someone for whom they feel affection, rather than with someone who merely gives them physical gratification.

Reiss says the introduction of the birth control pill in the 1960s had several social implications. He states that because the pill has placed contraceptive control in the females' hands, they value their sexuality more highly and are able to enjoy the physical aspects of sex to a much greater degree.

The change of sexual mores has produced a variety of social effects. Many schools now include sex education in the curriculum. Many parents live in anxiety that their teenaged daughter may lose her virginity or become pregnant. Earlier, in the 1970s, some parents objected to their young people being able to get the pill through Health Services on university and college campuses. In the late 1980s, we see students asking to have the pill included automatically in campus health plans, thus forcing everyone—sexually active or not—to pay the resulting higher premiums. At the same time, fear of AIDs has increased the use of condoms. It is estimated that 40 percent of condom consumers are females, many of whom insist that their male partners use them as a precaution against venereal disease.

Reiss does not see these changes as signs of a revolution toward sexual promiscuity. He summarizes the changes by stating that women today are more likely than before to value sex for its own sake and men are more likely to value sex with affection. The sexes still differ in that women are more oriented to affectionate sexuality and men more oriented to body-centred sexuality, but each sex has increasingly learned to appreciate the major orientation of the other.

Premarital sexuality in Canada now covers the full range of those who:

1. still use the double standard and are exploitative;
2. participate when there is affection;
3. participate when they are sure the relationship has some permanence (cohabitation or marriage);
4. do not initiate sex until the night of the wedding.

Marital Adjustment

Any intimate relationship is an ongoing process of adjustment. The satisfaction a couple experiences in their relationship depends upon three crucial considerations:

1. degree of commitment to the relationship;
2. willingness to work at the relationship;
3. external circumstances, which are less manageable, such as unanticipated illness, unemployment, or interference by relatives.

A good marriage requires effort as well as interpersonal skills, such as insight, sensitivity, and flexibility (Nass and McDonald, 1982, p. 221).

Little is known about the effect that our society's romantic and over-glamourous view of love in marriage has upon the young couple. Possibly, marital dissatisfaction and disillusionment is highest when romanticism has been excessively high during the courting period. At the same time, romantic love is an accepted and desirable characteristic of marriage in Western society.

Satisfaction in marriage varies through the family cycle. Carl Pineo of McMaster University states that loss of satisfaction is

FIGURE 10-1. Marital Satisfaction by Life Cycle

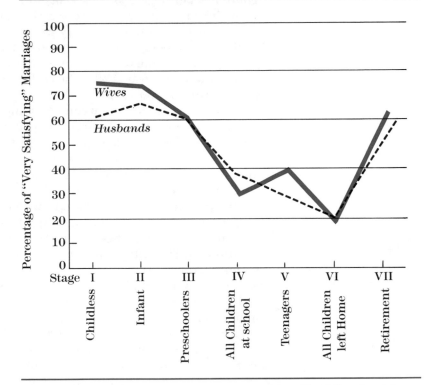

SOURCE: "The Quality of Marriage and the Passage of Time" by E. Lupri and J. Frieders, 1980, *Canadian Journal of Sociology*, 6(3).

"generally an unescapable consequence of the passage of time in a marriage" (1961, p. 11). In this regard, we might expect to see variance between the husband and the wife, because in a sense there is a "his" marriage and a "her" marriage. Mothers experience role incompatibility in that the prominent role of motherhood clashes with the companion role of wife (Lupri, 1986, p. 270). This role incompatibility is difficult to resolve and is heightened by the employee role that women are increasingly taking on.

At the same time it can be said that men have not done well in the employee-husband-father role complex. Researchers show that the North American family can be described as the father-absent family, because he is at work during so much of his children's awake time. The absence may be due to default, in that the father has no choice but to work long hours away from the family. On the other hand, the father may be absent by intent. He may prefer not to be involved in the family and therefore work long hours or spend time at the sports club—or the bar.

There is a fair degree of consensus in the research on satisfaction in the family cycle. Satisfaction is usually high at marriage, wanes with the presence of very young children, and climbs slightly when all children are in school. The lowest point in the family cycle is during the children's late adolescent years. Satisfaction abruptly increases after the children leave home and continues on through retirement.

But the relationship between husband and wife does not become static after the children leave home. This stage, often referred to as the empty nest period, requires more adjustments. The pair may welcome the time that belongs to the two of them, although some adjust poorly. After all, at least 20 years have passed since the first child intruded upon their marriage. Most welcome the grandparenting role, in which they can control the energy and time spent with demanding young children.

For men, the role change from employment to retirement is often difficult. Ties with employee friends may decline or end. In retirement, the wife must adapt to her husband being around the home for more hours of the day. It is at this stage that an increasing degree of role symmetry emerges among the more traditional couples. The man participates in house cleaning and shopping, especially if the wife continues her employment. His role definition changes and is reformulated. They have a greater opportunity to enrich their relationship with one another and with grandchildren. On the other hand, the couple's involvement with their married or single children may be limited at this stage because their lifestyles are different or because they live some distance apart.

Also during this stage, health becomes a major concern. Medical professionals are consulted more frequently. Ultimately, the end of the family cycle comes with the death of one of the spouses, requiring still further adjustments on the part of the survivor.

John Cuber and Peggy Harroff (1965) studied over 200 socially active and prominently successful Americans who considered themselves happily married. They found five distinct types or styles of marital adjustment:

1. conflict-habituated marriage;
2. devitalized marriage;
3. passive-congenial marriage;
4. vital marriage;
5. total marriage.

The conflict-habituated marriage has tension, but the tension is controlled. The partners seem to enjoy arguing, and they make no attempt to hide their arguments from children or the public. But the conflict is channelled and the hostility does have limitations.

In the devitalized marriage, the partners were at one time deeply in love and spent a lot of time with one another. But now life is dull. All that remains is the memory. Some adapt to this devitalized state, sensing that it might be normal for the middle years, while others long for the better years.

The passive-congenial marriage lacks emotional depth from the start. Marriage is viewed as a convenience, not as top priority. Other aspects of life, such as career, children, or community activity, are much more important.

All of these three views see marriage as utilitarian. Marriage serves a purpose and is really not sufficiently repulsive to warrant dissolution. It is a way of life.

The last two types of the Cuber and Haroff study, on the other

In what Cuber and Harroff (1965) refer to as a total marriage, spouses share all important aspects of life.

SOURCE: Canapress Photo Service

hand, involve couples who are intrinsically involved in the relationship. They are bound together psychologically and emotionally. There is keen sexual participation.

In the vital marriage, couples get great satisfaction from doing things together. They willingly give up more personal endeavours to spend time in the evenings or weekends together. Disagreements arise but are settled relatively quickly.

In the total marriage the spouses are even more closely meshed with one another. All important aspects of life are shared. There is no real private life. In most cases this means that the wife's activity becomes absorbed in the activity of the husband.

These types do not describe the person, but rather the relationship. These relationships tend to persist. They represent an adjustment to marriage: none of the couples in the study was on the verge of divorce. This research supports the symbolic-interaction view that the subjective meaning of the relationship is what counts. None of the first three types would be *considered* a good marriage in family textbooks, or possibly by friends of the couples; yet, the couples *said* they were either content or happy. It is worth noting that many marriages are not happy in the full sense of the word but persist and do not end in divorce.

There may be some limitation in how generally we can apply the results from this upper middle-class sample. A steady, reliable source of income contributes to stability in marriage, and there were ample resources in these marriages. This is a luxury that poor and lower middle-class families do not experience.

Divorce

One of the easier ways to recognize change in the Canadian family is by studying divorce. Such a study should look at the laws for dissolving marriage, the quality and expectation of marriage, and actual statistics of divorce, as well as the social attitudes of divorced people toward sex, children, and themselves.

Radical changes in the divorce laws were made in 1968, partly because the Roman Catholic Church recognized that it could no longer hold power to legislate marriage practices over non-Roman Catholic Canadians. For the first time, Newfoundland and Québec could issue their own divorces, whereas previously they had had to make application through the federal government in Ottawa. The new legislation also made some effort to produce a no-fault clause with the introduction of three-year separation as grounds for divorce. Compared to other Western countries these laws were overdue. The number of divorces jumped from 6563 to 11 343 in one year and there has been a slow upward trend ever since. Nonetheless, it would not be accurate to say that Canada had a record of stable marriages before these laws were passed. Societies find alternatives when the law is viewed as unreasonable or dated.

Under the Divorce Act of 1968, the grounds for divorce are adultery and mental or physical cruelty. About 29 percent of all divorces granted used adultery as grounds. Divorce because of marriage breakdown was granted on the grounds of three years separation, five years desertion, addiction to alcohol or drugs, or imprisonment. Thirty percent used the three-year separation as grounds for divorce.

Within a few years of the Divorce Act of 1968, there was a growing irritation that the law was not contemporary enough. Despite the supposed no-fault clause, litigation created a guilty and an innocent party and tended to punish the guilty in some way. Such a hostile exercise did not help to heal the wounds that the couple and sometimes their children experienced.

A new Divorce Act was passed in June, 1986. Once again, there was a sharp increase in divorce petitions, partly because some were already waiting for the new act to be passed. For others, the new grounds made the divorce process more attractive. The most significant change was a no-fault clause after one year of separation. Most divorce petitioners use these grounds. (Families under stress may still opt for a more immediate solution by using the grounds of physical or mental cruelty.)

FIGURE 10-2. Divorce Rates, Canada, 1952-1983

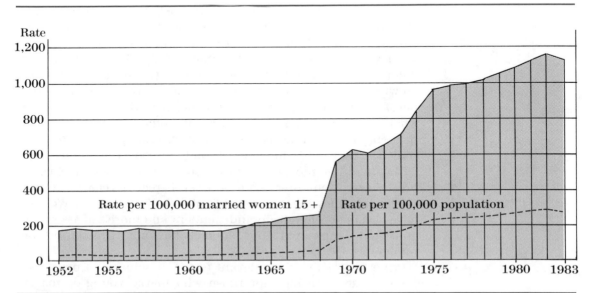

SOURCE: *Statistics Canada Daily*, p. 10, September 6, 1984. Cat. 11-001E.

TABLE 10-1. Number Divorces and Rate per 100,000, 1985

Province	Number	Rate
Canada	61,980	244
Newfoundland	561	97
Prince Edward Island	213	168
Nova Scotia	2,337	265
New Brunswick	1,360	189
Quebec	15,814	240
Ontario	20,854	230
Manitoba	2,314	216
Saskatchewan	1,927	189
Alberta	8,102	345
British Columbia	8,330	288
Yukon, Northwest Terr.	168	228

SOURCE: *Marriages and Divorces*, Vol. II (pp. 16-17) by Statistics Canada, 1985, Ottawa: Minister of Supply and Services.

In ten years, we are likely to see still further changes in divorce. The stigma of divorce may be reduced. It may become more acceptable that two people, who by choice initiated a union, can freely terminate that union—again by choice. Despite such changes, society is likely to continue to value the preservation of somewhat permanent heterosexual bonds, and the law will continue to be used to try to protect the "best interest" of children.

Sociologists attribute the rise in the divorce rate to societal causes. Marriage is less a sacred and more a secular institution than formerly. People are less constrained to act in a way acceptable to the larger community. There are fewer ties to extended family members. Leisure is more abundant. Families are smaller, and fewer activities involve the whole family. Marriage is viewed differently now than it was a generation ago. Most people wish to grow personally as well as to be intimately involved with a partner. A degree of conflict may arise between this search for the whole self and the demands of a marital relationship. When this happens, and marriage is viewed as restricting personal growth, some feel this to be sufficient reason to dissolve the union.

The feminist movement has also contributed to marriage breakdown. Women vacillate between career development and mothering, knowing that it is difficult to fulfil both roles. Women have become economically independent and more self-assertive, and some husbands find such behaviour threatening or intolerable.

Other factors are also relevant to the dissolution of marriage. Divorce rates are high for those who marry young or marry because of a pregnancy. The same is true of marriages resulting from brief courtships. Heterogeneous marriages are more likely to end in divorce than homogeneous unions. The poor are more likely to divorce than the middle class. People from a healthy and happy family, or people who are religious, are more likely to remain married, as are those people whose parents condone and affirm their marriages.

It has been said that young children are the greatest victims in divorce. In Canada, 50 000 children encounter divorce annually. They find the transition difficult and are likely to find stress from such questions as "Did I cause the separation?" "Who will care for me now?" "Where will we live?" Their daily family routine now lacks regularity and consistency. They want stability. They want assurance and love. Nonetheless, research proves that children from a hostile two-parent home environment do better in a single-parent home after the initial year of separation has passed (Hetherington, Cox & Cox, 1978). Adolescents are more likely than young children to understand the separation, and at times are even relieved at such a resolution to family stress. Many children of divorced parents take responsibility and mature in interpersonal relations at an earlier age than their counterparts in intact families.

Single Parents

There have always been single parents in the Canadian family. During most of our history, the proportion of single-parent families remained low and fairly constant. In 1981, 11.3 percent of all Canadian families were led by a single parent. Most of them were families in which one of the parents had died. A few were the result of separation or desertion. However, the composition of the single-parent family is different today (Table 10-2). The largest single group still consists of the widowed (32.7 percent). This group has a high proportion of children who are in their adolescence, and therefore are close to independence. Together, the separated single parents (31.3 percent) and the divorced single parents (26.3 percent) make up 57.6 percent of all single-parent families. These families generally have fewer young children than husband-wife families or single-parent families resulting from widowhood. The majority of divorcing parents have either one or two children (85 percent). There are approximately 70 000 single parents who were never married. Of this group, the mother is typically young with one child.

Several observations can be made about the single-parent family in the future. The number and proportion of single parents who are divorced, separated, and never married will grow. One reason for this growth is that individualism is valued in our society, often over social commitments. Divorce is accepted. As a result of the recent change in the divorce laws, the number of separated single parents will decrease and the number of divorced parents will rise. Changed attitudes toward sexuality are also related to single parenthood. The increasing acceptance of sex apart from marriage increases the likelihood of conception. The right of a single female to decide the destiny of the fetus in her womb also affects the number of single parents in our society. In addition, accepting that women can choose a single lifestyle and still be mothers will add to the number of single-parent families. Some argue that the availability of government financial aid encourages this family form, but that contention is not substantiated by research. It must also be remembered that many single parents are in a transition stage. Many eventually marry or remarry.

Another significant social change is the slow increase of males among single parents. Many people feel there is a special bond between the mother and her offspring. This bias is shown in court judgments about custody rights. The contention that mothers are better able to function as single parents is challenged by those who argue that single fathers receive much more community support in parenting than single mothers do. Mothers are *expected* to mother, while fathers get credit for stepping out of their instrumental role to mother. Usually fathers have better and more consistent financial resources to maintain their households than single mothers do.

Single-mother families are socially and economically vulnerable. On the average, their income is less than half the income of husband-wife families. Fathers are often either neglectful or sporadic with support payments. Adequate child-care facilities are difficult to find. And the income of women is comparatively low.

More recently Canadian family researchers have preferred to use the term *lone-parent* family rather than single-parent family. "Single parent" suggests that there is only one parent in the life of the child. But even though only one parent is living with the

TABLE 10-2. *Percent, Number and Type of Single Parents By Sex, 1981*

	Separated	Divorced	Widowed	Never-Married		
Male	40.5	25.7	29.5	4.3	124,237	(17.4%)
Female	29.3	26.4	33.3	11.0	589,773	(82.6%)
Total	31.3	26.3	32.7	9.8	714,010	

SOURCE: Statistics Canada, 1984, *Canada's Lone Parent Families*, Chart 2, Cat 99-933.

The number of single-parent families is growing in Canada. Most single parents are women.

SOURCE: Canapress Photo Service

child, the non-custodial parent often assists economically and in the care and nurturing of the child.

In 1984, Statistics Canada did a family history survey comparing lone-parent families with dual-parent families (1986). The study showed that female lone-parents bear their first child at a younger age, have a lower level of education, and start work at a later age than their married female counterparts. Lone parents are more likely to be in the labour force. Obviously the need for them to work is more urgent than it is for wives whose husbands are gainfully employed.

Most Single Mothers Live in Poverty

OTTAWA—More than a quarter million single-parent families headed by women were living in poverty in 1985, the National Council of Welfare reports.

The council said preliminary Statistics Canada data show six of every ten single-parent families headed by women were living in poverty and the figures have been growing year by year since 1981.

The poverty rates for other kinds of families and people living on their own were down slightly in 1985, as the unemployment rate continued falling and the economy as a whole continued to improve.

Council director Ken Battle estimates that a poverty rate of 60 percent among single mothers translates into 261 000 poor families that have been forced to fall back on welfare or low-paying jobs. It's not known how many children under 18 were living in those families.

"When a family breaks up, the mother still tends to have the kids," he said in an interview. "Even if she was employed before, her family income is going to be more than halved in all likelihood."

Men in the labour force earn substantially more on average than women.

The council's analysis of the latest statistics also shows that women in other family or non-family situations tend to be worse off than men in similar circumstances.

"I guess what we're saying is that women will always be more vulnerable to poverty regardless of the economic conditions," Battle said.

Havi Echenberg, executive director of the National Anti-Poverty Organization, said the latest poverty figures show the inadequacy of welfare programs and maintenance awards made by family courts following marriage breakdown.

"People don't want children living in poverty," she said, "And yet the levels of payments that have been established are below the poverty line."

Echenberg said maintenance awards are often inadequate and often ignored. And in many cases, they simply reduce a family's welfare entitlements.

"In every jurisdiction I can find, the amount of support is deducted from the social assistance levels," she said.

The National Council of Welfare is an advisory group to Welfare Minister Jake Epp. The National Anti-Poverty Organization is a private, non-profit group that speaks on behalf of the poor.

SOURCE: "Most Single Moms Live in Poverty," March 27, 1987, *Kingston-Waterloo Record*. Copyright Canadian Press.

Remarriage

Does the traumatic experience of a divorce turn a person away from marriage forever? Not for almost 67 000 brides and bridegrooms in Canada in 1985. In fact, the divorced are remarrying in increasing numbers, a trend which may continue.

The second marriage differs from the first in many ways. Second marriages are more apt to be heterogamous by age, religion, and social status. The couple often have financial assets, something few people have at the time of the first marriage. Behaviour patterns are more fixed. There are the memories of a former marriage—both positive and negative. The courtship period is briefer, and the ceremony is likely to be civil rather than religious.

On average, there is a three- or four-year period between marriages. In Canada, 53 percent of the formerly married men marry divorcees. Men have a greater likelihood of remarriage, and women over 35 years of age with children find it most difficult. Educated divorced women are least likely to remarry. Women with less than high school education are most likely to remarry. They tend to rush into remarriage because they are less employable and have less self-reliance. Divorce occurs more frequently among the remarried than among those married for the first time.

The family of a second marriage is likely to be different from the family of a first. Dependent children from a former marriage may be brought into the union. The result is the **blended** (or *reconstituted*, or *step*) **family**. The blended family involves transition for the children, but transition is not as stressful as the separation from their natural parent would be. The stress may be increased if arrangements to meet the other biological parent become more difficult. A child may not know how to relate to the step-parent, whose role is ill-defined in our society. Further, adjustments to stepsiblings may be difficult and complaints of favouritism a problem. On the positive side, some children welcome the blended family environment, because it means more attention and more stable emotional and economic resources.

Family Violence

Violence in the family has always existed, but it has received wide publicity only in recent years. In the past, what happened in the family was largely a private matter, often leaving the most vulnerable as victims. Now social workers and Canadian law have focused on the problem.

Family violence covers at least two broad topics—wife abuse and child abuse. Some would add a third—elder abuse (Nett, 1986, p. 376).

Spouse Abuse.   From our best available sources, one out of three women will be involved in a battering relationship at one time in her life. One out of five murders in Canada is committed by a husband against his wife (Nett, 1986, p. 277).

Eugen Lupri is a Calgary sociologist who specializes in the study of family issues. Professor Lupri set out to find the extent of violence in the homes of 562 couples. Each partner responded separately, to limit the influence by the other partner. The study showed that at least 20 percent of all women and 17 percent of all men admitted to initiating some violent act against their partners during the previous year. Since this was a self-administered questionnaire, Lupri estimates that actual figures of violence might in fact be twice those reported in the data (1986, p. 278).

We see by Lupri's data that abuse is not solely enacted by men against women, but the violence against wives is likely to be more serious. Family research shows that spouse abuse is definitely a *patterned* behaviour, learned in childhood and persisting in the adult household. In general, wives hesitate to initiate court proceedings and do so only after suffering over a prolonged period of time. Physical and mental cruelty are legal grounds for divorce, and, of the divorces granted in 1985, 14 percent were granted on the grounds of physical cruelty and 23 percent on the grounds of mental cruelty.

Child Abuse.   There are many forms of child abuse. Actual physical abuse might be inflicted on 60 000 children annually, but, if we include psychological abuse or neglect, this number would be multiplied many times. The effect of psychological abuse is often not detected until years later.

A peculiar type of psychological abuse associated with our high divorce frequency, is child-stealing. Since fathers are usually the non-custodial parents, they are most often the offenders. One study in the United States estimates that one child in each 22 divorces is subjected to this trauma (Agopian & Anderson, 1981).

Sexual abuse of children is the most publicized form of abuse. Fathers are often the offenders; 92 percent of the victims of incest are female (Herman and Hirschman, 1977).

Physical violence to an infant is revolting as well. Infants are sometimes victims of physical violence—cigarette burns, scalding water, hits, shoves, or slaps. Young children cannot comprehend the reason for such hurt. Parents often vent on children rage which actually comes from a totally different source. Anger at a marriage partner, frustration from the work place, or unemployment may find outlet in the punishment of helpless children. Research shows that a high percentage of abuser fathers have themselves been beaten as children.

Future of the Family

Some people voice concern that the family will cease to be a viable institution in the western world within another half century. They point to the rising divorce rate and the increased number of single-parent families in our society to substantiate their position. They remind us that cohabitation is on the increase and that gay and lesbian couples are seeking legal permission to rear children. How strong is their case?

There is no doubt that the family is changing. Historically, this has always been true. The Canadian family is obviously not what it was at the turn of the century, nor what it was in 1945, nor even in 1975. The function of marriage has changed. Possibly the primary function of marriage—or, more specifically, a heterosexual union—has changed from child rearing to companionship between two adult partners, especially for the first five years of their union. The family's relationship to other social institutions is changing, especially its relationship to the institutions of religion and law.

Discussion of fairly radical changes in the structure of the family has been in the literature for many years. Margaret Mead suggested that we adopt marriage in two steps. In the first stage, people would contract for a three- or five-year period for a childless union. This contract could be renewed. In the second stage, couples could opt to have children. Leo Davids of York University suggests that we would do well to require a licence for some people to have children—possibly 35 percent of the population (1976). Both these ideas emphasize the importance of children in our society. The degree of child abuse, sexual abuse, and incest supports the need for some changes in the existing system.

Two other alternatives will be noted. Robert Tyler feels that marriages could be saved if we addressed the differences of male and female sexual vigour (1970). Men appear to attain their greatest sexual vigour at about age 20, and women at about age 40. Tyler suggests that a man of 20 to 25 years of age should contract his first marriage with a woman who is between 40 and 45 years of age. Her first marriage would have been contracted with an older man, who has just left his first marriage. At age 60 to 65, men and women could initiate their third and final marriage.

As another alternative, Victor Kassel suggests polygamy for those over age 60, a time when there are many more living women than men. Kassel suggests that the aged in general would have better living conditions, would eat better, and would be less lonely if such a lifestyle were socially accepted.

The preceding four alternatives to the traditional family are fairly radical, and it appears unlikely that they will be readily accepted. Some less extreme changes are now in process. Several qualities of life found in the 1980s have a direct bearing upon the family in the future.

As a people, we are more secular than our forebears. In the past, religious teaching, community, and social norms had significant control over family and individual behaviour. In the process of secularization, we have become much more tolerant than we used to be of lifestyles that vary from the norm. As a society, we accept separation in a marriage, or two people cohabiting without marriage. We are not shocked when we hear of sex taking place between unmarried men and women. In a sense, we are saying , "I'll do what is right for me, and I expect that what you are doing is *right* for you, even though what you do is not *acceptable* to me." Our society has been accused of being narcissistic, preoccupied by looking after number one. The family, an institution based on mutual responsibility, is at risk in such an environment.

We cannot undervalue the effect that the increased independence of women is having on the family. Those who favour the traditional form of the family are in the minority. Women now see employment as their right. They expect to be employed for the same reasons as men are—for the sake of dignity, prestige, esteem, and a feeling of usefulness, along with autonomy, independence, identity, and financial gain (Scanzoni, 1983, p. 122). Canadian law increasingly views women as having these rights, and when a marriage is dissolved, the marital property is now divided equally.

Another contemporary pressure on the institution of marriage results from an increase in leisure for males and females of all ages. Some of this time is spent in heterosexual groups. Much of this leisure is experienced outside of the family, or apart from other family members. Television viewing has been accused of limiting family communication.

Having identified some specific qualities within our society that threaten the family, let us look more specifically at changes that are occurring in our family. It is well to see this as the *emerging family*, rather than the termination of one kind of family structure for an entirely new one.

Our society will have a larger percentage of single people in the population. Some of these will be socially active, travel a fair degree, and enjoy their careers. As is true today, there will also be singles in the future who are lonely. Singles bars will continue to exist, but will not be the answer to their social needs. A very few single women will also bear and rear a child. Cohabitation will increase from its current two percent of all couple households. It may even be seen as part of the courtship process—the last stop before marriage. Laws regarding property dispersement at the time of separating will be much more clearly articulated.

Marriage will on the average occur a little later in a person's life than it currently does. Marriage contracts will be more common, and these contracts will outline fairly clearly what the partners expect of each other, particularly concerning child care, household duties, and commitment to career and employment. There will be more dual parenting in the future. There will be more couples who are geographically separated because of job opportunities in separate regions. For these people, the marital experience will be centred on weekends, a time removed from the demands of work.

Though the Divorce Act of 1986 allows for a no-fault ruling, individuals must still remain apart for one year before the actual divorce is either processed or declared absolute. Canadian divorce laws may be changed to allow a married couple to terminate their union simply by mutual consent.

The state will continue to become involved in affairs that relate closely to the family. There is public and legal concern for children and their rights and a public indignation at the common occurrence of family violence in our society. The law will address other related matters related to child rights. Abortion, for example, continues to be a controversial political and legal topic throughout North America. A pregnant woman in the United States who had taken drugs was found guilty of child neglect and was charged after drugs were found in the brain of her dead newborn (Kitchener-Waterloo *Record*, 1986). Canadian courts are just now beginning to rule on matters such as *in vitro* fertilization, surrogate motherhood, embryo transplants, and sperm banks. The public and legislatures are not yet aware of the implication of these matters for the family or society.

In the future, families will be smaller. Further, the family will have a decreasing role in a child's development. Outside agencies will continue to play an important part in the socialization process of children and adolescents. The athletic coach, music teacher, computer instructor, and school counsellor—people outside the family system—will be important in raising Canadian citizens. We will see role-reversal occurring much more frequently between parents. Gender roles will be less stereotyped.

Summary

1. The family is a vital institution in our society. It has changed, sometimes because of forces outside and sometimes as a result of forces from within. We cannot assume that a contemporary Canadian family consists of an adult male, an adult female, and one or more children.

2. Despite change in the Canadian family, two very basic qualities persist. First, it is the basic institution in which children are born, nurtured, and socialized within our society. Second, the majority of adults seek a co-residential heterosexual union in which there is at least affective sharing. Many such unions include economic sharing, procreation, and the rearing of offspring as well.

3. Structural functionalists focus on the role of the family in society and the roles of the members within each family. Parsons claimed that men fulfil an *instrumental* role within the family, and women fulfil an *expressive* role.

4. The Scanzonis have identified four marriage patterns. They see an evolution toward the fourth of these, which they call the *equal-partner* pattern.

5. A nuclear family consists of a married man and woman and their offspring. An extended family consists of a nuclear family and one or more additional relatives.

6. Symbolic interactionists focus on communication among family members and on the roles that family members take and make in relation to one another.

7. Conflict theorists have lately become interested in the promotion of women's rights within the family.

8. Most Canadian marriages are homogamous for age and education. They are more likely to be heterogamous for ethnicity, religion, and class.

9. An increased emphasis on individualism is changing the way many couples adapt to marriage. More marriages are ending in divorce than in the past. There are more single-parent families, remarriages, and incidents of family violence. All these matters damage the traditional image of the family as a haven of security for its members.

Further Reading

Armstrong, P., & Armstrong, H. (1984). *The double ghetto: Canadian women and their segregated work.* Rev. ed. Toronto: McClelland and Stewart.
A well-documented discussion of the relationships between the two segments of labour, the home and the workplace.

Baker, M. (Ed.). (1984). *The family: Changing trends in Canada.* Toronto: McGraw-Hill Ryerson.
Eleven contributors discuss a variety of topics including industrialization and the origins of the modern family, changing views of child rearing and adolescence, patterns of power in family violence, divorce, ethnicity, aging, family law, social policies, and non-traditional living arrangements.

Johnson, L. C., & Dineen, J. (1981). *The kin trade: The day care crisis in Canada.* Toronto: McGraw-Hill Ryerson.
An examination of private day care in Canada.

Luxton, M. (1980). *More than a labour of love: Three generations of women's work in the home.* Toronto: Women's Press.
A case study of life in working-class families at three points in

time in a northern community, depicting women's domestic work in relationship to husbands and children.

MacLeod, L. (1980). *Wife battering in Canada: The vicious circle.* Hull, Québec: Canadian Government Publishing Centre.
Based on materials obtained from interviews with women in shelters across Canada, this book portrays the conditions in which family violence occurs and is institutionalized.

Russell, G. (1983). *The changing role of fathers.* Milton Keynes, England: Open University Press.
Report of research conducted in Australia comparing child care in a group of traditional couples (wife at home, husband sole income-earner) and non-traditional ones (both parents involved equally in child care at home). Findings are compared with those from other countries.

11
Religion

The purpose of this chapter is not to teach you about religion itself but to share with you some of the relationships between what people believe and the way they live and to show you what the functions and consequences of religions are for human society. A science cannot prove or disprove the existence of God; that is for the theologians. But a social scientist can observe what people say they believe about God, and we've already learned that society itself can be seen as a structure of beliefs (about values and norms, expectations of how people should and do behave).

When you are finished this chapter, you should be able to

1. briefly explain the ideas of Marx, Durkheim, and Weber concerning religion;

2. list the manifestations of personal religious commitment;

3. describe church organization in terms of
   (a) members,
   (b) goals,
   (c) norms;

4. describe the impact of religion on people and society;

5. make some predictions about the future of religion.

Religion has been present in virtually every society since the beginning of time. Its influence has varied with time and place—religion has known both its dark and golden ages. Since the rise of modern science, some observers have even predicted the disappearance of religion. And yet religion lives on into the present, embraced by at least a minority in all cultures. Therefore, sociologists have given it considerable attention.

Religion: A Definition

In defining religion for social scientific study, we might begin by noting that humans develop systems of meaning to interpret the world. As two of the foremost sociologists of religion, Americans Charles Glock and Rodney Stark (1965), have pointed out, some systems—commonly called **religions**—including Christianity, Judaism and Islam, take into account the supernatural. Others—

called humanist perspectives—including scientific and political disciplines, do not. Religion has a concern for the meaning of life. Religious perspectives imply the possibility that our existence has meaning beyond what we as humans decide to give it. They imply further that meaning lies with some supernatural reality.

The Nature of Religion

Bertrand Russell stated a central issue in this contrast in his summary of the humanist perspective, the point of view of someone who denies the existence or importance of god(s): "I do not think that life in general has any purpose. It just happened. But individual human beings have purposes" (quoted in Cogley, 1968). Religious perspectives imply that our existence has meaning that precedes any purpose we may impose upon it. If we accept Weber's contention that ideas have the power to influence behaviour, then we should expect to find a difference between the behaviour of religious people and non-religious people. We will begin to explore this by looking at some characteristics of religious people.

Sociology, as you will recall from Chapter 1, uses the scientific method of investigation to study social life. The scientific method relies on what we can perceive through our senses; that is, it relies on perceptions that are based on experience and can therefore be verified.

Religion, on the other hand, asserts that the world we know through our senses is only part of a greater reality and that this greater reality can only be known through faith. Thus, science and religion use two different approaches to knowledge: science deals with the perceivable, religion with the non-perceivable.

Sociology, following science, is unable to make statements about the faith claims of religion—for example, that there is a god. These are supernatural claims that cannot be resolved by science. Sociology's focus is on the social side of religion. While sociology cannot pass judgment on the *truth* of religious claims, it can explore questions relating to the *social aspects* of those claims—the beliefs people have, the relationship between individual commitment and group support, the factors influencing the inclination to be religious, and the impact that religious commitment has on a person's attitudes and behaviour. Thus, what is important for our purposes is not that religious beliefs are either true or false, but rather that they are presumed to be true and, therefore, have potential consequences for individual and social life.

Much of the work done in the sociology of religion has been influenced by the approaches of Marx, Durkheim, and Weber.

Theoretical Traditions

Marx and Conflict

Marx (1970; originally published in 1843) asserted, "Man makes religion; religion does not make man." Central to Marx's thought on religion is the belief that religion serves to hold in check the explosive tensions of a society. Religion is aligned with the interests of the dominant few. It soothes the exploited majority like an anaesthetic; it is "the opium of the people." Religion blinds people to the inequalities that surround them and bottles up their creative energies. The ruling class therefore encourages religion—it is yet another tool in the process of economic exploitation of the masses.

Marx, then, saw religion as an inadequate "salve" or "drug" for a sick society. When the sickness is remedied, there will be no need for the drug.

Durkheim and Collectivity

In *The Elementary Forms of the Religious Life*, Durkheim (1965; originally published in 1912) argued that religion has a social origin. Through living in community, people come to share common sentiments, with the result that a **collective conscience** is formed. It is experienced by each individual, yet is far greater than merely the sum of the individual consciences. Thus, when individuals have the religious feeling of standing before a higher power, they are in fact in the presence of a greater reality. But this reality is not a supernatural being; it is the collective conscience of society. So as humans experience society, they conceptualize the idea of a god; yet, in actuality, "God" is no more than a symbol for society itself.

Members of a society come together as a church for mutual support. In Durkheim's view, religion and church are inseparable. Even when religion seems to be entirely within the individual conscience, society is still the source that nourishes it. Besides meeting needs at the individual level, religion creates and reinforces social solidarity. Collective life is thus both the source and the product of religion. Accordingly, Durkheim defines religion as "a unified system of beliefs and practices relative to sacred things . . . which unite into one single moral community called a church, all those who adhere to them" (1965; originally published in 1912).

Durkheim readily acknowledged the decline of traditional Christianity. Unlike Marx, however, Durkheim did not predict the end of religion. Although the forms of expression might change, the social impetus that gives rise to religion will remain, and so will religion. Likewise, Durkheim argued that there will always be a place for religious explanations. He wrote that science is fragmentary and incomplete, advancing too slowly for impatient people. Religion will therefore continue to have an important role in providing explanations.

Weber and Ideas

Weber was trained in law and economics. His interest in the origin and nature of modern capitalism led him into extensive debate with Marx and stimulated much of his work in the sociology of religion. Weber did not concern himself with the question of whether or not religion is ultimately true or false. Rather, he recognized that it has a social dimension that can be studied according to its nature and relationship to the rest of life. Weber maintained that apart from its supernatural emphasis, religion is largely oriented toward this world. As a result, he argued that religious behaviour and thought must not be set apart from the range of everyday conduct.

Weber maintained that ideas, regardless of whether they are objectively true or false, represent one's definition of reality. Consequently, ideas about religion have the potential to influence behaviour.

Personal Religious Commitment

In recent years, sociologists have been inclined to view religious commitment as being multidimensional. Glock and Stark's proposed dimensions may offer the best scheme for analysing religious commitment. Briefly, they contend that there is considerable agreement among the religions of the world about how commitment is manifested. Glock and Stark cite four such manifestations, or dimensions of **personal religious commitment**:

1. belief;
2. practice;
3. experience;
4. knowledge.

Put briefly, the religiously committed typically hold certain *beliefs* (concerning, for example, the supernatural and life after death), engage in specific *practices* (such as prayer and worship), maintain they have *experienced* the presence of God or the supernatural, and possess a basic *knowledge* of the content of their faith.

In Canada, *Project Canada* national surveys have been carried out every five years since 1975. These surveys have provided pioneering, comprehensive data on personal religious commitment in this country. The surveys have found that Canadians exhibit relatively high levels of belief, practice, experience, and knowledge (see Table 11-1). Indeed, only four percent maintain that they do not believe in God, just 13 percent dismiss altogether the possibility of life after death, and only 23 percent claim they never pray. On the surface, late twentieth-century Canadians would, therefore, seem to be a highly religious people.

Important questions can, however, be raised concerning the

Hare Krishna followers are highly visible on city streets, but all such sects attract only a tiny proportion of the Canadian population.

SOURCE: Canapress Photo Service

TABLE 11-1. Religious Commitment, along Four Dimensions, Canada

Dimension		Percentage
BELIEF		
God	"I know God exists, and I have no doubts about it"	46
	"While I have doubts, I feel that I do believe in God"	20
	"I don't believe in a personal God, but I do believe in a higher power of some kind"	16
	"I don't believe in God"	4
	Other[1]	14
Jesus	"Jesus is the Divine Son of God, and I have no doubts about it"	46
	"While I have some doubts, I basically feel that Jesus is Divine"	22
	"I think Jesus was only a man, although an extraordinary one"	16
	Other[2]	16
Life after death	"There is life after death, with rewards for some people and punishment for others"	19
	"There must be something . . . but I have no idea what it may be like"	40
	"I am unsure whether or not there is life after death"	16
	"Reincarnation expresses my view"	7
	"I don't believe there is life after death"	13
	Other[3]	5
PRACTICE		
Private prayer	"Regularly, once a day or more"	28
	"Regularly, many times a week"	9
	"Sometimes"/"Only on special occasions"	40
	"Never or hardly ever"	23
EXPERIENCE		
God	"Yes, I'm sure I have"	20
	"Yes, I think I have"	23
	"No"	57
KNOWLEDGE		
Who denied	"Peter"	54
Jesus	"Judas"	19
	"I don't know"	20
	Other wrong answers	7

[1]I find myself believing in God some of the time, but not at other times," "I don't know whether there is a God, and I don't believe there is any way to find out," and a write-in option.
[2]"I feel that Jesus was a great man and very holy, but I don't feel him to be the Son of God;" "Frankly, I'm not entirely sure there really was such a person as Jesus," and a write-in option.
[3]"There is life after death, but no punishment;" and a write-in option.
SOURCE: Data derived from "Project Can80" by R. W. Bibby, 1982.

depth of this apparent commitment. The surveys have found that only about 38 percent of Canadians claim to be committed to Christianity and just two percent to some other religion. Fewer than half of these demonstrate the belief, practice, experience, and knowledge traits that Glock and Stark cite as central to commitment. Among the remaining 60 percent of Canadians,

some 40 percent indicate that they are interested in but not committed to any religion, while the remaining 20 percent simply
say that they are not religious (Bibby, 1987). In short, isolated
religious beliefs and practices flourish. Yet traditional and non-
traditional commitment to religion as an interpretive system for
living appears to characterize a minority of Canadians.

Collective Religious Commitment

It is frequently argued that one can be religious without having
anything to do with such religious organizations as churches,
synagogues, or temples. Most social scientists, however, would
maintain that personal religious commitment is highly dependent upon **collective religious commitment**, that is, group support of some kind. Such dependence is not unique to religion but
rather stems from a basic fact of life: the ideas we come to have
are largely the product of our interaction with other people.

Moreover, if we are to retain ideas, we need the continuing
endorsement of those ideas by other people—not necessarily a
lot of people, but at least a few who think as we do. This is not to
say that we as individuals are incapable of creativity, but rather
that, for the most part, the ideas we possess have been socially
imparted and are socially sustained.

In modern societies, where religious orientations compete
with non-religious ones, the existence of social groups that can
transmit and sustain religious ideas is essential to the maintenance of those ideas. And over the centuries, religion has not
lacked such supportive groups.

The Church-Sect Typology. Those who have examined religious groups in predominantly Christian settings have historically found themselves dealing with two major kinds of
organizations. On the one hand, there have been numerically
dominant groups—the Roman Catholic Church, the Church of
England, and the so-called mainline denominations in Canada
and the United States (the Episcopalian, Anglican, Methodist,
Presbyterian, and United Churches). On the other hand, there
have been smaller groups that have broken away from the dominant bodies. These smaller groups have ranged from the Wal-
densians of the twelfth century, through the Protestants four
centuries later, to the Baptist and Pentecostal splinter groups
found in virtually every major North American city today.

Not surprisingly, therefore, sociologists studying religious
groups have given considerable attention to a conceptual scheme
featuring these two major organization forms. The framework,
known as the **church-sect typology**, represents an attempt to

describe religious organizations in terms of the central characteristics of church and sect, as well as to account for the origin and development of the sect. In recent years, the church-sect typology has been discarded by a large number of sociologists because of its apparent limitations as an analytical tool.

Organizational Approaches.   There has been a growing tendency in sociology to study religious groups in the same manner that sociologists examine other groups—that is, by using *an organization approach* (see Chapter 9). The obvious advantage to this approach is that sociologists of religion can draw upon the extensive research already available on organizations and have access to well-developed concepts and analytic frameworks.

Viewed as an organization, a given congregation might be examined in the following terms:

1.   the nature and the sources of its members;
2.   its formal and informal goals;
3.   the norms and roles established to accomplish the group's purpose.

Organizational studies include Harrison's (1959) pioneering examination of the American Baptist Convention and Westhues's (1973; 1978) analyses of the Roman Catholic Church. Although such case studies are still relatively few, they can provide considerable insight into the nature of religious groups.

Kenneth Westhues (1978) is a sociologist at the University of Waterloo in Ontario. He has offered a stimulating analysis of the power organization of the Roman Catholic Church. He points out that the Catholic Church is a multinational religious body that both pre-dates nation-states and shares with them a high degree of organization. As a result, relations between the church and nation-states such as Canada and the United States essentially involve relations between equals. But the host countries do not always recognize the church as an equal, and they sometimes force it to make adaptions.

In the United States, for example, the Catholic Church was denied recognition in the founding of the country and was grouped into a common category with other religious bodies lacking official public authority. Tax money could not be used to build churches, pay clergy, or support schools. The church responded by trying to create a self-contained Catholic world, a subsociety within American life, which included schools, hospitals, welfare agencies, and senior-citizen homes.

Westhues (1978) writes that in Canada, there is no rigid principle of church-state separation. Rather, the creation and evolution of the country has seen the Catholic Church partially

Canadian history, for the most part, has seen a co-operative relationship between Church and State. Here, Pope John Paul II shakes hands with Prime Minister Brian Mulroney prior to his departure for a 12 day visit to Canada in 1984.

SOURCE: Canapress Photo Service

institutionalized in Québec. The church in that province has historically had the right to use tax money to support itself and its related educational and social service institutions. In all provinces but British Columbia and Manitoba (which account for less than five percent of Canadian Catholics), church schools receive legal recognition and public assistance. The barriers of region, language, ethnicity, and legal status have divided Canadian Catholics one from another, so that the national church is scarcely more integrated than the nation itself.

Religion in Canada

Affiliation with religious groups has been widespread in Canada since the founding of this country. Close ties have been apparent between British Canadians and the Church of England, Methodism, and Presbyterianism; between French Canadians and the

Roman Catholic Church; between other ethnic groups and the churches of their homelands. Such general affiliations continue to be very common in Canada. According to the 1981 census, Roman Catholics comprise 47 percent of the population and Protestants 41 percent. The remaining 12 percent consist of Jewish people (one percent), people with other religious preferences (three percent), and people who identify with no religious group (eight percent) (see Table 11-2).

It is an exaggeration, therefore, to think of Canada as a diversified religious mosaic. The reality is that almost 90 percent of Canadians identify with Christianity. The second largest category consists of those with no preference, but, as we will see shortly, many of these are only temporarily in that category. Only a small minority of Canadians are tied to non-Christian religions. While there is obviously diversity in the way people across the country express Christianity, it is clear that a Christian "monopoly" exists in Canada. More Canadians (over 50 percent) claim to belong to churches than to any other voluntary group. According to various polls, approximately one-third of Canadians say they attend services weekly, and roughly the same proportion of people with school-age children expose those children to church schools.

At the same time, however, there has been a considerable decline in church attendance in recent years, as indicated by the Gallup poll findings presented in Table 11-3. Since approximately the end of World War II, Protestant attendance has dropped off from about 60 percent to under 30 percent, levelling off in the last few years. For Roman Catholics, the decline appears to have started around 1965, moving downward from roughly 85 percent to 50 percent through the 1980s.

This attendance drop is further documented by the *Project Canada* national surveys. While one in three Canadians claim they currently attend service weekly, two in three maintain they were attending weekly when they were growing up (Bibby, 1987). Survey findings do not support the possibility that many people are substituting television "electronic churches" for service attendance. Only four percent of Canadians say that they regularly watch religious services on television or listen to them on radio—a decline from the 29 percent reported in a Gallup poll for 1957. Some 45 percent of those who regularly draw on media religious programs are weekly church-attenders, suggesting that the programs are largely a *supplement* for the church-committed rather than a *substitute* for the uninvolved.

Personal religious commitment depends on collective religious commitment; therefore this significant decrease in service attendance has likely been accompanied by a decline in the

TABLE 11-2. Religious Preference, Canada, 1981 (in rounded percentages)

Denomination	Canada	Nfld.	PEI	NS	NB	Que.	Ont.	Man.	Sask.	Alta.	BC	Yukon	NWT
	%	%	%	%	%	%	%	%	%	%	%	%	%
Anglican	10	27	6	16	9	2	14	10	8	9	14	20	33
Baptist	3	.	5	12	13	.	3	2	2	3	3	4	2
Greek Orthodox	.	.	.	.	.	.	2	2	2	2	.	.	.
Jehovah's Witnesses	.	.	.	.	.	.	.	.	1	.	1	.	.
Jewish	1	.	.	.	.	2	2	2	.	.	.	.	.
Lutheran	3	.	.	1	.	.	3	6	9	7	5	4	1
Mennonite	.	.	.	.	.	.	.	6	3	1	1	.	.
Pentecostal	1	7	1	1	3	.	1	2	2	2	2	2	3
Presbyterian	3	.	10	5	2	.	6	2	2	3	3	3	1
Roman Catholic	47	36	47	37	54	88	35	27	29	26	19	24	40
Salvation Army	.	8	.	1	.	1	1	1	.	.	.	.	.
Ukrainian Catholic	1	.	.	.	.	.	1	5	3	2	.	1	.
United Church	16	19	24	20	13	2	19	24	28	24	20	14	8
Other	7	3	4	3	3	3	6	4	5	9	11	8	6
No Religion	7	.	3	4	3	2	7	8	6	12	21	20	6
Totals	100	100	100	100	100	100	100	100	100	100	100	100	100

SOURCE: Computed from Statistics Canada, 1981 Census.

TABLE 11-3. Church Attendance for Roman Catholics and Protestants, Canada, Selected Years

"Did you happen to attend church (or synagogue) in the last seven days?

	1946	1956	1965	1975	1985
	%	%	%	%	%
Roman Catholics	83	87	83	61	43
Protestants	60	43	32	25	29
National	67	61	55	41	32

SOURCE: Canadian Institute of Public Opinion.

national level of personal religious commitment. Belief and practice fragments persist, but an erosion has undoubtedly been taking place in the proportion of Canadians who are committed to religion as a system that gives meaning to their lives.

The downward pattern, of course, may change. Indeed, some observers contend that it is changing, that there is a renewed interest in religion.

Religion: Its Consequences

From the standpoint of social scientist and layperson alike, one of the most significant questions about religion is its consequences. Does religion have an impact upon individuals that extends to how they live, or is it largely irrelevant? If such an influence exists, does religion tend to contribute to individual and societal well-being, or is it inclined to produce anxiety and guilt, social indifference, and bigotry? Further, if religion has an impact—positive or negative—to what extent is this impact unique to religion, and to what extent is it common to other institutions?

Religions, of course, claim to have consequences for individuals and hence for societies. Christians, for example, are likely to tell us that mature followers of the faith should find that it influences both themselves personally and their relations with others. Specifically, Christianity maintains that the committed will experience joy, satisfaction, peace, and hope. In addition, the tradition asserts that committed and mature Christians will be characterized by love in their relations with other people and that this love will be exhibited in such qualities as concern for others, acceptance, benevolence, forgiveness, self-control, honesty, and respect. In living out such a life of love, Christians are

The Voice of God or Human?

Social scientists cannot address the issue of whether or not God exists. However, they can explore the sources of the claims people make "in God's name." Sometimes human claims attributed to God are contradictory, suggesting that social rather than supernatural factors are involved. An example is the conflicting arguments of the former Roman Catholic archbishop of Toronto and Dr. Henry Morgentaler concerning abortion.

TORONTO—The archbishop of Toronto has urged his congregation of more than 1.1 million Roman Catholics to fight laws that "do not sufficiently protect the unborn."

Without referring specifically to the recent acquittal of Dr. Henry Morgentaler and two associates on abortion-related charges, Gerald Emmett Cardinal Carter declared: "Even where partial protection is afforded, the law is being flouted."

Carter's statement was in a letter read or distributed Sunday in the archdiocese's 196 parishes.

"This is not just a church matter," the letter said. "This is the killing of innocents."

"As citizens, as well as believers in God's law, we cannot stand idly by. Our position is without equivocation."

"I urge all Catholics, all Christians and all who respect human life to work together to curb and, if possible, eliminate this abomination."

EDMONTON—Dr. Henry Morgentaler said Thursday he has come to the conclusion that "God is guiding my hand" during abortion procedures.

"God told me to help women," Morgentaler told a wildly cheering crowd of about 700 at a fund-raising speech in Edmonton Thursday night. Gerard Liston, 25, an anti-abortionist, had asked him why he did not give up performing abortions.

"God is all-powerful," Morgentaler replied. "If He wanted to, He would have stopped me. I have come to the conclusion that God is guiding my hand."

The crowd howled with derision when one anti-abortionist asked: "How do you know you haven't aborted a Messiah?"

SOURCE: Canadian Press, November 25, 1984 (Carter) and January 17, 1985 (Morgentaler).

expected to follow ethical guidelines such as the Ten Commandments, the Sermon on the Mount, and the teachings of the Apostle Paul.

At the same time, religious groups certainly differ on specific issues (for instance, abortion). If an issue such as abortion is a religious issue, we would expect that a religious group's attitude would be influenced by its religion, rather than just reflect the same views as the population at large. Social scientists exploring the effects of Christianity, then, give their attention to three main areas:

1. individual consequences;
2. interpersonal consequences;
3. societal consequences.

Individual Consequences

Marx and Freud essentially conceded that religion contributed to positive personal characteristics such as happiness, satisfaction, and hope. Their adverse criticism rested in their belief that such qualities were based upon illusion rather than on reality. However, their views were based largely on speculation rather than on evidence.

Actual research on the consequences of individual commitment to religion is surprisingly limited. It is difficult to assess the consequences of someone's belief, and the studies that do exist suffer from serious methodological flaws. However, analyses to date suggest that Canadians who are religiously committed differ little from other people when it comes to happiness, satisfaction, leisure activities, and general well-being (Bibby, 1987).

In short, religious commmitment, by itself, appears to have a very limited influence upon personal characteristics. Moreover, it frequently is not as important as such variables as age, education, or employment—even among active church members—in predicting personal well-being.

Interpersonal Consequences

Research in the United States on the relationship between religious commitment and compassion has yielded inconsistent results (see, for example, Kirkpatrick, 1949 and Rokeach, 1969 versus Rushby and Thrush, 1973 and Nelson and Dynes, 1976). Considerable research has also been carried out exploring another facet of interpersonal relations—racial prejudice. Americans Richard Gorsuch and Daniel Aleshire (1974) reviewed all the published studies on the topic through the mid-1970s and concluded that the key to understanding conflicting findings is the way in which religious commitment is measured. If church membership is used as the measurement, members are more prejudiced than those who have never joined a church. If beliefs are used, the theologically conservative are more prejudiced than either the non-active or the most active members.

These researchers point out, however, that the precise role of organized religion in the influencing of prejudice is unclear. Sophisticated studies that measure the impact of churches on individuals over time simply have not yet been done.

An analysis of *Project Canada* data has found that the religiously committed in this country do not differ significantly

Pope Liked But Ignored

Two public opinion polls, one taken before Pope John Paul II's 1984 visit to Canada and the other after his departure, point to the selective use of Roman Catholicism by Canadian Catholics. While the Pope himself is respected, what he says is not necessarily taken seriously.

September 8, 1984

OTTAWA — A major pastoral goal of Pope John Paul's visit is doomed even before he sets foot in Québec on Sunday, according to a national opinion poll commissioned by Southam News.

The survey strongly suggests the Pope will be cheered as a media superstar, respected for his goodness, applauded for his engaging personality but ignored as irrelevant when he preaches on individual and public morality.

Preaching to the public on morality and humanity is one main goal of a papal visit, according to Vatican officials. The other is to strengthen the resolve of local bishops and priests.

Yet more than half the 1011 adults interviewed for the poll reject the pope's social thinking as "out of touch" and object to any religious figure taking strong stands on political and economic issues. Barely one in seven—rising to nearly one in five among Catholics only—consider John Paul's social thinking in line with Canadian society. Only a third of those interviewed even like the idea of religious leaders speaking out on politics and economics.

Such widespread opposition means the Pope will be preaching mostly to people with closed minds, whether restating his traditional views on contraception and abortion or outlining his progressive ideas on social justice and human work.

"He gets it from both sides," agreed a leading Catholic theologian who requested anonymity. "Liberals object to his moral traditionalism and the conservatives balk at his ideas for political and economic reform."

While Canadians may turn off the preaching, they will give a joyous and warm welcome to the "Pope for all Christians" on his 12-day visit.

Three out of every four interviewed this July said the papal visit was a good idea, rising to 88 percent approval among Roman Catholics. Only eight percent of Canadians think the visit is a bad idea, largely because of the expense, estimated from $50 million upward. Another seven percent say the visit is a good idea so long as taxpayers don't wind up with a big bill.

January, 31, 1985

OTTAWA — More than three-quarters of Canadians of all denominations approved of Pope John Paul's September visit, but they remember the man more than his message, a Gallup poll released today indicates.

The poll, commissioned by the Canadian Conference of Catholic Bishops, found 77 percent of respondents approved of the visit for a number of reasons, including the spirituality of the event and its unifying effect.

Of the 15 percent who disapproved of the Pope's presence, 82 percent cited the cost of the visit as the reason.

Residents of Atlantic Canada and Québec showed more interest and support for the visit than did the rest of the country, says the survey, conducted in October, a month after the Pope's departure.

The survey estimated ten percent of Canadian adults, fewer than two million, attended a papal event or watched motorcades. That number is far lower than was originally planned for by church and security officials.

But 63 percent of those surveyed said they followed the papal visit through television, newspapers or radio.

Father William Ryan, a general secretary for the conference, said the poll confirms that the visit "helped Canadians to take time out to think about important issues while at the same time enjoying an historic and spiritually renewing event."

It now is up to the church to foster this interest, Ryan said in a statement. "The long-range effects (of the visit) are harder to estimate."

SOURCE: Peter Calamai, September 8, 1984 and January 31, 1985.

from others with respect to their interpersonal relationships (Bibby, 1987). In comparison with other Canadians, the religiously committed hold a similar view of people, claim a comparable level of compassion, and appear to be no more or less tolerant of deviants, minority groups, or people of other religious faiths.

At this point it is important for us to pause and ask ourselves if we should really expect religion to be making a unique contribution in such areas as happiness and compassion at this stage in Canadian history? In a highly specialized industrialized society such as ours, religion is only one factor in a wide variety of influences on interpersonal norms. Characteristics such as compassion, integrity, and diligence are emphasized by virtually everyone—the family, the school, youth groups, voluntary associations, mass media. The influences on interpersonal norms—as on personal characteristics—are many, with religion being, at best, one influence affecting a decreasing number of people.

At the same time, there is one area in which the Christian religion still appears to speak with a fairly loud, if not unique, voice: the area of personal morality, notably sexuality. Here, Christian churches—some more explicitly than others—tend to function as opponents of moral innovation. Examples include opposition to the changing of sexual standards, to the increased availability of legal abortion, to the legalization of pornography distribution, and to the legalization of prohibited drugs. In recent years, these views have been underscored by Jerry Fallwell's high-profile Moral Majority movement in the United States and by its Canadian counterpart, Ken Campbell's Renaissance movement.

Table 11-4 reports findings that support the "opposition to moral innovation" argument. Religiously committed Canadians are more inclined than others to hold negative attitudes toward non-marital sexuality, homosexuality, abortion, pornography, and the use of marijuana. A national study of Canadian Mennonites has similarly found religious commitment to have an effect on moral attitudes rather than on social behaviour (Driedger *et al.*, 1981).

Religious commitment in Canada, then, appears to have its greatest influence, not so much in the areas of personal characteristics or interpersonal relations, in which alternatives from secular sources abound, but in the sphere of personal morality. Yet, even here, the influence of religion, while important, is generally no more significant than the year of one's birth (Bibby, 1979b). What this means is that the era in which a person was born is just as important in determining opposition to moral innovation as religious commitment, with opposition to change increasing with age.

TABLE 11-4. Commitment and Moral Attitudes

Percentage opposed to . . .

	Pre-Marital Sex[1]	Extra Marital Sex[1]	Homo-sexu-ality[1]	Abortion: Rape[2]	Abortion: Child Unwanted[3]	Porn-ography[4]	Marijuana[5]
	%	%	%	%	%	%	%
Service Attendance							
Weekly	38	76	83	29	81	55	87
Less than weekly	7	43	54	8	42	28	66
Religious Self-Image							
"Deeply committed"	33	71	81	27	75	51	86
"Not religious"	5	37	50	4	30	21	64
Other	7	46	53	9	47	30	65
Christian orientation							
Yes	38	72	84	35	85	55	92
No	11	49	58	10	46	32	68

All the above responses represent opposition to the following possibilities
[1]The responses on premaritial, extramarital, and homosexual relations are "Always wrong."
[2]The legal availability of abortion when "she became pregnant as a result of rape."
[3]The legal availability of abortion when "she is married and does not want to have any more children."
[4]The legal limitation of the distribution of pornographic materials to persons of all ages.
[5]The legalization of the use of marijuana.
SOURCE: Data derived from "Project Can80" by R. W. Bibby, 1982.

Societal Consequences

We have examined religion's influence on individuals and on social interaction. Does religion influence society as a whole? From at least the time of Marx and Durkheim, observers have argued that religion contributes to solidarity. Marx was particularly critical of the way in which, he believed, religion was fused with the interests of the powerful to keep the less powerful proletariat united in submission. Similarly, Durkheim saw the supernatural as both reflecting the nature of a society and functioning to unite it.

To be sure, however, religion can sometimes also be disruptive. From one vantage point, Roman Catholicism in Québec can be seen as having contributed to considerable ethnic and regional solidarity. From another point of view, though, such a solidifying function can be seen as having had the potential to disrupt Canadian unity. Fallwell's Moral Majority has become a right-wing Christian voice committed to altering the nature of American life through influencing the country's political, educational, and media realms.

The disruptive role of religion can further be seen in the Protestant-Catholic strife in Northern Ireland and in the Roman

On the set of Canada's most popular religious program, "100 Huntley Street." Evangelical movements tend to reinforce traditional, conservative moral values.

Catholic clergy's call for political and economic change in Poland and Latin America. Conflict also occasionally takes place over the dissenting views of Christian Scientists and Jehovah's Witnesses on blood transfusions, or over the pacifist stance of Mennonites and other groups.

Nevertheless, sociologist Peter Berger's (1961) observation still seems generally valid: while an adequate sociological theory of religion must be able to account for the possibility of disruption, Durkheim's assertion that religion integrates societies aptly describes religion in North America. Religion—at least the mainline segment of organized Christianity that embraces the largest number of members—appears largely to solidify culture, rather than to disrupt; that is, it appears to reinforce North American society as we know it, rather than to call for its reformation. As Calgary sociologist Harry Hiller (1976) has put it: "There are times then when religion can be a vital force in social change. . . . But as a general principle, we can say that in Canada organized religion has generally been a conservative force supporting the solidarity of the society." Significantly, North America's new Christian right wing is calling, not for revolution, but for a return to the values that made America great. The impact of their philosophy on an issue such as the reinstatement of the death penalty is examined in an accompanying article.

The primary reason for such a pattern has already been illustrated in our examination of the effects of religious commitment.

Death Penalty Debate

As Christians around the world commemorated Good Friday yesterday, members of a variety of denominations gathered outside Warkworth Penitentiary to protest efforts to reinstate capital punishment.

The afternoon Vigil for Life outside the Ontario prison presented a "unified witness" against the reinstatement of capital punishment, says Warkworth Presbyterian minister, Rev. Gunar Kravalis.

It was one of many events sponsored across the country as denominations representing 90 percent of Canadian Christians reaffirmed their long-standing opposition to the death penalty.

The opinion of most Christian churches, however, flies in the face of a recent national poll that showed about 70 percent of Canadians favoured a return of the death penalty. There is also a body of conservative, fundamentalist ministers who preach to their flocks that the Bible justifies state executions.

Like the 19th century debate among Christians over slavery, both sides in the capital punishment argument can appeal to biblical texts to support their stand. A recent poll in the evangelical magazine *Faith Today* showed

80 percent of those opposing the death penalty cited Scripture to support their position and 71 percent of those advocating its restoration did the same.

But among mainline church leaders, the weight of opinion is heavily against capital punishment. The religious bodies that have so far gone on record as supporting the continued abolition of the death penalty are the Anglican, United, and Presbyterian churches, Canada's Roman Catholic Bishops, the Baptist Convention of Ontario and Québec, the Canadian Unitarian Council, the Mennonite Central Committee, the Reformed Church of America and the Religious Society of Friends (Quakers).

"The teachings we give our people are not based on majority thinking," says Bishop Bernard Hubert of Longueuil, Québec, president of the Canadian Conference of Catholic Bishops.

The position of conservative evangelicals is less easy to define. Individual, independent fundamentalist churches and ministers take a strong pro-capital punishment stand, but there has been no collective statement in favour of reinstating the death penalty by a major evangelical group.

Rev. Brian Stiller, executive director of the

Culture seems to influence religion more commonly than the reverse. The result, in the words of one Canadian theologian, is that religion has difficulty saying something to the culture that the culture is not already saying to itself (Hordern, 1966), or, in the North American case, has not already said to itself. Rather than standing apart from culture, religion is commonly coloured by culture; it is culture's product rather than its source.

Religion: Its Future

Since social scientists first turned their attention to religion, they have been divided on the question of its future. Marx and Freud saw religion as being replaced by reason, an event that would usher in a superior quality of life. Durkheim, on the other hand, was among those who saw religion as persisting. Religious explanations, he said, may be forced to retreat, reformulate, and give ground in the face of the steady advance of science. Yet religion will survive because of both its social sources and its functions.

Evangelical Fellowship of Canada, an umbrella group for 23 conservative denominations, says most evangelicals likely support the death penalty but there is also a difference in positions.

"Some Mennonites have said that if you are against abortion, it follows logically that you have to be against capital punishment," Stiller says. "Other evangelical groups argue the reverse and say that human life is so sacred that to violate it means you suffer the consequences."

Stiller says based on responses to the poll by *Faith Today*, the evangelical position on capital punishment is not all that different from that of the larger community in Canada.

High support

The poll showed 76 percent of evangelicals responding favoured a return of the death penalty. Members of Christian and Missionary Alliance churches and Pentecostal churches recorded the highest support for capital punishment: 92 percent and 88 percent respec-

tively. Mennonites recorded the lowest support: 26 percent.

The coalition point out in an anti-capital punishment educational kit that the law of Moses in the Old Testament also called for the death penalty for nearly 30 crimes.

These included rebellion against parents, idolatory, incest, blasphemy, homosexuality, breaking of Sabbath laws, fornication and adultery. The law also called for the death penalty for anyone who kept an ox known to be dangerous if it caused a death.

Despite the number of capital crimes, the Jewish community of the Old Testament used technicalities to virtually eliminate capital punishment, the coalition says.

"They understood justice to go beyond revenge to reconciliation and healing," Rabbi Dow Marmur, senior rabbi at Holy Blossom Temple, Canada's largest Reform congregation, says he knows of no rabbinical authority, liberal or orthodox, that advocates capital punishment.

SOURCE: "Canadian Faiths Divided in Death Penalty Debate" by Michael McAteer, April 18, 1987, *Toronto Star*, p. A1.

The Secularization Argument

Secularization involves the adopting of a world view that rejects the supernatural and focuses on reality as known through the senses. According to the proponents of the **secularization argument**, traditional religion has experienced a decline parallel to modern industrialization. The increase in specialized activities has led to a reduction in the number of areas of life over which religion has authority, including meaning. Such a trend can be seen in the loss of influence of the church in Europe since the medieval period or in the similar loss of territorial authority experienced by the Roman Catholic church in Québec since approximately 1960.

Some of the factors contributing to secularization go along with social change—urbanization, urban growth, higher education, technological development, work force participation, an emphasis upon consumption, and the mass media.

The Persistence Argument

Other observers of religion have questioned the predicted decline of religion, arguing instead that it will persist. There are various forms of this **persistence argument**. Davis (1949) has contended that because of the functions religion performs, its future is not in question. According to Davis, there is a limit to which a society can be guided by sheer rationality. He therefore argued that while religion will certainly experience change, including the birth of new sects, it is unlikely to be replaced by science and technology.

In a well-known argument, Talcott Parsons (1964) noted that Christianity continues to flourish in the modern western world, "most conspicuously in the United States." Specialization, he maintained, does not necessarily mean a loss of significance for religion. On the contrary, religious values have now pervaded society, and religion is flourishing precisely because religious organizations can concentrate on religion. He further saw "the individualistic principle inherent in Christianity" as a strengthening factor. Individuals are responsible for deciding what to believe and with whom to associate. Far from being in a state of demise, then, Christianity, for Parsons, is thriving.

More recently, Stark and Bainbridge (1982; 1985) have argued that humans persist in having intense desires that require supernatural solutions. Consequently, secularization is countered by sect-inspired revival and cult-initiated innovation. The result is not the end of religion but the replacement of some faiths and groups with new ones. Religion constitutes an ever-changing marketplace. Rather than destroying religion, say Stark and Bainbridge, secularization stimulates it.

On the one hand, then, there are a number of social scientists who see industrialization as having a negative effect, largely irreversible, upon religious commitment. On the other hand, there are observers who deny such a relationship. The manner in which industrialization actually influences religious commitment is, therefore, still very much in question.

International Data

To evaluate modern industrialization's effect on religion, we need to study cross-cultural data. In a significant summary of international Gallup poll data, Lee Sigelman (1977) reported that religious commitment varies significantly among countries. Beliefs and their importance are highest in the developing countries and lowest in the highly industrialized western European countries, such as Scandinavia, West Germany, France, Britain, and Japan (see Table 11-5). The commitment level of an increasingly industrialized Canada lies between these two extremes.

While these international findings do not exclude the possibility of a return to religion, at this point in history the data appear to support the secularization thesis. A clear-cut, contrasting

TABLE 11-5. Religious Beliefs and Their Importance for Selected Countries and Areas

	Beliefs: Very Important	God	Life after Death
	%	%	%
India	81	98	72
Africa	73	96	69
Far East	71	87	62
Latin America	62	95	54
United States	56	94	69
Canada	36	89	54
Italy	36	88	46
Britain	23	76	43
France	22	72	39
West Germany	17	72	33
Scandinavia	17	65	35
Japan	12	38	18

SOURCE: Compiled from "Multi-nation surveys of religious beliefs" by Lee Sigelman, 1977, *Journal for the Scientific Study of Religion*, 16, p. 290.

"return to religion" pattern is not currently visible.

Even in the United States—an apparent exception to the industrialization-secularization rule—all is not well. American religion gives considerable evidence of being secularized from within as well as from without. Observers argue that religious organizations are being increasingly infiltrated by American secular culture. Furthermore, mainline denominations have known considerable membership losses since the 1960s. Some observers have argued that institutional religion in America prospered because the values held by Protestants, Catholics, and Jews were consistent with conservative political and family values (Nelsen and Potvin, 1980). But with the shift in values since the 1960s, religion is no longer experiencing its previous level of "establishment." Instead, an increasing level of dissatisfaction and disillusionment is being felt among the affluent young. Accordingly, the prosperous, well-educated, culture-affirming mainline denominations have been hit the hardest so far. But the trend may eventually spread to the more theologically conservative denominations as well. Relative to other countries, then, religion in the United States continues to flourish, although there is evidence that it is not escaping the secularizing tendencies of modern industrialization.

Canadian Data

We have already observed that to varying degrees Canadians assert belief in God and in the divinity of Jesus, claim to pray and to experience God, and maintain that there is life after death. The *Project Canada* surveys have further documented a more general widespread interest in supernatural phenomena.

Yet, as noted earlier, when asked point-blank, only about 40 percent of Canadians say that they are committed Christians. A mere two percent claim to be committed to religions other than Christianity. The remaining 60 percent of the population consists of the uncommitted (40 percent) and the non-religious (20 percent). It also will be recalled that only one in three people across the country attend services in churches and synagogues. In short, it appears on the surface that commitment to established religion is not high and that the religious situation in Canada represents fairly open territory for new competitors. Thus it is that Hexham *et al.* (1985) have written that "a market exists for new religious movements in Canada to fulfill needs which many people do not see traditional churches meeting."

TABLE 11-6. Religious Traits of Canadian Teens and Adults

	Teenagers	Adults
New Religions		
Strongly Interested	2	1
Belief		
God	85	82
Divinity of Jesus	85	68
Life after Death	80	69
Communication with Dead	36	38
Some have Psychic Powers	69	58
Astrology Claims Are True	37	45
Practice		
Pray Privately	20	37
Read the Bible	5	8
Attend Religious Services	23	28
Watch Religious Programs	2	6
Read Horoscope	25	13
Experience		
God	44	53
Knowledge		
Peter denied Jesus	41	54
Self-Image		
Religiously Committed	39	43

SOURCE: Derived from "Project Can80," 1982, and "Project Teen Canada," 1985, by R. W. Bibby.

But this analysis can be deceiving. Invariably, the question may be asked: Where are the drop-outs going? Some observers have said that they are joining new religions, while others have said they are turning to evangelical churches, television preachers, and even to no religion (see Bibby, 1987). The search for religious drop-outs in Canada yields an intriguing result: there are actually very few. Indeed, as noted earlier, almost 90 percent of Canadians with Catholic parents remain Catholics, as do some 90 percent of those with Protestant parents. By denomination, there is remarkable stability from one generation to another—about 80 percent for United Church affiliates, 70 percent for Anglicans, 55 percent for Conservatives , and 70 percent for other Protestants. The figure for other religious groups is about 80 percent (Bibby, 1984).

Clearly, identification with a religious group is valued in this country. But it is equally clear that individual Canadians differ considerably in the role they want religion to play in their lives. Some embrace it wholeheartedly, as a system of meaning that informs much of their lives. Others choose particular beliefs, particular practices, particular specialized services. Still others—a small minority—want nothing from religion or religious organizations.

It may well be that the significant religious decline associated with the industrialization of Canada is not the abandonment of religion. Rather, it is the tendency of Canadians to reject Christianity as an authoritative meaning system, in favour of drawing

These young people belong to the 40 percent of the population that claim to be committed Christians. Of these, most people select beliefs as consumers rather than using it as a system of meaning to shape their whole lives.

SOURCE: Miller Services

upon Christian fragments—select beliefs and practices—in a highly specialized, consumer-like fashion. In a similar manner, Canadians select fragments of other non-naturalistic systems (such as astrology or ESP) without adopting entire systems. In Stark and Bainbridge's words, these systems become "consumer cults."

The dominant tendency, then, is to draw selectively upon religion, rather than to allow it to become an all-embracing meaning system. Churches, whether they like it or not, are faced with the reality of being identification groups for large numbers of Canadians who want to choose selectively from what the churches have to offer.

It may well be that fragments are much more functional than all-encompassing religions in a society that requires one to compartmentalize in order to play a number of diverse roles. Religious systems may also frequently seem at odds with dominant cultural values, such as rationalism, consumption, and enjoyment.

If this is the case, then belief, practice, and service fragments are chosen over complete systems because they are more conducive to life in our present day, and not because there are no systems to choose from.

Summary

1. Sociology uses the scientific method to study religion. In contrast, religion explores reality beyond that which can be known through experience.

2. The sociology of religion has been strongly influenced by the theoretical contributions of Marx, Durkheim, and Weber. Marx stressed the role of religion as the "opium of the masses." Durkheim emphasized both the social origin of religion and its important function in holding society together. Weber gave considerable attention to the relationship between ideas and behaviour.

3. Religion can be defined as a system of meaning that assumes that there is more to the world than can be experienced through the senses.

4. Personal religious commitment has increasingly come to be seen as having many dimensions, with these four commonly noted: belief, practice, experience, and knowledge.

5. Collective religious commitment instills and sustains personal commitment. Organizational analyses examine religious collectivities in the same manner as other groups. In Canada, organized religion has experienced a considerable decline in participation during recent years, which has critical implications for commitment at the individual level.

6. Religion appears, at best, to be one of many paths leading to valued characteristics, such as personal happiness and compassion.

7. While religion sometimes has a disruptive impact, it more commonly seems to contribute to social solidarity, frequently mirroring the characteristics of groups and societies.

8. Historically, observers of religion have been divided on the question of religion's future, asserting both secularization and persistence hypotheses. Internationally, the secularization argument appears to have substantial support.

9. The search for alleged religious drop-outs in Canada reveals that few have turned to new religions, to privatized expressions, or to "no religion." Most are still identifying with the established groups.

10. The apparent paradox of widespread beliefs and practices existing alongside relatively low commitment suggests that many people in Canada prefer to draw selectively on religion, rather than to embrace it as an all-encompassing meaning system. Such a pattern is to be anticipated in highly industrialized societies more generally.

Further Reading

Bibby, R. W. (1987). *Fragmented Gods: The poverty and potential of religion in Canada*. Toronto: Irwin.
A comprehensive portrait of religion in contemporary Canada.

Chalfant, H. Paul, Beckley, Robert E., & Palmer. Eddie C. (1985). *Religion in contemporary society*. Palo Alto, CA: Mayfield Publishing Co.
A sociology of religion textbook, which succeeds in covering the field in a comprehensive and readable manner.

Clark, S.D. (1948). *Church and sect in Canada*. Toronto: University of Toronto Press.
A Canadian classic that examines the social factors contributing to the rise of different types of religious groups in this country.

Crysdale, Stewart, & Wheatcroft, Les (Eds.). (1976). *Religion in Canadian society*. Toronto: Macmillan of Canada.
One of the few works available dealing with the social scientific study of religion in Canada with articles by leading scholars in sociology, anthropology, and history.

Neibuhr, H. Richard. (1929). *The social sources of denominationalism*. New York: Henry Holt and Company.

A classic attempt to probe the role social factors (e.g., economics, nationality, race, region) had in creating denominationalism in Europe and America.

Robbins, Thomas, & Anthony, Dick (Eds). (1981). *In gods we trust: New patterns of religious pluralism in America.* New Brunswick, NJ: Transaction Books.

Essays examining the nature and significance of new religious movements in America by a wide variety of the nation's top social scientists.

Westhues, Kenneth (Ed.). (1978). *The Canadian Journal of Sociology 3* (Spring).

A valuable collection of articles by leading academics, comparing organized religion in Canada and the United States. Groups include mainline and conservative Protestants, Roman Catholics, Jews, Mennonites, and Mormons.

V Social Change

The world is changing, and the rate of change itself is accelerating. For example, it took more than a million years for the world's human population to reach about a quarter billion, in the year A.D. 1. It took an additional 1650 years for the population to double, to about one-half billion. But it took only about 200 years for it to double again, to one billion in 1850. Less than 100 years later, in 1930, it was two billion. It doubled again in 36 years, reaching four billion in 1976. By the year 2000 it will double again to eight billion. What will your world be like in 10 or 20 years?

Another example of accelerating change is the job market. Sociologists estimate that ten years from today, half the jobs now available to high school graduates will have faded out of existence. They will have been replaced by jobs that do not even exist today.

Social change is an essential ingredient of our society. Two fundamental causes of social change in the western world were

1. the industrial revolution;
2. urbanization.

It was no accident that sociology developed during the industrial revolution. The changes that this period brought about in society were a major concern of those early sociologists Durkheim, Weber, and Marx. Chapter 12 discusses what these changes were and how these three thinkers interpreted them. The chapter also looks at changes in the job market—now and in the future.

Chapter 13 explores one of the major areas of modern social change—the population shift from rural to urban. This chapter examines the extent, the causes, and the consequences of urbanization, emphasizing urban life in Canada.

Chapter 14, Social Movements, is a more general and theoretical treatment of social change, giving special attention to groups promoting or resisting change. The chapter focuses on the role of such social movements in Canada.

12
Industrialization and Work

Work is a central human activity; most of us spend close to a third of our day engaged in it. Much of our educational system is devoted to training us for work; our identity is greatly shaped by it; and, later in life, we search for activities to replace the work from which we have retired. After finishing this chapter, you should be able to

1. describe the inequalities resulting from industrialization;

2. describe the impact of industrialization on Canada;

3. describe the characteristics of unionism in Canada;

4. describe the basic attitudes toward work among Canadians;

5. describe what work may be like in the future.

"What do you do?" This is an important question, and it is almost always asked within a few minutes of strangers meeting. We all know what the question means—"What *work* do you do?" Work is such an integral part of our lives that the answer to the question reveals much more about a person than simply what he or she does for a living. It also allows us to estimate a person's educational level, probable income, prestige, and lifestyle. In other words, work is so central in our society that it is a major source of personal identity.

Work is the driving force of society. Work permits us to exist, and the type of work we do determines in large part the quality of that existence. In this chapter, we examine how the institution of work affects us, and how we in turn view the world of work.

The Industrial Revolution

The history of modern work can be traced to the *industrial revolution* that took place in England at the end of the eighteenth century. As a result of a number of technological developments, especially the invention of the steam engine by James Watt, the whole social structure of British and European societies began a process of radical change. Starting in the textile and agricultural-equipment industries, large factories utilizing mechanical power and employing hundreds of workers were built. The factories produced a volume of goods that no one in previous ages had dreamed possible. These goods were made more cheaply than by traditional methods, and more people in society were able to afford them. Thus, their production provided a great stimulus to the European economy.

The new agricultural equipment produced during this time contributed to higher food yields per hectare, thereby raising per capita income and freeing the people who had worked on the land to join the new industrial enterprise. It was now possible to produce more food with less labour. In this way, Britain became the first industrialized society.

Theoretical Perspectives

The events of the industrial revolution transformed the societies in which they occurred—first Britain and later Germany, France, the United States, and Canada. Durkheim, Weber, and Marx wrote major works on what they believed to be the most important issues arising out of the industrial revolution. They were each concerned about the relationship of the individual to society and how this relationship had changed as a result of the industrial revolution. Some of these changes are outlined in Table 12-1.

Durkheim

In writing about the effects of the industrial revolution, Durkheim (1964a, originally published in 1893) argued that changes in the division of labour were primarily responsible for changing the individual's relation to society. In the pre-industrial era, there was a very simple division of labour, and there were relatively few types of occupations. This meant that differences among individuals were minimized and the grounds for common interests were heightened. There was little difference between occupations, so the way in which individuals related to one another and to social groups was characterized by free and open interaction.

In this type of society—which is characteristic of pre-industrial, agrarian societies—social relations are based on what Durkheim termed *mechanical solidarity*. This concept assumes that people have common values, beliefs, and attitudes. Social relations occur primarily in the kinship system and through community networks. The family is the most important social institution in maintaining mechanical solidarity and also acts as the major agent of social control.

With the industrial revolution, the division of labour becomes more complex, and social relations change. The basis for society,

TABLE 12-1. The Great Dichotomy

From the time of Durkheim, Weber, and Marx to the present, sociologists have attempted to spell out the variety and types of social change that occurred as a result of the technological changes brought about by the industrial revolution. The list below is a simplified presentation; nevertheless, it shows that the effects of industrialization on the social structure are enormous in their impact.

Social Dimension	Pre-industrial Society	Industrial Society
Economy	Agricultural Subsistence production Simple division of labour Barter exchange	Industrial Market production Complex division of labour Money exchange
Culture	Homogeneous standards Bases on consensus	Heterogeneous standards Differentiation
Values	Traditional Sacred Ceremony and ritual	Innovative Secular Functional instrumental orientation
Social organization	Traditional Based on kinship	Rational-legal (bureaucratic) Based on merit
Social control	Informal moral pressure	Impersonal bureaucratic control mechanisms
Social relations	Informal Mechanical solidarity	Formal Organic solidarity
Mode of behaviour	Based on custom and tradition	Based on contract

then, according to Durkheim, becomes *organic solidarity*. Specialized work introduces differentiation into the social system; that is, people come into contact with others who do the same kind of work. In this occupationally diverse society, there is a corresponding need for co-ordination and control, which is satisfied through written procedures, contracts, and laws. Interaction is more impersonal, and the family is no longer the most important institution for maintaining social solidarity.

From this brief presentation, it may be seen that Durkheim's analysis is both structural and functional. It is structural because the independent variable, the division of labour, is an objective part of the social structure, which, when it changes, also causes changes in people's behaviour and their relations to one another. The analysis is functional because Durkheim was writing in terms of the needs of society. When one aspect of society changes, other changes occur to bring the system back into equilibrium.

Weber

Like Durkheim, Weber was interested in explaining the vast changes he was witnessing. In his book, *The Protestant ethic and the spirit of capitalism* (1958, originally published in 1905), he selects changing religious values as the most important independent variable to account for the rise of industrial capitalism. Before the Protestant Reformation, work had been regarded as the curse God placed on Adam and Eve when they were expelled from the Garden of Eden. However, the Protestant reformers reinterpreted work as a calling—that is, a duty and service to God. Consequently, in countries in which there is large proportion of Protestants, a strong value is placed on work. Following Weber, we refer to this value as the **Protestant work ethic.**

Weber asserted that the Protestant work ethic gave rise to conditions under which industrial capitalism would flourish. According to him, this explains why the Industrial Revolution began in Protestant Britain and why the current dominant industrial country (the United States) is also predominantly Protestant. Table 12-2 gives further support to Weber's thesis. Energy is the driving force of industrialization, so national per capita energy consumption can be used as a handy index to the level of industrialization in a country. Table 12-2 shows that Protestant countries have a much higher per capita energy consumption than do countries in which other religions are more heavily represented.

Marx

The major factor that Marx (1965; originally published between 1867 and 1895) used to explain the changes occurring in society and in the individual's relationship to it was ownership of the *means of production.* As you read in Chapters 1 and 7, two antagonistic classes are formed—those who own the means of industrial production (*bourgeoisie*) and those who do not and who

TABLE 12-2. *Median Energy Consumption for Groups of Nations Classified by Dominant Traditional Religion*

Dominant Traditional Religion	Median Energy Consumption	Number of Nations
Protestant	5,141	10
Eastern Orthodox	3,060	4
Roman Catholic	914	31
Islam	208	24
Eastern religions (Buddhism, Hinduism, etc.)	193	13
Pre-literate tribal faiths	70	25

NOTE: Consumption is based on kilograms of coal equivalent consumed per person per year in the median nation in each category.

SOURCE: From *Human Societies* (p. 270) by G. Lenski and J. Lenski, 1978, New York: McGraw-Hill.

therefore must sell their labour (*proletariat*). The bourgeoisie do not engage directly in the production process but extract profits from it, and therefore enjoy a privileged position in society. The proletariat, on the other hand, work at highly specialized tasks over which they have no control and in which they cannot produce entire products. The result, as you read in more detail in Chapter 9, is *alienation*, or personal feelings of both powerlessness and meaninglessness. Eventually, according to Marx, the proletariat will revolt against the bourgeoisie and seize the means of production. In turn, this will lead to a classless society.

Industrialization in the World Today

In 1850, when industrialization was well underway in both Europe and North America, per capita income was 70 percent higher in the industrialized, developed nations than it was in the developing countries of the world (Murdoch, 1980). In 1950, 100 years later, the difference in per capita income was 2242 percent, and by 1980 it had increased to 3838 percent. Per capita income in the developing nations in 1980 was $245 U.S., while in the rich, industrialized countries it had soared to $9648 U.S. (Seligson, 1984).

Industrialization has produced an inequality among the peoples of the world on a scale never before thought possible. This inequality is reflected in the figures describing health, education, welfare, and general quality of life. Table 12-3 presents 34 countries throughout the world ranked by per capita energy consumption, which is very often used as a measure of industrialization. By this measure, the United States is the most industrialized country in the world, while Chad in sub-Saharan Africa is the least.

Table 12-3 also presents data on eight social variables that are strongly related to this measure of industrialization. Generally,

TABLE 12-3. *Selected Countries Rank-Ordered by Industrialization, Which Is Related to the Quality of Life in These Countries*

| Selected Countries | Rank Order of Industrialization[1] | GNP per Capita 1982[2] | Life Expectancy at Birth[3] | Social Conditions Accompanying Industrialization | | | % Enrolled in Secondary School | | % Adults Illiterate[5] | | Average no. of Persons/Room |
				% Income Spent on Food	Percent Malnour- ished[4]	% with Access to Safe Water	Boys	Girls	M	F	
				%	%	%	%	%	%	%	
United States	10,204	$13,160	74	13	—[6]	—	95	96	1	1	0.6
Canada	10,070	11,320	74	15	—	—	89	90	1	1	0.6
West Germany	7,409	12,460	73	24	—	—	90	93	*[7]	1	1.5
Australia	5,987	11,140	75	17	—	—	77	79	*	*	0.7
USSR	5,738	5,940	69	—	—	—	77	82	1	2	1.3
Belgium	5,329	10,760	72	19	—	—	85	87	1	1	0.6
Bulgaria	5,261	—	72	—	—	—	69	69	3	7	1.2
Sweden	5,156	14,040	76	19	—	—	86	87	1	1	0.7
United Kingdom	4,641	9,660	73	18	—	—	76	78	1	1	0.6
Hungary	3,809	2,270	70	—	—	—	32	46	1	2	1.1
Japan	3,575	10,080	76	26	—	—	77	79	1	1	1.1
Italy	3,273	6,840	73	31	—	—	68	64	3	5	0.9
Venezuela	3,153	4,140	67	39	7	—	30	35	16	21	1.5
South Africa	2,694	2,670	61	24	—	—	87	81	43	43	1.3
South Korea	2,666	1,910	66	44	4	62	73	65	4	12	2.3
Yugoslavia	2,290	2,800	70	—	—	—	—	—	6	19	1.4
Israel	2,255	5,810	74	23	—	—	79	88	7	17	1.5
Argentina	1,718	2,520	70	—	2	66	68	70	4	6	1.4
Mexico	1,687	2,270	66	—	8	62	67	60	13	19	2.5
Malaysia	987	1,860	64	37	—	62	62	53	23	38	2.6
Brazil	757	2,240	63	—	13	77	—	—	25	28	1.1
Turkey	702	1,370	64	—	7	75	72	40	19	49	2.2
Peru	595	1,310	58	—	23	47	77	65	11	28	1.9
Egypt	516	690	56	—	8	66	49	29	44	72	1.8
Bolivia	365	570	50	—	45	34	17	13	21	42	—
Indonesia	242	580	49	—	30	12	23	16	22	42	1.5
Pakistan	221	380	51	—	26	29	20	7	61	82	2.8
India	199	260	50	58	30	33	35	18	44	72	2.8
Kenya	129	390	55	—	30	17	13	10	36	65	2.5
Sudan	89	440	48	65	30	46	24	16	62	86	2.5
Afghanistan	56	—	40	—	37	6	23	4	74	95	—
Bangladesh	46	140	47	—	38	53	24	9	56	81	—
Ethiopia	26	140	40	—	38	6	26	10	92	96	2.7
Chad	22	80	40	—	54	26	22	6	88	99	—

NOTES:
[1] Measured by per capita energy consumption in kilograms of coal equivalent, 1961.
[2] Gross National Product is the total value of goods and services produced within a country during one year.
[3] Life expectancy is the average number of years a newborn baby can expect to live given that country's mortality rate.
[4] Percent of the population below the critical minimum limit of nutrition as determined by the UN Food and Agricultural Organization.
[5] Literacy is defined according to the individual country's definition of "adult" and "literacy."
[6] Data not available.
[7] Less than one percent.

SOURCES: *1981 Statistical Yearbook.* New York: United Nations: table 169; *1984 World Population Data Sheet* and *1982 World's Children Data Sheet.* Washington, D.C.: Population Reference Bureau.

the more industrialized a country is, the greater is its per capita Gross National Product. Also, it will be noted that, by the standards of the least industrialized countries, those in the industrially advanced nations can expect to live almost two lifetimes. The average life expectancy in Afghanistan, Ethiopia, and Chad is 40 years, while in Sweden and Japan it is 76 years.

Another indicator of the quality of life is the proportion of income one has to spend on food. Although the data are not complete for this factor, they range from just over ten percent in the United States to nearly 65 percent in the Sudan. Quite clearly, if the bulk of one's income is spent on food, there is very little left for other essentials—not to mention luxuries. Malnourishment is a common condition of life, according to the United Nations Food and Agricultural Organization. Data for most of the industrialized countries are missing, probably because malnourishment does not constitute as much of a problem as it does in the developing countries. There, anywhere from one-quarter to over half of the population is officially designated as being below the critical minimum limit of nutrition required to be healthy.

A very surprising statistic is the proportion of the population who have no access to a safe water supply. Again, this does not constitute as much of a problem in the developed nations, but in some of the developing nations the figures are truly shocking. For example, in Indonesia—the fifth most populous country in the world (almost 175 million people)—only 12 percent of the population has access to safe water. The figures for Afganistan and Ethiopia are even lower, which explains in part why their death rates are among the highest in the world.

A further inequality appears in education. Virtually all of the population of boys and girls in the most industrialized countries are enrolled in secondary schools. However, in the developing nations, not only does the participation rate drop below one-quarter, but there is also a substantial increase in the participation of boys over girls.

The disparity between developing and developed nations also appears in the adult illiteracy rates. Formal education is a necessity; in order for a country to become industrialized, the general population must be able to read and write. By and large, this not so in the developing countries. However, in comparing the secondary school participation rates with the illiteracy figures in these countries, it may be concluded that the younger population is now receiving more education than the older generations did. Consequently, the adult illiteracy rates should drop in the next ten years as the effects of this education, although minimal, are more widely distributed throughout the population.

The final column in Table 12-3 reflects another aspect of the

Inadequate food and the lack of safe water lead to death rates in developing countries that are much higher than the death rates in industrialized countries.

SOURCE: Canapress Photo Service

quality of life—housing. In the developed nations, the average person has almost two rooms at his or her disposal, whereas in the developing nations the average person must share one room with two others.

All of these factors together back up the assertion that the growing gap between the rich, industrialized countries and the poor, developing ones is one of the most pressing social problems in the world today. Two former Canadian prime ministers, Lester B. Pearson and Pierre Elliot Trudeau, spent much of their terms in office attempting to persuade a substantial number of countries to help even up this imbalance, but did not have much success because the problems of co-operation are so complex.

The basis of the gap between the rich and poor nations lies in their different patterns of growth and development. During the original industrial revolution in Europe, population growth was high, thereby reducing much of the productivity gain achieved through industrialization. One solution to this was emigration. During the period from 1840 to 1930, at least 52 million Europeans (that is, more than double Canada's present population) emigrated (Davis, 1974). This emigration was of two basic types. The first type involved permanent settlement in the temperate regions of the world (Canada, the United States, Australia, New Zealand, and southern South America and Africa) and was an important safety valve in the control of European population growth.

The second type of emigration was to the tropical areas. Its main purpose was not settlement, but the acquisition of valuable raw materials (gold, silver, diamonds, and other goods not found in Europe). These riches were needed to help finance the industrialization process in Europe. Consequently, each of these migratory patterns contributed significantly to the development and modernization of the industrializing European nations.

Today, the problems are more complex, and it is not possible for industrialization in the developing nations to occur in the same fashion. For example, population growth in the poor, developing nations is now 2.1 percent per year (*1987 World Population Data Sheet*) economies of these nations must grow annually by this amount just to stay even. Furthermore, even though the present world migration pattern has changed, and there is now a general population movement from the poor to the rich nations, it is not enough to absorb the excess growth. The escape valve of emigration that existed for the industrializing European countries cannot be used by the developing nations.

Another major problem is the financing of the very expensive industrialization process. As mentioned above, this was largely achieved in the European industrial revolution through the exploitation of countries in the tropical regions. Some academics and politicians in the developed nations have suggested that it is now only fair for the industrialized countries to repay their debt to the developing nations by financially assisting in their industrialization (Tinbergen, 1976). But there has not been enough support to bring about the desired changes. Many of the developing nations are already heavily in debt to the developed nations—over $700 billion, according to the most recent World Bank estimates (World Bank, 1986, p. 32). Thus, it is impossible for these countries to accumulate independently the capital necessary to achieve industrialization.

These different patterns of growth and development between the industrialized and the industrializing nations more than likely mean that the gap between the rich and the poor will continue to increase. It seems inevitable that at some point this gap will be perceived as intolerable by the rapidly growing populations of the developing nations. Already they make up 76 percent of the world's population and, given present growth rates, by the year 2000 this figure will rise to 80 percent (*1987 World Population Data Sheet*). If the world's resources are not shared more equally, it is likely that social unrest in all forms will increase dramatically. As long as two decades ago, Lester Pearson noted: "Before long, in our affluent, industrial, computerized, jet society, we shall feel the wrath of the wretched people of the world. There will be no peace (quoted in Tinbergen, 1976). Already there are signs: mounting acts of terrorism and civil disobedience, massive illegal migration, rising crime rates, and internal disputes that escalate into international conflicts.

Industrialization in Canada

Table 12-3 indicates that Canada is the second most industrialized country of those listed. In terms of per capita energy consumption, this is true, but it is also true that all energy consumed does not drive industrial machinery. Canadians, as you well know, live in a cold climate and consume much energy just to keep warm. Also, Canada is a very large country, requiring high energy consumption for transportation. Consequently, Canada's apparent position in the rank order of industrialization is somewhat misleading when per capita energy consumption is used as the measure of industrialization.

In actual fact, many commentators have expressed concern about Canada's recent industrial performance (Economic Council of Canada, 1986; Royal Commission on the Economic Union and Development Prospects for Canada, 1985; Science Council of Canada, 1977; 1984). While it is true that Canada is among the leaders in per capita gross national product, the "product" is largely natural resources, agricultural products, and semi-finished manufactured goods such as lumber. According to another measure of industrialization—completely finished manufactured goods as a proportion of total exports—Canada lags behind such nations as Ireland, Mexico, Spain, Yugoslavia, and Portugal (Science Council of Canada, 1977). The Canadian manufacturing establishment is small, increasingly non-competitive in the international marketplace, and largely foreign-owned.

In order to understand industrialization in Canada, it is first necessary to realize how closely it is bound to the American economy. The United States is by far Canada's largest trading partner, accounting for approximately three-quarters of both Canadian exports and imports (Royal Commission on the Economic Union, 1985). Canada exports mainly natural resources and primary products, and imports finished manufactured goods (World Bank, 1984). Most of what Canada exports to the United States is also produced there. Traditionally, Canada has enjoyed favourable trade relations with the United States because of our relatively lower production costs and comparable productivity levels. However, within the last two decades, our competitive advantage relative to both the United States and Japan has eroded substantially (Kennedy, 1986), with the consequence that the Canadian dollar has fallen relative to American and Japanese currencies. This permits Canadian exports to remain competitive, but at the price of very expensive manufactured imports.

Another characteristic of Canadian industry is foreign ownership and control. Canada has been described as a branch-plant economy in that close to half of the mining, petroleum, and manufacturing industries are foreign controlled, mainly by American corporations (Royal Commission on the Economic Union, 1985). Because the foreign-controlled companies are branches of parent firms, they are often not complete manufacturing establishments; that is, not all aspects of the production process, including vital research and development, are represented in the Canadian branch plants. In many cases, the branch plants are only assembly or warehousing operations.

Most American exports to Canada are finished manufactured goods, and half of Canadian manufacturing firms are controlled by mainly American interests. As a result, the development of a complete, self-sufficient, and up-to-date industrial establishment in Canada is severely limited. Our proximity to the United States has limited Canada's ability to industrialize in a self-sufficient fashion.

Post-Industrialism

As you can see in Table 12-4, industrialization is not an all-or-nothing proposition. It is a gradual process and can vary substantially from one country to another, depending on when it is first introduced, as well as on the country's human and natural resources. Table 12-4 identifies the particular stages through which the developed nations have evolved. The column labelled "Emergent Post-Industrial Age" indicates some fairly recent changes that have taken place within these advanced industrial countries.

TABLE 12-4. Ages of Industrial Technology

Important Determiners of Technology in Dominant Ages	Pre-Industrial Age 1500–	Early Industrial Age 1785–	Mature Industrial Age 1870–	Emergent Post-Industrial Age 1953–
Power	Muscle, wind and water	Steam with the use of coal	Electricity and internal combustion machines with use of oil, gas, and coal	Atomic energy supplemented with solar, geothermal, and fusion energy
Tools	Hand	Machine	Automatic machine	Automatic factory
Work skills	All-around skilled craftsman and unskilled manual workers	Skilled craftspeople replaced by machine (semiskilled) operatives as a result of subdividing manufacturing processes	Skilled inspector, mechanic required as operations replace need for machine feeding or tending	Highly trained engineers as designers are required; skilled technicians required for monitoring controls and for maintenance of equipment
Materials	Wood, iron, bronze	Steel	Copper, alloyed steels, light alloys, aluminum	Plastics, superalloys, use of 32 new metals, notably magnesium and titanium
Transportation	Walking, or use of animals, via dirt roads; sailboat over seaways	Steam train via steel rails; the iron steamship via ocean way	Automobile, diesel train, or prop airplane via paved highway, railway, and airway	Road and rail track; jet airplane, rocket, and helicopter; turbine and atomic train via railway; atomic ships via ocean surface and subsurface
Communication	Word of mouth, newspaper, messenger	Mail moved faster by rail and water; newspaper printed on steam press	Telephone, telegraph, AM and FM radio, movie, television, microfilm, magnetic tape	Television telephone, video cassette, talking book or newspaper; universal two-way radio communication, highspeed computers, magnetictape photography, vocatypewriter; cable television

SOURCE: *Industrial Sociology* (pp. 40–41) by Delbert C. Miller and W. H. Form (1980). New York: Harper and Row.

Occupational Structure

According to sociologists and other social scientists, the definitions of *industrialization* and *post-industrialism* are directly linked to occupational structure—what people do in the labour force. There are three major sectors, or divisions, within the labour force: primary, secondary, and tertiary.

People in the **primary sector** work in agriculture, logging, mining, fishing, hunting, or trapping, although the vast majority in this sector are usually in agriculture. In each of these occupational groups, work involves some kind of extraction or harvesting; there is no transformation of raw materials into finished goods. If at least half of the workers in the labour force are in the primary sector, the society is defined as an **agricultural society.**

Industrialization involves the movement of workers out of the primary and into the **secondary sector**, as work activity is concentrated on the manufacture of goods for market. Thus, by this definition, those engaged in the logging industry are working in the primary sector (i.e. harvesting trees), but those working in sawmills are in the secondary sector (i.e. transforming trees into lumber). The construction industry is also classified as secondary, in that it too involves transforming basic materials into a finished product. When less than half of the workers in the labour force are in the primary sector, we have an **industrial society**.

The **secondary sector** involves the manufacture of finished and semifinished goods. People who work in the **tertiary sector** provide services. These include transportation, communication, the provision of public utilities, most professional work, and all occupations in commerce, finance, health, education, welfare, and recreation or leisure. If at least half of the labour force works in these two sectors combined, an **industrial society** exists. When at least half of the labour force works in the tertiary sector alone, that society is defined as a **post-industrial society** (Bell, 1967).

Today, the vast majority of those employed in Canada (70 percent) provide services rather than produce goods. Fewer than one-third of all workers are in the goods-producing primary and secondary sectors.

As an industrial society matures, it changes from being *labour intensive* to *capital intensive*. In the beginning stages of industrialization, human labour is cheaper than machines. But as the standard of living improves with industrialization (see Table 12-3), labour becomes increasingly expensive. This motivates owners and managers to substitute machines for labour. Thus, whereas early farms, mines, and factories swarmed with unskilled and semiskilled, poorly paid workers, today these same places of work are notable for their absence of workers and for the presence of highly complex equipment and machinery. The displacement of these workers from the primary and secondary sectors did not mean that they became unemployed, although at times there were serious dislocations. Rather, the whole occupational structure changed. Occupations previously unknown came into being (for example, all the service jobs in the computer and microprocessing industries), while other occupational groups expanded enormously (for example, professional consulting in finance, housing, health, education, welfare, management, interior design, landscaping, fashion, travel). The emphasis in society changed from production to consumption. It has been estimated by one expert that 90 percent of all new jobs created between 1969 and 1976 were in the services, or tertiary, sector (Ginzberg, 1982).

Labour Relations

Labour unions date back to before the industrial revolution, and the labour union movement represents a history of power, struggle, and conflict. It is a history of attempts to distribute more equally the material and symbolic rewards gained from work. By uniting, workers became a force to counteract the almost overwhelming power assumed by the early industrial capitalists.

The study and analysis of labour-management relations highlights most strongly the marked differences between the *consensus* and *conflict* perspectives (see Berg, 1979). The consensus perspective asserts that management and labour have common goals, while the conflict perspective sees these same goals as essentially in opposition. Consensus theorists argue that the distribution of power is shared, while conflict theorists state that it is extremely unequal. And finally, concerning the rewards received from work, the consensus theorists see the distribution as just and fair, reflecting differential contributions made, while conflict theorists are convinced that this distribution is grossly unjust.

In Canada, there are more than 800 unions, comprised of over 3.5 million members, which represent 38 percent of the non-agricultural work force (Directory of Labour Organizations in Canada, 1986). Sixteen of these unions have memberships of over of 50 000, accounting for just over half of all union members. Table 12-5 presents the ten largest of these unions.

There are three basic types of unions:

1. trade;
2. industrial;
3. public sector.

TABLE 12-5. Ten Largest Unions in Canada by Type of Union and Percentage Share of Total Union Membership, 1986

Union	Number of Members	Percentage of Total Membership	Type of Union
Canadian Union of Public Employees	304,300	8.2	Public
National Union of Provincial Government Employees	254,300	6.8	Public
Public Service Alliance of Canada	182,000	4.9	Public
United Steelworkers of America	160,000	4.3	Industrial
United Food and Commercial Workers	156,000	4.2	Industrial
International Union of United Automobile, Aerospace and Agricultural Implement Workers	140,000	3.8	Industrial
Social Affairs Federation	93,000	2.5	Public
International Brotherhood of Teamsters, Chauffeurs, Warehousemen and Helpers	91,500	2.5	Industrial
School Board Teachers' Commission	75,000	2.0	Public
Service Employees International Union	70,000	1.9	Public
TOTAL	1,526,000	41.1	

SOURCE: Adapted from *Directory of Labour Organizations in Canada 1986*, p. 15, Ottawa: Minister of Supply and Services, 1986.

Each of these types emerged at a particular historical period in the unionization of the labour force. Generally, unionism in Canada began with skilled blue-collar workers, spread to the semiskilled and unskilled workers, and, within the last few decades, has made significant inroads among lower white-collar workers and professionals.

Trade Unions.   The earliest type of union was a trade (or craft) union, in which workers organized on the basis of the specialized working skills they had in common. In Britain, for example, the first unions consisted of workers in the building and printing trades, and actually pre-dated the industrial revolution (Reynolds, 1959). These people formed the aristocracy of labour. They were able to organize themselves and protect their own interests because they possessed unique skills that were in high demand.

Industrial Unions.   With industrialization and increasing divisions of labour, semiskilled machine operators became the majority of the working class. These workers had no highly specialized skills the way the craft workers had before them and therefore could not organize in the same way. However, together, in industrial unions, they did constitute a powerful force that could challenge the privileges of management.

The efforts to organize industrial unions represented the most bloody and bitter period in the history of the labour union movement. Workers, attempting to organize on an industry-wide basis for the first time, posed a direct threat to the exclusive right of management to dictate the terms and conditions of work. Although craft workers had organized before industrial workers, the craft workers were not seen by management to be as serious a problem. They formed a very small proportion of the labour force and did not threaten the status quo. On the contrary, they wished to ensure their position within it. The unionization of the labouring masses, on the other hand, posed quite a different set of conditions. Management resisted extensively—and often violently—the attempts by workers to form industrial unions. The history of unions in the mining, textile, steel, and railroad industries is filled with bloody confrontations as the industrial workers of the world attempted and finally succeeded, to establish a new social, economic, and political contract.

Public-Sector Unions. From the industrial revolution until the middle of this century, the labour union movement increased both its membership and its acceptance within society. It was a movement made up of male blue-collar workers in the industrial labour force. In 1958 in Canada, its membership

The history of labour unions has been marked by sometimes violent confrontation, as with the six-week-long Winnipeg General Strike in 1919. On "Bloody Saturday" (June 21), a silent parade of war veterans supporting the strike was met by mounted charges of the Northwest Mounted Police. Two people were killed and 30 more were injured.

SOURCE: Manitoba Provincial Archives

peaked at slightly over one-third of non-agricultural workers (Chaison, 1982). Membership then remained constant and even declined somewhat, largely as a result of decreasing semiskilled jobs and increasing employment in the tertiary sector.

In 1972, there was a resurgence in union membership, associated with the formation of public sector unions. This time non-manual white-collar and professional workers were involved—particularly within the various levels of government. Today, although public sector workers make up only one-quarter of the labour force, they constitute almost half of all union members in Canada (Ponak, 1982). Table 12-5 reveals that the three largest Canadian unions are public-sector unions; furthermore, they constitute six of the top ten. Another interesting point with regard to these ten largest Canadian unions is that seven of them represent workers in the tertiary sector, a sector traditionally not associated with the labour movement. Finally, 28 percent of all Canadian union members today are female (Chaison, 1982). This figure has recently risen dramatically and will continue to grow as membership from the tertiary sector increases.

It is interesting to ask why at this particular time unionization has been successfully introduced in the tertiary sector in general and in public employment in particular. Most of those employed in the tertiary sector are non-manual white-collar workers. In the past, this group has largely rejected the notion of unionism and has, instead, endorsed the values and goals of management and attempted to imitate its lifestyle. However, as working conditions throughout the labour force are becoming more and more similar and as work is increasingly mechanized, the distinction between non-manual white-collar and manual blue-collar is becoming blurred.

Another important factor is financial. Many unionized blue-collar workers now earn wages far above what non-unionized white-collar workers earn. Also, a few white-collar unions that were in existence prior to the surge in tertiary sector unionism demonstrated that they could achieve not only economic benefits but also a stronger voice in their own self-determination (Ponak, 1982).

These recent developments have several very important implications for the labour union movement throughout the industrialized world. The whole strategy of unionism is built on the premise that if workers organize, they will be in an effective and powerful bargaining position with the employer. If the employer does not agree to the proposals put forward by the workers, their ultimate option is to withdraw their labour—that is, to strike.

This is an effective weapon against a *private* employer because, without labour, the employer cannot produce goods or provide services and, therefore, loses the opportunity to make a profit. However, this strategy becomes questionable when used against a *public* employer. In this case, the employer is the citizens of the municipality, province, or country. If workers strike, it is these citizens, and not industrial capitalists, who suffer. In fact, a strike can work to the economic advantage of government by saving its labour costs. The costs of a strike to government are not economic but political.

There are two related alternatives to the strike used in the public sector:

1. conciliation;
2. arbitration.

When labour and management cannot reach a negotiated settlement, the case is referred either to an independent *conciliation* board or to an independent *arbitration* board. A **conciliation** board examines all of the evidence and claims of both parties, then makes recommendations for a satisfactory compromise. However, these recommendations are not binding on either labour or management. An **arbitration** board engages in the same process, but its judgment is final and becomes the new collective agreement between labour and management. Conciliation does not necessarily eliminate the possibility of a strike, but arbitration does. While both conciliation and arbitration have been used in the public as well as the private sector, neither is seen as an ideal solution. Labour and management together have traditionally objected to outside interference in reaching a collective agreement. Each jealously guards the right to determine its own destiny.

The history of labour relations may be seen as one of increased recognition that both management *and* labour have rights in setting the conditions of work and the rewards to be gained from it. While management rights have never seriously been questioned, labour rights have. Today, the rights of labour have largely become recognized in law, as has the collective agreement upon which ultimately both management and labour agree.

Work Values

Much of the research on workers in industrial societies has been on how satisfied they are with what they actually do at work. From the first landmark study (Hoppock, 1935) to those most recently conducted, the results are consistent over time and from one country to another (see Table 12-6). As you will recall from Chapter 9, workers are largely satisfied with their jobs. Anywhere from two-thirds to three-quarters of the workers register satisfaction, while approximately 10 to 15 percent state that they are dissatisfied.

TABLE 12-6. Job Satisfaction of Industrial Workers in Britain, the United States, Australia, and Canada (1969–1979)

Job Satisfaction	Britain 1969	U.S.A. 1974	Australia 1977	Canada 1979
	%	%	%	%
Very satisfied	14	17	19	15
Satisfied	62	51	55	59
Indifferent	14	15	14	13
Dissatisfied	6	11	8	10
Very dissatisfied	3	6	4	3
Total	99	100	100	100
Number of workers	3,098	649	1,359	363

SOURCE: "Attachments to work: a cross-national examination" by R. Alan Hedley, 1981, *Comparative Research 9* (1), p. 12.

Whereas general orientations to work are similar, specific attachments to it vary. These variations may be explained with the help of three broad sets of factors:

1. work-related;
2. sociodemographic;
3. cultural.

Work-Related Factors

Of the many work-related factors explaining differing perceptions of work, occupational skill is especially important. Generally, those with higher skill place greater emphasis on intrinsic job features or the actual performance characteristics of work than do less-skilled workers. They value such features as the particular type of work they do (in terms of challenge, interest, variety, and responsibility), as well as the tools and equipment they work with. Less-skilled workers, on the other hand, focus more on features extrinsic to work performance than do those with greater skill. The actual hours they work, raises and bonuses, and holidays and vacations are valued more by less-skilled workers, as are interpersonal relationships with both co-workers and supervisors.

Another important factor is length of service, or the number of years spent with one's employer. Workers who have been with a company for a long time are likely to be concerned with the length of their employment and what this means in terms of their job security, company benefits, and familiarity with their jobs. As well, they attach greater importance to how the company is managed and how much profit it makes than do workers who have just begun working for a company. The latter group is more interested in social relations on the job and the opportunities existing within the company. They value the chance to meet new people, the ability to talk to others while working, and the relationship they have with their supervisor. They are also attracted to opportunities for advancement and promotion and the chance to learn more than one job.

Sociodemographic Factors

Gender and age also produce differences with regard to how people perceive work. For example, women are more attached to social relations at work than men are. Not only do they value meeting new people, talking to them at work, and getting together with them after work, they also want to get along with these same people (including supervisors) and are concerned with how the company judges them. In addition, women place more importance than do men on the hours they work, on how far they have to travel to work, on knowing in advance what they will do each day, and on holidays and vacations.

Men tend to value job security, employee benefits including retirement plans, and their chances for advancement and promotion more than women do. They also tend to be more intrinsically attached to their work than are female workers. They place greater importance on the type of work they do, on the quality of their equipment and tools, and on the chance to learn new things and to create new methods to do their jobs.

Older workers are concerned with having a job as a way of life, with their length of service with the firm, with being familiar with their job, and with knowing in advance what they will do each day. They are also interested in the amount of physical work they do, in controlling the number of things they do, and in the attention they have to pay to their work.

Younger workers, on the other hand, have a set of quite different priorities. They, too, are attached to their work, but through the challenge, interest, and variety of their jobs, creating new methods to do their jobs better, the usefulness of the company's products to society, familiarity with what goes on in the firm, teaching new employees, and their chances for advancement and promotion. Young workers are also attached to the social relations with other employees, both at the workplace and after work.

Cultural Factors

Comparisons of factory workers from Britain, the United States, Australia, and Canada reveal some interesting groupings of work attachments. British workers emphasize control over their work and their working conditions more than their co-workers in the other three countries. British workers value doing their jobs in their own way and exercising joint control over how the work is done. They value time for personal needs and a minimum of interference from the people they work with. They are concerned about the number of supervisors, about knowing enough to get by, about knowing tasks in advance each day, about how hard they have to work, and about how much attention they must pay. Their priorities regarding working conditions involve how clean the work area is, how well the facilities are kept, and how modern the firm is.

These work attachments contrast sharply with those specified by American workers. First and foremost, Americans are distinguished by their emphasis on the opportunity that work provides. While most workers from the other countries did not value highly their chances for advancement and promotion, Americans by and large attributed great importance to this aspect of work. Apparently, the American Dream is alive and flourishing. In general, Americans want respect from family and friends because of their jobs and are concerned about how the company judges them.

Intrinsic features of work are also important for U.S. workers. Challenge, interest, variety, and a chance to learn new things at work are emphasized, as are the value and usefulness of the products.

Australian workers present yet another picture of work attachments. They value social relations at work, in terms of getting along with fellow workers and supervisors, having a chance to help workmates, getting respect from people at work, and getting a good evaluation from the company. Australian workers also value extrinsic work features, such as holidays and vacations, hours worked, job security, and raises and bonuses.

Canadian workers also have distinct work attachments that set them apart. Intrinsically attached to their work, they rate as important work that is challenging and interesting, the sense of accomplishment they receive from work, and the particular tasks they perform. In addition, Canadians appear to be concerned about how much personal responsibility they have in their jobs, as well as how the company judges them.

Work-related, sociodemographic, and cultural factors all serve to produce differences in how people perceive the world of work.

However, it is also important to note that industrial workers of all types—skilled and unskilled, women and men, Americans and Canadians—also have a *common* core of work attachments that they perceive to be the most important of all. Generally, workers are concerned with achieving a sense of purpose in their work and also with achieving an economic security that will allow them to live their lives outside the workplace. In addition, they are attached to the obvious and immediate conditions and social relations at work that will permit them to perform their tasks with minimal personal cost. Thus, while diverse values and attitudes toward work can and do exist, there is an impressive consistency that is produced in individual assessments of the meaning of work.

Work in a Changing Society

While it is important to ascertain the value people place on work, it is also interesting to determine what influence, if any, employment has on workers' values and behaviour *outside* the workplace. Ever since Wilensky (1960, 1961) formalized some of the problems in this area of research, there have been many studies on the relationship between work and other activities. Generally, the results indicate that what people do for a living does exert influence on what they think and how they behave when they are not at work.

In this section, we will examine the substance of these findings and also explore the changing nature of work. If work does have an effect on non-work activities, and if it can be demonstrated that the world of work is in the process of change, then it will be interesting to speculate on what these changes will mean for our non-work values and behaviour in the future.

Work and Non-work

There are two models of the relationship between work and non-work:

1. holistic;
2. segmental.

The **holistic model** asserts that there is no essential division between work and non-work. We think and act in basically the same manner in both spheres of activity and, therefore, work attitudes spill over into non-work time. The **segmental perspective** states that there is a sharp line between work and non-work. Mentally, we partition our lives so that work does not interfere with non-work.

The research to date supports both models. Generally, the holistic model applies better in studies of upper white-collar professional and managerial workers, while the segmental model is better suited to blue-collar workers. The nature of the work performed in these two cases explains the different relationship.

In upper white-collar jobs, workers are given freedom to organize and carry out work in their own way. Because of their prior socialization and training, they have a strong commitment to working and to performing well. Consequently, it is unnecessary to supervise these workers closely. Also, again because of extensive socialization and training, the occupational roles of these upper white-collar workers have more to do with how they define themselves than do the roles of blue-collar workers. These factors together explain why white-collar workers take their work roles outside of work. One early study, *The organization man* (Whyte, 1956), documented how all-encompassing the spillover of work into non-work could be. He found that the management hierarchy at work extended into executives' non-work lives, dictating such things as the appropriate type of neighbourhood to live in, model of car to drive, and people to choose as friends.

Blue-collar jobs, on the other hand, are more specifically defined. Explicit job descriptions inform workers precisely what they are to do in each task, how they will perform it, and the time it will take them to complete it. They exercise little choice within their work roles. Because they have relatively little specialized training, and because it is assumed they have only limited organization loyalty, they are supervised closely.

Also, because the corporate enterprise is alien to their blue-collar culture, they make a sharp distinction between work and non-work (Hedley, 1982). As Dubin (1968) has noted: "Workers in modern industrial society do not make a living; they make money and buy a living." However, regardless of the distinction made between work and non-work, work does affect people's lives away from work.

One excellent study that spells out more fully the distinction between blue-collar and white-collar workers was conducted by Pearlin and Kohn (1966). They asked Italian and American mothers and fathers from both the middle and the working classes to choose 3 of 17 values that they considered most important for a boy or girl of their child's age. They analysed whether culture, gender, or class explained most of the variation in the ranking of values that the mothers and fathers chose. Overwhelmingly, they found that class, as measured by occupation, was the single most important variable. For example, working-class parents from both countries selected "obedience to parents" far more often than middle-class parents did, while the latter group chose "self-control" more frequently than did working-class parents.

Pearlin and Kohn explain this finding by stating that obedience and self-control are two aspects of one characteristic—control. Because much blue-collar work involves control by others, the characteristic of obedience becomes a value for blue-collar workers that they then transmit to their children. Similarly, because self-control and self-direction characterize white-collar occupations, this quality becomes internalized as a value by white-collar workers. The Pearlin and Kohn study suggests that regardless of whether we adopt holistic or segmental perspectives, the influence of work on values and behaviour is pervasive.

Work in a New Era

All the developments presented so far in this chapter have contributed to vast structural changes in society. In turn, these changes affect how we perceive work and what we actually do at work. In fact, very recent developments may cause us to re-evaluate what work is. Some experts have declared that we are currently experiencing a work revolution just as profound as the original industrial revolution, and with just as many far-reaching implications (see the insert on new work trends).

When industrialization first occurred in Britain 200 years ago, it caused us to redefine the concept of work. Work became an explicit set of obligations physically separated in time and space from the rest of life. Traditionally, work had not involved such a separation. It had taken place within the context of the family as and when the need dictated

Today, as a result of the electronic revolution, it is no longer necessary to perform much of what we do within explicitly defined space and time limits. While we are still responsible for achieving the goals of the organization, there is much more flexibility in the system. Most work today involves the manipulation of information rather than materials; therefore, former limitations of time and space are no longer necessary. Instead, workers are linked to each other in a free-floating electronic network. The portable computer is "the workplace". Where and (within certain limits) when we perform our duties are largely irrelevant.

It is important to ask what changes this new work arrangement will produce and how it will modify our existing attitudes toward work. One potentially far-reaching consequence is that work loses the importance it once held. It becomes instead, just one of many activities that must be fitted into personal time

New Work Trends

The following newspaper article presents some of the ways in which traditional work is changing. Brought about by structural pressures and individual worker demand, it is likely that we will have to redefine what it means to have a job.

Virtually everyone working at home, or at the home of a friend? Four-hour or even two-hour workdays? This new concept of work is steadily gaining ground. Does it represent progress? No one knows for sure.

You share your job with a neighbour. He alternates short assignments with periods of idleness. Another edits manuscripts on the family word processor in the morning and sells sweaters in the afternoon. All are new-era workers, with dreams of autonomy and self-improvement in an increasingly unstable world.

Work is not what it used to be. Not only are jobs difficult to find and to keep, but also the concept of full employment has gone out of fashion.

The current economic situation and increasing unemployment are reshaping the classical model of employment, which once was based on a full day's work and on lifetime employment with a single company, from training to retirement. The concept of total employment has been replaced by one of floating, uncertain work. In the past few years new and atypical forms of employment have flourished: tempo-rary jobs, substitutions, piecework, subcontracting, shared workplaces, short workdays, tailored hours.

The number of active workers who are content with this permanent precariousness is growing. Part-time employment, for example, has been gaining ground in all the industrial countries. Since 1974 half of the new jobs in Europe have been part-time.

In most industrial countries there is a nearly inexhaustible reserve of labour. It includes the unemployed, young people seeking their first jobs, housewives and mothers eager to resume working, and retirees who find it difficult not to work. This labour reserve creates a new situation that favours innovations. Flexibility has become the byword in both the private and public sector lately, as a means of reducing unemployment. And for many people flexibility means freedom. Who, especially among the younger generation, does not dream of throwing off the yoke of work restrictions?

New lifestyles and new values lead more and more people to doubt the sacrosanct value of work. Studies in France underscore this profound change. During the 1950s, nine out of every ten French workers were motivated by a need for economic security. In 1982, that ratio had fallen to three out of ten, and the "need for personal expression" had become of paramount importance for half of the country's potential work force.

SOURCE: From "Taking Work Home: A Comeback for Cottage Industry" by Michel Herteaux, January, 1985, *World Press Review*, 32(1) p. 38. Copyright 1984 by *Le Monde*.

schedules. Very likely this will result in a lessening of the value attributed to work, because increasingly it will have to compete with other important individual activities. No longer will work occupy its own separate space-time domain.

Another important implication of the electronic revolution is the reconstitution of the labour force. Because work is increasingly becoming an individualized activity, we can expect that the former solidarity of the physically united labour force will

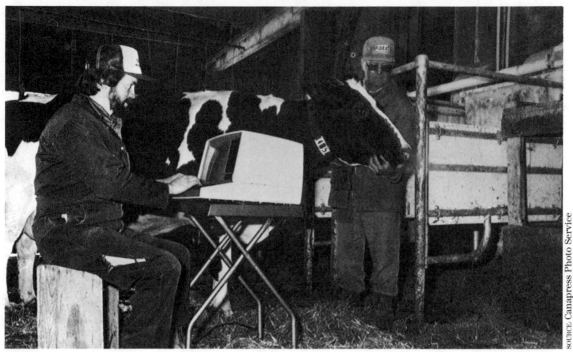

SOURCE: Canapress Photo Service

The electronic revolution is changing the way many people do their work. In this dairy farm, cows wear a computer chip that tells a sensor at the feed bin how much food to auger out. The computer also records production and breeding information.

become less. Labour-management relations are entering a new era, and the strength of labour unions to organize the labour force and to represent its interests is threatened. To the extent that unions adapt to the new conditions, they can maintain their function, but in a radically different form. Union "meetings" will occur electronically rather than physically. Since attendance at union meetings has traditionally been very low, this could actually increase membership involvement.

Finally, we should ask how extensive the changes we have been discussing will be. What proportion of the labour force will be affected? Farmers must still sow seeds; construction workers must still work at the building site; and surgeons must still appear in the operating room. While it is impossible at this stage to make an accurate estimate of how many people will be affected, technologically it is now feasible for a large proportion of conventionally employed workers in offices to switch to this new work arrangement.

As with so many other revolutionary events, the technology is changing before our norms and values are. While it is now possible for many workers to do their jobs without being bound by traditional time and space considerations, there is a resistance on the part of most—management and labour alike—to enter into a radically changed work structure. Nevertheless, change is occurring, and for you students about to enter the labour force, your experience with work and your reaction to it will likely be very different from the generation that preceded you.

Summary

1. The industrial revolution radically altered the organization of work. Changes in technology introduced the factory system of production, with goods being manufactured for large consumer markets.

2. Industrialization changed people's relationship to society. For Durkheim, the principal factor responsible for this change was the increased division of labour. For Weber, it was a change in the value people placed on work. For Marx, it was the ownership of the means of production by the bourgeoisie.

3. Industrialization has produced great inequality among the nations of the world, and the gap between the rich, developed nations and the poor, developing nations is increasing enormously. The industrialized nations enjoy a substantially higher per capita income and standard of living than do the developing countries.

4. While Canada has one of the highest per capita gross national products in the world, it is not as industrially developed as the United States, Japan, or the European nations. This is explained in part by Canada's special and unique relationship with the United States.

5. Post-industrial societies are those in which at least half the labour force is engaged in the service-producing tertiary sector. By this definition, Canada is post-industrial. Post-industrialism is accompanied by a transformation of the occupational structure and by more formal representation of workers by labour unions.

6. Generally, workers are satisfied with their jobs. Work-related, sociodemographic, and cultural factors all produce variations in how people are attached to their work.

7. The kind of work people do affects what they value and how they behave outside of the workplace. While some people attempt to maintain a sharp distinction between work and non-work (segmentalism), others do not (holism). Generally, higher occupational levels have a holistic perspective, while lower levels have a segmental orientation.

8. The new electronic revolution is changing popular conceptions of work. Work no longer need be confined in space and time. Rather, workers can be linked to their employment through interlocking electronic networks.

Further Reading

Anderson, J., & Gunderson, M. (Eds). (1982). *Union-management relations in Canada*. Don Mills, Ont.: Addison-Wesley.
A collection of 22 articles on all aspects of labour-management relations in Canada, including comparative data.

Chen, M. Y. T., & Regan, T. G. (1985). Work in the changing Canadian society. Toronto: Butterworths.
A Canadian text that concentrates mainly on the sociology of work and the workplace.

Lenski, G., & Lenski, J. (1982). *Human societies: An introduction to macrosociology*. New York: McGraw-Hill.
An examination of how societies have evolved over time. There are particularly good chapters on industrialization and the industrial revolution.

Miller, D. C., & Form, W. H. (1980). *Industrial sociology: Work in organizational life*. New York: Harper and Row.
A basic industrial sociology text now in its third edition, and written by noted experts in the field.

Murdoch, W. W. (1980). *The poverty of nations: The political economy of hunger and population*. Baltimore: The Johns Hopkins University Press.
An excellent treatment of the history and development of industrialization throughout the world, and an analysis of the reasons for the inequities that exist among nations.

Smucker, J. (1980). *Industrialization in Canada*. Scarborough, Ont.: Prentice-Hall.
A good treatment of industrialization and the labour union movement in Canada.

13
Urbanization and Urbanism

The purpose of this chapter is to help you explore some sociological ideas about cities. The first part of the chapter deals with the development of cities both historically and in the present. The second section focuses on the impact of cities upon those who live in them.

As a result of reading and studying this chapter, you should be able to

1. describe the forces affecting city development from the ancient period to modern times;

2. describe the pattern of urbanization in Canada;

3. explain the following ideas about urban development:
   - (a) the concentric-zone model,
   - (b) the sector model,
   - (c) the multiple-nuclei model;

4. evaluate the applicability of the above models to Canadian urban development;

5. explain the differences between the urban and rural ways of life with reference to the ideas of
   - (a) Tönnies,
   - (b) Wirth,
   - (c) Simmel,
   - (d) selection theory;

6. describe urban crime and explain its existence.

It is hard to define *city* in a way that will please everyone. Architects, planners, and civil engineers, for example, are mainly interested in planning, design, and physical factors; the way they define and view the city reflects those interests.

Since social scientists are concerned with social life, their view of the city and what they regard as its distinct features leads them to a somewhat different definition. Sociologists see **cities** as large concentrations of people whose work for the most part does not involve the primary production of food. Rather, it consists of a wide range of specialized and interdependent occupations.

The sociological view of cities is useful because it allows us to explain how cities grow and spread, and how and why people who live in them differ from people who live in rural areas. These are important issues for sociologists, especially in view of the recent and continuing rural-to-urban shift of the world's population.

Urbanization

Urbanization refers to an increase in the proportion of a population living in areas defined as urban. Increases have most often occurred through people migrating from rural to urban areas and, as noted in Chapter 6, to other countries.

The Ancient Period

Ancient cities were small by today's standards and contained only a tiny proportion of the world's population. Athens, the prime city of classical Greece, peaked with a population of from 120000 to 180000. Poor soil and simple agricultural technology, along with a cultural preference for small cities, combined to limit its growth (Davis, 1955; Palen, 1981).

The other great city of the ancient period was Rome. Several factors combined to push Rome far beyond the size of Athens: a more generous natural environment, a more complex division of labour, and a cultural interest in expansion. There were also certain technical advances—especially in agriculture and transport. Estimates of the size of ancient Rome, whose population peaked just before the birth of Christ, range between 250000 and 1.6 million (Palen, 1981).

De-Urbanization: The Middle Ages

Rome was the largest and most powerful city the world had ever seen, but when the Roman Empire fell (around the fifth century A.D.), neither the city nor its population could be maintained. When the Vandals cut the city off from its grain-producing areas in Africa, Rome was crippled, and its population dwindled to less than 25000 (Palen, 1981).

The demise of the Roman Empire, like the decline of Greece before it, involved the disorganization of an extensive social network, with a city at its centre. All roads led indeed to Rome. They carried raw materials, food, and labourers to the city and armies from it to collect taxes, maintain order in the provinces, and extend the empire's frontiers.

The fall of Rome was the start of a period of **de-urbanization**, the gradual return of much of the population to rural life. The vast network developed by Rome withered, and outlying localities were forced once again into isolation and self-sufficiency. During urban growth, people had flowed to the city on all the roads that led to Rome. In decline, the same roads took those people away. People returned to the land and to local rather than imperial domination. For a 600-year period, few European cities surpassed 100 000 in population.

Re-Urbanization: The Renaissance

In the eleventh century, Europeans began to return to the cities. Again, these were small by today's standards. According to Weber (1958, originally published 1921), each city had the following features:

1. a fortification;
2. a market;
3. a law court of its own;
4. a form of professional associations such as guilds;
5. at least partial political and administrative independence.

Weber thought that such cities were characteristic of Europe and had an important effect on the economy.

By the fourteenth century, the economy of Europe was becoming a city-centred, trade-oriented version of capitalism. Feudal self-sufficiency, characteristic of the medieval period, was in decline. Cities provided farm workers with a place to live, greater freedom, and a better occupational deal than the feudal manor did. As a result, serfs increasingly fled from the farms to the cities where, if they had the skills to persuade the city fathers and the guilds to allow them in and could escape capture for a year, they were considered to be free. Urbanization in Europe contributed to the destruction of the feudal economy and the concentration of capital in cities (Marx, 1965, originally published 1889). In this sense, then, the city affected the economic structure, as well as the culture, of western societies.

The development of cities in Europe during the Renaissance was associated with important changes in culture (such as the Protestant Reformation), as well as in the economy (such as the rise of modern capitalism). The major effects on cities during this period were the forces of urbanization and the opposing force of de-urbanization caused by several waves of the bubonic plague (the Black Death). In a three-year period, the plague killed about one-quarter of the population of Europe. By 1400, one-third of Europe's population was dead from the Black Death and over half of the residents of cities had died (Zinssen, 1965; Langer, 1973; and McNeill, 1976). The mortality rate from the bubonic plague was higher in cities than in rural areas, reflecting inadequate garbage and sewage disposal, as well as the greater ease with which communicable diseases can spread in high-density settings.

In the short run, then, the plague had a de-urbanizing effect on Europe. In the long run, however, the Black Death dealt the final blow to feudalism and actually accelerated urbanization. The death of large numbers of peasants lowered the already weakened supply of rural farm-workers. Those who survived left for the cities, where the plague had created a severe labour shortage. By the fifteenth century, the forces of urbanization had countered the forces of de-urbanization, and European cities began growing again.

Plagues continued into the seventeenth century, but never again affected the size or distribution of the population the way they had in the latter part of the fourteenth century. Still, the mortality rate from all causes continued to be higher in cities than in the countryside until the end of the nineteenth century. This mortality rate, combined with the typically lower rate of urban fertility, meant that heavy migration to the cities was required for urbanization to continue.

The Modern Era

The urbanization of Europe proceeded slowly until late in the eighteenth century, when the population grew quickly, partly because of a sudden drop in mortality rates. This drop probably resulted from Jenner's invention of the smallpox vaccine in 1792 and from a general improvement in health that resulted from significant increase in the amount and availability of food. This was made possible through several important advances in agricultural and transportation technology (McKeown, 1976). Extra food not only allowed a larger population to be better nourished, but released more people from agricultural occupations and rural areas. Many migrated to the cities and, for the first time in European history, close to ten percent of the human population lived in urban areas.

The development of a wide range of technologies freed increasing numbers of labourers from agricultural occupations, allowing them to take on other tasks in urban centres. The most important technical advance in this respect, as noted in Chapter 12, was industrialization.

In Europe, industrialization replaced animate sources of energy (humans, horses, oxen) with inanimate sources of energy (mainly oil and coal). This exchange involved the substitution of machines for tools as energy converters; for example, the horse collar and harness are tools that convert horse power into pulling power, but the tractor is a machine that converts inanimate energy into pulling power. Industrialization began in cottage industries (people working in their own homes) in nineteenth-century England, which became the centre of the "industrial revolution" and one of the most urbanized nations in the world (Bronowski, 1976).

Industrialization had at least three major effects on the city:

1. The application of new technology to agriculture greatly increased the efficiency of agricultural workers and the size of the surplus they could produce. This change released or forced many workers from farming and provided labourers for work in the cities elsewhere (McQuillan, 1980).

How many farmers would it take. . . ?

Between 50 and 90 farmers were required to produce sufficent food to sustain themselves and *one* other person in the first cities. This tiny surplus kept the population of the earliest cities small. As technology improved, the number of farmers required to sustain an urbanite decreased. By the beginning of the nineteenth century the number of farmers had been reduced to nine, and the second-largest city in the world was London with a population of 900 000. (The largest was Edo [Tokyo] at one million.) Industrialization has further decreased the number of farmers required to sustain an urbanite and increased the potential size of cities.

Today, in the United States, for example, one farmer can sustain himself of herself and approximately 45 other people. Fewer than five percent of the employed population are engaged in agricultural occupations, and the largest metropolitan area in the country is New York, with more than 16 million people.

SOURCES: "The origin and growth of urbanization in the world" by Kingsley Davis, March 1955, *American Journal of Sociology, 60*, p. 430; "Edo's importance in the changing Tokugawa society" by G. Rozman, 1975, *Journal of Japanese Studies, 1*(1), pp. 91-112; *The Urban World* by John Palen, 1975, New York: McGraw-Hill; *Urban Society*, 6th ed., New York: Thomas Y. Crowell, 1974.

2. The application of new technology to transportation greatly extended the territory on which an urban area could draw for food and raw materials and reduced the danger of starvation resulting from crop failure in a specific region. Such territorial extension affected Canada, because it allowed England to increase imports of wheat from its colony.

3. The building of factories resulted in a new type of city—the manufacturing city. Ironically, as industrialization made efforts to replace people and animals with machines, there was also a growth in demand for labourers as factory workers. So the industrial revolution was also a social revolution. People and capital, which had been dispersed throughout rural areas, became concentrated in factories, themselves concentrated in industrial cities. Labourers worked with machines, and what had once been relatively simple and family-oriented work was replaced by highly specialized occupations.

These effects combined to expand greatly the potential for the growth and spread of cities. Increased agricultural productivity meant that more food could be sent to cities. More efficient transportation meant that greater amounts of food could be sent faster and farther than before, and the urban promise of consumer goods and employment attracted millions of rural migrants.

Urban Futures

The last two centuries have seen a flood of people moving from rural to urban areas around the world. Urbanization has been most intense in industrialized countries, for the reasons outlined. For example, England was one of the first countries to industrialize and one of the first countries to experience a massive movement of people to the cities. As a result, England is now one of the most urbanized countries in the world, with about 70 percent of its population living in large cities and 80 percent in urban areas.

The rate of urbanization of the world's population is shown in Table 13-1. Between 1800 and 1950, the urban population of the world doubled every 50 years. Since 1950, however, the urban population has tripled every 50 years. The projected population of the urban areas of the world for the year 2000 is 61 percent, with 42 percent living in cities with populations greater than 100000. As for all projections, this one assumes that current trends will continue. However, there are signs that the rate of urbanization in some industrialized countries, including Canada, is starting to decline and may even reverse (Bourne, 1978).

TABLE 13-1. Percentage of World Urban Population, Actual and Projected, 1800-2000

	Urban (over 20,000)	Large Cities (over 100,000)
	%	%
1800	2	2
1850	4	2
1900	9	6
1950	21	13
1975	42	26
2000	61	42

NOTE: Percentages are rounded.

SOURCE: "The origin and growth of urbanization in the world" by Kingsley Davis, March, 1955, *American Journal of Sociology*, 60 p. 430; *World Urbanization*, 1950-70, vol. II, by Kingsley Davis, 1972, pp. 126-127.

Modern industrial countries are already heavily urbanized. Between 70 and 80 percent of the inhabitants of industrialized countries now live in urban areas. It is unclear whether a much greater proportion of these populations will be able to do so. Even now, some cities in industrialized countries have spread so much that their boundaries have merged. North American examples of this phenomenon include the urban belt extending from Massachusetts to Virginia along the eastern coast of the United States and the Golden Horseshoe stretching from Oshawa to Buffalo, around the western shore of Lake Ontario.

It is hard to predict future levels of world urbanization. Some projections suggest a highly urbanized world; however, projections are based on existing trends, such as the consumption of fossil fuels (oil, coal), which may not continue. De-urbanization is a definite possibility—as with ancient Rome and, in recent times, with the dramatic destruction of Phnom Penh and Kampuchia (Cambodia). It may also be starting in other developing countries (Szelenyi, 1981), as well as in North America.

Urbanization in Canada

Urbanization in what is now Canada began some time after French colonization in the seventeenth century. By the mid-1600s, the outpost towns of Québec, Montréal, and Trois-Rivières each contained fewer than 1000 people; by 1765, Québec and Montréal had grown into towns of more than 5000. At this time, New France was about 25 percent urban, while less than ten percent of the population of the 13 American colonies lived in urban areas. This reflects the fact that New France was more of a commercial centre—based on the fur trade—than an agricultural colony, like its southern neighbours.

By 1825, Fort York (Toronto) was a garrison of about 2000 people, while Québec and Montréal had each passed 20 000. By the mid-1800s, Montréal was a city of more than 50 000, and both Québec and Toronto had populations of over 30 000. In the Maritimes, both Saint John and Halifax had more than 20 000 people. In 1850, about seven percent of the populations of the Maritimes, Lower Canada (Québec), and Upper Canada (Ontario) lived in cities of 20 000 or more, compared with a world figure of five percent (Stone, 1967). In 1867, then, by world standards, Canada was an urbanized country.

Stone (1967) noted that "Canadian urban development probably had its take-off toward high levels of urbanization in the 10 to 15 years following Confederation in 1867." In this respect, Canada followed the pattern of urban growth in northwest Europe and the United States. In the twentieth century, the urbanization of Canada continued. Canada's pattern of urbanization, like that of the United States, moved from east to west.

When the first Europeans landed on the east coast of North America, European technology was not up to hacking through the forests. But native technology, in the form of the canoe, allowed rapid movement along rivers and lakes. So, during the exploration of the continent, water was the principal means of transportation.

As the Europeans pushed their frontier westward, gradually taming some of the wilderness, towns and cities were built behind them as forts or service centres. Most on the eastern coast began as ports—cities such as St. John's, Halifax, Saint John, and Charlottetown were built on natural harbours that gave ships protection from the sea. Québec, Montréal, and Trois-Rivières were situated on the St. Lawrence River in locations favouring defence and transportation. Montréal, for example, was built at the point where the St. Lawrence narrows. There, people and goods were transferred from ocean-going ships to vessels that could proceed westward on the St. Lawrence and Ottawa rivers, while furs and other raw materials travelled eastward on the St. Lawrence.

Generally, the largest cities in Canada and the United States were eastern ports for ocean-going ships. In the United States, such places as Boston, New York, and Philadelphia were, and still are, among the largest and most influential cities in the country. In Canada, however, the east coast was partly by-passed and developed differently from the United States coast. This was because the St. Lawrence River allowed ocean-going vessels to go much farther inland than they could go in the United States.

The westward movement of settlers in Canada was hampered to the north by climate, muskeg, and black flies and to the south by the political boundary with the United States. As a result, settlement was largely confined to a westward expansion along the United States border. Therefore, most Canadian cities are located both on waterways and also relatively near the United States border. In the last 20 to 30 years, however, developments in transportation and telecommunications have increased the technical ability to cope with the harsh Canadian environment. These advances, along with the lure of oil and other raw materials in the north, have produced increased movement away from the U.S. border.

Because Canada was colonized westward from the east to the Rockies, Canadian cities differ greatly in age. As a result, the city of Québec contains a wider range of old and new buildings than does a city such as Calgary. Some western cities tend to be built on grids, with numbered rather than named streets, and tend to have a car, rather than a pedestrian, orientation. Eastern cities (and B.C.'s coastal cities) seem more picturesque, established, and European than the newer western cities, which seem more modern, efficient, and American.

City populations, too, change and vary across the country. As you can see in Table 13-2, Canadian urbanization moved westward quickly. In 1851, Halifax, Saint John, and Kingston were the fourth, fifth, and sixth largest cities; within a century all three were surpassed by the western cities. The newer cities—Edmonton and Calgary—were the fastest growing in Canada between 1971 and 1981. This reflects the importance of wheat, cattle, and especially oil during that period.

Urban Ecology

Social scientists have a number of explanations for the ways in which individual cities grow. The most influential of these was developed by Ernest W. Burgess (1925) at the University of Chicago. His general orientation (developed by Burgess and his two colleagues, Robert E. Park and Roderick D. McKenzie) is known as **human ecology**, an application of ideas from plant and animal ecology to the study of the relationship between humans and their physical habitat (Park *et al.*, 1925; McKenzie, 1968).

The Concentric-Zone Model.   Burgess constructed a model of concentric zones for cities (see Figure 13-1) and applied to the model a number of concepts from natural ecology: segregation, natural areas, competition, invasion, and succession.

Segregation refers to a tendency for certain activity patterns (such as commercial or residential activities) or certain groups of people (such as income or ethnic groups) to cluster and to try to segregate themselves by excluding other activities or groups

TABLE 13-2. Population for Census Metropolitan Areas, Ranked by 1981 Population, Showing Percentage Change, 1976 and 1981

Rank	CMA	1976[1]	1981	Percentage Change
1	Toronto, Ont	2,803,101	2,998,947	7.0
2	Montréal, Qué.	2,802,547[2]	2,828,349	0.9
3	Vancouver, B.C.	1,166,348	1,268,183	8.7
4	Ottawa-Hull, Ont./Qué.	693,288	717,978	3.6
5	Edmonton, Alta.	556,270[2]	657,057	18.1
6	Calgary, Alta.	471,397[2]	592,743	25.7
7	Winnipeg, Man.	578,217	584,842	1.2
8	Québec, Qué.	543,158	576,075	6.3
9	Hamilton, Ont.	529,371	542,095	2.4
10	St. Catharines-Niagara, Ont.	301,921	304,353	0.8
11	Kitchener, Ont.	272,158	287,801	5.8
12	London, Ont.	270,383	283,668	4.9
13	Halifax, N.S.	267,991	277,727	3.6
14	Windsor, Ont.	247,582	246,110	−0.6
15	Victoria, B.C.	218,250	233,481	7.0
16	Regina, Sask.	151,191	164,313	8.7
17	St. John's, Nfld.	145,400[2]	154,820	6.5
18	Oshawa, Ont.	135,196	154,217	14.1
19	Saskatoon, Sask.	133,793[2]	154,210	15.3
20	Sudbury, Ont.	157,030	149,923	−4.5
21	Chicoutimi-Jonquière, Qué.	128,643	135,172	5.1
22	Thunder Bay, Ont.	119,253	121,379	1.8
23	Saint John, N.B.	112,974	114,048	1.0
24	Trois-Rivières, Qué.	106,031[3]	111,453	5.1

[1]Based on 1981 area.
[2]Adjusted figues due to boundary changes
[3]Defined as CMA for 1981 Census.
SOURCE: *Statistics Canada Daily*, Tuesday, March 30, 1982, p. 3.

from "their" territory. To the extent that they are successful, they form a **natural area**—a neighbourhood that is relatively homogeneous. Note that some people and activities can share the same physical environment, but do so at different times. Areas that are commercial by day are often recreational at night (see Tilly, 1974 and Melbin, 1978).

Burgess used the city of Chicago as the basis for his model of concentric zones, as shown in Figure 13-1. These concentric zones do not describe the actual *form* of a city; rather, they describe different patterns of urban activities and their tendency to concentrate, segregate, and create natural areas. The competition among activities for scarce space, as well as the territorial invasion and succession of activities and people, represent the growth patterns of urban areas.

FIGURE 13-1. Burgess's Concentric-Zone Model Applied to Chicago

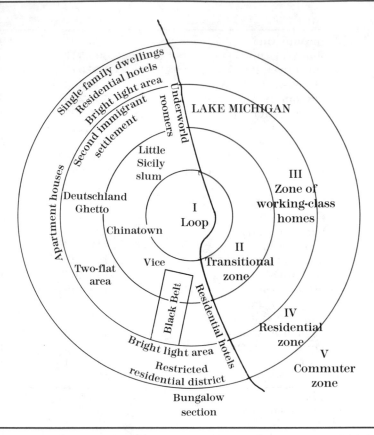

SOURCE: Redrawn from "The growth of the city: an introduction to a research project" by Ernest W. Burgess, in *Studies in Human Ecology* (p. 41) by George A. Theodorson (ed.), 1961, Evanston, IL: Row, Peterson.

Burgess's zones radiate from the centre of the city:

I.   the central business district (CBD), which in Chicago is known as the "Loop";

II. the zone of transition;

III. the working-class residential zone;

IV. the middle-class residential zone;

V.   the commuter zone.

Zone I, the CBD, is the commercial as well as the geographic centre of the city. This inner core contains retail shopping areas, entertainment and cultural centres (night clubs, restaurants, theatres, art galleries, museums, hotels), and office buildings. The edge of this zone includes wholesale businesses, markets, and warehouses. Because it is so central, the land in Zone I is the most valuable in the city. In fact, this land is so expensive that usually only commercial enterprises have the combination of motivation and money necessary to buy it. So commercial activities typically win over residential activities in competing for scarce space near the centre of the city. The result is a natural commercial area.

Zone II—the zone of transition—is the battle zone. **Competition** occurs when one activity or group attempts to invade the territory of another. In Zone II, competition occurs between residential and commercial activities, with the commercial activities often driving out the residents; that is, the commercial activities in the CBD expand into a sector that was formerly made up of homes and related residential activities (child rearing, house-related work, leisure activities, sleeping, and sports). The replacement of one form of activity by another is called **succession.** An important effect of this *invasion* is that the areas deteriorate and devalue as residential environments. As homes devalue, they become a source of cheap rental housing. Speculators hold them for the potential commercial value of the land they are situated on. In the interest of minimizing the costs of holding such property, they spend little or no money to maintain the buildings and at the same time attempt to maximize the number of renters. The result is crowded, deteriorated housing— slums.

To the extent that such an invasion is successful, the commercial activities will eventually result in succession, segregation, and a natural commercial area. Slums endure when an expected commercial expansion fails to occur.

The cheap housing in the transitional zone lets people with low incomes live in the city; this group includes the poor and unemployed, immigrants with little money, the physically and mentally handicapped, and some who survive through illegal commercial activities (muggings, thefts, drugs, and prostitution).

As immigrants arrive in the city, they often locate in the cheap housing of the transitional zone. And as members of alien ethnic groups invade the area, the people who had been living there before move out in order to maintain the integrity of their own ethnic group. Thus, just as commercial activities invade, compete with, and succeed residential activities, so ethnic groups invade the territories of others and succeed the original inhabitants of those neighbourhoods.

Zone III contains inexpensive houses often inhabited by the upwardly mobile children of immigrants in the transitional zone. In Chicago, these houses are typically semi-detached houses. Zone IV is the zone of better residences, where the middle class lives. Zone V, the commuter zone, consists of middle, upper-middle, and upper-class suburbs, where people with cars

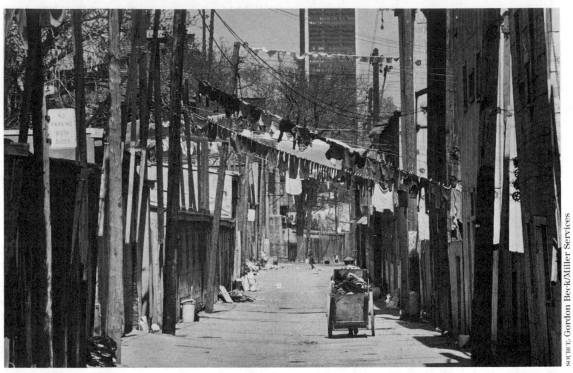

In transition zones, com-
mercial activity gradually
replaces residential use.

live. Most of the residences in Zones IV and V are single,
detached houses.

Although the concentric zone model was developed in Chicago
in the 1920s, it continues to be relevant. The patterns of segregation, competition, invasion, and succession that Burgess
described can still be observed in many North American cities.
However, application of the model is restricted. It does not fit pre-
industrial cities or smaller cities and towns. The model should
be applied with care, even in North America. Both cultural and
environment factors have occasionally produced incongruities
between the Burgess model and urban realities. For example, cultural constraints in the form of zoning laws have often kept commercial activities from pushing into residential areas. Also, in a
number of North American cities, there have recently been successful attempts by young urban professionals (Yuppies) to
reclaim deteriorated sections of both commercial and transitional areas for residential purposes—as in Toronto's Cabbage-
town. In this case, it is clear that commerce need not always
invade and succeed residential areas.

In other instances, the physical environment may prevent the
operation of the forces Burgess observed in Chicago. Vancouver,
for example, bounded on one side by mountains and on the
other by the ocean, appears to have developed an outer ring con-

taining both commercial and residential sections. These are connected and contain residents who neither work nor live "in town" (Hardwick, 1971).

The Sector Model.   Social scientists have produced other models of city growth in an attempt to improve on the concentric ring model. Hoyt (1939) proposed a **sector model** of urban expansion that emphasized transportation arteries rather than concentric rings. Like Burgess, Hoyt believed that activities and groups are segregated into natural areas and that cities expand outward. But Hoyt argued that the commercial and residential areas and the different ethnic and income groups expanded from

FIGURE 13-2. Sector Analysis Applied to Calgary, 1961

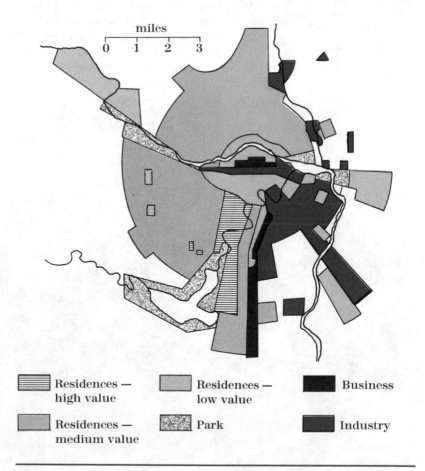

Residences — high value
Residences — low value
Business
Residences — medium value
Park
Industry

SOURCE: "Calgary: a study in urban pattern" by P. J. Smith, 1962, *Economic Geography, 38*, pp. 318-28.

the centre of cities in wedge-shaped sections, along natural boundaries and transportation arteries (see Figure 13-2).

The sector model accounts for the existence of high-priced residential areas near the centre of cities (such as Forest Hill in Toronto and Westmount in Montréal) and underscores the importance of traffic arteries. In this way, the sector model is an improvement over the concentric-zone model, which was developed at a time when traffic arteries, especially highways, were less important.

The Multiple-Nuclei Model. Like Burgess and Hoyt, Harris and Ullman (1945) believed that activities and groups were segregated within areas of cities. But Harris and Ullman rejected the idea that these natural areas radiated from the centre of the city in either concentric rings or sectors. Instead, they developed the **multiple-nuclei model**, which explains the city as a series of nuclei that attract similar activity patterns or social groups and repel others. This model is illustrated in Figure 13-3.

For example, the University of Western Ontario in northwest London and the University of Alberta in south-central Edmonton

Since about 1950, the world's urban population has been tripling every 50 years. In Canada, many of these new urbanites live in highrise apartment buildings, such as these in Vancouver's inner-city West End. As land prices rise, many of these buildings are being sold as expensive condominiums.

SOURCE: Richard Harrington/Miller Services

FIGURE 13-3. Multiple-Nuclei Model of a City

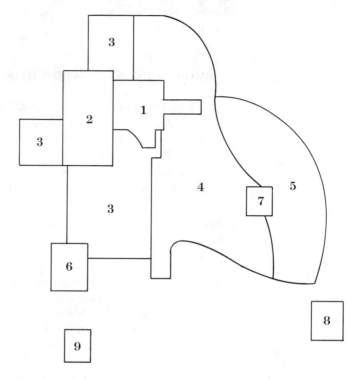

1 CBD
2 Wholesale light manufacturing
3 Lower-class residential
4 Middle-class residential
5 High-class residential

6 Heavy manufacturing
7 Outlying business
8 Residential suburb
9 Industrial suburb

SOURCE: "The nature of cities" by Chauncey D. Harris and Edward L. Ullman, 1945, *Annals of the American Academy of Political and Social Science, 242,* pp. 7-17.

are each a nucleus for several smaller colleges and schools, a number of research institutes, a university hospital (related to the medical school), a variety of student-related service centres (such as bookstores, recreational facilities, and pubs or taverns), and both faculty and student housing. Other nuclei emerge around mutually supporting commercial activities (such as law firms, insurance companies, and real estate offices), industrial activities, and residences.

The multiple-nuclei model is the most recently developed of the three models of urban expansion. Perhaps that is why it seems most applicable to cities that have developed with the automobile as a major means of transportation; the car has allowed a much greater degree of decentralization of facilities and city sectors.

Canadian and American Cities

It is always tempting for sociologists to generalize from the observations they have made; after all, general statements are the goal of social science, rather than specific ones. Most of the published work on urban sociology is about American rather than Canadian cities. Certainly, the similarities between the two societies outweigh the differences, but some of the differences do count, especially the following three:

1. density;
2. core areas;
3. public transit.

First among the differences is that Canadian cities are higher in density, since the U.S. cities contain a much higher proportion of single, detached houses. Probably because of tax breaks on mortgage interest, a higher proportion of people in the United States live in their own single, detached houses (Goldberg and Mercer, 1980). While Canadian cities are more compact, cities in the United States are more troubled by urban sprawl.

Second, like their U.S. counterparts, Canadian cities have lost population from their core areas in recent years. But in Canada, the growth of suburbs has not involved a widespread departure of inner-city taxpayers or an outright abandonment of residential housing. As a result, the centres of Canadian urban areas have stayed economically, physically, and socially viable. In fact, the core areas typically contain some of the most desirable and expensive housing.

In contrast, the core areas of many U.S. cities contain a visible lower class who cannot leave because they are either unemployed or poorly paid. The rate of violent crime is six times greater in the United States than in Canada, and much of the criminal activity occurs in these areas. For their part, Canadian cities are relatively safe and are perceived as such by their residents (Bourne, 1975). The socio-economic status will be higher and the crime rate noticeably lower in the suburbs of American cities than in the city centre. These differences are much less pronounced in Canadian cities.

Third, Canadian city-dwellers use public transit much more than Americans do. The lower rate of crime and the compact form of Canadian cities probably has much to do with this. However, as Mumford noted, the American way of life may be more car-oriented—"based on the religion of the motor car" (Mumford, 1968). There are more cars and, accordingly, more highways in and around American cities. These federally funded freeways are a distinctive feature of U.S. urban areas (Goldberg and Mercer, 1980). Whether this orientation to cars reflects a cultural difference or whether it is manifestation of the higher standard of living in the United States is unclear.

These differences indicate that all three models of city growth, developed in the United States, probably fit their cities better than they fit Canadian cities. This is not to say that the models are irrelevant for Canadian cities; it simply means that these models should be applied with care and modified for the Canadian context. Even within Canada, cities differ dramatically in form, so a particular model will fit some better than others. Montréal, for example, constrained by its geographical location on an island, is a compact city of apartments and renters (Linteau and Robert, 1977). In contrast, Toronto is a sprawling city of single, detached houses, distinct neighbourhoods, and highways.

Urbanism

Urbanism refers to the attitudes, beliefs, and behaviours or lifestyles of people who live in cities. Many sociologists believe there is a great difference between the lifestyles of urban and those of rural residents. Furthermore, the changes required of people who move from one to the other can produce a variety of sociopsychological problems. Some social scientists believe that urbanism itself, rather than the change from a rural lifestyle to city living, causes psychological disorders or other social disorganization among urban dwellers.

Gemeinschaft and Gesellschaft

In 1885, German sociologist Ferdinand Tönnies produced one of the first analyses of rural-urban differences. He argued that rural social organization involves

1. small populations;
2. close, personal relationships between people, most of whom share common values;
3. a collective orientation or sense of identity;
4. informal social control;
5. strong kinship ties to extended families;
6. a strong respect for tradition as the basis for these patterns and social obligations.

Tönnies referred to rural systems as **Gemeinschaft** ("community ") organizations (1957, originally published in 1887).

On the other side, urban systems involve

1. many people with various values and more individualistic
    attitudes;
2. interpersonal relationships that tend to be temporary, imper-
    sonal, and specifically focused;
3. nuclear families predominating over extend families;
4. formal social control, with laws, courts, and police.

Tönnies called this type of organization **Gesellschaft**
("association").

In rural areas and small towns, people are likely to know one
another in a variety of contexts and statuses. For example, your
dentist may also be a client or customer of yours, belong to the
same clubs or friendship groups as you do, live in the same
neighbourhood, and be married to your cousin. When you go to
the dentist, then, your relationship is more than just as dentist
and patient. You have a number of common interests and lots to
talk about (around that hand in your mouth).

In contrast, in large cities, a visit to your dentist is likely to be
the only time you see each other in a six-month period. You are
not likely to know each other in other contexts and, apart from
the weather and sports, have little to talk about. Harris (1981)
argues that because of this you will get better service in the rural
setting, where people are more likely to care. A botched extraction or filling may deprive a dentist of a golfing partner as well
as a patient.

Cities are highly specialized organizations and, as we have
seen, this is typically reflected physically, especially in larger cities. The extreme segregation of different types of activities from
each other can give individuals a distorted view of the nature of
the community and its life. For example, rural residents in pre-
industrial societies are more likely to be familiar with all stages
of the life cycle, including death. Meat-eaters may not only have
seen their latest meal on the hoof, but may have assisted in its
birth, as well as its slaughter and preparation for the table. In
contrast, urban carnivores who order a Big Mac are unlikely to
have been near, let alone inside, the slaughterhouse that provided the meat they intend to consume.

Urbanism as a Way of Life

The most important intellectual offspring of Tönnies's work is
Louis Wirth's article, "Urbanism as a Way of Life" (1938). Wirth

drew heavily on the ideas of Georg Simmel (1950b), as well as those of Tönnies, in developing his argument. Simmel argued that urban environments produce a continuous and intense bombardment of stimuli. The sounds, sights, and smells of the city combine with the press of large numbers of people to assault the nervous systems of its residents. According to Simmel, urbanites cope with such high levels of stimulation by developing filter techniques. People in cities learn to ignore irrelevant information as they engage in their routine work and leisure activities. Urbanites can sleep with traffic noise in the background, can ignore intimate conversations occurring between other people within listening distance, and do not get interpersonally involved with most of the people they interact with.

As noted before, cities contain large numbers of people in specialized and interrelated roles. According to Simmel, co-ordination and planning are necessary to bring the right people together in a particular place at a specific time. For example, the removal of tonsils usually requires the co-ordinated efforts of at least one physician, an anaesthetist, several nurses, and a number of technicians and workers to prepare the equipment, the patient, and the operating room for the event at a specific time. Such co-ordination of specialists and locations puts pressure on urbanites to be punctual.

Urban dwellers learn to ignore anything that does not directly concern them. Passerby takes no notice of a naked man strolling in the South Granville area of Vancouver.

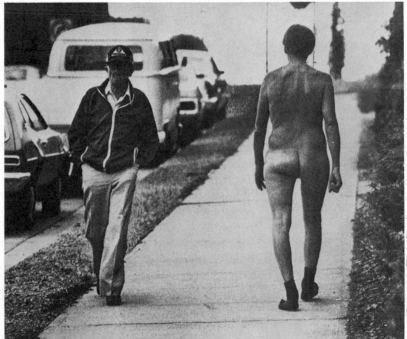

SOURCE: Canapress Photo Service

Because of this pressure, urban residents are more often in a hurry than their country cousins are. If city-dwellers invested emotion and time in every person encountered, took notice of every sound made, and paid attention to every new or different sight, they would always be behind schedule. Both individuals and social systems would break down. People in cities, therefore, move and think quickly; they learn to act on little information and to avoid becoming bogged down with details.

According to Simmel, then, the more relaxed, personal, and spontaneous way of living in rural societies simply does not allow one to cope effectively with the demands of the city. Those who migrate from rural to urban areas must adapt by learning to live the way urbanites do.

Wirth (1938) extended Simmel's argument and focused more on the social than on the psychological side of urban life. He believed that the elements of the urban environment that have the greatest impact on social life are the size, density, and social mix of the urban population. Wirth based his model of the city on these three variables. He argued that extensive exposure to large numbers of socially different people causes urbanites to withdraw psychologically, reducing the intensity of their social interactions (cf. Gillis and Hagan, 1984). This leads to superficial, impersonal, and segmented social relationships, increased individualism, self-interest, and anomie (normlessness), low morale, and reduced community integration. Wirth's picture of life in the city, then, is largely negative.

Selection

The views of Simmel and Wirth are examples of **environmental determinism**—the idea that the physical environment can affect or determine people's attitudes, behaviours, or conditions. The urban environment is believed to cause city people to be different from country people. This is not, however, the only way sociologists explain rural-urban differences in lifestyle. Other sociologists believe that differences between people in one environment and those in another reflect cultural or structural factors and selection, rather than the impact of the particular environment on the inhabitants.

Selection theory allows that situations or behaviours and places may be related, but holds that the physical environment need not necessarily be a cause. Instead, people with particular shared characteristics choose to live in some areas and to avoid others. Certain people have access to some areas, but are denied access to others. The denial may take the form of direct discrimination, but in industrial, capitalist societies, the means is usually more indirect and persuasive—income.

Earlier we saw that some areas of the city, such as the transitional zone, contain cheap, high-density housing and socially heterogeneous populations. Most of the people who live there are poor. Few choose to live in these physical or social circumstances, but low income prevents them from moving elsewhere.

Housing the Nation's Seniors

Better provision for the elderly is among the challenges facing today's Canadian cities. The problem is not, of course, exclusively urban, but it is obvious and grave in the cities.

The needs are many: public transport that has easy access (a single step can be a barrier), suitable recreation facilities, food and clothing stores that sell items the elderly can afford and want to buy. And, above all, housing, for where people live often determines the quality of their lives.

The time is drawing near when Gladys Gillie, 81, will have to move from her one-bedroom apartment in North Toronto. Her daughter is worried because Gillie, though healthy, is starting to become forgetful. "I'm scared she'll leave a burner on or lose her key," said Gwen Iveson.

Gillie, like many of the elderly, doesn't require full-time medical supervision. For her to enter a nursing home or a home for the aged would be a classic example of what critics call "inappropriate placement."

On the other hand, she has reached the stage of needing some support and monitoring. In the past, she might have moved in with her daughter and grandchildren, but like many women today, Iveson works full time and both she and her mother feel the emotional strains on the entire family would be too great.

One problem for Gillie is cost. She has a nest egg but like many seniors, she's hesitant to break into it. She's looking for a retirement home, costing no more than $600 to $700 a month with meals. It won't be easy. Commercially run homes in Toronto charge twice to three times that rate.

One non-profit complex Gillie likes is the Baptist-run Fellowship Towers. It's a 300-unit home geared to reasonably healthy seniors. It offers 24-hour nursing and a physician who visits twice a week, though it is not set up to accommodate those with failing mental health or memory impairment. Self-sufficient apartments run $690 a month, while one of the 230 rooms which offer full dining-room service is $925.

Another problem, said Iveson, who has helped her mother look for months, is that "there isn't that much available for the stage my mother is at. This situation is obviously threatening to an older person's dignity."

Metro Toronto has more than 30 000 subsidized apartments for the elderly, but they're aimed at self-sufficient seniors.

Housing with access to on-site medical care is hard to find, though its need has been emphasized recently in dozens of government and seniors groups' reports.

So has the need for a whole variety of housing options. Planners know that while the elderly make up only 10 percent of the population now, in 12 years they'll account for 13 percent. And by the time the baby-boom generation finishes retiring between 2010 and 2030, one in every four Canadians will be a senior citizen.

If the housing needs of future seniors are to

be met, the groundwork has to be laid now, at the beginning of the demographic boom, while there's still time.

Winnipeg-based Farley Cates, like many of his fellow community planners, condemns the current bricks-and-mortar approach that ignores seniors' special requirements. Barren highrises with scores of elderly people living anonymous lives in subsidized apartments are neither a social nor an economic answer.

Under study are a variety of housing approaches used elsewhere. Several European countries which already have elderly populations of 16 and 17 percent are coping well with shelter needs, says Brian Gray, senior researcher with the Central Mortgage and Housing Corp.

Both seniors groups and housing experts agree that the elderly who can should be encouraged to stay in the community as long as possible. That will mean an increase in home-based social and medical services, visiting nurses, homemakers and meals-on-wheels and the like. It will also require a complete redefinition of what housing is.

Innovations being tried in Ontario, elsewhere in Canada and in the United States include:

Home sharing:
Two seniors, or one senior and a younger person share an existing house that one of them owns. It reduces costs, provides companionship and increases a sense of security.

"But," said Nina Herman, director of a Canadian pilot project in Toronto," it's not always easy to bring two strangers together. We've had more luck with inter-generational pairings." The Americans report their greatest success is in linking single-parent families to older people.

Granny flats:
Self-contained, removable prefab homes can be installed in a relative's yard, serving as temporary living quarters for an elderly relative. More than 4500 units are in place in Australia where they were developed 13 years ago.

Ontario currently has 11 experimental units. The building cost averages $35 000; each unit rents at $300 to $336 a month plus an installa-tion fee of $7 to $9 000. So it's not a cheap option, and many current zoning laws won't allow it. But the province has received more than 700 inquiries.

House rehabilitation:
For example, self-contained units attached to an existing family home. Two households can live close enough to provide companionship and services, but each retains independence.

Again, municipal regulations could be a problem, but pilot studies are under way and convert-to-rent grants are already available.

Group homes:
Large family homes are converted into cluster residences—six to 10 seniors living in their own rooms with communal dining and activities. Supporters say they are preferable to large-population, subsidized high-rises.

Financial supports:
A variety of financial incentives that would help more seniors remain in their own homes.

For example, municipalities could allow property taxes to accumulate as a charge to a senior's estate, thus alleviating the year-to-year financial burden on elderly homeowners. The City of Toronto already provides a $100 tax credit to homeowners who receive Guaranteed Annual Income benefits and the province an additional $500 property tax grant.

Another fiscal option may be the use of reverse mortgages: a homeowner could sell or mortgage the property to a third party but remain in the house, receiving monthly cash payments until death or a pre-negotiated date.

Lawrence Crawford, board member of St. Hilda's Towers, an Anglican Church-run seniors complex, believes private developers should be playing a bigger part than they have in the past. St. Hilda's is planning to build a retirement community with an adjoining nursing home and Crawford would like to see a joint enterprise between his non-profit church group and a commercial homebuilding company.

That's good news to Norman Godfrey, president of the Canadian Homebuilders Association, who says developers are well aware of the coming seniors boom and have no intention of ignoring it. "You're already seeing condos aimed at seniors who are downsizing from the family home. But before much else can be done . . . there's the regulatory problem."

Obtaining municipal approval is a lengthy process and may prove impossible, especially for anyone wanting to build something other than a subsidized seniors apartment or a nursing home for the chronically ill.

Bob Hart knows all about zoning impediments. When his Stay-at-Home-in-Leaside group first approached East York with the idea of building a seniors condo, the city executive was bluntly opposed—despite the fact that the elderly make up 25 percent of the Toronto borough's population. "Then we called a meeting and 300 supporters showed up. Anyone who'd opposed it at that point would have been lynched."

Hart's project began with a survey of Leasiders which found that seniors who lived alone were concerned about loneliness, security and the loss of a sense of purpose. Those still living with spouses wondered what they'd do when they were on their own. Said Hart, "People wanted to stay in the community among people who care about them. Our condo will provide everything from recreational facilities and pastoral counselling to housekeeping, nursing and dental services."

The 103-unit Leaside Gate will open next spring. Prices range from $190 000 to $240 000—not inexpensive, Hart admits, but within the means of Leasiders selling houses on today's market. After downsizing to a condo, he says, most will have a nest egg of at least $30 000.

Meanwhile Gillie continues to look at Fellowship Towers. "Time and again," said Grace Sweatman, its administrator, "new residents tell me they've made the decision to come here while they still can. Loneliness is the big enemy and no amount of community services can really overcome that. Once they're here, and involved in everything, they say "Thank God, I've found you.""

"There is no one answer," said Gray. "We will have to come up with a wide range of options that reflect the differences among the elderly."

SOURCE: "Bold Alternatives Sought To House Nation's Seniors" by Linda Hurst, *The Toronto Star*, June 1, 1987.

In contrast, the suburbs are typically homogeneous, are low in density, and contain middle or upper income populations with few of the income-related troubles of slum-dwellers. There is a tendency to associate slum-dwellers' problems with slum environments, but income is the important factor in determining both where people live (through selection) and what types of problems they have. We should not conclude that density or heterogeneity is *causing* the problems of slum-dwellers. From a selection standpoint, the physical environment is merely a place where action occurs; it is not important as an independent variable.

The selection argument can also be used to explain differences in rural and urban behaviour. According to Simmel (1950) and Wirth (1938), cities cause people to behave in particular ways. A selection argument, on the other hand, would say that it is not the physical environment, but demographic, cultural, and socioeconomic variables, that cause people to behave in specific ways and that determine whether they live in rural areas or migrate to cities.

Most people who migrate from rural to urban areas do so for economic reasons (Fischer, 1983). This includes people with specialized skills, who are pulled to the more lucrative markets in urban areas and people with low skills, who are surplus labour in rural areas, this second group are pushed out and carry their hopes to urban areas, where they also find little demand for their skills. S.D. Clark (1978) calls this latter category the "new urban poor."

Urban areas tend to attract migrants from the top and the bottom of the range of marketable skills. Thus, rural areas lose a portion of their most talented and ambitious young people. At the same time, rural areas also lose those members of their population who are most likely to experience "instability and deviance" (Fischer, 1983). The combined effect is a stabilization of the skill levels of rural populations along with a decline in the proportion of young people and misfits. Urban areas, on the other hand, gain a young population with a wide range of skill levels and a higher proportion of unemployables and deviants.

To the extent that this selective migration occurs, then, we would expect to find differences between rural and urban areas in rates of crime as well as other forms of deviance. But it is selection and composition—not differences in the physical nature of the rural and urban environments—that cause the association (see Fischer, 1983; Butterworth and Chance, 1981; Gordon, 1976; Laub, 1983; and Romanos, 1979).

These, then, are the major arguments that social scientists have about the effects of the urban environment on people. Some, such as Simmel and Wirth, argue that the urban environment actually shapes and determines human attitudes and behaviours. Others argue that social and cultural factors, rather than the physical environment, affect the lives of people.

Cities and Social Networks

Although social scientists have several explanations for rural-urban differences in attitudes, behaviours, and conditions, it is unclear exactly what differences between rural and urban lifestyles in fact exist. For example, the social isolation, psychological withdrawal, and anomie that Wirth (1938) attributed to urbanites is also found in rural populations (Leighton, 1959). Furthermore, it is not at all clear that psychological withdrawl or other disorders are more prevalent among urban than among rural populations (Webb and Collette, 1977; 1979; Crothers, 1979). Like life in the city, life for many people in rural areas is no bed of roses. The strain of the assembly line may be more than matched by the physical and mental strain of farming, fishing, and the limited facilities associated with rural areas. The belief that life is somehow better in the countryside may reflect romantic nostalgia for a rural past, an ignorance of many of the harsher aspects of rural life, and a tendency to take for granted many urban conveniences, such as high pay and access to specialized medical care, dental care, and education.

If descriptions of rural life have been too favourable, most descriptions of urban life have been too unfavourable (White and White, 1962). Urban life is less normless than Wirth and the Chicago school believed. Gans (1962a; 1967), Jacobs (1961), Reiss (1959), Wellman (1979), and others note that city-dwellers have friends, too, and are involved in important social networks that function like those in rural communities. The fact that these networks are not physically segregated in the way that neighbourhoods, small towns, and villages are does not mean that they do not exist as social entities. Extended families with frequent and intense interaction are often maintained in cities, although residences may be physically distant (Young and Willmot, 1957; Pineo, 1971).

People in cities may indeed be less likely to be friends with their next-door neighbours. But the reasons for this unneighbourly behaviour may have less to do with the size, density, and social mix of the urban population than with the fact that city people frequently change residence (Sorokin and Zimmerman, 1929). This results in friends and relations being widely dispersed and also gives people less time to get to know their neighbours. People in cities seem to draw their friends more from their place of work or their voluntary associations (recreational clubs) than from their neighbourhoods.

City-dwellers are not as friendly or as helpful to strangers as rural residents are (Fischer, 1981; Franck, 1980). This fact, coupled with the fact that urbanites are not very friendly with their neighbours, could lead one to conclude that the city is socially cold. But it is not. Urbanites may draw a sharper distinction between friends and strangers and have a larger proportion of friends who do not live close to them, but these represent important differences in the form of rural and urban friendship ties, rather than differences in their number or strength.

Differences in individual and group life in rural and urban areas may have been more dramatic when Wirth published "Urbanism as a Way of Life" in 1938. At that time, many of the residents of Chicago had been raised in rural areas, and the urbanism Wirth described may have been their way of adapting to what, for them, was an unfamiliar environment. Most North Americans are now considerably more familiar with urban environments, both from first and second hand experience. The mass media, especially television, bring urban values, beliefs, and behaviours to rural regions. So we see rural residents adopting urban lifestyles without actually spending much time in cities. Similarly, many urbanites are fans of "country" music. As a result, rural and urban belief systems and lifestyles may have converged over the last few decades.

Finally, there is evidence that North-American cities have changed in important ways since Wirth's time. More and more people are moving to smaller, socially homogeneous suburbs, and the centres of cities are declining in population size and density. This reduced size, density, and heterogeneity of urban (and suburban) environments may have all but eliminated the social and psychological impact of these variables (Guterman, 1969). However, for some city-dwellers, density and heterogeneity may still cause malaise; for example, people who have little money and few housing alternatives often have to live in areas where density and heterogeneity are high. When this happens, they are more likely to suffer from psychological strain (Gillis, 1983). So the combination of Wirth's factors and an inability to escape may produce in limited areas of Canada the effects he observed in Chicago on a more widespread basis.

Crime in the Streets

There are several reasons for the proliferation and distribution of urban crime. One viewpoint, drawn from the arguments of Simmel and Wirth, centres on the freedom and anonymity found on city streets. Urbanites seem more tolerant of non-conformity (Stephen and McMullin, 1982; Wilson, 1985) and are less likely to get involved in the problems of strangers. Furthermore, bystander indifference not only allows deviants to get away with their behaviours, it may even *provoke* deviance. Many of the strange sights and activities seen in the city may be expressions of individualism and attempts to gain recognition—to be a "somebody" (Rainwater, 1966). Because this is hard to do with an audience of blasé urbanites, some efforts go beyond the merely bizarre, to damaging property or to shocking or injuring passersby.

Although Thrasher (1927) argued that deviance can be expressive, most of his colleagues in the Chicago school believed that deviance was the result of the breakdown of social order. In 1972, Newman produced an interesting variant of this argument. He suggested that some types of urban architecture prevent surveillance and control in neighbourhoods, even within apartment buildings. High walls, underground parking areas, long corridors, and hidden spaces, such as stairwells, discourage or physically prevent residents from feeling responsible for what happens in these places. Criminals can lurk behind walls or in stairwells or loiter in hallways, where they are bothered by neither the police nor the residents. These design factors, which are associated with high-density housing, foster higher rates of crime in some areas of the city than in others (Gillis, 1974).

In Newman's (1972) view, the physical environment—in this case urban architecture—prevents or permits action, rather than motivates it. Law-abiding people are not driven to thoughts of mayhem by the *presence* of a stairwell. But someone with mugging or sexual assault in mind may be prevented by the *absence* of such a secluded space. It is when residents are either unable or unwilling to provide informal surveillance that urban spaces become crime sites (see also Gillis and Hagan, 1983).

Although Newman's view accounts for differences in crime rates between buildings, neighbourhoods, and areas of the city, other explanations also fit the data. One of these is drawn from the symbolic-interactionist tradition. Areas of the city with high-density housing by definition contain large numbers of people. Because of this, the police pay more attention to them than other places as likely trouble spots. In contrast, it makes little organizational sense to deploy many police in low density areas. There are neither many potential victims nor many potential offenders in these locations. Some areas are overpatrolled; others are underpatrolled. Because of this, incidents in high-density areas are more likely to be detected and processed as criminal offences than those in low-density areas. This occurs independently of the socio-economic status of the populations involved. On the basis of "seek and ye shall find" rather than actual differences in rates of criminal behaviour, then, some areas have higher rates of crime than others (Hagan *et al.*, 1978).

A similar argument can be used to explain differences in rural and urban crime rates. In rural or smaller urban areas, the police are usually informal and are not likely to process minor offences as crimes. In larger cities, with modern, more bureaucratic police forces, minor offences are more likely to be processed as crimes (Wilson, 1968). It is interesting to see that both the "under" and "over" control viewpoints give logical explanations of these differences in crime rates. In fact, recent studies show that both views may be accurate, depending on the nature of the offense (Gillis and Hagan, 1982).

At present, it is difficult to determine just what the relationship between urbanization and crime really is. If we focus on rates of serious crime (such as homicide, sexual assault, and aggravated assault) and long-term trends, there is little doubt that urbanization is related to crime. But the relationship is negative. Historical analyses show that, in western countries, rates of serious crime have been in decline over the last several centuries (see, for example, Archer *et al.*, 1978; Gillis, 1984; Gurr, 1981; Lane, 1980). At the same time, these countries have become more urbanized. In many countries, rural areas continue to be more dangerous than urban areas. In some parts of rural Mexico, for example, residents are more likely to be murdered than war-time Londoners were likely to die from the blitz. Even in Canada, rates of homicide continue to be somewhat higher in rural than in urban areas (Nettler, 1982; see also Wilkinson, 1984).

Before we decide that urbanization does not cause crime and reject all the theories outlined earlier, two points should be examined. The first is that rates of minor crimes have been dramatically increasing over the last several centuries. The second concerns very recent trends in serious crime. Historically, serious crimes most often involved family members and friends. For example, women had more to fear from their husbands and male friends than from anyone else; only a minority of homicides, sexual assaults, and aggravated assaults involved victims and offenders who were strangers. This continues to be the case in Canada and other western countries.

But recent trends suggest that important changes may be taking place. Over the last several decades, the homicide rates have stopped declining and have begun to increase. This is largely a result of an increased incidence of people killing strangers (Gillis, 1985). Since this has only been going on for a few decades, it is hard to decide whether the pattern represents a new trend or a short-term fluctuation or drift.

Brown's (1984) observations of his native Harlem over 20 years led him to believe that social life in cities is indeed deteriorating. Many of the young residents of large cities are frustrated and feel insignificant. They place little value on themselves or others. Killing someone, especially a stranger, may not be repugnant to these urbanites. In addition, homicide frequently involves material gain for the killer, and even if he or she is caught, the notoriety conferred by peers and the press may be regarded as better than no attention at all (Brown, 1984).

Several of the theories of urban crime fit with Brown's description of the situation in Harlem; however, Harlem may not be representative of other urban centres. Whether the patterns described by Brown will be observed in other places remains to be seen. Meanwhile, the public's fear of urban crime may reflect the preoccupation of the media with such places as Harlem and/ or a recognition of short-run trends (Fischer, 1983). Urbanization in the United States is now matched directly by increases in violent crime (Nettler, 1982), and this may become true of Canada in the near future.

Summary

1. Sociologists define a city as a large concentration of people engaged in a wide range of interdependent occupations that, for the most part, do not involve the primary production of food.
2. The shift of the human population of the world from rural to urban areas has been associated with technical, organizational, and cultural developments that have allowed the development of large agricultural surpluses. Industrialization seems to have had the largest effect on urbanization.
3. The urbanization of Canada followed temporarily the patterns in industrial Europe and the United States and generally proceeded from east to west.
4. At present, about three-quarters of the Canadian population live in urban areas. In recent years, the most obvious change in the Canadian urban population has been that many cities have stopped growing or are even declining in population, while their suburbs have grown dramatically.
5. Several perspectives have been developed that incorporate ecological principles to explain the growth of an individual city. The concentric-zone, sector, and multiple-nuclei models are three of these. All apply more to the large cities in the United States than to those in Canada.
6. Social scientists have developed various explanations for the existence of a distinctly urban way of life, or urbanism. The most important of these theories is Wirth's. He focused on the size, density, and social heterogeneity of urban populations and argued that these factors cause segmented social relationships, social isolation, and psychological withdrawal. But recent evidence suggests that the current impact of these variables may not be as great as it was in the past.
7. A number of arguments have been developed to explain urban deviance; however, except for recent trends, the overall relationship between urbanization and serious crimes is negative, and people are still safer in Canadian cities than in rural areas.

Further Reading

Bronowski, J. (1976). *The ascent of man.* London: British Broadcasting Corporation.
Chapter 2, "The Harvest of the Seasons;" Chapter 3, "The Grain in the Stone;" and Chapter 8, "The Drive for Power" are particularly relevant to the study of cities. (*The ascent of man* is also available on film.)

Clairmont, D., & Magill, D. (1974). *Africville: The life and death of a Canadian black community.* Toronto: McClelland and Stewart.

    A detailed account of the destruction of Africville, a settlement of blacks in the north end of Halifax, the motivations behind this "urban renewal," and the effects of relocation on community members.

Clark, S. D. (1966). *The suburban society.* Toronto: University of Toronto Press.

    This monograph discusses the forces affecting the suburbanization of Toronto.

Fischer, C. (1983). *The urban experience.* (2nd ed.) New York: Harcourt, Brace, Jovanovitch.

    A good review of current work in American urban sociology. The author also presents his views on the importance of city size, subcultures, and social networks.

Kennedy, L. W. (1982). *The urban kaleidoscope.* Toronto: McGraw-Ryerson.

    An examination of most of the models and theories developed by urban sociologists, with special attention given to Canada.

Lucas, R. A. (1971). *Minetown , milltown, railtown: Life in Canadian communities of single industry.* Toronto: University of Toronto Press.

    A detailed account of the impact of small, single-industry towns on the institutions and lives of their inhabitants. A classic in the study of Canadian communities.

Marsh, L. (1970). *Communities in Canada.* Toronto: McClelland and Stewart.

    Another Canadian classic. Marsh gives a broader portrayal than does Lucas and presents an interesting argument on the importance of the physical environment.

Melbin, M. (1978). Night as Frontier. *American Sociological Review, 43*(1), 3-22.

    An excellent and readable account of the "civilization" of the night and its implications.

Palen, J. J. (1981). *The urban world* (2nd ed.). New York: McGraw-Hill.

    An excellent general text in urban sociology.

Westhues, K., & Sinclair, P. R. (1974). *Village in crisis.* Toronto: Holt, Rinehart and Winston.

    An interesting study of community life and change in a small Ontario town (Elora) on the fringe of larger urban centres.

14
Social Movements and Social Change

In this chapter you will be learning about social change, especially change purposefully attempted by social movements. After reading this chapter, you should be able to

1. define social movements and categorize the different types;

2. explain the existence of social movements from the viewpoints of
    (a) collective behaviour theory,
    (b) deprivation theories,
    (c) resource mobilization theory;

3. explain the factors that both help and hinder the development and success of social movements;

4. outline the basic tactics used by social movements.

300 Stage Rally at Peace Bridge to Protest New Policy on Refugees
The Globe and Mail, February 23, 1987

Students at [University of Toronto] Sit-In to Protest School's Holdings in South Africa
Toronto Star, March 5, 1987

34 Arrested as Crowd Hits Military Ties
Vancouver Sun, April 6, 1987

120 000 [petitioners] Want Non-Profit Day Care
The Globe and Mail, June 16, 1987

Many people think that the era of social protest died with the 1960s. But as the headlines above suggest, this popular view falls short of reality. The marches, demonstrations, sit-ins, and other protest tactics associated with the 1960s have since been adopted by social movements advocating a wide range of social changes. Organized shows of discontent come from a variety of single-issue movements, such as those promoting peace, environmental concerns, women's rights, minority rights, and gay rights, as well as those protesting against seal hunts, pornography, cut-backs in social services, smoking in public places, and abortion.

What are Social Movements?

Social movements are collective attempts to promote, maintain, or resist social change. Frequently, social movements are associated with demands for a change in the status quo to improve a disadvantaged group's material circumstances—Canada's native people, for example. Other groups seek what they see as improvements in the established order—social, ideological, or political. Peace activists, for instance, demand that policies to avert a nuclear disaster be made a government priority. Gay-rights groups ask that their lifestyle be treated as a legitimate alternative, not as a deviant activity. Religious sects seek the same freedom as established churches to recruit converts. Whether the goals involve changes in the class, social, or political status quo, all such groups constitute social movements.

Change-Seekers, Change-Resisters

Social movements are not necessarily change-seekers. They may also be change-resisters, or **counter-movements**, which are efforts to resist or to reverse some of the changes brought about by social movements. The movement and counter-movement phenomenon is quite common. It is, for example, a prominent feature of the debate over Canada's abortion laws (see box). Another counter-movement is the push to return to capital punishment, which was abolished in the 1970s after much agitation. Police associations protested to restore the death penalty and swung public opinion to their side. When Parliament was forced to reconsider its vote in 1987, it again supported abolition, and the restoration counter-movement was left to regroup.

Notice, too, that both change-seekers and change-resisters can be described as either reformist or radical. Movements are said to be **reformist** when they seek adjustments in society's current way of doing particular things while maintaining the overall existing system. The movement listed in the headlines at the beginning of this chapter would be described as reformist. But change-seekers and resisters do not always have such limited goals. A group may aim to change the basic established order—that is, to replace existing elites, institutions, or values with other arrangements that seem likely to make the protesting group's aims society's central aims. Movements pursuing such a displacement of the established order are described as **radical**. The many independence movements that overthrew colonial rule after World War II qualify as radical change-seekers. Fundamentalist groups who want to restore religious authority to

The Cost of Dissent

The pro-choice and pro-life movements involved in Canada's abortion debate are striking examples of the movement and counter-movement process. Here is an account of the high costs of mounting such a challenge for social change.

1984

To the man whose name is synonymous with abortion in Canada—Dr. Henry Morgentaler—his Toronto abortion trial was "a fight between light and darkness, democracy and totalitarianism."

To Joseph Borowski of Winnipeg, the country's best known anti-abortionist, it was "a charade, a perversion of justice, a waste of money."

But if there is anything the two symbols agree on, it is that the emotion-laden abortion issue is not about to go away just because Dr. Morgentaler and two associates were acquitted in Ontario of a charge of conspiring to commit a miscarriage.

The future of his crusade to open clinics across the country is as clouded as it ever was. Worn out and $250 000 poorer, Dr. Morgentaler faces the distinct possibility of more criminal charges, more expenses and an increasingly hostile anti-abortion lobby.

"Probably the anti-abortion people will step up their attacks," he said in an interview during the trial. "They're pretty desperate—they have lost the battle. In desperation they might do what they did in the United States: commit violence against clinics and slander me even more than they have."

Mr. Borowski agrees: "If that man walks away free, the Government of Canada will be sowing the seeds of violence," he said last week. "There are extremists everywhere. Morgentaler was saying it is justified to break the law in order to change the law. Well, what's sauce for the goose is sauce for the gander."

As the legal scorecard stands now, Dr. Morgentaler has won three acquittals in Québec and one in Toronto. He faces trial in Winnipeg, and says he plans to challenge the law in other provinces whenever he gets enough money to open clinics there.

The court battles "are like an absurd piece of theatre each time—a doctor being prosecuted for helping people," Dr. Morgentaler said.

In each of his legal battles, he has sought out prosecution, and then during the trial he virtually admits guilt, but appeals to the social conscience of the jury. The challenges have written a new page in Canadian legal history.

Dr. Morgentaler, who needed seven years to pay the legal debts incurred during his three jury trials in Québec in the mid-1970s, now acknowledges his forays into Toronto and Winnipeg may have been premature. He is in financial trouble. "I did overextend myself. From a business point of view, this is sheer madness."

And worse for his cause is the fact that Dr. Morgentaler's supporters have not donated enough money to pay for his recent cases, let alone the ones to come.

1985

Dr. Henry Morgentaler has launched a personal appeal to the public for donations to meet legal and security costs in the fight to keep his Toronto abortion clinic open.

In an advertisement which appeared on Saturday in *The Gazette* in Montréal, Dr. Morgentaler said he cannot personally afford to pay for his legal battles and the high cost of extra security at the Harbord Street clinic in Toronto.

No such advertisement appeared in Toronto newspapers. However, an advertisement asking for donations to the Pro-Choice Defence Fund appeared in *The Globe and Mail* on December 20, the day after Dr. Morgentaler's associate, Dr. Robert Scott, was arrested and charged with conspiring to procure a miscarriage at the clinic. The same charge was laid against Dr. Morgentaler on December 20.

Readers were also asked to send a coupon to Ontario Attorney General Roy McMurtry demanding an end to prosecutions against Dr. Morgentaler.

Dr. Morgentaler also plans to go on a five-day tour of Calgary, Edmonton, and Winnipeg late this month to drum up support and raise funds.

Anti-abortionists in Calgary say they will demonstrate against Dr. Morgentaler's announced intention to open at least one abortion clinic in Alberta within the next year.

Judy Rebick, spokesperson for the Ontario Coalition for Abortion Clinics, said that a personal appeal from Dr. Morgentaler is the "most effective vehicle" to deal with the "ongoing problem" of financing his defence fund. The target is $150 000 "over the next month or so."

Ms. Rebick said publicly solicited money goes into the "war chest" to cover legal fees and not to operate the clinic, which is financed by Dr. Morgentaler and his backers. The fund has managed to raise about $150 000 so far, she said.

"If they continue the legal harassment and continue with charges in Winnipeg," Ms. Rebick said, legal costs could reach $500 000. Although most of the costs for past court battles have been paid, she said lawyers in Toronto are still owed $50 000 and $20 000 is still outstanding for the defence against abortion-related charges at Dr. Morgentaler's Winnipeg clinic.

Meanwhile, the Calgary Coalition for Life promised to hold protests similar to those held in Toronto against Dr. Morgentaler when he visits Calgary on Jan. 15.

SOURCES: Makin, Kirk. *The Globe and Mail*. November 9, 1984; and Marotte, Bernard. *The Globe and Mail*. January 7, 1985.

dominance in Western society would qualify as radical change-resisters.

The distinction between reformist and radical groups can be difficult to see. In practice, social movements tend to be rated on a reformist-to-radical scale according to the degree of change they advocate in the status quo. Groups seeking moderate changes or step-by-step solutions are generally regarded as reformist. Those groups devoted to extensive or immediate changes are generally regarded as radical.

Non-routine Group Action

Social movements are distinguished from other change-related activities by three features:

1. group action;
2. shared goals;
3. non-institutionalized activity.

By definition, a social movement must have some degree of group action and shared goals. Sometimes change is brought about through isolated individual acts, but then it is not classified as a social movement. For instance, many parents may object to violent television programs and restrict their own children's television viewing to non-violent shows. Such separate, unrelated acts would not constitute a movement against televised violence. However, if some objectors grouped together to raise people's awareness of the problem and to promote a boycott of violent programs as a means of changing network practices, this shared commitment to change would take on the character of a social movement. While shifts in individual attitudes and tastes often contribute to social change, the people involved constitute a social movement only when they consciously support a shared cause.

Another distinguishing characteristic of social movements is that their activities are non-institutionalized. Members' interests have to be met outside society's established institutions and conventions. They do not have ready access to authority in the social sphere that concerns them. Thus, in order to advance their goals, they must explore channels of influence that are out of the ordinary.

To say that social movement activity is not institutionalized does not mean that it cannot be tightly organized. Some social movements have a high level of formal organization, with a distinct hierarchy of authority, well-defined operating procedures, and membership criteria. The National Action Committee on the Status of Women is an example of such an organization. Other movements are loosely organized, such as riots sparked by a particular incident of discrimination. Thus, in terms of internal organization, social movements range from the highly to the loosely structured. It is in terms of their external relations with the larger society that social movements are always non-institutionalized , because their goals are not routinely treated as rights by society's established institutions. For instance, until recently, Canadians' right to smoke was taken for granted, and non-smokers' rights were not institutionally backed. In the last few years, many localities and workplaces have responded to the pressure to put limits on smoking, and the federal government has introduced legislation that would ban all tobacco advertising by 1989. All such moves make the anti-smoking movement's goals more institutionalized now than when it was formed in the 1970s. But the movement still has a long way to go to institutionalize its main goal of a smoke-free society.

Success and Institutionalization

Even though a social movement begins with non-institutionalized interests, to be successful it must achieve institutionalization. Success has several dimensions and degrees. A movement attains partial success when society recognizes and accepts its representatives as the defenders of a legitimate set of concerns. Another kind of partial success is attained when a movement achieves some of its stated goals. But a movement gains full success only when its interests are fully institutionalised—that is, when society recognizes and enforces the movement's goals as rights.

So many movements achieve partial success that it is often difficult to decide where social movements stop and mainstream interest groups or political parties begin. The Parti québécois (PQ) provides a good example of partial success and the difficulties this phenomenon causes for activists involved in a movement. During the 1960s, political independence for Québec was the goal of what was clearly a social movement in that province. From that movement sprang the PQ. The party's twin goals of getting elected and gaining Québec's independence were both certainly non-institutionalized when it was created in 1968, but it attained some success in the provincial elections of 1970 and 1973, gaining only a handful of seats in the legislature but 23 and 30 percent, respectively, of the popular vote.

During the next campaign, the party modified its stance to separate its twin goals. It announced that, if elected, it would seek sovereignty association (a form of partial independence), but only after using a referendum to obtain voters' specific backing for the move. This strategy led to electoral success; in November 1976 the PQ formed the Québec government. But the referendum on sovereignty-association, held in May 1980, was defeated by almost 60 to 40 percent. In campaigning for the provincial

The Parti Québécois began as a popular social movement but became a mainstream political party.

SOURCE: Canapress Photo Service

elections of the next year, the party again downplayed its goal of independence, and won again with an even larger majority.

Thus, the PQ gained electorial success for a number of years, but it failed to institutionalize its original main goal of independence. This contradiction created obvious conflicts for many of the party's activists, who had devoted time, money, and expertise to the PQ because they were committed to the independence cause. While it was in office, the party retained a strong social-movement character frequently conflicted with its more routine, vote-seeking character. The tensions inherent in this dual character eventually led to a split in early 1985. When René Lévesque responded to low voter support by persuading the party to drop independence from its election platform, many of the strongly pro-independence activists—the so-called orthodox wing of the party—left the PQ. In the resulting struggle to define the true nature of the PQ, Lévesque himself resigned as leader.

When the next election came, the opposition Liberals swept to power, stripping the PQ of even the partial success it had gained by having the movement's representatives in power. Some of the orthodox activists have gone on to found other pro-independence movements. But most former activists have not joined these movements, and the two-thirds decline in the PQ's membership seems to indicate that many have become disenchanted with electoral politics as well.

Social movements are not a prominent preoccupation of the other classical viewpoints.

Traditional Approaches

Structural Functionalism and Breakdown Theory

Structural functionalists are not much interested in social movements. When movements do receive attention in this tradition, they are attributed to the temporary disorientation and disorganization provoked by changing times, an approach called **breakdown theory**.

Functionalists see the discontent that spawns social movements as caused by a disequilibrium in the social system when society changes too fast. Usually, this disturbing change is caused by too rapid economic development, but other major dislocations, such as serious economic depressions, massive rural-urban migration, and rapid bureaucratization, can also prove disruptive.

Whatever the cause of the change, all parts of the social system do not adapt immediately: some lag behind. These lags lead to societal breakdown, since the social structures no longer fit the social values that legitimize them. Social values no longer make sense of the individual's everyday reality. The inappropriate values loosen society's hold over the individual's behaviour. People begin to indulge in unrealistic hopes, fears, and beliefs in utopian solutions for their new social problems. These generate disorder and social movements.

For structural functionalists, therefore, social movements are only transitory phenomena that disappear once changing social structures and legitimizing values catch up to one another. Such brief bouts of disorganization are not a major concern for functionalists.

Marxism

Classical Marxism does focus on conflict and social change but only on a very limited range of workers' protests and revolutionary movements. As you read in earlier chapters, Marx argued that the working class in capitalist societies had an inherent interest in revolution because capitalist development led inevitably to the deterioration of the workers' economic position and the gradual destruction of the independent middle class. Thus society became polarized into two, clearly opposed classes of workers and owners. By concentrating the working class in cities and factories, the capitalist system also promoted a consciousness of common class interests and working-class solidarity against oppressive conditions. Therefore, in the Marxist approach, it is not the disorganization of the discontented but their solidarity that leads to workers' movements for revolutionary change.

Collective-Behaviour Theories

The most widespread traditional approach to the study of social movements treats them as part of collective behaviour. They are thus grouped with such phenomena as panics, crazes, fads, fashions, and crowds—all group outbursts, whether change-related or not. The usual justification for this grouping is that all collective outbursts are distinctive as deviations from everyday behaviour. Unlike everyday behaviour, collective behaviour is not seen as having a rational base. Thus, all group action that is unconventional is also seen as somewhat irrational.

LeBon's Theory.   The collective-behaviour tradition was deeply influenced by the work of a nineteenth-century French analyst,

Gustave LeBon (1960, originally published in 1895). LeBon was appalled by the intensity of the riots and the erosion of aristocratic authority during the century encompassing the French Revolution and the subsequent industrial revolution. LeBon branded this era "the Age of the Crowd," as it seemed to him that unruly mobs and the masses had taken over the power to direct society. LeBon attributed to crowds a distinct psychological state—a uniform group mind—a kind of herd instinct that erodes and replaces individual differences and moral judgment. Having suspended the ability to think critically, he said, people in crowds are suggestible, ideas spread by contagion, and behaviour is easily manipulated by emotional leaders. Thus, LeBon argued, crowds are amoral and dangerous.

Blumer's Theory.   LeBon's notion that people massed in crowds catch a common irrationality became widely applied in sociological research. It is most clearly visible in the work of the symbolic interactionist Herbert Blumer (1951). Blumer held that collective behaviour differs from normal everyday behaviour because the usual process of symbolic interaction is suspended in crowds. Rather than interpreting one another's actions and responding on the basis of rational thought, people in crowds bypass interpretations and directly copy one another's reactions in a state of circular reaction. Social movements are the more organized forms that spring from this epidemic of group unrest.

Criticisms of Collective-Behaviour Theories

Although the collective-behaviour approach to social movements was widely accepted for many years, there is little compelling evidence to support its view of collective irrationality. Collective action at times is indeed violent or disorderly, and everyday rules of behaviour are often inadequate guides in exceptional circumstances, such as a spontaneous protest. But that does not mean collective action is necessarily irrational or that a special psychological state is needed to explain crowd dynamics. An alternative view—the **emergent norm** view—is that people in special circumstances tend to generate new norms to guide and contain their behaviour. Individuals in a disorderly setting may have difficulty getting the information needed to assess their personal situation fully, but people do the best they can to make rational choices with the information available, just as they do in other aspects of life.

Much of the initial research challenging the collective-irrationality thesis sprang from observation of the race riots that hit several American cities in the 1960s. The rioters' goals and targets were chosen neither at random nor strictly on impulse. The riots focused on long-standing grievances that community representatives had been articulating through more conventional channels for years, with little success. For instance, after persistent community complaints about police practices, one Los Angeles riot was sparked by the arrest of a black youth, for which police were accused of using undue force. The targets of most personal attacks during the rioting were the Los Angeles police officers who were directly linked to the grievance, not the other law-enforcement officers attempting to control the riot scene. Targets for burning and looting were also narrowly chosen; residences, government and social service agencies, and black-owned businesses were spared, while white-owned businesses were more likely to be attacked. Even in a disorderly bout of collective action, then, we find much evidence of strategic thinking and individual rationality.

Contrary to the "swept-away" aspect of an irrational crowd psychology, bystanders are not automatically pulled into participation in protest action. Among the people who do participate, not all play the same role; most stop short of action they disapprove of and scatter if someone else's the action threatens their well-being. In a study of several incidents of violence and protest in Canada, Frank (1984) found that the disruption planned by Québec's pro-independence RIN (Rassemblement pour l'indépendence nationale) at the 1968 Saint-Jean Baptiste Day parade in Montréal did not drag in large numbers of crowd members. Although the Québec holiday is a traditional time of national pride, and the site was crowded with celebrants, the parade-goers resisted involvement in the RIN's tactics, which were widely considered to be risky and illegitimate.

Although collective-behaviour theorists maintain that social movements evolve from bouts of collective unrest, the evidence shows the oppposite; that is, protest action usually springs from existing social movements. Most demonstrations are planned by and recruit participants from organizations that are already linked with the cause at issue. For instance, Frank reports that the 1970 Toronto demonstrations against the Vietnam War attracted members from 50 associations with pacifist leanings, ranging from middle-class citizen groups to Yippies and Maoists. Most of the demonstrators were veterans of other quality-of-life and peace protests. In other words, protest action generally attracts people who already have personal or organizational links to groups concerned about a social problem; it does not often recruit converts at random off the streets.

There is a special factor operating in large crowds that can promote disorderly acts because it makes them appear to be cost-free. Individuals may do violent things because being in a large

Like most protests, this Toronto peace march was organized by existing social groups.

crowd makes it more rational to do so (in that they are less likely to face individual detection and punishment), not irrational, as collective behaviourists maintain. This temptation to disorder results from the safety-in-numbers anonymity operating in big crowds; that is, the larger the number of people involved in an action, the less the blame for that action can be placed on any one individual. The fact that individuals in a crowd can get away with behaviour that would be punished in another setting can encourage disorder, especially in spontaneous collective action, such as a riot, in which there are few official leaders to be held responsible for the group. But the evidence shows that most collective action is not disorderly, because participants are already socially linked and not anonymous, or because disorder might hurt the cause.

Sources of Discontent

Current research approaches treat social movements as rational activities, the normal outgrowth of conflicting interests in the distribution of rewards by society's various institutions. The types of conflicts that may generate social movements are extremely diverse. Most frequent are those that follow the lines of the major status and income inequalities in complex societies: inequalities based on occupation, ethnicity, race, gender, region, and age (see Chapter 7). Other movement-provoking conflicts relate to access to decision making or power in any of society's institutions, large or small.

Analysts who focus on underlying conflicts of interest to explain social movements ask the questions: Why are these people dissatisfied? What makes them believe that change is needed or must be prevented? Not all agree on the nature or the level of the grievances most likely to foster social movements.

Two general explanations for discontent are

1. absolute deprivation;
2. relative deprivation.

Absolute Deprivation

Disadvantages rooted in either bad life-conditions or unequal opportunities are known as **absolute deprivations**. Analysts who rely on absolute deprivation to explain social movements hold that the greater the disadvantage a group faces, the greater the likelihood that a social movement will be formed. Absolute deprivations are concrete and deeply rooted in the social structure.

Among the most studied protests in Canada are the prairie farmers movements that surfaced during the 1920s and 1930s. Prominent explanations for the emergence of the Farmers' Union, the Progressives, the Social Credit League, and the Co-operative Commonwealth Federation (the CCF—the parent of today's New Democratic Party) point to economic and political discontent that originated in the structure of the farm economy at that time (Skogstad, 1980). All of these agrarian protest movements appeared during depressed economic times. Compounding the problems of hard times was the farmers' heavy dependence on banks, railways, elevator companies, the Grain Exchange, and the eastern manufacturers of agricultural tools and supplies.

Given this structure of financial dependence, western farmers had developed a deep distrust of eastern banks, railways, and

Rural Alienation

Rural life is often more socially isolated and competitive than people think. That is why current self-help movements to ease the pain of farm loss have had to organize through Church resources, like rural protest movements in the past.

It seemed odd at the time to Margaret Kirkland that people knew of farm families in crisis but no one, including friends, felt free to call on them.

Fresh from Toronto as a Presbyterian minister in the small village of Duart, she set up the area's Neighbour Network, one of a growing number of small self-help groups that have sprung up independently in Southwestern Ontario to help families cope with the trauma of farms lost in an agriculture crisis largely obscured by the general prosperity in Ontario.

Agriculture officials estimate that 11 000 to 15 000 of Ontario's 40 000 farm operations are in financial difficulty and Southwestern Ontario is the worst-hit region.

The number of farm loans in arrears is growing and many farmers who have been struggling for several years with overwhelming debts are losing their farms.

But, though rural areas have long been regarded as tightly knit communites where neighbours help neighbours, most of those falling victim to insolvency seem to struggle alone, keeping financial and ensuing family problems behind the farmhouse kitchen curtains.

Henk and Joanne deWit of Highgate, who have finally come to grips with the slow, inevitable loss of their own farm properties, helped found Neighbour Network in nearby Ridgetown.

Mr. deWit said the problem is that most farmers will not go to neighbours or friends when they fall into desperate financial trouble and it begins to disrupt family life.

"As the situation gets worse, they get into a shell and they can't seem to break out until it's too late."

He knows the pattern well. The farmer loses himself in work in the barn, trying to shut out what is happening. His wife struggles alone in the house with fears and uncertainty. Slowly, anger and stress begins to intrude on their relationship and spills over in outbursts at the children.

Last spring, Mr. deWit saw an advertisement placed by Mrs. Kirkland who was appealing for public interest in the problems of farmers. With the help of a United Church lay minister who had lost his farm, Mrs. Kirkland organized the public meeting that gave birth to Neighbour Network.

Among the calls they responded to was one by friends of a farmer who was threatening suicide because he was faced with the loss of his farm. Mrs. Kirkland said two volunteers drove to the farm to talk to him and "went through the steps" of liquidation with him. The result, she said, was that he did not carry out his threat of suicide.

But the stories of suicide persist in rural areas.

Rev. Barrie Bain, a Hanover United Church minister who has been working with farm families said that when a farmer loses his land, "so much of their identity, self-esteem and sense of pride is lost that they no longer feel a whole person."

He said the bond with the family farm is so strong that "there are some who have taken their own life in suicide 10 years after leaving that farm."

He said many farmers in trouble avoid going to neighbours or friends, not only because of a sense of independence, but also because of the competitive form that farming has taken.

"You don't go to other farmers because you feel they are out there waiting to grab your land—like vultures," he said.

SOURCE: "Farmers often struggle alone" by Rudy Platiel, June 16, 1987, *The Globe and Mail*, p. A3.

other commercial institutions, which they felt were exploiting them. This distrust was transferred to the federal political parties, which seemed to favour the eastern interests. When falling prices for their product forced a drop in farm incomes, the sum of the farmers' grievances incited them to reject the national parties and to launch local protest parties.

History is full of revolts, rebellions, and political protests that fit this model: direct response to a bad and worsening position. Yet the immediate cause of many movements is not so clear cut. For example, the women's movement surfaced in the 1960s just when women had made educational gains that were beginning to bring them status and income gains. But although women's economic conditions actually improving in some ways, their overall situation was still far from equal to that of men (see Chapter 3). Whatever the gains they had made, women were still not getting the better paying jobs as often as men were, even when they were as qualified. This type of discontent, based on unequal opportunities rather than on deteriorating conditions, is also the source of many ethnic and racial movements.

Relative Deprivation

The notion of relative deprivation adds a social-psychological dimension to discontent. Some theorists stress that disadvantage alone is not enough to stir discontent strong enough to incite social movements. They maintain that to provoke protest, a disadvantage must be perceived as unfair or unjust and that this perception depends on individual experiences and beliefs. People feel deprived relative to their expectation of fair treatment. It is feelings of relative, not absolute, deprivation that are thought to stir discontent.

Relative deprivation occurs when people get less than they think they should. When people don't get the rewards they feel they are entitled to, they are likely to rebel.

The relative deprivation approach to the study of social movements was proposed by James Davies (1962) to explain the outbreak of revolutions and rebellions. He maintained that revolutions are most likely to occur when a prolonged period of economic growth and well-being is followed by a period of sharp decline. This rise-and-drop pattern, he said, generates, a sense of relative deprivation because the period of improving fortunes raises expectations that are dashed when a depression, war, or some other crisis brings a sudden downturn. (In contrast, a steady downward drift of economic conditions does not generate conflict, in this view, because people's expectations have time to deflate gradually.) According to Davies, the sharper the gap between the original economic success and the later failure, the greater the relative deprivation and the more violent the ensuring political conflict.

Several analysts have expanded this relative deprivation explanation to a more general theory that emphasizes perceived institutional deficiencies as the source of discontent leading to social movement. In this view, a large gap between the way people expect to be treated and the way they really are treated makes them see institutional practices as unfair. When institutions fail to measure up to expectations and standards of fairness, people's dissatisfaction turns into restlessness and the urge to do something to change the situation. This frustrating gap can result from a sudden deterioration of treatment or the growth of new expectations, or both at the same time. For instance, the discontent behind the 1960s youth movement has been attributed to the clash between new expectations of personal freedom, resulting from liberalized child-rearing practices, and the personal restrictions imposed by increasingly bureaucratized universities and work settings (Clark, *et al.*, 1975; Westhues, 1975). According to this view, the frustration of holding do-your-own-thing ideals in live-by-the-book institutions sparked a sense of relative deprivation and the youth revolt.

Absolute versus Relative Deprivation

The debate over the relative or absolute nature of the deprivations most likely to spark social movements has raged in research literature for years. In many of the situations studied, a case can be made for either. For instance, relative deprivation theory has commonly been used to explain the emergence of civil rights movement and race riots in the United States. There is surely some truth in the view that the source of racial discontent was relative deprivation because in the 1960s blacks' expectation of equality grew much faster than did the actual improvements in their life conditions. In this sense, the black revolt was a revolt of rising expectations. Yet it also seems that the racial discontent was based on real instances of discrimination and absolute, structurally based inequalities, which would seem to argue in favour of absolute deprivation as the cause. Data on educational and income levels, housing conditions, and residential segregation have been used to argue both sides of this case.

Much of the choice of interpretation depends on whether the analyst sees protest action as a means of releasing pent-up frustrations—the relative relative deprivation perspective—or as a means of combatting real conflicts of interest and deeply-rooted disadvantages—the absolute deprivation perspective. The tendency among social movement analysts has been to blame absolute deprivation, especially when serious inequalities are involved. Many analysts reserve the notion of relative deprivation for the unfulfilled ideals that give rise to social movements not based on obvious material disadvantages—for example, lifestyle movements such as the Moonies and other religious cults.

Resource Mobilization

The currently dominant approach to the study of social movements does not concentrate on absolute, relative, or any other kind of deprivation to explain collective action. Instead, it focuses on the ways in which personal, organizational, and political resources encourage people to take group action for social change. This is not because conflicts of interest and deprivations are not considered to be prominent parts of society. Rather, conflicts and discontent are thought to be so commonplace that knowing that people are dissatisfied is not enough to tell you what, if anything they are going to do about it. How can a severe disadvantage directly explain why one group unites to protest for social change, when another equally disadvantaged group suffers in silence?

Not only are serious disadvantages not enough to explain the appearance of social movements, they are not even necessary. The dissatisfaction behind movements is based on any group's desire to keep or obtain more of the good things in life, whether the group is privileged or underprivileged. Dissatisfaction is pervasive because of the conflicts of interest driving social life. The "good things in life"—wealth, prestige, the power to control one's life circumstances—are in short supply in any society. Those who have these advantages want to keep them and to obtain more, while the disadvantaged want a greater share. This conflict over scarce rewards maintains the major social disadvantages, but it also operates throughout society's institutions to create a set of insiders, who use the institution for their own ends, and a set of outsiders, who are dependent on but have little say in the institution. For example, student governments are at times controlled by a clique or a social set (the insiders), who spend the student budget to their own advantage. The student body (the outsiders) may become dissatisfied with the slant of the campus newspaper, with travel expenses, or with other insider perks that tend to displace the services that they have paid for. Also, bureaucracies tend to work more to the advantage of the officials entrenched in them than of the clients and users whose needs they are supposed to meet but who are treated as outsiders. The dissatisfaction generated by such insider-outsider conflict has led to student referenda, welfare rights protests, tax revolts, and self-help groups, among other movements, in the last few years.

But, in an affluent, "have-it-all" society such as ours, any want can be defined as a need, and its absence as a social problem. The spate of upper-income movements to achieve the perfect body or inner peace show that the potential for dissatisfaction is almost infinite in society, whether based on deprivations or on high aspirations. This dissatisfaction is likely to lead to social movements when it seems that those affected can improve their situation by acting together.

Dissatisfaction may be at the root of social movements, but it cannot explain why some groups look for collective solutions, while others fall back on individual solutions or fatalistically accept their social problems. Wanting social change is not enough. Taking collective action requires a great number of resources. It takes time, money, expertise, leadership, and a host of other resources to put together the kind of challenge that can convince society to accept change. Before an assortment of concerned people can act together, they must put a lot of effort into obtaining enough resources under the group's control to challenge their opponents. This process of attracting, co-ordinating, and applying resources for a shared goal is called **resource mobilization**.

In the resource-mobilization approach, a group's capacity to act together and its chances of making gains through group action are the factors most directly related to social-movement formation. If group action for change seems likely to provoke more costs than benefits, no social movement will emerge. When collective action is too costly to organize or is hopeless, people will look for individual means of solving or escaping their social problems—whatever their level of dissatisfaction. Rather than ask why people are dissatisfied, the resource mobilization analysts ask: What chance do these people have of organizing a collective demand for change? What makes them think that collective demands can overcome the opposition to change? The answer lies in the group's access to resources that lower the cost of organizing an effective response to problems.

The Obstacles to Mobilization

Ironically, research findings show that it is not the less but the more privileged who are likely to launch protest to overcome their dissatisfaction. Both Pinard (1971) and Lipset (1966) found that the poor—the most discontented—were late joiners of the Social Credit Party of Québec and the Saskatchewan CCF. The poor threw their support behind these movements only when the better-off farmers had built the protest parties into viable political forces. Likewise, the participants in the American black ghetto riots were more likely to be residents with jobs and strong neighbourhood links than the unemployed and socially isolated. These are just a few of a long list of cases in which it is the dissatisfied who have the most resources—not those with the most discontent—who initiate collective action. The poverty-stricken may endure the most miserable living conditions until leaders emerge who can afford to organize their cause, until outside sympathizers pour resources into their cause, or until some event weakens the authorities' ability to punish their rebellion.

Raising enough resources for social change is such a dilemma because of the three major obstacles that social movements face:

1. their opponents' resources to resist change are usually formidable and well-institutionalized;
2. the personal costs of participating in group action for change are high;
3. individuals tend to downplay their personal responsibility for group problems and solutions.

Organization of women on the issue of abortion is facilitated because the groups do not depend for support on those who are economically and culturally disadvantaged.

Demand for change in any society's institutions are likely to be resisted by those groups who benefit from existing arrangements. These opponents' advantages are enforced as rights by

their institutions and often by the rest of society as well. Their privileged position is seen as legitimate. Thus, those who want change start with few established resources or means of influence, but they must face opponents who have low-cost, institutionalized means of defending their position. For instance, when anti-nuclear activists picket a nuclear plant, the plant's owners and people who support nuclear power do not have to go into the streets to stop the blockade. Their rights are protected by law; law enforcement agencies bear the cost of keeping the demonstration under control, and the state bears the cost of prosecuting disorderly protestors. But the movement has to directly bear the costs of its ongoing organization, the demonstration, and its activists' legal defense. Since its goals are not institutionally protected as rights, a movement has to bear higher direct costs than do the well-established opponents to change.

Social movements also face mobilization problems that result from the collective nature of the good a movement pursues. Unlike a private good, which benefits a particular person exclusively, a *collective good* benefits all members of a group, whether or not they contribute to attaining it. If an anti-pollution drive wins a reduction in acid rain, everyone benefits from the clean environment—not just the people who took part in the movement.

It is difficult to mobilize support for a collective good, because it is not always in an individual's own immediate interest to invest in such a group interest. A person who invests in a social movement entails *opportunity costs*; he or she commits resources, such as money or time, that could otherwise have been used for leisure, career, or other personal goals. Social movements also entail direct participation costs—such as involvement in meetings or the risk of arrest or of being branded a troublemaker—which few people are anxious to bear. Since any benefits of social change will be shared by everyone anyway, individuals have an interest in letting other people take on the major costs of procuring that change. The concerned student who spends three years getting a degree and a job benefits as much from a clean environment as the dropout who spends all that time protesting to stop acid rain. People who benefit from a collective good without contributing to it are called *free riders*. Free riders get the best of both worlds. Others pay to improve their group position, while they pour all of their own resources into personal advancement. This tension between individual and collective interests leads to the familiar cry, "Why doesn't somebody do something about it? But don't look at me—I'm too busy."

The tension between individual and group interests has another dimension. An individual has no reason to make sacrifices for a collective cause if those sacrifices do not seem to make a noticeable difference to advancing the cause. In a classic example, Olson (1965), an economist, argued that an individual would not be likely to cut personal spending to bring down inflation, since one such effort would not have much impact on the overall economic situation. Still less could an individual be expected to volunteer for a pay cut to fight inflation for the good of all. People ask: "Why should I be the one to pay? What harm could my little raise do anyway?" This logic also applies to social movements.

Few people have an interest in increasing the level of lead pollution in the environment. But people have difficulty seeing how personally switching to lead-free gasoline would improve the overall pollution problem. They, themselves, would pay more for their gas, and that one gesture is not going to end pollution. Their single contribution appears to be an insignificant drop in the bucket. An individual's sacrifice is even less likely to seem worthwhile if people have no reason to expect that enough others would make a similar sacrifice to solve their shared problem. Why should one person pay the cost of pursuing change, if others who would benefit are not going to do the same? Since one person's contribution can't possibly pay the full cost of social change, people usually don't see how their own action makes a significant difference to a shared problem.

Given the high costs imposed by the opponents, the free-rider syndrome, and individuals' low sense of responsibility for group problems, it is not surprising that many deprived groups never overcome mobilization obstacles to form social movements. People can be expected to invest in collective action only when the personal costs involved are lower than the value of the benefits that collective action is likely to bring them. This cost-benefit reasoning explains why the better-off members of dissatisfied groups are frequently the ones who launch social movements; an investment in collective action is less of a sacrifice for them than for the more deprived. People who have many resources—money, free time, respectability—can afford to take risks for potential gains. The very deprived, on the other hand, have few resources that are not devoted to survival. They are not only powerless but nearly resourceless. The severely deprived have to know that real benefits can be won before they will risk the enormous costs of collective action to go after them.

Selective Incentives

The better-off may be more prone to form social movements, but simply having the resources doesn't guarantee that people will invest them in collective action. The better off people are, the more they can afford individual ways of solving or escaping their problems. Such people are just as likely as anyone else to engage in the free-rider behaviour and to downplay their personal responsibility for group problems.

Highly institutionalized groups that pursue collective goods have found a solution to attracting such individuals' resources. They provide **selective incentives**, personal rewards that are available only to people who contribute to the collective cause. For instance, professional associations that lobby for the interests of a whole occupational group provide such personal benefits as professional journals, conventions, certification, and other career enhancements only to those who pay their membership dues. Thus, although all members of, say, a nurses' association benefit from its lobbying, only paid-up members get to participate in its meetings—an activity that can be an important step in career advancement. Similarly, political parties promise patronage appointments and other plums to those who contribute heavily to building and maintaining the party, particularly to those who keep the party going when it is out of power. Giving separate, personal rewards is the chief means that organizations use to ensure that individuals contribute to the group. If only a few people are going to pay for the whole group's benefits, they want to know the answer to the question, "What's in it for me?" The more personal resources they put into the group, the more personal payoffs they will need in return. the chief means that voluntary organizations use to ensure that individuals contribute to group efforts.

Organizational Resources

Social movements can solve their mobilization problems by giving activists selective incentives. However, they are seldom in a position to hand out the kind of material rewards that institutionalized groups use to assure participation. Their non-routine and unconventional nature means that they have to mobilize a great number of resources before they can hope to maintain support through material payoffs or penalties. At the same time, their mobilization costs are higher than those of other voluntary groups because of the opposition provoked by the movements' challenge to the status quo. Luckily for social movements, some social conditions and arrangements can help to overcome the serious obstacles to mobilization. For example, a social movement can escape heavy mobilization costs if it can avoid building its organization from scratch. In fact, discontented groups that manage to put together something more than off-and-on, short-term protests are usually built on resources transferred from established organizations. Recruiting support individual by individual is extremely costly and forbidding. **Bloc recruitment** is the attraction of groups of people who already have existing links and means of co-ordinating their actions. It makes collective action much more affordable. If people experiencing a problem have already set up ways of pooling their resources—a farming co-operative, for example—there is a strong chance that they will pursue a collective solution to that problem.

Pre-established links reduce the costs of collective action in several ways. If the individuals facing a threat have a long-lasting shared identity, they are more likely to feel that the group problem is also their problem and to contribute accordingly. Thus, a television show that is seen as an insult or threat to a distinct ethnic community is more likely to elicit a group response than is a show that is similarly perceived by anonymous viewers. When people share a strong group identity, they are more inclined to act in a group-oriented way.

People are even more likely to act in a group-oriented way if they are tied together by shared networks of communication and friendship. Numerous studies have shown the mobilizing effect of established information and friendship networks. When Pinard (1971) examined the Créditistes, a right-wing movement that grew in rural and small-town Québec during the late 1930s and 1940s and eventually became a political party of some importance in the early 1960s, he found that the discontented farmers and workers who were involved in friendship networks with similarly discontented people were highly likely to know about and support the Créditiste movement. The most socially active among the discontented joined early and gave strong support to the cause, while the socially isolated gave little support. In Alberta, Social Credit support rapidly spread through the rural areas among the listeners of religious leader William Aberhart's radio show (Irving, 1959). In both the Alberta and Québec cases, the new political movement spread along the lines of informal friendship networks—clear instances of bloc recruitment.

But the strongest incentive to collective action comes when a group has existing formal organizational links. If there are a large number of associations within a group sharing a problem, many individuals' resources will already be committed to group action, and there will already be established leaders with both the experience and the organizational backing needed to promote the group. When pre-established leaders, participants, and associations throw their resources behind efforts for social change, a movement's mobilization costs are dramatically reduced.

Pinard (1971) found that participants in farmers' and labour unions were even more likely than those who were only part of informal networks to support the Créditiste cause. This mobilization effect was so strong that even union members who were not dissatisfied with the status quo supported the protest movement once their leaders backed it.

Likewise, Lipset's (1966) study of Saskatchewan shows that the first major backers of the CCF's protest platform were the already established leaders of the province's many consumer and marketing co-operatives. These co-operatives had been set up in response to earlier economic problems in order to eliminate farmers' dependence on middlemen and unstable prices. On average, each Saskatchewan farmer was a member of four or five such co-operatives, according to one estimate. The rural areas of the province also had a dense network of voluntary associations offering the social, health, and other community services otherwise available only in distant cities. The active participants in these co-operatives and community associations gave early and strong backing to their leaders' sponsorship of CCF protest. The structures, meeting places, and other physical and social facilities controlled by the associations were turned to building the protest party. The movement's rapid and extensive mobilization depended heavily on the support these existing organizations made available.

Social Incentives

Established networks and associations are such strong mobilizers because they are in a good position to apply **social incentives**—including social pressure and the threat of lost social and career contacts, as well as the social pleasure of shared activities—to ensure that individuals recognize their personal interest in supporting group interests. In fact, some theorists maintain that highly integrated groups frequently generate social movements because they so thoroughly blend their members' individual and group interests. The individual is not left free to pursue purely personal interests with no concern for the group.

Leaders of such groups usually have their personal power and status so closely tied to the group's position that they have built-in incentives for group defense. Leaders stand to lose more than others if the group's interests suffer and to gain more than others if the group's position improves. For instance, being the leader of an ethnic community that is losing rights, population, and social standing is not a very rewarding position, either financially or socially. Being the leader of an ethnic community that stands to gain in wealth or social and political recognition, on the other hand, can be distinctly rewarding. The leaders' personal career, power, and prestige are so tied to the group's standing, that they cannot afford to act like free riders and hope someone else stands up for the group.

Once a cohesive group's leaders have thrown their personal and associational resources behind a cause, members of the group may not find it easy to ignore that cause. In a highly integrated social structure, a good part of a person's social life or even livelihood depends on maintaining good relations with other group members. Earning approval in the group means doing your share for group goals. There can be powerful social pressures for conformity to group ends, as well as sanctions for non-conformity. It is hard to be a free rider when your close friends and colleagues feel you are disloyal if you do not turn up for meetings. But sanctions are not the only reason people participate. There can also be a great deal of fun in working for a cause with people you know and like. Groups, then, also use positive incentives, such as the personal pleasure of friendship and new social experiences, to reward participants in its cause.

Social Segmentation

Every social movement has to be built on some kind of organizational base. If the movement can borrow that base from existing structures, the cost of mobilizing the movement will be significantly reduced. But existing social networks and associations can work against the formation of a social movement, as well as for it. If the leaders of existing groups oppose a movement, the same social incentives and constraints that are frequently used to encourage a movement can be used to suppress it. If a group you are closely tied to actively resists a movement, it may be difficult for you to speak out for its cause, even if you believe in it personally.

To know how easily a group's organizational base can be mobilized for protest, it is important for analysts to know about the group's external links with those whose interests would be challenged by the protest. For this reason, people who study social movements are interested in social segmentation. A society is said to have high levels of **social segmentation** when there is great social distance and few ties of interdependence between at least two of its groups. The level of social segmentation indicates how tied to or cut off from one another groups are. Under conditions of extreme segmentation, a single society's groups may be so cut off from one another that each is almost a complete mini-societies, controlling a wide range of institutions and linked to the other groups only by a few overarching political and economic structures.

The more segmented a social group, the more cut off its leaders and active participants will be from outside opponents' reward-and-approval structures. Consequently, a high level of segmentation encourages a sense of alienation from outside groups and makes it affordable for leaders to take the risk of challenging a powerful outside opponent because they have nothing to lose by doing so. Conversely, the more links that unite a group's leaders and active participants with its potential opponents, the less likely it is that the group's organizational base will be made available for challenging action.

Studies on the American civil rights movement illustrate this point. While active participation in other social movements and dissident political groups increased the likelihood of civil rights involvement, participation in mainstream political parties discouraged it. People active in political parties were linked to the reward-and-approval structures of institutions that were threatened by the movement's demands, so the risks of open protest were unacceptable to them.

Weak ties between a group and any specific institutional elite may facilitate a challenge to that institution. But strong social movements are most likely to be sustained when an aggrieved group has few links and little interaction with any outside group or institutions—that is, when the group's social and economic life is almost totally limited to its own members.

External Breaks, Internal Bonds

The previous subsections suggest that it is possible to gain a fairly accurate idea of the groups most likely to engage in ongoing protest by examining the nature of the social breaks between groups and the social bonds within them. For example, Canada's provinces have only weak links to one another and a great deal of independent control over their own institutions. The food- and resource-producing provinces—Alberta and Saskatchewan, for example—have few direct co-operative links with the more industrialized regions. Even higher segmentation exists for Québec, since its extensive set of Francophone social networks and institutions add language barriers to the already weak links between the provinces.

This combination of weak external ties to potential opponents and extensive internal organization gives the provinces, regions, and Francophone Québec a high capacity to mobilize against threats to their separate interests. Not surprisingly, matters of

Band-aid?

Canada's native leaders have turned to staging media events to embarrass the government into bargaining with them. These new tactics may be more sophisticated than the old, but they have mainly brought symbolic improvements in native rights.

The media consultants are back from Los Angeles and London where they met rock groups, concert promoters and television producers.

Now they are meeting their client—a group of Manitoba Indian chiefs.

This is the new reality of Canada's Indian movement.

The violent confrontations of the early seventies are long forgotten. Today, Indian organizations are hiring professionals, broadening their tactics and breaking into the international arena as they seek the full extent of their rights.

The media specialists have produced films, worked in the video business, and co-ordinated publicity for a U.S. tour by Archbishop Desmond Tutu, the head of the Anglican Church in South Africa.

For the confederacy, they have concentrated on capturing the attention of politicians and the national media.

They lobby television networks, leak federal reports, arrange news conferences, and invent new ways of publicizing the needs of Indian bands.

When a news conference is held, they try to persuade the chiefs to wear business suits instead of their usual T-shirts and baseball caps.

One of their successes came when they helped assemble a long list of allegations of financial misconduct by the federal Indian Affairs Department.

The allegations prompted the department to order an independent audit. The audit confirmed many of the allegations, and they fed the information to opposition politicians.

Their latest scheme is a benefit concert for Indians, modelled on the Live Aid fund-raiser for African famine relief. They say they found a "tremendous response" in their meetings with rock groups in Britain.

"Within moments of sitting down in a studio, local groups were saying they'll do a concert and donate their services and send the money back to help the Indian people."

"The chiefs would have more impact over there than they do here. These guys would be stars over there. They're from another land."

Executives from MTV music network in the United States assured the specialists that a benefit concert for the Canadian Indians could get blanket coverage on television.

Richard Ponting, a University of Calgary sociologist who specializes in native issues, said the Indian leaders are adopting a multi-faceted approach today.

"There's a greater reliance on media strategies. The sophistication is much greater now. The leaders of the Indian organizations are moving up the political learning curve."

Mr. Pointing noted that Indians are not rich in political resources, for they represent only 2 percent of eligible voters in Canada and cannot afford to make large campaign donations to political parites.

"One of the few resources they have is the ability to embarrass the federal Government, especially internationally."

Indian groups are becoming more imaginative as they begin to hire professional specialists such as pollsters, lobbyists and consultants, Mr. Ponting said.

Native leaders have learned that the Indian Affairs Department tends to respond to bands that apply pressure through politicians and the media, Mr. Ponting said.

Demonstrations and protests have not disappeared from the Indian movement, but other tactics are becoming more common. The Assembly of First Nations, the major national Indian group, has commissioned public opinion polls and placed large advertisements in national media.

Raoul McKay, former head of the University of

Manitoba's native studies department, said Indian leaders have learned to be careful in their use of demonstrations and sit-ins.

"If you do it too often, you lose the media attention," he said.

"They know how to handle the media and how to push the government. There's more breadth and depth in what they're doing."

During constitutional debates in the early eighties, Indians realized that they could influence Ottawa by gaining publicity in the international arena.

By traveling across the Atlantic to lobby British parliamentarians, a delegation of Indian chiefs helped secure an aboriginal-rights clause in the Constitution.

The chief of the Lubicon Lake Indians has travelled to Europe, and the Alberta band is now supported by a network of 23 organizations in nine foreign countries.

Petitions from cities such as Bonn and Berlin, urging aid for the Lubicon Indians, arrive regularly in the Prime Minister's Office in Ottawa.

The Lubicon band has enjoyed the support of the World Council of Churches since 1983. The churches provide an annual grant to the Lubicon.

Fred Lennarson, a Chicago management consultant, has advised the Lubicon Indians since the seventies.

Indians turned to Europe out of desperation, Mr. Lennarson said. Other tactics, such as legal action, were not succeeding.

"While they were before the courts, their traplines were being bulldozed. They became increasingly cynical. The activity in Europe has a greater impact on the Canadian Government.

SOURCE: "Natives learning to use media skillfully in quest for rights" by Geoffrey York, March 23, 1987, *The Globe and Mail*, p. A4.

provincial control, regional development, and Québec autonomy have been the central and recurrent themes of Canada's major political protest movements.

Other groups also have weak ties to outsiders. For instance, Canada's native peoples are highly segmented from non-natives. However, the native peoples themselves are divided internally by language and by differences among bands. In addition, they have little independent control over the organizational and political resources needed to mobilize a social movement; consequently, native peoples don't have readily available, low-cost means of maintaining a strong movement organization. Because of these organizational difficulties, native protests throughout the 1960s and 1970s were sporadic, even though native grievances are serious and chronic. In the 1980s, native protestors have aimed their modest resources at gaining media coverage, a move that has raised their profile, but not their payoffs to any great extent (see the accompanying article "Band-Aid"). Only when a group's weak links to opponents are matched by extensive internal organizational resources is the capacity to act collectively for social change at its highest (Oberschall, 1973).

The Québec independence movement provides an interesting example of how segmentation affects support for a cause. Francophone Québec is highly segmented from Anglophone Canada, but it is not completely segmented. There are still enough political and economic ties between the two segments that most Québécois have to balance their cultural interest in increased Québec autonomy with their interest in maintaining an economic link to Canada. A 1980 pre-referendum poll shows how the Francophone Québécois balance these conflicts interests. While only 16 percent of Francophones supported the federal status quo, not more than one-third supported the PQ's sovereignty—association option (Pinard and Hamilton, 1984). The majority of Francophone Québécois wanted a compromise option—renewed federalism—that would give the Québec government greater cultural and social powers while maintaining strong economic and political ties to Canada.

Most Québécois found sovereignty-association too risky because it would disturb their economic link to Canada, even though they were dissatisfied with their cultural and language situation. The strongest supporters of the sovereignty option were the Francophone intellectuals—that occupational group that includes professors, teachers, scientists, artists, journalists, and writers who may be classified as cultural workers. Their economic status and cultural status were both more closely tied to Québec's separate Francophone institutions and more cut off from Anglophone control than any other group in the province. Almost half the Francophone intellectuals supported the sovereignty option, while only one-third of the professionals, technicians, and clerical workers did. Just one-fifth of the managers and owners supported sovereignty, the same fraction of support as was found among blue-collar workers and farmers.

The cultural workers' strong sovereignist commitment is further demonstrated by the fact that over one-half of the Parti québécois' elected representatives and two-thirds of its cabinet ministers were intellectuals during its years in power. In this segmented setting, it was the intellectuals who had the weakest ties to outside opponents and the strongest ties to the group's own organizations. These cultural workers could best afford and were most active in the challenge for Québec independence.

Opportunities for Success

As we have noted, the resource-mobilization approach holds that social movements will emerge when the costs of pursuing challenging action are lower than the gains to be made through that action. No matter what kind of organizational base a group has, it is not likely to push demands for change if its actions achieve nothing but heavy losses. Thus, groups seeking social change have to have reason to believe that their opponents will be vulnerable to collective action. Before engaging in such action, people ask, "What good will it do?" Since the state is the main target and mediator for such demands, the answer to this question must usually be that the state or some part of it will eventually give in to the movement's pressure tactics (Tilly, 1978).

In this sense, social movements are directly dependent on expectations. It is the expectation that the movement will be a success (that it really will make a difference in overcoming problems) that incites participation in collective action. This expectation can be raised by the group's past experience, by the success of other social movements, or by a shift in the balance of power that makes opponents seem vulnerable. Social-movement success breeds other social movements. Social-movement failure breeds hopelessness and demobilization.

In seeking to have their opponents accept social change, social movements adopt three types of tactics (Turner & Killian, 1972):

1. **Persuasive tactics** rely on the authorities' holding certain values that can be activated in favour of the movement's goals. Any group whose demands for social change represent a major challenge to established interests isn't likely to achieve success by persuasion alone.

2. **Bargaining tactics** rely on having something valuable to trade with authorities, such as votes or a potential impact on their image. Bargaining can depend on gaining broad public support or at least the support of some powerful allies who are important to authorities.

3. **Coercive tactics** depend on the symbolic or actual disruption of institutional life in order to pressure authorities to make concessions. Most coercive tactics, such as marches, demonstrations, or sit-ins, are designed to cause only minor, non-violent upsets to routine. They are aimed at gaining public attention and sympathy or at showing the movement's already considerable support in order to build bargaining power. Other coercive tactics are more directly disruptive: for instance, Greenpeace has attempted to stop—not simply to protest—the seal hunt by chasing herds away from the hunt site and putting coloured marks on baby seals to reduce the value of their fur. Highly coercive tactics, such as threats of violence, rioting, or terrorist tactics, depend on directly inflicting damage in order to force a response from authorities.

Highly coercive tactics are extremely risky because they can provoke both repression and backlash. In many circumstances,

SOURCE: Canapress Photo Service

The coercive tactics used by students in Canada are designed to gain public support, not to cause major changes in the social system.

violence raises the risks of movement participation without increasing the likelihood of success; violent protest is not often adopted by social movements. But, as the many hijackings, hostage-takings, and terrorist bombing show, if violent or illegal acts promise to get results with few risks for those involved, they may become attractive means of dissent. This can be the case even for supposedly humanistic causes, such as the Animal Liberation Front, which used illegal breaking-and-entering and vandalism to rescue animals being used for scientific experiments. These violent tactics have given the movement a great deal of free media coverage, have thrown doubts on the researchers' ethics, and have raised universities' insurance, security, and research costs. At the same time, the movement's secret cell organization, copied from radical political movements, has allowed its activists to escape getting caught or punished for their acts.

Even though most movements purposely avoid violent protest, most do use some kind of coercive strategy in their challenge to overcome the opposition to their demands. In western democracies, a format of protest etiquette has evolved that tolerates the orderly, disciplined expression of discontent. Demonstrations that follow this format inflict mainly symbolic disruption.

Protest is a dynamic process depending as much on the authorities' as on the movement's actions. This point is well illustrated in Frank's previously mentioned study (1984) of four Canadian protest efforts that ended in violence: a Ukrainian-Canadian demonstration against the USSR (Toronto, 1971), an

anti-Vietnam War demonstration (Toronto, 1970), the Saint-Jean
Baptiste Day demonstration (Montreal, 1968), and a Yorkville sit-
in (Toronto, 1967) by hippies who wanted traffic blocked and
youth hostels subsidized to preserve Yorkville as Canada's anti-
materialistic, countercultural centre.

In each of these four cases, Frank shows violence was a police
response to the kind of action that the police considered deviant.
These protests that became violent had three points in common.
First, the activities did not follow standard protest tactics; the
action was disorganized, chaotic, or, as in the Yorkville sit-in,
spontaneous and police found the behaviour unpredictable and,
therefore, difficult to control. Second, the police judged the
protesters to be of low, marginal, or countercultural status (not
"respectable"). Third, police officers resorted to beating and
other violent acts to break up what they considered to be illegitimate protest.

In three of the four cases, the movement lost credibility and
bargaining power because of the violent outcome. The Ukrainian-
Canadian protesters, however, gained sympathy because of what
a later inquiry termed the "police riot"—the obvious loss of
police officers' control over their own actions.

Notice that Frank, like many other analysts, found that police
perceptions of respectability play an important role in the reaction to protest activities. Authorities allow middle-class protesters, a great deal of leeway for letting off steam. The irony is that
disadvantaged and marginal groups, who are least likely to have
the organizational resources for anything but spontaneous protest, are the very ones whose protest activities are least likely to
be tolerated or taken seriously. The difficulty involved in finding
protest strategies that are both affordable and effective has a
strong demobilizing effect on social movements.

Affordable Effective Action

In deciding what kinds of tactics are most likely to bring results,
movements are highly constrained by their own resource base,
as well as by their opponents' and the public's likely reactions.
For example, Canadian native people engaged in a wide range of
persuasive, bargaining, and coercive protest tactics during the
1960s and 1970s, yet they were largely ignored by most Canadians. Even the confrontational and violent tactics that many
feared would cause backlash against the native people's cause
remained irrelevant to the Canadian public. Ponting and Gibbins
(1981) conclude that the movement was ignored because it was
so sporadic and regionally isolated that neither the protest nor

the native people's problems really registered with the non-native population.

In their choice of strategies, the protesters faced a dilemma. They did not have the organizational base to sustain the persuasive and bargaining tactics and the protest marches that most Canadians approve of. They could manage to mobilize resources for other highly disruptive tactics, such as attacks on logging or pipeline operations, but some of these tactics are not acceptable to most Canadians, and they threatened to provoke backlash if they ever raised enough interest to make the national news. This tactical dilemma is very common to resource-poor groups and severely hampers their chances of gaining support for their demands.

Even among groups with many resources, the difficulty of finding effective collective action tactics can inhibit the formation of social movements. A good illustration of this phenomenon comes again from Québec, where the non-Francophone minority has adopted mainly individual rather than collective solutions to language grievances. At first glance, Québec's non-Francophones seem to have textbook-perfect conditions for putting together a collective challenge. The various measures taken by the Québec government to reduce the use of English (culminating in the mid-1970s in Bill 101) presented open targets for discontent. Furthermore, the non-Francophone minority is divided from the Francophone majority by language and separate social networks and institutions—the kind of segmented social arrangements that we have seen tend to encourage the mobilization of a collective stand.

But a close look shows that these conditions weren't as well structured to promote collective action as they appeared to be. For one thing, non-Francophones are a collection of very socially diverse groups, divided internally by ethnicity, race, language, and religion. Their community associations and service institutions also divide along these lines, and most are dependent on the Francophone-dominated Québec government for funding and continued survival. A survey of non-Francophone leaders' opinions showed that the difficulties involved in getting the diverse minority representatives and organizational resources united in a common cause was a major drawback to collective action (Fitzsimmons-LeCavalier and LeCavalier, 1984).

Heavy organizational costs were magnified by the leaders' belief that making collective demands would do little to improve the minority situation. When language tensions were very high in Québec, any defense of minority rights could have been interpreted as a threat to the rights of Francophones, themselves an embattled minority in the wider Canadian setting. Since non-

Francophones had such limited opportunities for collective action, they tended to adopt individual solutions to overcome their minority situation. The main individual solution was to master French; by 1981, nearly two-thirds of the non-Francophone labour force was bilingual. Another individual solution was to escape the minority situation; almost 15 percent of non-Francophones left Québec between 1971 and 1981.

As the position of the French language has strengthened in Québec, however, the Francophones' language grievances have been reduced, and people have begun to be more open to minority problems. In response to this greater openness, non-Francophones have started to take co-ordinated stands for changes in the conditions of their integration to French life, such as mounting court challenges for limited adjustment in Bill 101. As in many other cases, it is a time of increasing political opportunities, not at the time of greatest crisis and discontent, that the mobilization of a movement for social change has surfaced. But a collective anti-French backlash—like that of some Ontario municipalities against their provincial government's extension of French-language services—would be political suicide in Québec and is not likely ever to be sustained there.

Overcoming the Obstacles to Mobilization

Currently, the most widespread approach to the study of social movements focuses on the ways discontented groups overcome the obstacles to mobilization. As we have seen, discontent, frustration, and unfulfilled ideals are considered too common to explain the appearance of a protest group, when so many other dissatisfied groups suffer in silence. Making collective demands for social change requires many resources and much co-ordination, and persistence in the face of opposition. Social movements are most likely to emerge when the people sharing a problem already form a united, solidary group. The more a discontented group has binding traits—pre-established leaders, shared outlooks, friendship networks, formal organizations, and other mechanisms for encouraging commitment to group ends—the more likely the individual members are to support collective solutions to their problems.

Of course, discontented groups seldom have a perfect, pre-established base. But there are often many distinct, well-organized groups within the larger collection of people who share a social problem. Movements frequently mobilize by recruiting the most central leaders and the most active participants from these various organizations, overcoming the high costs of mobilization by building a coalition of subgroups within the larger discontented group. These groups' resources are then transferred to backing the cause.

Calling in the Cult-Busters

Even social movements professing to be non-political—those mainly concerned with personal transformation—face high organizational costs and the need for sustained funding. The Moonies are a religious cult, whose highly successful financial operations—based on the free labour of devoted followers—have sparked as much opposition as the cult's unconventional ideals.

Grand Manan Island, NB — On Grand Manan Island, the traditional adversary of the local population has two claws and turns a flaming orange when placed in boiling water.

It never buys up businesses with a bottomless international fund, does not proselytize their children, and steadfastly refuses to undermine established religion.

Unlike lobsters, however, the followers of Reverend Sun Myung Moon, popularly known as Moonies, are believed to do all those things; that is why this island fishing community 32 km off the southeastern coast of New Brunswick has called in the cult-busters.

At the invitation of the Grand Manan Ministerial Association, an umbrella group for the island's seven different religious denominations, a representative of the Toronto-based Council On Mind Abuse will pay a visit to the island on Saturday.

The purpose of the four-day visit is to teach this very religious community (15 churches for 2700 inhabitants) about the dangers of cult groups like the Holy Spirit Association for the Unification of World Christianity, also known as the Unification Church.

Sun Myung Moon, the founder of the Unification Church, is now serving a 15 month jail term in the United States for tax evasion.

The arrival of Moonies on Grand Manan has created an atmosphere of mistrust and taciturn bitterness as residents try to decide what should be done about the newcomers they believe are a threat to the way of life here.

One of the pastors who thinks the Moonies are bad for Grand Manan nevertheless concedes that the impact they are creating may be getting out of hand.

"One of my parishioners was a little late getting home one day," she said, "and when she got there, she found her daughter hiding in a cupboard. She told her mother she was afraid the Moonies were going to get her."

"Everyone knows the Moonies are bad, but no one knows exactly why. We've been trying to educate people as to why the Moonie approach is wrong, why they are not to be tolerated."

So far, the four Moonies who rent a large white house up the hill from Cronk's grocery store in Seal Cove have been tolerated—more or less.

Although the island's established churches have been vociferous in their opposition to the Moonies, business leaders are just as upset. The major of Seal Cove, who operates lobster pounds as well as a fish processing plant, said that free labour and the enormous financial resources of the Unification Church could spell disaster for island business people.

Four Moonies arrived in Grand Manan a few months ago to run two lobster pounds purchased by Ocean Fresh Sea Foods, a Moonie-owned company based in Portland, Maine. The two lobster pounds, operated by another Moonie firm called Ocean Pounds Ltd., are capable of storing $750 000 worth of lobster, 20 percent of the total pound capacity on Grand Manan.

Grand Manan's harbourmaster and chairman of the Chamber of Commerce agrees the Moonies pose a business threat. He said that in Gloucester, Massachusetts, the Moonies quickly built up a financial and commercial empire despite repeatedly saying they were not interested in expanding their business interests.

The Moonies say that, if their initial investment on Grand Manan is a success, they intend to expand their interests on the island.

SOURCE: Harris, Michael. *The Globe and Mail*. October 29, 1984.

Another way in which movements overcome their high organizational costs is to move beyond their own members' resources and to build on the donations of outside sympathizers—better-off people or organizations willing to support the cause as a matter of conscience. In prosperous times, when many individuals and organizations have free time and money at their disposal, causes that defend important social ideals may attract considerable backing from allies.

At times, movements get enough outside financial support for leaders and organizers to make a full-time career of pursuing social change. Movements maintained by a small, full-time core of activists dependent on the financial backing of outside sympathizers are called **professional social movements**. Pollution Probe is one example of a movement that has been highly subsidized by outside agencies. Professional movements can be built with very little support from the discontented base itself and in this way avoid heavy mobilization costs. However, such movements are vulnerable to changing economic conditions, to shifting fashions, and to the changing financial priorities of well-off sympathizers. A cause may be "in" one month and "out" the next, and the leaders' salaries disappear with the changing trendiness of social problems.

A full-time leadership core is more likely to be sustained by conscience money when there is a large number of well-off people who are part of the discontented group itself. In fact, in very affluent groups, a movement may even be maintained by a small core of unpaid activists who donate their leadership resources out of ideological commitment to the cause.

Still, highly committed people who work only for the pleasure of doing what they believe in tend to suffer burnout if the challenging action is too risky, time-consuming, or drawn-out. Movements led by people obtaining only ideological rewards are also prone to split into warring ideological factions—splinter groups whose ideals of social change are incompatible. With everyone working for different ideological rewards, the movement disintegrates long before the battle for social change has been won.

Although there are many ways to mobilize for collective action, social movements built on a solid organizational base are more likely to endure through the highs and lows of a major challenge for social change.

Summary

1. Social movements are collective attempts to promote, maintain, or resist social change. The changes may relate to the material, social, ideological, or political status of a dissatisfied group.

2. Change-seekers (and change-resisters) are considered to form a social movement only when the individuals involved consciously support a shared cause. Social change brought about by a series of unrelated individual decisions does not constitute a social movement.

3. Social-movement action is essentially non-institutionalized action to promote interests that are not met through society's established institutions or conventions.

4. In the traditional collective behaviour approach, social movements are seen as part of a wide range of unconventional crowd behaviour that has an irrational base.

5. Current approaches treat social movements as a normal outgrowth of conflicts of interest regarding the distribution of rewards in society.

6. In the resource-mobilization approach—the currently dominant perspective—discontent, frustration, and unfulfilled ideals are all considered too common to explain directly the appearance of a social movement.

7. Making collective demands for social change requires sizable resources—time, money, leadership, co-ordination, and persistence in the face of opposition. Groups advocating social change have heavy mobilization costs, since they start with few established resources or means of influence and face opponents who have low-cost, institutionalized means of defending the status quo.

8. Dissatisfied groups are most likely to overcome the high costs of mobilizing a social movement if they have a long-standing shared identity, established leadership, friendship networks, and organizational links, as well as weak ties to opponents. Such an organizational base offers built-in incentives for individuals to support group action.

9. Movements may also overcome the obstacles to mobilization by relying on well-off individuals and agencies to donate enough resources out of sympathy to the cause to sustain full-time leadership. Such movements, however, are vulnerable to the shifting priorities of their backers and are not as likely as those built on an institutional base to maintain a long-term challenge.

10. No matter what a social movement's organizational base consists of, it is not likely to push collective demands for social change if those demands provoke nothing but heavy losses. Social movements are sensitive to the opportunities for success and adapt their actions to the response expected from authorities and opponents.

Further Reading

Clark, S. J., Grayson, P., & Grayson, L. M. (Eds.). (1975). *Prophecy and protest: Social movements in twentieth-century Canada.* Toronto: Gage Educational Publishing

A collection of articles covering a wide range of such Canadian social movements as the social gospel, the CCF, and the union and western protest movements in English Canada, as well as Québec's nationalist and Social Credit movements.

Freeman, J. (Ed.). (1983). *Social movements of the sixties and seventies.* New York: Longman.

A reader presenting analyses of typical 1960s and 1970s movements, such as the women's, environmental, anti-war, civil rights, disabled, and countercultural movements, from a resource-mobilization perspective.

Lipset, S. M. (1950; rev. ed. 1968). *Agrarian socialism.* Berkeley: University of California Press.

A classic study of the social conditions that enabled the agrarian movement to succeed in Saskatchewan. The updated edition contains five new chapters by sociologists who studied later party developments in that province.

McRoberts, K., & Posgate, D. (1980). *Québec: Social change and political crisis.* Toronto: McClelland and Stewart.

A study of the development and social alignments behind the Québec independence movement.

Oberschall, A. (1973). *Social conflict and social movements.* Englewood Cliffs, NJ: Prentice-Hall.

The first major theoretical outline of the resource-mobilization perspective, this study documents the way in which prior social organization and the dynamics of conflict with opponents affect the identity and course of social movements.

Pinard, M. (1971). *The rise of a third party.* Englewood Cliffs, NJ: Prentice-Hall.

A study of the emergence of the Social Credit Party in Québec. This work draws on a wide range of data to show how the grievances, available organizational base, and political opportunities came together to shape a specific movement.

Appendix

You have just been assigned an essay, research paper, or project. If you approach it the right way, you should find it a positive learning experience. This appendix will try to help you to achieve that goal.

Time Management

The big secret of successful time management is to learn how to break your work into manageable units, make use of all of the time available, and set up a schedule to keep you on the right track. Instead of setting aside a huge block of time to work on your essay, divide the task into small jobs and work on one at a time. If you have time between classes, drop into the library to find the books you'll need. If you have time during your lunch period, work on your outline. Even devoting some time to thinking about the structure of your essay or the argument you want to present can be valuable. Once you start using your time effectively, you will be surprised by what you can accomplish.

To *stay* organized, develop a good schedule. At the beginning of the term, sit down with your calendar, timetable, and the list of due dates for assignments, and formulate a *critical path* schedule detailing the time you require to finish all of your assignments and to complete your studying.

As you calculate the time you need to complete an essay, remember to schedule time for research, reading, writing, editing, and preparation of the final copy. Allow time also for your regular course work. Don't cut yourself short. Expect that some of the tasks will take longer than you anticipate. Don't let the work pile up.

Use your schedule to finish sections of your essay in advance of the due date. See if your instructors will agree to read an outline or draft of your essay and point out weaknesses in your structure, argument, or research. This will give you time to revise and edit your essay before it is submitted. Almost all students could improve their grades if they would only leave adequate time to edit and proofread essays. When you manage your time effectively, you reduce the stress caused by deadlines and increase the quality of the work you produce.

Choosing the Right Topic

Topics and Research

A research assignment allows you to thoroughly investigate and gain a great deal of knowledge about a specific area, but it is important to choose your topic carefully. Even if the instructor has assigned a topic, you will have to determine the specific focus of your research. For example, if you are to investigate "Social Inequality," you will have to decide if you are going to concentrate on the structural functionalist, symbolic interactionist, or conflict perspective. You might decide to compare these points of view or examine factors contributing to inequality of opportunity. You could discuss how the factors of ascribed status affect someone's position in the class structure. Although it may appear that you do not have any choice of topic, you will see that you still have to choose a specific area within the assigned topic.

One way to help you to understand what you are required to include in an essay is to look for *key words* in the essay topic. Key words appear in most assigned essay topics and help to define the approach to be taken and indicate what information to include in an essay on that topic. An essay will be easier to organize once you learn how to recognize key words. A few typical key words and the action they require are listed below:

Agree or Disagree	– choose one side of the issue – give your observations or opinions supported by logically organized or factual evidence
Analyze	– examine in detail – separate the whole into parts – show the relationships
Compare	– point out similarities and differences
Criticize	– discuss the merits and faults
Discuss	– consider from various points of view like a debate – give reasons, pro and con – be complete and give details
Examine	– look closely to find information, relationships, etc.
Explain	– give reasons for or account for – tell how to do – tell the meaning or interpret – clarify
Prove	– establish that something is true by citing research evidence or by giving clear and logical reasons
Summarize	– give only the main points – briefly recount the important fact or ideas

Once you have chosen your topic, do some preliminary research to make sure that you'll have access to information about your subject. List all of the sources you may want to use for your research. Books will contain valuable information, but do not overlook journals and periodicals which contain more current information. Films, radio, and television shows can also be good sources of information. Newspapers and news magazines are good sources of examples of the theories you are trying to explain. When you have done preliminary research, consult your instructor if you feel that your topic should be narrowed further or if you would like suggestions for additional research sources.

Defining Your Topic: The Thesis Statement

To narrow and define your topic, you must formulate a thesis. This statement of your purpose is often included in the opening paragraph of your essay. The thesis should be a precise statement of your position, rather than a general observation. For example, tell your reader that you are going to prove that "the ritual of marriage demonstrates the importance of rites of passage from a structural functionalist perspective" rather than saying that you are going to "discuss rituals."

In order to develop your thesis, examine your topic carefully. Does it have separate "parts" that must be discussed? For example, examine the "parts" in this topic:

Explain what is meant by the term 'ritual' and show how rituals are important aspects of human life.

First, "ritual" will have to be defined in sociological terms, which might differ from a dictionary definition. Explain how the definitions differ. Once you have defined a ritual, you should apply this definition to several activities to show how they are ritualistic. You might choose to explain how weddings, funerals, or graduations fall into the category of rituals. Including these examples will show that you are able to apply the theoretical definition. Finally, you must explain how these rituals are "important aspects of human life." What demonstrates the importance of these rituals? What would life be like if these rituals were eliminated? What research has been done to demonstrate the importance of these rituals to the individual or to society?

By breaking your topic into parts or separate units, you begin to develop a plan which will help you through both your research and writing stages. It is much easier to find information when you know exactly what you are looking for, and it is easier to write your essay if you know what information you must include.

Research

It is useful to be familar with the reference works which are commonly used in the field of sociology.

Reference Books

A dictionary of the social sciences—J. Gould and W. L. Kolb, Eds.

A modern dictionary of sociology—G. A. Theodorson & A. G. Theodorson

International encyclopedia of the social sciences—D. L. Sills, Ed. (18 volumes)

Sources of information in the social sciences: A guide to literature—W. H. Webb *et al.*

Journals

American Journal of Sociology

American Sociological Review

British Journal of Sociology

Canadian Review of Sociology and Anthropology

Journal of Abnormal and Social Psychology

Journal of Marriage and the Family

Sociology of Education

Bibliographies

International Bibliography of the Social Sciences

International Bibliography in Marriage and the Family 1900-1964

Other Useful Reference Sources

Statistics Canada

Facts on file

Gallup opinion index

Taking Research Notes

Begin your research by scanning the books or other reference works you have selected. Look through the "Table of Contents" and the "Index" to see how much of the work is devoted to your topic. Quickly skim through the material to determine if the book is of value for your research. If the book does not relate to your topic or is too general, return it. Once you have collected the books, journals, newspapers, and other sources that will be useful to you, read them and take good research notes.

Many writers use index cards to take and organize their notes. For each source, an index card is prepared listing the title, author, publisher, place of publication, and date of publication. Then, notes about that book are kept on that card. This system works well for extended research, such as the type that would be required to complete a university thesis or a textbook.

Each sheet is given a heading with the same information that would be on an index card. This information is important, because you will need it later to document your essay. As you read each book (or other source), take notes about the ideas or concepts that will help you to support your thesis.

It is crucial that you have a way of distinguishing three separate things in your notes—direct quotations, summaries, and your own ideas. Unless you make a distinction at this stage, you are liable to get confused and end up in the dangerous territory of plagiarism. Direct quotations can be indicated in your notes with the use of quotation marks. Remember if you are noting a direct quotation, you must not change the original at all. Do not forget to include a note about the page number. You will need the page number for documentation.

Dealing with the Ideas of Others

Summaries of the author's ideas are useful, especially if the original passage is long or if you want to present a summary of the findings of a study or other research. You must still make it clear, especially in your notes, that the ideas you are recording are the author's, not your own. Even if you change the author's words, you are still presenting information or ideas developed by someone else, and that person must be given credit. In your notes, you could write "SUMMARY " beside your entry, or you could begin (as you will later in your essay) with an entry such as *"Smith and Brown discovered in their 1984 survey of students at Honour Academy that 93 percent of undergraduates felt a marriage must be monogamous."* In addition, always make a complete note of your source.

You also want to make note of the ideas that occur to you as you are taking your notes. Distinguish them from the source material by writing them in pencil, putting an asterisk beside them, or boxing them in. Since the essay will be a presentation of *your* ideas supported by the views and research or others, your ideas are extremely important and should be recorded at this stage.

When you complete your notes, organize them before you

begin to write your essay. Review all of the notes you have taken to give yourself an overview of your topic.

The Writing Process

Your research has given you information about your topic; now you need to concentrate on presenting that information clearly. Writing the essay is not an impossible task, as long as you remember to apply your time management skills to this phase as well. Divide the work into small sections and stay on schedule. It is better to finish ahead of time than to rush at the last minute.

Outlining

Writing an essay does not begin with inspiration; it begins with an outline. An outline works like a blueprint for your essay, so you will know exactly what shape the final version will take.

Many social science works that present original studies use this pattern:

1. Identify the issue or problem.
2. State thesis, objectives and information needs.
3. Identify the research methodology you are using.
4. Summarize and analyse data collected.
5. Draw conclusions and recommendations.

Other sociology essays, including many college essays which depend on the use of secondary research, use this pattern:

1. introduction (including the thesis statement);
2. summary of important research relevant to your thesis;
3. observations and analysis;
4. summary and conclusions.

The pattern you choose will depend on the purpose of your essay, the topic you have been assigned, and the nature of your research.

As you write your outline, list the major ideas that you want to cover in your paper as you think of them. Use point-form notes. Do not worry about organizing your information in this initial outline; just get your ideas down on paper. Index cards are very handy for this purpose, because you can sort them later into a logical structure without rewriting.

Once your ideas are recorded, examine the list and see if you can arrange them in a logical manner which is appropriate for your essay. Write another point form outline listing the ideas in the order you want them to be discussed. For each idea that you list, decide what evidence you are going to offer to support your observation.

Your outline will guide you through the writing of your essay, so keep it handy as you progress. One of the main advantages of an outline is that it helps you to get back on track quickly if you are interrupted or if you cannot finish writing your essay in one sitting.

The First Draft

The first draft of your essay allows you to expand your point-form essay into sentences and paragraphs. As you compose your essay, write sentences that are clear and precise, and keep each paragraph organized around one central idea. On the other hand, do not get so tied up with details of composition that you neglect to include all of the necessary information or allow yourself to become frustrated when you cannot find the right words to express yourself. Charge through the first draft, forcing yourself to get the "meat on the bones" by expanding your outline and writing your ideas in sentences and paragraphs.

At the draft stage, the important task is to get your essay written out in full while recognizing that this draft is not intended to be the final version of the essay and will need to be edited.

Essay Style

An academic essay is also considered to be a formal piece of writing, so the style of your writing must reflect this formality.

Eliminate unnecessary words. Your sentences should only contain words that contribute to the clear communication of your ideas. Always express your ideas in the most concise and direct manner. If you do not choose words carefully, your ideas can become lost. A good essay style comes from the direct expression of ideas. Instead of trying to impress your reader with "fancy" writing, present your information clearly and concisely. You will be able to control your essay more easily, and the result will be more successful.

Your essay could also be weakened by the use of overly general words and phrases. Writing "many students believe" is less effective than explaining "22 of the 30 students in the class believe." Instead of writing "some theorists found," write "Cliff (1964), Lane (1979), Wesolowski (1969) and Lenski (1966) found." Whenever you give specific information, provide your reader with support for your position—in doing so, you will make your essay more interesting and authoritative.

Be aware of sexist language in essays. It might offend your reader. For example, the sentence "In this situation, a doctor should prescribe rest for his patient" gives the impression that a doctor is expected to be male. Writing "A doctor should prescribe rest for his or her patient" is awkward. Often the problem can be solved be using the plural—"Doctors should prescribe rest for their patients." However, you should specify an individual's sex if it is relevant to the information you are discussing.

Abbreviations should be avoided because they can be confusing. Your reader might not recognize MMPI as the short form for the Minnesota Multiphasic Personality Inventory, or RT as the short form for reaction time, or CS as the short form for conditioned stimulus. Write all words out in full, including common abbreviations such as "e.g.," and "etc".

Figures

Figures (charts, graphs, drawings, photos, or diagrams) may be effectively used to explain information, depict the results of a survey, or summarize a process. However, they should not be used to repeat information you have already presented in your essay, nor should they be used to substitute for a complete explanation. A figure should not exist in isolation; instead, it should be tied to the text of your essay. For example, the text of your essay could include a reference such as:

Figure A (page 12) illustrates the relationship between arrest and conviction rates.

Editing

When you have finished writing the first draft, take a break from your essay. Putting some distance between you and the work will help you to edit your essay with a clear head and a critical eye.

Your writing skills will be just as important as your research and analytical abilities to the success of your essay. Divide your editing into several steps. Begin by examining the essay as a whole. Then examine each section, each paragraph, each sentence and each word. Use these editing guidelines:

The Essay

1. Is the essay well organized? Your essay should have a strong opening and conclusion. The opening paragraph creates the initial impression of your work in the reader's mind, and you want that impression to be good. Similarly, the conclusion leaves the reader with your final statement on the topic, and you want your summation and conclusion to represent accurately the research you have presented. The body of your essay must develop your observations and ideas in a logical sequence so your reader understands your argument.

2. Is all of your material relevant to your thesis? Review your thesis and your outline to ensure that every idea you present

is vital to the development and explanation of your position. It is easy to fall into the trap of including information which is interesting but not relevant to the topic you are discussing. As well, never try to pad an essay which is too short with irrelevant information. Instead, do some additional research so you can include relevant information to strengthen your essay.

3. Have you included all of the necessary information? As you edit your essay, try to anticipate all of the questions your reader could ask. Do not assume that the reader shares your point of view or understands the way you have used sociological terms. Give complete explanations of your ideas, and clarify any terms you use in your explanations.

4. Have you supported every major idea? Your essay will be convincing to your reader only if you give evidence to support the ideas you are presenting. What have the experts written on the subject? Do their findings correspond with your own? Support the general information you present with specific examples.

5. Does your essay conform to the assigned requirements? In addition to adequately covering the assigned topic, your essay must conform to the instructor's requirements regarding length, research methodology, style, and documentation. Your instructor is expecting a work which meets certain guidelines. Don't expect to get a favourable reaction if you ignore those guidelines.

The Paragraphs

1. Does each paragraph develop one central idea? Do not try to cover too much territory in a single paragraph. Each paragraph should focus on one idea and develop that idea fully so the reader can understand it before going on to the next paragraph and the next idea. Each paragraph should be a "mini-essay" complete with an opening sentence to introduce the idea, and a final sentence to conclude your observations. If you cram too much into each paragraph, the reader will become mired in the ideas you present.

2. Are the paragraphs coherent? Each paragraph should follow naturally from the preceding one and lead naturally to the next. Writers use several methods to achieve this coherence. Often, a word from the concluding sentence of one paragraph is repeated in the opening sentence of the following

paragraph. For example, in Chapter 7, you'll find a paragraph ends:

"The high fertility of pre-transitional societies is upheld by social beliefs and values that run counter to the behavioural changes reduced fertility implies."

The next paragraph begins:

"Nevertheless, modernization eventually operates to lower fertility."

Note the use of the transitional word "nevertheless" and the repetition of the word "fertility". These techniques help the writer to achieve coherence.

3. Have you eliminated unnecessary sentences? Unnecessary sentences are excess baggage in your paragraphs. Develop ideas; don't repeat them. If your sentences are repetitious, your reader will feel as though he has been subjected to reruns and will become bored.

Sentences

1. Does the structure of each sentence make your idea clear? Strong sentence structure allows you to emphasize important ideas. In general, place the most important idea in the sentence first. Do not use long introductory phrases which can weaken what you are trying to say. For example, it is more effective to write, "Brothers and sisters play an important role in socializing one another" than to write, "In socializing one another, brothers and sisters play an important role."

2. Are your sentences varied in length? Sentence length should be varied so your writing does not become monotonous.

3. Are your sentences strong? Try to use active verbs ("Davis and Moore conducted the study") rather than passive verbs ("The study was conducted by Davis and Moore"). When you use active verbs, you eliminate much of the wordiness caused by the need for auxiliary verbs such as "was," "were," "has been," or "have been."

Words

Have you eliminated unnecessary words? Cut out all words or expressions that are not needed. Get the greatest value out of every word without sacrificing the ideas you want to present.

Documentation

When you write your essay and use the ideas, research, and observations of others in order to support your own ideas, it is crucial that you give full credit to your sources. When you give credit, you assist your reader in recognizing your own ideas as opposed to the ideas you have taken from other sources.

If you attempt to include material which is not your own in your essay without giving credit to the proper sources, you are plagiarizing. Plagiarism is the act of representing the words or ideas of others as your own. In effect, plagiarism is theft and can result in severe penalties that may adversely affect your academic future.

Word for word copying is not the only kind of plagiarism. You must give proper credit, even if you change the original author's words into your own. As well, you must give proper credit if you summarize someone else's ideas, observations, or research.

Remember that the purpose of the essay is not to merely summarize the work of others. Your essay must present your own analyses, observations, examples, and ideas. The source material you use should support your own original ideas, not be a substitute for them.

Documentation

Always check with your instructor to find out what system of documentation you should use. Follow the instructor's directions exactly; every documentation system is extremely precise. Although the Modern Languages Association (MLA) documentation system is often required for English essays, most sociology instructors prefer the documentation system devised by the American Psychological Association. This system is usually referred to as the APA system. Since this system is the one most widely used for sociology essays and reports, the following information will give you examples of documentation using the APA style.

Two major areas of your essay require documentation. You must document specific information you have taken from sources and included in your essay. You must also properly document a complete list of all of the source material to which you have referred in your essay.

References Within the Essay

Whenever information from another source is used in your essay, the source of that information must be properly acknowledged. The information could include a quotation, a summary, a theory, or facts which have been borrowed to support your own observations or ideas.

In the APA format, parenthetical references are used to give the reader a description of the work. Then, the reader can refer to the "Works Cited" list at the end of the essay to get complete information about the source. For example, if you want to include the definition of "culture" given in Chapter Two you could write:

"Culture refers to shared symbols and their meaning prevailing in any society or parts of society" (Hagedorn, 1986, p. 31).

Or you could write:

Hagedorn (1986, p. 31) sees culture as "shared symbols and their meaning prevailing in any society or parts of society."

You will notice that if the author's name is not included in the body of the essay, it is added in the parentheses along with the date of publication. If the name is included, then only the date of publication is given. In this case, you are also using a direct quotation, so the page number is included. Your reader can then refer to the references or works cited list at the end of your essay to find complete information about the Hagedorn reference.

Guidelines for Parenthetical References: APA Style

1. If you include the name of the author in your narrative, only the date of the publication is given.
    S. D. Clark (1976) found that social expectations rose in the post-war period.

2. If the name of the author is not included in the narrative, include both the author's name and the date of publication.

    In a recent sociological study (Clark, 1976) found that expectations rose.

3. If the work has two authors, give both names in every reference.

    Bowes and Gintis (1976) conducted studies to show that students were rarely rewarded for emotional behaviour.

    If the names are given in parentheses, join them with an ampersand (&).

    Students were rarely rewarded for emotional behaviour (Boles & Gintis, 1976).

4. If the work has more than two authors, give only the name of the first author, followed by "et al.".

Hagen et al. (1978) found that crime rates are poor indicators of this problem.

This problem is not indicated by examining crime rates (Hagen et al., 1978).

5. If two authors have the same last name, include the author's initials in all references.

    S. Wilson (1984) and R. Wilson (1978) disagree with these theories.

    Other writers (S. Wilson, 1984, & R. Wilson, 1978) disagree with these theories.

6. If the author's name is not known, give a few words from the title of the work.

    These problems are avoided in many nursing homes ("Health Care for the Aged").

7. Include the page number for quotations.

    "Culture refers to shared symbols and their meaning prevailing in any part of a society" (Hagedorn, 1986, p. 31).

    If the quotation is long, indent the quotation five spaces from the left margin. Using too many long quotations can be distracting and can weaken your essay. Try to keep quotations short and precise.

8. Interviews are documented within the essay, but they are not listed in the "Works Cited" list.

    S. Attwell (personal interview, Nov. 1986) pointed out that a general education is essential.

Works Cited: APA Style

At the end of your essay, you must provide a complete list of all of the works to which you have referred in your essay. This list is called "Works Cited" or "References." It does *not* include sources which might have been useful to you but have not been specifically referred to in your essay.

The "Works Cited" list should be arranged alphabetically by author. If you are listing two works by the same author, list the works in chronological order. If two or more authors have the same last name, alphabetize according to the authors' first names. If no author is given, use the first major word in the title to determine alphabetical order.

The first line of each entry is flush to the left margin. Subsequent lines in the entry are double spaced and indented three spaces from the left margin. Also, double space between each entry in the list.

The list provided below will help you to find the correct format for the type of references you need to include under "Work Cited":

Book—1 author

Charon, J. M. (1979). *Symbolic interaction.* Englewood Cliffs, NJ: Prentice-Hall.

Book—2 authors

Turner, R. H., & Killian, L. M. (1972). *Collective behavior.* Englewood Cliffs, NJ: Prentice-Hall.

Book—author & editor

Simmel, G. (1950). *The sociology of Georg Simmel* (K. Wolff, Ed.). Glencoe, IL: Free Press.

Book—editors

Block, W. E., & Walker, M. A. (Eds.). (1982). *Discrimination, affirmative action, and equal opportunity.* Vancouver: The Fraser Institute.

Book—Translation

Durkheim, E. (1964). *Suicide* (J. A. Spaulding & G. Simpson, Trans.). Gencoe, IL: Free Press. (Original work published 1897)

Book—Edition

Smith, H. W. (1981). *Strategies of social research.* (2nd ed.) Englewood Cliffs, NJ: Prentice Hall

Reference to chapter in a book

Wood, P. (1982). The environmental movement: Its crystallization, development and impact. In J. L. Wood & M. Jackson (Eds.), *Social movements: Development, participation and dynamics* (pp. 201-220). Belmont, CA: Wadsworth.

Reference to a Work in a Collection or Anthology

Archer, J. (1976). Biological explanations of psychological sex differences. In B. Lloyd & J. Archer (Eds.), *Exploring sex differences* (pp. 83-87). New York, Academic Press.

Book Review

Goldsen, R. K. (1979). [Review of Marie Winn, *The plug-in drug: Television, children and the family*]. *American Journal of Sociology, 84,* 1054-1056.

Magazine article

Blaunt, R., Jr. (1984, June). Erma Bombeck gets the dirt out. *Esquire* (pp. 208-210).

Journal article—one author

Power, M. (1975). Woman's work is never done—by men: A socio-economic model of sex-typing in occupations. *Journal of Industrial Relations, 17,* 225-239.

Journal article—two authors

Driedger, L., & Mezoff, R. (1980). Ethnic prejudice and discrimination in Winnipeg high schools. *Canadian Journal of Sociology, 6,* 1-17.

Newspaper article—author

Ford, C. (1983, July 23). Leave-me-alone group tunes out. *The Calgary Herald,* p. 16.

Newspaper article—no author

Deadline set for claiming make-work funds. (1979, July 19). *The Globe and Mail,* p. 8.

Report—University

Marshall, V. W. (1981). *The changing family relationships of older people* (Research report 5). Hamilton, Ontario: McMaster University, Program for Quantitative Studies in Economics and Population.

Conference Report

Coale, A. (1973). The demographic transition reconsidered. *International Population Conference.* Liège, Belgium: International Union for the Scientific Study of Population.

Government Report

Statistics Canada (1985). *Current demographic analysis: Report of the demographic situation in Canada 1983.* Ottawa: Ministry of Supply and Services.

Encyclopedia

Hexham, I., Currie, R., & Townsend, J. (1984). The new religions. *New Canadian Encyclopedia* (pp. 412-414). Edmonton: Hurtig.

Presenting Your Essay

A typed essay is preferable to a handwritten one. Use a good quality paper and type on one side of the page only. Leave 1½ inch (4 cm) margins at the top, bottom and sides of the page. Indent paragraphs five spaces, and indent long quotations ten spaces. Remember to leave two spaces after the period at the end of each sentence. Don't divide words at the end of the line.

Your essay should have a front title page with the title of your essay in the centre of the page. In the lower right corner type in your name, your class, the instructor's name and the date of submission. The "Works Cited" list should begin on a separate page at the end of the essay.

Proofreading

Before handing in your essay, proofread it to catch errors in spelling or grammar. Read slowly and carefully, checking each word, each sentence and each paragraph. It is also a good idea to have a friend read your essay. Sometimes, someone who reads an essay for the first time will catch errors the author has missed.

Keep your research documents and a copy of your essay until you receive your final and official transcript. In fact, your records can prove to be a valuable reference for writing other essays in future. As you review your old work, you will be able to see the progress you have made and learn from your own experience.

Further Reading

American Psychological Association (1985). *Publication manual of the American Psychological Association.* (3rd. ed.) Hyattsville, MD: Author.

Bailey, E. P., Jr., Powell, P., & Shuttleworth, J. (1986). *The practical writer.* (3rd. ed.) New York: Holt, Rinehart and Winston.

Gibaldi, J., & Achtert, W. S. (1984). *MLA handbook for writers or research papers* (2nd. ed.) New York: Modern Languages Association.

Hubbuch, S. M. (1985). *Writing research papers across the curriculum.* New York: Holt, Rinehart and Winston.

Millward, C. (1983). *Handbook for writers* (2nd. ed.) New York: Holt, Rinehart and Winston.

Norton, S., & Green, B. (1985). *The bare essentials* (Form A, 2nd. ed.) New York: Holt, Rinehart and Winston.

Walter, T., & Siebert, A. (1984). *Student success.* (3rd. ed.) New York: Holt, Rinehart and Winston.

Wood, N. (1986). *College reading and study skills.* (3rd. ed.) New York: Holt, Rinehart and Winston.

Glossary

Absolute deprivation. Structured disadvantage rooted in concrete inequalities of wealth, status, or power.

Adult socialization. Socialization that takes place after childhood to prepare people for adult roles, e.g., husband, mother, computer technician.

Age structure. Pertaining to population, the proportion of people in each age category.

Age-specific birth rate. Incidence of births in a given year per 1000 women of a given age group. The rates are calculated for five-year age groups.

Agricultural society. A society in which at least half the labour force is engaged in the primary sector.

Alienation. Workers' feelings that they are small, meaningless parts of an insensitive production system over which they have little control.

Androgeny. The presence of both feminine and masculine elements within people of both sexes.

Anomie. Term originally used by Durkheim to refer to an absence of social regulation, or normlessness. Merton revived the concept to refer to the consequences of a faulty relationship between goals and the legitimate means of attaining them.

Anticipatory socialization. Role learning that occurs in advance of the actual playing of roles.

Arbitration. The process whereby a third party intervenes between management and labour and passes binding judgment on the new collective agreement.

Assimilation. Process by which ethnic or cultural diversity declines as ethnic or minority group members are absorbed into the larger society.

Authority. The recognized right to make binding decisions.

Bargaining tactics. Strategies that rely on having something valuable to trade with authorities.

Blended family. A family resulting from a remarriage in which dependent children from a previous marriage have been brought into the union.

Bloc recruitment. The attraction to an organization or movement of sets of supporters already linked by friendship or organizational ties.

Bourgeoisie. The dominant class, which consists of those who own capital and are thus able to employ others.

Breakdown theory. An approach that attributes social-movement formation to disorganization and disorientation caused by rapid social change.

Bureaucracy. A formal organization based on the application of legal-rational principles.

Charismatic authority. Authority that is based on the belief that the individual leader is special and possesses some exceptional ability or magic, which inspires loyalty in the followers.

Church-sect typology. A framework, dating back to Weber, that examines religious organizations in terms of ideal-type, church, and sect characteristics.

Circular reaction. A process through which people in crowds directly copy one anothers' excited moods and actions, leading to disorderly, irrational group behaviour.

City. Large concentration of people engaged in a wide range of interdependent occupations that, for the most part, do not involve the primary production of food.

Class conflict. Antagonism between social classes, especially between the class that owns the means of production and the classes that do not.

Class consciousness. Awareness, particularly among the working class, of common economic conditions.

Classical design. Experimental design in which two equivalent groups are selected, one of which is subjected to the independent variable, the other (the control group) of which is not.

Closed system. Theoretical perspective of organizations as relatively self-contained units in which particular structural arrangements and individual behaviour patterns may be accounted for by factors internal to the organization.

Coercive tactics. The symbolic or actual disruption of institutional routines in order to attract support or exert pressure for movement demands.

Cohesiveness. Conditions whereby individuals identify themselves as members of the group, members want the group to remain together, and members have a high regard for each other.

Collective conscience. Durkheim's term, referring to the awareness that the group is more than the sum of its individual members; norms, for example, appear to exist on a level beyond the individual consciences of group members.

Collective good. A benefit available to all members of a group, whether or not they contribute to the cost of gaining it.

Commodity production. Goods and services created for exchange in the marketplace.

Competition. Action of two or more groups or activities that attempt to occupy the same area.

Composition. The characteristics of people in a population, particularly age and sex.

Concentric-zone model. Model of the city in which economic and residential activity patterns and social groups are segregated in concentric zones, with economic activities located at the centre of the city and residential activities located toward the periphery.

Conciliation. The process whereby a third party intervenes between management and labour, and makes recommendations regarding a new collective agreement.

Conflict crimes. Acts that are defined by law as criminal, are often severely punished, but are usually regarded as only marginally harmful; typically they are subjects of conflict and debate.

Conflict perspective. A sociological view emphasizing that conflict, power, and change are permanent features of society.

Conflict subculture. Illegal group activity that is prone to violence and is common in settings (e.g., "disorganized slums") where legitimate and illegitimate spheres are not integrated.

Consensus crimes. Acts defined by law as criminal that are widely regarded as extremely harmful, are severely punished, and are consensually identified as deviant.

Conservative perspective on social inequality. Normative theory that inequality is necessary, inevitable, and just.

Consociational democracy. A nation-state that acknowledges and encourages its multicultural character.

Corporation. Legal entity created for purposes of conducting business, which has an existence separate from that of its members and provides them with limited liability.

Counterculture. A subculture that is consciously opposed to certain central aspects or values of the dominant culture.

Counter-movements. Collective attempts to resist or reverse change or the demands for change made by some other social movement.

Crime control model. Model of law enforcement that places heavy emphasis on the repression of criminal conduct, because insuring order is seen as the only way to guarantee individual freedom.

Crude rate. Frequency of an event per unit of the total population, usually 1000. Applied especially to deaths and births.

Cultural diversity. Differences in cultural values between societies.

Cultural relativism. The view that all cultures are equally valid and valuable and that each culture must be judged by its own standards.

Cultural universals. Behaviour patterns found in many cultures.

Culture. Shared set of symbols and their meanings that prevail in a society.

Deliquent subculture. Collective response of working-class adolescents to their failure to satisfy middle-class expectations; the result is an inversion of middle-class values.

Demographic transition theory. Description and explanation of the three-stage transition from high birth and death rates to low birth and death rates.

Demography. Scientific study of population.

Dependent variable. See *Variable*.

Deviance. Variation from a norm, made socially significant through the reaction of others.

De-urbanization. A decrease in the proportion of population inhabiting urban areas.

Differential association. Process by which criminal behaviour is learned in conjunction with people who define such behaviour favourably and in insolation from those who define it unfavourably.

Dimensions of religious commitment. Glock and Stark identify four: belief, experience, practice, and knowledge.

Discrimination. The practice by which a majority group deprives a minority group of equal access to opportunities, privileges, or resources.

Distribution. The geographical location of people.

Division of labour. Process whereby general tasks and roles become increasingly specialized.

Doubling time. Number of years it would take for a population to double its present size, given the current rate of population growth.

Due process model. Model of law enforcement that emphasizes procedural safeguards thought useful in protecting accused person from unjust applications of criminal penalties.

Dynamic equilibrium. Parson's term for the orderly change that constantly occurs among the interrelated parts of a social system.

Dysfunctional. Adjective applied to an element or part of a system that disrupts or is harmful to the system.

Ego. The director of the Freudian personality. The Ego attempts to mediate among the demands of the Id, the Super-ego, and the external world. The Ego encompasses the cognitive functions and the defence mechanisms.

Endogamy. Formal and informal rules that require that marriage be within one's group or community.

Environmental determinism. The idea that the physical environment can affect or determine people's attitudes, behaviour, or conditions.

Ethnic boundary. Unwritten codes and customs that define a person as a member or non-member of a particular group.

Ethnic group. A group with a shared sense of identity based upon culture, religion, national origin, or race.

Ethnicity. The shared cultural characteristics of an ethnic group.

Ethnocentrism. Tendency to use one's own culture as the only valid standard for evaluating other cultures, societies, and peoples.

Exogamy. Formal and informal rules that require that marriage be outside one's group or community.

Exploitation. Unequal social relations resulting in the acquisition of a valued commodity by the dominant individual or group. In Marxist theory, exploitation is inherent in capitalist economic relations.

Expressive role. The role that focuses on the home and the nurturing and raising of children.

Extended family. A family comprised of a nuclear family plus other relatives.

Fact. An observation that has been verified after several qualified observers have achieved the same results.

Factions. Splinter organizations within a movement that hold conflicting views on the degree, nature, or tactics of social change to be pursued.

False consciousness. Lack of awareness of common and economic conditions, especially among the working class. It is usually associated with non-economic factors such as race, ethnicity, or gender.

Family. Refers to any group of people considered to be related to each other by blood (genetically) or marriage. Also refers to the social arrangements that tie together this group of people, normatively establishing the relationships between the people who fill various positions and defining boundaries, rights, and duties.

Family of orientation. The family into which people are born and in which the major part of their socialization takes place.

Family of procreation. The family people create when they marry and have children.

Fertility. Actual childbearing performance of a woman or group of women; an important component of population change.

Folkways. Traditional rules about customary ways of behaving that are informally enforced and of mild concern to society members.

Formal organization. Relatively enduring or continuing social collectivity in which roles and resources are co-ordinated through a division of labour in the use of a technology to achieve a goal or goals. Co-ordination, control, and problem-solving are facilitated through communication, leadership, and varying degrees of written rules and procedures.

Formalization. Process by which the informality of relationships is gradually replaced by varying degrees of rules, codes and conduct, laws, and other means of regulation.

Functional. Adjective applied to parts of a social system that contribute to the overall stability of the system.

Gemeinschaft. Tönnies' term for relatively small organizations that are characterized by a commitment to tradition, informal social control, intimate interpersonal contact, a collective orientation, and group consciousness.

Gender. Societal definitions of appropriate female and male traits and behaviours.

Gender assignment. The designation of a person as female or male.

Gender identity. The individual's conviction of being male or female.

Gender roles. Culturally defined positions and activities that are considered appropriate for the male or the female within the family (or society).

Gender script. The details of a society's ideas about masculinity and femininity contained, for example, in gender stereotypes and gender attitudes.

Gender socialization. The lifelong processes through which people learn to be feminine or masculine according to the expectations current in their society.

General fertility rate. The incidence of births in a given year per 1000 women between the ages of 15 and 49.

Gesellschaft. Tönnies' term for relatively large organizations that are characterized by formal social control, impersonal contact, an orientation to individualism, and little commitment to tradition.

Growth rate. Number of people added to or subtracted from a population in a given period for every 100 or 1000 total population. A positive rate is for an increasing population; a negative rate is for a decreasing population.

Heterogamy. Marriage of two people who share very few common characteristics.

Holistic model of work. A perspective asserting that there is no essential division between work and non-work.

Homogamy. Marriage of two people who share characteristics such as age and education.

Homophobia. Fear and hostility toward homosexuals that is expressed in prejudicial attitudes and discriminatory behaviour.

Human ecology. Application of such ecological principles as competition, invasion, and succession to the scientific study of human behaviour.

Hypothesis. An idea expected to be true, but which remains to be proven as a result of scientific research.

I. Mead's dimension of the self which is acting, spontaneous, creative, and unpredictable. The "I" is seen as a component of a process, not as a concrete entity.

Id. The reservoir of inborn, biological propensities in the Freudian personality structure. The selfish, impulsive Id operates according to the pleasure principle.

Independent variable. See *Variable.*

Indicators. The empirical measurements used for variables.

Industrial revolution. Technological change first brought about by the invention of the steam engine at the end of the eighteenth century, which resulted in a radical restructuring of work.

Industrial society. A society in which less than half the labour force is engaged in the primary sector.

Industrial union. A formal organization of non-trade workers based on the private-sector industry in which they work.

Industrialization. Involves the movement of workers out of the primary sector into the secondary manufacturing sector.

Inequality of condition. Inequality in the overall structure of rewards (for example, money, prestige) in a society.

Inequality of opportunity. Inequality in the chances that members of a society have to obtain socially valued resources such as money, prestige, and power.

Institutionalized discrimination. Indirect discrimination that occurs as a by-product of the ordinary functioning of social institutions.

Labour theory of value. Theory that the value of a commodity is determined by the labour that goes into it, in contrast to the utility theory of value, which holds that the value of a commodity is determined by what people are willing to pay for it.

Laws. Norms that have been formally promulgated by a legislative body and are enforced by an executive body of government.

Legal-rational authority. Authority based on belief in the legality of formally specified rules and relationships.

Lobbying. Activities by special interest groups aimed at influencing government legislation.

Looking glass self. Cooley's formulation of the self as the interpreted reflection of others' attitudes. It consists of "the imagination of our appearance to the other person, the imagination of his judgment of that appearance, and some sort of self-feeling, such as pride or mortification."

Marginal. Disassociated from the principal values and norms of the society.

Marriage. Socially approved and relatively permanent heterosexual relationship, usually involving a public ceremony and economic co-operation.

Marxism. A conflict theory that emphasizes the material basis of social inequality.

Mass culture. Cultural elements transmitted by mass media and therefore shared in standardized form by large numbers of people.

Material culture. Physical artifacts or products of a society embodying cultural meanings.

Me. That dimension of Mead's notion of self that represents internalized societal attitudes and expectations. The "Me" is an aspect of a process, not a concrete entity.

Mechanical solidarity. Feeling of people in primitive societies that they are held together by kinship, neighbourliness, and friendliness.

Migration Movement of people from one geographical locale to another, either within a country or from one country to another.

Minority group. A social category that occupies a subordinate rank in a social hierarchy. Members view themselves as objects of discrimination.

Moral autonomy. Later stage of moral thought, according to Piaget, in which children over age eight judge wrongdoing in terms of intentions and extenuating circumstances, as well as consequences, and view rules as social conventions that can be changed.

Moral realism. Early stage of moral development, according to Piaget, in which children four to eight years old judge wrongdoing strictly in terms of its consequences and believe all rules are immutable absolutes.

Mores. Traditional rules about how the individual must or must not behave, invested with strong feelings and informally enforced.

Mortality. Occurrence of deaths in a population; an important component of population change.

Mosaic. The unity that is achieved through a collection of diverse components.

Multiculturalism. An affirmation of the belief in cultural pluralism; a situation in which numerous groups maintain different cultures, ideologies, or interests within a framework of mutual respect and tolerance.

Multiple nuclei model. Model of a city as several specialized areas located along and connected by major traffic arteries, such as highways. Unlike the concentric zone and the sector models, the multiple nuclei model does not suggest that zones radiate from the centre of the city.

Nation. An ethnic group that occupies a homeland or is associated with a particular territory.

Natural increase. Excess of births over deaths in a population during a given time period.

Net migration. Difference between the number of in-migrants and the number of out-migrants.

Neutralization techniques. Linguistic expressions that, through a subtle process of justification, allow individuals to drift into deviant lifestyles.

Non-functional. A part that is of no importance to the system.

Non-institutionalized activity. Non-routine action taken to promote interests that are not met by society's established institutions and conventions.

Normative beliefs. Ideas about what should or should not be, referring especially to goodness, virtuousness, or propriety.

Normative theory. Any theory concerned mainly with moral evaluation and the question of justice.

Norms. Formal or informal rules stating how categories of people are expected to act in a particular situation, the violation of which is subject to sanction.

Nuclear family. Family group of a wife and her husband and their unmarried children or, alternatively, a single parent and dependent children, or a heterosexual couple without children.

Objective ethnicity. Parentage.

Observation. Method of gathering data without direct questioning. See also *participant observation.*

Occupational prestige. A measure of the material and political rewards that go with an occupational role.

Occupational segregation. The concentration of members of one sex in a relatively few occupations in which they greatly outnumber the other sex.

Occupational sex-typing. The societal view that certain occupations are more appropriate work for one sex than the other.

Official minority. The English mother-tongue population in Québec or the French mother-tongue population in all provinces except Québec and New Brunswick. (New Brunswick accords equal status to French and English.)

Open system. Theoretical perspective of organizations in which particular structural arrangements and individual behaviour patterns may be accounted for by a combination of factors internal to the organization and its external environment.

Organic solidarity. Dependencies among people in developed societies created as a result of a more specific division of labour.

Organization. A collectivity in which people and resources are co-ordinated through a division of labour in the use of a technology to achieve a goal. Co-ordination , control, and problem-solving are facilitated through communication and leadership.

Participant observation. Observation in which observer is part of the social setting being observed.

Passing. The act of publicly presenting oneself with an identity contrary to one's own personal assessment in order to avoid minority group stigma or to gain societal reward.

Patriarchy. Family arrangement in which only the males (father, husband, sons) have legitimate power or authority vested in their positions.

Persistence argument. Assertion that religion will continue to have a significant place in the modern world, either because it has never actually declined or because people can absorb only so much rationality and materialism.

Persuasive tactics. Strategies based on the authorities' holding certain values that can be activated in favour of the movement's goals.

Population. The total body of people being studied.

Post-industrial society. A society in which at least half the labour force is engaged in the provision of services.

Power. The ability to control the behaviour of others.

Prejudice. Prejudging people on the basis of characteristics assumed to be shared by all members of their social category.

Primary deviance. Deviant behaviours that precede a societal or legal response and have little impact on the individual's self-concept.

Primary sector. That division of the occupational structure in which employment involves either harvesting or extraction of goods (e.g., agriculture, logging, mining, fishing, hunting, and trapping).

Primary socialization. Socialization that occurs during childhood.

Production of use-values. Goods and services produced in the home.

Professional social movements. Movements maintained by a small, full-time core of activists, dependent on the financial donations of unrelated sympathizers or outside agencies.

Proletariat. The working class.

Protestant work ethic. An ideology that states that work is service to God that one's duty is to work hard, and that success in work is measured by money and property.

Public-sector union. A formal organization of workers employed in some type of government enterprise.

Race. An arbitrary social category whose membership is based upon inherited physical characteristics, such as skin colour and facial features, which are defined as socially meaningful.

Racism. The belief in the genetically based inferiority and superiority of different human populations.

Radical. Pursuing the displacement of the established order.

Radical perspective on social inequality. Normative theory that inequality is unnecessary and unjust.

Random sample. Sample in which each person within the population has an equal chance of being selected.

Rate of natural increase. Frequency of increase in population arrived at by subtracting crude death rate from crude birth rate.

Reformist. A person who seeks adjustments in society, but want to maintain the overall existing system.

Relative deprivation. A feeling of unfairness provoked by a gap between the rewards that people expect to receive and those they actually do receive.

Religions. Systems of meaning used to interpret the world that have a supernatural referent (e.g., Christianity, Hinduism, astrology).

Resocialization. Replacement of established attitudes and behaviour patterns.

Resource mobilization. The process of attracting, co-ordinating, and applying resources to achieve a collective goal.

Retreatist subculture. Group-supported forms of escapist behaviour, particularly drug abuse, that result from failure in both legitimate and illegitimate spheres of activity.

Role taking. Process of imaginatively putting oneself in the role of another and seeing the world from that person's perspective.

Safety in numbers. A factor, operative in large gatherings, whereby the larger the crowd is, the less the blame for disorder is likely to be attached to any one person, allowing a potentially rational base for disorder.

Sample. A smaller group chosen to represent the whole population. See also *Random sample*.

Scientific law. A hypothesis that has been repeatedly supported by empirical tests.

Scientific management Taylor's term for achieving perfection in productivity by finding the one best way to do each and every task.

Secondary deviance. Deviant behaviours that follow a societal or legal response and involve a transformation of the individual's self-concept.

Secondary sector. That division of the occupational structure in which employment involves the transformation of raw materials into semi-finished or finished manufactured goods. The secondary sector includes all manufacturing and construction industries in the private sector.

Sector model. Model of a city as a series of wedge-shaped sectors radiating from the centre of the city, each containing different activities or land use and separated by major traffic arteries or natural boundaries.

Secularization argument. Assertion that religion, as it has been traditionally known, is declining continuously and irreversibly.

Segmental model. A perspective asserting that there is an essential division between work and non-work.

Segregation. Tendency of specific activities or race, class, or ethnic groups to cluster and exclude other activities or groups from occupying a region or neighbourhood at the same time.

Selection. Viewpoint that relationships between the physical environment and behaviour reflect the migration or movement of people with particular characteristics to particular places.

Selective incentives. Personal rewards that are available only to individuals who contribute to a collective cause, not to free riders.

Self-report survey. Paper and pencil questionnaires used with adolescents and adults to obtain first-person accounts of behaviour.

Serial monogamy. Societally accepted pattern of more than one spouse in a person's lifetime, as long as that person is married to only one spouse at a time; that is, divorce and remarriage are required.

Sex. Physiological differences between females and males.

Sex ratio. Number of males per 100 females in a population.

Sexism. A belief in gender-based oppression.

Size. The number of people (i.e., the population) in a given area.

Social base. Factors determining what life will be like in a society.

Social democracy. Normative theory of inequality that holds that ownership consists of a divisible bundle of rights and that satisfactory progress toward equality can be achieved through non-violent, gradual reform within the political institutions of democratic capitalist societies.

Social deviation. Non-criminal variation from social norms that is nonetheless subject to frequent official control.

Social distance. Differences in levels of tolerance toward minorities.

Social diversion. Variations of lifestyle, including fads and fashions of appearance and behaviour.

Social facts. Durkheim's term to indicate things that are external to and coercive or constraining upon the individual.

Social incentives. The built-in rewards and penalties solidary groups have available to assure that individual members act in a group-oriented way.

Social inequality. State resulting from various members of a society having unequal amounts of socially valued resources (e.g., money, power) and unequal opportunities to obtain them.

Social mobility. Upward or downward movement of individuals or groups into different positions in the social hierarchy.

Social movements. Collective attempts with varying degrees of formal organization to promote, maintain, or resist social change.

Social segmentation. A deep break between social groups, in which there are few co-operative ties to bind the groups and separate sets of social institutions to maintain the division between them.

Social systems. Within the consensus or structural-functionalist perspective, a series of interrelated parts in a state of equilibrium, with each part contributing to the maintenance of other parts.

Socialization. Complex learning process through which an individual develops selfhood and acquires the knowledge, skills, and motivations required to participate in social life.

Sociology. The description and explanation of social behaviour, social structures, and social interaction in terms of these social structures, and/or in terms of people's perceptions of the social environment.

Spontaneous organization. Temporary coordination of people and resources that disbands when its task or mission has been completed.

Stable criminal subculture. Illegal group enterprises made more persistent by the protection they receive from people in legitimate social roles (e.g., politicians and police).

Stereotype. A mental cartoon that exaggerates what are presumed to be characteristics of the typical member of a particular social group.

Structural-functionalist perspective. A perspective that stresses what the parts of the system do for the system. This perspective is usually classified with the consensus perspective.

Subculture. Group that is part of dominant culture but differs in some important values and norms.

Subjective ethnicity. Personal belief in ethnic culture.

Succession. Replacement of one form of activity by another.

Super-ego. The Freudian conscience, or internalization of societal values and behavioural standards.

Surplus value. The value remaining for the capitalist after the workers have received their share.

Symbol. Anything, such as a word, gesture, or object, taken by people as a matter of convention to stand for something else, to have a meaning.

Synthesis. A theoretical approach to the study of social inequality that attempts to use insights from both the radical and the conservative perspectives and that attempts to be scientific in its methodology.

Task environment. Those elements in an organization's environment that are relevant or potentially relevant to setting goals and attaining goals.

Technology. Application of a body of knowledge through the use of tools and processes in the production of goods and/or services.

Tertiary sector. That division of the occupational structure in which employment involves the provision of services.

Trade union. A formal organization of workers based on their specialized skills (also called a craft union).

Traditional authority. Authority that is based on followers' belief that the monarch has a divine right to rule that is transferred down through eligible descendents.

Unbiased observation. Observation during which the researcher's values can be controlled.

Urbanism. Set of attitudes, beliefs, and behaviours that are thought to be characteristic of city-dwellers.

Urbanization. Increase in the proportion of a given population inhabiting areas designated as urban.

Validity. Property of measurement whereby what is measured is what was intended to be measured.

Value judgment. A moral or ethical judgment about what is right or wrong, good or bad, desirable or undesirable that can be contrasted with a scientific judgment.

Values. Cultural conceptions about what are desirable goals and what are appropriate standards for judging actions.

Value-free sociology. The position that personal judgments and biases can and should be excluded from social observations and interpretations.

Variable. Measurable characteristic that takes on two or more values (such as age, gender, or violent behaviour). There are two types of variables:

a) **Dependent variable.** A factor that depends on or is caused by some other factor.

b) **Independent variable.** The factor that causes the dependent variable.

Verifiability. Characteristic of a conclusion or factual statement by which it can be subjected to more than one observation or test.

Verstehen. Weber's term for the subjective interpretation of social behaviour and intentions, usually based on empathy. In German, literally "understanding."

Visible minority. A term that loosely describes people who are non-white and who are distinct from the British, French, aboriginal peoples, and other so-called white ethnic groups.

Work. An activity that permits one a livelihood. Work includes conventional, paid employment, illegal employment, and homemaking.

Zero population growth. Rate at which births and deaths are equal, resulting in a stationary population.

References

Abella, I. (Ed.) (1974). *On strike*. Toronto: Lorimer.

Aberle, D., & Naegele, K. (1952). Middle-class fathers' occupational role and attitudes toward children. *American Journal of Orthopsychiatry, 22,* 366-378.

Abu-Laban, S. M. (1980). Social supports in older age: The need for new research directions. *Essence, 4,* 195-210.

Adams, I., et al. (1971). *The real poverty report.* Edmonton: Hurtig.

Agopian, M. W., & Anderson, G. L. (1981). Characteristics of parental child stealing. *Journal of Family Issues* 2(4), 471-484.

Aird, J. S. (1978). Fertility decline and birth control in The People's Republic of China. *Population and Development Review, 4,* 225-253.

Al-Issa, I. (1980). *The psychopathology of women.* Englewood Cliffs, NJ: Prentice-Hall.

Allen, R. (1971). *The social passion: Religion and social reform in Canada, 1914-1928.* Toronto: University of Toronto Press.

Allport, G. (1958). *The nature of prejudice.* New York: Doubleday.

Ambert, A. (1976). *Sex structure* (2nd ed.). Don Mills, Ont.: Longman Canada.

Ambert, A. (1980). *Divorce in Canada.* Toronto: Academic Press.

Amirault, E., & Archer, M. (1976). *Canadian business law.* Toronto: Methuen.

Anderson, G. M., & Alleyne, J.M. (1979). Ethnicity, food preferences and habits of consumption as factors in social interaction. *Canadian Ethnic Studies, 11,* 83-87.

Archer, D., Gutner, R., Akert, R., & Lockwood T. (1978). Cities and homicide: A new look at an old paradox. *Comparative Studies in Sociology, 1,* 73-95.

Armstrong, D. (1970). *Education and economic achievement.* Ottawa: Information Canada.

Armstrong, P., & Armstrong, H. (1978). *The double ghetto: Canadian women and their segregated work.* Toronto: McClelland and Stewart.

Armstrong, P., & Armstrong, H. (1983). *A working majority: What women must do for pay.* Ottawa: Canadian Advisory Council on the Status of Women.

Armstrong, P., & Armstrong, H. (1984). *The double ghetto: Canadian women and their segregated work* (rev. ed.). Toronto: McClelland and Stewart.

Asch, M. (1984). *Home and native land: Aboriginal rights and the Canadian Constitution.* Toronto: Methuen.

Atkinson, T., & Murray, M. A. (1980). *Values, domains and the perceived quality of life: Canada and the United States.* York University, Toronto: Institute for Behavioral Research.

Bandura, A., Ross, D., & Ross, S. A. (1963). Imitation of film-mediated aggressive models. *Journal of Abnormal and Social Psychology, 66,* 3-11.

Bardwick, J. M. (1979). *In transition.* New York: Holt, Rinehart and Winston.

Barnard, C. (1938). *The functions of the executive.* Cambridge, MA: Harvard University Press.

Barth, F. (Ed.). (1969). *Ethnic groups and boundaries.* Oslo: Universitetsforlaget.

Beattie, C., & Spencer, B. (1971). Career attainment in Canadian bureaucracies. *American Journal of Sociology, 77,* 472-490.

Beaujot, R. P. (1978). Canada's population: Growth and dualism. *Population Bulletin, 33*(2), 36.

Becker, H. (1963). *Outsiders: Studies in the sociology of deviance.* New York: Free Press.

Bell, D. (1967). The post-industrial society: A speculative view. In Elizabeth Hutchings (Ed.), *Scientific progress and human values.* New York: Elsevier.

Bem, S. L. (1981). Gender schema theory: A cognitive account of sex typing. *Psychological Review, 88,* 354-364.

Bem, S. L. (1983). Gender schema theory and its implications for child development: Raising gender-aschematic children in a gender-schematic society. *Signs, 8,* 598-616.

Benston, M. (1969). The political economy of women's liberation. *Monthly Review, 21,* 13-27.

Berg, I. (1970). *Education and jobs: The great training robbery.* New York: Beacon Press.

Berg, I. (1979). *Industrial sociology.* Englewood Cliffs, NJ: Prentice-Hall.

Berger, P. (1961). *The noise of solemn assemblies.* New York: Doubleday.

Berk, R. (1974). *Collective behavior.* Dubuque, IA: Wm. C. Brown.

Bernard, J. (1971). The paradox of the happy marriage. In Vivian Gornick & Barbara K. Moran (Eds.). *Woman in sexist society.* New York: Mentor Books.

Bernard, J. (1975). *Women, wives, mothers: Values and options.* Chicago: Aldine.

Bernard, J. (1981). *The female world.* New York: Free Press.

Best, R. (1983). *We've all got scars: What boys and girls learn in elementary school.* Bloomington, IN: Indiana University Press.

Beuf, A. (1974). Doctor, lawyer, household drudge. *Journal of Communication, 24,* 142-145.

Bibby, R. W. (1979a). The state of collective religiosity in Canada. *Canadian Review of Sociology and Anthropology, 16,* 105-116.

Bibby, R. W. (1979b, October). Consequences of religious commitment: The Canadian case. Paper presented at the Annual Meeting of The Society for the Scientific Study of Religion, San Antonio, TX

Bibby, R. W. (1983). Religionless Christianity. *Social Indicators Research, 13,* 1-16.

Bibby, R. W. (1985). Religious encasement in Canada: An argument for Protestant and Catholic entrenchment. *Social Compass.*

Bibby, R. W., & Brinkerhoff, M. B. (1973). The circulation of the saints: A study of people who join conservative churches. *Journal for the Scientific Study of Religion, 12,* 273-283.

Bibby, R. W., & Brinkerhoff, M. B. (1982). Circulation of the saints revisited: A longitudinal look at conservative church growth. *Journal for the Scientific Study of Religion, 22,* 253-262.

Bibby, R. W., & Mauss, A. (1974). Skidders and their servants: Variable goals and functions of the skid road rescue mission. *Journal for the Scientific Study of Religion, 13,* 421-436.

Bibby, R. W., & Posterski, D. C. (1985). *The emerging generation* (pp. 17, 21, 82, 124). Toronto: Irwin Publishing.

Bird, F., & Reimer, B. (1982). Participation rates in new religious movements and para-religious movements. *Journal for the Scientific Study of Religion, 21,* 1-14.

Black, D. J., & Reiss, A. J., Jr. (1970, February). Police control of juveniles. *American Sociological Review, 35,* 63-77.

Blauner, R. (1964). *Alienation and freedom.* Chicago, IL: University of Chicago Press.

Blishen, B., & Atkinson, T. (1980). Regional and status differences in Canadian values. York University, Toronto: Institute for Behavioral Research.

Block, W. E., & Walker, M. A. (Eds.). (1982). *Discrimination, affirmative action, and equal opportunity.* Vancouver: The Fraser Institute.

Blumberg, A. S. (1967). *Criminal justice.* Chicago: Quadrangle Books.

Blume, J. (1972). *Tales of a fourth grade nothing.* New York: Dell Publishing.

Blumer, H. (1951). Collective behavior. In Alfred McLung Lee (Ed.), *New outline of the principles of sociology.* New York: Barnes & Noble.

Bodemann, Y. M. (1984). Elitism, fragility, and commoditism: Three themes in the Canadian sociological mythology. In S. D. Berkowitz (Ed.), *Models and myths in Canadian sociology* (p. 212). Toronto: Butterworths.

Bogardus, E. S. (1928). *Immigration and race attitudes.* Boston: D.C. Heath.

Bogatz, G. A. & Ball, S. (1972). *The second year of Sesame Street: A continuing evaluation.* Princeton, NJ: Educational Testing Service.

Bonnie, R. J. & Whitebread, C. H. (1974).*The marihuana conviction.* Charlottesville: University Press of Virginia.

Bossen, M. (1971). Manpower utilization in Canadian chartered banks (Study No. 4). Ottawa: The Royal Commission on the Status of Women in Canada.

Bottomore, T. B. (1964). *Karl Marx, selected writings in sociology and social philosophy.* New York: McGraw-Hill.

Bottomore, T. B., & Rubel, M. (Eds.). (1956). *Selected writings in sociology and social philosophy.* New York: McGraw-Hill.

Boulet, J. A. & Laval, C., with C. Pader & M. Poulin. (1983). *L'évolution des disparités linguistiques de revenu de travail au Canada de 1970 á 1980* (Document No. 245). Ottawa: Economic Council of Canada.

Bourne, L. S. (1975). *Urban systems: Strategies for regulation.* London: Oxford University Press.

Bourne, L. S. (1978). Emergent realities of urbanization in Canada: Some parameters and implications of declining growth (Research Paper No. 96). Toronto: University of Toronto, Centre for Urban and Community Studies.

Boyd, M. (1977). The forgotten minority: The socioeconomic status of divorced and separated women. In P. Marchak (Ed.), *The working sexes.* Vancouver: University of British Columbia.

Boyd, M. (1984). *Canadian attitudes toward women: Thirty years of change.* Ottawa: Women's Bureau, Labour Canada.

Braithwaite, J. (1981). The myth of social class and criminality reconsidered. *American Sociological Review, 46*(1), 36-57.

Brandwein, R. A., Brown, C. A., & Fox, E. M. (1974). Women and children last: The social situation of divorced mothers and their families. *Journal of Marriage and the Family, 36,* 498-514.

Brannon, R. (1971). Organizational vulnerability in modern religious organizations. *Journal for the Scientific Study of Religion, 10,* 27-32.

Brenton, M. (1974). *Friendship.* New York: Stein and Day.

Breton, R. (1964). Institutional completeness of ethnic communities and the personal relations of immigrants. *American Journal of Sociology,70*(2), 193-205.

Breton, R. (1972). *Social and academic factors in the career decisions of Canadian youth.* Ottawa: Information Canada.

Brim, O. G., Jr. (1966). Socialization through the life cycle. In O. G. Brim, Jr. & S. Wheeler (Eds.), *Socialization after childhood: Two essays.* New York: Wiley.

Brim, O. G., Jr., & Kagan, Jerome. (1980). Constancy and change: A view of the issues. In O. G. Brim, Jr. & J. Kagan (Eds.), *Constancy and change in human development.* Cambridge, MA: Harvard University Press.

Brinkerhoff, M. B., & Mackie, M. (1985). Religion and gender: A comparison of American and Canadian student attitudes. *Journal of Marriage and the Family.*

Briskin, L. (1983). Women and unions in Canada: A statistical overview. In L. Briskin & Lynda Yanz (Eds.), *Union sisters: Women in the labour movement* (pp. 28-43). Toronto: Women's Press.

Britton, J. N. H., & Gilmour, J. M. (1978).*The weakest link: A technological perspective on Canadian industrial underdevelopment* (Background Study 43). Ottawa: Science Council of Canada.

Brodzinsky, D. M., Barnet, K., & Aiello, J. R. (1981). Sex of subject and gender identity as factors in humor appreciation. *Sex Roles, 7,* 561-573.

Brofenbrenner, U. (1970). *Two worlds of childhood: U.S. and U.S.S.R.* New York: Sage.

Broverman, I. K., Vogel, S. R., Broverman, D. M., Clarkson, F. E., & Rosenkrantz, P. S. (1972). Sex-role stereotypes: A current appraisal. *Journal of Social Issues, 28,* 59-78.

Brown, C. (1984, September 16). Manchild in Harlem. *The New York Times Magazine,* pp. 36-44, 54, 76-78.

Brown, L., & Brown, L. (1973). *An unauthorized history of the R.C.M.P.* Toronto: Lewis and Samuel.

Bruce, C. J. (1978). The effect of young children on female labor force participation rates: An exploratory study. *The Canadian Journal of Sociology, 3,* 431-439.

Burgess, E. W. (1925). The growth of the city. In R. E. Park, E. W. Burgess, & R. D. McKenzie (Eds.), *The city.* Chicago: University of Chicago Press.

Bush, D. M., & Simmons, R. G. (1981). Socialization processes over the life course. In M. Rosenberg & R. H. Turner (Eds.), *Social psychology: Sociological perspectives* (pp. 133-163). New York: Basic Books.

Butler, M., & Paisley, W. (1980). *Women and the mass media.* New York: Human Sciences Press.

Butterworth, D., & Chance, J. K. (1981). *Latin American urbanization.* New York: Cambridge University Press.

Cahalan, D. (1970). *Problem drinkers.* San Francisco: Jossey-Bass.

Campbell, C., & Szablowski, G. (1979). *The superbureaucrats.* Toronto: Macmillan.

Campbell, E. Q. (1975). *Socialization: Culture and personality.* Dubuque, IA: Wm. C. Brown.

Canadian Advisory Council on the Status of Women. (1979). *Ten years later: An assessment of the federal government's implementation of the recommendations made by the Royal Commission on the status of women.* Ottawa: Queen's Printer.

Carroll, M. (1980, Fall). *The gap between male and female income in Canada. Canadian Journal of Sociology, 5,* 359-362.

Canadian Radio-Television and Telecommunications Commission (1982). *Images of women: Report of the task force on sex-role stereotyping in the broadcast media.* Ottawa: Ministry of Supply and Services.

Cardinal, H. (1969). *The unjust society.* Edmonton: Hurtig.

Chafetz, J. S. (1974). *Masculine/feminine or human?* Itasca, IL: Peacock.

Chaison, G. N. (1982). Unions: Growth, structure, and internal dynamics. In J. Luderson & M. Gunderson (Eds.), *Union-management relations in Canada.* Don Mills, Ont.: Addison-Wesley.

Chalfant, P. H., Beckley, R. E., & Palmer, C. E. (1981). *Religion in contemporary society.* Palo Alto, CA: Mayfield.

Chambliss, W., & Seidman, R. (1971). *Law, order, and power.* Reading, MA: Addison-Wesley.

Chappell, N. L., & Colwill, N. L. (1981). Medical schools as agents of professional socialization. *Canadian Review of Sociology and Anthropology, 18,* 67-81.

Charon, J. M. (1979). *Symbolic interactionism.* Englewood Cliffs, NJ: Prentice-Hall.

Clairmont, D., & Magill, D. (1974). *Africville: The life and death of a Canadian black community.* Toronto: McClelland and Stewart.

Clark, B. R. (1956). *Adult education in transition.* Berkeley, CA: University of California Press.

Clark, L. (1976). *The offense of rape and the concept of harm.* Unpublished manuscript. University of Toronto.

Clark, S., Grayson, J. P., & Grayson, L. M. (1975). *Prophecy and protest: Social movements in the twentieth century.* Toronto: Gage.

Clark, S. D. (1978). *The new urban poor.* Toronto: McGraw-Hill Ryerson.

Clark, S., & Harvey, A. (1976). The sexual division of labour: The use of time. *Atlantis, 2,* 46-66.

Clausen, J. A. (1968). Perspectives on childhood socialization. In J. A. Clausen (Ed.), *Socialization and society.* Boston: Little, Brown.

Clement, W. (1975). *The Canadian corporate elite.* Toronto: McClelland and Stewart.

Clement, W. (1977). *Continental corporate power.* Toronto: McClelland and Stewart.

Cloward, R., & Ohlin, L. (1960). *Delinquency and opportunity: A theory of delinquent gangs.* New York: Free Press.

Coale, A. (1973). The demographic transition reconsidered. *International population conference.* Liege, Belgium: International Union for the Scientific Study of Population.

Cohen, A. (1955). *Delinquent boys.* New York: Free Press.

Cohn, W. (1978). On inequality in Canada. *Canadian Review of Sociology and Anthropology, 15,* 399-401.

Colwill, N. J. (1982). *The new partnership: Women and men in organizations.* Palo Alto, CA: Mayfield Publishing.

Committee of Inquiry into the National Broadcasting service. (1977, July). A content analysis of the Canadian Broadcasting Corporation: Similarities and differences of French and English news (Background Research Paper). Ottawa.

Condry, J. C., & Douglas, K. (1983). Educational and recreational uses of computer technology. *Youth & Society, 15,* 87-112.

Condry, J. C., Siman, M. L., & Bronfenbrenner, V. (1968). *Characteristics of peer- and adult-oriented children.* Ithaca NY: Cornell University. Unpublished manuscript.

Connelly, P., & Christiansen-Ruffman, L. (1977). Women's problems: Private troubles or public issues? *Canadian Journal of Sociology, 2,* 167-178.

Connor, W. (1979). *Socialism, politics and equality.* New York: Columbia University Press.

Cook, S. (1969). Canadian narcotics legislation, 1908-23: A conflict model interpretation. *Canadian Review of Sociology and Anthropology, 6*(1), 36-46.

Cooley, C. H. (1902). *Human nature and the social order.* New York: Scribner's.

Corwin, R. G. (1965). *A sociology of education.* New York: Appleton-Century-Crofts.

Coser, R. Laub, & Rokoff, G. (1971). Women in the occupational world: Social disruption and conflict. *Social Problems, 18,* 535-554.

Cottrell, W. F. (1951, June). Death by dieseliation. *American Sociological Review, 16,* 358-365.

Cousi neau, D., & Veevers, J. E. (1972, January). Incarceration as a response to crime: The utilization of Canadian prisons. *Canadian Journal of Criminology and Corrections, 14,* 10-31.

Cronan, S. (1978). Marriage. In A. Jagger & P. Struhl (Eds.), *Feminist frameworks* (pp. 252-257). New York: McGraw-Hill.

Crothers, C. (1979). On the myth of rural tranquility: Comment of Webb and Collette. *American Journal of Sociology, 84*(6), 1441-1445.

Crysdale, S. (1961). *The industrial struggle and Protestant ethics in Canada.* Toronto: Ryerson Press.

Cuber, J. F., & Harroff, P. (1965). *The significant Americans.* Baltimore: Penguin.

Cumming, E., & Lazar, C. (1981). Kinship structure and suicide: A theoretical link. *Canadian Review of Sociology and Anthropology, 18,* 271-282.

Cuneo, C. J., & Curtis, J. E. (1975). Social ascription in the educational and occupational status attainment of urban Canadians. *Canadian Review of Sociology and Anthropology, 6,* 6-254.

Dahrendorf, R. (1959). *Class and class conflict in industrial society.* Palo Alto, CA: Stanford University Press.

David, D. S., & Brannon, R. (1976). *The forty-nine percent majority: The male sex role.* Reading, MA: Addison-Wesley.

Davids, L. (1976). North American marriage: 1990. *The futurist.* Washington, DC: World Future Society.

Davies, J. C. (1962). Toward a theory of revolution. *American Sociological Review, 27,* 5-19.

Davis, K. (1949). *Human society.* New York: Macmillan.

Davis, K. (1955). The origin and growth of urbanization in the world. *American Journal of Sociology, 60,* 429-437.

Davis, K. (1974). The migration of human populations. *The Human Population.* San Francisco: W. H. Freeman.

Deaux, K. (1984). From individual differences to social categories: Analysis of a decade's research on gender. *American Psychologist, 39,* 105-116.

DeFleur, M. L., & DeFleur, L. B. (1967). The relative contribution of television as a learning source for children's occupational knowledge. *American Sociological Review, 32,* 777-789.

Dill, W. W. (1958, March). Environment as an influence on managerial autonomy. *Administrative Science Quarterly, 23,* 409-443.

Directory of Labour Organization in Canada. (1986). Ottawa: Minister of Supply and Services.

Dofny, J. (1970). *Les ingenieurs Canadiens-français et Canadiens-anglais á Montréal.* Ottawa.

Dominick, J. R. (1979). The portrayal of women in prime time, 1953-1977. *Sex Roles, 5,* 405-411.

Downs, A. (1957). *An economic theory of democracy.* New York: Harper.

Doyle, J. A. (1983). *The male experience.* Dubuque, IA: Wm. C. Brown.

Driedger, L. (1974, Winter). Doctrinal belief: A major factor in the differential perception of social issues. *Sociological Quarterly,* 66-80.

Dubbert, J. L. (1979). *A man's place: Masculinity in transition.* Englewood Cliffs, NJ: Prentice-Hall.

Dubin, R. (1968). Workers. *International encyclopedia of the social sciences.* New York: Macmillan and Free Press.

Dubin, R., Hedley, R. A., & Taveggia, T. C. (1976). Attachment to work. In R. Dubin (Ed.), *Handbook of work, organization, and society.* Chicago: Rand McNally.

Dulude, L. (1978). *Women and aging: A report on the rest of our lives.* Ottawa: Canadian Advisory Council on the Status of Women.

Durkheim, E. (1938). *The rules of sociological method* (S. A. Solway & J. H. Mueller, Trans., G.E.G. Catlin, Ed.). Glencoe, IL: Free Press. (Original work published in 1895).

Durkheim, E. (1964a). *The division of labor in society* (G. E. G. Catlin, Ed.). Glencoe, IL: Free Press. (Original work published in 1893)

Durkheim, E. (1964b). *Suicide* (J. A. Spaulding, & G. Simpson, Trans.). Glencoe, IL: Free Press. (Original work published in 1897)

Duck, N. (Ed.), (1985). *Indigenous peoples and the nation-state.* St. John's: Memorial Universtiy of Newfoundland, Institute of Social and Economic Research.

Eagly, A. H., & Carli, L. L. (1981). Sex of researchers and sex-typed communications as determinants of sex differences in influence ability: A meta-analysis of social influence studies. *Psychological Bulletin, 90,* 1-20.

Eagly, A. H., & Steffen, V. J. (1984). Gender stereotypes stem from the distribution of women and men into social roles. *Journal of Personality and Social Psychology, 46,* 735-754.

Eakins, B. W., & Eakins, R. G. (1978). Sex differences in human communication. Boston: Houghton Mifflin.

Economic Council of Canada (1986). *Changing times. Twenty-third annual review.* Ottawa: Minister of Supply and Services.

Eder, D., & Hallinan, M. T. (1978). Sex differences in children's friendships. *American Sociological Review, 43,* 237-250.

Eichler, M. (1975). The egalitarian family in Canada? In S. P. Wakil (Ed.), *Marriage, family and society: Canadian perspectives* (pp. 223-235). Toronto: Butterworths.

Eichler, M. (1978). Women's unpaid labour. *Atlantis, 3,* Part II, 52-62.

Eichler, M. (1983). *Families in Canada today.* Toronto: Gage.

Elder, G. H., Jr. (1974). *Children of the great depression,* Chicago: University of Chicago Press.

Ellis, G. J. (1983). Youth in the electronic environment: An introduction. *Youth & Society, 15,* 3-12.

Employment and Immigration Canada. (1984). Background paper on future immigration levels. Ottawa: Ministry of Supply and Services.

Engels, F. (1942). *The origin of the family, private property and the state.* New York: International Publishers. (Original work published in 1884)

Espenshade, T. J. (1980) Raising a child can now cost $85 000. *Intercom, 8*(9), 1, 10-11.

Eysenck, H. J., & Nias, D. K. B. (1978). *Sex, violence and the media.* New York: Harper and Row.

Fasteau, M. F. (1975). *The male machine.* New York: Delta.

Featherman, D., & Hauser, R. (1976a). Changes in the socioeconomic stratification of the races, 1962-1973. *American Journal of Sociology, 82,* 621-651.

Featherman, D., & Hauser, R. (1978). *Opportunity and change*. New York: Academic Press.

Fink, A., & Kosecoff, J. (1977). Girls' and boys' changing attitudes toward school. *Psychology of Women Quarterly, 2*, 44-49.

Firestone, M. M. (1978, April). Socialization and interaction in a Newfoundland outport. *Urban life, 7*, 19-110.

Fischer, C. S. (1981). The public and private worlds of city life. *American Sociological Review, 46*, 306-316.

Fischer, C. S. (1983). *The urban experience* (2nd ed.). New York: Harcourt, Brace, Jovanovich.

Fitzsimmons-LeCavalier, P., & LeCavalier, G. (1984). Individual versus collective action: The minority response of Québec's nonfrancophones. Paper presented at the annual meeting of the Canadian Sociology and Anthropology Association in Guelph.

Flacks, R. (1979). Growing up confused. In P. I. Rose (Ed.), *Socialization and the life cycle*. New York: St. Martin's Press.

Forcese, D. (1980). *The Canadian class structure* (2nd ed.). Toronto: McGraw-Hill Ryerson.

Foreign Investment Review Agency. (1980). Increased domestic control of Canadian industry. *Foreign Investment Review, 3*(2), 2-3.

Fouts, G. T. (1980). Parents as censors of TV content for their children. *Journal of the Canadian Association for Young Children, 6*, 20-31.

Fox, B. (Ed.). (1982). *Hidden in the household: Women's domestic labour under capitalism*. Toronto: Women's Press.

Franck, K. A. (1980). Friends and strangers: The social experience of living in urban and non-urban settings. *The Journal of Social Issues, 36*(3), 52-71.

Frank, J. A. (1984). La dynamique des manifestations violentes. *Canadian Journal of Political Science, 17*(2), 325-350.

Frazer, C. F., & Reid, L. N. (1979). Children's interaction with commercials. *Symbolic Interaction, 2*, 79-96.

Friedl, E. (1978, April). Society and sex roles. *Human Nature*, 70.

Friedland, M. (1981). Gun control in Canada: Politics and impact. Presented to seminar on Canadian-U.S. relations, Harvard Center for International Affairs: University Consortium for Research on North America.

Fullan, M. (1970, December). Industrial technology and worker integration in the organization. *American Sociological Review, 35*, 1028-1039.

Galbraith, J. K. (1967). *The new industrial state*. Boston: Houghton Mifflin.

Gans, H. (1962). Urbanism and suburbanism as ways of life. In A. M. Rose (Ed.), *Human behavior and social processes*. Boston: Houghton Mifflin.

Gans, H. (1967). *The Levittowners: Way of life and politics in a new suburban community*. New York: Pantheon.

Gans, H. (1972). The positive functions of poverty. *American Journal of Sociology, 78*, 275-289.

Garn, S. M. (1966). Body size and its implications. In L. W. Hoffman & M. I. Hoffman (Eds.), *Review of child development research 2* (pp. 529-561). New York: Sage.

Garrison, H. H. (1979). Gender differences in the career aspirations of recent cohorts of high school seniors. *Social Problems, 27*, 170-185.

Gecas, V. (1976). The socialization and child care roles. In F. I. Nye (Ed.), *Role structure and analysis of the family*. Beverly Hills, CA: Sage.

Gecas, V. (1981). Contexts of socialization. In M. Rosenberg & R. H. Turner (Eds.), *Social psychology: Sociological perspectives*. New York: Basic Books.

Gee, E. M. Thomas. (1980). Female marriage patterns in Canada: changes and differentials. *Journal of Comparative Family Studies, 11*, 457-473.

Gerbner, G. *et al.* (1979, Summer). The demonstration of power: Violence profile no. 10. *Journal of Communications, 29*, 177-196.

Gerbner, G., & Cross, L. (1976, April). The scary world of TV's heavy viewer. *Psychology Today, 9*, 41-45, 89.

Gerth H., & Mills, C. W. (1958). *From Max Weber: Essays in sociology*. New York: Oxford University Press.

Gillis, A. R. (1974). Population density and social pathology: the case of building type, social allowance, and juvenile delinquency. *Social Forces, 53*(2), 306-314.

Gillis, A. R. (1983). Strangers next door: an analysis of density, diversity and scale in public housing projects. *Canadian Journal of Sociology, 8*(1), 1-20.

Gillis, A. R. (1984). Violent crime, policing, and urbanization in nineteenth century France: An analysis of trends. Paper presented to the Social Science and History Association in Toronto.

Gillis, A. R. (1985). Domesticity, divorce, and deadly quarrels: A macro analysis. In T. F. Hartnagel & R. A. Silverman (Eds.). *Critique and explanation: Essays in honour of Gwyne Nettler*. NJ: Transaction.

Gillis, A. R., & Hagan, J. (1982). Density, delinquency and design: formal and informal control and the built environment. *Criminology, 19*(4), 514-529.

Gillis, A. R., & Hagan, J. (1984). Delinquent samaritans: A study of group conflict, subcultural sentiment, and the willingness to intervene (Research Paper 150). Toronto: University of Toronto, Centre for Urban and Community Studies.

Ginzberg, E. (1982). The mechanization of work. *Scientific American, 247*(3), 67-75.

Glazer, N. (1977). Introduction to part two. In N. Glazer & H. Y. Waehrer (Eds.), *Woman in a man-made world* (2nd ed.). Chicago: Rand McNally.

Glock, C., Ringer, B., & Babbie, E. (1967). *To comfort and to challenge*. Berkeley, CA: University of California Press.

Glock, C., & Stark, R. (1965). *Religion and society in tension*. Chicago: Rand McNally.

Goffman, E. (1977). The arrangement between the sexes. *Theory and Society, 4*, 301-331.

Goldberg, M. A., & Mercer, J. (1980). Canadian and U.S. cities: Basic differences, possible explanations, and their meaning for public policy. *Papers of the Regional Science Association, 45*, 159-183.

Gordon, R. A. (1976). Prevalence: The rare datum in delinquency measurement and its implications for the theory of delinquency. In M. Klein (Ed.), *The juvenile justice system* (pp. 201-284). Beverly Hills, CA: Sage.

Gorsuch, R., & Aleshire, D. (1974). Christian faith and ethnic prejudice: A review and interpretation of research. *Journal for the Scientific Study of Religion, 13,* 281-307.

Gould, M., & Kern-Daniels, R. (1977). Toward a sociological theory of gender and sex. *The American Sociologist, 12,* 182-189.

Gove, W. R., Hughes, M., & Galle, O. R. (1979). Overcrowding in the home: An empirical investigation of its possible consequences. *American Sociological Review, 44,* 59-80.

Goyder, J. C., & Curtis, J. E. (1979). Occupational mobility in Canada over four generations. In J. Curtis & W. Scott (Eds.), *Social stratification: Canada* (2nd ed.). Scarborough, Ont.: Prentice-Hall.

Grayson, J. P., & Grayson, L. M. (1978). The Canadian literary elite: A socio-historical perspective. *Canadian Journal of Sociology, 3*(3), 291-308.

Greenglass, E. R., & Devins, R. (1982). Factors related to marriage and career plans in unmarried women. *Sex Roles, 8,* 57-71.

Grindstaff, C. F. (1975). The baby bust: Changes in fertility patterns in Canada. *Canadian Studies in Population, 2,* 15-22.

Grossman, B. A. (1969). *The prosecutor.* Toronto: University of Toronto Press.

Gunderson, M. (1976). Work patterns. In G. C. A. Cook (Ed.), *Opportunity for choice: A goal for women in Canada.* Ottawa: Information Canada.

Guppy, N., Mikicich, P. D., & Pendakur, R. (1984). Changing patterns of educational inequality in Canada. *Canadian Journal of Sociology, 9,* 319-331.

Gurr, T. R. (1981). Historical trends in violent crime: A critical review of the evidence. In N. Morris & M. Tonry (Eds.), *Crime and justice: An annual review of research.* Chicago: University of Chicago Press.

Gusfield, J. (1963). *Symbolic crusade.* Urbana, IL: University of Illinois Press.

Guterman, S. S. (1969). In defence of Wirth. *American Journal of Sociology, 74*(5), 492-499.

Hagan, J. (1974, August). Criminal justice and native people: A study of incarceration in a Canadian province. *Canadian Review of Sociology and Anthropology, Special Issue,* 220-236.

Hagan, J. (1985). Toward a structural theory of crime, race and gender: The Canadian case. *Crime and Delinquency, 31,* 129-146.

Hagan, J., & Albonetti, C. (1982). Race, class and the perception of criminal injustice in America. *American Journal of Sociology, 88,* 329-355.

Hagan, J., Gillis, A. R., & Chan, J. (1978, Summer). Explaining official delinquency: A spatial study of class, conflict, and control. *Sociology Quarterly,* 386-398.

Hagan, J., & Leon, J. (1977). Rediscovering delinquency: Social history, political ideology, and the sociology of law. *American Sociological Review, 42*(4), 587-598.

Hagan, J., Nagel, I., & Albonetti, C. (1980). The differential sentencing of white-collar offenders in ten federal district courts. *American Sociological Review, 45,* 802-820.

Hagedorn, R. (Ed.). (1986). *Sociology.* (3rd ed.). Toronto: Holt, Rinehart and Winston.

Haller, A., & Bills, D. (1979). Occupational prestige hierarchies: Theory and evidence. *Contemporary Sociology, 8,* 721-734.

Hamilton, R., & Pinard, M. (1977). Poverty in Canada: Illusion and reality. *Canadian Review of Sociology and Anthropology, 14*(2), 247-252.

Hardwick, W. G. (1971). Vancouver: The emergence of a 'core-ring' urban pattern. In R. L. Gentilcore (Ed.), *Geographical approaches to Canadian problems.* Scarborough, Ont.: Prentice-Hall.

Harris, C. D., & Ullman, E. L. (1945, November). The nature of cities. *Annals of The American Academy of Political and Social Science, 242,* 7-17.

Harris, M. (1981). *America now: Why nothing works.* New York: Simon and Schuster.

Harrison, J. B. (1978). Warning: The male sex role may be dangerous to your health. *Journal of Social Sciences, 34,* 65-86.

Harrison, P. (1959). *Authority and power in the free church tradition: A social case study of the American Baptist convention.* Princeton, NJ: Princeton University Press.

Hartley, R. E. (1959). Sex-role pressures in the socialization of the male child. *Psychological Reports, 5,* 457-468.

Hazelrigg, L., & Garnier, M. (1976). Occupational mobility in industrialized societies: A comparable analysis of differential access to occupational rank in seventeen countries. *American Sociological Review, 41,* 498-511.

Hedley, R. A. (1982). Work, life, and the pusuit of happiness: A study of Australian industrial workers. *Journal of Industrial Relations, 23*(3), 397-404.

Hedley, R. A. (1984). Work-nonwork contexts and orientations to work: A crucial test. *Work and Occupations, 11*(3), 353-376.

Hedley, R. A., Dubin, R., & Taveggia, T. C. (1980). The quality of working life, gender and occupational status: A cross-national comparison. In A. Szalai & F. M. Andrews (Eds.), *The quality of life.* Beverly Hills, CA: Sage.

Herberg, W. (1960). *Protestant, Catholic, Jew* (rev. ed.). New York: Doubleday.

Herman, J., & Hirschman, L. (1977). Father-daughter incest. *Signs, 2*(4), 735-756.

Hewill, C. (1977). The effect of political democracy on equality in industrial societies: A cross-national comparison. *American Journal of Sociology, 42,* 450-464.

Hiller, H. H. (1976). The sociology of religion in the Canadian context. In G. N. Ramu & S. D. Johnson (Eds.), *Introduction to Canadian society.* Toronto: Macmillan.

Hindelang, M. J. (1978). Race and involvement in common law personal crimes. *American Sociological Review, 43*(1), 93-109.

Hobart, C., & Brent, C. (1966). Eskimo education Danish and Canadian, a comparison. *Canadian Review of Sociology and Anthropology, 3*, 47-66.

Hogan, D., & Featherman, D. (1977). Racial stratification and socioeconomic change in the American North and South. *American Journal of Sociology, 83*, 100-126.

Hogarth, J. (1971). *Sentencing as a human process.* Toronto: University of Toronto Press.

Hoge, D. (1976). *Division in the Protestant house.* Philadelphia: Westminster Press.

Hoppock, R. (1935). *Job satisfaction.* New York: Harper and Brothers.

Hordern, W. (1966). *New directions in theology, introduction, 1.* Philadelphia: Westminster Press.

Houghland, J. G., & Wood, J. R. (1979). Inner circles in local churches. *Sociological Analysis, 40*, 226-239.

House of Commons Debates. (197', October 8). Statement of P. E. Trudeau.

Howe, F. (1974). Sexual stereotypes and the public schools. In R. B. Kundsin (Ed.), *Women and success: The anatomy of achievement.* New York: William Morrow.

Hoyt, H. T. (1939). *The structure and growth of residential neighbourhoods in American cities.* Washington, D.C.: Federal Housing Authority.

Huggins, M. D., & Straus, M. A. (1978). Violence and the social structure as reflected in children's books from 1850 to 1970. In M. A. B. Gammon (Ed.), *Violence in Canada.* Toronto: Methuen.

Hunter, A. A. (1981). *Class tells: On social inequality in Canada.* Toronto: Butterworths.

Innis, H. A. (1930). *The fur trade in Canada: An introduction to Canadian economic history.* New Haven, CT: Yale University Press; (Original work published in 1927, Toronto: Oxford University Press)

Innis, H. A. (1940). *The cod fisheries: The history of an international economy.* New Haven, CT: Yale University Press.

Irving, J. (1959). *The Social Credit movement in Alberta.* Toronto: University of Toronto Press.

Isajiw, W. W. (1978). Olga in Wonderland: Ethnicity in a technological society. In L. Driedger (Ed.), *The Canadian ethnic mosaic.* Toronto: McClelland and Stewart.

Ishwaran, K. (Ed.). (1976). *The Canadian family* (rev. ed). Toronto: Holt, Rinehart and Winston.

Jacobs, J. (1961). *The death and life of great American cities.* New York: Random House.

Jenkins, J. C. (1981). Sociopolitical movements. In S. L. Long (Ed.), *The handbook of political behavior* (pp. 81-153). New York: Plenum Press

Jenson, G. F., Strauss, J. H., & Harris, V. W. (1977). Crime delinquency and the American Indian. *Human Organization, 36*, 252-257.

Johnson, L. A. (1974). *Poverty in wealth.* Toronto: New Hogtown Press.

Johnson, L. A. (1977). Illusions or realities: Hamilton and Pinards approach to poverty. *Canadian Review of Sociology and Anthropology, 14*(3), 341-346.

Johnson, L. A. (1979a). Income disparity and the structure of earnings in Canada, 1946-74. In J. Curtis, and W. Scott (Eds.), *Social stratification: Canada* (2nd ed.). Scarborough, Ont.: Prentice-Hall.

Johnson, L. A. (1979b). Class, status, and power. In J. Fry (Ed.), *Economy, class, and social reality.* Toronto: Butterworths.

Johnson, L. A. (1979c). The capitalist labour market and income inequality in Canada. In J. Fry (Ed.), *Economy, class and social reality.* Toronto: Butterworths.

Johnson, N. (1970). *How to talk back to your television set.* Boston: Little, Brown.

Jourard, S. M. (1964). *The transparent self.* New York: Van Nostrand Reinhold.

Joy, L. A. *et al.* (1986). Television and children's aggressive behavior. In T. Macbeth Williams (Ed.), *The Impact of Television* (pp. 140-174). Toronto: The Academic Press.

Kahn, R. L. (1975). In search of the Hawthorne effect. In E. L. Cass & F. G. Zimmer (Eds.), *Man and work in society.* Toronto: Van Nostrand Reinhold.

Kalbach, W. E., & McVey, W. W. (1979). *The demographic bases of Canadian society* (2nd ed.). Toronto: McGraw-Hill Ryerson.

Kando, T. M. (1980). *Leisure and popular culture in transition* (2nd ed.). St. Louis: The CV Mosby Company.

Katz, F. E. (1967). Explaining informal work groups in complex organizations: The case for autonomy. In W. A. Faunce (Ed.), *Readings in Industrial Sociology.* New York: Appleton-Century-Crofts.

Keesing, R. (1976). *Cultural anthropology: A contemporary perspective.* New York: Holt, Rinehart and Winston.

Kelly, W., & Kelly, N. (1976). *Policing in Canada.* Toronto: Macmillan Company of Canada.

Kelner, M. 1970. Ethnic penetration into Toronto's elite structure. *Canadian Review of Sociology and Anthropology, 7*, 128-137.

Kennedy, M. (1986, December). Measuring Canada's international competitiveness. *Quarterly Economic Review*, 37-45.

Kessler, S. J., & McKenna, W. (1978). *Gender: An ethnomethodological approach.* New York: John Wiley and Sons.

Komarovsky, M. (1976). *Dilemmas of masculinity.* New York: W. W. Norton.

Kome, P. (1983). *The taking of twenty-eight: Women challenge the constitution.* Toronto: Women's Press.

Kunkel, J. H. (1977). Sociobiology vs. biosociology. *The American Sociologist, 12*, 69-73.

Lambert, W. E., Hamers, J. F., & Frasure-Smith, N. (1979). *Child-rearing values: A cross-national study.* New York: Praeger.

Lambert, W. E., Yackley, A., & Hein, R. N. (1971). Child training values of English-Canadian and French-Canadian parents. *Canadian Journal of Behavioural Science, 3*, 217-236.

Landsberg, M. (1982). *Women & children first*. Markham, Ont.: Penguin Books.

Lane, R. (1980). Urban homicide in the nineteenth century: Some lessons for the twentieth. In J. Inciardi & C. Faupel (Eds.), *History and crime: Implications for criminal justice policy*. Beverly Hills, CA: Sage.

Langer, W. (1973). The black death. Cities: Their origin, growth and human impact. *Scientific American*. San Francisco: W. H. Freeman.

Laub, J. H. (1983, July). Urbanism, race, and crime. *Journal of Research on Crime and Delinquency*, 183-198

Lautard, E. H., & Loree, D. J. (1984). Ethnic stratification in Canada, 1931-1971. *Canadian Journal of Sociology 9*,(3) 333-343.

Laws , J. L. (1979). *The second X: Sex role and social role*. New York: Elsevier.

LeBon, G. (1960). *The crowd*. New York: Viking Press. (Original work published in 1895)

Lee, D. (1974). *Alligator pie*. Toronto: Macmillan Company of Canada.

Lee, J. A. (1982). Three paradigms of childhood. *Canadian Review of Sociology and Anthropology, 19*, 591-608.

Leighton, A. (1959). *My name is legion*. New York: Basic Books.

Lemert, E. (1967). *Human deviance, social problems, and social control*. Englewood Cliffs, NJ: Prentice-Hall.

Lenski, G. (1961). *The religious factor*. New York: Doubleday.

Lenski, G. (1966). *Power and privilege*. New York: McGraw-Hill.

Lenski, G., & Lenski, J. (1978). *Human societies*. (pp. 249-277) New York: McGraw-Hill.

Lever, J. (1978). Sex differences in the complexity of children's play. *American Sociological Review, 43*, 471-483.

Levinson, D. J., *et al.* (1978). *The seasons of a man's life*. New York: Ballantine.

Levitt, K. (1970). *Silent surrender*. Toronto: Macmillan.

Levy, J. (1979). In search of isolation: The Holdeman Mennonites of Linden, Alberta and their school. *Canadian Ethnic Studies, 2*, 115-130.

Lewis, M. (1972, May). Culture and gender roles: There's no unisex in the nursery. *Psychology Today, 5*, 54-57.

Liebert, R. M., Sprafkin, J. N., & Davidson, E. (1982). *The early window: Effects of television on children and youth* (2nd ed.). New York: Pergamon Press.

Linteau, P., and Robert, J. (1977). Land ownership and society in Montréal: An hypothesis. In G. A. Stelter & A. F. J. Artibise (Eds.), *The Canadian city: Essays in urban history*. Toronto: McClelland and Stewart.

Lipman-Blumen, J. (1984). *Gender roles and power*. Englewood Cliffs, NJ: Prentice-Hall

Lippmann, W. (1922). *Public opinion*. New York: Harcourt and Brace.

Lips, H. M. (1983). Attitudes towards childbearing among women and men expecting their first child.

International Journal of Women's Studies, 6, 119-129.

Lipset, S. M. (1966). *Agrarian socialism*. New York: Doubleday Anchor.

Litwak, E. (1968). The use of extended family groups in achievement of social goals. In M. Sussman (Ed.), *Sourcebook in marriage and the family* (pp. 82-88). Boston, Houghton Mifflin.

Lone Parenthood. (1986). Ottawa: Ministry of Supply and Services.

Lowe, G. D., & Hodges, H. E. (1972, Fall). Race and treatment of alcoholism in a southern state. *Social Problems*, 240-252.

Lowe, G. S. (1980). Women, work and office: the feminization of clerical occupations in Canada, 1901-1931. *Canadian Journal of Sociology, 5*, 361-381.

Lucas, R. A. (1971). *Minetown, milltown, railtown: Life in Canadian communities of single industry*. Toronto: University of Toronto Press.

Luckmann, T. (1967). *The invisible religion*. New York: Macmillan.

Lupri, E. (1986). The family. In K. Ishwaran (Ed.), *Sociology: An introduction*. Don Mills, Ont.: Addison-Wesley Publishers, 253-284.

Lupri, E., & Mills, D. L. (1982). The changing roles of Canadian women in family and work: An overview. In E. Lupri (Ed.), *The changing roles of women in family and society: A cross-cultural comparison*. Leiden, Neth.: E. J. Brill.

Luxton, M. (1980). *More than a labour of love: Three generations of women's work in the home*. Toronto: The Women's Press.

Lynn, D. B. (1959). A note on sex differences in the development of masculine and feminine identification. *Psychological Review, 66*, 126-135.

Lynn, D. B. (1969). *Parental and sex-role identification: A theoretical formulation*. Berkeley: McCutchan.

Maccoby, E. E. (1980). *Social development: Psychological growth and the parent-child relationship*. New York: Harcourt Brace Jovanovich.

Maccoby, E. E., & Jacklin, J. N. (1974). *The psychology of sex differences*. Stanford, CA: Stanford University Press.

Maccoby, E. E., & Jacklin, C. N. (1974). *The psychology of sex differences*. Stanford, CA: Standard University Press.

Maccoby, E. E., & Jacklin, C. N. (1980). Sex differences in aggression: A rejoinder and reprise. *Child Development, 51*, 964-980.

Mackie, M. (1975). Defection from Hutterite colonies. In R. M. Pike & E. Zureik (Eds.), *Socialization and values in Canadian society* (Vol. 2). Toronto: McClelland and Stewart.

Mackie, M. (1983). *Exploring gender relations: A Canadian perspective*. Toronto: Butterworth.

Mannheim, K. (1952; 1953). The sociological problem of generations. In P. Kecskemeti (Eds.), *Essays on the sociology of knowledge*. New York: Oxford University Press/London: Routledge and Kegan Paul.

Manvel, G., & Poslums, M. (1974). *The fourth world:*

Indian Reality. Toronto: Collier-MacMillan.

Manzer, R. (1974). *Canada: A socio-political report.* Toronto: McGraw-Hill Ryerson.

Marchak, P. (1975). *Ideological perspectives on Canada.* Toronto: McGraw-Hill Ryerson.

Marini, M. M., & Greenberger, E. (1978). Sex differences in occupational aspirations and expectations. *Sociology of work and occupations, 5,* 147-175.

Markle, G. E. (1974). Sex ratio at birth: Values, variance, and some determinants. *Demography, 11,* 131-142.

Martin, W. B. W., & Macdonell, A. J. (1978). *Canadian education: A sociological analysis.* Scarborough, Ont.: Prentice-Hall.

Martyna, W. (1980). Beyond the 'he/man' approach: The case of nonsexist language. *Signs, 5,* 482-493.

Marx, K. (1965). *Capital: A critical analysis of capitalist production 1.* New York: International Publishers. (Original work published in 1867-1895)

Marx, K. (1969). On class. In C. Heller (Ed.), *Structured social inequality.* New York: Macmillan.

Marx, K. (1970). *Critique of Hegel's 'Philosophy of right.'* (A. Jolin, & J. O'Malley, Trans.). Cambridge, MA: Harvard University Press. (Original work published in 1843)

Matras, J. 1980. Comparative social mobility. *Annual Review of Sociology, 6,* 401-431.

Matthews, A. M. (1980). Women and widowhood. In V. W. Marshall (Ed.), *Aging in Canada: Social perspectives.* Don Mills, Ont.: Fitzhenry and Whiteside.

Mayo, E. (1945). *The social problems of an industrial civilization.* Cambridge, MA: Harvard University Press.

McKenzie, R. D. (1968). *On human ecology.* Chicago: University of Chicago Press.

McKeown, T. (1976). *The modern rise of population.* New York: Academic Press.

McKie, D. C., Prentice, B., & Reed, P. (1983). *Divorce: Law and the family in Canada.* Ottawa: Ministry of Supply and Services.

McNeill, W. H. (1976). *Plagues and peoples.* Garden City, NY: Doubleday.

McNulty, F. (1983, December 5). Children's books for Christmas. *The New Yorker.* 191-208.

McQuillan, K. (1980). Economics factors and internal migration: The case of nineteenth-century England. *Social Science History, 4*(4), 479-499.

McRoberts, H. A., et al. (1976). Différence dans la mobilité professionnelle des francophones et des anglophones. *Sociologie et sociétés, 8*(2), 61-79.

Mead, G. H. (1934). *Mind, self, and society.* Chicago: University of Chicago Press.

Meissner, M., Humphreys, E. W., & Meis, S. M., & Scheu, W. J. (1975). No exit for wives: Sexual division of labour and the cumulation of household demands. *Canadian Review of Sociology and Anthropology 12,* Part I:424-439.

Melbin, M. (1978). Night as frontier. *American Sociological Review, 43*(1), 3-22.

Meltzer, B. N. (1978). Mead's social psychology (C. W. Morris, Ed.). In J. G. Manis & B. N. Meltzer, (Eds.),

Symbolic interaction: A reader in social psychology (3rd ed.). Boston: Allyn and Bacon.

Menzies, H. (1984). Women and microtechnology. In G. S. Lowe & H. J. Krahn (Eds.), *Working Canadians* (pp. 290-297). Toronto: Methuen.

Merton, R. (1957). *Social theory and social structure.* Glencoe, IL: Free Press.

Metz, D. (1967). *New congregations: Security and mission in conflict.* Philadelphia: Westminister Press.

Miliband, R. (1973). *The state in capitalist society.* London: Weidenfeld and Nicalson; Quartet Books. (Original work published in 1969)

Mitchell, J. (1973). *Women's estate.* Toronto: Random House.

Mitchell, R. (1966). Polity, church attractiveness, and ministers' careers. *Journal for the Scientific Study of Religion, 5,* 241-258.

Mols, H. (1976). Major correlates of church going in Canada. In S. Crysdale & L. Wheatcroft (Eds.). *Religion in Canadian society.* Toronto: Macmillan Company of Canada.

Money, J., & Ehrhardt, A. A. (1972). *Man and woman, boy and girl: The differentiation and dimorphism of gender identity from conception to maturity.* Baltimore: Johns Hopkins University Press.

Money, J., & Tucker, P. (1975). *Sexual signatures: On Being a man or a woman.* Boston: Little, Brown.

Morris, C. (1980). Determination and thoroughness: The movement for a royal commission on the status of women in Canada. *Atlantis, 5,* 1-21.

Morris, R., & Lamphier, C. M. (1977). *Three scales of inequality: Perspectives on French-English relations.* Don Mills, Ont.: Longman.

Mortimer, J. T., & Simmons, R. G. (1978). Adult socialization. *Annual Review of Sociology, 4* 421-454.

Morton, F. L. (1985). Group rights versus individual rights in the charter: The special cases of Natives and Québécois. In N. Nevitte & A. Kornberg (Eds.), *Minorities and the Canadian state.* Oakville: Mosaic.

Morton, P. (1972). Women's work is never done. In *Women unite! An anthology of the Canadian women's movement.* Toronto: Canadian Women's Educational Press.

Mumford, L. (1968). *The urban prospect.* New York: Harcourt, Brace and World.

Murdock, G. P. (1931). Ethnocentrism. In E. R. A. Seligman (Ed.), *Encyclopedia of the Social Sciences, 5.* New York: Macmillan.

Murdock, G. P. (1949). *Social structure.* New York: Macmillan.

Murdock, W. W. (1980). *The poverty of nations.* Baltimore: Johns Hopkins University Press.

Murphy, E. F. (1920). The grave drug menace. *Maclean's Magazine, 33*(3), 1.

Murphy, E. F. (1922). *The black candle.* Toronto: Thomas Allen.

Murray, J. P., & Kippax, S. (1979). From the early window to the late night show: International trends in the study of television's impact on children and adults. *Advances in Experimental Social Psychology, 12,* 253-320.

Murstein, B. I. (1980). Mate selection in the 1970s. *Journal of Marriage and the Family, 42,* 777-792.

Myrdal, G. (1944). *An American dilemma.* New York: McGraw Hill.

Nelsen, H. M., & Potvin, R. H. (1980). Toward disestablishment: New patterns of social class, denomination, and religiosity among youth? *Review of Religious Research, 22,* 137-154.

Nelson, L. D., & Dynes, R. (1976). The impact of devotionalism and attendance on ordinary and emergency helping behavior. *Journal for the Scientific Study of Religion, 15,* 47-59.

Nemerowicz, G. M. (1979). *Children's perceptions of gender and work roles.* New York: Praeger.

Nett, E. M. (1986). The Family. In R. Hagedorn (Ed.), *Sociology* (3rd ed.). Toronto: Holt, Rinehart and Winston of Canada.

Nettler, G. (1978). *Killing one another.* Cincinnati, OH: Anderson Publishing Co.

Newman, O. (1972). *Defensible space.* New York: Macmillan.

Nichols, J. (1975). *Men's liberation.* New York: Penguin.

Nielsen, J. McCarl (1978). *Sex in society: Perspectives on stratification.* Belmont, CA: Wadsworth.

Oberschall, A. (1973). *Social conflict and social movement.* Englewood Cliffs, NJ: Prentice-Hall.

Ogburn, W. F. (1922). *Social change with respect to culture and original nature.* New York: B. W. Huebsch.

Ogburn, W. F. (1933). The family and its function. In W. F. Ogburn (Ed.), *Recent social trends* (chap. 13). New York: McGraw-Hill.

Ogmundson R. (1976). Mass-elite linkages and class issues in Canada. *Canadian Review of Sociology and Anthropology, 13*(1), 1-12.

Olsen, D. (1977). The state elites. In L. Panitch (Ed.), *The Canadian state: Political economy and political power.* Toronto: University of Toronto Press.

Olson, M. (1965). *The logic of collective action.* Cambridge, MA: Harvard University Press.

Ostry, S. (1968). *The female worker in Canada.* Ottawa: Queen's Printer.

Packer, H. (1964). Two models of the criminal process. *University of Pennsylvania Law Review, 113,* 1-68.

Palen, J. (1981). *The urban world* (2nd ed.). New York: McGraw-Hill.

Pappert, A. (1983, December). The one and only. *Quest,* 38-42.

Park, R. E., Burgess, E. W., & McKenzie, R. D. (1925). *The city.* Chicago: University of Chicago Press.

Parker, G. (1976). The juvenile court movement. *University of Toronto Law Journal, 26,* 140.

Parsons, H. M. (1974, March). What happened at Hawthorne? *Science, 8,* 922-932.

Parsons, T. (1951). *The social system.* Glencoe: Free Press.

Parsons, T. (1960). *Structure and process in modern societies.* New York: Free Press.

Parsons, T. (1964). Christianity and modern industrial society. In L. Schneider (Ed.), *Religion, culture, and society.* New York: Wiley.

Parsons, T., & Bales, R. F. (Eds.). (1955). *Family socialization and interaction process.* Glencoe, IL: Free Press.

Pearlin, L. I., & Kohn, M. L. (1966). *Social class, occupation, and parental values: A cross-national study. American Sociological Review, 31*(4), 466-479.

Peters, J. F. (1980). High school dating, implications for equality. *International Journal of Comparative Sociology, 21*(3), 109-118

Peters, J. F. (1986). Adolescents as socialization agents to parents. *Adolescence, 20,* 621-633.

Peters, J. F. (1987). Youth, family and employment. *Adolescence, 22,* 465-473.

Peterson, G. W., & Peters, D. F. (1983). Adolescents' construction of social reality: The impact of television and peers. *Youth & Society, 15,* 67-85.

Piaget, J. (1928). *Judgment and reasoning in the child.* New York: Harcourt.

Piaget, J. (1932). *The moral judgment of the child.* New York: Harcourt.

Pike, R. M. (1975). Introduction and overview. In R. M. Pike, & E. Zureik (Eds.), *Socialization and values in Canadian society* (Vol. 2). Toronto: McClelland and Stewart.

Pinard, M. (1971). *The rise of a third party.* Englewood Cliffs, NJ: Prentice-Hall.

Pinard, M., & Hamilton, R. (1984). The class bases of the Québec independence movement: Conjectures and evidence. *Ethnic and Racial Studies, 7*(1), 19-54

Pineo, C. (1961). Disenchantment in later years of marriage. *Marriage and Family Living, 23,* 3-11.

Pineo, P. C. (1971). The extended family in a working-class area of Hamilton. In B. Blishen, *et al.* (Eds.), *Canadian society.* Toronto: Macmillan.

Pineo, P. (1976). Social mobility in Canada: The current picture. *Sociological Focus, 9*(2), 109-123.

Pineo, P. C. (1983). Stratification and social class. In M. M. Rosenberg, *et al.* (Eds.), *An introduction to sociology* (pp. 339-374). Toronto: Methuen.

Pineo, P. C., & Looker, D. (1983). Class conformity in the Canadian setting. *Canadian Journal of Sociology, 8,* 293-317.

Platt, A. M. (1969). *The child savers.* Chicago: University of Chicago Press.

Ponak, A. (1982). Public sector collective bargaining. In J. Anderson & M. Gunderson (Eds.), *Union-management relations in Canada.* Don Mills, Ont.: Addison-Wesley.

Ponting, J. R., & Gibbins, R. (1981). The reactions of English Canadians and French Québecois to native Indian protest. *Canadian Review of Sociology and Anthropology, 18*(2), 222-238.

Porter, J. (1965). *The vertical mosaic: An analysis of social class and power in Canada.* Toronto: University of Toronto Press.

Porter, M., Porter, J., & Blishen, B. (1973). *Does Money Matter?* Toronto: York University, Institute for Behavioural Research.

Prus, R., & Styllianoss, I. (1980). *Hookers, rounders and desk clerks.* Toronto: Gage Publishing Limited.

Pyke, S. W. (1975). Children's literature: Conceptions of sex roles. In R. M. Pike & E. Zureik (Eds.), *Socialization and values in Canadian society* (Vol. 2). Toronto: McClelland and Stewart.

Pyke, S. W., & Stewart, J. C. (1974). This column is about women: women and television. *The Ontario Psychologist, 6*, 66-69.

Quinney R. (1970). *The social reality of crime*. Boston: Little, Brown.

Radcliffe-Brown, A. R. (1929). Age organisation — terminology. [Letter to the editor]. *Man, 29*, 21.

Rainwater, L. (1966). Work and identity in the lower class. In S. Bass Warner Jr. (Ed.) *Planning for a nation of cities*. Cambridge: M.I.T. Press.

Reiss, A. J. (1971). *The police and the public*. New Haven, CT: Yale University Press.

Reiss, A. J., Jr. (1959). The sociological study of communities. *Rural Sociology, 24*, 118-130.

Reiss, I. (1980). *Readings in the family system*. New York: Holt, Rinehart and Winston.

Reitz, J. G. (1980). *The survival of ethnic groups*. Toronto: McGraw-Hill.

Reuber, G. (1978). The impact of government policies on the distribution of income in Canada: A review. *Canadian Public Policy, 4*, 505-529.

Reynauld, A., et al. (1967). La re-partition des revenus selon les groupes ethniques au Canada. *Report to the Royal Commission on Bilingualism and Biculturalism*. Ottawa: Queen's Printer.

Rich, H. (1976). The vertical mosaic revisited. *Journal of Canadian Studies*, 14-31.

Richardson, L. W. (1981). *The dynamics of sex and gender* (2nd ed.). Boston: Houghton Mifflin.

Richer, S. (1979). Sex-role, socialization and early schooling. *Canadian Review of Sociology and Anthropology, 16* 195-205.

Richmond-Abbott, M. (1983). *Masculine and feminine: Sex roles over the life cycle*. Reading, MA: Addison-Wesley.

Rioux, M. (1971). Québec in question. Toronto: James, Lewis and Samuel.

Robb, A. L., & Spencer, B. G. (1976). Education: Enrolment and attainment. In G. C. A. Cook (Ed.), *Opportunity for choice*. Ottawa: Information Canada.

Robson, R., & Lapointe, M. (1971). *A comparison of men's and women's salaries and employment fringe benefits in the academic profession*. Ottawa: Queen's Printer.

Roethlisberger, F. J., & Dickson, W. J. (1947). *Management and the worker*. Cambridge, MA: Harvard University Press.

Rohner, R. P., & Rohner, E. C. (1970). *The Kwakiutl: Indians of British Columbia*. New York: Holt, Rinehart and Winston.

Rokeach, M. (1969). Religious values and social compassion. *Review of Religious Research, 11*, 3-23.

Romanos, M. C. (1979). Forsaken farms: The village-to-city movement in Europe. In M. C. Romanos (Ed.), *Western European cities in crisis* (pp. 3-19). Lexington, KY: Lexington Press.

Rosaldo, M. Z. (1974). Woman, culture, and society: A theoretical overview. In M. Zimbalist Rosaldo & L. Lamphere (Eds.), *Woman, culture, and society*. Stanford, CA: Stanford University Press.

Rosaldo, M. Z. (1980). The use and abuse of anthropology: Reflections on feminism and cross-cultural understanding. *Signs, 5*, 389-417.

Rosenburg, M. (1965). *Society and the adolescent self-image*. Princeton, NJ: Princeton University Press.

Rosenberg, M. M., & Weinfeld M. (1983). Ethnicity. In M. M. Rosenberg, *et al.* (Eds.), *An introduction to sociology* (pp. 543-586). Toronto: Methuen.

Rosenhan, D. L. (1973). On being sane in insane places. *Science, 179*(19), 250-258.

Ross, A. D. (1982). *The lost and the lonely: Homeless women in Montréal*. Montréal: Canadian Human Rights Foundation.

Rossi, A. S. (1980). Life-span theories and women's lives. *Signs, 6*, 4-32.

Rossi, A. S. (1984). Gender and parenthood. *American Sociological Review, 49*, 1-19.

Roy, D. (1952). Efficiency and 'the fix': Informal intergroup relations in a piece-work machine shop. *American Journal of Sociology, 57*, 427-442.

Royal Commission on the Economic Union and Development Prospects for Canada (1985). *Report, 1*, 237-233. Ottawa: Minister of Supply and Services.

Royal Commission on the Status of Women in Canada (1970). *Report*. Ottawa: Information Canada.

Rubin, J. Z., & Provenzano, F. J., & Luria Z. (1974). The eye of the beholder: Parents' views on sex of newborns. *American Journal of Orthopsychiatry, 44*, 512-519.

Ruether, R. R. (Ed.). (1974). *Religion and sexism: Images of woman in the Jewish and Christian traditions*. New York: Simon and Schuster.

Rushby, W., & Thrush, J. (1973). Mennonites and social compassion. *Review of Religious Research, 15*, 16-28.

Safilios-Rothschild, C. (1974). *Women and social policy*. Englewood Cliffs, NJ: Prentice-Hall.

Saunders, E. (1982). Women in Canadian society. In D. Forcese & S. Richler (Eds.), *Social issues: Sociological view of Canada* (pp. 211-257). Scarborough, Ont.: Prentice-Hall.

Sayers, J. (1982). *Biological politics: Feminist and anti-feminist perspectives*. London: Tavistock.

Scanzoni, J. (1983). *Shaping tomorrow's family*. Beverly Hills: Sage.

Scanzoni, L. D., & Scanzoni, J. (1981). *Men, women, and change: A sociology of marriage and family*. New York: McGraw-Hill.

Scheff, T. (1966). *Being mentally ill: A sociological theory*. Chicago: Aldine.

Schneider, F. W., & Coutts, L. M. (1979). Teacher orientations towards masculine and feminine: Role of sex of teacher and sex composition of school. *Canadian Journal of Behavioral Science, 11*, 99-111.

Schellenberg, J. A. (1974). *An introduction to social psychology* (2nd ed.). New York: Random House.

Schmidt, W., Smart, R., & Moss, M. (1968). *Social class and the treatment of alcoholism* (Monograph No. 7). Toronto: The University of Toronto: Addiction Research Foundation.

Science Council of Canada. (1977). *Uncertain prospects: Canadian manufacturing industry, 1971-1977.* Ottawa: Ministry of Supply and Services.

Science Council of Canada. (1984). *Canadian industrial development: Some policy directions.* Ottawa: Ministry of Supply and Services.

Seashore, S. E. (1954). *Group cohesiveness in the industrial work group.* Ann Arbor, MI: (University of Michigan) Survey Research Center,

Seligson, M. A. (1984). The dual gaps: An overview of theory and research. In M. A. Seligson (Ed.), *The gap between rich and poor.*

Selznick, P. (1949). *TVA and the grass roots.* Berkeley, CA: University of California Press.

Shaw, M.Œ., & Costanzo, P. R. (1970). *Theories of social psychology.* New York: McGraw-Hill.

Sheehy, G. (1976). *Passages* . Toronto: Clarke, Irwin.

Sheinin, R. (1981). The rearing of women for science, engineering and technology. *International Journal of Women's Studies, 4,* 339-347.

Sheppard, H. L. (1970). *Toward an industrial gerontology.* Cambridge, MA: Schenkman.

Sigelman, L. (1977). Multi-nation surveys of religious beliefs. *Journal for the Scientific Study of Religion, 16,* 289-294.

Simmel, G. (1950). The metropolis and mental life. In R. Gutman & D. Popenoe (Eds.), *Neighborhood, city, and metropolis.* New York: Random House.

Singer, J. L., & Singer, D. G. (1981). *Television, imagination, and aggression: A crucial appraisal.* Chicago: Rand McNally.

Singer, J. L., & Singer, D. G. (1981b). *Television, imagination and aggression: A study of pre-schoolers.* Hillsdale, NJ: Lawrence Erlbaum.

Skipper, J. K., Jr., & Nass, G. (1966). Dating behavior: A framework for analysis and an illustration. *Journal of Marriage and the Family, 23,* 412-420.

Skogstad, G. (1980). Agrarian protest in Alberta. *Canadian Review of Sociology and Anthropology, 17*(1), 55-73.

Smith, D. E. (1977). *Feminism & marxism.* Vancouver: New Star Books.

Smyth, J. E., & Soberman, D. A. (1976). *The law and business administration.* Toronto: Prentice-Hall.

Sorokin, P., & Zimmerman, C. C. (1929). *Principles of rural urban sociology.* New York: Holt, Rinehart and Winston.

Stanovnik, J. (1984). A web of peril. *World Press Review, 31*(3), 35-36.

Stark, R., & Bainbridge, W. S. (1979). Of churches, sects, and cults. *Journal for the Scientific Study of Religion, 18.* 117-118.

Stark, R., & Bainbridge, W. S. (1985). *The future of religion.* Berkeley, CA: University of California Press.

Starks, R. (1978). *Industry in decline.* Toronto: James Lorimer.

Statistics Canada. (1984). *Charting Canadian incomes, 1951-1981.* Ottawa: Ministry of Supply and Services.

Statistics Canada. (1985). *Current demographic analysis: Report of the demographic situation in Canada 1983.* Ottawa: Ministry of Supply and Services.

Statistics Canada. (1984). *Canada's lone-parent families.* Ottawa: Supply and Services.

Statistics Canada. (1985). *Family expenditure in Canada.* Ottawa: Supply and Services.

Statistics Canada. (1986). *Marriages and divorces* (Vol. 2). Ottawa: Supply and Services.

Stephen, G. E., & McMullin, D. R. (1982). Tolerance of sexual nonconformity: City size as a situational and early learning determinant. *American Sociological Review, 47,* 411-415.

Stephens, W. (1963). *The family in cross-cultural perspective.* New York: Holt, Rinehart and Winston.

Stolnitz, G. J. (1964). The demographic transition: From high to low birth rates and death rates. In R. Freedman (Ed.), *Population: The vital revolution.* New York: Anchor.

Stone, L. O. (1967). *Urban development in Canada.* Ottawa: Dominion Bureau of Statistics.

Sudnow, D. (1965, Winter). Normal crimes: Sociological features of the penal code in a public defender office. *Social Problems,* 255-276.

Sullivan, T. A. (1983). Family morality and family mortality: Speculation on the demographic transition. In W. V. D'Antonio & J. Aldous (Eds.), *Families and religions* (pp. 49-66). Beverly Hills, CA: Sage.

Sumner, W. G. (1906). *Folkways.* New York: Ginn.

Sutherland, E. (1924). *Criminology.* Philadelphia: Lippincott.

Sutherland, E. (1949). *White collar crime.* New York: Dryden.

Sydie, R. A. (1983). Sociology and gender. In M. M. Rosenberg, *et al.* (Eds.), *An introduction to sociology* (pp. 185-223). Toronto: Methuen.

Sykes, G., & Matza, D. (1957). Techniques of neutralization: A theory of delinquency. *American Sociological Review, 22,* 664-670.

Symons, G. L. (1981). Her view from the executive suite: Canadian women in management. In K. Lundy & B. Warme (Eds.), *Work in the Canadian context* (pp. 337-353). Toronto: Butterworth.

Szelenyi , I. (1981). *Structural changes and alternatives to capitalist development in the contemporary urban and regional system.*

Tannenbaum, F. (1938). *Crime and the community.* Boston: Ginn.

Tausig, C. (1982, January). At Royal Military College: Days filled with challenge. *University Affairs,* 3-5.

Taylor, I., Walton, P., & Young, J. (1973). *The new criminology: For a social theory of deviance.* London: Routledge & Kegan Paul.

Taylor, I., Walton, P., & Young, J. (1975). *Critical criminology.* London: Routledge & Kegan Paul.

Tepperman, L. (1975). *Social mobility in Canada.* Toronto: McGraw-Hill Ryerson.

Terry, C., & Pellens, M. (1970). *The opium problem.* Montclair, NJ: Patterson Smith.

Thatcher, T. C. (1978). Report of the Royal Commission on violence in the communications industry. In M. A. Beyer Gammon (Ed.), *Violence in Canada.* Toronto: Methuen.

Thomlinson, R. (1965). *Population dynamics: Causes and consequences of world demographic change.* New York: Random House.

Thompson, M. K., & Brown, J. S. (1980). Feminine roles and variations in women's illness behaviors. *Pacific Sociological Review, 23* 405-422.

Thorne, B., & Henley, N. (1975). Difference and dominance: An overview of language, gender, and society. In B. Thorne & N. Henley (Eds.), *Language and sex: Difference and dominance.* Rowley, MA: Newburg House Publishers.

Thrasher, F. (1927). *The gang.* Chicago: University of Chicago Press.

Tilly, C. (1974). Ecological triangle. In C. Tilly (Ed.), *An urban world.* Boston: Little, Brown.

Tilly, C. (1978). *From mobilization to revolution.* Reading, MA: Addison-Wesley.

Timberlake, J. H. (1963). *Prohibition and the progressive movement, 1900-1920.* Cambridge, MA: Harvard University Press.

Tinbergen, J. (1976). *Reshaping the international order.* New York: Dutton.

Toby, J. (1974). The socialization and control of deviant motivation. In D. Glazer (Ed.), *Handbook of criminology.* Chicago: Rand McNally.

Tönnies, F. (1957). *Gemeinschaft [Community and society] Gemeinschaft und Gesellschaft.* New York: Harper Torchbooks. (Original work published in 1887)

Townsen, M. (1980). *Women and money in the eighties: Facing up to the crisis.* Unpublished paper.

Treiman, D. (1978). *Occupational prestige in comparative perspective.* New York: Academic Press.

Tresemer, D. (1975). Assumptions made about gender roles. In M. Millman & R. Moss Kanter (Eds.), *Another voice: Feminist perspectives on social life and social sciences.* Garden City, N.Y.: Doubleday Anchor.

Troyer, W. (1979). *Divorced kids.* Toronto: Clarke Irwin.

Truzzi, M. (Ed.). (1968). *Sociology and everyday life.* Englewood Cliffs, NJ: Prentice-Hall.

Tsui, A. O., & Bogue, D. J. (1978). Declining world fertility: Trends, causes, implications. *Population Bulletin, 33*(4). Washington, D.C.: Population Reference Bureau, Inc.

Tuchman, G. (1978). Introduction: The symbolic annihilation of women by the mass media. In G. Tuchman, A. Kaplan Daniels, & J. Benet (Eds.), *Hearth and home: Images of women in the mass media* (pp. 3-38). New York: Oxford University Press.

Tumin, M. (1953). Some principles of stratification: A critical analysis. *American Sociological Review, 18,* 387-394.

Turk, A. T. (1969). *Criminality and the legal order.* Chicago: Rand McNally.

Turner, R. H. (1962). Role-taking: Process versus conformity. In A. M. Rose (Ed.), *Human behavior and social processes: An interactionist approach.* Boston: Houghton Mifflin.

Turner, R. H., & Killian, L. M. (1972). *Collective behavior.* Englewood Cliffs, NJ: Prentice-Hall.

Turrittin, A. H., Anisef, P., & MacKinnon, N. J. (1983). Gender differences in educational achievement: A study of social inequality. *Canadian Journal of Sociology, 8,* 395-419.

Tyree, A., *et al.* (1979). Gaps and glissandos: Inequality, economic development, and social mobility. *American Sociological Review, 44,* 410-424.

Van den Berghe, P. L. (1981). *The ethnic phenomenon.* New York: Elsevier.

Veevers, J. E., & Cousineau, D. F. (1980). The heathen Canadians: Demographic correlates of nonbelief. *Pacific Sociological Review, 23,* 199-216.

Waller, I., & Chan, J. (1975). Prison use: A Canadian and international comparison. *Criminal Law Quarterly, 47-71.*

Ward, D., & Balswick, J. (1978). Strong men and virtuous women: A content analysis of sex roles stereotypes. *Pacific Sociological Review, 21,* 45-53.

Warnock, J. (1970). *Portner to Behemoth.* Toronto: New Press.

Waters , H. F., & Malamud, P. (1975, March). Drop that gun, Captain Video. *Newsweek , 85*(10), 81-82.

Watkins, M. (1973). The trade union movement in Canada. In R. Laxer (Ed.), *Canada Ltd.* Toronto: McClelland and Stewart.

Weaver, S. M. (1981). *Making Canadian Indian policy.* Toronto: University of Toronto Press.

Webb, S. D., & Collette, J. (1977). Rural-urban differences in the use of stress-alleviative drugs. *American Journal of Sociology, 83,* 700-707.

Webb, S. D., & Collette, J. (1979). Rural-urban stress: New data and new conclusions. *American Journal of Sociology, 84*(6), 446-452.

Weber, M. (1930). *The protestant ethic and the spirit of capitalism.* London: George Allen and Unwin.

Weber, M. (1947). *The theory of social and economic organization.* (A. M. Henderson and T. Parsons). New York: Free Press.

Weber, M. (1958). *The city.* D. Martindale and G. Neuwirth (trans.). New York: Free Press.

Weinstein, E. A. (1969). The development of interpersonal competence. In D. A. Goslin (Ed.), *Handbook of socialization theory and research.* Chicago: Rand McNally.

Wellman, B. (1979). The community question: The intimate networks of East Yorkers. *American Journal of Sociology, 84*(5), 201-231.

Wesolowski, W. (1969). Some notes on the functional theory of stratification. In C. Heller (Ed.), *Structured social inequality.* New York: Macmillan.

Westhues, K. (1973). The established church as an agent of change. *Sociological Analysis, 34,* 106-123.

Westhues, K. (1978). Stars and stripes, the maple leaf, on violence in the communications industry. In M. A. Beyer Gammon (Ed.). *Violence in Canada*. Toronto: Methuen.

Westhues, K. (1978). Stars and stripes, the maple leaf, and the papal coat of arms. *Canadian Journal of Sociology, 3*, 245-261.

White, M., & White, L. (1962). *The intellectual versus the city*. Cambridge, MA: Harvard University Press and Militi Press.

White, T. H. (1978). *Power or pawns: Boards of directors in Canadian corporations*. Toronto: C.C.H.

Whyte, W. H., Jr. (1956). *The organization man*. New York: Simon and Schuster.

Wilensky, H. L. (1960). Work, careers, and social integration. *International Social Science Journal, 12*, 543-560.

Wilensky, H. L. (1961). Orderly careers and social participation: The impact of work history on social integration in the middle class. *American Sociological Review, 26*, 521-539.

Wiley, N. 1967. America's unique class politics: The interplay of the labor, credit, and commodity markets. *American Sociological Review, 32*, 529-541.

Williams, J. E., & Best, D. L. (1982). *Measuring sex stereotypes: A thirty-nation study*. Beverly Hills, CA: Sage.

Williams, T. M., & Boyes, M. C. (1986). Television viewing patterns and use of other media. In T. M. Williams (Ed.). *The impact of television* (p. 241). Toronto: The Academic Press.

Williams, T. R. (1983). *Socialization*. Englewood Cliffs, NJ: Prentice-Hall.

Wilson, J. Q. (1968). The police and the delinquent in two cities. In S. Wheeler (Ed.), *Controlling delinquents*. New York: John Wiley.

Wilson, S. J. (1981). The image of women in Canadian magazines. In E. Katz & T. Szecsko (Eds.), *Mass media and social change* (pp. 231-245). Beverly Hills, CA: Sage.

Wilson, S. J. (1982). *Women, the family and the economy*. Toronto: McGraw-Hill Ryerson.

Wilson, T. C. (1985). Urbanism and tolerance: A test of some hypotheses drawn from Wirth and Stouffer. *American Sociological Review, 50*(1), 117-123.

Wimberley, R. C. (1971). Mobility in ministerial career patterns: Exploration. *Journal for the Scientific Study of Religion, 10*, 249-253.

Winn, M. (1977). *The plug-in drug: Television, children and the family*. New York: Viking.

Winn, M. (1983). *Children without childhood*. New York: Pantheon.

Wirth, L. (1938). Urbanism as a way of life. *American Journal of Sociology, 44*, 3-24.

Wirth, L. (1945). The problem of minority groups. In R. Linto (Ed.), *The science of man in the world crisis*. New York: Columbia.

Wolf, W. C., & Fligstein, N. D. (1979). Sex and authority in the workplace: The causes of sexual inequality. *American Sociological Review, 44*, 235-252.

Women's Bureau, Labour Canada. (1980). Women in the labour force, 1978-1979. Part I: Participation. Ottawa: Minister of Supply and Services Canada.

Women's Bureau, Labour Canada. (1983). *Women in the labour force. Part I: Participation*. Ottawa: Ministry of Supply and Services.

World Bank (1984). *World development report 1984*. New York: Oxford University Press.

World Bank. (1986). *World development report 1986*. New York: Oxford University Press.

Wright, E. O. (1978). *Class, crisis and the state*. London: New Left Books.

Yinger, J. M. (1976). Ethnicity in complex societies. In L. A. Coser & O. N. Larsen (Eds.), *The uses of controversy in soiology*. New York: Free.

Yinger, J. M. (1985). Ethnicity. In R. H. Turner & J. Short (Eds.), *Annual Review of Sociology, 2*. Palo Alto, CA: Annual Reviews.

Yoels, W. C., & Karp, D. A. (1978). A social psychological critique of 'over-socialization': Dennis Wrong revisited. *Sociological Symposium, 24*, 27-39.

Young, M., & Willmot, P. (1957). *Family and kinship in east London*. London: Routledge & Kegan Paul.

Zinssen, H. (1965). *Rats, lice and history*. New York: Bantam.

Photo Credits

The publishers thank the following sources of material used in this book. We have attempted to trace the ownership of copyright for all materials used and will gladly receive information enabling us to rectify any errors in references or credits.

Index

To the Owner of This Book

We are interested in your reaction to **Fundamentals of Sociology**. Through feedback from you, we may be able to improve this book in future editions.

1. What was your reason for using this book?

_____ community college course

_____ preparation for a professional examination

_____ reference text

_____ other (specify)

2. What was the best feature of this book?

3. Can you suggest any improvements?

4. Should any topics be added to this book?

Fold here

Tape shut